S0-DRG-042

DATE DUE

WOMEN IN MUSIC:
A Biobibliography

by
DON L. HIXON
and
DON HENNESSEE

The Scarecrow Press, Inc.
Metuchen, N.J.   1975

CALIFORNIA INSTITUTE
OF THE ARTS LIBRARY

Library of Congress Cataloging in Publication Data

Hixon, Donald L
    Women in music.

    "List of sources indexed": p.
    1. Women musicians--Biography. 2. Music--Bio-
bibliography--Indexes. I. Hennessee, Don, joint author.
II. Title.
ML105.H6   780'.92'2   75-23075
ISBN 0-8108-0869-2

1/30/78 Ka

For

LURA SODERSTROM

Musician, teacher, friend

CONTENTS

v

This volume was compiled with two purposes in mind.
Most obviously, it serves as an index to the biographies of
women musicians of all periods and countries, as found in a
representative selection of significant music dictionaries and
encyclopedias. Equally important, however, by providing
relatively detailed entries for each of the musicians, this
volume is capable of standing by itself as a brief-identifica-
tion type of biographical dictionary. It must be noted that
only those musicians whose efforts have been directed toward
"classical" music have been included; "popular" performers, jazz
musicians, cabaret performers, and others whose chief interest
and expertise lie exclusively within the realm of "popular"
music, have been omitted.

Each entry consists of the following information.
    1. *Musician's name*, including appropriate pseudonyms,
maiden name, stage name, and variant forms and spellings, from
each of which references have been made. Compound surnames are
alphabetized as one word, and references are made from each part
of the compound. In German names, ä is alphabetized as ae, ö as
oe, and ü as ue; umlauts in other languages do not affect alpha-
betization. No effort has been made to reconcile the different
transliteration systems encountered among the sources treating
Slavic names.
    2. *Place and date of birth and death*. When this
information varies from one source to another, the most commonly
recurring date or place has been selected, unless scholarship
more recent than the sources containing the biography has pro-
vided data to the contrary. Variations in place and date found
among the sources follow the entry in *italics*.
    3. *Field(s) of musical activity or specialization*
(flutist, composer, etc.), arranged whenever possible to ascer-
tain in order of prominence.
    4. *Coded list of sources in which biographies may be
found*. The "codes" are, in general, derived from the last name
of the editor or compiler of the work containing the biography;
occasionally, codes based on the title of the work are employed.
Complete bibliographical detail will be found in the *List of
Sources Indexed* which follows this preface. When an entry
contains reference to more than one source, the sources have
been arranged in alphabetical order without regard for the
significance or length of the biographies contained therein.
Since the biographies contained in each of the sources are
arranged in alphabetical order, page number references have not

been supplied except when necessary to direct the reader to internal biographies under a form different from the entry chosen in this volume, or to separately-alphabetized sections within the sources, generally supplements and appendices.

5. *An asterisk (*) preceding a source code* indicates that the source contains an illustration of the musician. Page number references are made only when the illustration does not fall on the same or adjacent page as the biography itself.

In order to provide citations as complete as possible, it was often necessary to seek information lying outside the sources indexed. This was particularly true when establishing dates and places of death for those individuals who had died since the publication of the sources in which their biographies appear. While time constraints prohibited an exhaustive search, the following sources were utilized in attempts to provide the additional data: the annual "Index to Music Necrology" appearing in the June issues of *Notes; the Quarterly Journal of the Music Library Association*; *The New York Times Obituaries Index, 1858-1968* (New York, New York Times, 1970), in addition to annual and biweekly volumes and issues of *The New York Times Index* covering the period subsequent to 1968; and the "Necrology" section (pp.995-1101) of *The Biographical Encyclopedia and Who's Who of the American Theatre*, ed. Walter Rigdon (New York, Heineman, 1966).

Gratitude must be extended to the Acquisitions, Catalog, and Reference Departments of the University of California Library, Irvine, for providing released time during which to pursue research related to portions of this volume; to Vincent Duckles and John A. Emerson of the Music Library, University of California, Berkeley, for their keen interest in and support of this project; to Vernon Sternberg and Marilyn Hails of the Southern Illinois University Press in Carbondale for their gracious willingness to provide access to the galley proofs of the then-unpublished third and fourth volumes of Philip Highfill's *Biographical Dictionary*; to Herbert Ahn and Carol Jackson of the UCI Library Systems Analysis Office for providing the computer software from which the "Classified List of Women Musicians" which concludes this volume was produced; and to Bob Bates, Sara Eichhorn, Fred Forbes, and Dora Jones of the UCI Library Reference Department for their valuable assistance with instances of last-minute verification.

In any volume of this type, it seems that errors are inevitable, regardless of the pains taken in its preparation. The authors would be grateful if errors, misinterpretations, and inconsistencies were brought to their attention so that subsequent editions might profit from the increased accuracy.

Donald L. Hixon
Don A. Hennessee

Summer 1975

Descriptions of these sources are available in
Vincent Duckles' *Music Reference and Research
Materials; an Annotated Bibliography*, third ed.
(New York, Free Press, 1974). References to
such annotations are found in brackets at the
end of each of the citations below.

ARIZAGA   Arizaga, Rodolfo. *Enciclopedia de la música
Argentina*. Buenos Aires, Fondo Nacional de
las Artes, 1971. [Duckles 103]

BAKER 1   Baker, Theodore. *A biographical dictionary of
musicians...with portraits from drawings in
pen and ink by Alex Gribayédoff*. New York,
G. Schirmer, 1900. [Duckles 65]

BAKER 5   -----. -------. 5th ed., completely rev. by
Nicolas Slonimsky. New York, G. Schirmer,
1958. [Duckles 65]

BAKER 1971   -----. -------. -----. *Supplement*. By Nicolas
Slonimsky. New York, G. Schirmer, 1971.
[Duckles 65]

BLOM   Blom, Eric. *Everyman's dictionary of music*.
Revised by Sir Jack Westrup, with the colla-
boration of [others]. New York, St. Martin's
Press, 1971. [Duckles 5]

BROWN BIO   Brown, James Duff. *Biographical dictionary of
musicians; with a bibliography of English
writings on music*. Hildesheim, New York,
Georg Olms, 1970 (reprint of 1886 ed.)
[Duckles 68]

BROWN BRIT   -----. *British musical biography: a dictionary
of musical artists, authors and composers,
born in Britain and its colonies*. By James D.
Brown...and Stephen S. Stratton. Birmingham,
Stratton, 1897. [Duckles 129]

CBC   Canadian Broadcasting Corporation. *Catalogue of
Canadian composers*. Ed. Helmut Kallmann. Rev.
and enl. ed. [Ottawa? 1952?] [Duckles 111]

CELLETTI   Celletti, Rodolfo. *Le grandi voci; dizionario
                critico-biografico dei cantanti con disco-
                grafia operistica.* Rome, Istituto per la
                Collaborazione Culturale, 1964. [Duckles 84]

CLAYTON   Clayton, Ellen Creathorne. *Queen of song: being
                memoirs of some of the most celebrated female
                vocalists who have performed on the lyric
                stage from the earliest days of opera to the
                present time.* New York, Harper & Brothers,
                1864. [Not in Duckles]

COOPER   Cooper, Martin. *The concise encyclopedia of
                music and musicians.* 2nd ed., rev. London,
                Hutchinson, 1971. [Duckles 10]

CORTE   Corte, Andrea della. *Dizionario di musica* [di]
                A. della Corte e G. M. Gatti. 6th ed.   Torino,
                G. B. Paravia, 1959. [Duckles 11]

COSMA   Cosma, Viorel. *Compozitori si muzicologi români;
                mic lexicon.* Bucuresti, Editura Muzicala a
                Uniunii Compozitorilor din R. P. R., 1965.
                [Duckles 164]

DICT MUS   *Dictionnaire de la musique.* Publié sous la
                direction de Marc Honegger. Paris, Bordas,
                1970. 2v. [Duckles 25]

ENCI MUS   *Enciclopedia della musica.* Direttore: Claudio
                Sartori; vice-direttore: Riccardo Allorto.
                Milano, Ricordi, 1963-64. 4v. [Despite
                citation in index, inadvertently omitted from
                Duckles 3rd ed.; no. 16 in 2nd ed.]

ENCI SALVAT   *Enciclopedia Salvat de la música.* Barcelona,
                Salvat, 1967. 4v. [Duckles 15]

ENCY MUS   *Encyclopedie de la musique.* [Publié sous la
                direction de François Michel en collaboration
                avec François Lesure et Vladimir Fédorov et
                un comité de rédaction composé de Nadia Bou-
                langer et al.] Paris, Fasquelle, 1968-61.
                3v. [Duckles 16]

EWEN LIVING   Ewen, David. *Living musicians.* New York, H. W.
                Wilson Co., 1940. [Duckles 80]

EWEN LIV SUP   -----. -------. *Supplement.* New York, H. W.
                Wilson Co., 1957. [Duckles 80]

EWEN NEW   -----. *The new encyclopedia of the opera.* New
                York, Hill and Wang, 1971. [Duckles 348]

GARDAVSKY   Gardavský, Čeněk. *Contemporary Czechoslovak
               composers*. Prague, Panton, 1965. [Duckles
               115]

GROVE 1   Grove, *Sir* George. *A dictionary of music and*
               *musicians (A.D. 1450-1889) by eminent
               writers, English and foreign*. With illus-
               trations and woodcuts. Ed. by Sir George
               Grove...with appendix, ed. by J. A. Fuller
               Maitland (and index, by Mrs. Edmond Wode-
               house). London, New York, Macmillan, 1879-90.
               4v. and index. [Duckles 21]

GROVE 1 APP   -----. -------. *Appendix*, v.4, pp.517-818.
               [Duckles 21]

GROVE 5   -----. -------. 5th ed., ed. by Eric Blom.
               New York, St. Martin's Press, 1954. 9v.
               [Duckles 21]

GROVE 5 SUP   -----. -------. -----. *Supplementary volume*,
               ed. by Eric Blom; associate editor, Denis
               Stevens. New York, St. Martin's Press, 1961.
               [Duckles 21]

HIGHFILL   Highfill, Philip H. *A biographical dictionary
               of actors, actresses, musicians, dancers,
               managers & other stage personnel in London,
               1660-1800*. By Philip Highfill, Jr., Kalman
               A. Burnim and Edward A. Langhans. Carbondale,
               Southern Illinois University Press, 1973- .
               In progress: v.1-4 (A-D) indexed in this
               bibliography. [Duckles 132]

KUTSCH   Kutsch, K. J. *A concise biographical dictionary
               of singers; from the beginning of recorded
               sound to the present*. By K. J. Kutsch and
               Leo Riemens. Translated from the German,
               expanded and annotated by Harry Earl Jones.
               Philadelphia, Chilton Book Co., 1969. (A
               translation of the author's *Unvergängliche
               Stimmen: Kleines Sängerlexikon*. [Duckles 88]

MARIZ   Mariz, Vasco. *Dicionario bio-bibliográfico
               musical (brasileiro e internacional)*. Rio de
               Janeiro, Livraria Kosmos, 1948. [Duckles 154]

MGG   *Die Musik in Geschichte und Gegenwart; all-
               gemeine Enzyklopädie der Musik*...Von Fried-
               rich Blume. Kassel, New York, Bärenreiter,
               1949-68. 14v. [Duckles 38]

MGG SUP   -----. *Supplement*, 1969- . In progress:
               fascicles A-F indexed. [Duckles 38]

MURDOCH

Murdoch, James. *Australia's contemporary composers*. Melbourne, Macmillan, 1972. [Not in Duckles]

NAPIER

Napier, Ronald. *A guide to Canada's composers*. Willowdale, Ontario, Avondale Press, 1973. [Not in Duckles]

PALMER

Palmer, Russell. *British music; an encyclopedia of British musicians*. London, S. Robinson, 1948. [Duckles 133]

PAVLAKIS

Pavlakis, Christopher. *The American music handbook*. New York, Free Press, 1974. Only portions containing relatively complete biographical sketches indexed in this bibliography. [Duckles 1829]

PRATT

Pratt, Waldo Selden. *The new encyclopedia of music and musicians*. New and rev. edition. New York, Macmillan, 1929. [Duckles 43]

REIS

Reis, Claire Raphael. *Composers in America; biographical sketches of contemporary composers with a record of their works*. Rev. and enl. edition. New York, Macmillan, 1947. [Duckles 190]

RIEMANN

Riemann, Hugo. *Riemann Musik-Lexikon*. 12. völlig neubearbeitete Auflage in drei Bänden. Hrsg. von Wilibald Gurlitt. Mainz, B. Schotts Söhne, 1959-67. 3v. Only v.1-2 (Personenteil) indexed. [Duckles 46]

RIEMANN ERG

-----. -------. *Ergänzungsbände*. Hrsg. C. Dahlhaus. Mainz, B. Schotts Söhne, 1972- . In progress: v.1 (A-K) indexed. [Duckles 46]

ROSENTHAL

Rosenthal, Harold D. *Great singers of today*. London, Calder & Boyars, 1966. [Not in Duckles]

SANDVED

Sandved, Kjell Bloch. *The world of music; an illustrated encyclopedia*. New York, Abradale Press, 1963. 4v. [Not in Duckles]

SCHOLES

Scholes, Percy Alfred. *The Oxford companion to music*. Ed. by John Owen Ward. 10th ed., completely rev. and reset and with many additions to text and illustrations. London, New York, Oxford University Press, 1970. [Duckles 52]

SCHUH   Schuh, Willi. *Schweizer Musiker-Lexikon, 1964.*
                     Im Auftrag des Schweizerischen Tonkünstler-
                     vereins. Bearb. von Willi Schuh [et al.]
                     Zürich, Atlantis Verlag, 1964. Bound with
                     Nachtrag (1965). [Duckles 170]

SCHUH NACH   -----. -------. Nachtrag 1965. Zürich,
                     Atlantis Verlag, 1965. [Duckles 170]

SLONIMSKY   Slonimsky, Nicolas. *Music of Latin America.*
                     New York, Thomas Y. Crowell, 1945. [Not
                     in Duckles]

THOMPSON   Thompson, Oscar. *The international cyclopedia
                     of music and musicians.* 9th ed. New York,
                     Dodd, Mead, 1964. [Duckles 58] The tenth
                     (1975) edition of this work was received
                     after the research for this volume had been
                     completed, and therefore too late for
                     inclusion. It should be noted, however,
                     that a spot-check of a representative
                     selection of letters revealed that the
                     number of new names of women musicians
                     added in the tenth edition was minimal
                     indeed, while an average of ten percent
                     of the names of women musicians appearing
                     in the ninth was omitted from the tenth
                     edition.

ULLSTEIN   *Ullstein Musiklexikon.* Von Friedrich Herzfeld.
                     Mit 4500 Stichwörtern, 600 Notenbeispielen,
                     1000 Abbildungen und 32 Tafelseiten. Berlin,
                     Frankfurt/M., Ullstein, 1965. [Duckles 24]

VINTON   Vinton, John. *Dictionary of contemporary music.*
                     New York, E. P. Dutton, 1974. [Not in
                     Duckles]

VODARSKY   Vodarsky-Shiraeff, Alexandria. *Russian com-
                     posers and musicians; a biographical
                     dictionary.* New York, Da Capo, 1969. "An
                     unabridged republication of the first
                     edition published in 1940." [Duckles 175]

AARBURG, Ursula. Lübeck, Germany, Jan 13 1924-May 15 1967, Bremen, Germany. Musicologist, writer. RIEMANN ERG.

ABARBANELL, Lina. Berlin, Jan 3 1879-Jan 6 1963, New York City. Soprano. KUTSCH.

ABBADIA, Luigia. Genoa, 1821-Jan 1896, Rome. Mezzo-soprano, voice teacher. BAKER 1, ENCI MUS, MGG SUP, PRATT, THOMPSON.

ABBOTT, Bessie Pickens see Abott, Bessie Pickens

ABBOTT, Emma. Chicago, Dec 9 1850-Jan 5 1891, Salt Lake City. Soprano. BAKER 1, BAKER 5, BLOM, ENCI MUS, EWEN NEW, GROVE 5, GROVE 5 SUP, PRATT, THOMPSON.

ABEGG, Mrs. fl.1758-63. English actress, soprano. HIGHFILL.

ABEL, Jenny. Bredstedt/Husum, Schleswig-Holstein, Germany, Nov 23 1942- . Violinist. RIEMANN ERG.

ABEL-STRUTH, Sigrid. Breitscheid, Dillkreis, Germany, Jul 24 1924- . Teacher, writer. RIEMANN ERG.

ABENDROTH, Irene (stage name of Irene Thaller von Draga). Lemberg, Austria, Jul 14 1872-Sep 1 1932, Weidling, nr. Vienna. Soprano. CELLET-

TI, ENCI SALVAT, ENCY MUS, KUTSCH, PRATT. [CELLETTI= d. Sep 2 1932]

ABERT, Anna Amalie. Halle, Germany, Sep 19 1906- . Musicologist, editor, writer. BAKER 5, CORTE, DICT MUS, ENCI MUS, ENCI SALVAT, ENCY MUS, GROVE 5, MGG, RIEMANN, RIEMANN ERG, ULLSTEIN.

ABOTT (Abbott), Bessie Pickens. Riverdale, New York, 1878-Feb 9 1919, New York City. Soprano. KUTSCH, MARIZ, THOMPSON.

ABRAMS, Eliza. London?, c1763-?. Singer. BROWN BRIT, GROVE 1, GROVE 5, HIGHFILL, THOMPSON.

ABRAMS, Flora. fl.1778. English singer. HIGHFILL.

ABRAMS, Miss G. fl.1778-80. English singer, actress. HIGHFILL.

ABRAMS, Harriet. London?, 1760-c1825, London? Composer, soprano. BROWN BIO, BROWN BRIT, GROVE 1, GROVE 5, *HIGHFILL, THOMPSON.

ABRAMS, Jane. fl.1799. English singer?. HIGHFILL.

ABRAMS, Theodosia (later Mrs. Thomas Fisher & Mrs. Joseph Garrow). ?, c1761-Nov 4 1849, Braddons, England. Contralto. BROWN BRIT, GROVE 1, GROVE 5, HIGHFILL, THOMPSON.

ACHSEL, Wanda. Berlin, Oct 12
1891- . Soprano, voice
teacher. KUTSCH.

ACHTE, Aïno see Ackte, Aïno

ACHTÉ, Emmy (Emma Charlotta,
born Strömer). Uleåborg,
Finland, Nov 14 1850-Dec 2
1924, Helsinki. Soprano.
GROVE 5.

ACKLAND, Jeanne Isabel Dorothy.
Calgary, ?- . 20th-century
Canadian pianist, composer,
organist, violinist. CBC.

ACKLAND, Jessie Agnes. Ontario, ?- . 20th-century
Canadian pianist, piano
teacher, composer, teacher.
CBC.

ACKTÉ, Aïno (orig. Achte).
Helsinki, Apr 23 1876-Aug 8
1944, Nummela, Finland.
Soprano. BAKER 5, ENCI MUS,
ENCI SALVAT, GROVE 5, GROVE
5 SUP, KUTSCH, PRATT, RIE-
MANN, RIEMANN ERG, THOMPSON.

ACKTÉ, Irma see Tervani,
Irma

ACQUA, Teresa del' see
Del'Acqua, Teresa

ADAÏEWSKA (Adajewska), Ella
(Elisabeth) von (born von
Schultz). St. Petersburg,
Jan 29 or Feb 10 1846-Jul 26
1926, Bonn. Composer, pia-
nist. CORTE, ENCI MUS, MGG
SUP, RIEMANN, RIEMANN ERG,
THOMPSON.

ADAMI CORRADETTI, Iris. Milan,
Mar 14 1909- . Soprano.
ENCI MUS.

ADAMOWSKA, Antoniette see
Szumowska, Antoniette

ADAMS, Mrs. fl.1750. English
actress, singer. HIGHFILL.

ADAMS, Miss E. fl.1800-08.
English dancer, singer.
HIGHFILL.

ADAMS, Miss H. fl.1800-08.
English dancer, singer.
HIGHFILL.

ADAMS, Miss S. fl.1800-08.
English dancer, singer.
HIGHFILL.

ADAMS, Sara Flower see Flower, Sara

ADAMS, Suzanne. Cambridge,
Mass., Nov 28 1872-Feb 5 1953,
London. Soprano. BAKER 5,
ENCI MUS, ENCI SALVAT, ENCY
MUS, EWEN NEW, GROVE 5, GROVE
5 SUP, KUTSCH, PRATT, SANDVED,
THOMPSON, ULLSTEIN. *[PRATT=
b.1873]*

ADANI, Mariella (stage name of
Laura Tadeo Adani). Palan-
zano, Parma, Italy, Dec 27
1934- . Soprano. ENCI MUS.

ADCOCK, Miss. fl.1782-83.
English singer. HIGHFILL.

ADDISON, Adele. New York, Jul
24 1925- . Soprano. PAVLAKIS=
p. 285, *SANDVED, THOMPSON.

ADDISON, Elizabeth (Mrs. John,
born Willems). fl.1785-1840.
English actress, singer.
BROWN BRIT, GROVE 5, HIGHFILL,
PRATT.

ADER, Rose (Ader-de-Trigona).
Oderberg, Germany, Apr 28
1890-Mar 28 1955, Buenos
Aires. Soprano, voice teacher. KUTSCH.

ADINI (Adiny), Ada (Mrs. Anto-

3 *AHNA*

nio Aramburo, born Chapman).
Boston, 1855-Feb 1924,
Dieppe, France. Soprano,
voice teacher. ENCI MUS=v.1
p.92, KUTSCH, THOMPSON.

ADLER, Agnes Charlotte Dagmar
(born Hansen). Copenhagen,
Feb 19 1865-Oct 11 1935,
Copenhagen. Pianist, piano
teacher. PRATT, THOMPSON.

ADRIEN, Atale see Wartel,
Atale

AFFABILI, Barbara see
Westenholz, Barbara

AFFERNI, Mary (May; Mrs. Ugo,
born Bramner or Brommer).
Great Grimsby, England,
May 2 1872-?. Violinist.
ENCI MUS, PRATT.

AGABEG, Mrs. see Wynne,
Sarah Edith

AGAI, Karola. Budapest, Mar 30
1932- . Soprano. RIEMANN
ERG.

AGASJEWNA, Sara see Dolu-
chanowa, Sara

AGNESI PINOTTINI, Maria Teresa
d'. Milan, Oct 17 1720-Jan
19 1795, Milan. Composer,
pianist, opera composer.
BAKER 1, ENCI MUS=v.2 p.1,
ENCI SALVAT, ENCY MUS,
GROVE 1, GROVE 5, MGG SUP,
PRATT, RIEMANN, RIEMANN ERG,
THOMPSON. *[BAKER 1=1724-80;
GROVE 1=b.1724; PRATT=1724-
1780?]*

AGNETTA, Signora. fl.1747-51.
Singer. HIGHFILL.

AGOSTINELLI QUIROLI, Adelina.
Verdello, Bergamo, Italy,
Nov 23 1882-Jul 6 1954,
Buenos Aires. Soprano, voice

teacher. CORTE, ENCI MUS,
KUTSCH.

AGRICOLA, Benedetta Emilia
(born Molteni). Modena,
1722-1780, Berlin. Soprano.
BLOM, ENCI MUS, ENCI SALVAT,
ENCY MUS, GROVE 5, THOMPSON.

AGTHE, Rosa see Milde, Rosa

AGUIAR, Luiza Rosa d' see
Todi, Luiza Rosa

AGUILAR, Maria Asuncion see
Ros, Maria

AGUJARI (Ajugari), Lucrezia
(later Mme. Giuseppe Colla;
known as La Bastardina or
Bastardella). Ferrara, c1743-
May 18 1783, Parma. Soprano.
BAKER 1, BAKER 5, BLOM, BROWN
BIO, COOPER, CORTE, ENCI MUS,
ENCI SALVAT, ENCY MUS, GROVE
1, GROVE 5, HIGHFILL, MARIZ=
p.22, MGG SUP, PRATT, RIE-
MANN, RIEMANN ERG, SCHOLES=
p.1096, THOMPSON.

AHLEFELDT, Maria Theresia.
Regensburg, Germany, Feb 28
1755-Nov 4 1823, Prague.
Composer, light-opera composer. GROVE 5, MGG SUP.

AHLES, Rosina see Lortzing,
Rosina

AHLGRIMM, Isolde. Vienna, Jul
31 1914- . Cembalist. RIE-
MANN, RIEMANN ERG, ULLSTEIN.

AHLIN, Cvetka. Ljubljana, Yugoslavia, Sep 8 1928- . Contralto. KUTSCH, RIEMANN ERG.

AHNA, Eleanora de see De
Ahna, Eleanora

AHNA, Pauline de see De Ahna,
Pauline

AHNGER, Alexandra. Kuopio, Finland, May 15 1859-Nov 9 1940, Helsinki. Singer, voice teacher. THOMPSON.

AIMARO, Lina. Turin, Feb 6 1914- . Soprano, voice teacher. KUTSCH.

AINSWORTH, Clara see West, Clara

AÏTOFF, Irène. St. Caast, France, 1904- . Pianist. ENCI SALVAT, ENCY MUS.

AJUGARI, Lucrezia see Agujari, Lucrezia

ALAIN, Marie-Claire. St. Germain-en-Laye, France, Aug 10 1926- . Organist. DICT MUS, ENCI MUS, ENCI SALVAT, ENCY MUS, RIEMANN, RIEMANN ERG, ULLSTEIN.

ALARIE, Pierrette (Mrs. Leopold Simoneau). Montréal, 1922- . Soprano. KUTSCH.

ALBAN-WILK, Judith. 20th-century American soprano. PAVLAKIS=p.285.

ALBANESE, Licia. Bari, Italy, Jul 22 1913- . Soprano. BAKER 5, BAKER 1971, BLOM, CELLETTI, COOPER, CORTE, ENCI MUS, ENCI SALVAT, ENCY MUS, *EWEN LIV SUP, EWEN NEW, GROVE 5, GROVE 5 SUP, KUTSCH, MARIZ, RIEMANN, RIEMANN ERG, *ROSENTHAL=illus.p.9, *SANDVED=another illus.p.786, THOMPSON, ULLSTEIN. *[BLOM=b. Jul 23 1909; ENCI SALVAT & ENCY MUS=b.1914; MARIZ=b. 1908]*

ALBANI, Emma (stage name of Marie Louise Cecilia Emma Lajeunesse). Chambly, nr. Montréal, Nov 1 1847-Apr 3 1930, London. Soprano, voice teacher. BAKER 1, BAKER 5, BLOM, BROWN BIO=p.372, BROWN BRIT=p.236, CBC, CELLETTI, *COOPER=illus.p.53, *ENCI MUS=illus.fac.p.31, ENCI SALVAT, ENCY MUS, EWEN NEW, GROVE 1, GROVE 1 APP=v.2 p.85, GROVE 5, GROVE 5 SUP, KUTSCH, MGG SUP, PRATT, RIEMANN, RIEMANN ERG, SANDVED, THOMPSON. *[GROVE 1 APP=b. 1850; BROWN BIO=b.1851; BAKER 1, CELLETTI, & PRATT= b.1852]*

ALBERGHETTI, Anna Maria. Rodi, Italy, May 5 1936- . Soprano. BAKER 5, SANDVED.

ALBERGOTTI, Vittoria. fl.1713. Singer. HIGHFILL.

ALBERT, Hermine d' see Finck, Hermine

ALBERTAZZI, Emma (born Howson). London, May 1 1814-Sep 25 1847, London. Contralto. BAKER 1, BROWN BIO, BROWN BRIT=pp.5 & 463, ENCI MUS, GROVE 1, PRATT, THOMPSON.

ALBERTINI-BAUCARDÉ, Augusta. Florence, ?-Jan 1898, Florence. Soprano. ENCI MUS.

ALBERTS, Eunice. 20th-century American contralto. PAVLAKIS= p.297.

ALBITES, Marietta see Gazzaniga Malaspina Albites, Marietta

ALBONI, Marietta (real name= Maria Anna Marzia Alboni). Cesena or Città di Castello, Italy, Mar 6 1823-Jun 23 1894, Ville d'Avray, nr. Paris. Contralto. BAKER 1, BAKER 5, BLOM, BROWN BIO, *CLAYTON=p.439, CORTE, *ENCI

MUS=illus.fac.p.34, ENCI SALVAT, ENCY MUS, EWEN NEW, GROVE 1, GROVE 1 APP, GROVE 5, GROVE 5 SUP, MARIZ, MGG SUP, PRATT, RIEMANN, THOMPSON. *[GROVE 1 APP=b. Mar 10]*

ALBORE, Lilia d' see D'Albore, Lilia

ALBRICI, Leonora. fl.1662-71. Singer. HIGHFILL.

ALBRIZZI-TODESCHINI, Teresa. Milan, Dec 26 1723-Jun 30 1760, Prague. Contralto. GROVE 5, THOMPSON.

ALCOCK, Merle. Andover, Mo., 1890?-Mar 1 1975, Phoenix, Ariz. Contralto, voice teacher. *EWEN LIVING, THOMPSON. *[Death date from obituary in Variety, Mar 19 1975, p.87]*

ALDA, Frances (born Davies). Christchurch, New Zealand, May 31 1883-Sep 18 1952, Venice. Soprano, voice teacher. BAKER 5, CELLETTI, ENCI MUS, ENCI SALVAT, ENCY MUS, *EWEN LIVING, EWEN LIV SUP, EWEN NEW, KUTSCH, MARIZ, PRATT, RIEMANN, SANDVED, THOMPSON.

ALDIGHIERI, Maria (Mrs. Gottardo, born Spezia). Villafranca Veronese, Italy, 1828-Aug 3 1907, Colognola ai Colli, Verona. Soprano. ENCI MUS.

ALDRICH, Mariska. Boston, Feb 7 1881- . Soprano. PRATT, THOMPSON.

ALDROVANDI GATTI, Clelia see Gatti, Clelia Aldrovandi

ALEMÁN, Fedora. Caracas, Oct 11 1917- . Soprano. RIEMANN ERG.

ALEOTTI, Raffaela. Ferrara,

c1570-after 1638, Ferrara. Composer, organist. ENCI SALVAT, ENCY MUS, GROVE 5, MGG SUP, THOMPSON.

ALEOTTI, Vittoria. Ferrara, c1575-?. Composer, harpsichordist. GROVE 5, THOMPSON.

ALESSANDRA, Caterina. fl.1609. Italian church composer. GROVE 5, THOMPSON.

ALESSANDRI, Lavinia Maria see Guadagni, Lavinia Maria

ALESSIO, Aurora d'. Valencia, 1897-Jul 1965, Florence. Contralto. KUTSCH.

ALEXANDRE, Charlotte (Mrs. Dreyfuss). 19th-century French harmonium player. ENCI MUS, RIEMANN.

ALFANI-TELLINI, Ines see Tellini, Ines Alfani-

ALFORD, Violet. Bristol, England, Mar 1881- . Writer and lecturer on folk dancing. BAKER 5.

ALFTHAN, Margarete see Kilpinen, Margarete

ALHEIM, Marie Olénine d' see Olénine d'Alheim, Marie

ALIÓ, Myriam. Buenos Aires, ?- . 20th-century Argentine mezzo-soprano. ENCI SALVAT.

ALLAN, Jean Mary. Channelkirk Manse, Oxton, Scotland, Sep 27 1899- . Music librarian. MGG SUP.

ALLEGRANTI, Teresa Maddalena (later Mrs. Harrison). Florence, c1750-c1802, Ireland. Soprano. BLOM, BROWN BIO, ENCI MUS, GROVE 5, *HIGHFILL, THOMPSON.

ALLEMAND, Pauline d' see
L'Allemand, Pauline

ALLEN, Betty. Campbell, Ohio,
1930- . Mezzo-soprano. PAV-
LAKIS=p.293, *SANDVED,
THOMPSON.

ALLEN, Dinah see Farmer,
Dinah

ALLEN, Lilian Stiles- see
Stiles-Allen, Lilian

ALLEN, Mildred. Akron, Ohio,
?- . 20th-century American
soprano. THOMPSON.

ALLINSON, Mrs. fl.1699. English singer. HIGHFILL.

ALLISON, Maria. fl.1698-99.
English actress, singer.
HIGHFILL.

ALLITSEN, Emma. 19th-century
English contralto, voice
teacher. BROWN BRIT.

ALLITSEN, Frances. ?, 1849-
Oct 2 1912, London. Composer,
singer. BAKER 1, BROWN BRIT,
GROVE 5.

ALONSO, Alicia (born Martinez).
Havana, Dec 21 1921- . Dan-
cer and ballet director.
RIEMANN ERG.

ALPAR, Gitta. Budapest, Mar 5
1903- . Soprano, actress.
KUTSCH, RIEMANN ERG.

ALPENHEIM, Ilse von. Innsbruck,
Feb 11 1927- . Pianist.
SCHUH.

ALSEN, Elsa. Obra, Poland, Apr
7 1880-Jan 31 1975, New York.
Soprano, voice teacher. *EWEN
LIVING, KUTSCH, MARIZ, THOMP-
SON. *[Date & place of death
from Los Angeles Times obi-*

*tuary, Feb 3 1975, pt.3,
p.7]*

ALSOP, Ada. Darlington, England, Mar 19 1915- . Soprano. PALMER.

ALTEN, Bella. Zaxaczewc, Poland, Jun 30 1877-Dec 31
1962, London. Soprano, voice
teacher. KUTSCH.

ALTER, Martha. New Bloomfield,
Pa., 1904- . Composer,
teacher, pianist. REIS.

ALTMAN, Karen. 20th-century
American soprano. PAVLAKIS=
p.285.

ALVARENGA, Oneyda. Varginha,
Brazil, Dec 6 1911- . Musi-
cologist, folklorist, poet.
ENCI MUS, ENCI SALVAT, ENCY
MUS, GROVE 5, MARIZ, RIEMANN
ERG.

ALVAREZ, Carmen. Madrid, 1905-
. Pianist. ENCY MUS, THOMP-
SON.

ALVAREZ, Marguerite d'. Liver-
pool, c1886-Oct 18 1953,
Alassio, Italy. Contralto.
EWEN NEW=p.160, GROVE 5,
GROVE 5 SUP, KUTSCH, MARIZ,
SANDVED, THOMPSON.

ALVEAR, Regina de see Pacini,
Regina

ALVSLEBEN, Melitta see Otto,
Melitta

AMADIO, Florence Mary see
Austral, Florence Mary

AMALIA, Anna see Anna Amalia

AMALIA CATHARINA (Princess of
Erbach). Arolsen, Germany,
Aug 8 1640-Jan 4 1697, Cuy-

lenburg, Holland. Music
amateur. MGG SUP.

AMALIA, Friederike see
Amalia, Marie A. Friederike

AMALIA, Marie A. Friederike
(Princess of Saxony). Dresden., Aug 10 1794-Sep 18
1870, Dresden. Light-opera
composer, church composer,
opera composer. BAKER 1,
BAKER 5, RIEMANN.

AMARA, Lucine (orig. Lucy
Armaganian). Hartford,
Conn., Mar 1 1927- . Sopra-
no. EWEN NEW, KUTSCH, PAV-
LAKIS=p.285, *ROSENTHAL=
illus. p. 10, *SANDVED=
another illus. p. 417,
THOMPSON.

AMAYA, Carmen. Barcelona, Nov
2 1913-Nov 19 1963, Bagur,
Spain. Dancer. *ENCI SALVAT,
ENCY MUS.

AMBLER, Sarah see Brereton,
Sarah

AMBREVILLE, Anna Maria Lodovica d'. Modena, Jul 21
1693-c1760, Vienna?. Soprano. ENCI MUS, GROVE 5=v.6
p.675.

AMBREVILLE, Rosa Teresa Gio-
vanna Lodovica d' (later
Mrs. Borosini). Modena,
Jun 27 1698-after 1740,
Vienna?. Soprano. BLOM=p.76,
ENCI MUS, GROVE 5=v.1 p.825.

AMBROSCH, Wilhelmine see
Ambrož, Wilhelmine

AMBROSE, Mrs. (born Mahon).
fl.1770-89. English soprano.
GROVE 5=v.5 p.518, HIGHFILL.

AMBROSINI, Antonia. fl.1754.
Singer. HIGHFILL.

AMBROŽ (Ambrosch), Wilhelmine.
Berlin, 1791-?. Soprano, pianist. GROVE 5.

AMELING, Elly (orig. Elisabeth
Sara Ameling; Mrs. Belder).
Rotterdam, Feb 8 1938- .
Soprano. RIEMANN ERG.

AMES, Marie Mildred. England,
Jun 20 1867-?. Composer.
BROWN BRIT=p.9.

AMICIS (Buonsollazzi), Anna
Lucia de. Naples, c1733-1816,
Naples. Soprano. BLOM, BROWN
BIO, CORTE=p.175, ENCI MUS=
v.2 p.18, ENCI SALVAT, ENCY
MUS, GROVE 1, GROVE 5, MGG
SUP, PRATT, RIEMANN, RIEMANN
ERG, THOMPSON. [Most sources
=b.c1740, which RIEMANN ERG
corrects to c1733]

AMICIS (Buonsollazzi), Rosalba
Baldacci. Atri, Italy, c1716-
?. Singer. ENCI MUS=v.2 p.18.

AMIET, Doris. Zürich, Oct 12
1923- . Soprano. SCHUH=p.418.

AMORETTI, Giustina. fl.1748-49.
Singer. HIGHFILL.

AMPARAN, Belen. El Paso, ?- .
20th-century American contralto. THOMPSON.

AMSTAD, Marietta. Beckenried,
Switzerland, May 31 1892- .
Soprano, voice teacher.
GROVE 5.

AMSTAD, Martha. Beckenried,
Switzerland, Mar 11 1895- .
Soprano, voice teacher.
GROVE 5.

ANASTASI POZZONI, Antonietta.
Venice, 1846-Apr 8 1917,
Genoa. Soprano. ENCI MUS.

ANCELL, Sarah. Buenos Aires,

Aug 4 1896- . Pianist. ENCI
SALVAT, ENCY MUS, THOMPSON.

ANDAY, Rosette. Budapest, Dec
22 1903- . Contralto. ENCI
SALVAT, ENCY MUS, KUTSCH,
RIEMANN, RIEMANN ERG,
THOMPSON, ULLSTEIN.

ANDERSEN, Hildur. Christiania,
Norway, May 25 1864-?.
Pianist. THOMPSON.

ANDERSEN, Lale. Bremerhaven,
Germany, Mar 23 1908- .
Singer. RIEMANN ERG.

ANDERSEN (Anderson), Lucy
(born Philpot). Bath, England, Dec 12? 1790 or 1797-
Dec 24 1878, London. Pia-
nist, piano teacher. BAKER
1, BROWN BIO, BROWN BRIT,
GROVE 1, GROVE 1 APP, GROVE
5, PRATT, THOMPSON.

ANDERSEN, Stell. Linn Grove,
Iowa, Feb 28 1897- . Pia-
nist, piano teacher. BAKER
5, *EWEN LIVING, SANDVED,
THOMPSON.

ANDERSON, Emily. Galway, Ireland, Mar 17 1891-Oct 26
1962, London. Musicologist,
editor, translator. BAKER
1971, BLOM.

ANDERSON, Josephine (born
Bartolozzi). London, 1806-
May 1 1848, London?. Mezzo-
soprano. BROWN BIO, BROWN
BRIT.

ANDERSON LUCAS, Mary see
Lucas, Mary Anderson

ANDERSON, Lucy see Ander-
sen, Lucy

ANDERSON, Marian. Philadelphia, Feb 17 1902- . Con-

tralto. BAKER 5, CORTE, *ENCI
MUS=illus.fac.p.70, ENCI
SALVAT, ENCY MUS, *EWEN LIV-
ING, EWEN LIV SUP, EWEN NEW,
GROVE 5, GROVE 5 SUP, KUTSCH,
MARIZ, RIEMANN, RIEMANN ERG,
SANDVED, THOMPSON, *ULLSTEIN=
illus.p.24. *[EWEN LIVING=b.
1908]*

ANDRADE, Graciela Patiño see
Patiño Andrade, Graciela

ANDRADE, Janine. Besançon,
France, Nov 13 1918- .
Violinist. ENCI SALVAT, ENCY
MUS, RIEMANN.

ANDREA, Clara Natalia see
Mac Farren, Clara Natalia

ANDRÉE, Elfrida. Visby, Sweden,
Feb 19 1841-Jan 11 1929,
Göteborg, Sweden. Organist,
composer, opera composer.
BAKER 5, BLOM, GROVE 5, PRATT,
RIEMANN, RIEMANN ERG, THOMP-
SON. *[Some sources=d. in
Stockholm, which RIEMANN ERG
corrects to Göteborg]*

ANDRÉE, Fredrika see Stenhammar, Fredrika

ANDREIDES, Rosalie see Holzbauer, Rosalie

ANDREINI, Virginia (Mrs. Giovanni Battista, born Ramponi).
Milan, Jan 1 1583-1630, Bologna. Singer, actress. ENCI
MUS, ENCI SALVAT, RIEMANN.

ANDREOLI, Maria. Mirandola,
Modena, Italy, Mar 1 1860-
Dec 3 1927, Modena, Italy.
Pianist, organist. ENCI MUS.

ANDREOLI, Rosa. Mirandola,
Modena, Italy, Apr 13 1843-
Mar 27 1925, Modena, Italy.
Pianist, piano teacher.
ENCI MUS.

ANDREOZZI, Anna (Mrs. Gaetano, born De Santi). Florence, 1772-?. Soprano. ENCI MUS, RIEMANN.

ANDREWS, Miss. fl.1796-98. English singer, actress. HIGHFILL.

ANDREWS, Jenny (Mrs. John Holman, born Constant). London?, 1817-Apr 29 1878, London. Singer, voice teacher, composer. BROWN BRIT.

ANDRIESSEN, Pelagie (later Mrs. von Sthamer, Mrs. Walter Ende, and Mrs. Paul Greef). Vienna, Jun 20 1860 or 1862-1937, Frankfurt. Soprano. BAKER 1=p.564, KUTSCH=p.169, THOMPSON=p.2109.

ANFOSSI, Gioconda see Rinaldi, Gioconda

ANGELELLI, Augusta (stage name of Mrs. Vittorio Correr, born Wynne). fl.1798. Singer. HIGHFILL.

ANGELES, Maria Morales de los. Malaga, Spain, Jan 2 1929- . Soprano. CORTE, ENCI SALVAT= v.3 p.386. [CORTE=b.in Madrid]

ANGELES, Victoria de los see De los Angeles, Victoria

ANGELICA, Mrs. fl.1785. English singer. HIGHFILL.

ANGELICI, Mart(h)a. Cargèse, Corsica, 1916-Sep 1973, Ajaccio, Corsica. Soprano. ENCI SALVAT, ENCY MUS, KUTSCH. [Date and place of death based on obituary in Opera News, Mar 23 1974, p.37]

ANGELO, Signora. fl.1714-15. Singer?. HIGHFILL.

ANGELO, Gianna d'. Hartford, Conn., Nov 18 1934- . Soprano. KUTSCH, RIEMANN ERG, SANDVED, THOMPSON=p.486, *ULLSTEIN. [KUTSCH=b.1928; RIEMANN ERG=b.1929; SANDVED= b.1930]

ANGELO, Pauline Sant see Sant Angelo, Pauline

ANGERER, Margit (real name= Margit von Rupp; also sang under name Angerer-Schenker). Budapest, Nov 6 1902- . Soprano. KUTSCH, MARIZ, THOMPSON. [KUTSCH=b.1903]

ANGERI, Anna d' see D'Angeri, Anna

ANGERMAYER DE REDENBURG, Anna see D'Angeri, Anna

ANGIOLINI, Mme. Turin, ?-?. 18-19th-century Italian dancer. ENCI MUS.

ANGIOLINI, Carolina see Pitrot, Carolina

ANGIOLINI, Fortunata. 18-19th-century Italian dancer. ENCI MUS.

ANGIOLINI, Teresa see Fogliazzi, Teresa

ANGRI, Elena. Corfu, May 14 1824-?. Contralto. ENCI MUS.

ANIDA, María Luisa. Morón, Argentina, 1909- . Guitarist, composer. ARIZAGA.

ANITÚA, Fanny. Durango, Mexico, Jan 22 1887- . Soprano, voice teacher. CELLETTI, ENCI MUS, KUTSCH, RIEMANN ERG.

ANLAUF, Julia see Hamari, Julia

ANNA, Signora. fl.1703. Singer. HIGHFILL.

ANNA AMALIA (Duchess of Saxe-
Weimar). Wolfenbüttel, Ger-
many, Oct 24 1739-Apr 10
1807, Weimar. Composer.
BAKER 1, BAKER 5, DICT MUS,
GROVE 1, GROVE 5, MGG, RIE-
MANN, THOMPSON, ULLSTEIN.
*[GROVE 1=d. Apr 12 1807 in
Brunswick; THOMPSON=d. in
Brunswick]*

ANNA AMALIA (Princess of
Prussia). Berlin, Nov 9
1723-Sep 30 1787, Berlin.
Composer, clavecinist.
BAKER 1, BAKER 5, BAKER 1971,
BLOM, DICT MUS, GROVE 1,
MGG, PRATT, RIEMANN, RIEMANN
ERG, THOMPSON, ULLSTEIN.
*[BAKER 1 & BLOM=d. Mar 30
1787]*

ANSBACH, Elizabeth see
Anspach, Elizabeth

ANSORGE, Margarethe. Halle,
Germany, Dec 14 1872-Oct 4
1944, Berlin. Pianist.
ENCI MUS.

ANSPACH (Ansbach), Elizabeth
(Margravine of). London,
Dec 17 1750-Jan 13 1828,
Naples. Composer, music
amateur. GROVE 5.

ANTIER, Maria. Lyons, c1687-
1747, Paris. Singer. ENCI
SALVAT, ENCY MUS, PRATT,
THOMPSON.

ANTOINE, Josephine. Denver,
Oct 27 1908-Oct 30 1971,
Jamestown, New York. Sopra-
no, voice teacher. BAKER 5,
*EWEN LIVING, MARIZ, SANDVED,
THOMPSON.

ANTONELLI, Pina. 20th-century
American pianist. PAVLAKIS=
p.259.

ANTTI, Aune. Lappeenranta,

Finland, Dec 23 1901- . Soprano. RIEMANN.

ANUNCIATI, Signora. fl.1766-67.
Singer. HIGHFILL.

APPELDOORN, Dina. Rotterdam,
Feb 26 1884-Dec 4 1938, The
Hague. Composer, pianist,
piano teacher. BAKER 5,
THOMPSON.

APPIGNANI, Adelaide see
Aspri, Orsola

ARAMBURO, Ada see Adini, Ada

ARANGI-LOMBARDI, Giannina.
Marigliano, nr. Naples,
Jun 20 1891-Jul 9 1951, Milan.
Contralto, soprano, voice
teacher. CELLETTI, *ENCI MUS=
illus. v.3 fac. p.311, KUTSCH.
[KUTSCH=b.1890, d.Jul 6 1951]

ARÁNYI, Adila d' see Fachiri,
Adila

ARÁNYI, Jelly (Yelly) d'.
Budapest, May 30 1893-Mar 30
1966, Florence. Violinist.
BAKER 5, BAKER 1971, ENCI
MUS=v.2 p.159 (brief mention
in article on Adila Fachiri),
ENCI SALVAT, *EWEN LIVING,
GROVE 5, GROVE 5 SUP, MARIZ=
p.64, PALMER=p.74, RIEMANN,
RIEMANN ERG, THOMPSON. *[Most
sources=b.1895, which RIEMANN
ERG corrects to 1893]*

ARAUJO, Gina de. Rio de Janeiro,
1890- . Composer, singer.
ENCI MUS, GROVE 5, MARIZ.

ARBLAY, Frances d' (Fanny).
King's Lynn, England, Jun 13
1752-Jan 6 1840, London.
Editor. ENCI MUS=v.1 p.344
(brief mention in article on
father, Charles Burney).

ARCADA, Ermelinda Talea Pas-

torella see Maria Antonia
Walpurgis

ARCHER, Violet Balestreri.
Montreal, Apr 24 1913- .
Pianist, composer, teacher.
BAKER 1971, CBC, NAPIER,
VINTON.

ARCHILEI, Vittoria (born Con-
carini, called "La Romani-
na"). Rome, 1550-1618, Rome.
Singer, dancer, lutenist.
ENCI MUS, ENCI SALVAT, ENCY
MUS, MGG SUP.

ARCHIPOVA, Irina. Sverdlovsk,
USSR, 1929- . Contralto.
KUTSCH.

ARCO, Annie d'. Marseilles,
1920- . Pianist. ENCI SAL-
VAT, ENCY MUS.

ARETZ DE RAMÓN Y RIVERA
(Aretz-Thiele), Isabelle.
Buenos Aires, Apr 13 1909- .
Pianist, musicologist, com-
poser, ethnomusicologist.
ARIZAGA, ENCI SALVAT, ENCY
MUS, GROVE 5, MGG SUP, RIE-
MANN ERG, SLONIMSKY.

ARGENTINA, LA (pseud. for
Antonia Mercé). Buenos
Aires, Sep 4 1890-Jul 18
1936, Bayonne. Dancer,
choreographer. *ENCI SALVAT=
v.3 p.324, RIEMANN, RIEMANN
ERG.

ARGERICH, Martha. Buenos
Aires, Jun 5 1941- . Pia-
nist. ARIZAGA, RIEMANN ERG.

ARGILAGÓ, Rosita Mauri see
Mauri Argilagó, Rosita

ARIZTI, Cecilia. Loma del
Angel, Cuba, Oct 28 1836-
Jun 30 1930, Havana. Compo-
ser, teacher. RIEMANN ERG.

ARKEL, Teresa. Lemberg, Aus-

tria, 1861-?. Soprano, voice
teacher. KUTSCH.

ARKWRIGHT, Marian Ursula.
Norwich, England, Jan 25
1853-Mar 23 1922, Highclere,
nr. Newbury, England. Composer. GROVE 5, MGG SUP, THOMP-
SON.

ARKWRIGHT, Mrs. Robert. ?-1849,
England?. Actress, composer,
song-writer. BROWN BIO,
BROWN BRIT.

ARMAGANIAN, Lucine see
Amara, Lucine

ARMHOLD, Adelheid. Hamburg,
1902- . Soprano. THOMPSON.

ARMITT, Mary Louisa. Salford,
England, Sep 24 1851-?.
Writer. BROWN BRIT.

ARMSTRONG, Helen Porter see
Melba, Nellie

ARMSTRONG, Karen. 20th-century
American soprano. PAVLAKIS=
p.285.

ARNAUD, (Germaine) Yvonne.
Bordeaux, Dec 20 1890-Sep 20
1958, London. Pianist, actress. GROVE 5, GROVE 5 SUP.

ARNDT-OBER, Margaret see
Ober, Margaret Arndt

ARNE, Ann (Mrs. Michael III,
born Venables). fl.1772-1820.
English singer. ENCI MUS,
HIGHFILL.

ARNE, Cecilia (Mrs. Thomas
Augustine, born Young). Lon-
don, 1711-Oct 6 1789, London.
Soprano. BAKER 5=p.1830,
BLOM=p.785, BROWN BRIT, ENCI
MUS=v.4 p.599, GROVE 5=v.9
p.383, HIGHFILL.

ARNE, Elizabeth (Mrs. Michael

II, born Wright). London?,
1751 or 1752-May 1 1769?,
Bristol, England. Soprano.
BROWN BRIT, HIGHFILL.
[BROWN BRIT=b.c1743]

ARNE, Susanna Maria see
Cibber, Susanna Maria

ARNHEIM, Amalie. Berlin, Dec
29 1863-May 26 1917, Berlin.
Musicologist, writer. RIE-
MANN.

ARNIM, Bettina von see
Brentano, Bettina

ARNOLD, Elizabeth see also
Clendining, Elizabeth

ARNOLD, Elizabeth (Mrs. Henry,
later Mrs. Charles Tubbs,
born Smith). fl.1784-99.
English actress, singer.
HIGHFILL.

ARNOLD, Irmgard. Lippe, Bavaria, ?- . 20th-century
soprano. RIEMANN ERG.

ARNOLD, Josephina Huguet de
see Huguet de Arnold,
Josephina

ARNOLD, Mary Sophia see
Bailey, Mary Sophia

ARNOLDSON, Sigrid. Stockholm,
Mar 20 1861-Feb 7 1943,
Stockholm. Soprano, voice
teacher. BAKER 1, BLOM,
CELLETTI, GROVE 5, GROVE 5
SUP, KUTSCH, PRATT, RIE-
MANN, RIEMANN ERG, THOMP-
SON, ULLSTEIN. *[BAKER 1=*
b.c1865; KUTSCH=d.Feb 2]

ARNOULD, Madeline Sophie.
Paris, Feb 13 1740-Oct 22
1802, Paris. Soprano.
BAKER 5, BROWN BIO, CLAY-
TON=p.80, DICT MUS, ENCI
MUS, ENCI SALVAT, ENCY MUS,

EWEN NEW, GROVE 1, GROVE 5,
MGG SUP, PRATT, RIEMANN, RIE-
MANN ERG, THOMPSON, ULLSTEIN.

ARRAL, Blanche. Liège, 1865-
1945, New York City. Soprano.
KUTSCH.

ARRIEU, Claude. Paris, Nov 30
1903- . Composer, light-opera
composer, pianist. BAKER 1971.

ARROYO, Martina. New York City,
Feb 2 1940- . Soprano. BAKER
1971, EWEN NEW, PAVLAKIS=p.
285, RIEMANN ERG, ULLSTEIN.
[ULLSTEIN=b.1936]

ARTHUR, Fanny see Robinson,
Fanny

ARTHUR, Grace (Mrs. John II,
later Mrs. Daniel Williams,
born Read). fl.1760-74.
English actress, singer.
HIGHFILL.

ARTNER, Josephine von. Prague,
Nov 10 1867-Sep 7 1932, Leip-
zig. Soprano, voice teacher.
KUTSCH.

ARTÔT, Marguerite-Joséphine-
Desirée (born Montagney).
Paris, Jul 21 1835-Apr 3
1907, Berlin. Mezzo-soprano,
voice teacher. BAKER 1,
BAKER 5, BLOM, BROWN BIO,
DICT MUS, ENCI MUS, ENCY
MUS, EWEN NEW, GROVE 5,
PRATT, RIEMANN, RIEMANN ERG,
THOMPSON, ULLSTEIN. *[Some*
sources=d. in Vienna, which
RIEMANN ERG considers in-
correct]

ARTÔT DE PADILLA, Lola. Sèvres,
nr. Paris, Oct 5 1876-Apr 12
1933, Berlin. Soprano, voice
teacher. BAKER 1=p.1196,
CORTE=p.452, ENCI MUS, KUTSCH,
PRATT=p.632, RIEMANN, RIEMANN
ERG, THOMPSON=p.1563, *ULL-

STEIN. *[Some sources=b.1885, which RIEMANN ERG considers incorrect]*

ASCHIERI, Caterina, "la Romanina." Rome, c1710-?. Singer. ENCI MUS.

ASHKENASI, Catherine see Gayer, Catherine

ASHTON, Diana Uvedale. Durham, England, Oct 21 1840-Dec 21 1873, New York City. Pianist?. BROWN BRIT.

ASHTON, Gertrude Cave- (born Holman Andrews). London, Apr 17 1855-?. Soprano. BROWN BIO=p.151, BROWN BRIT.

ASOW, Hedwig Müller von see Müller von Asow, Hedwig

ASPERI, Orsola see Aspri, Orsola

ASPRI (Asperi), Orsola (stage name of Adelaide Appignani). Rome, c1807-Sep 30 1884, Rome. Composer, singer, conductor. ENCI MUS.

ASSANDRA, Caterina. 16-17th-century Italian composer. MGG SUP.

ASTRUA, Giovanna. Graglia, Vercelli, Italy, c1720-Oct 28 1757, Turin. Soprano. BROWN BIO, ENCI MUS. *[BROWN BIO=1725-1758]*

ASTRUC, Yvonne. Asnieres, France, 1889- . Violinist. ENCI SALVAT, ENCY MUS.

ATHERTON, Miss. fl.1732-44. English dancer, singer, actress. HIGHFILL.

ATKINS, Eliza (Mrs. William, later Mrs. Hill, born Warrell). fl.1787-1808. Singer, actress. *HIGHFILL.

ATTWOOD, Miss. fl.1794. English harpsichordist. HIGHFILL.

ATTWOOD, Martha (Mrs. G. R. Baker). Wellfleet, Cape Cod, Mass., 1887?-Apr 6 1950, Eastham, Mass. Soprano. THOMPSON.

AUBERT, Isabella. fl.1715-20. Singer. HIGHFILL.

AUBERT, Pauline. Paris, 1894- . Clavecinist. ENCI SALVAT, ENCY MUS.

AUBERVAL, Mme. Jean d' see D'Auberval, Mme. Jean

AUBIGNY, Madame d' see Maupin, Madame

AUDINOT, Mlle. 18th-century French singer. ENCI MUS.

AUERBACH, Cornelia see Schröder, Cornelia

AUERBACH, Nanette (born Falk). Danzig, Poland, c1838-after 1917, ?. Pianist, voice teacher. PRATT, THOMPSON.

AUERNHAMMER, Josepha Barbara von (really Bessenig). Vienna, Sep 25 1758-Jan 30 1820, Vienna. Composer. MGG SUP.

AULIN, Laura Valborg. Gävle, Sweden, Jan 9 1860-Jan 11 1928, Örebro, Sweden. Pianist, composer. ENCI MUS, GROVE 5.

AUS DER OHE, Adele. Hanover, Dec 11 1864-Dec 7 1937, Berlin. Pianist, composer. *BAKER 1=p.649, BAKER 5, MARIZ=p.170, PRATT, THOMPSON.

AUSTEN, Augusta Amherst (Mrs. T. Anstey Guthrie). London, Aug 2 1827-Aug 5 1877, Glasgow. Composer, organist. BROWN BRIT.

AUSTER, Lidia Martinowna. Petropawlowsk, Kasachstan, Russia, May 17 or May 30 1912- . Composer. RIEMANN ERG.

AUSTIN, Miss. fl.1794. English pianist. HIGHFILL.

AUSTIN, Florence. Galesburg, Mich., Mar 11 1884-Aug 1926, Fairchild, Wis. Violinist, violin teacher. BAKER 5, THOMPSON.

AUSTIN, Leily (Mrs. Richard, born Howell). 20th-century English violoncellist. GROVE 5.

AUSTRAL, Florence Mary (Mrs. Amadio, born Wilson). Richmond, nr. Melbourne, Australia, Apr 26 1892-May 15 1968, Newcastle, N.S.W. Soprano, voice teacher. BAKER 5, BAKER 1971, BLOM, COOPER, *EWEN LIVING, EWEN LIV SUP, EWEN NEW, GROVE 5, GROVE 5 SUP, KUTSCH, MARIZ, RIEMANN, RIEMANN ERG, THOMPSON. *[Some sources=b.1894, which RIEMANN ERG corrects to 1892]*

AVELLONI, Margherita see Durastanti, Margherita

AVERINO, Olga. Moscow, Nov 15 1895- . Soprano. THOMPSON.

AVOGLIO (Avolio), Christina Maria. fl.1740-44. Singer. BLOM, GROVE 1, HIGHFILL, THOMPSON.

AXENFELD, Edith Picht- see

Picht-Axenfeld, Edith

AXTENS, Florence E. London, ?- . 20th-century English composer. THOMPSON.

AYLIFF, Mrs. fl.1690-97. English singer, actress. HIGHFILL.

AYLWARD, Amy. fl.1880. English soprano. BROWN BRIT.

AYLWARD, Gertrude. 19th-century English soprano. BROWN BRIT.

AYLWARD, Janetta. England?, 1837?-Jun 7 1853, London?. Pianist. BROWN BRIT.

AYLWARD, Leila J. 19th-century English pianist, contralto. BROWN BRIT.

AYRES, Cecile see Horvath, Cecile

AYTON, Fanny. Macclesfield, England, 1806-after 1832, England?. Soprano. BROWN BRIT, GROVE 1, GROVE 5, THOMPSON.

B

BABAÏAN, Marguerite. Gotha, Germany, 1884- . Folklorist, singer, writer. ENCI SALVAT, ENCY MUS.

BABBI, Giovanna. fl.1739. Italian singer. ENCI MUS.

BABBI, Giovanna. fl.1797. Italian singer. ENCI MUS.

BABER, Miss Colbourne (Mrs. Harrison White). 19-20th-century English soprano. BROWN BRIT.

BABIN, Vitya see Vronsky, Vitya

BACCARA, Luisa. Venice, Jan 14
1894- . Pianist. ENCI MUS.

BACCHELLI, Signora see
Corri, Signora Domenico

BACCOLINI, Bruna see
Castagna, Bruna

BACEWICZ (Bacevičius), Graz-
yna. Łódź, Poland, May 5
1913-Jan 17 1969, Warsaw.
Composer, violinist, tea-
cher. BAKER 5, BAKER 1971,
BLOM, DICT MUS, ENCI MUS,
ENCI SALVAT, ENCY MUS,
GROVE 5, MGG SUP, RIEMANN,
RIEMANN ERG, THOMPSON,
VINTON. [Some sources=b.
May 5 1909, others Feb 5
1909; RIEMANN ERG corrects
these to May 5 1913]

BACH, Maria. Vienna, Mar 11
1896- . Composer. ULLSTEIN.

BACH, Maria Barbara. Gehren,
Germany, Oct 20 1684-Jul 7
1720, Köthen, Germany.
Musician. BLOM, ENCI MUS,
ENCI SALVAT, ENCY MUS,
ULLSTEIN.

BACHAUER, Gina. Athens, May
21 1913- . Pianist. BAKER 5,
ENCI SALVAT, ENCY MUS, *EWEN
LIV SUP, GROVE 5, RIEMANN,
RIEMANN ERG, *SANDVED,
THOMPSON.

BACHE, Constance. Birmingham,
England, Mar 11 1846-Jun 28
1903, Montreux, Switzerland.
Pianist, writer, translator,
teacher. BAKER 1=p.649,
BAKER 5, BROWN BRIT, GROVE
5, PRATT, SCHOLES, THOMPSON.

BACHMANN, Charlotte Karoline
Wilhelmine (born Stöwe).
Berlin, Nov 2 1757-Aug 19
1817, Berlin. Pianist,
singer, composer. BAKER 1,

GROVE 5.

BACHMANN, Karoline Günther-
see Günther-Bachmann,
Karoline

BACKER-GRØNDAHL, Agathe
Ursula. Holmestrand, Norway,
Dec 1 1847-Jun 4 1907, Or-
möen, nr. Oslo. Composer,
pianist. BAKER 1, BAKER 5,
BLOM, GROVE 5, GROVE 5 SUP,
PRATT, RIEMANN, SCHOLES,
THOMPSON. [RIEMANN=d.Jun
16 1907]

BACON, Katherine (Mrs. Arthur
Newstead). Chesterfield,
England, Jun 2 1896- . Pia-
nist, piano teacher. *EWEN
LIVING, THOMPSON.

BACON, Louisa Mary. Norwich,
England, Mar 4 1800-Feb 2
1885, ?. Musician. BROWN
BRIT=p.21 (in article on
father, Richard Mackenzie
Bacon).

BADARZEWSKA-BARANOWSKA, Tekla.
Warsaw, 1834-Sep 29 1861,
Warsaw. Composer. BAKER 1,
BAKER 5, BAKER 1971, BROWN
BIO, ENCI SALVAT, GROVE 5,
MGG SUP, RIEMANN, RIEMANN
ERG, SCHOLES, THOMPSON.
[Some sources=b.1838, which
RIEMANN ERG corrects to 1834]

BADDELEY, Sophia (Mrs. Robert,
born Snow). Westminster,
England, 1745?-Jul 1 1786,
Edinburgh. Actress, singer.
*HIGHFILL.

BADIA, Anna Maria Lisi see
Lisi, Anna Maria

BADIA, Anna Maria Sofia see
Novelli, Anna Maria Sofia

BADINGS, Olly Folge see
Fonden, Olly Folge

BADINI, Signora. fl.1792.
Italian singer. HIGHFILL.

BADURA-SKODA, Eva (Mrs. Paul,
born Halfar). Munich, Jan
15 1929- . Musicologist,
pianist, writer. ENCI MUS,
RIEMANN ERG.

BAER, Kathi Meyer- see
Meyer-Baer, Kathi

BÄUMER, Margaret. ?, May 26
1898-Dec 1969, Inning, Germany. Soprano, voice tea-
cher. KUTSCH.

BAGDASARJANZ, Ursula. Winterthur, Switzerland, Jun 30
1934- . Violinist. SCHUH.

BAGDASARJANZ-WEISS, Margrit.
?, Feb 19 1905- . Violinist.
SCHUH.

BAGLIONI, Camilla. 18th-cen-
tury Italian singer. ENCI
MUS=v.1 p.443 (brief men-
tion in article on the
Cavos family).

BAGLIONI, Clementina. 18th-
century Italian singer.
ENCI MUS.

BAGLIONI, Costanza. 18th-cen-
tury Italian singer. ENCI
MUS.

BAGLIONI, Giovanna. 18th-cen-
tury Italian singer. ENCI
MUS.

BAGLIONI, Rosina. 18th-cen-
tury Italian singer. ENCI
MUS.

BAGLIONI, Vincenza. 18th-cen-
tury Italian singer. ENCI
MUS.

BAGNOLESI, Anna (stage name
of Signora Giovanni Battista

Pinacci). fl.1731-32. Contralto. GROVE 1, HIGHFILL.

BAHR-MILDENBURG, Anna (born von
Mildenburg). Vienna, Nov 29
1872-Jan 27 1947, Vienna. So-
prano, voice teacher, writer.
BAKER 5=p.1089, BLOM, CELLET-
TI, COOPER, CORTE, ENCI MUS,
EWEN NEW, GROVE 5, GROVE 5
SUP, KUTSCH, MARIZ=p.155,
MGG=v.9 col.294, PRATT=p.588,
RIEMANN=v.2 p.221, THOMPSON=
p.1353, ULLSTEIN. *[CELLETTI=
d.Feb 3 1947; ENCI MUS=
mezzo-soprano]*

BAILEY, Lilian June see
Henschel, Lilian June   .

BAILEY, Mary Sophia (Mrs.
William, stage name of Mrs.
William O'Reilly, born
Arnold). fl.1778-82. Actress,
singer. HIGHFILL=p.214-15
(in article on husband
William Bailey).

BAILEY APFELBECK, Marie Louise.
Nashville, Tenn., Oct 24
1873-Jan 12 1927, Minneapolis. Pianist. BAKER 1, PRATT,
RIEMANN, RIEMANN ERG. *[Some
sources=b.1876, which RIEMANN
ERG corrects to 1873]*

BAILLIE, Isobel. Hawick, Rox-
burghshire, Scotland, Mar 9
1895- . Soprano. GROVE 5,
GROVE 5 SUP, PALMER, THOMP-
SON.

BAINI, Cecilia. fl.1763-64.
English singer. HIGHFILL.

BAIRD, Martha (later Mrs. John
D. Rockefeller, Jr.). Madera,
Calif., Mar 15 1895-Jan 24
1971, New York City. Pianist,
patron. BAKER 1971, THOMPSON.
[BAKER 1971 & THOMPSON=b.1898]

BAKER, Mrs. ?-Oct 10 1760?, Co-

ventry, England. Singer,
actress, dancer. HIGHFILL.

BAKER, Miss?. fl.1766-67.
English singer. HIGHFILL.

BAKER, Elizabeth (Mrs. Thomas,
born Miller). fl.1761-92.
English actress, singer,
dancer. HIGHFILL.

BAKER, Mrs. J. S. fl.1785-1800.
English actress, singer,
dancer. HIGHFILL=v.1 p.224.

BAKER, Janet Abbott. Hatfield,
Yorkshire, England, Aug 21
1933- . Mezzo-soprano.
BAKER 1971, BLOM, KUTSCH,
RIEMANN ERG.

BAKER, Martha see Attwood,
Martha

BALBI, Rosina. fl.1748-60.
English dancer, court
musician. HIGHFILL.

BALCELLS, Rosa. Barcelona,
1914- . Harpist. ENCI
SALVAT.

BALDACCI, Rosalba see
Amicis, Rosalba Baldacci

BALDANZA, Romana. Tropea,
Italy, ?- . 20th-century
Italian soprano, voice
teacher. THOMPSON.

BALDASSARE-TEDESCHI, Giuseppina. Trani, nr. Bari,
Italy, Oct 28 1881- . So-
prano, voice teacher. ENCI
MUS, KUTSCH.

BALDUCCI, Maria (stage name of
Maria Bertaldi). Genoa,
1758-?. Soprano. ENCI MUS.

BALDWIN, Marcia. 20th-century
American mezzo-soprano.
PAVLAKIS=p.293.

BALDWIN, Mary. fl.1703-06.
English singer. HIGHFILL.

BALESTRI, Itala see Del
Corona, Itala

BALFE, Lina (Mrs. Michael
William, born Rosa). Hungary,
1806-Jun 11 1888, London.
Soprano. BAKER 5, BROWN BRIT,
ENCI MUS.

BALFE, Victoire (Duchesse de
Frias). Paris, Sep 1 1837-
Jan 22 1871, Madrid. Soprano.
BROWN BRIT.

BALFOUR, Margaret. 20th-century
English contralto. THOMPSON.

BALGUERIÈ, Suzanne Madeleine.
Le Havre, 1888-Feb 1973,
Grenoble. Soprano. ENCI
SALVAT, ENCY MUS, GROVE 5.

BALL, Mrs. fl.1789. English
singer. HIGHFILL.

BALLEK, Daniela. Troppau,
Czechoslovakia, May 29 1931-
. Pianist. RIEMANN ERG.

BALLOU, Esther Williamson.
Elmira, New York, Jul 17
1915-Mar 1973, ?. Composer,
teacher. BAKER 1971, PAV-
LAKIS=p.320 & 750.

BALLS, Eliza. 19th-century
music engraver, seller, and
publisher. GROVE 5.

BALMER, Lucie see Dikenmann-
Balmer, Lucie

BALY, Adelaide C. see Byrn,
Adelaide C.

BAMBERGER, Johanna see
Hitzelberger, Johanna

BAMBRIDGE, Mrs. fl.1757-67.
English dancer. HIGHFILL.

BAMPTON, Rose E. (Mrs. Wilfred Pelletier). Cleveland, Nov 28 1909- . Soprano, at first contralto. BAKER 5, ENCI SALVAT, ENCY MUS, *EWEN LIVING, EWEN LIV SUP, EWEN NEW, GROVE 5, GROVE 5 SUP, KUTSCH, MARIZ, RIEMANN, RIEMANN ERG, *SANDVED, THOMPSON.

BANDIERA, Anna. fl.1756. Singer. HIGHFILL.

BANDIN, Sofía. Argentine soprano. ENCI SALVAT.

BANDROWSKA-TURSKA, Ewa. Cracow, Poland, May 20 1899- . Soprano, voice teacher. GROVE 5, RIEMANN, RIEMANN ERG.

BANG, Maia (Mrs. Baronin Hohn). Tromsö, Norway, Apr 24 1879-Jan 3 1940, New York City. Teacher, violinist. BAKER 5, MARIZ, RIEMANN. *[MARIZ= b.in Bergen]*

BANTI, Signora. fl.1756-58. Dancer. HIGHFILL.

BANTI, Brigitta (Mrs. Zaccaria, born Giorgi). Crema, Italy, 1759-Feb 18 1806, Bologna. Soprano. BAKER 1, BAKER 5, BLOM, BROWN BIO, CORTE, ENCI MUS, ENCI SALVAT, GROVE 1, GROVE 5, GROVE 5 SUP, *HIGHFILL, PRATT, THOMPSON. *[BAKER 5, CORTE, GROVE 5, & HIGHFILL= b.in Monticelli d'Ongina, Italy]*

BANTI, Felicità. fl.1777-88. Dancer. HIGHFILL.

BARABAS, Sari. Budapest, Mar 14 1920- . Soprano. KUTSCH, RIEMANN ERG. *[KUTSCH=b.1918]*

BARATTA, María de. San Salva-dor, Feb 27 1894- . Composer, folklorist. RIEMANN ERG, *SLONIMSKY=illus.fac.p.281.

BARBANY, María Rosa. Granollers, Barcelona, Aug 30 1928- . Soprano. ENCI SALVAT.

"BARBARINA, La" see Campanini, Barbarina

BARBATO, Elisabetta. Barletta, nr.Bari, Italy, Sep 11 1921- . Soprano. ENCI MUS, KUTSCH.

BARBERIIS, Lya de see De Barberiis, Lya

BARBI, Alice. Modena, Jun 1 1862-Sep 4 1948, Rome. Mezzo-soprano. BAKER 5, BLOM, CORTE, ENCI MUS, GROVE 5, GROVE 5 SUP, PRATT, THOMPSON.

BARBIER, Jane. London?, 169?-1757, London?. Singer. HIGHFILL.

BARBIERI, Fedora. Trieste, Jun 4 1920- . Mezzo-soprano. CELLETTI, COOPER, CORTE, ENCI MUS, *EWEN LIV SUP, EWEN NEW, GROVE 5, KUTSCH, RIEMANN ERG, *ROSENTHAL=illus. p.12, *SANDVED, *ULLSTEIN.

BARBIERI-NINI, Marianna. Florence, c1820-Nov 27 1887, Florence. Soprano. ENCI MUS.

BARBIROLLI, Evelyn (Mrs. John, born Rothwell). 20th-century English oboist. ENCI MUS, RIEMANN.

BARBLAN-OPIENSKA, Lydia. Morges, Vaud, Switzerland, Apr 12 1890- . Composer, writer. RIEMANN, RIEMANN ERG, SCHUH.

BARBOUR, Florence Newell. Providence, R.I., Aug 4 1866-Jul 24 1946, Providence, R.I.

Composer, pianist. BAKER 5,
THOMPSON.

BARCAVELLE, Mrs.?. fl.1786.
Dancer?. HIGHFILL.

BARDA, Camilla see Mandl,
Camilla

BARENTZEN, Aline van see
Van Barentzen, Aline

BARFOOT, Mrs. see Bates,
Miss

BARILLI, Marianna Bondini.
Dresden, Oct 18 1780-Oct 25
1813, Paris. Soprano.
ENCI MUS.

BARKER, Laura W. see Taylor,
Laura W.

BARLOW, Catherine see
Hamilton, Catherine

BARLOW, Klara. 20th-century
American soprano. PAVLAKIS=
p.285.

BARNARD, Charlotte (Mrs.
Charles, born Alington;
"Claribel"). ?, Dec 23 1830-
Jan 30 1869, Dover, England.
Composer, poet. BAKER 1,
BAKER 5, BROWN BIO, BROWN
BRIT, GROVE 1 APP, GROVE 5,
PRATT, THOMPSON.

BARNES, Miss. fl.1781-82.
English actress, singer,
dancer. HIGHFILL.

BARNES, Philippa. Holmer
Green, Bucks, England, Nov
5 1931- . Pianist. PALMER.

BARNET, Mrs.; possibly Cathe-
rine Barnett, q.v. fl.1795.
English actress, singer.
HIGHFILL.

BARNETT, Alice. Lewiston, Ill.,

May 26 1886- . Composer.
BAKER 5.

BARNETT, Alice (Mrs. Dickons
or Dickens). 19th-century
English contralto. BROWN
BRIT=p.324 (in article on
sister Fanny Kemble Poole).

BARNETT, Catherine (possibly
Mrs. Barnet, q.v.). fl.1786-
1800. English actress, singer. HIGHFILL.

BARNETT, Clara Kathleen see
Rogers, Clara Kathleen

BARNETT, Emma. 19th-century
English pianist, composer.
BROWN BRIT.

BARNETT, Fanny Kemble see
Poole, Fanny Kemble

BARNI, Contessa see Grisi,
Giuditta

BARNS, Ethel. London, 1880-
Dec 31 1948, Maidenhead,
England. Composer, violinist.
BAKER 5, ENCI SALVAT, ENCY
MUS, GROVE 5, RIEMANN,
THOMPSON.

BARON SUPERVIELLE, Susana.
Buenos Aires, 1910- . Composer. ARIZAGA.

"BARONESS, THE" see Lindelheim, Joanna Maria

BARONI (or Basile-Baroni),
Andriana (Åndreana), "la
belle Adriana." Posillipo,
Italy, c1580-1640, Rome.
Contralto. ENCI MUS=v.1
p.199, ENCI SALVAT, GROVE 5,
THOMPSON.

BARONI (or Basile-Baroni),
Caterina. Mantua, after 1620-
?. Singer, harpist, poet.
ENCI MUS=v.1 p.199, ENCI MUS,
GROVE 5, THOMPSON.

BARONI (or Basile-Baroni),
Eleanora (Leonora), "l'Ad-
rianetta." Mantua, Dec 1611-
Apr 1670, Rome. Singer,
theorbist, viola da gambist.
CORTE, ENCI MUS=v.1 p.199,
ENCI SALVAT, GROVE 5, THOMP-
SON.

BARONI-CAVALCABO, Julie. Vienna, 1805-?. Pianist, com-
poser. BROWN BIO.

BAROWBY, Miss. fl.1766.
Actress, dancer. HIGHFILL.

BARRAINE, Jacqueline Elsa.
Paris, Feb 13 1910- .
Composer, opera composer,
motion-picture composer.
BAKER 5, BLOM, CORTE, DICT
MUS, ENCI MUS, ENCI SALVAT,
ENCY MUS, GROVE 5, MGG SUP,
RIEMANN, RIEMANN ERG,
THOMPSON, ULLSTEIN.

BARRÉ, Mlle. fl.1795-96.
Dancer. HIGHFILL.

BARRE, Anna la see La Barre,
Anne

BARRE (Barrett), Catherine?
(Mrs. Joseph?, born Groce).
fl.1768-97. Actress, singer.
HIGHFILL.

BARRERA, Giulia. Brooklyn,
?- . 20th-century soprano.
PAVLAKIS=p.285.

BARRETT, Miss. fl.1776. English actress or singer.
HIGHFILL.

BARRETT, Mrs. fl.1790-1816.
English actress, dancer,
singer. HIGHFILL.

BARRETT, Catherine see
Barre, Catherine

BARRETT, Georgiana Ansell see
Weiss, Georgiana

BARRIENTOS, María. Barcelona,
Mar 10 1884-Aug 8 1946, Ci-
boure, nr.St.-Jean-de-Luz,
France. Soprano. BAKER 1,
BAKER 5, CELLETTI, CORTE,
*ENCI MUS=illus.fac.p.191,
*ENCI SALVAT=another illus.
v.3 p.347, ENCY MUS, GROVE 5,
KUTSCH, MARIZ, MGG SUP, PRATT,
RIEMANN, SANDVED, THOMPSON.

BARRISFORD, Mary see Bulkley,
Mary

BARRO, Mathilde. 19th-century
German singer. ENCI MUS=v.2
p.519 (brief mention in
article on son Heinrich
Kaminski).

BARSANTI, Jane (later Mrs. John
Richard Kirwan Lyster, later
Mrs. Richard Daly, sometime
stage name=Mrs. Lisley).
?-1795, ?. English actress,
singer. *HIGHFILL.

BARSOVA, Valeria Vladimirovna.
Astrakhan, Russia, Jun 13
1892-Nov 1967, Sochi, Russia.
Soprano, voice teacher.
KUTSCH. *[KUTSCH=b.in Sochi,*
d.Dec 15 1967]

BARSTOW, Vera. Celina, Ohio,
Jun 3 1891-Jun 10 1975, Long
Beach, Calif. Violinist,
teacher. BAKER 5, BAKER 1971,
PRATT, THOMPSON. *[PRATT=b.*
1893. Death date based on
obituary in Los Angeles Times,
Jun 12 1975, pt.IV, p.31]

BARTELMAN, Mrs. fl.1767. Singer.
HIGHFILL.

BARTH, Anna Maria Wilhelmine
see Hasselt-Barth, Anna
Maria Wilhelmine

BARTHÉLEMON, Cecilia Maria
(later Mrs. Henslowe). ?,
1770?-?. Singer, harpsichordist, harpist. HIGHFILL.

BARTHÉLEMON, Polly (or Mary)
see Young, Polly

BARTHOLOMEW, Ann Sheppard
see Mounsey, Ann Sheppard

BARTLETT, Ethel (Mrs. Rae
Robertson). London, Jun 6
1900- . Pianist, harpsichord-
dist, piano teacher. BAKER
5, COOPER, ENCI SALVAT, ENCY
MUS, *EWEN LIVING, GROVE 5,
PALMER, RIEMANN, SANDVED,
THOMPSON. [EWEN LIVING=b.
1901]

BARTOLOMASI, Valentina. Milan,
1889-1932, Milan. Soprano.
KUTSCH.

BARTOLOZZI, Josephine see
Anderson, Josephine

BARTOLOZZI, Lucia Elizabeth
see Vestris, Lucia Eliza-
beth

BASABILBASO DE CATELIN, Henriette. 20th-century Argentine soprano. THOMPSON.

BASILE BARONI, Andriana see
Baroni, Andriana

BASILE BARONI, Caterina see
Baroni, Caterina

BASILE BARONI, Eleanora see
Baroni, Eleanora

BASILIER-MAGELSSEN, Ida. Pidis-
järvi, now Nivala, Finland,
Sep 10 1846-May 23 1928,
Hegra, Norway. Soprano.
GROVE 5.

BASSAN, Miss. fl.1773-80.
Dancer. HIGHFILL.

BASSETT, Karolyn Wells. Derby,
Conn., Aug 2 1892-Jun 8 1931,
New York City. Soprano, com-
poser. THOMPSON.

BASSI, Carolina (born Manna).
Naples, Jan 10 1781-Dec 12
1862, Cremona. Contralto.
CORTE, ENCI MUS.

BASSINI, Rita Gabussi de see
De Begnis, Rita

"BASTARDELLA, LA" see
Agujari, Lucrezia

"BASTARDINA, LA" see
Agujari, Lucrezia

BASTER, Eleanor (Mrs. John,
born Green). fl.1799-1809.
English actress, singer.
HIGHFILL.

BASTON, Miss. fl.1732-35.
English dancer, harpsichord-
dist. HIGHFILL.

BATCHELOR, Miss. fl.1750-54.
English dancer. HIGHFILL.

BATE, Mrs. J. D. fl.1886.
English tune-book compiler.
BROWN BRIT.

BATEMAN, Mary? (Mrs., born
Humphry?). ?, 1765?-1829, ?.
English actress, singer.
HIGHFILL.

BATES, Miss (later Mrs. Barfoot). fl.1793-1820. English
dancer, singer. HIGHFILL.

BATES, Mary see Dibdin, Mary

BATES, Mona. Burlington, nr.
Hamilton, Ontario, Canada,
c1895- . Pianist, piano
teacher. THOMPSON.

BATES, Sarah (Mrs. Joah, born
Harrop). Lancashire, England,
c1756-Dec 11 1811, London.
Soprano, actress. BROWN BIO=
p.304, BROWN BRIT=p.185,
GROVE 5, *HIGHFILL.

BATH, Maid of see Linley, Eliza Ann

BATHORI, Jane (orig. Jeanne-Marie Berthier; Mrs. Pierre Émile Engel). Paris, Jun 14 1877-Jan 21 1970, Paris. Soprano, voice teacher. BAKER 1971, DICT MUS, ENCI MUS=v.2 p.130, ENCI SALVAT, ENCY MUS, GROVE 5, KUTSCH, RIEMANN ERG.

BATTISHILL, Elizabeth see Davies, Elizabeth

BAU BONAPLATA, Carmen. Barcelona, 1890- . Soprano. ENCI SALVAT.

BAUCARDÉ, Augusta see Albertini-Baucardé, Augusta

BAUER, Emilie Frances. Walla Walla, Wash., Mar 5 1865-Mar 9 1926, New York City. Composer, critic, pianist, piano teacher, editor. THOMPSON.

BAUER, Marion Eugenie. Walla Walla, Wash., Aug 15 1887-Aug 9 1955, South Hadley, Mass. Composer, writer, teacher, musicologist. BAKER 5, ENCY MUS, GROVE 5, GROVE 5 SUP, REIS, SANDVED, THOMPSON.

BAUERMEISTER, Mathilde. Hamburg, 1849-Oct 15 1926, Kent, England. Soprano, contralto. KUTSCH, THOMPSON.

BAULD, Alison. Sydney, Australia, 1944- . Composer. *MURDOCH=illus.preceding p.35.

BAUR, Bertha. Ann Arbor, Mich., before 1890-Sep 18 1940, Cincinnati. Teacher, music administrator. THOMPSON.

BAWR, Alexandrine Sophie Coury (Goury) de Champgrand, Comtesse de Saint-Simon (later Baronne de Bawr; pseud.= M. François). Paris, Oct 8 1773-Dec 31 1860, Paris. Singer, composer. ENCI SALVAT, MGG SUP, RIEMANN.

BAYAN, Daria. 20th-century Russian soprano. *PALMER= illus.p.134.

BAYLEY, Mrs. fl.1780-81. English singer. HIGHFILL.

BAYLIS, Lilian. London, May 9 1874-Nov 25 1937, London. Violinist, theater manager. ENCI SALVAT, ENCY MUS, GROVE 5.

BAYON, Mme. Louis. fl.1770. French clavecinist, singer, composer. ENCI SALVAT, ENCY MUS.

BAYZAND, Elizabeth (Mrs. William, born Taylor). fl.1792-96. Singer. HIGHFILL.

BEACH, Amy Marcy (born Cheney; known as Mrs. H. H. A. Beach). Henniker, N.H., Sep·5 1867-Dec 27 1944, New York City. Composer, pianist. *BAKER 1, BAKER 5, BLOM, ENCI MUS, GROVE 5, GROVE 5 SUP, MARIZ, MGG, PRATT, REIS, RIEMANN, RIEMANN ERG, *SCHOLES=illus. p.1056, THOMPSON.

BEARDMORE, Maria Hester see Parke, Maria Hester

BEARDSLEE, Bethany. Lansing, Mich., Dec 25 1927- . Soprano. BAKER 1971, KUTSCH, PAVLAKIS=p.285, RIEMANN ERG.

BEATON, Isabella. Grinnell, Iowa, May 20 1870-Jan 19 1929, Mt. Pleasant, Iowa.

Pianist, composer, opera composer. BAKER 5, PRATT, THOMPSON.

BEATTY, Louise Dilworth see Homer, Louise

BEAUCÉ, Delphine see Ugalde, Delphine

BEAUFORT, Miss?. fl.1794-95. Singer. HIGHFILL.

BEAUHARNAIS, Hortense de see Hortense, Queen

BEAUJON, Marise. Lyons, Oct 12 1890- . Soprano. KUTSCH.

BEAULIEU, Mrs. fl.1783-85. Dancer. HIGHFILL.

BEAUMESNIL, Henriette Adélaide Villard de. Paris, Aug 31 1758-1813, Paris. Singer, composer. ENCI SALVAT, ENCY MUS, GROVE 5.

BEAUMONT, Mrs. fl.1769-73. Singer. HIGHFILL.

BEAUMONT, Adelaide see Mullen, Adelaide

BECKER, Helen see Tamiris, Helen

BECKER, Jeanne. Mannheim, Jun 9 1859-Apr 6 1893, Mannheim. Pianist. BAKER 1, ENCI MUS.

BECKER-GLAUCH, Irmgard (born Klein). Bochum, Germany, Nov 16 1914- . Musicologist, music librarian, writer. ENCY MUS, GROVE 5, RIEMANN, RIEMANN ERG. [GROVE 5=b. in Cologne]

BECKERATH, Lulu see Schultz von Beckerath, Lulu

BECKMANN, Friedel. ?, 1904- .

German contralto. KUTSCH.

BÉCLARD D'HARCOURT, Marguerite see D'Harcourt, Marguerite Béclard

BEDFORD, Liza see Lehmann, Liza

BEDINI, Signora. fl.1787-88. Dancer. HIGHFILL.

BEEBE, Carolyn (Mrs. Henry H. Whitehurst). Westfield, N.J., ?-Sep 23 1950, Mystic, Conn. Pianist. THOMPSON.

BEECHAM, Betty (Mrs. Thomas, born Humby). 20th-century English pianist. GROVE 5.

BEERCROFT, Norma (Marian). Oshawa, Ontario, Canada, Apr 11 1934- . Composer, electronic music composer. NAPIER, VINTON.

BEESLEY, Mattie see Spinney, Mattie

BEETH, Lola. Cracow, Poland, Nov 23 1862-Mar 18 1940, Berlin. Soprano, voice teacher. BAKER 1, BAKER 5, GROVE 5, KUTSCH, PRATT, THOMPSON. [PRATT=b.1864]

BEEZ, Maria Anna see Franziska, Maria Anna

BEGNIS, Giuseppina Ronzi de (born Ronzi). Milan, Jan 11 1800-Jun 7 1853, Florence. Soprano. BLOM, BROWN BIO, *ENCI MUS=v.4 p.51, GROVE 1, GROVE 5. [GROVE 1=d.Jul 3 1853 in Paris]

BEGNIS, Rita de see De Begnis, Rita

BEHR, Therese see Schnabel, Therese

BEHREND, Jeanne. Philadelphia, May 11 1911- . Pianist, composer, teacher. *EWEN LIVING, REIS.

BEHRENDT, Lydia Hoffmann- see Hoffmann-Behrendt, Lydia

BEILKE, Irma Käthe Else. Berlin, Aug 24 1904- . Soprano, voice teacher. KUTSCH, RIEMANN, RIEMANN ERG.

BELCE, Luise Reuss- see Reuss-Belce, Luise

BELDER, Elly see Ameling, Elly

BELFORT, Mrs. fl.1760-61. English dancer. HIGHFILL.

BELISANI, Cecchina (Cecilia). 18th-century Italian singer. ENCI MUS=v.1 p.337 (brief mention in article on husband Giuseppe Maria Buini).

BELL, Miss see Farren, Mrs. William

BELL, Mrs. fl.1791. English dancer. HIGHFILL.

BELL, Susanne Weber- see Weber-Bell, Susanne

BELLAMY, Harriet see Grist, Harriet

BELLARY, Marie-Luce see Bohé, Marie-Luce

"BELLE ESPAGNOLE, LA" see Redigé, Mme. Paulo

BELLEVILLE, Anna Caroline de see Oury, Anna Caroline

BELLINCIONI, Bianca (Stagno-Bellincioni). Budapest, Jan 23 1888- . Soprano. ENCI MUS= v.1 p.225 & v.4 p.271.

BELLINCIONI, Carlotta (later Soroldoni). 19th-century Italian contralto. ENCI MUS.

BELLINCIONI, Gemma Cesira Matilda. Como (not Monza), Aug 18 1864-Apr 23 1950, Roccabelvedere, nr. Naples. Soprano, voice teacher. BAKER 5, BLOM, *CELLETTI=illus.foll. col.96, CORTE, *ENCI MUS= illus.fac.p.219, ENCI SALVAT, ENCY MUS, EWEN NEW, GROVE 5, GROVE 5 SUP, KUTSCH, MARIZ, MGG SUP, PRATT, RIEMANN, RIEMANN ERG, THOMPSON, ULLSTEIN. *[CELLETTI, EWEN NEW, & MGG SUP=b.Aug 17; KUTSCH=b.Aug 19; CELLETTI & MGG SUP=d. Apr 24]*

BELLING, Susan. 20th-century American soprano. PAVLAKIS= p.286.

BELLOC, Maria Teresa (Georgi-Trombetta-Belloc). San Benigno, Canavese, nr. Turin, Jul 2 1784-May 13 1855, San Giorgio, Canavese, nr. Turin. Mezzo-soprano. BAKER 1, BAKER 5, BLOM, CORTE, *ENCI MUS= illus.fac.p.226, GROVE, PRATT, THOMPSON. *[BAKER 1= b.Aug 13; BLOM & GROVE 5= soprano]*

BELLOLI, Marianna. fl.1793. Singer. HIGHFILL.

BELMAS, Xenia. Kiev, 1896- . Soprano, voice teacher. KUTSCH.

BELOCCA, Anna de. St. Petersburg, Jan 1854-?. Mezzo-soprano. BROWN BIO.

BEMBO, Antonia. Venice?, c1670-

?, Italy?. Composer, court
musician. BAKER 5, RIEMANN.

BENAVENTE, Regina. Buenos
Aires, Jan 22 1932- . Composer. RIEMANN ERG.

BENDA, Mme. fl.1790-92. Singer. HIGHFILL.

BENDA, Anna Franciska. Staré
Benatky, Bohemia, May 26
1728-1781, Gotha, Germany.
Soprano. DICT MUS, ENCI
MUS, GROVE 1, MGG. *[GROVE
1=b.1726; ENCI MUS & GROVE
1=d.1780]*

BENDA, Juliana. Potsdam, 1752-
May 9 1783, Berlin. Composer. DICT MUS, ULLSTEIN.

BENDA, Maria Carolina. 18th-
century Bohemian singer and
cembalist. ENCI MUS, THOMP-
SON.

BENDAZZI, Ernestina (Ernestina
Secchi Bendazzi Garulli).
Naples, Apr 18 1864-May 12
1931, Trieste. Soprano.
CELLETTI, ENCI MUS.

BENDAZZI, Luigia. Ravenna,
Italy, 1833-Mar 5 1901,
Nice, France. Soprano. ENCI
MUS.

BENDIDIO, Isabella. 16th-cen-
tury Italian singer. ENCI
MUS=v.2 p.370 (brief mention
in article on Battista Gua-
rini).

BENDIDIO, Lucrezia. 16th-cen-
tury Italian singer. ENCI
MUS=v.2 p.370 (brief mention
in article on Battista Gua-
rini).

BENE, Adriana Ferrarese del
see Gabrieli, Adriana

BENEDICTS, Sara see Bos-

mans, Sara

BENINI, Anna (Signora Bernardo
Mengozzi). fl.1784-91. Ita-
lian soprano. GROVE 1, HIGH-
FILL, THOMPSON.

BENNET, Elizabeth. London?,
1714-Sep 15 1791, London.
Singer, actress, dancer.
HIGHFILL.

BENNETT, Maria. fl.1752.
English singer. HIGHFILL.

BENOIS, Marie. St. Petersburg,
Jan 1 1861-?. Pianist. BAKER
1.

BENOIT, Francine (Germaine
van Gool). Périgueux, France,
Jul 30 1894- . Critic, composer. GROVE 5.

BEN-SEDIRA, Leila. Algiers,
1909- . Soprano. ENCI SALVAT,
KUTSCH.

BENSON, Mrs. fl.1675. English
singer, court musician.
HIGHFILL.

BENSON, Mrs. fl.1784-86. English singer, actress. HIGH-
FILL=v.2 p.43 (in article on
husband Mr. Benson).

BENTI BULGARELLI (not Bulga-
rini), Marianna, "La Romanina." Rome, 1684-Feb 26
1734, Rome. Soprano. CORTE,
ENCI MUS.

BENZA NAGY, Ida. ?-Mar 10 1880,
Budapest. Soprano. ENCI MUS.

BENZELL, Mimi. Bridgeport,
Conn., Apr 6 1923-Dec 23
1970, Manhasset, Long Is-
land, New York. Soprano.
BAKER 1971, *EWEN LIV SUP,
SANDVED, THOMPSON. *[BAKER
1971=b.1922; EWEN LIV SUP &
SANDVED=b.1924]*

BERALTA, -----. fl.1757.
Italian soprano. GROVE 1.

BÉRAT, Louise. France?, 1882-
?. Contralto. GROVE 5.

BERBERIAN, Cathy. Attleboro,
Mass., Jul 4 1925- . So-
prano, composer. BAKER
1971, KUTSCH, PAVLAKIS=
p.293, RIEMANN ERG. [RIEMANN
ERG=b.1928]

BERCKMAN(N), Evelyn. Phila-
delphia, Oct 18 1900- .
Composer, writer. ENCI
SALVAT, ENCY MUS, REIS,
THOMPSON.

BERG, Anna Lisa. 20th-century
Austrian singer. ENCI MUS=
v.1 p.270 (brief mention in
article on Björling family).

BERG, María. London, 1888- .
Pianist. ENCI SALVAT, ENCY
MUS, THOMPSON.

BERGANZA, Teresa. Madrid,
Mar 16 1935- . Mezzo-soprano.
CELLETTI, ENCI SALVAT, EWEN
NEW, KUTSCH, *ROSENTHAL=
illus.p.14, SANDVED, *ULL-
STEIN. [EWEN NEW=b.Mar 14
1934]

BERGÉ, Laure. ?, 1892-May 4
1961, Brussels. Soprano.
KUTSCH.

BERGER, Erna. Cossebaude, nr.
Dresden, Oct 19 1900- . So-
prano, voice teacher. BAKER
5, BLOM, ENCI SALVAT, ENCY
MUS, *EWEN LIV SUP, EWEN
NEW, GROVE 5 SUP, KUTSCH,
MGG, RIEMANN, RIEMANN ERG,
SANDVED, THOMPSON, *ULL-
STEIN. [SANDVED=b.1906]

BERGER, Ludmilla Kupfer- see
Kupfer-Berger, Ludmilla

BERGER, Marie see Rappold,
Marie

BERGER, Rita see Streich,
Rita

BERGHAUS, Ruth see Dessau,
Ruth

BERGHOUT, Sophie Rose. Rotterdam, 1909- . Harpsichordist.
ENCI SALVAT, ENCY MUS.

BERGLUND, Ruth. Amal, Sweden,
Apr 12 1897- . Contralto.
KUTSCH.

BERGMANN, Maria. Höchst, Oden-
wald, Germany, Feb 15 1918- .
Pianist. RIEMANN, RIEMANN
ERG, ULLSTEIN.

BERGMANN, Valentine Semenovna
see Serov, Valentine Semenovna

BERIOSOVA, Svetlana (Mrs. Khan).
Kaunus, Lithuania, Sep 4
1932- . Dancer. RIEMANN ERG.

BERLENDI, Livia. ?, c1875-?.
Italian soprano. ENCI MUS.

BERNARD, Annabelle. New Orleans,
La., Oct 11 1934- . Soprano.
RIEMANN ERG.

BERNARD, Caroline see Richings-Bernard, Caroline

BERNARD, Claire. Rouen, France,
Mar 31 1947- . Violinist.
RIEMANN ERG.

BERNARDI, Signora. fl.1770.
Singer. HIGHFILL.

BERNASCONI, Antonia Wagele.
Stuttgart, 1741-1803, Stutt-
gart. BLOM, BROWN BIO, DICT
MUS, ENCI MUS, GROVE 1,
GROVE 5, HIGHFILL, PRATT,

RIEMANN, THOMPSON.

BERNÁTHOVÁ, Eva. Budapest,
Dec 4 1922- . Pianist.
RIEMANN ERG.

BERNAU-GALLIGNANI, Chiara
see Gallignani-Bernau,
Chiara

BERNETTE, Yara. Boston, Mar
14 1920- . Pianist. RIE-
MANN ERG.

BERNSDORFF, Christiane see
Engelbrecht, Christiane

BERREY, Mabel see Smith,
Mabel

BERRY, Sarah. Bamford, nr.
Manchester, England, ?-?.
19-20th-century English
contralto. BROWN BRIT.

BERT, Miss see Birt, Miss S.

BERTALDI, Maria see Bal-
ducci, Maria

BERTANA, Luisa. Buenos Aires,
Jan 11 1898-Jul 27 1933,
Buenos Aires. Mezzo-soprano.
ARIZAGA, *ENCI MUS=illus.
fac.v.3 p.311, KUTSCH.
[KUTSCH=d. Jul 23]

BERTHIER, Jeanne-Marie see
Bathori, Jane

BERTHON, Mareille. Paris, Aug
6 1889-Jan 19 1955, Paris.
Soprano. KUTSCH.

BERTIN, Louise-Angélique.
Les Roches, nr. Bièvres,
France, Feb 15 1805-Apr 26
1877, Paris. Composer, pia-
nist, opera composer, con-
tralto. BAKER 1, BAKER 5,
BLOM, BROWN BIO, ENCI MUS,
ENCI SALVAT, ENCY MUS, GROVE
1, GROVE 5, PRATT, RIEMANN,
THOMPSON.

BERTINOTTI-RADICATI, Teresa.
Savigliano, Piedmont, Italy,
1776-Feb 12 1854, Bologna.
Soprano, voice teacher.
BROWN BIO, CORTE, ENCI MUS,
GROVE 1, GROVE 5, PRATT,
THOMPSON.

BERTLES, Miss see Dighton,
Mrs. Robert

BERTLOVÁ, Ludmila see
Kubelik, Ludmila

BERTOLLI, Francesca. fl.1729-
39. Italian contralto. BROWN
BIO, ENCI SALVAT, GROVE 1,
GROVE 5, HIGHFILL, PRATT,
THOMPSON.

BERTON, Liliane. Brunoy, France,
1924- . Singer. ENCI SALVAT,
ENCY MUS.

BERTRAND, Aline. Paris, 1798-
Mar 13 1835, Paris. Composer,
harpist. BAKER 5, PRATT,
THOMPSON.

BERWALD, Astrid Maria Beatrice.
Stockholm, Sep 8 1886- .
Pianist. ENCI SALVAT, ENCY
MUS, GROVE 5, RIEMANN, RIE-
MANN ERG.

BESANZONI, Gabriella. Rome,
Nov 20 1890-Jun 6 1962,
Rome. Contralto, voice tea-
cher, actress. BAKER 1971,
KUTSCH, MARIZ, RIEMANN ERG,
THOMPSON. *[BAKER 1971=b.Sep
20 1890, d.Jul 8 1962]*

BESFORD, Esther. England?,
c1757-?. Dancer, actress.
HIGHFILL.

BESFORD, Mrs. Joseph?. fl.1767-
68. English dancer. HIGHFILL.

BESSENIG, Josepha Barbara see

Auernhammer, Josepha Barbara von

BESTWICK, Lavinia see Fenton, Lavinia

BESVILLE, Elise see Landouzy, Lise

BESWICK, Mrs. fl.1787. Dancer. HIGHFILL.

BETTAQUE, Katharina see Senger-Bettaque, Katharina

BETTENDORF, Emmy. Frankfurt, Jul 16 1895-Oct 20 1963, Berlin. Soprano. KUTSCH.

BETTI, Carolina Navone- see Navone-Betti, Carolina

BETTINI, Signora. fl.1744-45. Dancer. HIGHFILL.

BETTINI, Zelia Trebelli- see Trebelli (-Bettini), Zelia

BEYRON, Olga Brita Lovisa Hertzberg- see Hertzberg-Beyron, Olga Brita Lovisa

BIALKIEWICZ DE LANGERON, Irena. Poland?, 1890- . Soprano, pianist, composer. GROVE 5.

BIANCHI, Cecilia see Giuliani, Cecilia

BIANCHI, Jane (Mrs. Francesco, later Mrs. John Lacy, born Jackson). London, 1776-Mar 19 1858, Ealing, England. Soprano. BROWN BIO=p.370, BROWN BRIT=p.235, HIGHFILL.

BIANCHI, Valentine. Vilna, Lithuania, 1839-Feb 28 1884, Candau, Kurland, Latvia. Soprano. BAKER 5.

BIANCHI CHARITAS, Bianca (real name=Bertha Schwarz).

Heidelberg, Jun 27 1855-Feb 1947, Salzburg. Soprano, voice teacher. BAKER 1, BAKER 5, ENCI MUS, GROVE 1, GROVE 5, THOMPSON. *[BAKER 1=b. 1858]*

BIANCO-LANZI, Maria. Turin, Oct 3 1891- . Pianist. THOMPSON.

BIANCOLINI RODRIGUEZ, Marietta. Fermo, Italy, Sep 20 1846-May 31 1905, Florence. Contralto. ENCI MUS.

BIBLE, Frances. Sackets Harbor, New York, 1925- . Mezzo-soprano. PAVLAKIS=p.294, *SANDVED, THOMPSON.

BICKING, Ada Elizabeth. Evansville, Ind., Feb 17 1886-Feb 22 1953, Evansville, Ind. Teacher, writer. THOMPSON.

BICKNELL, Mrs. fl.1755. Singer. HIGHFILL.

BICKNELL, Margaret (born Younger). Scotland, c1680-May 24 1723, London. Dancer, actress. HIGHFILL.

BIDAL, Denise. Nyon, France, Sep 4 1913- . Pianist, writer. ENCY MUS, SCHUH.

BIDDY, Miss. fl.1728-29. Dancer. HIGHFILL.

BIENENFELD, Elsa. Vienna, Aug 23 1877-? (died in concentration camp, time and place unknown). Critic, writer. PRATT, RIEMANN, RIEMANN ERG.

BIGGS, Anne (later Mrs. Samuel Young). Debenham, Suffolk, 1775-Jun 28 1825, Islington (or Hampstead), England. Singer, actress. *HIGHFILL.

BIGI, Giacinta. fl.1791-96.

Singer. HIGHFILL.

BIGOT DE MOROGNES, Marie
(born Kiéné). Colmar,
France, Mar 3 1786-Sep 16
1820, Paris. Pianist,
piano teacher. BAKER 1,
BAKER 5, BLOM, BROWN BIO,
DICT MUS, ENCI MUS, ENCY
MUS, GROVE 1, GROVE 5,
MGG, PRATT, RIEMANN, RIE-
MANN ERG, THOMPSON.

BILGRAM, Hedwig. Memmingen,
Bavaria, Mar 31 1933- .
Organist, cembalist,
teacher. RIEMANN ERG.

BILINGTHON, Mme. see Bil-
lington, Elizabeth

BILLINGTON (Bilingthon),
Elizabeth (born Weichsel).
London, 1765 or 1768-Aug 25
1818, nr. Venice. Soprano,
composer. BAKER 1, BAKER 5,
BLOM, BROWN BIO, BROWN BRIT,
*CLAYTON, COOPER, *ENCI MUS=
illus.fac.p.259, ENCY MUS,
GROVE 1, GROVE 1 APP, GROVE
5, *HIGHFILL, RIEMANN, SAND-
VED, THOMPSON.

BILLINGTON, Maria see
Hawes, Maria

BILSINGHAM, Miss. fl.1786.
Dancer. HIGHFILL.

BILTCLIFFE, Florence. Yorkshire, ?- . 20th-century
English pianist, teacher,
composer. CBC.

BINDERNAGEL, Gertrude. Magdeburg, Germany, Jan 11 1894-
Nov 3 1932, Berlin. Soprano.
KUTSCH, THOMPSON. [THOMPSON=
b.1895 in Berlin, d.Oct 23]

BINET, Jocelyne. East Angus,
Québec, Sep 27 1923- .
Violinist, composer, tea-

cher. CBC.

BINETY, Anna. fl.1761-63. Dancer. HIGHFILL.

BINFIELD, Fanny Jane. ?-Sep 3
1881, Reading, England.
Pianist. BROWN BRIT.

BINFIELD, Hannah Rampton.
Reading, England, 1810-May 2
1887, Reading, England.
Pianist, harpist, organist.
BROWN BRIT.

BINFIELD, Louisa. 19th-century
English concertina player.
BROWN BRIT.

BINFIELD, Louisa. ?-Nov 26
1856, Reading, England.
Musician. BROWN BRIT.

BIRCH, Charlotte Ann. London,
c1815-Jan 26 1901, London.
Soprano. BROWN BRIT, GROVE 1
APP, GROVE 5, THOMPSON.

BIRCH, Eliza Ann. England,
c1830-Mar 26 1857, London.
Soprano. GROVE 1 APP,
GROVE 5, THOMPSON.

BIRET, Idil. Ankara, Nov 22
1941- . Pianist. RIEMANN ERG.

BIRT (Bert), Miss S. (later
Mme. Frederic). fl.1791-1813.
Dancer. HIGHFILL.

BISCACCIANTI, Eliza (born
Ostinelli). Boston, 1824 or
1827-Jul? 1896, Paris. Sin-
ger, voice teacher. BAKER 1,
BROWN BIO, ENCI MUS=v.2 p.420
(brief mention in article on
Hewitt family), THOMPSON.
[BROWN BIO=b.1825]

BISCHOF, Marie see Brandt,
Marianne

BISGAARD, Astri Udnaes. Bel-

lingham, Wash., Jan 22
1891- . Singer. THOMPSON.

BISHOP, Mrs. fl.1741-42.
English dancer, actress,
singer. HIGHFILL.

BISHOP, Adelaide (Mrs. Schur).
New York City, Jun 23
1928- . Soprano. RIEMANN
ERG.

BISHOP, Ann(a) (Mrs. Henry
Rowley, later Mrs. Martin
Schultz, born Rivière).
London, Jan 9 1810-Mar 18
1884, New York City. So-
prano. BAKER 5, BLOM, BROWN
BIO, BROWN BRIT, ENCI MUS,
GROVE 1 APP, GROVE 5, GROVE
5 SUP, SANDVED, THOMPSON.
*[BROWN BRIT=b.1812 or 1814-
15, d.Mar 18 or 20 1884;
GROVE 1 APP=b.1814]*

BISSET, Catherine. London,
1795-Feb 1864, Barnes,
England. Pianist. BROWN
BIO, BROWN BRIT.

BISSET, Elizabeth Anne. London, 1800-?, London? Harpist,
composer. BROWN BRIT.

BITHMERE, Mme. Augustine Louis.
fl.1784-87. Dancer. HIGHFILL.

BITHMERE, Marie Françoise.
fl.1784-88. Dancer, actress.
HIGHFILL.

BIZZOZERO, Julieta. 20th-cen-
tury Uruguayan pianist.
ENCI SALVAT.

BJONER, Ingrid. Kraakstad,
Norway, Nov 8 1927- .
Soprano. EWEN NEW, KUTSCH,
RIEMANN ERG, *SANDVED=
illus.only p.826, THOMPSON,
ULLSTEIN. *[KUTSCH=b.1929 in
Oslo; ULLSTEIN=b.in Oslo]*

BJÖRLIN, Elli Rangman- see
Rangman-Björlin, Elli

BJÖRLING, Heddy (Mrs. Karl
Gustaf, born Petersen).
20th-century Norwegian
singer. GROVE 5.

BJÖRNSON, Bergljot see
Ibsen, Bergljot

BLACHER, Gerty (Mrs. Boris,
born Herzog). Aachen, Jul 14
1922- . Pianist. ENCI MUS,
*ULLSTEIN=p.236.

BLAES, Elisa (born Meerti).
Antwerp, c1820-after 1875, ?.
Soprano, voice teacher.
BROWN BIO, GROVE 1, GROVE 5.

BLAESI, Emmy Troyon- see
Troyon-Blaesi, Emmy

BLAGDEN, Miss. fl.1759-62.
Dancer. HIGHFILL.

BLAHETKA (Plahetka), Marie
Léopoldine. Guntramsdorf,
Baden, nr. Vienna, Nov 15
1811-Jan 12 1887, Boulogne,
France. Composer, pianist,
opera composer, physharmonica
player. BAKER 1, BAKER 5,
BROWN BIO, ENCI SALVAT, GROVE
1, GROVE 5, MGG SUP, PRATT,
THOMPSON. *[BAKER 1=d.Jan 17
1887; BROWN BIO=b.Nov 15
1809; MGG SUP=b.Nov 16 1811]*

BLAKE, Mrs. fl.1761. Dancer.
HIGHFILL.

BLAKE, Dorothy Gaynor. St.
Joseph, Mo., Nov 21 1893- .
Composer, teacher. BAKER 5,
THOMPSON.

BLANCARD, Jacqueline. Paris,
Apr 6 1909- . Pianist. SCHUH.

BLANCHARD, the Misses. fl.1789-

91. Dancer. HIGHFILL.

BLANCHARD, Charlotte (Mrs. Thomas, born Wright). ?, 1761-after 1834, ?. Singer, actress. HIGHFILL.

BLANCHET, Elisabeth-Antoinette see Couperin, Elisabeth-Antoinette

BLAND, Dora see Jordan, Dora

BLAND, Elsa. Vienna, Apr 16 1880-Sep 27 1935, Vienna. Soprano, voice teacher. KUTSCH.

BLAND, Maria Theresa Catherine (Mrs. George, born Tersi, called "Romani" and "Romanzini"). London?, Sep 12 1770-Jan 15 1838, Westminster, England. Soprano. BLOM, BROWN BIO, BROWN BRIT, GROVE 1 APP, GROVE 5, *HIGHFILL, PRATT, THOMPSON. *[BLOM=b.1769 in Italy?; PRATT=b.1769]*

BLASIS, Teresa de see De Blasis, Teresa

BLASIS, Virginia de see De Blasis, Virginia

BLAUMAUER, Karoline see Lenya, Lotte

BLAUVELT, Lillian Evans. Brooklyn, New York, Mar 16 1874-Aug 29 1947, Chicago. Soprano, voice teacher. BAKER 5, GROVE 5, KUTSCH, PRATT, THOMPSON. *[KUTSCH= b.1873, d.Aug 27 1947]*

BLEGEN, Judith. 20th-century American soprano. PAVLAKIS= p.286.

BLISS, Ilsa Foerstel. 20th-

century German harpsichordist, music administrator. PAVLA-KIS=p.278.

BLISS, Mrs. J. Worthington, born Lindsay. 19th-century English song-writer. BAKER 1= p.356, BROWN BIO, BROWN BRIT.

BLIUDZ, Julia see Stucevski, Julia

BLOCH, Suzanne. Geneva, Aug 7 1907- . Harpsichordist, virginal player, lecturer. BAKER 5, *EWEN LIVING, RIEMANN ERG, THOMPSON. *[RIEMANN ERG=b.Aug 9 1907]*

BLOMFIELD-HOLT, Patricia. Lindsay, Ontario, Canada, Sep 15 1910- . Composer, pianist, teacher. CBC, NAPIER.

BLOOMFIELD, Fannie see Zeisler, Fannie Bloomfield

BLUME, Bianka. Reichenbach, Silesia, May 4 1843-1896, Buenos Aires. Soprano. ENCI MUS.

BLURTON, Mary (Mrs. James). fl.1793-1800. Singer, actress. HIGHFILL.

BLYTH, May. London, Feb 12 1899- . Soprano. GROVE 5, THOMPSON.

BOATRIGHT, Helen. 20th-century American soprano. PAVLAKIS= p.286.

BOBESCO, Lola-Anna-Maria. Craiova, Romania, Aug 9 1920- . Violinist. ENCI SALVAT, ENCY MUS, RIEMANN ERG.

BOBILLIER, Antoinette Christine Marie see Brenet, Michel

BOCCABADATI, Luigia. Modena
or Parma, 1799 or 1800-Oct
12 1850, Turin. Soprano,
voice teacher. BROWN BIO,
CORTE, ENCI MUS, GROVE 1,
GROVE 5, THOMPSON.

BOCCABADATI CARIGNANI, Virginia. Turin?, Apr 29 1828-
Aug 6 1922, Turin. Soprano.
CORTE, *ENCI MUS=illus.fac.
p.275.

BOCCABADATI FRANCALUCCI,
Augusta. ?-Dec 1875, Santi-
ago de Chile. Singer. ENCI
MUS.

BOCCABADATI GAZZUOLO, Cecilia.
?-1906, Florence. Singer.
ENCI MUS.

BOCCABADATI VARESI, Elena.
Florence, 1854-Jun 5 or 15
1920, Chicago. Soprano.
ENCI MUS=v.1 p.278 & v.4
p.465, GROVE 5. *[ENCI MUS:
v.1 p.278=d.Jun 15, v.4
p.465=d.Jun 5]*

BOCCABADATI VARESI, Giulia.
19-20th-century Italian
singer. ENCI MUS.

BOCCHERINI, Anna Matilda.
18th-century Italian bal-
lerina. ENCI MUS.

BOCCHERINI, Maria Ester.
18th-century Italian bal-
lerina. ENCI MUS.

BOCCOLINI, Ebe. Ancona, Italy,
1889- . Soprano. KUTSCH.

BODANYA, Natalie. New York
City, c1914- . Soprano.
*EWEN LIVING, EWEN LIV SUP.

BODDA, Louisa Fanny see
Pyne, Louisa Fanny

BODMAN, Karin see Vretblad,
Karin

BÖHM CARTELLIERI, Elisabeth.
Riga, Latvia, 1756-1797,
Berlin. Soprano, actress.
ENCI MUS=v.1 p.419 (brief
mention in article on son
Casimiro Antonio Cartel-
lieri), GROVE 1, THOMPSON.
[GROVE 1=b.1736]

BÖHME, Hedwig see Müller von
Asow, Hedwig

BOERNER, Charlotte. Leipzig,
Jun 22 1900- . Soprano.
KUTSCH.

BOESE, Helen. Toronto, 1896- .
Composer, pianist, music
administrator. CBC.

BOESE, Ursula. Hamburg, Jul 27
1933- . Contralto. RIEMANN
ERG.

BOGARD, Carole. 20th-century
American soprano. PAVLAKIS=
p.286.

BOGUE, Christina W. see
Morison, Christina W.

BOHÉ, Marie-Luce (stage name=
Marie-Luce Bellary). Rouen,
France, Jan 8 1937- . Mezzo-
soprano. RIEMANN ERG.

BOHRER, Sophie. Paris, 1828-
1849, St. Petersburg. Pianist. ENCY MUS, GROVE 5.

BOÏELDIEU, Jenny (Mrs. François
Adrien, born Phillis). 19th-
century French singer. ENCI
MUS.

BOIMAISON, Mrs. fl.1793-96.
Singer, actress. HIGHFILL.

BOISGÉRARD, Mme. fl.1791.
Dancer. HIGHFILL.

BOK, Mary Louise see
Curtis, Mary Louise

BOKESOVÁ-HANÁKOVÁ, Zdeňka.
Bedihošť, Moravia, Nov 28
1911- . Musicologist, writer, critic. ENCI SALVAT,
GROVE 5.

BOKOR, Margit. Losoncz, nr.
Budapest, 1905-Nov 9 1949,
New York City. Soprano.
KUTSCH.

BOLLA, Maria. fl.1799-1804.
Singer, actress. GROVE 1,
HIGHFILL, THOMPSON.

BOLOGNA, Barbara. fl.1786-
1804. Dancer. HIGHFILL.

BOLOGNA, Mrs. Louis. fl.1799-
1800. Dancer. HIGHFILL.

BOLOGNA, Mrs. Pietro. fl.1786-
98. Dancer, singer. HIGH-
FILL.

BOLSKA, Adelaida Yulianovna.
19th-century Russian so-
prano of Polish origin.
GROVE 5.

BOLTON, Duchess of see
Fenton, Lavinia

BOLTON, Eliza. 19th-century
English soprano. BROWN
BRIT=p.53 (in article on
father (?) Thomas Bolton`.

BOLTON, Mary Catherine (Lady
Thurlow). London, 1790-
Sep 28 1830, Southampton.
Soprano. BROWN BRIT=p.53
(in article on her father
(?) Thomas Bolton).

BOMAN, Mrs. fl.1716-56. English singer, dancer, act-
ress. HIGHFILL.

BOMAN, Elizabeth (Mrs. John,

born Watson). England, 1677?-
1707?, England. Singer, actress. HIGHFILL.

"BOMBASTINI, Signora." fl.1759.
Dancer?. HIGHFILL.

"BOMBASTINI, Signorina." fl.
1759. Hornist. HIGHFILL.

BONAZZI, Elaine. 20th-century
American mezzo-soprano.
PAVLAKIS=p.294.

BOND, Carrie Jacobs (born
Jacobs). Janesville, Wis.,
Aug 11 1862-Dec 28 1946,
Glendale, Calif. Composer.
BAKER 5, BAKER 1971, MARIZ,
THOMPSON.

BOND, Jessie. 19th-century
English contralto, actress.
BROWN BRIT.

BONDINI, Marianna Barilli see
Barilli, Marianna Bondini

BONINSEGNA, Celestina. Reggio
Emilia, Italy, Feb 26 1877-
Feb 14 1947, Milan. Soprano.
CELLETTI, ENCI MUS, KUTSCH,
THOMPSON.

BONIS, Mélanie (Mme. Albert
Domange). Paris, Jan 21
1858-Mar 18 1937, Sarcelles,
Seine-et-Oise, France.
Composer. BAKER 5.

BONNEAU, Jacqueline. St.-
Astier, France, 1917- .
Pianist. ENCI SALVAT, ENCY
MUS.

BONNEVAL, Mlle. fl.1741-44.
Dancer. HIGHFILL.

BONOMI, Giac(inta?). fl.1757-
59. Dancer. HIGHFILL.

BONURA, Giustina Gentili see
Gentili Bonura, Giustina

BONWICK, Miss. fl.1794. Organist, soprano. HIGHFILL.

BOORN-COCLET, Henriette van den see Van den Boorn-Coclet, Henriette

BOOTH, Miss. fl.1715. Singer. HIGHFILL.

BOOTH, Hester (Mrs. Barton II, born Santlow). London?, c1690-Jan 15, 21, or 31 1773, London. Dancer, actress. *HIGHFILL.

BOOTH, Ursula Agnes (Mrs. John). London?, 1740-Aug 1803, London?. Singer, actress. HIGHFILL.

BORDES-PÈNE, Léontine Marie (born Péne). Lorient, France, Nov 25 1858-Jan 24 1924, Rouen, France. Pianist, piano teacher. BAKER 5, BLOM, GROVE 5, THOMPSON.

BORDEWIJK ROEPMAN, Johanna. Rotterdam, Aug 4 1892- . Composer. THOMPSON.

BORDINO, Maria. 19-20th-century Italian pianist. ENCI MUS=v.1 p.424 (brief mention in article on son Alfredo Casella).

BORDOGNI-WILLENT, Luisa. ?-c1855, ?. Italian singer, voice teacher. ENCI MUS.

BORDONI, Faustina see Hasse, Faustina

BOREK, Minuetta. Calgary, Canada, ?- . 20th-century Canadian pianist, teacher, composer. CBC.

BORELLI ANGELINI, Medea. Costantinia, Algeria, c1860-Jul 2 1924, Florence. So-

prano. ENCI MUS.

BORGATTI, Renata. Bologna, Mar 2 1894- . Pianist, piano teacher. BAKER 5, ENCI MUS, GROVE 5.

BORGHI, Adelaide see Borghi-Mamo, Adelaide

BORGHI-MAMO, Adelaide (born Borghi). Bologna, Aug 9 1826-Sep 10 1901, Bologna. Mezzo-soprano. BAKER 1, BAKER 5, CORTE, *ENCI MUS=illus.fac. p.295, GROVE 1 APP, GROVE 5, PRATT, RIEMANN, RIEMANN ERG, THOMPSON. *[BAKER 1, BAKER 5, GROVE 1 APP, & GROVE 5=b. 1829; GROVE 5=d.Sep 29 1901. Most sources=d.sep 28 1901, which RIEMANN ERG corrects to Sep 10 1901]*

BORGHI-MAMO, Erminia. Paris, Feb 18 1855-Jul 29 1941, Bologna. Soprano. BAKER 1, CORTE, GROVE 5=v.1 p.816, PRATT, RIEMANN, RIEMANN ERG.

BORI, Lucrezia (real name= Lucrezia Borja y Gonzales de Riancho). Valencia, Spain, Dec 24 1887-May 14 1960, New York City. Soprano. BAKER 5, BAKER 1971, CELLETTI, *ENCI MUS=illus.fac.p.299, ENCI SALVAT, ENCY MUS, *EWEN LIVING, EWEN NEW, KUTSCH, MARIZ, PRATT, RIEMANN, RIEMANN ERG, *SANDVED, THOMPSON.

BORKH, Inge (Ingeborg Wellitsch). Mannheim, May 26 1917- . Soprano. CELLETTI, ENCI MUS, ENCI SALVAT, ENCY MUS, *EWEN LIV SUP, EWEN NEW, GROVE 5 SUP, KUTSCH, RIEMANN, RIEMANN ERG, *ROSENTHAL=illus.p.26, *SANDVED=illus.p.403, SCHUH NACH, THOMPSON, *ULLSTEIN.

BORKOWICZÓWNA, Maria. Warsaw,

35   *BOUDET*

1886- . Composer. GROVE 5,
RIEMANN, RIEMANN ERG.

BORNEMANN, Eva. Wuppertal,
Germany, ?- . 20th-century
German contralto. RIEMANN
ERG.

BORONAT, Olimpia. Genoa, 1867-
1934, Warsaw. Soprano, voice
teacher. KUTSCH.

BORONAT FABRA, Teresina.
Barcelona, 1904- . Dancer.
ENCI SALVAT.

BOROSINI, Rosa see Ambre-
ville, Rosa Teresa Giovanna
Lodovica d'

BORSELLI, Elisabetta (Signora
Fausto). fl.1789-90. Singer.
HIGHFILL.

BORSI, Teresa de Giuli see
De Giuli Borsi, Teresa

BORTON, Alice. 19th-century
English pianist, composer.
BROWN BRIT.

BOSCH, Betty van den see
Van den Bosch, Betty

BOSCHETTI, Signora Mengis.
fl.1770-72. Soprano. GROVE
1, HIGHFILL.

BOSCHETTI, Teresa. Prague,
1847-?. Organist, court
musician. ENCI MUS.

BOSCHI, Francesca (Mrs.
Giuseppe Maria, born Vanini).
fl.1710-11. Italian singer.
GROVE 5, HIGHFILL.

BOSCHI, Hélène. Lausanne,
1917- . Pianist. ENCI SAL-
VAT.

BOSELLO, Anna Morichelli- see
Morichelli-Bosello, Anna

BOSETTI, Hermine (orig.=Hermine
von Flick). Vienna, Sep 28
1875-May 1 1936, Hohenrain,
Bavaria. Soprano, voice
teacher. GROVE 5, GROVE 5
SUP, KUTSCH, RIEMANN ERG,
THOMPSON.

BOSIO, Angiolina. Turin, Aug 22
1830-Apr 12 1859, St. Peters-
burg. Soprano. BLOM, BROWN
BIO, CLAYTON=p.451, ENCI MUS,
GROVE 1, GROVE 5, PRATT,
THOMPSON. *[ENCI MUS=d.Apr 13]*

BOSMANS, Henriëtta. Amsterdam,
Dec 6 1895-Jul 2 1952, Am-
sterdam. Composer, pianist.
BAKER 5, ENCI SALVAT, GROVE
5, MGG SUP, RIEMANN ERG,
THOMPSON.

BOSMANS, Sara (Mrs. Henri, born
Benedicts). Amsterdam, Oct
23 1861-?. Pianist, piano
teacher. GROVE 5.

BOSSI, Mme. Cesare see Del
Caro, Mlle.

BOTARELLI, Mrs. fl.1778-84.
Singer. HIGHFILL.

BOTEZ, Manya. Sulina, Romania,
?- . 20th-century pianist.
THOMPSON.

BOUCHER, Céleste (Mrs. Alexan-
der Jean, born Gallyot). ?-
Feb 1841, Paris. Harpist.
ENCI MUS.

BOUCHER, Lydia (Soeur Marie
Thérèse). St. Ambrose de
Kildare, Canada, Feb 28
1890- . Composer, teacher,
instrumentalist. CBC.

BOUDET, Mme. fl.1726. Dancer.
HIGHFILL.

BOUDET, Mlle. fl.1726. Dancer.
HIGHFILL.

BOUÉ, Géorgi. Toulouse, Oct
16 1918- . Soprano. KUTSCH,
*SANDVED=illus.only p.266.

BOUGIER, Mlle. fl.1791. Dancer. HIGHFILL.

BOULANGER, Lili Juliette Marie
Olga. Paris, Aug 21 1893-Mar
15 1918, Mézy, Yvelines, nr.
Paris. Composer. BAKER 5,
BLOM, COOPER, CORTE, DICT
MUS, ENCI MUS, ENCI SALVAT,
ENCY MUS, GROVE 5, MGG SUP,
PRATT, RIEMANN, RIEMANN ERG,
THOMPSON.

BOULANGER, Marie Julie(nne)
(born Hallinger). Paris,
Jan 29 1786-Jul 23 1850,
Paris. Soprano. ENCI MUS,
GROVE 1, GROVE 5, MGG SUP,
PRATT, THOMPSON.

BOULANGER, Nadia Juliette.
Paris, Sep 16 1887- . Com-
poser, conductor, teacher,
opera composer, writer,
choral conductor, organist.
BAKER 5, BLOM, COOPER, CORTE,
DICT MUS, ENCI MUS, ENCI SAL-
VAT, ENCY MUS, *EWEN LIVING,
EWEN LIV SUP, GROVE 5, GROVE
5 SUP, MARIZ, MGG SUP, RIE-
MANN, RIEMANN ERG, *SANDVED,
THOMPSON, *ULLSTEIN, VINTON.

BOURGEOIS, Mlle. fl.1793.
Dancer. HIGHFILL.

BOURGES, Clementine de. ?-
Sep 30 1581, Lyons. Com-
poser, poet. GROVE 1,
GROVE 5. *[GROVE 5=d.1561]*

BOURGIGNON, Jane. Bordeaux,
1894- . Contralto, voice
teacher. KUTSCH.

BOURK, Elizabeth (Mrs. William, born Bradshaw). fl.
1779-93. Dancer. HIGHFILL.

BOUVIER, Hélène. Paris, Jun 20
1905- . Contralto. ENCI SAL-
VAT, ENCY MUS, KUTSCH.

BOVY, Vina (Malvina Bovi).
Ghent, May 22 1900- .
Soprano, manager. BAKER 5,
ENCI MUS, ENCI SALVAT, ENCY
MUS, *EWEN LIVING, EWEN LIV
SUP, EWEN NEW, GROVE 5,
GROVE 5 SUP, KUTSCH, RIEMANN,
RIEMANN ERG, SANDVED, THOMP-
SON.

BOWDEN, Pamela. Rochdale, Lancashire, England, Apr 17
1925- . Contralto. RIEMANN,
RIEMANN ERG.

BOWEN, Catherine Drinker.
Haverford, Pa., Jan 1 1897-
Nov 1 1973, Haverford, Pa.
Writer. MGG SUP=col.1850.

BOWER, Mrs. fl.1721. Singer.
HIGHFILL.

BOYCE, Ethel Mary. Chertsey,
Surrey, England, Oct 5
1863-?. Composer, pianist.
BROWN BRIT.

BOYCE, Mrs. Thomas. fl.1790-
96. Dancer. HIGHFILL.

BOYD, Anne. Sydney, Australia,
?- . 20th-century composer,
electronic music composer,
teacher. *MURDOCH=illus.foll.
p.50.

BOYDE, Hesther see Colles,
Hesther

BOYLE, Elise (Mrs. George
Frederick, born Heuvel).
19-20th-century Dutch
singer. ENCI MUS.

BOYS, Margaret. Burnley, Lancashire, England, Oct 6
1908- . Contralto. PALMER.

BOZZI LUCCA, Irma. Buenos Aires, Sep 30 1920- . Soprano. ENCI MUS.

BRACEGIRDLE (Brasgirdle), Anne. Northamptonshire?, England, c1663-Sep 12 1748, London. Singer, actress. *HIGHFILL.

BRADFORD, Mrs. fl.1775. Singer. HIGHFILL.

BRADLEY, Mrs. M. fl.1772-77. Singer. HIGHFILL.

BRADSHAW, Anna Maria see Tree, Anna Maria

BRADSHAW, Elizabeth see Bourk, Elizabeth

BRADSHAW, Lucretia (later Mrs. Martin Folkes). ?-c1755, London. Singer, actress. HIGHFILL.

BRAGARD, Anne-Marie. Huy, Belgium, May 7 1932- . Musicologist, writer. ENCI MUS.

BRAITHWAITE, Ann. fl.1775-90. Dancer, actress. HIGHFILL.

BRAMBILLA, Amalia. Milan, ?-Aug 1880, Castellamare di Stabia, Italy. Soprano. ENCI MUS.

BRAMBILLA, Annetta. 19th-century Italian singer. ENCI MUS.

BRAMBILLA, Francesca, "Farinella." fl.1774. Italian singer. ENCI MUS.

BRAMBILLA, Giuseppina. Cassano, Italy, 1819-1903, Milan. Soprano. ENCI MUS, MGG SUP. [ENCI MUS=contralto]

BRAMBILLA, Laura. 19th-century Italian singer. ENCI MUS.

BRAMBILLA, Maria see Fuoco, Sofia

BRAMBILLA, Marietta. Cassano d'Adda, Italy, Jun 6 1807-Nov 6 1875, Milan. Contralto, voice teacher. BAKER 1, BAKER 5, CORTE, *ENCI MUS= illus.fac.p.311, GROVE 1, GROVE 1 APP, GROVE 5, MGG SUP, PRATT, RIEMANN, RIEMANN ERG.

BRAMBILLA, Teresa (Teresina). Cassano d'Adda, Italy, Oct 23 1813-Jul 15 1895, Milan. Soprano. BAKER 1, BAKER 5, *ENCI MUS=illus.fac.p.311, MGG SUP, PRATT. [MGG SUP= b.Dec 23 1813]

BRAMBILLA, Teresa (Mrs. Amilcare Ponchielli). Cassano d'Adda, Italy, Apr 15 1845-Jul 1 1921, Vercelli, Italy. Soprano. BROWN BIO=p.479 (brief mention in article on husband), CORTE, ENCI MUS= v.1 p.313 & v.3 p.470 (latter in article on husband), MGG SUP, RIEMANN=v.2 p.425 (brief mention in article on husband).

BRAMNER, Mary see Afferni, Mary

BRAMWELL, Georgiana. fl.1791-1804. Singer, actress. HIGHFILL.

BRANCATO, Rosemarie. Kansas City, Mo., ?- . 20th-century American soprano. THOMPSON.

BRANDES, Emma. Nr.Schwerin, Germany, Jan 20 1854-?. Pianist. BAKER 1, GROVE 1 APP, GROVE 5, THOMPSON.

BRANDT, Carolina see Weber, Carolina

BRANDT, Marianne (real name=
Marie Bischof). Vienna, Sep
12 1842-Jul 9 1921, Vienna.
Contralto, voice teacher.
BAKER 1, BAKER 5, ENCI MUS,
ENCI SALVAT, ENCY MUS,
GROVE 1 APP, GROVE 5, KUTSCH,
MARIZ, PRATT, RIEMANN, *SAND-
VED, THOMPSON, ULLSTEIN.

BRANDT-FORSTER, Ellen. Vienna,
Oct 11 1866-1921, Vienna.
Soprano. KUTSCH.

BRANÈZE, Maria. Étampes,
France, 1910- . Singer.
ENCI SALVAT, ENCY MUS.

BRANSCOMBE, Gena (Mrs. John
Ferguson Tenney). Picton,
Ontario, Canada, Nov 4
1881- . Composer, teacher,
choral conductor, conductor,
pianist. BAKER 5, CBC, ENCI
MUS, GROVE 5, NAPIER, PRATT,
REIS, RIEMANN, RIEMANN ERG,
SANDVED, SCHOLES, THOMPSON.

BRANSCOMBE, Marie (born
Hooton). 19th-century English contralto. BROWN BRIT.

BRANSDEN, Lillie Aileen.
London, May 31 1905- .
Organist. GROVE 5.

BRANZELL REINSHAGEN, Karin
Maria. Stockholm, Sep 24
1891-Dec 15 1974, Altadena,
Calif. Contralto, voice
teacher. BAKER 5, BAKER
1971, CELLETTI, CORTE=p.713,
ENCI MUS, *EWEN LIVING, EWEN
LIV SUP, EWEN NEW, GROVE 5,
GROVE 5 SUP, KUTSCH, RIEMANN,
RIEMANN ERG, SANDVED, THOMP-
SON. *[Date and place of death
based on obituary in Opera
News, Jan 25 1975, p.30]*

BRASGIRDLE, Anne see Bracegirdle, Anne

BRASLAU, Sophie. New York City,
Aug 16 1892-Dec 22 1935, New
York City. Contralto. BAKER 5,
EWEN NEW, KUTSCH, RIEMANN,
SANDVED, THOMPSON.

BRASSEUR, Élisabeth. Verdún,
1896-Nov 23 1972, Versailles.
Choral conductor, teacher.
ENCI SALVAT, ENCY MUS.

BRAUN, Helena (Mrs. Ferdinand
Frantz). Düsseldorf, 1903- .
Soprano. KUTSCH, RIEMANN
ERG=v.1 p.378 (brief mention
in article on husband).

BRAWN, Miss see Brown, Miss

BRAY, Anna Eliza (born Kempe).
St. Mary, Newington, Surrey,
England, Dec 25 1790-Jan 21
1883, London. Writer. BROWN
BIO, BROWN BRIT.

BRÉJEAN-SILVER, Georgette.
Paris, Sep 22 1870-?. So-
prano, voice teacher. KUTSCH.

BRELET, Gisèle. Fontenay-de-
Comte, Vendée, France, Mar 6
1915- . Writer. ENCI MUS,
ENCI SALVAT, ENCY MUS, MGG
SUP, RIEMANN ERG.

BREMA, Marie (orig. Bremer; real
name=Minny Fehrman). Liverpool,
Feb 28 1856-Mar 22 1925, Man-
chester, England. Contralto,
voice teacher. BAKER 5, BLOM,
BROWN BRIT, ENCI MUS, GROVE 5,
PRATT, RIEMANN, SANDVED, THOMP-
SON. *[BLOM, GROVE 5, RIEMANN,
& SANDVED=mezzo-soprano; ENCI
MUS=contralto & mezzo-soprano]*

BREMER, Marie see Brema, Marie

BRENET, Michel (pseud.; real
name=Antoinette Christine
Marie Bobillier). Lunéville,
France, Apr 12 1858-Nov 4

1918, Paris. Musicologist, writer. BAKER 5, BLOM, CORTE, DICT MUS, ENCI MUS, ENCI SALVAT, ENCY MUS, GROVE 5, MGG, PRATT, RIEMANN, SCHOLES, THOMPSON.

BRENNING, Marie see Krebs, Marie

BRENT, Charlotte (Mrs. Thomas Pinto). London, c1735-Apr 10 1802, London. Soprano. BLOM, BROWN BIO=p.474 (in article on husband), BROWN BRIT=p.321 (in article on husband), GROVE 1 APP, GROVE 5, PRATT, THOMPSON.

BRENTANO, Bettina (Elisabeth) (Mrs. Achim von Arnim). Frankfurt, Apr 4 1785-Jan 20 1859, Berlin. Composer, poet. DICT MUS, RIEMANN, RIEMANN ERG.

BRERETON, Sarah (born Ambler). 19th-century English soprano. BROWN BRIT.

BRESSLER-GIANOLI, Clotilde. Geneva, Jun 3 1875-May 12 1912, Geneva. Mezzo-soprano. BAKER 5, ENCI SALVAT, ENCY MUS, KUTSCH, PRATT, SANDVED, THOMPSON. *[BAKER 5 & SAND-VED=contralto; KUTSCH=b. 1874]*

"BRÉTET, Mlle." see Haynes, Elizabeth

BRETT, Anne see Chetwood, Anne

BRETT, Elizabeth (Mrs. Dawson, born Cibber). London, bapt. Mar 16 1701-?, London?. Dancer, actress. HIGHFILL.

BRETT, Frances see Hodgkinson, Frances

BRETT, Frances R. see Chapman, Frances R.

BRETT, Hannah (Mrs. William). ?-c1804, London?. Singer, actress. HIGHFILL.

BREUNING-STORM, Gunna. Copenhagen, Jan 25 1891-Apr 24 1966, Copenhagen. Violinist. RIEMANN, RIEMANN ERG.

BRÉVAL, Lucienne (orig. Berthe Agnes Lisette Schilling). Männedorf (not Berlin), Nov 4 1869-Aug 15 1935, Neuilly-sur Seine, nr.Paris. Soprano, voice teacher. BAKER 5, BLOM, CELLETTI, ENCI SALVAT, ENCY. MUS, EWEN NEW, GROVE 5, KUTSCH, PRATT, RIEMANN, RIEMANN ERG, SANDVED, THOMPSON.

BRICE, Carol. Sedalia, N.C., Apr 16 1918- . Contralto. *EWEN LIV SUP.

BRICKLAYER, Miss. fl.1756-57. Singer. HIGHFILL.

BRICKLER, Miss. fl.1758-67. Singer. HIGHFILL.

BRICO, Antonia. Rotterdam, Jun 26 1902- . Conductor, choral conductor. BAKER 5, BAKER 1971, *EWEN LIVING, EWEN LIV SUP, RIEMANN, RIEMANN ERG, THOMPSON.

BRIDA, Marie Catherine see Dorival à Corifet

BRIDE, Elizabeth (later Mrs. Lefevre, later Mrs. Samworth?). ?-Sep 1826, ?. 18-19th-century English dancer, actress. HIGHFILL.

BRIDER, Miss. fl.1765. Dancer. HIGHFILL.

BRIDGE, Elizabeth see
Stirling, Elizabeth

BRIDGES, Mrs. fl.1744-49.
Singer, actress. HIGHFILL.

BRIDGMAN, Nanie. Angoulême,
Charente, France, Feb 2
1907- . Musicologist,
librarian, contralto,
writer. ENCI MUS, ENCI
SALVAT, ENCY MUS, GROVE 5
SUP, MGG, RIEMANN, RIEMANN
ERG. *[MGG=b.Feb 6 1910]*

BRIEM, Tilla. Morhange,
Lothringen, Germany, Mar 31
1905- . Soprano. RIEMANN,
RIEMANN ERG.

BRIGG, Mrs. fl.1790-1802.
Dancer, singer, actress.
HIGHFILL.

BRIGHENTI, Maria (real name=
Geltrude Giorgi-Righetti).
Bologna, 1792-1862, Bologna.
Soprano, contralto, mezzo-
soprano. BLOM=p.242, ENCI
MUS=v.4 p.16 (under Righet-
ti Giorgi), GROVE 1, PRATT,
THOMPSON.

BRIGHI, Mimi see Coertse,
Mimi

BRIGHT, Dora Estella. Sheffield, England, Aug 16
1863-Nov 16 1951, Babing-
ton, Somerset (not London).
Composer, opera composer,
pianist. BLOM, BROWN BRIT,
ENCI SALVAT, ENCY MUS,
GROVE 5, PRATT, RIEMANN
ERG, THOMPSON. *[Some sources=
d.Dec 1951, which RIEMANN
ERG corrects to Nov 16]*

BRIGLIA, Antonietta. 19-20th-
century Italian violinist.
ENCI MUS=v.2 p.307 (brief
mention in article on the
Giannini family).

BRINKERHOFF, Clara M. (born
Rolph). England, before
1830?-?. Soprano. BROWN
BIO, THOMPSON.

BRIOUSSOVA, Nadejda Yakovleva
see Brjussowa, Nadeschda
Jakowlewna

BRISSAC, Jules (pen name) see
Macfarren, Emma Marie Bennett

BRISTOW, Mrs. (later Mrs. Robert
Skinner). fl.1797-1804. Singer.
HIGHFILL.

BRITAIN, Radie. Amarillo, Tex.,
Mar 17 1903- . Composer.
BAKER 5, BAKER 1971, ENCI MUS,
PAVLAKIS=p.323, REIS, THOMP-
SON. *[PAVLAKIS=b.1907]*

BRITTON, Mrs. fl.1729-31. Dancer, actress. HIGHFILL.

BRIXI, Dorota (Dorothea).
Skalsko, Bohemia, Jan 15
1686-1762, Nová Ves, Bohemia.
Musician. ENCI MUS=v.1 p.230
(brief mention in article on
Benda family), MGG SUP.

BRIZZI GIORGI, Maria. Bologna,
Aug 7 1775-Jul 26 1811,
Bologna. Organist, pianist,
composer. ENCI MUS.

BRJUSSOWA (Brioussova, Bryusova),
Nadeschda (Nadejda, Nadezhda)
Jakowlewna (Yakovleva, Yakov-
levna). Moscow, Nov 19 1881-
Jun 28 1951, Moscow. Composer,
writer. ENCY MUS, MGG SUP,
RIEMANN, RIEMANN ERG, VODAR-
SKY.

BROAD, Elizabeth see Haynes,
Elizabeth

BROADFOOT, Eleanora see
Cisneros, Eleanora de

BROADHURST, Miss. London?,

c1775-after 1803, USA?.
Singer, actress. *HIGHFILL.

BROADWOOD, Lucy E. London,
Aug 9 1858-Aug 22 1929,
London. Folksong collector,
editor, composer. BROWN
BRIT, GROVE 5, GROVE 5 SUP.

BROCKHOFF, Maria Elisabeth.
Ludwigsburg, Germany, Apr 2
1922- . Musicologist,
writer. RIEMANN ERG.

BRODSKY, Vera. Norfolk, Va.,
Jul 1 1909- . Pianist.
BAKER 5.

BROGGINI, Cesy. San Giuliano
Terme, Pisa, Italy, Jun 5
1928- . Soprano. ENCI MUS.

BROGUE, Roslyn. Chicago, Feb
16 1919- . Composer.
BAKER 1971.

BROHLY, Suzanne. France,
1882- . Contralto. KUTSCH.

BROMMER, May see Bramner,
Mary

BRONDI, Maria Rita. Rimini,
Italy, 1889-1941, Rome.
Guitarist, lutenist, writer.
CORTE.

BRONSART VON SCHELLENDORF,
Ingeborg von (born Starck).
St. Petersburg, Aug 24 1840-
Jun 17 1913, Munich. Pia-
nist, composer, opera com-
poser. BAKER 1, BAKER 5,
BLOM=p.660, DICT MUS, ENCI
MUS, GROVE 5, RIEMANN,
THOMPSON=p.2094.

BRONSKAJA, Eugenia. St. Petersburg, Feb 2 1884- . Soprano,
voice teacher. KUTSCH.

BROOKES, Miss. fl.1774-75.
Dancer. HIGHFILL.

BROOKS, Patricia. New York City,
Nov 7 1937- . Soprano, act-
ress. PAVLAKIS=p.286, RIEMANN
ERG.

BROTHIER, Yvonne. St. Julien
l'Ars, France, Jun 6 1880-
Jan 22 1967, Paris. Soprano,
voice teacher. ENCI SALVAT,
ENCY MUS, KUTSCH. [ENCI
SALVAT=d.Jan 29; ENCY MUS=
b.1895]

BROUGH, Annie see Romer,
Annie

BROUWENSTIJN, Gré (orig. Gérar-
da Demphina van Swol). Den
Helder, Netherlands, Aug 26
1915- . Soprano. CELLETTI,
ENCI SALVAT, ENCY MUS, GROVE
5 SUP, KUTSCH, MGG SUP, RIE-
MANN, RIEMANN ERG, *ROSEN-
THAL=illus.p.28, SANDVED,
THOMPSON, ULLSTEIN.

BROUWER, Geneviève see Vix,
Geneviève

BROWN (Brawn), Miss. fl.1767-78.
Dancer, actress. HIGHFILL.

BROWN, Mrs. fl.1786-87. Singer.
HIGHFILL.

BROWN, Mrs. fl.1790-97. Singer,
actress. HIGHFILL.

BROWN, Ann (Mrs. R.) see
Cargill, Ann

BROWN, Claudia Anne Russell-
see Russell, Anna

BROWN, Mrs. J. (born Mills,
formerly Mrs. William Ross).
?-1823, ?. English singer,
actress. *HIGHFILL.

BROWN, Sarah. London?, 1757-
Dec 5 1806, London?. Dancer.
HIGHFILL.

BROWN, Sophia see De Camp, Sophia

BROWNING, Miss. fl.1785-86. English singer, dancer. HIGHFILL.

BROWNING, Jean see Madeira, Jean

BRUCE, Mrs. fl.1705-06. Dancer. HIGHFILL.

BRUCE, Janet see Winston, Jeannie

BRUCE CLARKE, Marian see Somigli, Franca

BRUCH, Clara (Mrs. Max, born Tuczek). Berlin, ?-Aug 1919, Friedenau, Germany. Singer. ENCI MUS, RIEMANN.

BRUCHOLLERIE, Monique de la. Paris, Apr 20 1915-Dec 13 1972, Paris. Pianist. BAKER 1971, ENCI SALVAT=v.3 p.130.

BRUCKSHAW, Kathleen. London, Jan 5 1877-Oct 10 1921, London. Pianist, composer. GROVE 5.

BRÜGELMANN, Hedy Iracema- see Iracema-Brügelmann, Hedy

BRUCKARD, Martha see Leffler-Bruckard, Martha

BRUMAIRE, Jacqueline. Paris, ?- . 20th-century French singer. ENCI SALVAT, ENCY MUS.

BRUMEN, Miss. fl.1794. English singer. HIGHFILL.

BRUN, Antoinette Laute- see Laute-Brun, Antoinette

BRUNA-RASA, Lina. Milan, Sep

24 1907- . Soprano. ENCI SAL- VAT, ENCY MUS, KUTSCH.

BRUNETTE, Miss. fl.1734-42. English dancer, actress. HIGHFILL.

BRUNO, Joanna. 20th-century soprano. PAVLAKIS=p.286.

BRUNSKILL, Muriel. Kendal, England, Dec 18 1899- . Contralto. CELLETTI, KUTSCH, PALMER, THOMPSON.

BRYHN-LANGAARD, Borghild. Kongsvinger, Norway, Jul 23 1883-Nov 20 1939, Oslo. Soprano. KUTSCH.

BRYUSOVA, Nadezhda Yakovlevna see Brjussowa, Nadeschda Jakowlewna

BRZEZIŃSKA, Filipina (born Szymanowska). Warsaw, Jan 1 1800-Nov 10 1886, Warsaw. Pianist, composer. GROVE 5, RIEMANN.

BUCHANAN, Annabel Morris. Grossbeck, Tex., Oct 22 1889- Composer, pianist, organist, writer. THOMPSON.

BUCHANAN, Jessie Niven see McLachlan, Jessie Niven

BUCHARDO, Brigida (Mrs. Carlos López, born Frías). Buenos Aires, 1896- . Soprano. ARIZAGA=p.201, GROVE 5.

BUCK, Era Marguerite. Manitou- lin Island, Ontario, Canada, ?- . 20th-century Canadian pianist, organist, violinist, composer. CBC.

BUCK, Heather see Harper, Heather

BUCKEL, Ursula. Lauscha, Thür-

inger Wald, Germany, Feb 11
1926- . Soprano. RIEMANN
ERG.

BUCKINGER, Miss. fl.1761-69.
Dancer. HIGHFILL.

BUCKLEY, Beatrice Barron.
Sarnia, Ontario, Canada,
?- . 20th-century Canadian
pianist, composer, writer,
singer. CBC.

BUCKLEY, Olivia see Dussek,
Olivia

BUCKMAN, Rosina. Blenheim, New
Zealand, ?-Dec 31 1948, Lon-
don. Soprano. GROVE 5,
THOMPSON.

BUCKNALL, Margaret see
Eyre, Margaret

BUDGELL, Anne Eustace. London?,
c1726-c1755, Bath, England.
Singer, actress. HIGHFILL.

BÜLTEMANN, Margarete Frida
see Klose, Margarete Frida

BÜRDE-NEY, Jenny (born Ney).
Graz, Dec 21 1826-May 17
1886, Dresden. Soprano.
BAKER 1, BLOM, GROVE 1 APP,
GROVE 5, PRATT, THOMPSON.

BÜRGER, Marie see Paur,
Marie

BUGAMELLI, Teresita. 19-20th-
century Italian singer.
ENCI MUS.

BUGG, Madeleine. Rheims, 1894?-
1936, Paris. Soprano. KUTSCH.

BUGIANI, Elizabetta. fl.1752-
57. Dancer. HIGHFILL.

BUINI, Cecchina see Belisani,
Cecchina

BUKOWSKA, Barbara Hesse- see
Hesse-Bukowska, Barbara

BULKLEY, Mary (Mrs. George,
later Mrs. Ebenezer Barrisford, born Wilford). London?,
1748-Dec 19 1792, Dumfries,
Scotland. Dancer, actress.
*HIGHFILL.

BULLOCK, Miss. fl.1777-78.
Dancer. HIGHFILL.

BULLOCK, Ann (Mrs. Hildebrand,
born Russell). fl.1714-48.
Dancer. HIGHFILL.

BULLOCK, Harriet see Dyer,
Harriet

BULLOCK, Henrietta Maria (later
Mrs. John Ogden). fl.1719-48.
Dancer, actress. HIGHFILL.

BUMBRY, Grace Ann (Mrs. Jaeckel).
St. Louis, Mo., Jan 4 1937- .
Mezzo-soprano. BAKER 1971,
EWEN NEW, KUTSCH, PAVLAKIS=
p.286, RIEMANN ERG, *SANDVED,
THOMPSON, *ULLSTEIN.

BUNLET, Marcelle (Marie Hen-
riette Jeanne). Fontenay-le-
Comte, Vendée, France, Oct 4
1900- . Soprano. ENCI SALVAT,
ENCY MUS, GROVE 5, KUTSCH.
[KUTSCH=b.Oct 9, 1900 at
Strasbourg]

BUONSOLLAZZI, Anna Lucia see
Amicis, Anna Lucia de

BUONSOLLAZZI, Rosalba Baldacci
see Amicis, Rosalba Baldacci

BURCHELL, H. Louise. Sydney,
Nova Scotia, Canada, ?- .
20th-century Canadian composer, teacher, organist,
choral conductor. CBC.

BURCHELL, Isabella see
Vincent, Isabella

BURDEN, Kitty (born White).
fl.1757-83. English singer,
actress. HIGHFILL.

BURDINO, Elen see Dosia,
Elen

BURGUET DÍAZ, Iris Zenaida.
Víbora, Cuba, Oct 23 1928- .
Soprano. RIEMANN ERG.

BURKE, Hilda. Baltimore, Md.,
?- . 20th-century American
soprano. *EWEN LIVING,
EWEN LIV SUP.

BURLIN, Natalie Curtis see
Curtis, Natalie

BURN, Miss. fl.1759. Dancer,
actress. HIGHFILL.

BURNETT, Miss. fl.1783-1822.
English singer, actress.
HIGHFILL.

BURNETT, Mrs. William? (born
Goodman?). London?, ?-
c1822?, London?. English
singer, actress. HIGHFILL.

BURNEY, Esther (Mrs. Charles
Rousseau, born Burney).
?, 1749-1832, Bath, England.
Harpsichordist. *HIGHFILL.

BURNS, Georgina (Mrs. Leslie
Crotty). London, 1860-?.
Soprano. BROWN BRIT.

BURONI, Signora. fl.1777.
English singer. HIGHFILL.

BURR, Mrs. fl.1694. English
singer. HIGHFILL.

BURRELL, Mary. England, 1850-
1898, England. Writer.
SCHOLES.

BURROWES, Katharine. Kingston,
Ontario, Canada, ?-Nov 5
1939, Detroit. Teacher,

pianist, piano teacher.
PRATT, THOMPSON.

BURSTEIN, Rosa see Raisa,
Rosa

BURY, Miss. fl.1783-89.
Dancer. HIGHFILL.

BURZIO, Eugenia. Poirino,
Turin, Jun 20 1879-May 18
1922, Milan. Soprano.
CELLETTI, CORTE, ENCI MUS,
KUTSCH. [CORTE=b.1882;
KUTSCH=b.1872]

BUSCH-WEISE, Dagmar von.
Kulmbach, Germany, Jan 2
1926- . Musicologist,
writer. RIEMANN ERG.

BUSHNELL, Catherine see
Hayes, Catherine

BUSI, Leonida. Bologna, May 4
1835-Dec 27 1900, Bologna.
Writer. CORTE, ENCI MUS.

BUSSANI, Carolina. fl.1815.
Italian singer. ENCI MUS.

BUSTABO, Guila. Manitowoc,
Wis., Feb 25 1919- . Vio-
linist, teacher. BAKER 5,
BAKER 1971, ENCI MUS, ENCI
SALVAT, *EWEN LIVING, RIE-
MANN, RIEMANN ERG, THOMPSON,
ULLSTEIN. [ENCI SALVAT=
b.1918]

BUTCHER, Sarah see Ward,
Sarah

BUTLER, Mrs. fl.1746-50. Singer, actress. HIGHFILL.

BUTLER, Antonia. London, Jun 1
1909- . Violoncellist.
GROVE 5, THOMPSON.

BUTLER, Charlotte. fl.1673-95.
Singer, dancer, actress.
HIGHFILL.

BUTLER, Joan. West Bromwich, England, May 2 1923- . Soprano. PALMER.

BUTLER, Mrs. William. fl. 1789-1812. English singer. HIGHFILL.

BUTT, Dame Clara. Southwick, nr. Brighton, Sussex, Feb 1 1873-Jan 23 1936, Worthsloke, Oxford. Contralto. BAKER 5, BLOM, BROWN BRIT, COOPER, GROVE 5, KUTSCH, MARIZ, PRATT, SANDVED, THOMPSON.

BUTTERWORTH, Annie. ?, 1852?- Dec 9 1885, Hendon, England. Contralto. BROWN BRIT.

BUXTON, Eugenia. Memphis, Tenn., ?- . 20th-century American pianist. *EWEN LIVING.

BYRN, Adelaide C. (later Mrs. William Baly). 19-20th-century English pianist. BROWN BRIT=p.23 (in article on husband).

BYRNE, Mrs. London?, ?-Sep 1782, London?. Dancer. HIGHFILL.

BYRNE, Miss. fl.1784-87. English dancer. HIGHFILL.

BYRNE, Mrs. fl.1785-1800. English singer, dancer, actress. HIGHFILL.

C

CABALLÉ, Montserrat. Barcelona, Apr 12 1933- . Soprano. ENCI SALVAT, EWEN NEW, KUTSCH, RIEMANN ERG.

CABANEL, Eliza. fl.1792-1800. English dancer. HIGHFILL.

CABANEL, Harriot (later Mrs. Helme). fl.1791-1806. English dancer. HIGHFILL.

CABEL (Cabu), Marie Josephe (born Dreulette). Liége, Belgium, Jan 31 1827-May 23 1885, Maisons Lafitte, nr. Paris. Soprano. BROWN BIO, GROVE 1, GROVE 1 APP, GROVE 5, PRATT, THOMPSON.

CABRERA, Ana S. de. Simoca, Argentina, 1897-1970, ?. Folklorist, guitarist. ARIZAGA.

CABU, Marie Josephe see Cabel, Marie Josephe

CACCAMISI, Baroness Andre see · Marchesi de Castrone, Blanche

CACCINI, Francesca, "La Cecchina." Florence, Sep 18 1587-c1640, Lucca?, Italy. Opera composer, singer, composer. BAKER 5, BLOM, CORTE, DICT MUS, ENCI MUS, ENCI SALVAT, ENCY MUS, GROVE 5, RIEMANN, RIEMANN ERG.

CACCINI, Settimia. Florence, c1590-after 1640, Florence. Singer. DICT MUS, ENCI MUS.

CADORET, Charlotte (Soeur Saint-Jean-du-Sacre-Coeur). Newark, N.J., Feb 29 1908- . Composer, pianist. CBC, NAPIER.

CADZOW, Dorothy. Edmonton, Alberta, Canada, Aug 9 1916- . Composer, arranger, teacher. BAKER 5, CBC, NAPIER.

CAFFARET, Lucie. Paris, 1893- . Pianist. ENCI SALVAT, ENCY MUS.

CAHIER, Sarah-Jane (Mrs. Char-

les, born Layton Walker).
Nashville, Tenn., Jan 8
1870-Apr 15 1951, Manhattan
Beach, Calif. Contralto,
voice teacher. BAKER 5,
ENCI SALVAT, ENCY MUS,
EWEN NEW, KUTSCH, SANDVED,
THOMPSON. *[EWEN NEW &
THOMPSON=b.Jan 6; ENCI SAL-
VAT=b.1875, d.Los Angeles]*

CALAND, Elisabeth. Rotterdam,
Jan 13 1862-Jan 26 1929,
Berlin. Pianist, piano
teacher, editor, writer.
BAKER 5, CORTE, ENCI MUS,
PRATT, RIEMANN, THOMPSON.

CALARI, Angiola see Calori,
Angiola

CALCAGNO, Elsa. Buenos Aires,
Oct 19 1910- . Composer,
pianist. ARIZAGA, ENCI MUS.

CALEGARI, Maria Caterina.
Bergamo, Italy, 1644-1662?,
Milan. Composer, organist,
singer. GROVE 5, MGG SUP,
THOMPSON.

CALLAS, Maria Meneghini
(born Anna Sofia Cecilia
Kalogperopoulous). New York
City, Dec 3 1923- . Soprano.
BAKER 5, BLOM, *CELLETTI=
illus.foll.col.96 & 352,
*COOPER=p.64, CORTE, *ENCI
MUS=illus.p.366, *ENCI SAL-
VAT=v.1 p.430, ENCY MUS,
*EWEN LIV SUP, EWEN NEW,
GROVE 5, GROVE 5 SUP,
KUTSCH, MGG SUP, PAVLAKIS=
p.286, RIEMANN=v.2 p.197,
RIEMANN ERG, *ROSENTHAL=
illus.p.2 & 38, *SANDVED,
THOMPSON, *ULLSTEIN. *[CEL-
LETTI, KUTSCH, & ULLSTEIN=
b.Dec 4; MGG SUP=b.Dec 2;
EWEN LIV SUP=b.1924]*

CALLAULT, Marie Sophie see
Ponchard, Marie Sophie

CALLCOTT, Maria Hutchins.
London?, 1799-Apr 3 1859,
London. Writer. BROWN BIO,
BROWN BRIT.

CALLE, Isabel de la. Madrid,
1878-?. Teacher. ENCI SALVAT=
v.1 p.430.

CALLIARI, Isabella see
Girardeau, Isabella

CALLOW, Harriet Anne see
Smart, Harriet Anne

CALORI (Calari), Angiola.
Milan, 1732-c1790, Milan.
Soprano. GROVE 1, GROVE 5,
HIGHFILL, MGG SUP, PRATT,
THOMPSON.

CALVÉ, Rosa-Noémie-Emma (orig.
Calvé de Roquer). Décaze-
ville, Aveyron, France, Aug
15 1858-Jan 6 1942, Millau,
Aveyron, France. Soprano.
BAKER 5, BLOM, CELLETTI,
COOPER, CORTE, *ENCI MUS=
illus.fac.p.366, ENCI SALVAT,
ENCY MUS, *EWEN LIVING, EWEN
LIV SUP, EWEN NEW, GROVE 5,
KUTSCH, MARIZ, MGG SUP,
PRATT, RIEMANN, RIEMANN ERG,
THOMPSON.

CALVERT, Mrs. fl.1772. English
singer. HIGHFILL.

CALVESI, Teresa. fl.1783-92.
Singer. HIGHFILL.

CAMAITI, Corella Provvedi.
Siena, Italy, Sep 11 1916- .
Pianist, piano teacher.
ENCI MUS=v.3 p.497 (in
article on the Provvedi
family).

CAMAL, Maria see Camati,
Maria

CAMARGO, Sophie? (or Marie-
Anne Charlotte de?) Cupis de

(or Capi, Cappi, or Cuppi).
Brussels, Apr 15 1710-Apr
28 1770, Paris. Dancer.
DICT MUS=under Cupis, *ENCI
SALVAT, *ENCY MUS, HIGHFILL,
RIEMANN ERG.

CAMATI (Camal), Maria, "la
Farinella." Venice, ?-?.
18th-century Italian singer.
ENCI MUS.

CAMBERT, Marie-Anne. 17th-
century clavicembalist.
ENCI MUS=v.2 p.167 (brief
mention in article on husband Michel Farinel).

"CAMILLA" see Tofts,
Catherine

CAMINALS, Rosa Maria. Barcelona, 1932- . Pianist.
ENCI SALVAT.

CAMMARANO, Rosalia (later
Vitellaro). 19th-century
Italian singer. ENCI MUS.

CAMP, Adelaide de see
De Camp, Adelaide

CAMP, Sophia de see De
Camp, Sophia

CAMPANINI, Barbarina, "la
Barbarina." Parma, 1721-Jun
7 1799, Barschau, Germany.
Dancer. ENCI SALVAT, *HIGH-
FILL.

CAMPANINI, Miriamne see
Domitilla, Miriamne

CAMPBELL, Mrs. fl.1751.
Singer, actress. HIGHFILL.

CAMPBELL, Lady Archibald.
19th-century English
writer, musician. BROWN
BRIT.

CAMPBELL, Edith May. St. Luc,

Québec, Canada, Sep 1 1912- .
Composer, organist, choral
conductor. CBC.

CAMPBELL, Ellen (born De Fonblanque). Gloucester?, ?-?.
19th-century English soprano.
BROWN BRIT.

CAMPBELL, Helen see Kennedy,
Helen

CAMPBELL, Helen Dudley see
Del Puente, Helen

CAMPBELL, Mary Maxwell.
Fife, Pitlour House, Scot-
land, 1812-Jan 15 1886,
St. Andrews, Scotland.
Composer. BROWN BRIT.

CAMPI, Antonia (born Miklaszewicz). Lublin, Poland, Dec
10 1773-Sep 30 1822, Munich.
Soprano. CORTE, ENCI MUS,
ENCI SALVAT, ENCY MUS, GROVE
5. *[CORTE=d. 1821]*

CAMPIÑA, Fidela. Tijola, Spain,
1897- . Soprano. ENCI SAL-
·VAT, ENCY MUS.

CAMPION, Mary Anne. England,
c1687-May 19 1706, Devon-
shire. Singer, dancer,
harpsichordist. HIGHFILL.

CAMPIONI, Signora. fl.1744-54.
Dancer. HIGHFILL.

CAMPMANY, Montserrat. Barcelona, Mar 7 1901- . Composer,
teacher. ARIZAGA, RIEMANN
ERG.

CAMPO, Sofia del see Del
Campo, Sofia

CAMPOBELLO, Clarice see
Sinico, Clarice

CAMPODONICO, Armanda (Amanda).
Rosario, Argentina, Nov 17

1879-Jul 14 1933, Buenos
Aires. Mezzo-soprano, voice
teacher. ENCI SALVAT, ENCY
MUS, THOMPSON.

CAMPOLINI, Signora. fl.1767-68.
Singer. HIGHFILL.

CAMPORESE, Violante. Rome,
1785-1839, Rome. Soprano.
BAKER 1, BLOM, BROWN BIO,
CLAYTON=p.228, GROVE 5,
PRATT, THOMPSON. *[BROWN BIO=
d. after 1860 (1839?)]*

CAMPREDON, Jeanne. 20th-cen-
tury French soprano. ENCI
SALVAT, ENCY MUS.

CANAL, Marguerite. Toulouse,
France, Jan 29 1890- .
Composer. BAKER 5, DICT MUS,
ENCI SALVAT, ENCY MUS, RIE-
MANN, THOMPSON.

CANALES, Marta. 20th-century
Chilean violinist, composer.
THOMPSON.

CANALI, Isabella. Padua, 1562-
1604, Lyons, France. Singer.
ENCY MUS, RIEMANN=v.1 p.36
(brief mention in article
on son Giovanni Battista
Andreini).

CANALS, María R. Barcelona,
?- . 20th-century Spanish
pianist. ENCI SALVAT.

CANASI, Ida. Buenos Aires,
1899- . Mezzo-soprano.
ARIZAGA.

CANAVASSO, Genoveffa (Mrs.
Alessandro, born Garnier).
17-18th-century Italian
singer. ENCI MUS.

CANDEILLE (Simons), Amélie-
Julie. Paris, Jul 31 1767-
Feb 4 1834, Paris. Soprano,
actress, composer, light-

opera composer, teacher.
BAKER 1, BLOM, ENCI MUS,
GROVE 5, PRATT, RIEMANN,
RIEMANN ERG, THOMPSON.

CANELA, María. 20th-century
Spanish pianist. ENCI SALVAT.

CANIGLIA, Maria. Naples, May
3 1905- . Soprano. CELLETTI,
CORTE, ENCI MUS, ENCI SALVAT,
ENCY MUS, GROVE 5, KUTSCH,
MARIZ, RIEMANN ERG. *[Sources
give various birth dates
ranging from 1902 to 1906;
the date found in RIEMANN
ERG, given above, assumed
correct]*

CANNABICH, Josephine (Mrs.
Carl, born Woraleck). 18-19th-
century German soprano.
GROVE 5.

CANNABICH, Rosine Therese
Petronelle (Rosa). Mannheim,
Aug 18 1764-?. Pianist.
ENCI MUS, GROVE 5.

CANNE MEYER, Cora. Amsterdam,
Aug 11 1929- . Mezzo-soprano.
ENCI SALVAT, ENCY MUS,
KUTSCH. *[KUTSCH=contralto]*

CANNON, Ellen Beach see
Yaw, Ellen Beach

CANTADOR, Maria Cäcilia see
Philippi, Maria Cäcilia

CANTELO, Annie (Mrs. Harry
Cox). Nottingham, ?-?.
19th-century English pianist,
composer. BROWN BRIT.

CANTELO, April, 20th-century
English soprano. KUTSCH.

CANTRELL, Mrs. fl.1716-37.
English singer, actress.
HIGHFILL.

CANTRELL, Miss. fl.1736-39.

English dancer, actress.
HIGHFILL.

CANTRELL, Miss. fl.1766-71.
English singer. HIGHFILL.

CAPDEVILLE, Mlle. fl.1754-71.
English dancer, proprietor.
HIGHFILL.

CAPDEVILLE, Miss. fl.1762.
English dancer. HIGHFILL.

CAPI, Sophie see Camargo,
· Sophie

CAPITANI, Polly. fl.1759-66.
English dancer. HIGHFILL.

CAPLAN, Joan. 20th-century
American mezzo-soprano.
PAVLAKIS=p.294.

CAPPELLETTI, Theresa Poggi.
fl.1791. Italian soprano.
HIGHFILL.

CAPPER, Miss. fl.1798-1810.
English singer. HIGHFILL.

CAPPI, Sophie see Camargo,
Sophie

CAPSIR-TANZI, Mercedes.
Barcelona, Jul 20 1895-Mar
13 1969, Suzzara, Lombardy,
Italy. Soprano, composer.
CELLETTI, ENCI MUS, ENCI
SALVAT, ENCY MUS, KUTSCH,
MARIZ, RIEMANN, RIEMANN ERG.

CAPUANA, Maria. Nr. Pesaro,
Italy, 1891-Feb 22 1955,
Cagliari, Sardinia. Con-
tralto. CORTE, KUTSCH.
[CORTE=d. Naples]

"CAPUCHINO, Signora." fl.1746.
Dancer. HIGHFILL.

CARA, Giovanna (Mrs. Marco,
born de Mareschi). 16th-
century Italian singer.
ENCI MUS.

CARACCIOLO, Juanita. Ravenna,
Italy, Oct 25 1888-Jul 5
1924, Milan. Soprano.
CELLETTI, ENCI MUS, THOMPSON.
[CELLETTI=b.c1890, ENCI MUS=
b.1888, THOMPSON=b.1889]

CARADORI- (CARRADORI-) ALLAN,
Maria Caterina Rosalbina
(born de Munck). Casa Pala-
tina, Milan, 1800-Oct 15
1865, Surbiton, Surrey, England. Soprano. BLOM, BROWN
BIO, ENCI MUS=v.1 p.418,
GROVE 1, GROVE 1 APP, GROVE
5, PRATT, THOMPSON.

"CARAMBA, La" see Fernández,
María Antonia

CARARA, Signora Antonio. fl.
1768-78. Italian singer.
HIGHFILL.

CARBONE ROSSINI, Maria. Castellamare di Stabia, Naples,
Jun 15 1908- . Soprano.
ENCI MUS, KUTSCH. [KUTSCH=
b. Jun 12 1912]

CARBONELL, María. Barcelona,
1911- . Pianist. ENCI SALVAT.

CARDARELLI (Cardelli), Signora.
fl.1775-76. Singer. GROVE 1,
HIGHFILL.

CARDELLI, Signora see
Cardarelli, Signora

CARDI, Signora. fl.1773-74.
Singer. HIGHFILL.

CARDIGAN, Cora. fl.1880-90.
English flutist, BROWN BRIT.

CARELESS, Elizabeth (Betty).
England?, ?-Apr 22 1752,
London. Singer, actress.
*HIGHFILL.

CARELLI, Emma. Naples, May 12
1877-Aug 17 1928, nr. Monte-
fiascone, Italy. Soprano.

CELLETTI, CORTE, ENCI MUS,
KUTSCH, RIEMANN ERG,
THOMPSON.

CARENA, Maria. Turin, 1894- .
Soprano. ENCI MUS, KUTSCH.

CAREW, Miss?. London, Oct 16
1799-?. Soprano. BROWN
BIO, BROWN BRIT.

CAREY, Mrs. George Saville
(born Gillo). fl.1789-98.
English singer. HIGHFILL.

CARGILL, Ann (Mrs. R., born
Brown). London, c1759-Mar
12 or Feb 24 1784, Scilly,
England. Singer, actress.
*HIGHFILL.

CARIAGA, Marvellee. 20th-
century contralto. PAVLA-
KIS=p.297.

CARIGNANI, Virginia see
Boccabadati Carignani,
Virginia

CARIVEN-MARTEL, Edith. Paris,
1906- . Harpist. ENCI
MUS, ENCY MUS.

CARLEY, Nathalie see Dol-
metsch, Nathalie

CARLI, Miss. fl.1762-70.
Singer. HIGHFILL.

CARLINI, Rosa. fl.1758-59.
Dancer. HIGHFILL.

CARLSTEDT, France Marguerite
see Ellegaard, France
Marguerite

CARMICHAEL, Mary Grant. Bir-
kenhead, England, 1851-Mar
17 1935, London. Composer,
pianist, light-opera composer. BAKER 1, BAKER 5, BROWN
BRIT, PRATT, THOMPSON.

CARMIGNANI, Giovanna. fl.1763.
English singer. GROVE 1,
HIGHFILL.

CARMIRELLI, Pina. Varzi,
Italy, Jan 23 1914- . Vio-
linist. PAVLAKIS=p.271,
RIEMANN ERG.

CARNE, Miss. fl.1799-1802.
English dancer. HIGHFILL.

CARNER, Helen (Mrs. Mosco,
born Pyke). ?-Jul 13 1954,
?. Pianist. GROVE 5.

CARNEVALE, Signora Pietro.
fl.1783-92. Singer, actress.
HIGHFILL.

CARO, Mlle. del see Del
Caro, Mlle.

CARO, Giulia de see De Caro,
Giulia

CAROLI, Ersilde Cervi see
Cervi Caroli, Ersilde

"CAROLINA, Signora" see
Pitrot, Carolina

CARON, Rose Lucille (born
Meuniez). Monerville, nr.
Paris, Nov 17 1857-Apr 9
1930, Paris. Soprano, voice
teacher. BAKER 5, BLOM,
CELLETTI, ENCI MUS, ENCY MUS,
GROVE 5, KUTSCH, PRATT,
THOMPSON.

CAROSIO, Margherita. Genoa,
Jun 7 1908- . Soprano.
CELLETTI, ENCI MUS, ENCI
SALVAT, ENCY MUS, GROVE 5
SUP, KUTSCH, RIEMANN ERG.
[KUTSCH=b. Jun 4 1908]

CARR, Mrs. fl.1741. Dancer.
HIGHFILL.

CARRACCIOLO, Juanita. Palermo,

1890-Jul 6 1924, Milan.
Soprano. KUTSCH.

CARRADORI-ALLAN, Maria see
Caradori-Allan, Maria

CARRÉ, Marguerite. Bordeaux,
1881-1947, Paris. Soprano,
voice teacher. KUTSCH.

CARRÉ, Marie-Thérèse. Paris,
1757-?. Dancer. HIGHFILL.

CARREÑO, Maria Teresa. Carácas,
Dec 22 1853-Jun 12 1917, New
York City. Pianist, composer,
singer. BAKER 1, BAKER 5,
BLOM, BROWN BIO, COOPER,
CORTE, DICT MUS, ENCI MUS,
ENCI SALVAT, ENCY MUS, GROVE
5, MARIZ, MGG, PRATT, RIE-
MANN, RIEMANN ERG, *SANDVED,
THOMPSON, ULLSTEIN.

CARRERA, Avelina. Barcelona,
Jan 2 1871-?. Soprano.
ENCI MUS.

CARRERAS, Maria Avani. Rome,
1877-Apr 15 1966, New York
City. Pianist, piano tea-
cher. *EWEN LIVING, THOMP-
SON. *[THOMPSON=b.c1872;*
information in entry from
New York Times obituary,
Apr 18 1966, p.29, col.5]

CARRILLO, Inés Gómez see
Gómez Carrillo, Inés

CARRINGTON-THOMAS, Virginia.
Bristol, Conn., Oct 27
1899- . Composer, organist,
teacher. THOMPSON.

CARRIQUE, Ana. Buenos Aires,
1886- . Composer. ARIZAGA.

CARROLL, Joan. Philadelphia,
Jul 27 1939- . Soprano.
RIEMANN ERG.

CARSTAIRS, Miss see Molesworth, Lady

CARTELL, Mrs. see Castelle,
Mrs.

CARTELLIERI, Elisabeth see
Böhm Cartellieri, Elisabeth

CARTER, Mrs. fl.1728-36.
English singer, dancer.
HIGHFILL.

CARTER, Miss. fl.1741-42.
English singer, actress.
HIGHFILL.

CARTER, Miss. fl.1759-65.
English singer. HIGHFILL.

CARTER, Helen see Leidy,
Helen

CARTER, Mary. Redhill, England,
Apr 30 1917- . Violinist.
PALMER.

CARTERI, Rosanna. Verona, Dec
14 1930- . Soprano. CELLETTI,
ENCI MUS, KUTSCH, RIEMANN
ERG, *ROSENTHAL=illus.p.37,
ULLSTEIN.

CARTWRIGHT, Mrs. fl.1772.
English singer. HIGHFILL.

CARTWRIGHT, Miss. fl.1800.
Player on musical glasses.
HIGHFILL (in article on
husband John Cartwright).

CARVALHO, Caroline (born
Félix Miolan). Marseilles,
Dec 31 1827-Jul 10 1895,
Seine-Inférieure, nr.Dieppe.
Soprano. BAKER 5, BLOM,
BROWN BIO, CORTE, ENCI MUS,
ENCI SALVAT, ENCY MUS, EWEN
NEW=p.450, GROVE 1 APP,
GROVE 5=v.5 p.789, MARIZ,
PRATT, RIEMANN, RIEMANN ERG,
THOMPSON.

CARVALHO, Dinorá de. Uberaba
Minas Gerais, Brazil, Jul 1
1905- . Composer, pianist.
ENCI MUS, RIEMANN ERG.

CARWITHEN, Doreen. Haddenham,
Bucks., England, 1922- .
Composer, pianist, piano
teacher. PALMER.

CARY, Annie Louise. Wayne,
Me., Oct 22 1842-Apr 3
1921, Norwalk, Conn. Con-
tralto. BAKER 1, BAKER 5,
BLOM, BROWN BIO, ENCI MUS,
EWEN NEW, GROVE 5, PRATT,
RIEMANN, SANDVED, THOMPSON.
[GROVE 5=mezzo-soprano]

CASA, Lisa della see Della
Casa-Debeljevic, Lisa

CASACCIA, Gaetana. ?, 1737-?.
Italian singer. ENCI MUS.

CASADESUS, Gaby (Mrs. Robert,
born L'Hote). Marseilles,
Aug 9 1901- . Pianist.
ENCI MUS, ENCI SALVAT, ENCY
MUS, MGG, MGG SUP, *SANDVED.

CASADESUS, Gladys (later
Thibaud). 20th-century
French pianist. ENCI MUS.

CASADESUS, Jacqueline, "Pianiavia." 20th-century French
singer. ENCI MUS, ENCI SAL-
VAT, ENCY MUS, MGG, MGG SUP.

CASADESUS, Lucette Laffitte
see Laffitte, Lucette

CASADESUS, Marie-Louise.
20th-century French harpist.
ENCI MUS.

CASADESUS, Regina Patorni.
Paris, 1886- . Pianist,
piano teacher, clavecinist,
composer. ENCI MUS, ENCI
SALVAT, ENCY MUS, MGG,
MGG SUP.

CASADESUS, Rose. Paris, Mar
28 1873-Jul 17 1944, Paris.
Pianist, piano teacher. ENCI

MUS, ENCI SALVAT, ENCY MUS,
MGG, MGG SUP.

CASAGLI, Serafina. 19th-century
Italian ballerina. ENCI MUS=
v.1 p.444 (brief mention in
article on son Enrico Cec-
chetti).

CASAIA, Miss. fl.1766-67.
Dancer. HIGHFILL.

CASALS, Pilar. Barcelona,
1922- . Violoncellist.
ENCI MUS, ENCI SALVAT.

CASARINI, Signora. fl.1746-
48. Italian soprano. HIGH-
FILL.

CASARINI, Domenica (Mrs.
Gaetano Latilla). 18th-
century Italian soprano.
ENCI MUS=v.2 p.573, GROVE 1.

CASAZZA, Elvira. Ferrara,
Nov 15 1887-Jan 1965, Milan.
Contralto, voice teacher.
ENCI MUS, KUTSCH.

CASAZZA, Rosina Gatti- see
Galli, Rosina

CASE, Anna. Clinton, N.J.,
Oct 29 1889- . Soprano.
KUTSCH, PRATT, THOMPSON.

CASE, Grace see Egerton,
Grace

CASEI, Nedda. Baltimore,
1935?- . Contralto. KUTSCH,
PAVLAKIS=p.294. *[PAVLAKIS=
mezzo-soprano]*

CASELLI, Signora. fl.1743-44.
Singer. HIGHFILL.

CASEY, Polly. fl.1741. English
singer. HIGHFILL.

CASIMERE, Mme. fl.1787. Dancer.
HIGHFILL.

CASPAR, Helene. Zittau, Germany, Sep 3 1857-Jul 1918, Leipzig. Pianist, piano teacher, writer. PRATT, RIEMANN.

CASSON, Margaret. London?, c1775-?. Composer, harpsichordist, singer. BROWN BIO, BROWN BRIT, HIGHFILL.

CASTAGNA, Bruna (Mrs. Baccolini). Bari, Italy, Oct 15 1905- . Contralto, voice teacher. BAKER 5, ENCI MUS, *EWEN LIVING, EWEN LIV SUP, EWEN NEW, KUTSCH, MARIZ, RIEMANN, RIEMANN ERG, THOMPSON. *[ENCI MUS=mezzosoprano. Most sources=b. 1908, which RIEMANN ERG corrects to 1905]*

CASTAGNERI, Marie-Anne. ?, 1722-Oct 6 1787, Paris. Music publisher. MGG SUP.

CASTELLAN, Jeanne Anaïs. Beaujeu, Rhône, France, 1819-?. Soprano. GROVE 1 APP, GROVE 5, PRATT, THOMPSON. *[PRATT=b.Mâcon]*

CASTELLE (Cartell, Castelli), Mrs. fl.1787-1804. Singer. HIGHFILL.

CASTELLI, -----. fl.1825. Italian singer. GROVE 1.

CASTELLI, Mrs. see Castelle, Mrs.

CASTELLI, Anna. fl.1754-55. Italian singer. HIGHFILL.

CASTRONE, Blanche Marchesi de see Marchesi de Castrone, Blanche

CASTRONE, Mathilde Marchesi de see Marchesi de Castrone, Mathilde

CASULANA, La see Mezari, Maddalena

CATALANI, Angelica. Sinigaglia, Italy, May 10 1780-Jun 12 1849, Paris. Soprano, voice teacher, manager. BAKER 1, BAKER 5, BROWN BIO, CLAYTON= p.183, COOPER, CORTE, DICT MUS, *ENCI MUS=illus.fac.p. 430, ENCI SALVAT, ENCY MUS, EWEN NEW, GROVE 1, GROVE 5, MARIZ, *MGG, PRATT, RIEMANN, RIEMANN ERG, THOMPSON, ULLSTEIN. *[BAKER 1 & GROVE 1= b. Oct 1779; MARIZ=d. Milan]*

CATENACCI, Signora Maria. fl.1783-86. Singer. GROVE 1, HIGHFILL.

"CATERINUCCIA" see Martinelli, Caterina

CATLEY, Ann(e) (later Mrs. Francis Lascelles). London, 1745-Oct 14 1789, Little Ealing, nr. Brentford, England. Singer, actress, dancer. BROWN BIO, BROWN BRIT, GROVE 1, GROVE 5, GROVE 5 SUP, *HIGHFILL, THOMPSON.

CATLEY, Gwen(doline Florence). London, Feb 9 1911- . Soprano. GROVE 5, PALMER. *[GROVE 5=b. 1910]*

CATTNEO, Irene Minghini- see Minghini-Cattaneo, Irene

CATUNDA, Eunice. Rio de Janeiro, Mar 14 1915- . Composer. BAKER 5.

"CATUJA, La" see Palomino, Catalina

CATZONI, Francesca see Cuzzoni, Francesca

CAUVINI, -----. fl.1812. English musician. GROVE 1.

CAVALIER, Franziska see
Cavalieri, Katharina

CAVALIERI, Katharina (pseud.
of Franziska Cavalier).
Währing, nr.Vienna, Feb 19
1760-Jun 30 1801, Vienna.
Soprano. BAKER 1, BAKER 5,
BLOM, BROWN BIO, ENCI MUS,
ENCI SALVAT, ENCY MUS, GROVE
1, GROVE 5, PRATT, THOMPSON.
[BAKER 1 & GROVE 1=b.1761]

CAVALIERI, Lina (Natalina).
Viterbo, Italy, Dec 25
1874-Feb 8 1944, Poggio
Imperiale, Florence.
Soprano, actress. BAKER 5,
BLOM, *CELLETTI=illus.fol.
col.224, CORTE, *ENCI MUS=
illus.fac.p.435, ENCI SAL-
VAT, ENCY MUS, EWEN NEW,
GROVE 5, GROVE 5 SUP,
KUTSCH, MARIZ, PRATT, *SAND-
VED, THOMPSON. [CELLETTI &
ENCI MUS=d.Feb 7; KUTSCH &
MARIZ=b.in Rome]

CAVALLI, Floriana. Bologna,
Feb 16 1930- . Soprano.
ENCI MUS.

CAVALLO, Enrica Gulli (Mrs.
Franco Gulli). Milan, May
19 1921- . Pianist. ENCI
MUS=v.2 p.379.

CAVAN, Marie (stage name of
Mary Edith Cawein). New
York City, Feb 6 1889- .
Soprano, voice teacher.
BAKER 5, PRATT, THOMPSON.

CAVE-ASHTON, Gertrude see
Ashton, Gertrude-Cave

CAVELTI, Elsa. Rorschach,
Switzerland, May 4 1914- .
Contralto, soprano. CORTE,
ENCY MUS, KUTSCH, RIEMANN,
RIEMANN ERG, SCHUH, THOMP-
SON, ULLSTEIN. [ENCY MUS &
KUTSCH=b.1915]

CAVOS, Camilla Baglioni see
Baglioni, Camilla

CAWEIN, Mary Edith see
Cavan, Marie

CEBOTARI, Maria. Kishinev
(Chisinău), Bessarabia,
Feb 10 1910-Jun 9 1949,
Vienna. Soprano. BAKER 5,
CORTE, ENCI MUS, ENCY MUS,
EWEN NEW, GROVE 5, KUTSCH,
MGG SUP, RIEMANN, SANDVED,
THOMPSON, *ULLSTEIN.

"CECCHINA, La" see Caccini,
Francesca

CECCO, Disma de see De Cecco,
Disma

CECIL, Theophania. London,
1782-Nov 15 1878, London.
Organist, editor. BROWN BRIT.

CECILIA, Saint. Sicily?, ?-
c178, Sicily. Patron saint
of music. BLOM, *ENCY MUS,
GROVE 1, GROVE 1 APP, GROVE 5,
*SANDVED.

CELEMENTINA, Signora see
Cremonini, Clementina

"CELESTE" or "Celestina" see
Gismondi, Celeste

CELESTINO, Signora Eligio.
fl.1780-92. Italian singer.
HIGHFILL.

CELLOTT, Juliana see Celotti,
Ziuliana

CELOTTI, Ziuliana (Juliana
Cellott). fl.1705-14.
Singer. HIGHFILL.

CELSON, Miss fl.1798. Singer.
HIGHFILL.

CEMMITT, Miss. fl.1785-91.
Singer. HIGHFILL.

CERAIL (Crail), Mlle. ?-Nov 1723, Paris. Dancer, singer. HIGHFILL.

CERNAY, Germaine (orig.=Germaine Pointu). Le Havre, France, 1900-1943, Paris. Contralto. ENCY MUS, KUTSCH.

CERQUETTI, Anita. Montecòsaro, nr. Macerata, Italy, Apr 13 1931- . Soprano. ENCI MUS, GROVE 5 SUP, KUTSCH, RIEMANN ERG, ULLSTEIN.

CERRI, Giannina see Russ, Giannina

CERRITO, Fanny. Naples, 1817-1909, Paris. Dancer, choreographer. *ENCI MUS=illus. only fac.p.451, ENCI SALVAT, ENCY MUS.

CERTAIN, Marie-Françoise. Paris?, 1661 or 1662-Feb 1 1711, Paris. Clavecinist. DICT MUS, ENCI SALVAT, RIEMANN.

ČERVENÁ, Sona. Prague, Sep 9 1925- . Contralto. KUTSCH, RIEMANN ERG. [KUTSCH=b.Sep 5 1925]

CERVERA, Montserrat. 20th-century Spanish violinist. *ENCI SALVAT.

CERVI CAROLI, Ersilde. Casumaro, Ferrara, Italy, Apr 24 1884- . Soprano. ENCI MUS.

CÉSAR, Sara. Lincoln, Argentina, 1896- . Mezzo-soprano. ARIZAGA.

CESBRON-VISEUR, Suzanne. Paris, 1878-Dec 1967, Paris. Soprano, voice teacher. KUTSCH.

CHABRAN, Margherita. fl.1806. Italian singer. ENCI MUS= v.1 p.467 (in article on the Chiabrano family).

CHABRAN, Marianna (born Albani). fl.1791-1806. Italian singer. ENCI MUS=v.1 p.467 (in article on the Chiabrano family).

CHAILLEY, Marie-Thérèse. Paris, 1921- . Singer, voice teacher. ENCI SALVAT, ENCY MUS.

CHAILLEY-RICHEZ, Céliny. Lille, France, 1894- . Pianist, piano teacher. ENCI SALVAT.

CHAILLON, Paule see Guiomar, Paule

CHALABALA, Běla (Rozumová). Příbram, Moravia, Feb 8 1903- . Soprano. ENCI MUS.

CHALIA, Rosalia. Havana, 1866-1961, Havana. Soprano. KUTSCH.

CHALMERS, Eleanor (Mrs. James, born Mills). ?-May 22 1792, Dublin. Singer, actress. HIGHFILL.

CHAMBERLAINE, Elizabeth see Von Hoff, Elizabeth

CHAMBERLAYNE, Miss E. A. fl.1895. English composer. BROWN BRIT.

CHAMBERS, Elizabeth (Mrs. William, born Davis?). ?-1792, Chiswick?, England. Singer, actress. *HIGHFILL.

CHAMBERS, Isabella. fl.1722-41. Singer, actress. HIGHFILL.

CHAMBERS, Lucy. Sydney, N.S.W., Australia, ?-1894, Melbourne. Contralto. BROWN BRIT.

CHAMBURE, Comtesse de   see
Thibault, Geneviève

CHAMINADE, Cécile-Louise-
Stéphanie. Paris, Aug 8
1857-Apr 13 1944, Monte
Carlo. Composer, pianist.
*BAKER 1, BAKER 5, BLOM,
COOPER, CORTE, DICT MUS,
ENCI MUS, ENCY MUS, GROVE 5,
PRATT, RIEMANN, RIEMANN ERG,
SANDVED, THOMPSON. [BAKER 1,
DICT MUS, & PRATT=b.1861.
Most sources give date of
death as Apr 18 1944, which
RIEMANN ERG corrects to
April 13 1944]

CHAMPION, Marguerite Roesgen-
see   Roesgen-Champion,
Marguerite

CHANOT, Florentine (born
Demoliens). ?-1858, ?.
French lutenist. ENCI MUS,
GROVE 5.

CHAPLIN, Kate. London, Jul 3
1865-Dec 9 1948, London.
Viola d'amore player,
violinist. BROWN BRIT,
THOMPSON.

CHAPLIN, Mabel. fl.1890.
English violoncellist.
BROWN BRIT.

CHAPLIN, Nellie. London, Feb
11 1857-?. Harpsichordist,
writer, pianist. BROWN
BRIT, THOMPSON.

CHAPMAN, Charlotte Jane
(formerly Mrs. Morton).
USA, 1762-Feb 14 1805,
London. Singer, actress.
*HIGHFILL.

CHAPMAN, Frances R. (Mrs.
George, born Brett). ?-
Apr 1804, Liverpool.
Singer, actress. HIGHFILL.

CHAPMAN, Hannah (Mrs. Thomas).
?-c1756, Richmond?, England.
Dancer, actress. HIGHFILL.

CHARON, Mme. fl.1755-56.
French dancer. HIGHFILL.

CHARPENTIER, Mme. fl.1734-35.
French dancer?. HIGHFILL.

CHARRAT, Janine. Grenoble,
Jul 24 1924- . Dancer,
choreographer, teacher.
*ENCI SALVAT, RIEMANN,
RIEMANN ERG.

CHARTON-DEMEUR, Anne Arsène
see   Demeur, Anne Arsène

CHASE, Mary Wood. Brooklyn,
New York, Jan 21 1868-?.
Pianist, piano teacher,
writer. PRATT, THOMPSON.

CHATEAUNEUF (Chatin), Marie.
France, Apr 15 1721-?.
Dancer, singer, manager.
HIGHFILL.

CHATFIELD, Eliza Rebecca   see
Large, Eliza Rebecca

CHATIN, Marie   see Chateauneuf, Marie

CHATTERLEY, Miss. fl.1791-98.
Singer, actress. HIGHFILL.

CHAUVIRÉ, Yvette. Paris, Apr
22 1917- . Dancer. ENCI
SALVAT, ENCY MUS, RIEMANN,
RIEMANN ERG.

CHAVANNE, Irene von. Graz,
Apr 18 1868-Dec 26 1938,
Dresden. Contralto. BAKER 1,
BAKER 5, KUTSCH, PRATT.

CHAVARRI, Emperatriz   see
Sumac, Yma

CHAZAL, Mrs.   see   De Gambarini, Elisabetta

CHEMET, Réné. Boulogne-sur-
Seine, France. c1888-?.
Violinist. *EWEN LIVING.

CHENAL, Marthe. Saint-Maurice,
nr. Paris, Aug 24 1881-Jan
29 1947, Paris. Soprano.
KUTSCH, THOMPSON.

CHENEY, Amy Marcy see
Beach, Amy Marcy

CHENOWETH, Vida. Enid, Okla.,
?- . 20th-century American
marimbist. THOMPSON.

CHERRIER, Miss. fl.1708.
Dancer. HIGHFILL.

CHETWOOD, Anne (Mrs. William
Rufus II, born Brett).
London, May 8 1720-?.
Dancer, actress. HIGHFILL.

CHEVÉ, Nanine (Mrs. Emile,
born Paris). Paris, 1800-
Jun 28 1868, Paris. Writer.
ENCI MUS, MGG SUP, RIEMANN.

CHEVIGNY, Mlle. ?, c1770-?.
French dancer. ENCI SALVAT,
ENCY MUS.

CHÉZY, Helmina (orig. Wilhelmine Christiane) von (born
von Klencke). Berlin, Jan
26 1783-Jan 28 1856, Geneva.
Poet, librettist. BLOM,
MGG SUP.

CHIANTI, Margaret see
Chimenti, Margherita

CHIESA, Maria Tibaldi see
Tibaldi Chiesa, Maria

CHILDE, Ann see Seguin, Ann

CHIMENTI, Margherita (Margaret Chianti; called "La
Droghierina"). fl.1736-38.

Singer. GROVE 1, HIGHFILL.

CHIPPENDALE, Mrs. William.
fl.1797-1820. English singer.
HIGHFILL.

CHIRINGHELLI, Signora. fl.
1774. Dancer. HIGHFILL.

CHISE, Mme. fl.1757. Dancer.
HIGHFILL.

CHISSELL, Joan Olive. Cromer,
England, May 22 1919- .
Musicologist, teacher,
writer, critic. ENCI SALVAT,
ENCY MUS, GROVE 5.

CHITTENDEN, Kate Sara. Hamilton, Ontario, Canada, Apr 17
1856-Sep 16 1949, New York
City. Teacher, composer,
writer. THOMPSON.

CHLADEK, Rosalia. Brno, Czechoslovakia, May 21 1905- .
Dancer, choreographer, teacher. RIEMANN ERG.

CHOIŃSKA-MIKORSKA, Ludmila
Jeske- see Jeske-Choińska-
Mikorska, Ludmila

CHOLLET, Constance. fl.1771.
Dancer. HIGHFILL.

CHOMEL, Adelaide see Rubini,
Adelaide

CHOOKASIAN, Lili. Chicago, ?- .
20th-century American contralto. PAVLAKIS=p.297,
THOMPSON.

CHRISTIANE, Wilhelmine see
Chézy, Helmina

CHRISTIANI, Élise. Paris, Dec
24 1827-1853, Tobolsk, Russia. Violoncellist. BAKER 1.

CHRISTIE, Audrey see Mildmay, Audrey

CHRISTIE, Winifred. Stirling,
England, Feb 26 1882- .
Pianist. BAKER 5=p.1109,
THOMPSON.

CIAMPI, Cécile Ritter- see
Ritter-Ciampi, Cécile

CIAMPI, Gabrielle Ritter- see
Ritter-Ciampi, Gabrielle

CIAMPOLI, Elena Fioretti see
Fioretti Ciampoli, Elena

CIANCHETTINI, Veronica Eliza-
beth (born Dussek; not to
be confused with Veronica
Rosaria Dussek). Časlav,
Bohemia, 1779-1833, London.
Pianist, piano teacher,
composer. BROWN BIO, BROWN
BRIT, ENCI SALVAT, ENCY
MUS, GROVE 1, THOMPSON.

CIBBER, Catherine (Mrs. Col-
ley, born Shore). London,
c1669-Jan 17 1734, Knights-
bridge, England. Singer,
actress. BLOM=p.635, BROWN
BIO=p.560, BROWN BRIT=
p.372, GROVE 1, HIGHFILL,
MGG. [BLOM, BROWN BIO, &
BROWN BRIT=b.1668, d.1730]

CIBBER, Elizabeth see
Brett, Elizabeth

CIBBER, Jane (Mrs. Theophilus
I, born Johnson). ?, 1706-
Jan 25 1733, London. Sin-
ger, actress. *HIGHFILL.

CIBBER, Susanna Maria (Mrs.
Theophilus II, born Arne).
London, Feb 28 1714-Jan 30
1766, London. Contralto,
actress, playwright. BLOM=
p.27, BROWN BIO, BROWN
BRIT, ENCI MUS=v.1 p.114
(in article on Arne family),
GROVE 1, GROVE 5, *HIGH-
FILL, MGG=v.1 col.659,
THOMPSON.

CIGNA, Gina (born Sens).
Angères, nr. Paris, Mar 6
1900 (not 1904)- . Soprano,
voice teacher. BAKER 5,
BAKER 1971, CELLETTI, ENCI
MUS, *EWEN LIVING, EWEN LIV
SUP, EWEN NEW, KUTSCH,
MARIZ, RIEMANN, RIEMANN ERG,
SANDVED, THOMPSON.

CIMAGLIA-ESPINOSA, Lía. Buenos
Aires, 1906- . Pianist,
composer, teacher. ARIZAGA.

CINTI-DAMOREAU, Laure see
Damoreau, Laure Cinthie

CIOMAC, Muza Germani- see
Germani-Ciomac, Muza

CIONCA-PIPOS, Aurelia. 20th-
century Romanian pianist.
THOMPSON.

CISNEROS, Eleanora de (born
Broadfoot). New York City,
Nov 1 1878-Feb 3 1934, New
York City. Mezzo-soprano,
voice teacher. BAKER 5,
ENCI MUS, EWEN NEW, GROVE 5,
KUTSCH, PRATT, SANDVED,
THOMPSON. [PRATT=b.1880]

CLAESSENS, Maria. Brussels,
May 20 1881- . Mezzo-
soprano. THOMPSON.

CLAIRBERT, Clara (orig.Impens).
St.-Gilles-lez-Bruxelles,
Feb 21 1899-Aug 5 1970,
Brussels. Soprano. KUTSCH,
RIEMANN ERG.

CLAIRE, Marion. Chicago, Feb
25 1904- . Soprano, actress.
KUTSCH.

CLAMAKIN, Mrs. fl.1731.
Dancer. HIGHFILL.

CLAMAN, Dolores Olga. Vancouver, Canada, Jul 6 1927- .
Composer, pianist. CBC.

"CLARA, Signora" see Dixon, Clara Ann

"CLARIBEL" see Barnard, Charlotte Alington

CLARK, Mrs. fl.1695-1723. Singer, dancer, actress HIGHFILL.

CLARK, Miss. fl.1736. Singer, actress. HIGHFILL.

CLARK, Miss. fl.1736-47. Singer, actress. HIGHFILL.

CLARK, Mrs. fl.1789. Singer. HIGHFILL.

CLARK, Florence Durell. Rochester, New York, Apr 29 1891- . Composer, pianist, organist, violinist, viola player. CBC, NAPIER.

CLARKE, Amelia see Creser, Amelia

CLARKE, Jane. fl.1808. English organist. BROWN BRIT.

CLARKE, Marian Bruce see Somigli, Franca

CLARKE, Mary Cowden see Novello, Mary Victoria

CLARKE, Mrs. Nathaniel?. fl.1727-47. Singer, actress. HIGHFILL.

CLARKE, Rebecca. Harrow, England, Aug 27 1886- . Composer, violinist, viola player. BAKER 5, BAKER 1971, BLOM, CORTE, ENCI MUS, ENCI SALVAT, ENCY MUS, GROVE 5, RIEMANN, SCHOLES, THOMPSON.

CLARY, Mme. fl.1757-58. Dancer. HIGHFILL.

CLAUSS-SZARVADY, Wilhelmine. Prague, Dec 13 1834-Sep 1

1907, Paris. Pianist. BROWN BIO=p.168, 583-84, GROVE 1, GROVE 1 APP, GROVE 5, PRATT, THOMPSON.

CLAUSSEN, Julia (born Ohlson). Stockholm, Jun 11 1879-May 1 1941, Stockholm. Mezzo-soprano, voice teacher. BAKER 5, EWEN NEW, GROVE 5, KUTSCH, PRATT, RIEMANN, SANDVED, THOMPSON.

CLAVEL, Antoinette Cécile see Saint-Huberty, Antoinette Cécile

CLAYTON, Eleanor Creathorne (Mrs. Needham). Dublin, 1832-?. Writer. BROWN BIO, BROWN BRIT.

CLEGG, Miss see Davis, Mrs.

CLEGG, Edith Kate. London, ?- . 20th-century mezzo-soprano. PRATT, THOMPSON.

CLEMENS, Clara (Mrs. Ossip Gabrilowitsch; later Mrs. Jacques Alexander Samossound). Elmira, New York, 1874-Nov 19 1962, San Diego, Calif. Contralto, writer. PRATT, THOMPSON. *[Death date supplied from obituary in Los Angeles Times, Nov 21 1962, p.1]*

CLEMENTINE, Frances Maria see Dubellamy, Frances Maria

CLENCH, Leonora. St. Mary's, Canada, ?-?. 19th-century violinist. BROWN BRIT.

CLENDINING, Elizabeth (Mrs. William, born Arnold). Stourhead, England, 1768-Jul 16 1799, Edinburgh. Singer, actress. HIGHFILL.

CLERC, Germaine Vaucher- see Vaucher-Clerc, Germaine

CLERCX-LEJEUNE, Suzanne (born Clercx). Houdeng-Aimeries, Hennegau, Belgium, Jun 7 1910- . Editor, musicologist, writer. BAKER 5, DICT MUS, ENCI MUS, ENCI SALVAT, ENCY MUS, GROVE 5, MGG, MGG SUP, RIEMANN, RIEMANN ERG, THOMPSON.

CLÉRICY BLANC DU COLLET, Marie Camille Joséphine. Puget-Théniers, Alpes-Maritimes, France, Jun 24 1850-Feb 26 1921, Nice. Singer, voice teacher. RIEMANN, RIEMANN ERG.

CLEVE, Berit. Vestre Aker, nr. Christiania, Norway, Feb 10 1878- . Pianist. THOMPSON.

CLINTON, Florence Edith see Sutro, Florence Edith

CLIVE, Catherine ("Kitty"; Mrs. George, born Raftor or Rafftor). London, Nov 15 1711-Dec 6 1785, London. Singer, actress. BLOM, BROWN BIO, BROWN BRIT, GROVE 1, *HIGHFILL, PRATT, THOMPSON. [BLOM & GROVE 1= b. Twickenham, Middlesex]

CLOSSON, Mlle. fl.1740. Dancer. HIGHFILL.

CLOSTRE, Adrienne. Thomery, Seine-et-Marne, France, Oct 9 1921- . Composer. DICT MUS.

COATES, Mrs. fl.1797-1822. Singer, actress. HIGHFILL.

COATES, Edith Mary. Lincoln, England, May 31 1908- . Contralto, mezzo-soprano, actress. *CELLETTI=illus. fol.col.224, GROVE 5, THOMPSON.

COATS, Miss. fl.1779-80. Singer. HIGHFILL.

COBELLI, Giuseppina. Salò, Italy, Sep 1 1898-Aug 10 1948, Salò, Italy. Soprano. ENCI MUS, KUTSCH, RIEMANN ERG.

COCCIA, Maria Rosa. Rome, Jan 4 1759-Nov 1833, Rome. Composer. BLOM, ENCI SALVAT, ENCY MUS, GROVE 5, THOMPSON.

"COCHETTA, La" see Gabrielli, Caterina

COCLET, Henriette van den Boorn- see Van den Boorn-Coclet, Henriette

COCORASCU, Madeleine. Botosani, Romania, Jul 22 1893- . Pianist, piano teacher. THOMPSON.

COCQ-WEINGAND, Amelia. Santiago de Chile, 1884- . Pianist. THOMPSON.

"CODGERINO, Signora." fl.1752. Dancer. HIGHFILL.

COELHO, Olga Praguer. Manaus, Brazil, 1909- . Folklorist, guitarist, soprano. GROVE 5, MARIZ, SANDVED, THOMPSON.

COEN, Anna Seppilli. Brescia, Italy, Jun 18 1906- . Pianist. ENCI MUS=v.4 p.200 (in article on the Seppilli family).

COERTSE, Mimi (Mrs. Diego Brighi). Durban, Natal, Union of South Africa, Jun 12 1932- . Soprano. KUTSCH, RIEMANN ERG.

COETMORE, Peers. Lincolnshire, England, ?- . 20th-century English violoncellist. PALMER.

"COGHETTA, La" see Gabrielli, Caterina

COHEN, Dulcie. 20th-century Australian composer. THOMPSON.

COHEN, *Dame* Harriet. London, Dec 2 1895-Nov 13 1967, London. Pianist. BAKER 5, BAKER 1971, BLOM, ENCI MUS, *EWEN LIVING, EWEN LIV SUP, GROVE 5, GROVE 5 SUP, PALMER, RIEMANN, RIEMANN ERG, SANDVED, THOMPSON. *[Some sources=b.1901, which RIEMANN ERG corrects to 1895]*

COHRONE, Lenore see Corona, Leonora

COINTRIE, Mme. de la see De la Cointrie, Mme.

COLBRAN, Isabella Ángela. Madrid, Feb 2 1785-Oct 7 1845, Castenaso, nr. Bologna. Soprano, composer. BLOM, BROWN BIO, CORTE, *ENCI MUS=illus.fac.p.503, ENCI SALVAT, ENCY MUS, EWEN NEW, GROVE 1, GROVE 5, PRATT, RIEMANN, SANDVED, THOMPSON. *[BLOM & SANDVED= mezzo-soprano]*

COLE, Miss. ?, 1729-?. Singer, dancer, actress. HIGHFILL.

COLE, Belle. Chautauqua, New York, 1845-Jan 5 1905, London. Contralto. PRATT. *[Death date based on New York Times obituary, Jan 6 1905, p.9, col.3]*

COLE, Blanche (later Mrs. Sidney Naylor). Portsmouth, England, 1851-Aug 31 1888, London. Soprano. BROWN BRIT=p.294, GROVE 5, PRATT, THOMPSON.

COLE, Charlotte. Tarrington, England, ?-?. 19th-century English soprano, voice teacher, composer. BROWN BRIT.

COLE, Susanna. 19th-century English mezzo-soprano, voice teacher. BROWN BRIT.

COLERIDGE-TAYLOR, Avril (Gwendolen). Upper Norwood, London, Mar 8 1903- . Conductor, composer. ENCY MUS, GROVE 5, PALMER.

COLINETTE, Rose see Didelot, Marie-Rose

COLLA, Mrs. Giuseppe see Agujari, Lucrezia

COLLAULT, Marie Sophie see Ponchard, Marie Sophie

COLLES, Hesther (Mrs. Joseph, born Boyde). fl.1776-80. Singer, actress. *HIGHFILL.

COLLET, Mrs. Ann?. fl.1765-71. Singer, actress. HIGHFILL.

COLLET, Catherine (later Mrs. Tetherington). fl.1767-1800. Dancer, actress. HIGHFILL.

COLLET, Sophia Dobson. London, 1822-Mar 27 1894, Highbury Park, England. Composer. BROWN BRIT.

COLLIER, Joan. Barnes, London, Sep 24 1917- . Soprano. PALMER.

COLLIER, Marie Elisabeth. Ballarat, Australia, Apr 16 1927-Dec 8 1971, London. Soprano. RIEMANN ERG. *[RIEMANN ERG=b.1926. Birth and death dates obtained from New York Times obituary, Dec 8 1971, p.40, col.1]*

COLOMBARI DE MONTÈGRE, Gabriella see Ferrari, Gabriella

COLOMBATI, Elisabetta. fl. 1791-1811. Singer. HIGHFILL.

COLOMBE, Émilie. fl.1788-89. Dancer. HIGHFILL.

COLON, Marguerite. Boulogne-sur-Mer, France, Nov 5 1808-Jun 5 1842, Paris. Singer. BROWN BIO.

COLONNA, Vittoria (Duchess of Amalfi and Marchesa of Pescara). Marino, Italy, 1490-Feb 25 1547, Rome. Church composer. *MGG SUP=illus. fac.col.1568.

COLONNE, Eugénie Elise (Mrs. Édouard, born Vergin). Lille, France, Mar 21 1854-?. Soprano, voice teacher. GROVE 5, THOMPSON.

COLONNESE, Elvira. Naples, 1860-?. Soprano, voice teacher. THOMPSON.

COLTELLINI, Anna (Annetta). fl.1782-94. Italian singer. ENCI MUS.

COLTELLINI, Céleste. Leghorn, Italy, Nov 26 1760-Jul 24 1828, Capodimonte, nr. Naples. Mezzo-soprano. BLOM, CORTE, *ENCI MUS=illus.fac. p.510, GROVE 1, THOMPSON. [GROVE 1 & THOMPSON=b.1764, d.1817; CORTE=d.1829]

COMANESTI, Ioana Ghika- see Ghika-Comanesti, Ioanna

COMO, Signora Antonio. fl. 1775. Dancer. HIGHFILL.

COMPTON, Louisa see Gray, Louisa

CONANT, Isabel see Pope, Isabel

CONCARINI, Vittoria see Archilei, Vittoria

CONCATO, Augusta. ?, 1895-Jun 1964, Carate Brianza, Italy. Soprano. KUTSCH.

CONNARD, Miss. fl.1794. Singer, actress. HIGHFILL.

CONNELLY, Miss. fl.1799. Dancer. HIGHFILL.

CONNER, Nadine. Compton, Calif., Feb 20 1914- . Soprano. *EWEN LIV SUP, EWEN NEW, SANDVED.

CONRAD, Barbara Smith. Texas, ?- . 20th-century American soprano. PAVLAKIS=p.287.

CONRAD-AMBERG, Margrit. Lucerne, Switzerland, Sep 21 1918- . Contralto. SCHUH.

CONSTANCE, Mlle. fl.1784-87. Dancer. HIGHFILL.

CONSTANT, Jenny see Andrews, Jenny

CONSTANTINI, Signora. fl.1726-27. Dancer. HIGHFILL.

CONTI, Anna. fl.1754-55. Dancer. HIGHFILL.

CONTINI, Giovanna. fl.1742-43. Singer. HIGHFILL.

COOK, Mrs. fl.1740-41. Dancer. HIGHFILL.

COOK, Mrs. fl.1763. Dancer. HIGHFILL.

COOK, Alice Aynsley. 19th-century English singer. BROWN BRIT=p.98.

COOK, Mrs. Aynsley (born
Payne). 19th-century Eng-
lish contralto. BROWN
BRIT=p.98.

COOK, Linda see Scates,
Linda

COOKE, Alicia see Daniels,
Alicia

COOKE, Harriet see Waylett,
Harriet

COOKE, Mary. ?, 1666?-Mar 18
1745, London?. Singer,
actress. HIGHFILL.

COOLIDGE, Elizabeth Sprague
(Mrs. Frederick Shurtleff).
Chicago, Oct 30 1864-Nov 4
1953, Cambridge, Mass.
Composer, patron, pianist.
BAKER 5, BLOM, GROVE 5,
RIEMANN, RIEMANN ERG,
SANDVED.

COOMBES, Miss. fl.1795-1802.
Dancer. HIGHFILL.

COONS, Minnie. New York City,
1882?- . Pianist. THOMPSON.

COOPER, Miss. fl.1785-87.
Dancer. HIGHFILL.

COOPER, Miss. fl.1793. Singer, actress. HIGHFILL.

COOPER, Margaret. ?-Dec 27
1922, London. Singer.
THOMPSON.

COPE, Mrs. fl.1770-71. Dancer. HIGHFILL.

COPELAND, Mrs. fl.1729.
Dancer. HIGHFILL.

COPIN, Elizabeth (Mrs. Roger).
fl.1733-73. Singer, actress.
HIGHFILL.

COPPERWHEAT, Winifred. London,
?- . 20th-century English
viola player. PALMER.

CORADINI, Signora. fl.1767-68.
Dancer. HIGHFILL.

CORNELYS, Teresa (born Imer).
Venice, 1723-Aug 19 1797,
London. Singer, entrepreneur.
BLOM, GROVE 1 APP, GROVE 5,
HIGHFILL, THOMPSON.

CORONA, Itala del see Del
Corona, Itala

CORONA, Leonora (real name=
Lenore Cohrone). Dallas,
Oct 14 1900- . Soprano.
BAKER 5, ENCI SALVAT, RIE-
MANN, RIEMANN ERG, THOMPSON.

CORREA, Lorenza. Malaga, Spain,
1773-after 1831, Spain?.
Singer, actress. ENCI MUS.

CORREIA, Arminda. Lagos, Portugal, Dec 26 1903- . Soprano.
GROVE 5.

CORREIA, Lourença Nunes.
Lisbon, 1771 or Málaga,
1773-after 1831, ?. Portu-
guese or Spanish singer.
RIEMANN, RIEMANN ERG.

CORRER, Augusta see Ange-
lelli, Augusta

CORRI, Signora Domenico (born
Bacchelli). fl.1771-1810.
Singer. HIGHFILL.

CORRI, Fanny (Francesca) see
Corri-Paltoni, Frances(ca)

CORRI, Ghita. 19th-century
Italian soprano, composer.
ENCI SALVAT, GROVE 5.

CORRI, Rosálie. ?, 1803-?.
Soprano. GROVE 5.

CORRI, Sophia Giustina see
Dussek, Sophia Giustina

CORRI-PALTONI, Frances(ca)
(Fanny). Edinburgh, 1795
or 1801-?. Mezzo-soprano.
BROWN BIO, BROWN BRIT,
DICT MUS=v.1 p.234, ENCI
MUS, ENCI SALVAT, GROVE 1,
GROVE 5, PRATT, THOMPSON.

CORRIDORI, Lucia. Lucerne,
Switzerland, ?- . 20th-
century soprano, voice
teacher. SCHUH.

CORSI, Emilia. Lisbon, Jan
21 1870-Sep 17 1927,
Bologna. Soprano. ENCI MUS.

CORTESI, Adelaide. Milan,
Oct 1828-1889, Milan.
Soprano. ENCI MUS.

CORTINI, Zaira Falchi see
Falchi Cortini, Zaira

COSMI, Emanuela (Mrs. Giuseppe Giordani). 18th-
century Italian singer.
ENCI MUS=v.2 p.315.

COSSIRA, Emma. 19-20th-century
mezzo-soprano. ENCI MUS.

COSSOTTO, Fiorenza. Crescen-
tino, Vercelli, nr. Turin,
Apr 22 1935- . Contralto.
BAKER 1971, CELLETTI, ENCI
MUS, KUTSCH, RIEMANN ERG,
*ULLSTEIN.

COSTA, Margarita de (called
"Ferrarese.") Ferrara,
c1600-?. Singer, poet.
CORTE, ENCY MUS, MGG.

COSTA, Mary. Knoxville, Tenn.,
Apr 5 1930- . Soprano.
PAVLAKIS=p.287, THOMPSON.

COSTANTINI, Signora. fl.1726.
Italian singer. GROVE 1,

HIGHFILL.

COSTANZA, Signora. fl.1742-43.
Dancer. HIGHFILL.

COSTANZO, Irma. Buenos Aires,
1938- . Guitarist. ARIZAGA.

CÔTE, Hélène (Soeur Marie-
Stéphane). St. Barthelemi,
Québec, Canada, Jan 9
1888- . Composer, pianist,
writer, administrator. CBC.

COTTEREL, Miss. fl.1750.
Singer. HIGHFILL.

COTTLOW, Augusta. Shelbyville,
Ill., Apr 2 1878-Apr 11
1954, White Plains, New
York. Pianist. BAKER 5,
BAKER 1971, PRATT, THOMPSON.

COULOMBE-SAINT-MARCOUX,
Micheline. Québec, Canada,
1938- . Composer, electronic
music composer. NAPIER.

COULON, Anne Jacqueline (later
Mme. Pierre Gabriel Gardel
I). fl.1787-92. Dancer.
HIGHFILL.

COULTHARD, Jean. Vancouver,
Feb 10 1908- . Pianist,
composer. BAKER 1971, CBC.

COUPERIN, Antoinette Victoire.
?, c1760-1812, Paris. Singer, organist, harpist.
DICT MUS, ENCI MUS.

COUPERIN, Céleste-Thérèse.
Paris, 1793-Feb 14 1860,
Belleville, France. Pianist,
piano teacher, singer, voice
teacher. BAKER 5, BLOM, DICT
MUS, ENCI MUS, ENCI SALVAT,
ENCY MUS, GROVE 5, MGG,
RIEMANN, RIEMANN ERG, THOMP-
SON. [ENCY MUS=d.1862;
THOMPSON=d.1850]

COUPERIN, Elisabeth-Antoinette (born Blanchet). Paris, Jan 14 1729-1815, St. Louis, France. Organist, clavecinist. BAKER 1, BAKER 5, ENCI MUS, MGG.

COUPERIN, Marguerite-Antoinette. Paris, Sep 19 1705-c1778, Paris. Harpsichordist, teacher, court musician, clavecinist. BLOM, DICT MUS, ENCI MUS, ENCI SALVAT, ENCY MUS, GROVE 5, MGG, RIEMANN, RIEMANN ERG, THOMPSON.

COUPERIN, Marguerite-Louise. Paris, c1676-May 30 1728, Versailles. Singer, harpsichordist. BAKER 5, BLOM, DICT MUS, ENCI MUS, ENCI SALVAT, ENCY MUS, GROVE 5, MGG, RIEMANN, THOMPSON.

COUPERIN, Marie-Madeleine-Cécile. Paris, Mar 11 1690-Apr 16 1742, Maubisson, France. Organist. BAKER 5, BLOM, DICT MUS, ENCI MUS, ENCI SALVAT, ENCY MUS, MGG, RIEMANN, RIEMANN ERG.

COURT, Joséphine-Thérèse see Lefébure-Wély, Joséphine-Thérèse

COURTENAY, Miss (stage name of Miss Crawley). fl.1777. Singer, actress. HIGHFILL.

COUVAND, Chérie. ?-1880, ?. French singer. ENCI MUS= v.1 p.18 (brief mention in article on the Adam family).

COWARD, Hilda. 19th-century English soprano. BROWN BRIT.

COWPER, Miss. fl.1771-80. English soprano. HIGHFILL.

COX, Mrs. fl.1760. English singer. HIGHFILL.

COX, Mrs. fl.1781-82. English singer, actress. HIGHFILL.

COX, Miss. fl.1795-1804. English actress, dancer, singer?. HIGHFILL.

COX, Mrs. fl.1798. English dancer?. HIGHFILL.

COX, Annie see Cantelo, Annie

COZZOLANI, Chiara Margherita. Milan, ?-c1653, Milan. Composer, singer. ENCI MUS.

CRADER, Jeannine. 20th-century American soprano. PAVLAKIS= p.287.

CRAFORD, Mrs. see Crawford, Mrs.

CRAFT, Marcella. Indianapolis, Aug 11 1880-Dec 12 1959, Riverside, Calif. Soprano, voice teacher. BAKER 5, BAKER 1971, KUTSCH, PRATT, RIEMANN, RIEMANN ERG, THOMPSON.

CRAIG, Elizabeth (born Noble). 19th-century Scottish singer, voice teacher. BROWN BRIT.

CRAIL, Mlle. see Cerail, Mlle.

CRAMERER, Mlle. fl.1779-80. Dancer. HIGHFILL.

CRANE, Lois see Russell, Louise

CRANFIELD, Mrs. fl.1790-98. Dancer. HIGHFILL.

CRANFORD, Miss. fl.1784-94. Singer, actress. HIGHFILL.

CRAUFORD, Mrs. fl.1765.
Dancer. HIGHFILL.

CRAWFORD (Craford), Mrs.
fl.1760-61. Dancer. HIGH-
FILL.

CRAWFORD, Miss. fl.1785-94.
Singer. HIGHFILL.

CRAWFORD, Beatrice see
Parkyns, Beatrice

CRAWFORD, Ruth Porter (Mrs.
Charles Seeger). East
Liverpool, Ohio, Jul 3 1901-
Nov 18 1953, Chevy Chase,
Md. Composer, pianist,
piano teacher. BAKER 5,
ENCI MUS, ENCI SALVAT, ENCY
MUS, GROVE 5, RIEMANN,
RIEMANN ERG, THOMPSON,
VINTON.

CRAWLEY, Miss see Courtenay,
Miss

CRAWLEY, Sybil see Nielsen,
Flora

CREMONINI, Clementina (Signora
Celementina). fl.1763-66.
Singer. HIGHFILL.

CRÉPÉ, Mlle. see D'Auberval,
Mme. Jean

CRESER, Amelia (born Clarke).
19th-century English con-
tralto. BROWN BRIT.

CRESPI, Signora. fl.1773-86.
Dancer. HIGHFILL.

CRESPIN, Régina (Régine).
Marseilles, Mar 23 1927- .
Soprano. BLOM, CELLETTI,
ENCI SALVAT, ENCY MUS,
EWEN NEW, KUTSCH, RIEMANN
ERG, *ROSENTHAL=illus.p.42,
THOMPSON, *ULLSTEIN.

CREWS, Lucille (Mrs. Lucille

Marsh). Pueblo, Colo., Aug
23 1888- . Composer. BAKER 5.

CRISP, Henrietta Maria (Mrs.
Samuel, born Tollett).
London?, 1709-1780, ?.
Actress, dancer, singer.
HIGHFILL.

CRISTOFOREANU, Florica.
Bucarest, c1890- . Soprano.
ENCI MUS.

CROFTS, Miss. fl.1786-90.
Dancer, singer, actress.
HIGHFILL.

CROIX, Mlle. de la see
De la Croix, Mlle.

CROIZA, Claire (Conelly).
Paris, Sep 14 1882-May 15
1948, Paris. Contralto,
voice teacher. BLOM, ENCY
MUS, GROVE 5, KUTSCH.
[*BLOM & ENCY MUS=d.1946*]

CROSBY, Miss. fl.1800.
Singer. HIGHFILL.

CROSS, Mrs. John Cartwright?
(stage name of Mrs. Gilbert
Hamilton?). fl.1790-93.
Singer, actress. HIGHFILL.

CROSS, Frances (Mrs. Richard,
born Shireburn). ?, 1707-
Jun 29 1781, London. Singer,
actress. HIGHFILL.

CROSS, Joan. London, Sep 7
1900- . Soprano, administrator. *CELLETTI=illus.foll.
col.224, ENCI MUS, GROVE 5
SUP, KUTSCH, *PALMER=illus.
p.151, RIEMANN, *SANDVED,
THOMPSON.

CROSS, Letitia. ?, 1677-1737,
London. Singer, actress,
dancer. HIGHFILL.

CROSSLEY, Ada (Jessica). Tarra-

ville, Gippsland, Australia,
Mar 3 1874-Oct 17 1929,
London. Contralto, voice
teacher. BAKER 5, BLOM,
GROVE 5, KUTSCH, PRATT,
THOMPSON. [THOMPSON=mezzo-
soprano]

CROTTY, Georgina see Burns,
Georgina

CROUCH, Anna Maria (Mrs.
Rawlings Edward, born
Phillips). London, Apr 20
1763-Oct 2 1805, Brighton,
England. Soprano, actress.
BROWN BIO, BROWN BRIT,
CLAYTON=p.125, GROVE 1,
GROVE 1 APP, GROVE 5,
*HIGHFILL, THOMPSON.

CROWE, Jane (Mrs. William,
born Rowson). fl.1791-99.
Dancer. HIGHFILL.

CROXFORD, Eileen. Leighton
Buzzard, England, 1924- .
Violoncellist. *PALMER=
illus.p.187.

CROZIER, Miss. fl.1742.
Dancer, singer. HIGHFILL.

CROZIER, Catherine. USA?,
1914- . Organist, teacher.
PAVLAKIS=p.282.

CRÜWELL see Cruvelli

CRULL, Johanna Frederika see
Siboni, Johanna Frederika

CRUVELLI (Crüwell), Friederike
Marie. Bielefeld, Germany,
Aug 29 1824-Jul 26 1868,
Bielefeld, Germany. Singer.
ENCI MUS, GROVE 5, PRATT,
THOMPSON.

CRUVELLI (Crüwell), Johanne
Sophie Charlotte. Biele-
feld, Germany, Mar 12 1826-
Nov 6 1907, Monte Carlo.

Soprano. BLOM, BROWN BIO,
CLAYTON=p.483, ENCI MUS,
GROVE 1, GROVE 5, PRATT,
THOMPSON.

CRUZ, Maria Antonieta de Lima
see Lima Cruz, Maria
Antonieta de

CRUZ-ROMO, Gilda. 20th-century
Mexican soprano. PAVLAKIS=
p.287.

CSERFALVI, Elise. Budapest,
Feb 23 1929- . Violinist.
SCHUH.

CULLBERG, Birgit. Nyköping,
Sweden, Aug 3 1908- .
Dancer, choreographer.
RIEMANN ERG.

CULLEN, Rose (Mrs. Albert
Tench). Nr. London, ?-Dec
1888, England?. Singer,
actress. BROWN BRIT.

CULP, Julia Bertha (Mrs. von
Ginzkey). Groningen, Netherlands, Oct 6 1880-Oct 13
1970, Amsterdam. Mezzo-
soprano. BAKER 5, BAKER
1971, *EWEN LIVING, EWEN LIV
SUP, GROVE 5, KUTSCH, MGG
SUP, PRATT, RIEMANN, RIE-
MANN ERG, SANDVED, THOMPSON.

CUNEY-HARE, Maud. Galveston,
Texas, ?-Feb 13 1936,
Boston. Pianist, writer,
teacher. THOMPSON.

CUNITZ, Maud. London, 1911- .
Soprano. KUTSCH.

"CUOCHETINA, La" see
Gabrielli, Caterina

CUPIS DE CAMARGO, Sophie
see Camargo, Sophie

CUPPI, Sophie see Camargo,
Sophie

CURIONI, Rosa. fl.1754-62.
English singer. ENCI MUS,
GROVE 1, GROVE 5, HIGHFILL.

CURRAN, Pearl Gildersleeve.
Denver, Jun 25 1875-Apr 16
1941, New Rochelle, New
York. Composer. BAKER 5,
THOMPSON.

CURRY, Corinne. 20th-century
American mezzo-soprano.
PAVLAKIS=p.294.

CURTIN, Phyllis (born Smith).
Clarksburg, W.Va., Dec 3
1922- . Soprano. BAKER 1971,
EWEN NEW, KUTSCH, PAVLAKIS=
p.287, RIEMANN ERG, *SAND-
VED=another illus.p.1194,
THOMPSON. *[Some sources=b.
1927, which RIEMANN ERG
corrects to 1922]*

CURTIS, Mary Louise (Mrs.
Edward Bok, later Mrs.
Efrem Zimbalist, Sr.).
Boston, Aug 16 1876-Jan 4
1970, Philadelphia. Patron,
writer. BAKER 1971=p.28,
ENCI MUS=v.4 p.620, MGG=
v.14 col.1288, MGG SUP,
RIEMANN, RIEMANN ERG,
SANDVED=v.4 p.1512.

CURTIS, Natalie (Mrs. Paul
Burlin). New York City,
Apr 26 1875-Oct 23 1921,
Paris. Writer. BAKER 5,
ENCI MUS, ENCI SALVAT,
ENCY MUS, PRATT=p.261,
RIEMANN, THOMPSON.

CURTIS-VERNA, Mary. Salem,
Mass., May 9 1927- .
Soprano. *SANDVED, THOMP-
SON. *[SANDVED=b.1926;
THOMPSON=b.1927]*

CURTISS, Mina (real name=
Kirstein). Boston, Oct 13
1896- . Musicologist,
writer. BAKER 5, BAKER 1971,

MGG, MGG SUP, THOMPSON.

CURTZ, Mlle. fl.1769-76.
Dancer. HIGHFILL.

CURUBETO GODOY, María Isabel.
San Juan, Argentina, 1904-
Aug 23 1959, Buenos Aires.
Pianist, composer. ARIZAGA,
ENCI MUS. *[ARIZAGA=b.1898]*

CURWEN, Annie Jessy (Mrs. John
Spencer, born Gregg). Dublin,
Sep 1 1845-Apr 22 1932,
Matlock, England. Writer,
teacher, pianist, piano
teacher. BLOM, BROWN BRIT,
GROVE 5, SCHOLES.

CURZON, Lucille see Wallace,
Lucille

CUSHMAN, Charlotte Saunders.
Boston, Jul 23 1816-Feb 18
1876, Boston, Contralto.
THOMPSON. *[THOMPSON=d.1886.
Death date in entry based on
The Biographical Encyclopedia
and Who's Who of the American
Theatre (Rigdon), which indi-
cates death at the age of 59]*

CUSTONELLI, Signora. fl.1752.
Singer. HIGHFILL.

CUYLER, Louise Elvera. Omaha,
Neb., Mar 14 1908- . Musico-
logist, teacher, writer.
GROVE 5, RIEMANN ERG,
THOMPSON.

CUZZONI (Catzoni), Francesca
(later Signora Pietro Giu-
seppe Sandoni and/or Signora
San-Antonio Ferre, called
"la Parmigiana.") Parma,
1700-1770, Bologna. Soprano.
BAKER 1, BAKER 5, BLOM, BROWN
BIO=p.538, CLAYTON=p.52,
CORTE, *ENCI MUS, ENCI SAL-
VAT, EWEN NEW, GROVE 1 APP,
GROVE 5, *HIGHFILL, *MGG,
PRATT, RIEMANN, THOMPSON,
ULLSTEIN.

CVEJIĆ (Tzveych), Biserka
(born Katušić). Jesenice,
nr. Split, Yugoslavia,
Nov 5 1923- . Mezzo-soprano.
KUTSCH=p.444, RIEMANN ERG,
THOMPSON.

CZANYI, Cornelia see
Schmitt, Cornelia

CZARTORYSKA, Marcelline (born
Princess Radziwill). Vienna,
May 18 1817-Jun 8 1894, nr.
Cracow. Pianist. ENCI SAL-
VAT, ENCY MUS, GROVE 5,
RIEMANN, THOMPSON.

CZEKANOWSKA, Anna. Lemberg,
Poland, Jun 25 1929- .
Musicologist, ethnomusi-
cologist, writer. RIEMANN
ERG.

CZERNY-STEFAŃSKA, Halina.
Cracow, Dec 30 1922- .
Pianist. GROVE 5=v.8 p.64,
RIEMANN ERG, *ULLSTEIN.

D

DABADIE, Zulmé (born Leroux).
Boulogne-sur-Mer, France,
Mar 20 1804-Nov 1877,
Paris. Soprano. ENCI MUS.

DACH, Charlotte von. Lyss,
Switzerland, Apr 29 1913-
Composer, writer. SCHUH.

DACOSTA, Janine. Bordeaux,
1923- . Pianist. ENCI SAL-
VAT, ENCY MUS.

D'AGNESI PINOTTINI, Maria
Teresa see Agnesi Pinot-
tini, Maria Teresa d'

D'AGUIAR, Luiza Rosa see
Todi, Luiza Rosa

DAHLMAN, Berta see Sjögren,
Berta

DAHMAN, Mona (born Scholte).
Haarlem, Netherlands,
1894- . Pianist, composer.
ENCI SALVAT.

D'ALBERT, Hermine see Finck,
Hermine

D'ALBORE, Lilia (orig. Emilia).
S. Maria Capua Vetere, nr.
Caserta, Italy, Jan 4 1914- .
Violinist. ENCI MUS, RIEMANN,
RIEMANN ERG.

DALE, Kathleen (born Richards).
London, Jun 29 1895- .
Pianist, musicologist, com-
poser, teacher, writer.
ENCI SALVAT, ENCY MUS,
GROVE 5, THOMPSON.

D'ALESSIO, Aurora see
Alessio, Aurora d'

D'ALHEIM, Marie Olénine see
Olénine d'Alheim, Marie

DALIS, Irene. San Jose, Calif.,
Oct 8 1925- . Mezzo-soprano.
EWEN NEW, KUTSCH, PAVLAKIS=
p.294, SANDVED, THOMPSON.
[KUTSCH=b.1929; SANDVED=
b.1927]

DALL, Miss. fl.1776-94.
Singer, actress, composer.
HIGHFILL.

DALLA-RIZZA, Gilda (Ermene-
gilda). Verona, Oct 12
1892- . Soprano, voice
teacher. CELLETTI, *ENCI
MUS=illus.fac.p.2, EWEN NEW,
KUTSCH, MARIZ, THOMPSON.
[CELLETTI=b.Oct 13; KUTSCH=
b.Oct 2]

DALL'OCCA, Sophie see
Schoberlechner, Sophie

DAL MONTE, Toti (stage name of
Antonietta Meneghelli or

Meneghel, Mrs. Enzo de Muro Lomanto). Mogliano Veneto, nr. Treviso, Jun 27 1893-Jan 26 1975, Treviso. Soprano, voice teacher. BAKER 5=p.1106, BLOM, *CELLETTI, CORTE=p.715, *ENCI MUS, *ENCI SALVAT, GROVE 5 SUP, KUTSCH, RIEMANN, RIEMANN ERG, THOMPSON. *[Many sources=b.1899, which RIEMANN ERG corrects to 1893]*

D'ALVAREZ, Marguerite see Alvarez, Marguerite d'

DALY, Jane see Barsanti, Jane

D'AMBREVILLE, Anna see Perroni, Anna

D'AMBREVILLE, Rosa see Borosini, Rosa

DAMIAN, Grace. 19th-century English contralto. BROWN BRIT.

DAMOREAU, Laure Cinthie (born Montalant; first known as Mlle. Cinti). Paris, Feb 6 1801-Feb 25 1863, Paris. Soprano, voice teacher. BAKER 1, BAKER 5, BLOM=p.122, BROWN BIO, CLAYTON=p.221, DICT MUS, ENCI MUS=v.1 p.485, GROVE 1, GROVE 5= v.2 p.309, GROVE 5 SUP= p.76, MGG, PRATT, RIEMANN, THOMPSON. *[BAKER 1 & BAKER 5=b.in Chantilly]*

DAMROSCH, Clara see Mannes, Clara

DANCLA, Alphonsine-Geneviève-Lore (later Mme. Deliphard). Bagnères-de-Bigorre, France, Jun 21 1824-Mar 22 1880, Tarbes, France. Composer, teacher. MGG.

DANCEY, Mrs. fl.1732-39. Dancer, actress. HIGHFILL.

DANCEY, Miss. fl.1731-40. Dancer, actress. HIGHFILL.

DANCO, Suzanne. Brussels, Jan 22 1911- . Soprano. BAKER 5, BLOM, COOPER, CORTE, ENCI MUS, ENCI SALVAT, ENCY MUS, GROVE 5, KUTSCH, RIEMANN, RIEMANN ERG, SANDVED, THOMPSON, *ULLSTEIN. *[ENCI SALVAT= b.1914]*

DANEAU, Suzanne. Tournai, France, Aug 17 1901- . Pianist, composer. ENCI MUS, ENCI SALVAT, ENCY MUS, RIEMANN, RIEMANN ERG.

D'ANGELO, Gianna see Angelo, Gianna d'

D'ANGERI, Anna (stage name of Anna Angermayer de Redenburg). Vienna, Nov 14 1853-Dec 14 1907, Trieste. Soprano. ENCI MUS.

DANIELS, Alicia (later Mrs. George Frederick Cooke II and Mrs. Windsor). ?-Apr 30 1826, Bath, England. Singer, actress. *HIGHFILL.

DANIELS, Mabel Wheeler. Swampscott, Mass., Nov 27 1878-Mar 10 1971, Boston. Composer. BAKER 5, BAKER 1971, ENCI MUS, ENCI SALVAT, ENCY MUS, SANDVED, SCHOLES, THOMPSON.

DANILOVA, Alexandra Dionisjewna. Peterhof (Petrodworez), nr. Leningrad, 1904- . Dancer. RIEMANN, RIEMANN ERG.

DANZI, Franziska see Lebrun, Franziska

71   *DAVIES*

DANZI, Margarete (born Mar-
chand). Frankfurt?, 1768-
Jun 11 1800, Munich.
Soprano. ENCI MUS, ENCI
SALVAT=v.3 p.278, ENCY
MUS=v.3 p.148, GROVE 5,
MGG=v.8 col.1621.

DA PONTE, Giulia. Cesena,
Italy, 1810-1836, Trieste.
Soprano. ENCI MUS.

D'ARÁNYI, Jelly see Arányi,
Jelly d'

D'ARBLAY, Frances see
Arblay, Frances d'

DARBO, Erica. Christiania,
Norway, May 23 1891- .
Soprano. THOMPSON.

DARCLÉE, Hariclea (stage name
of Hariclea Haricly de
Hartulary). Bucharest,
1868-Jan 12 1939, Bucharest.
Soprano. CELLETTI, *ENCI
MUS=illus.fac.p.15, KUTSCH.
[KUTSCH=b.1860]

DARLEY, Anne (Mrs. William
John?). ?-1758?-1838?,
London?. Singer, actress.
HIGHFILL.

"DARLING MARIA" see Kil-
pinen, Margarete

DARRÉ, Jeanne-Marie. Givet,
France, Jul 30 1905- .
Pianist. BAKER 1971, ENCI
SALVAT, ENCY MUS.

DA SILVA, Marcia Salaverry
Pereira see Haydee,
Marcia

D'AUBERVAL, Mme. Jean (born
Crépé, called Mme. Théo-
dore). Paris?, ?-1798,
Paris?. Dancer. HIGHFILL.

D'AUBIGNY, Madame see Maupin, Madame

DAUSE, Mrs. fl.1760. Dancer.
HIGHFILL.

DAVELLI, Marthe. Lille, ?- .
20th-century French soprano.
THOMPSON.

DAVENPORT, Marcia. New York
City, Jun 9 1903- . Writer.
BAKER 5, THOMPSON.

DAVENPORT, Mary Ann (Mrs.
George Gosling, born Harvey).
Launceston, England, 1759-
May 8 1843, Brompton, Eng-
land. Singer, actress.
*HIGHFILL.

DAVENPORT GOERTZ, Gladys.
Croydon, England, Oct 11
1895- . Composer, violinist.
CBC.

DAVID, Annie Louise. Boston,
Oct 11 1891-May 7 1960,
San Francisco. Harpist.
THOMPSON.

DAVID, Marie Luise see
Dulcken, Marie Luise

DAVIDOVA, Vera. Nishnii
Novgorod, Russia, Sep 3
1906- . Contralto. KUTSCH.

DAVIDSON, Joy. 20th-century
American mezzo-soprano.
PAVLAKIS=p.294.

DAVIES, Miss. fl.1794-95.
Singer. HIGHFILL.

DAVIES, Cecilia. London, 1752-
Jul 3 1836, London. Soprano.
BLOM, BROWN BRIT, ENCI MUS,
GROVE 1, GROVE 1 APP, GROVE
5, HIGHFILL.

DAVIES, Clara (Mrs. Ben, born
Perry). 19th-century English
soprano. BROWN BRIT=p.117.

DAVIES, Clara Novello- see
Novello-Davies, Clara

DAVIES, Dotie see Temple, Hope

DAVIES, Elizabeth (later Mrs. Jonathan Battishill and Mrs. Anthony Webster). ?-Oct 1777, Cork, Ireland. Singer, actress. BROWN BRIT=p.35 (in article on husband Jonathan Battishill), HIGHFILL.

DAVIES, Fanny. Guernsey, England, Jun 27 1861-Sep 1 1934, London. Pianist. BAKER 1, BAKER 5, BLOM, BROWN BRIT, GROVE 1 APP, GROVE 5, PRATT. *[BAKER 1= b.Jun 17 1863?]*

DAVIES, Joan (Mrs. Ivor Walsworth). Isleworth, Middlesex, England, Apr 29 1912- . Pianist. ENCI MUS=v.4 p.555, GROVE 5, PALMER.

DAVIES, Llewela. Brecon, South Wales, ?-?. 19th-century Welsh pianist, composer. BROWN BRIT.

DAVIES, Margaret. Dowlais, South Wales, ?-?. 19th-century Welsh soprano. BROWN BRIT.

DAVIES, Marianne. London?, 1744-1792, London?. Harpsichordist, pianist, piano teacher, harmonica player, glass harmonica player. BROWN BIO, BROWN BRIT=p.117, ENCI MUS, GROVE 1, GROVE 1 APP, GROVE 5. *[BROWN BIO & BROWN BRIT=b.1736]*

DAVIES, Marianne. ?, 1744-1816?, ?. English singer. HIGHFILL.

DAVIES, Mary. London, Feb 27 1855-Jun 22 1930, Hamp-

stead, England. Mezzo-soprano, soprano. BROWN BIO, BROWN BRIT, GROVE 5, PRATT, THOMPSON. *[GROVE 5=d.in London]*

DAVIES, Ruth (Mrs. Tudor, born Packer). 20th-century English soprano. GROVE 5.

DAVIS, Mrs. (born Clegg). fl. 1726-45. Singer. HIGHFILL.

DAVIS, Miss. ?, c1736-?. Harpsichordist. HIGHFILL.

DAVIS, Miss. fl.1739-62. Singer?, dancer, actress. HIGHFILL.

DAVIS, Miss. fl.1794. Singer. HIGHFILL.

DAVIS, Miss. fl.1795. Singer?, dancer?. HIGHFILL.

DAVIS, Mrs. fl.1799-1803. Singer, actress. HIGHFILL.

DAVIS, Miss. 19th-century English composer. BROWN BRIT.

DAVIS, Agnes. Colorado Springs, Colo., ?- . 20th-century American soprano. *EWEN LIVING.

DAVIS, Elizabeth see Chambers, Elizabeth

DAVIS, Ellabelle. New Rochelle, New York, Mar 17 1907-Nov 11 1960, New Rochelle, New York. Soprano. *EWEN LIV SUP, KUTSCH, *SANDVED. *[SANDVED=b.1920]*

DAVIS, Jessie Bartlett. Nr. Morris, Ill., 1860-May 14 1905, Crown Point, Ind. Contralto. THOMPSON.

DAVIS, Mrs. K. fl.1789-92. Dancer. HIGHFILL.

DAVIS, Marianne (later Mrs. Gabriel). ?-Jul 18 1888, Littlemore, Oxford. Composer. BROWN BRIT.

DAVIS, Mary (later Mrs. James Paisible). fl.1660-98. Dancer, singer, actress. *HIGHFILL.

DAVIS, Sarah (Mrs. William). London?, ?-Dec 1797, at sea. Singer, actress. HIGHFILL.

DAVISON, Arabella see Goddard, Arabella

DAVRATH, Netania. 20th-century Israeli soprano. KUTSCH.

DAVY, Gloria. Brooklyn, Mar 29 1931- . Soprano. KUTSCH, PAVLAKIS=p.287, RIEMANN, RIEMANN ERG, *SANDVED, THOMPSON, *ULLSTEIN.

DAVY, Ruby Claudia Emily. Salisbury, Australia, Nov 22 1883-Jul 12 1949, Melbourne. Composer, pianist. THOMPSON.

DAW, Miss. fl.1760-68. Dancer. HIGHFILL.

DAWIDOWITSCH, Bella Michajlowna. Baku, Russia, Jul 16 1928- . Pianist. RIEMANN ERG.

DAWSON, Miss. fl.1779-82. Singer, actress. HIGHFILL.

DAWSON, Elizabeth see Brett, Elizabeth

DAWSON, Nancy. London?, c1730-Jun 9 1767, London. Dancer. *HIGHFILL.

DAWSON, Nancy. fl.1785. Dancer. HIGHFILL.

DAY, Ellen. London, Mar 3 1828-?. Pianist, organist. BROWN BRIT.

DAYAS, Karin Elin. Helsinki, May 13 1892-Mar 4 1971, Cincinnati. Pianist, piano teacher. PRATT, RIEMANN, RIEMANN ERG, THOMPSON.

DEACON, Marie Conner. Johnson City, Tenn., Feb 22 1907- . Composer, pianist, organist. CBC.

DEACON, Mary Ann. Leicester, England, Jun 26 1821-?. Pianist, organist, teacher. BROWN BRIT.

DE AHNA, Eleanora (Eleonore). Vienna, Jan 8 1838-May 10 1865, Berlin. Mezzo-soprano. BAKER 1, GROVE 5, RIEMANN= v.1 p.14, THOMPSON=p.27.

DE AHNA, Pauline see Strauss, Pauline

DE ALVEAR, Regina see Pacini, Regina

DE AMICIS, Anna Lucia see also Amicis, Anna Lucia de

DE AMICIS, Anna Lucia (Signora Domenico). fl.1755-89. Singer, dancer. HIGHFILL.

DEARL, Mrs. fl.1765. Dancer. HIGHFILL.

DE ARNOLD, Josephine Huguet see Huguet de Arnold, Josephine

DE BASSINI, Rita see De Begnis, Rita

DE BEAUHARNAIS, Hortense see Hortense, Queen

DE BEGNIS, Rita (born Gabussi;

Rita Gabussi de Bassini).
Bologna, c1815-Jan 26 1891,
Naples. Soprano. ENCI MUS,
ENCY MUS=v.2 p.195 (in
article on husband Vincenzo
Gabussi).

DEBELJEVIC, Lisa see Della
Casa-Debeljevic, Lisa

DE BELLEVILLE, Anna Caroline
see Oury, Anna Caroline

DEBICKA, Hedwig von. Warsaw,
1890- . Soprano, voice
teacher. KUTSCH.

DE BLASIS, Teresa. Naples,
May 27 1797-Apr 20 1868,
Florence. Pianist. ENCI
MUS.

DE BLASIS, Virginia. Mar-
seilles, Aug 5 1804-May 11
or 12 1838, Florence.
Soprano. ENCI MUS, RIEMANN
ERG=v.1 p.120.

DEBOGIS, Marie Louise. Geneva,
Aug 15 1879- . Soprano.
THOMPSON.

DECAIX, Marianne Ursule
(called "l'aînée."). ?,
1715-1751, ?. French
church composer. ENCY MUS.

DE CAMP, Adelaide. France,
Dec 1780-Apr 1834, Niagara
Falls, New York. Dancer,
actress. HIGHFILL.

DE CAMP, Sophia. fl.1776-77.
Dancer. HIGHFILL.

DE CAMP, Sophia (later Mrs.
Frederick Brown). ?, 1785-
?. Dancer. HIGHFILL.

DÉCARIE, Reine (Soeur Johane
d'Arcie). Montréal, Jan 4
1912- . Voice teacher,
composer. CBC.

DE CARO, Giulia (Ciulla).
Naples, Jul 13 1646-Nov 17
1697, Naples. Singer. ENCI
MUS.

DE CASTRONE, Blanche Marchesi
see Marchesi de Castrone,
Blanche

DE CASTRONE, Mathilde Marchesi
see Marchesi de Castrone,
Mathilde

DE CECCO, Disma. Udine, Italy,
Oct 4 1926- . Soprano. ENCI
MUS.

DECEUNINCK, Marguerite see
Heldy, Fanny

DECORNE, Jeanne Marguerite
Marcelle see Demougeot,
Marcella

D'EDLA, Countess see Hen-
sler, Elise

DE FESCH, Mrs. William?. fl.
1732. Singer. HIGHFILL.

DE FESTENBOURG, Stefania
Gérard see Lobaczewska,
Stefania

DE FILIPPI, Giuseppina (Mrs.
Luigi Mercantini). ?-1912,
Palermo. Pianist. ENCI MUS=
v.3 p.156.

DE FOMPRÉ, Mme. fl.1734-35.
Dancer, actress. HIGHFILL.

DE FONBLANQUE, Ellen see
Campbell, Ellen

DE FRANO, Mlle. fl.1737.
Dancer. HIGHFILL.

DE FRIDMAN-KOTSCHEWSKOJ, Sophie
Carmen see Eckhardt-Gramatté, Sophie Carmen

DE GAMBARINI, Elisabetta (later

Mrs. Chazal). ?, 1731-?.
Soprano, composer, organist.
GROVE 1=v.1 p.580, HIGHFILL.

DE GARMO, Tilly see Garmo,
Tilly de

DE GIULI BORSI, Teresa (stage
name of Maria Teresa Pippeo).
Mondovi, Italy, Oct 26 1817-
Nov 18 1877, Naples. Soprano. ENCI MUS.

D'EGVILLE, Miss. fl.1794.
Singer. HIGHFILL.

D'EGVILLE, Fanny. fl.1779-
1800. Dancer. HIGHFILL.

D'EGVILLE, Sophia. fl.1791-95.
Dancer. HIGHFILL.

DE HARTULARY, Hariclea Haricly
see Darclée, Hariclea

DE HENNEY, Mme?. fl.1753.
Dancer. HIGHFILL.

DE HIDALGO, Elvira see
Hidalgo, Elvira de

DELABORDE, Élie Miriam.
Chaillot, France, 1839-1913,
?. Pianist, piano teacher,
composer. ENCI SALVAT, ENCY
MUS, PRATT. *[ENCY MUS=b.
in Paris]*

DE LA BRUCHOLLERIE, Monique
see Bruchollerie, Monique
de la

DE LA COINTRIE, Mme. fl.1749-
52. Dancer. HIGHFILL.

DEL'ACQUA, Teresa. fl.1790.
Singer. HIGHFILL.

DE LA CROIX, Mlle. fl.1790-99.
Dancer. HIGHFILL.

DELAGARDE, Mrs. Charles?. fl.
1710-11. Dancer. HIGHFILL.

DELAGARDE, Mrs. J. (born
Oates). fl.1730-51. Dancer,
actress. HIGHFILL.

DE LA GUERRE, Élisabeth Jacquet
see La Guerre, Élisabeth
Jacquet de

DE LARA, Adelina (real name=
Tilbury). Carlisle, England,
Jan 23 1872-?. Pianist,
composer. BROWN BRIT=p.238,
GROVE 5, GROVE 5 SUP.
*[BROWN BRIT notes that her
father's name was Tilbury
and that De Lara was the
maiden name of her mother,
Mrs. Henry Russell]*

DE LARROCHA, Alicia see
Larrocha, Alicia de

DE LA VALLE, Mme. fl.1790-96.
Pianist, harpist. HIGHFILL.

DEL BENE, Adriana Ferrarese
see Gabrieli, Adriana

DEL CAMPO, Sofia. Chile, 1884-
Jun 24 1964, Santiago de
Chile. Soprano. KUTSCH.

DEL CARO, Mlle. (later Mme.
Cesare Bossi). fl.1794-1803.
Dancer. HIGHFILL.

DEL CARO, Mlle. fl.1790-1815.
Dancer. HIGHFILL.

DEL CORONA, Itala (born Balestri). 20th-century Italian
pianist. ENCI MUS.

DE L'ÉPINE, Francesca Margherita see L'Épine, Fran-
cesca Margherita

DELFEVRE, Mme. fl.1786-87.
Dancer. HIGHFILL.

DELICATI, Margherita (Signora
Luigi). fl.1789. Singer.
GROVE 1, HIGHFILL.

DELIGNY, Louise. fl.1791.
Dancer. HIGHFILL.

DELIPHARD, Madame see
Dancla, Alphonsine-Gene-
viève-Lore

DE L'ISLE, Mlle. fl.1735-36.
Dancer. HIGHFILL.

DE L'ISLE, Jeanne Marié see
Marié de L'Isle, Jeanne

DELLA CASA-DEBELJEVIC, Lisa.
Burgdorf, Switzerland, Feb
2 1919- . Soprano. BLOM,
CELLETTI, ENCI MUS, ENCI
SALVAT=p.611, ENCY MUS,
EWEN NEW, GROVE 5, GROVE 5
SUP, KUTSCH, MGG SUP, RIE-
MANN, RIEMANN ERG, *ROSEN-
THAL=illus.p.43, SCHUH,
THOMPSON, *ULLSTEIN=p.106.
[THOMPSON=b.1921]

DELLA MOREA, Vincenza Garelli
see Garelli Della Morea,
Vincenza

DELLA SANTA, Marcella see
Lotti della Santa, Marcella

DELLE SEDIE, Margherita
(Mrs. Enrico, born Tizzoni).
?-Mar 23 1888, ?. Italian
teacher. ENCI MUS.

DELLERA, Helen see Jepson,
Helen

DELMAS, Solange. ?, 1907?- .
Soprano, administrator.
KUTSCH.

DELNA, Marie (real name=Marie
Ledan). Meudon, nr. Paris,
Apr 3 1875-Jul 24 1932,
Paris. Contralto. BAKER 5,
CELLETTI, ENCI MUS, ENCI
SALVAT, ENCY MUS, KUTSCH,
PRATT, SANDVED, THOMPSON.
*[KUTSCH=d.Jun 24; CELLETTI &
ENCI MUS=d.Jul 3; BAKER 5=
d. Jul 23]*

DELORME, Mme. fl.1730-37.
Dancer. HIGHFILL.

DELORME, Mlle. fl.1730-37.
Dancer, actress. HIGHFILL.

DELORME, Isabelle. Montréal,
Nov 14 1900- . Pianist,
violinist, composer, teacher.
CBC.

DE LOS ANGELES, María see
Angeles, María Morales de los

DE LOS ANGELES, Victoria (real
name=Victoria Gomez Cima).
Barcelona, Nov 1 1923- .
Soprano. BAKER 5, BLOM=p.384,
*CELLETTI=col.487, illus.foll.
col.480, COOPER=p.282, DICT
MUS=v.2 p.649, ENCI MUS=v.3
p.44, ENCI SALVAT=v.3 p.230,
ENCY MUS=v.3 p.100, *EWEN LIV
SUP=p.13, EWEN NEW, GROVE 5=
v.5 p.403, GROVE 5 SUP=p.277,
KUTSCH=p.15, MGG SUP=col.217,
RIEMANN=v.2 p.100, *ROSEN-
THAL=illus.p.54-55, *SAND-
VED=another illus.p.800,809,
THOMPSON, *ULLSTEIN=p.24.

DELPINI, Signora Carlo Antonio.
fl.1784-1828. Singer, actress.
HIGHFILL.

DEL PUENTE, Helen (Mrs. Giuseppe, born Helen Dudley
Campbell). 19-20th-century
mezzo-soprano. ENCI MUS.

DEL RIEGO, Teresa Clotilde
(Mrs. Leadbetter). London,
Apr 7 1876-Jan 23 1968,
London. Composer. SCHOLES=
p.877, THOMPSON.

DE LYS, Edith (born Edith Ely).
Boston, 1886-Jul 3 1961, New
York City. Soprano, voice
teacher. THOMPSON. *[Dates
in entry taken from obituary
in Opera News, vol.26, p.36,
Dec 30 1961]*

DELYSSE, Jean (pseud.) see
Roesgen-Champion, Mar-
guerite

DE MACCHI, Maria see Macchi,
Maria de

DE MARESCHI, Giovanna see
Cara, Giovanna

DEMARQUEZ, Suzanne. Paris,
Jul 5 1899-Oct 23 1965,
Paris. Composer, teacher,
critic, writer. BAKER 1971,
ENCI MUS, ENCI SALVAT, ENCY
MUS, GROVE 5, RIEMANN, RIE-
MANN ERG.

DE MENDI, Antonia Sitcher
see Hubert, Antonia

DEMERA, Signora. fl.1771.
Singer. HIGHFILL.

DEMESSIEUX, Jeanne. Mont-
pellier, France, Feb 14
1921-Nov 11 1968, Paris.
Organist, composer, teacher.
BAKER 5, BAKER 1971, DICT
MUS, ENCI MUS, ENCI SALVAT,
ENCY MUS, MGG, RIEMANN,
RIEMANN ERG, THOMPSON.

DEMEUR, Anne Arsène (born
Charton). Sanjon, Charente,
nr. Saintes, France, Mar 5
1824 or 1827-Nov 30 1892,
Paris. Soprano. BAKER 1,
BLOM=p.115, BROWN BIO=p.
154, ENCI MUS=v.1 p.461,
ENCI SALVAT, ENCY MUS,
GROVE 1 APP, GROVE 5=v.2
p.189, PRATT, THOMPSON.
*[ENCI MUS & ENCI SALVAT=
b.Mar 15 1824]*

DE MICHELI, Mary Ann (Signora
Leopoldo). fl.1775-78.
Singer. HIGHFILL.

DE MILLE, Agnes. New York
City, 1908- . Dancer.
RIEMANN=v.2 p.223.

DEMOLIENS, Florentine see
Chanot, Florentine

DE MONTÈGRE, Gabriella Colombari see Ferrari, Gabriella

DE MONTMOLLIN, Marie-Lise see
Montmollin, Marie-Lise de

DE MOSS, Mary Hissem- see
Hissem-De Moss, Mary

DEMOUGEOT, Marcella (orig.=
Jeanne Marguerite Marcelle
Decorne). Dijon, France,
1876-1931, Paris. Soprano.
KUTSCH.

DE MURO LOMANTO, Toti see
Dal Monte, Toti

DE MURSKA, Ilma see Murska,
Ilma de

DENERA, Erna. Pila Castle, nr.
Posen, Germany, Sep 4 1881-
Mar 3 1938, Berlin. Soprano,
voice teacher. KUTSCH.

DENÉRÉAZ, Marguerite. Lausanne,
1894- . Teacher. ENCY MUS.

DEN HOVEN, Cacteau van see
Van den Hoven, Cacteau

DENIS, Agnes see Stavenhagen,
Agnes

DENNETT, Miss B. fl.1799-1820.
Dancer, actress?. *HIGHFILL.

DENNETT, Eliza (later Mrs.
Robert O'Neill). fl.1799-
1820. Dancer, actress?.
*HIGHFILL.

DENNETT, Miss F. fl.1799-1820.
Dancer, actress?. *HIGHFILL.

DENNIS, Mrs. fl.1720. Singer.
HIGHFILL.

DENNIS, Mrs. fl.1752-70. Singer, dancer. HIGHFILL.

DENNISON, Mrs. fl.1752.
Singer, dancer. HIGHFILL.

DENSMORE, Frances. Red Wing,
Minn., May 21 1867-Jun 5
1957, Red Wing, Minn.
Musicologist, ethnomusico-
logist, writer, folklorist.
BAKER 5, BAKER 1971, RIE-
MANN, RIEMANN ERG, THOMPSON.

DENTS, Miss?. fl.1723.
Dancer. HIGHFILL.

DENTS, De Long. fl.1723.
Dancer. HIGHFILL.

DENYA, Marcelle. ?, 1900- .
French soprano. ENCI SALVAT,
ENCY MUS.

DE PACHMANN, Maggie see
Oakey, Maggie

DE PASQUALI, Bernice (born
James). Boston, 1880-Apr 3
1925, New York City.
Soprano. KUTSCH=p.327,
THOMPSON.

DE REDENBURG, Anna Angermayer
see D'Angeri, Anna

DE RESZKE, Josephine see
Reszke, Josephine de

DE RHIGINI, Countess see
Russell, Ella

DERING, Lady see Harvey,
Mary

DERNESCH, Helga (Mrs. Landzettel). Vienna, Feb 3
1939- . Soprano. RIEMANN
ERG.

DE ROQUER, Calvé see
Calvé, Rosa-Noémie-Emma

DEROUBAIX, Jeanne. Brussels,
Feb 16 1927- . Contralto.
ENCI SALVAT, ENCY MUS,

ULLSTEIN. *[ENCI SALVAT &
ENCY MUS=b.1917]*

DERP, Clotilde von. Berlin,
1895- . Dancer. ENCI MUS=
v.4 p.94 (in article on the
Sakharoff family).

DERSHINSKAYA, Xenia. Kiev,
Jan 25 1889-Jun 9 1961,
Moscow. Soprano, voice
teacher. KUTSCH.

DE SANTI, Anna see Andreozzi,
Anna

DESBARQUES, Mlle. fl.1707.
Dancer. HIGHFILL.

DESBARQUES, Mme. fl.1708.
Dancer. HIGHFILL.

DESCAVES, Lucette. Paris,
1909- . Pianist, piano
teacher. ENCI SALVAT, ENCY
MUS.

DESCHALLIEZ, Louise (later
Louise Deschalliez de Vau-
renville). fl.1720-22.
Dancer. HIGHFILL.

DESCHAMPS-JEHIN, Blanche.
Lyons, Aug 18 1875-Jun 1923,
Paris. Contralto. KUTSCH.

DESDECHINA, Signora. fl.1749.
Dancer. HIGHFILL.

DE SISLEY, Mme. fl.1794.
Singer. HIGHFILL.

DE SIVRAI, Jules (pen-name)
see Roeckel, Jane

DESMOND, Astra. Torquay, England, Apr 10 1898-Aug 16
1973, London. Contralto.
GROVE 5, GROVE 5 SUP,
PALMER, THOMPSON. *[THOMPSON=
b.1893]*

DESPORTES, Yvonne Berthe Melit-

ta. Coburg, Saxony, Jul 18
1907- . Composer, teacher.
DICT MUS, ENCI MUS, ENCI
SALVAT, GROVE 5, RIEMANN
ERG.

DES ROSIERS, Roede Lima Fran-
chère- see Franchère-
DesRosiers, Roede Lima

DESSOFF, Margarete (Margar-
ethe). Vienna, Jun 11 1874-
Nov 27 1944, Locarno.
Choral conductor, teacher.
BAKER 5, ENCI MUS, ENCY
MUS, *EWEN LIVING, EWEN LIV
SUP, RIEMANN, SANDVED,
THOMPSON.

DESSOIR, Susanne (Mrs. Max,
born Triepel). Grünberg,
Silesia, Jul 23 1869-Jun 24
1953, Königstein, Taunus,
Germany. Soprano, voice
teacher, pianist. ENCI MUS=
v.4 p.421, KUTSCH, THOMPSON.
[KUTSCH=b.Jul 21]

DESTINN, Emmy (stage name of
Ema Pavlína Kittlová or
Ema Kittl, at first used
Czech name Ema Destinnová).
Prague, Feb 26 1878-Jan 28
1930, České Budějovice,
Bohemia. Soprano, actress,
writer. BAKER 5, BLOM,
CELLETTI, *COOPER=illus.
p.91, CORTE=p.184, *ENCI
MUS=illus.fac.p.39, EWEN
NEW, GROVE 5, KUTSCH,
MARIZ, *MGG SUP=illus.fac.
col.1728, PRATT, RIEMANN,
RIEMANN ERG, *SANDVED=
illus.p.518, THOMPSON.
[COOPER=d.1932]

DESTINNOVÁ, Ema see
Destinn, Emmy

DESZNER (Teschner), Salomea.
Bialystok, Poland, 1759-
1809, Grodno, Poland. Actress, singer. GROVE 5.

DE TARELLI, Elsa Piaggio see
Piaggio de Tarelli, Elsa

DE TRÉVILLE, Yvonne see
Tréville, Yvonne de

DETTEY, Miss. fl.1794. Singer.
HIGHFILL.

DEVALLIER, Lucienne. Geneva,
Apr 11 1928- . Contralto.
RIEMANN ERG, SCHUH.

DE VAURENVILLE, Louise Deschalliez see Deschalliez,
Louise

DE VEGA, Silvia Eisenstein
see Eisenstein de Vega,
Silvia

DE VELASCO, María Sánchez see
Thompson, Marquita Sánchez de

D'EVELYN, Miss. fl.1797-98.
Singer, actress. HIGHFILL.

DE VERNEUIL, Mimi. fl.1733-35.
Dancer, actress?. HIGHFILL.

DEVÈZE, Germaine. Paris, 1921- .
Pianist. ENCI SALVAT, ENCY
MUS.

DE VITO, Gioconda. Martina
Franca, Puglia, Italy, Jul
26 1907- . Violinist.
BAKER 5, CORTE, ENCI MUS,
RIEMANN, RIEMANN ERG,
*ULLSTEIN.

DEVRIENT, Therese (Mrs. Eduard,
born Schlesinger). 19th-
century German singer.
ENCI MUS.

DEVRIENT, Wilhelmine see
Schröder-Devrient, Wilhelmine

DEVRIÈS, Fidès. ?, Apr 22 1851-
1941?, ?. French soprano.
ENCI MUS, ENCY MUS.

DEVRIÈS, Jeanne. 19th-century French soprano. ENCI MUS.

DE VRIES, Rosa van Os. Deventer, Netherlands, 1828-1889, Rome. Soprano. ENCI MUS.

DEWS, Elizabeth. Wolverhampton, England, ?-?. 19th-century English contralto. BROWN BRIT.

DEYO, Ruth Lynda. Poughkeepsie, New York, Apr 20 1884-Mar 4 1960, Cairo, Egypt. Pianist, opera composer, composer. BAKER 5, BAKER 1971, PRATT, THOMPSON.

D'HARCOURT, Marguerite Béclard see Harcourt, Marguerite Béclard d'

D'HARDELOT, Guy see Hardelot, Guy d'

D'HERVIGNI, Mlle. fl.1735-36. Dancer. HIGHFILL.

"DIAMANTINA, La" see Scarabelli Diamante, Maria

DIANDA, Hilda. Córdoba, Argentina, Apr 13 1925- . Composer, writer, teacher, conductor. BAKER 1, BAKER 1971, RIEMANN ERG, VINTON. *[BAKER 1=b.1917]*

DIBDIN, Miss. fl.1799-1804. Dancer. HIGHFILL.

DIBDIN, Anne (Mrs. Thomas John, born Hilliar). London?, ?-Aug 29 1828, London. Singer, actress. *HIGHFILL.

DIBDIN, Isabelle Perkins (Mrs. James Robert William, born Palmer). Southwold, Suffolk, Jan 19 1828-?.

Church composer, soprano. BROWN BRIT.

DIBDIN, Mary (Mrs. Charles Isaac Mungo, born Bates). London?, 1782-Aug 16 1816, ?. Singer, actress. *HIGHFILL.

DIBDIN, Mary Anne (later Mrs. Tonne). England, c1800-?. Harpist, teacher. BROWN BIO, BROWN BRIT.

DICKENS, Maria see Dickons, Maria

DICKINSON, Helen Adell. Port Elmsley, Ontario, Canada, Dec 5 1875-Aug 25 1957, Tucson. Writer. BAKER 5, BAKER 1971.

DICKONS (Dickens), Maria (born Poole). London, c1770-May 4 1833, London. Soprano. BROWN BIO, BROWN BRIT, GROVE 1, GROVE 5, THOMPSON.

DICKSON, Ellen ("Dolores.") Woolwich, England, 1819-Jul 4 1878, Lyndhurst, England. Composer. BROWN BIO, BROWN BRIT.

DICKSON, Joan. Edinburgh, Dec 21 1921- . Violoncellist. RIEMANN ERG.

DICKSON, Muriel. Edinburgh, c1910- . Soprano. THOMPSON.

DIDELOT, Marie-Rose (Mme. Charles-Louis, born Paul). ?-1803, Russia. Dancer. *HIGHFILL.

DIDIÉE, Constance Betzy Rosabella Nantier- see Nantier-Didiée, Constance Betzy Rosabella

DIDIER, Margaret (Mrs. Abra-

ham J., born Evans). ?,
1741-1829, Bristol, England.
Singer, actress. HIGHFILL.

DIE, Comtesse de. 12th-cen-
tury French troubadour.
ENCI SALVAT, ENCY MUS.

DIEMAN, Ursula Van. Schwerin,
Germany, 1897- . Soprano,
voice teacher. KUTSCH.

DIEREN, Frieda van (Mrs.
Bernard, born Kindler).
19-20th-century Dutch
pianist. GROVE 5.

DIETRICH, Marie. Weinsberg,
Germany, Jan 27 1867-Dec 14
1940, Berlin. Soprano,
voice teacher. KUTSCH.

DIEUDONNÉ, Blanche see
Donadio, Bianca

DIEZ, Sophie (born Hartmann).
Munich, Sep 1 1820-May 3
1887, Munich. Soprano.
BAKER 1.

DIGHTON, Mrs. Robert (born
Bertles). fl.1787-94.
Singer. *HIGHFILL.

DIKENMANN-BALMER, Lucie.
Berne, Switzerland, Oct 21
1902- . Musicologist,
writer. ENCI SALVAT, ENCY
MUS, GROVE 5, MGG, RIEMANN,
SCHUH.

DILLER, Angela. Brooklyn,
Aug 1 1877-Apr 30 1968,
Stamford, Conn. Teacher,
writer, pianist, editor,
administrator. BAKER 5,
BAKER 1971, THOMPSON.

DILLING, Mildred. Marion,
Ind., Feb 23 1894- . Harpist, teacher, writer. BAKER
5, *EWEN LIVING, PAVLAKIS=
p.281, RIEMANN ERG, THOMPSON.

DILLON, Fannie Charles. Denver,
Mar 16 1881-Feb 21 1947,
Altadena, Calif. Composer,
pianist. BAKER 5, THOMPSON.

DI MARIA, Geltrude (Mrs.
Fedele Fenaroli). 18-19th-
century Italian singer.
ENCI MUS=v.2 p.178.

DI MURSKA, Ilma see Murska,
Ilma de

DINGELSTEDT, Jenny (born Lut-
zer). Prague, Mar 4 1816-
Oct 3 1877, Vienna. Soprano.
BAKER 1, THOMPSON.

DINKELA, Lilly Johanna Maria
Hafgren- see Hafgren-
Dinkela, Lilly Johanna Maria

DIRKENS, Annie. Berlin, Sep 25
1869-Nov 11 1942, Vienna.
Soprano. KUTSCH.

DITTERS VON DITTERSDORF, Nicolina (Mrs. Karl, born Trenck,
"Mlle. Nicolini"). 18th-cen-
tury singer. ENCI MUS.

DIXON, Clara Ann (later Mrs.
Smith, then Mrs. Sterling).
fl.1795-1822. Singer, actress.
*HIGHFILL.

DIXON, Mrs. Cornelius?. fl.1787.
Dancer. HIGHFILL.

DJURIĆ-KLAJN, Stana. Belgrade,
May 5 1908- . Pianist, piano
teacher, writer. MGG SUP.

DLUGOSZEWSKI, Lucia. Detroit,
Jun 16 1925- . Composer,
pianist, teacher. THOMPSON,
VINTON. [VINTON=b.1931]

DOBBS, Mattiwilda. Atlanta,
Jul 11 1925- . Soprano.
ENCI MUS, *EWEN LIV SUP, EWEN
NEW, GROVE 5, KUTSCH, PAVLA-
KIS=p.287, RIEMANN ERG,

*ROSENTHAL=illus.p.57,
· *SANDVED, THOMPSON. *[KUTSCH=
b.in Tennessee]*

D'OBIGNY DE FERRIÈRES, Amélie
Alexandrine see Obigny de
Ferrières, Amélie Alexan-
drine d'

DODD, Martha (Mrs. James
William). ?-Nov 28 1769,
Bury St. Edmunds, England.
Singer, actress. HIGHFILL.

DODSON, Miss. fl.1740-42.
Dancer, actress. HIGHFILL.

DODSON, Mrs. fl.1740-49.
Singer, actress. HIGHFILL.

DOE, Doris. Bar Harbor, Me.,
Mar 23 1899- . Contralto.
BAKER 5, *EWEN LIVING,
THOMPSON.

DOHRN, Ellinor von der Heyde-
see Heyde-Dohrn, Ellinor
von der

DOLBY, Charlotte Helen see
Sainton-Dolby, Charlotte
Helen

DOLMETSCH, Cécile. Dorking,
Surrey, Mar 22 1904- .
Mezzo-soprano. ENCI MUS,
MGG, SCHOLES.

DOLMETSCH, Hélène. Nancy,
France, Apr 14 1880-1924,
?. Viola da gamba player,
violoncellist. ENCI MUS,
ENCY MUS, GROVE 5, MGG,
THOMPSON.

DOLMETSCH, Mabel Johnston
(Mrs. Arnold). London, Aug
6 1874-Aug 12 1963, Hasle-
mere, Surrey. Viola da
gamba player, dancer. DICT
MUS, ENCI MUS, ENCY MUS,
GROVE 5, MGG, RIEMANN, RIE-
MANN ERG, SCHOLES.

DOLMETSCH, Marie. Glasgow,
Feb 16 1916- . Viola da
gamba player, flutist.
ENCI MUS, MGG, RIEMANN.

DOLMETSCH, Nathalie (Mrs.
Carley). Chicago, Jul 31
1905- . Viola player. DICT
MUS, ENCI MUS, MGG, RIEMANN,
RIEMANN ERG, SCHOLES.

"DOLORES" see Dickson, Ellen

· DOLORES, Antonia see Trebelli, Antoinette

DOLUCHANOWA (Dolukhanova),
Sara (Zara) (Sarui Agas-
jewna). Moscow, Mar 5 1918- .
Mezzo-soprano. KUTSCH, MGG
SUP, RIEMANN ERG.

DOMANGE, Mélanie see Bonis,
Mélanie

DOMANÍNSKÁ, Libuše. Brno,
Moravia, Jul 4 1924- .
Soprano. RIEMANN ERG.

DOMINGUEZ, Oralia. San Luis
Potosí, Mexico, Oct 15
1928- . Contralto. ENCI MUS,
KUTSCH, RIEMANN ERG, *ULL-
STEIN.

DOMINIQUE, Mme. fl.1748.
Singer, dancer. HIGHFILL.

DOMITILLA, Miriamne (born
Campanini). fl.1741-48.
Dancer. HIGHFILL.

DONÀ, Mariangela. Piove di
Sacco, Padua, Italy, May 23
1916- . Musicologist, writer.
RIEMANN ERG.

DONADIEU, Miss. fl.1775. Singer. HIGHFILL.

DONADIO, Bianca (stage name of
Blanche Dieudonné). Nizza
Italy, c1855- . Soprano.
ENCI MUS.

DONALDA, Pauline (orig.Light-
stone or Lichtenstein).
Montréal, Mar 5 1882-Oct 22
1970, Montréal. Soprano,
voice teacher. BAKER 5,
BAKER 1971, GROVE 5, KUTSCH,
SANDVED, THOMPSON.

DONATH, Helen (born Erwin).
Corpus Christi, Tex., Jul
10 1940- . Soprano. PAVLA-
KIS=p.287, RIEMANN ERG.

DONÁTOVÁ, Narcisa. Uherské
Hradiště, Czechoslovakia,
May 8 1928- . Composer,
opera composer, teacher.
GARDAVSKY.

DORDA, Martha Winternitz-
see Winternitz-Dorda,
Martha

DORFMANN, Ania. Odessa, Rus-
sia, Jul 9 1899- . Pianist.
BAKER 5, *EWEN LIVING,
*SANDVED, THOMPSON.

DORIA, Clara see Rogers,
Clara Kathleen

DORIVAL, Anne Marguerite.
Paris?, ?-1788, Marseilles.
Dancer. HIGHFILL.

DORIVAL À CORIFET (stage name
of Marie Catherine Brida).
Paris?, c1754-?. Dancer.
HIGHFILL.

DORMAN, Elizabeth (Mrs. Ridley, born Young). ?-Apr 12
1773, London. Singer,
actress. ENCI MUS=v.4 p.599,
GROVE 5=v.9 p.384, HIGHFILL.

DORSION, Mlle. fl.1792.
Dancer. HIGHFILL.

D'ORTA, Rachele (later Signora
Giorgi). fl.1784-85. Singer.
HIGHFILL.

D'ORTA, Rosina. fl.1784.
Singer. HIGHFILL.

DORUS-GRAS, Julie-Aimée-
Josèphe (born van Steenkiste).
Valenciennes, France, Sep 7
1805-Feb 6 1896, Paris.
Soprano. BAKER 1, BROWN BIO=
p.287, CLAYTON=p.313, ENCI
MUS, ENCY MUS, GROVE 1=v.1
p.619, GROVE 1 APP=v.4 p.654,
GROVE 5, PRATT, THOMPSON.
[ENCI MUS=b.Sep 9, d.Feb 9;
GROVE 1 APP=b.1804]

DOSIA, Elen (Mrs. André Burdino). Athens, 1915?- .
Soprano. KUTSCH.

DOTTI, Anna. fl.1724-27.
Singer. GROVE 1, HIGHFILL.

DOUBLEDAY, Leila (Mrs. Max
Pirani). Australia, c1894- .
Violinist. GROVE 5=v.6, p.779,
THOMPSON.

DOUGALL, Lilly. 19th-century
English contralto. BROWN
BRIT.

DOVE, Elizabeth (Mrs. Michael).
fl.1731-47. Dancer, actress.
HIGHFILL.

DOW, Dorothy. Houston, Oct 8
1920- . Soprano. BAKER 5,
ENCI MUS, GROVE 5, RIEMANN
ERG, THOMPSON.

DOWDING, Emily. fl.1796-1814.
English organist. GROVE 5.

DOWIAKOWSKA, Karolina. Warsaw,
Feb 9 1840-Feb 3 1910,
Warsaw. Soprano. GROVE 5.

DOWSON, Ann. fl.1765-79.
Singer. HIGHFILL.

DOYLE, Ada. 19th-century
English contralto. BROWN BRIT.

DRAGONETTE, Jessica. Calcutta,
?- . 20th-century American
soprano. *EWEN LIVING,
EWEN LIV SUP, SANDVED,
THOMPSON.

DRAKE, Miss. fl.1798-1801.
Dancer, singer. HIGHFILL.

DRAPER, Miss. fl.1776-82.
Dancer, singer. HIGHFILL.

DRÉGE-SCHIELOWA, Lucja.
Warsaw, Feb 13 1893- .
Pianist, composer. GROVE 5.

DRESSER, Marcia van see
Van Dresser, Marcia

DREULETTE, Marie Josephe see
Cabel, Marie Josephe

DREWETT, Nora. Sutton, Surrey,
Jun 14 1882- . Pianist,
piano teacher. BAKER 5,
THOMPSON.

DREYFUSS, Charlotte see
Alexandre, Charlotte

DREYSCHOCK, Elisabeth (born
Nose). Cologne, 1832-Jul
1911, Cologne. Contralto,
administrator. BAKER 1,
DICT MUS, ENCI MUS.

DRINKER, Catherine see
Bowen, Catherine Drinker

DRINKER, Sophie Hutchinson
(Mrs. Henry S.). Haverford,
Pa., Aug 24 1888-Sep 5 1967,
Philadelphia. Music amateur,
writer. GROVE 5.

"DROGHIERINA, La" see
Chimenti, Margherita

DROMAT, Marianne?. fl.1792-95.
Dancer. HIGHFILL.

DROUCKER, Sandra. Petrograd,
1876-?. Pianist, piano

teacher, writer. PRATT,
VODARSKY.

DROZ, Eugènie. La Chaux-de-
Fonds, Switzerland, Mar 21
1893- . Musicologist,
writer. BAKER 5, ENCI SALVAT,
ENCY MUS, RIEMANN, RIEMANN
ERG, THOMPSON.

DRUCKER, Sandra see Droucker,
Sandra

DRYNAN, Margaret. Toronto,
Dec 10 1915- . Composer.
NAPIER.

DUBELLAMY, Frances Maria (Mrs.
Charles Clementine I).
London?, ?-1773, London.
Singer, actress. HIGHFILL.

DUBISKA, Irena. Inowroclaw,
nr. Bydgoszcz, Poland,
Sep 26 1899- . Violinist.
GROVE 5, RIEMANN, RIEMANN
ERG.

DUBOIS, Claudie Marcel- see
Marcel-Dubois, Claudie

DUCHAMBGE, Charlotte Antoinette
Pauline (born du Montet).
Martinique, cl778-Apr 23
1858, Paris. Composer,
pianist, piano teacher.
DICT MUS, ENCY MUS, RIEMANN.

DUCHEMIN, Mlle?. fl.1789.
Dancer. HIGHFILL.

DUCHÊNE, Maria. ?, 1880- .
French contralto. KUTSCH.

DUCHESNE, Mme. fl.1791.
Dancer. HIGHFILL.

DUCLAIRFAIT, Claudine see
Lacombe, Claudine

DUCRAST, Mme. fl.1794. Singer.
HIGHFILL.

DUDLEY, Miss. fl.1778-83.
Dancer, actress. HIGHFILL.

DUDLEY CAMPBELL, Helen see
Del Puente, Helen

DUFAU, Jenny. Rothau, Alsace,
?-Aug 29 1924, Pau, France.
Soprano. PRATT, THOMPSON.

DUFFERIN, Helen Selina (born
Sheridan). Ireland, 1807-
Jun 13 1867, ?. Composer.
BROWN BRIT, THOMPSON.

DUFFEY, Johanna Beula see
Harris, Johanna Beula

DUFOUR, Camilla (later Mrs.
Jacob Henry Sarratt).
fl.1796-1809. Singer,
actress. HIGHFILL.

DUFOUR, Marie. Lausanne,
Nov 20 1912- . Organist,
pianist. SCHUH.

DUGAL, Madeleine. Chicoutimi,
Québec, Jun 3 1926- . Pianist, composer. CBC.

DUGAZON, Louise-Rosalie (born
Lefèvre). Berlin, Jun 18
1755-Sep 22 1821, Paris.
Singer, actress. BAKER 5,
BLOM, ENCI MUS, *ENCY MUS,
GROVE 1, GROVE 5, MGG SUP,
PRATT, THOMPSON. [PRATT &
THOMPSON=b.1753]

DULCKEN, Marie Luise (Louise;
born David). Hamburg, Mar
29 1811-Apr 12 1850, London.
Pianist, piano teacher.
BAKER 5, BROWN BIO, GROVE 1,
GROVE 1 APP, GROVE 5, GROVE
5 SUP, PRATT, RIEMANN, RIE-
MANN ERG, THOMPSON. [BROWN
BIO & THOMPSON=b.Mar 20]

DULCKEN, Sophie (born Lebrun).
London, Jun 20 1781-?.

Pianist, composer. GROVE 1=
v.2 p.109-110.

DULISSE, Mme. fl.1757-58.
Dancer. HIGHFILL.

DULISSE, Mlle. fl.1757-59.
Dancer. HIGHFILL.

DUMESNIL, Suzanne (Zaïde).
LeHavre, Nov 6 1884- .
Soprano. PRATT, THOMPSON.

DUMONT, Mme. fl.1738-48.
Dancer. HIGHFILL.

DUMONT, Mlle. fl.1748.
Dancer. HIGHFILL.

DUMONT, Mlle. fl.1781.
Dancer. HIGHFILL.

DUMONT, Mrs. fl.1799-1800.
Singer. HIGHFILL.

DU MONTET, Charlotte Antoinette
Pauline see Duchambge,
Charlotte Antoinette Pauline

DUNCAN, Isadora. San Francisco,
May 27 1878-Sep 14 1927,
Nice, France. Dancer, writer.
ENCI MUS, *ENCI SALVAT,
RIEMANN, RIEMANN ERG, THOMP-
SON, ULLSTEIN.

DUNCKER, Sylvia see Geszty,
Sylvia

DUNLOP, Isobel (Violet Skelton).
Edinburgh, Mar 4 1901- .
Violinist, composer. BAKER 5,
GROVE 5.

DUNN, Mignon. Memphis, Tenn.,
Jun 17 1931- . Mezzo-soprano.
PAVLAKIS=p.294, THOMPSON.

DUNNING, Carre Louise. New York
City, Apr 6 1860-Sep 8 1929,
?. Pianist, piano teacher.
ENCI SALVAT, THOMPSON.

DUNSTALL, Mary (Mrs. John).
London?, ?-May 28 1758,
London. Singer, actress.
HIGHFILL.

DU PAIN, Mlle?. fl.1789.
Dancer. HIGHFILL.

DUPARC, Elizabeth (called
"La Francescina.") fl.
1736-44. English soprano.
BLOM, GROVE 1=v.1 p.558,
GROVE 5, GROVE 5 SUP,
THOMPSON.

DU PARK, Miss. fl.1800.
Harpist. HIGHFILL.

DUPONT, Gertrude Pitzinger-
see Pitzinger-Dupont,
Gertrude

DUPORT, Miss. fl.1770.
Singer. HIGHFILL.

DUPRÉ, Mme. fl.1735-55.
Dancer?. HIGHFILL.

DUPRÉ, Éléonore (Caroline?).
fl.1776-87. Dancer.
HIGHFILL.

DUPRÉ, Jacqueline. Oxford,
England, Jan 26 1945- .
Violoncellist. BAKER 1971.

DUPREE, Miss. fl.1797.
Harpist. HIGHFILL.

DUPUY, Hilaire (known as
Mlle. Hilaire). 17th-century
French singer. ENCI MUS=
v.2 p.562 (in article on
Michel Lambert).

DURAND, Mlle. fl.1791.
Dancer. HIGHFILL.

DURAND, Marie. Charleston,
S.C., ?-?. 19th-century
American soprano. BROWN BIO.

DURANSTANTI (Durastanti),

Margherita (Signora Casimiro
Avelloni). Italy, c1685-
after 1734, Italy?. Soprano.
BLOM, BROWN BIO, ENCI MUS,
ENCI SALVAT, ENCY MUS, GROVE
1, GROVE 5, HIGHFILL.

DURET, Mme. see Saint-
Aubin, Anne-Cécile-Dorlise

DURHAM, Miss. fl.1757-58.
Dancer. HIGHFILL.

DURIGO, Ilona. Budapest, May 13
1881-Dec 25 1943, Budapest.
Mezzo-soprano, voice teacher.
CORTE, GROVE 5, KUTSCH, RIE-
MANN, SCHUH, THOMPSON.

DURNO, Jeannette. ?, Jul 12
1876-?. Pianist. THOMPSON.

DURONCERAY, Marie-Justine-
Benoîte see Favart,
Marie-Justine-Benoîte

DU RUEL, Mme. fl.1704-06.
Dancer. HIGHFILL.

DUŠEK see Dussek

DUSSEAU, Jeanne (born Ruth
Thom). Elgin, nr. Edinburgh,
c1900- . Soprano. THOMPSON.

DUSSEK, Josepha (Josephine or
Josefina, born Hambacher).
Prague, Mar 6 1753-after
1798, ?. Singer, pianist,
composer. BLOM, DICT MUS,
ENCI MUS, ENCI SALVAT, ENCY
MUS, GROVE 1, GROVE 5,
GROVE 5 SUP, *MGG, THOMPSON.
[DICT MUS=b.Mar 7]

DUSSEK, Olivia (later Mrs.
Buckley). London, Sep 29
1801-1847, London. Pianist,
harpist, organist, composer,
writer. BROWN BIO=p.125,
BROWN BRIT=p.67, ENCI MUS,
GROVE 1, GROVE 5, PRATT.

DUSSEK, Sophia Giustina (Mrs.
Jan Ladislav, later Mrs.
John Alvis Moralt, born
Corri). Edinburgh, May 1
1775-1847, London. Singer,
pianist, harpist, composer.
BLOM, BROWN BRIT, DICT MUS=
v.1 p.234, ENCI SALVAT=v.1
p.530&646, GROVE 1, GROVE 1
APP, GROVE 5=v.2 p.456, HIGH-
FILL, MGG, THOMPSON. [HIGH-
FILL=d.c1830]

DUSSEK, Veronica (later
Štěbetova). 18-19th-century
Bohemian harpist. ENCI MUS.

DUSSEK, Veronica Elizabeth
see Cianchettini, Veronica
Elizabeth

DUSSEK, Veronica Rosaria (Rosa-
lie; not to be confused with
Veronica Elizabeth Cianchet-
tini, born Dussek). Časlav,
Bohemia, Mar 8 1769-1833,
London. Pianist. BROWN BRIT,
ENCI MUS, ENCI SALVAT, ENCY
MUS, MGG.

DUSTMANN, Marie Luise (born
Meyer). Aix la Chapelle,
Aug 22 1831-Mar 2 1899,
Charlottenburg, Berlin.
Soprano, voice teacher.
BAKER 1, BAKER 5, GROVE 5,
GROVE 5 SUP, PRATT, THOMPSON.

DUVAL, Mlle. French 18th-cen-
tury singer, composer.
GROVE 5.

DUVAL, Mlle. fl.1740-44.
Dancer. HIGHFILL.

DUVAL, Mme. fl.1741-45.
Dancer. HIGHFILL.

DU VAL, Lorraine. Saskatoon,
Canada, Aug 3 1917- .
Violinist. PALMER.

DUVAL, Marie see Worrell,
Marie

DUX, Claire. Witkowicz, nr.
Bydgoszcz, Poland, Aug 2
1885-Oct 8 1967, Chicago.
Soprano. BAKER 5, GROVE 5,
KUTSCH, MARIZ, RIEMANN,
RIEMANN ERG, THOMPSON,
ULLSTEIN.

DVOŘÁKOVÁ, Ludmila. Kolín,
Czechoslovakia, Jul 11
1923- . Soprano. KUTSCH,
RIEMANN, ULLSTEIN. [ULLSTEIN=
b.1928]

DYER, Mrs. fl.1692-93. Singer.
HIGHFILL.

DYER, Harriet (Mrs. Michael,
born Bullock). ?, 1721?-?.
English dancer, actress.
HIGHFILL.

DYER, Lorely. England?, Dec 17
1910- . Soprano. PALMER.

DYER, Louise (Mrs. Louise B.
M. Hanson). Melbourne, Jul 16
1890-Nov 9 1962, Monaco.
Patron, publisher. BAKER
1971, RIEMANN=v.2 p.340
(brief mention in article on
L'Oiseau Lyre).

E

E. T. P. A. (pseud.) see
Maria Antonia Walpurgis

EADIE, Noël. Paisley, Scotland,
Dec 10 1901-Apr 11 1950,
London. Soprano. BLOM, GROVE
5, THOMPSON.

EAMES, Emma Hayden (Mme. Eames-
Story). Shanghai, Aug 13
1865-Jun 13 1952, New York
City. Soprano. BAKER 1,
BAKER 5, CELLETTI, ENCI MUS,
*EWEN LIVING, EWEN LIV SUP,
EWEN NEW, GROVE 5, MARIZ,
PRATT, *SANDVED, THOMPSON.
[BAKER 1=b.1867; SANDVED=
d.1932]

EASTLAKE, Lady Elizabeth.
England, 1816-1852, Eng-
land. Writer. BROWN BIO,
BROWN BRIT.

EASTON, Florence Gertrude.
Middleboro-on-Tees, York-
shire, Oct 24 1884-Aug 13
1955, New York City. So-
prano. BAKER 5, ENCI MUS,
*EWEN LIVING, EWEN LIV SUP,
EWEN NEW, GROVE 5, GROVE 5
SUP, RIEMANN, RIEMANN ERG,
SANDVED, THOMPSON.

EATON, Sybil Evelyn. Ketton,
Rutland, England, Feb 17
1897- . Violinist. GROVE 5.

EBEL-WILDE, Minna. Germany,
Sep 27 1890- . Soprano.
THOMPSON.

EBERHART, Constance. York,
Neb., ?- . 20th-century
American mezzo-soprano.
THOMPSON.

EBERLIN, Maria Cäcilia Barbara. Salzburg, Nov 17
1728-?. Composer. ENCI MUS.

EBERLIN, Maria Francisca
Veronika. Salzburg, Jan 31
1735-Jan 13 1766, Salzburg.
Singer. ENCI MUS.

EBERLIN, Maria Josepha
Catharina. Salzburg, Nov 14
1730-May 14 1755, Salzburg.
Musician. ENCI MUS.

EBERS, Clara. Karlsruhe, Germany, Dec 26 1902- .
Soprano. RIEMANN ERG.

EBERT, Maria Anna see
Wegmann, Maria Anna

EBERWEIN, Henriette (born
Hassler). Erfurt, Germany,
1797-Aug 6 1849, Weimar.
Soprano. ENCI MUS.

EBNER, Suzanne Renate (later
Krauss). 17th-century
Austrian musician. ENCI MUS.

ECKERT, Johanna see Holm,
Hanya

ECKHARDT-GRAMATTÉ, Sophie
Carmen (born de Fridman-
Kotschewskoj, since 1939
known as Sonia Friedman-
Gramatté). Moscow, Dec 24
1901 or Jan 6 1902- .
Violinist, composer, pianist.
BAKER 5, BAKER 1971, ENCI
MUS, ENCI SALVAT, ENCY MUS,
GROVE 5, GROVE 5 SUP, MGG
SUP, NAPIER, RIEMANN, RIE-
MANN ERG, THOMPSON.

EDEL, Katharina Fleischer-
see Fleischer-Edel, Katharina

EDER, Josephine see Vieuxtemps, Josephine

EDINGER, Christiane. Potsdam,
Mar 20 1945- . Violinist.
RIEMANN ERG.

EDLA, Countess d' see
Hensler, Elise

EDSTROM, Liva see Järnefelt,
Liva

EDUARDSEN, Karin Maria see
Branzell, Karin Maria

EDVINA, Marie Louise Lucienne
Juliette Martin. Québec,
c1885-Nov 13 1948, London.
Soprano. GROVE 5, SANDVED,
THOMPSON. [THOMPSON=b.in
Vancouver]

EDWARDS, Clara (born Gerlich).
Mankato, Minn., Apr 18
1879?-Jan 17 1974, New York
City. Composer. BAKER 5,
BAKER 1971, THOMPSON. [BAKER
5, BAKER 1971, THOMPSON=

b.1887; dates in entry based
on obituary in New York
Times (Jan 19 1974, p.34,
col.5 & Jan 20 1974, p.57,
col.1) indicating that she
died at the age of 95]

EDWARDS, Philippine (born
Siedle). England, 1851-May 7
1930, New York City. So-
prano. THOMPSON.

EDWIN, Elizabeth Rebecca
(born Richards). 19th-cen-
tury English actress,
singer. BROWN BRIT.

EGERTON, Grace (later Mrs.
George Tinkler Case).
19th-century English so-
prano. BROWN BRIT=p.81
(in article on husband).

EGGAR, Katharine Emily.
London, Jan 5 1874-?.
Pianist, composer. GROVE 5,
THOMPSON.

EGGERTH, Marta (Mrs. Jan
Kiepura). Budapest, Apr 17
1912- . Soprano, actress.
CORTE, ENCI MUS=v.2 p.531
(in article on husband),
*SANDVED=illus.only p.842.

EGGLESTON, Anne. Ottawa,
Sep 6 1934- . Composer.
NAPIER.

EGVILLE, d' see D'Egville

EHLERS, Alice. Vienna, Apr 16
1887- . Pianist, harpsi-
chordist, piano teacher,
teacher. BAKER 5, BAKER
1971, CORTE, ENCI MUS,
EWEN LIVING, GROVE 5,
RIEMANN, RIEMANN ERG,
THOMPSON. [Some sources=
b.1890, others=b.1893;
RIEMANN ERG corrects these
to 1887]

EHRENBERG, Alexandra see
Warwick, Alexandra

EHRENBERG, Eleanora (Baroness).
Prague, 1832-?. Soprano.
BROWN BIO.

EHRHARDT, Dorothy see
Erhart, Dorothy

EIBENSCHÜTZ, Ilona. Budapest,
May 8 1872-May 21 1967,
London. Pianist. BAKER 1,
GROVE 5, PRATT, THOMPSON.
[GROVE 5 & PRATT=b.1873]

EIPPERLE, Trude. Stuttgart,
Aug 12 1910- . Soprano.
RIEMANN ERG.

EISBEIN, Adrienne see
Kraus, Adrienne

EISENSTEIN DE VEGA, Silvia.
Buenos Aires, Jan 5 1917- .
Ethnomusicologist. ARIZAGA,
RIEMANN ERG.

EISSLER, Emma. 19th-century
Moravian pianist. BAKER 1.

EISSLER, Marianne. Brno,
Moravia, Nov 18 1865-?.
Violinist. BAKER 1.

EKMAN, Ida (born Mordauch).
Helsinki, Apr 22 1875-Apr
14 1942, Helsinki. Soprano.
GROVE 5, THOMPSON.

ELFRIEDA WINN, Mary see
Williams, Mary Lou

ELÍA, Magdalena Bengolea de
Sánchez see Sánchez Elía,
Magdalena Bengolea de

ELIAS, Rosalind. Lowell, Mass.,
Mar 13 1931- . Mezzo-soprano.
EWEN NEW, PAVLAKIS=p.295,
RIEMANN ERG, *SANDVED=illus.
p.809, THOMPSON. [RIEMANN
ERG=b.1929; THOMPSON=b.1932]

ELIZALDE, Elena Sansinena de. Buenos Aires?, 1889-1970, ?. Patron. ARIZAGA.

ELLEGAARD, France Marguerite (Mrs. Birger Carlstedt). Paris, Oct 10 1912 (not 1913)- . Pianist. BAKER 5, RIEMANN, RIEMANN ERG.

ELLICOTT, Rosalind Frances. Cambridge, England, Nov 14 1857-Apr 5 1924, London. Composer, pianist. BAKER 5, BROWN BRIT, GROVE 5, PRATT, RIEMANN, THOMPSON.

ELLINGER, Désirée. Manchester, England, 1894?-Apr 30 1951, London. Soprano. GROVE 5.

ELLIOTT, Carlotta. 19th-century English soprano. BROWN BRIT.

ELLIOTT, Victoria. Newcastle-on-Tyne, England, Mar 7 1922- . Soprano. *PALMER= illus.p.187.

ELLIS, Catherine Joan. Birregura, Victoria, Australia, May 19 1935- . Musicologist, ethnomusicologist, writer, teacher. MGG SUP.

ELMO, Cloe. Lecce, Italy, Apr 9 1910-May 24 1962, Ankara. Mezzo-soprano. CORTE, ENCI MUS, GROVE 5 SUP.

ELSSLER, Fanny (orig.=Franziska). Gumpendorf, nr. Vienna, Jun 23 1810-Nov 27 1884, Vienna. Dancer. CORTE, DICT MUS, *ENCI MUS= illus.only v.1 fac.p.354, RIEMANN, RIEMANN ERG.

ELSSLER, Therese. Vienna, Apr 5 1808-Nov 19 1878, Merano, Italy. Dancer.

DICT MUS, RIEMANN, RIEMANN ERG.

EL-TOUR, Anna. Odessa, Russia, Jun 4 1886-May 30 1954, Amsterdam. Soprano, voice teacher. BAKER 5, THOMPSON.

ELY, Edith see De Lys, Edith

ENCK-GOTTSCHALL, Liselotte. Linz, Jul 16 1918- . Soprano. RIEMANN, RIEMANN ERG.

ENDE, Pelagie see Andriessen, Pelagie

ENDERSSOHN, Mary Ann see Graham, Mary Ann

ENDICH, Saramae. Steubenville, Ohio, Nov 20 1928-Jun 12 1969, New York City. Soprano. RIEMANN ERG, SANDVED. [SAND-VED=b.1930]

ENDORF, Cäcilie Rüsche- see Rüsche-Endorf, Cäcilie

ENGEL, Jane see Bathori, Jane

ENGELBRECHT, Christiane (Mrs. Bernsdorff). Erwinen, East Prussia, Jan 6 1923- . Musicologist, writer. MGG SUP, RIEMANN, RIEMANN ERG.

ENGLE, Marie. St. Louis, Mo., c1860-?. Soprano. THOMPSON.

"EOS CYMRU PENCERDDES" see Wynne, Sarah Edith

ÉPINE, Francesca Margherita de l' see L'Épine, Francesca Margherita de

ERDMANNSDÖRFFER, Pauline (born Oprawnik, called Fichtner after her adoptive father). Vienna, Jun 28 1847-?. Pianist, court musician. BAKER 1=p.651.

ERHART, Dorothy Agnes Alice.
London, Jan 5 1894-Apr
1971, England. Harpsichordist, conductor, composer,
writer. GROVE 5.

ERIKSON, Märta Greta. Stock-
holm, Dec 20 1919- .
Pianist, piano teacher.
RIEMANN ERG.

ERKIN, Ferhunde. Istanbul,
Jul 8 1909- . Pianist.
RIEMANN, RIEMANN ERG.

ERMELINDA TALEA PASTORELLA
ARCADA see Maria Antonia
Walpurgis

ERNST, Anna Katherina. Mün-
ster, Alsace, Sep 13 1894- .
Singer, voice teacher.
SCHUH.

ERTMANN, Catharina Dorothea
(born Graumann). Frankfurt
(not Offenbach), May 3
1781-Mar 16 1849, Vienna.
Pianist. CORTE, ENCI MUS,
ENCI SALVAT, ENCY MUS,
GROVE 1, MGG SUP, PRATT,
RIEMANN, RIEMANN ERG,
THOMPSON.

ERWIN, Helen see Donath,
Helen

ESCOBAR, Maria Luísa. Valen-
cia, Spain, Dec 5 1903- .
Composer. RIEMANN, RIEMANN
ERG, SLONIMSKY, THOMPSON.

ESIPOVA, Anna Nikolaevna
see Essipova, Anna Niko-
laevna

ESSEX, Countess of see
Stephens, Catherine

ESSIPOVA (Esipova, Essipoff,
Essipow), Anna (Annette)
Nikolaevna (Nikolajewna,

Nicolayevna). St. Petersburg,
Feb 12 1851-Aug 18 1914,
St. Petersburg. Pianist,
piano teacher, court musician.
BAKER 1, BAKER 5, BLOM, BROWN
BIO, COOPER, CORTE, ENCI MUS,
ENCI SALVAT, ENCY MUS, GROVE
1 APP, GROVE 5, GROVE 5 SUP,
PRATT, RIEMANN, RIEMANN ERG,
THOMPSON, VODARSKY.

ESTCOTT, Lucy (born Grant).
Springfield, Mass., ?-?.
19th-century soprano.
THOMPSON.

ESTCOURT, Mary Jane. 19th-
century English writer,
editor. BROWN BIO.

ESTORF, Franziska Meyer- see
Martienssen-Lohmann,
Franziska

ESTRELLA, Blanca. Sanfelipe,
Venezuela, Sep 5 1915- .
Composer, teacher. RIEMANN
ERG.

EVANS, Fanny see Frickenhaus,
Fanny

EVANS, Margaret see Didier,
Margaret

EVANS, Nancy. Liverpool, Mar
19 1915- . Mezzo-soprano.
BAKER 5, GROVE 5, *PALMER=
illus.p.188, THOMPSON.

EVELYN, Miss d' see D'Evelyn,
Miss

EVEREST, Eleanor see Freer,
Eleanor

EVERS, Katinka. Hamburg, 1822-
?. Singer. GROVE 5.

EVRARD, Jane. Neuilly-Plaisance,
France, 1898- . Conductor.
ENCI SALVAT, ENCY MUS.

EYRE, Margaret (Mrs. Alfred
James Eyre, born Bucknall).
19th-century English
pianist. BROWN BRIT.

EYTH, Johanna see Pohl,
Johanna

F

FABBRI, Flora. 19th-century
Italian dancer. ENCY MUS.

FABBRI, Guerrina. Ferrara,
Jun 21 1868-Feb 21 1946,
Turin. Contralto. CELLETTI,
ENCI MUS, ENCY MUS, KUTSCH.
*[CELLETTI=b.1866, d.Feb 15;
KUTSCH=b.1886 (undoubtedly
misprint)]*

FABBRI, Vittorina. 19-20th-
century Italian mezzo-
soprano. ENCI MUS.

FABRI, Anna Maria. 18th-cen-
tury Italian singer. ENCI
MUS.

FABRIS, Amanda. New York City,
c1865-Sep 27 1950, New York
City. Soprano. THOMPSON.

FABRIZIO, Margaret. 20th-
century American harpsichordist, teacher. PAVLAKIS=
p.279.

FACCIO, Chiarina. Verona,
Jun 15 1846-Apr 23 1923,
Trieste. Soprano. ENCI MUS.

FACHIRI, Adila (born d'Arányi).
Budapest, Feb 26 1886 (not
1888)-Dec 15 1962, Florence.
Violinist. BAKER 5, BAKER
1971, BLOM, ENCI MUS, GROVE
5, GROVE 5 SUP, RIEMANN,
RIEMANN ERG, THOMPSON.

FAHBERG, Antonia. Vienna,
May 19 1928- . Soprano.
RIEMANN ERG.

FAHRBACH, Henriette. Vienna,
Jan 22 1851-Feb 24 1923,
Vienna. Choral conductor,
composer, teacher. ENCI MUS,
ENCI SALVAT, ENCY MUS.

FAHRBACH, Johanna (Jenny).
Vienna, Jun 3 1842-Jul 19
1911, Vienna. Pianist, piano
teacher. ENCI SALVAT, ENCY
MUS.

FAHRBACH, Josephine. Vienna,
1831-Dec 2 1854, Vienna.
Pianist, piano teacher.
ENCI SALVAT, ENCY MUS.

FAHRBACH, Maria Johanna.
Padua, Oct 6 1843-Mar 8
1866, Vienna. Singer.
ENCI SALVAT, ENCY MUS.

FAHRINI, Helene. Thun, Switzerland, Nov 12 1901- . Soprano.
ENCI MUS, GROVE 5, SCHUH.

FAIRLESS, Margaret. Newcastle-
on-Tyne, England, Nov 10
1901- . Violinist. THOMPSON.

FAISST, Clara Mathilde. Karlsruhe, Jun 22 1872-Nov 22
1948, Karlsruhe. Composer.
ENCI SALVAT, ENCY MUS,
RIEMANN.

FALCHI CORTINI, Zaira. Rome,
Sep 4 1859-Jun 12 1944,
Rome. Soprano. ENCI MUS.

FALCON, Marie-Cornélie. Paris,
Jan 28 1814-Feb 25 1897,
Paris. Soprano. BAKER 1,
BAKER 5, BLOM, CLAYTON=p.323,
CORTE, DICT MUS, ENCI MUS,
*ENCI SALVAT, *ENCY MUS,
EWEN NEW, GROVE 1 APP, GROVE
5, GROVE 5 SUP, *MGG=illus.
only v.9 col.257, PRATT,
RIEMANN, RIEMANN ERG, SAND-
VED, THOMPSON. *[BAKER 1,
BLOM, CORTE, GROVE 1 APP, &
PRATT=b.1812]*

FALK, Anna see Mehlig, Anna

FALK, Lina. Geneva, Jan 29 1889-Jun 25 1943, Geneva. Contralto, voice teacher. SCHUH.

FALK, Nanette see Auerbach, Nanette

FALL, F. Ethel see Norbury, F. Ethel

FALTIS, Evelyn. Trautenau, Bohemia, Feb 20 1890-May 19 1937, Vienna. Composer. RIEMANN, THOMPSON. [THOMP-SON=d.May 13]

"FARINELLA" see Brambilla, Francesca

FARINELLA, La see Camati, Maria

FARLEY, Carole. Iowa, ?- . 20th-century American soprano. PAVLAKIS=p.288.

FARMER, Anna Maria. ?-Apr 11 1846, London. Singer. BROWN BRIT.

FARMER, Dinah (later Mrs. De Lisle Allen). ?-Apr 10 1884, London. Pianist. BROWN BRIT.

FARMER, Emily Bardsley (Mrs. Arthur W. Lambert). 19th-century English composer. BROWN BRIT.

FARNADI, Edith. Budapest, Sep 25 1921-Dec 12 or 14 1973, Graz. Pianist. RIEMANN, RIE-MANN ERG, THOMPSON. [Date and place of death based on obituary in Neue Zeitschrift für Musik, Mar 1974, p.198]

FARNESE, Marianna. fl.1776-77. English singer. GROVE 1.

FARNETI, Maria. Forlì, Italy,

Dec 8 1877-Oct 17 1955, S. Varano, nr. Forlì, Italy. Soprano. CELLETTI, CORTE, *ENCI MUS=illus.fac.p.167, ENCI SALVAT, ENCY MUS, KUTSCH, THOMPSON. [KUTSCH= b.1878, d.in Milan; THOMPSON= b.c1875]

FARNOL, Eleanor see Moir, Eleanor

FARRAR, Geraldine. Melrose, Mass., Feb 28 1882-Mar 11 1967, Ridgefield, Conn. Soprano. BAKER 5, BAKER 1971, BLOM, *CELLETTI=illus.fol. col.352, COOPER, CORTE, ENCI MUS, ENCI SALVAT, ENCY MUS, *EWEN LIVING, EWEN NEW, GROVE 5, KUTSCH, MARIZ, *MGG, MGG SUP, PRATT, RIEMANN, RIEMANN ERG, *SANDVED, THOMPSON, *ULLSTEIN.

FARRELL, Eileen. Willimantic, Conn., Feb 13 1920- . So-prano. BAKER 1971, *EWEN LIV SUP, EWEN NEW, KUTSCH, PAV-LAKIS=p.288, RIEMANN, *SANDVED, THOMPSON.

FARRENC, Jeanne Louise (Mrs. Jacques-Hippolyte-Aristide, born Dumont). Paris, May 31 1804-Sep 15 1875, Paris. Pianist, piano teacher, composer. BAKER 1, BLOM, BROWN BIO, ENCI MUS, GROVE 1, GROVE 5, PRATT, THOMPSON.

FARRENC, Victorine Louise. Paris, Feb 23 1826-Jan 3 1859, Paris. Pianist, com-poser. BROWN BIO, GROVE 5.

FASSBÄENDER, Brigitte. Berlin, ?- . 20th-century German contralto. RIEMANN ERG.

FASSBÄENDER (Fassbender), Zdenka (Mrs. Felix Mottl). Děčin, Bohemia, Nov 12 1880-

Mar 14 1954, Munich. Soprano. ENCI SALVAT, ENCY MUS, EWEN NEW, PRATT=p.599. *[ENCI SALVAT=b.Dec 12 1873; PRATT=b.1879]*

FAULL, Ellen. 20th-century American soprano. SANDVED.

FAURE, Constance Caroline Lefebvre (Mrs. Jean Baptiste). Paris, Dec 21 1828-1905, ?. Soprano. ENCI MUS, ENCY MUS, PRATT.

FAUSTINA see Hasse, Faustina

FAUSTO, Signora see Borselli, Elisabetta

FAVART, Marie-Justine-Benoîte (born Duronceray). Avignon, Jun 14 1727-Apr 21 1772, Paris. Singer, actress. BLOM, BROWN BIO, ENCI MUS, GROVE 5, THOMPSON. *[BLOM, BROWN BIO, & ENCI MUS= b.Jun 15; BROWN BIO=d.Apr 20]*

FAVEL, Andrée see Lacombe, Claudine

FAVERO, Mafalda. Portomaggiore, nr.Ferrara, Jan 6 1905- . Soprano. CELLETTI, ENCI MUS, ENCI SALVAT, ENCY MUS, KUTSCH, RIEMANN ERG.

FAY, Amy. Bayou Goula, Miss., May 21 1844-Feb 28 1928, Watertown, Mass. Pianist, piano teacher, writer. BAKER 1, BAKER 5, BROWN BIO, PRATT, RIEMANN, THOMPSON. *[BROWN BIO=b. Bayou Goula, La.]*

FAY, Maude. San Francisco, Apr 18 1883-Oct 7 1964, San Francisco. Soprano. BAKER 1971, ENCI SALVAT, ENCY MUS, KUTSCH, PRATT,

THOMPSON. *[KUTSCH=b.1878; BAKER 1971=b.1879; ENCY MUS= b.Apr 8 1883]*

FÉART, Rose. Saint-Riquier, France, Mar 26 1878-Oct 5 1954, Geneva. Soprano, voice teacher. ENCI SALVAT, ENCY MUS, SCHUH NACH. *[ENCI SALVAT & ENCY MUS=b.1881 in Lille, d.1957]*

FEATHERSTONE, Isabella see Paul, Isabella

FEHRMAN, Minny see Brema, Marie

FEI-LIU-LI. Hangchow, 1925- . Singer. ENCY MUS.

FEIRING, Bertha see Tapper, Bertha

FEL, Marie. Bordeaux, Oct 24 1713-Feb 2 1794, Chaillot, nr. Paris. Soprano. BLOM, DICT MUS, ENCI MUS, ENCI SALVAT, ENCY MUS, GROVE 5, THOMPSON.

FEL, Marie Antoinette Françoise. fl.1780. French singer. GROVE 5.

FELBERMAYER, Annie (Anny). Vienna, Jul 24 1924- . Soprano. KUTSCH, RIEMANN, RIEMANN ERG, ULLSTEIN. *[ULLSTEIN=b.1929]*

FÉLIX-MIOLAN, Caroline see Carvalho-Miolan, Caroline-Marie-Félix

FELLINGER, Imogen. Munich, Sep 9 1928- . Musicologist, writer. RIEMANN ERG.

FENAROLI, Geltrude see Di Maria, Geltrude

FENNINGS, Sarah. Essex, England, c1873-?. Violinist, teacher. THOMPSON.

FENTON, Lavinia (Duchess of Bolton; real name=Bestwick). London, 1708-Jan 24 1760, Greenwich. Soprano, actress. BLOM, BROWN BIO, BROWN BRIT, CLAYTON=p.35, ENCI SALVAT, ENCY MUS, GROVE 1, GROVE 5, THOMPSON.

FENTUM, Catherine (Katherine). fl.1780-85. English music publisher and seller. GROVE 5.

FENTUM, Mary Ann. 19th-century English music publisher and seller. GROVE 5.

FÉRALDY, Germaine. Toulouse, 1894- . Soprano, voice teacher. KUTSCH.

FÉRÈS, Maria Simone. Pelle- voisin, France, 1920- . Singer. ENCI SALVAT, ENCY MUS.

FERLENDIS, Signora. Rome, c1778-after 1810, ?. Contralto. GROVE 1, GROVE 5.

FERLOTTI, Claudia. ?-Apr 1868, Paris. Singer. ENCI MUS.

FERLOTTI, Giuseppina. Odessa, c1855-Feb 1915, Rome. Soprano. ENCI MUS.

FERLOTTI, Santina (later Sangiorgi). Cesena, Italy, Feb 13 1805-Sep 25 1853, Cesena, Italy. Soprano. ENCI MUS.

FERNÁNDEZ, Josefa see Gassier, Josefa

FERNÁNDEZ, María Antonia ("La Caramba"). Motril, Granada, 1751-1787, Madrid.

Singer. ENCI SALVAT, ENCY MUS=v.1 p.489, GROVE 5= v.2 p.57, THOMPSON.

FERNI, Carolina. Como, Aug 20 1839-Jun 4 1926, Milan. Soprano, violinist. CORTE, ENCI MUS, ENCY MUS. [CORTE=b.1846]

FERNI, Vincenzina. Como, c1837- 1926, Turin. Soprano, vio- linist. ENCI MUS, ENCY MUS.

FERNI GERMANO, Virginia. Turin, 1849-Feb 4 1934, Turin. Soprano. ENCI MUS, ENCY MUS.

FERON, Elizabeth see Glossop, Elizabeth

FERRABOSCO, Elizabeth. Green- wich, bapt.Dec 3 1640-?. English singer. BLOM, GROVE 5.

FERRANDINI (Ferradini), Anna Maria Elisabetta. 18th- century Italian singer. ENCI MUS.

FERRANI, Cesira (stage name of Cesira Zanazzio). Turin, May 8 1863-May 4 1943, Pollone (Biella), Italy. Soprano, voice teacher. CELLETTI, *ENCI MUS=illus. fac.p.178, KUTSCH. [CELLETTI= d.May 6]

FERRARESE DEL BENE, Adriana see Gabrieli, Adriana

FERRARI, Carlotta. Lodi, Jan 27 1837-Nov 23 1907, Bologna. Composer, opera composer. BAKER 1, BAKER 5, BROWN BIO, CORTE, ENCI MUS, ENCY MUS, PRATT, RIEMANN, THOMPSON.

FERRARI, Francisca. Christiania, Norway, c1800-Oct 5 1828,

Gross-Salzbrunn, Silesia.
Harpist. BAKER 1.

FERRARI, Gabriella (born
Colombari de Montègre).
Paris, Sep 14 1851-Jul 4
1921, Paris. Composer,
pianist. BAKER 5, BAKER
1971, ENCI MUS, PRATT,
RIEMANN, THOMPSON.

FERRARI, Sofia. 19th-century
Italian singer. ENCI MUS=
v.2 p.184 (brief mention in
article on father-in-law
Giacomo Goffredo Ferrari).

FERRARIS, Amalia. Voghera,
Italy, c1828-Feb 8 1904,
Florence. Dancer. ENCI
SALVAT, ENCY MUS.

FERRARIS, Ines Maria. Turin,
May 6 1883-Dec 11 1971,
Milan. Soprano, voice
teacher. *ENCI MUS=illus.
fac.v.4 p.326, KUTSCH.

FERRIER, Kathleen Mary.
Higher Walton, Lancashire,
Apr 22 1912-Oct 8 1953,
London. Contralto. BAKER 5,
BLOM, *CELLETTI=illus.fac.
col.352, COOPER, CORTE=p.
716, *ENCI MUS=illus.fac.
p.182, ENCI SALVAT, ENCY
MUS, *EWEN LIV SUP, EWEN
NEW, GROVE 5, GROVE 5 SUP,
KUTSCH, MGG SUP, PALMER,
RIEMANN, RIEMANN ERG,
*SANDVED, THOMPSON, ULLSTEIN.

FESCH, Mrs. William? de see
De Fesch, Mrs,. William?

FESCHOTTE, Colette (Mrs.
Jacques, born Wyss). La
Neuveville, Switzerland,
Nov 21 1893- . Singer.
ENCI MUS, SCHUH.

FESTA, Francesca (known as
Signora Festa-Maffei).

Naples, 1778-Jan 1836, St.
Petersburg. Singer. BAKER 1,
CORTE, ENCI MUS, THOMPSON.

FESTENBOURG, Stefania Gérard
de see Lobaczewska,
Stefania

FEUDEL, Elfriede Antonie
(born Thurau). Prussian
Stargard, West Prussia,
Oct 30 1881-Mar 30 1966,
Freiburg im Breisgau,
Germany. Teacher, writer.
MGG SUP, RIEMANN, RIEMANN ERG.

FEUGE, Elisabeth. Dessau,
Germany, 1902-Jul 4 1942,
Munich. Soprano. KUTSCH.

FEUGE-GLEISS, Emile. Rhenish
Palatinate, 1863-1923,
Dessau, Germany. Soprano.
KUTSCH.

FÈVRE, Caroline le see
Spivacke, Caroline

FICHTNER, Pauline see
Erdmannsdörffer, Pauline

FIELD-HYDE, Margaret. Cambridge,
England, May 4 1905- .
Soprano. GROVE 5, THOMPSON.

FIERSOHN, Reba see Gluck,
Alma

FIGNER, Medea Mei- see
Mei-Figner, Medea Ivanovna

FIGNER-GERARD, Lidia Nikolaievna. 19-20th-century
Russian soprano, voice teacher. ENCI MUS.

"FILIPPI, Signora" see
Phillipps, Adelaide

FILIPPI, Giuseppina de see
De Filippi, Giuseppina

FILIPPI, Pauline (Mrs. Filippo,

born Vaneri). 19th-century
Italian singer, voice
teacher. ENCI MUS.

FILIPPONE-SINISCALCHI, Tina.
Rome; Feb 1903-Sep 14 1926,
Resina, Italy. Pianist.
ENCI SALVAT.

FILLUNGER, Marie. Vienna,
Jan 27 1850-Dec 1930, ?.
Soprano. ENCI SALVAT,
ENCY MUS, PRATT, THOMPSON.

FINCK, Hermine (Mrs. Eugen
d'Albert). Baden-Baden,
Germany, Jan 1 1872-Nov 1
1932, Berlin. Singer.
ENCI MUS=v.1 p.35, RIEMANN.

FINE, Vivian. Chicago, Sep 28
1913- . Composer, pianist,
teacher. BAKER 5, ENCI MUS,
REIS, RIEMANN ERG, SANDVED,
THOMPSON, VINTON.

FINESCHI, Onelia. Florence,
Apr 5 1924- . Soprano.
ENCI MUS, KUTSCH.

FINNEBERG, Laelia. Liverpool,
May 1908- . Soprano. PALMER.

FINNILÄ, Birgit. Falkenberg,
Sweden, Jan 20 1931- .
Contralto. RIEMANN ERG.

FINZI-MAGRINI, Giuseppina.
Turin, May 5 1878-Nov 30
1944, Turin. Soprano.
KUTSCH.

FIORETTI CIAMPOLI, Elena.
Macerata, Italy, 1830?-?.
Soprano. ENCI MUS.

FIRENZE (stage name) see
Florence, Amy

FISCHER, Annie. Budapest,
Jul 5 1914- . Pianist.
ENCI SALVAT, ENCY MUS,
MGG SUP, RIEMANN, RIEMANN
ERG, SANDVED, *ULLSTEIN.

*[ENCI SALVAT & ENCY MUS=
b.1916]*

FISCHER, Barbara (Mrs. Ludwig,
born Strässer). Mannheim,
1758-?. Singer. ENCI MUS.

FISCHER, Elsa see Stralia,
Elsa

FISCHER, Else Gentner- see
Gentner-Fischer, Else

FISCHER, Ivana. Zagreb, Jun 13
1905- . Conductor. THOMPSON.

FISCHER, Josepha (later Vernier). Vienna, 1782-?.
Singer. ENCI MUS.

FISCHER, Lore. Stuttgart, May 27
1911- . Contralto. KUTSCH,
RIEMANN, RIEMANN ERG, ULL-
STEIN.

FISCHER, Louise. 18-19th-century
German singer. ENCI MUS.

FISCHER, Res (Maria Theresia).
Berlin, Nov 8 1896-Oct 4 1974,
Stuttgart. Contralto. ENCI
SALVAT, ENCY MUS, KUTSCH,
RIEMANN, RIEMANN ERG, ULL-
STEIN. *[Date and place of
death based on obituary in
Opera, Dec 1974, p.1098]*

FISCHER, Therese Wilhelmine.
?, 1785-?. German singer.
ENCI MUS.

FISHER, Charlotte E. (Carlotta).
London, ?-?. 19th-century
violinist, pianist, composer,
editor. CBC.

FISHER, Esther. Christchurch,
New Zealand, ?- . 20th-century
pianist. PALMER.

FISHER, Susanne. Sutton, W. Va.,
?- . 20th-century American
soprano. *EWEN LIVING, THOMP-
SON.

FISHER, Sylvia. Melbourne,
Australia, 1911- . Soprano.
GROVE 5, KUTSCH, *ROSENTHAL=
illus.p.59, THOMPSON.

FITZIU, Anna (born Powell).
Huntington, W.Va., 1888-
Apr 20 1967, Hollywood.
Soprano, voice teacher.
KUTSCH, THOMPSON.

FITZWILLIAM, Kathleen Mary
(Mrs. C. Withall). England,
1826-?. Singer, actress.
BROWN BRIT.

FJODOROWA, Jelisaweta Semjonowna see Sandunowa,
Jelisawetz Semjonowna

FLACHOT, Reine. Santa Fé,
France, 1922- . Violon-
cellist. ENCI SALVAT, ENCY
MUS.

FLAGSTAD, Kirsten Malfrid
(Mrs. Henry Johansen).
Hamar, nr.Oslo, Jul 12
1895-Dec 7 1962, Oslo.
Soprano. BAKER 5, BAKER
1971, BLOM, CELLETTI,
*COOPER=illus.p.96, CORTE,
ENCI MUS, ENCI SALVAT, ENCY
MUS, *EWEN LIVING, EWEN LIV
SUP, EWEN NEW, GROVE 5,
GROVE 5 SUP, KUTSCH, MARIZ,
MGG, MGG SUP, RIEMANN, RIE-
MANN ERG, *SANDVED=another
illus.p.1143, THOMPSON,
*ULLSTEIN. [CELLETTI &
ULLSTEIN=d.Dec 8]

FLAVEL, Andrée see Lacombe,
Claudine

FLEISCHER, Editha (Edytha).
Falkenstein, Germany, Apr 5
1898- . Soprano, voice
teacher. ARIZAGA, BAKER 5,
KUTSCH, SANDVED, THOMPSON.

FLEISCHER, Eva. Breslau,
Germany, May 5 1922- . Sin-

ger. RIEMANN, RIEMANN ERG.

FLEISCHER-EDEL, Katharina.
Mülheim, Germany, Sep 25
1875-Aug 18 1928, Dresden.
Soprano. KUTSCH, PRATT,
THOMPSON. [KUTSCH=b.Sep 27
1873; PRATT=b.1873]

FLEITES, Virginia. Melena del
Sur, Cuba, Jul 10 1916- .
Composer. ENCI SALVAT, ENCY
MUS, GROVE 5, SLONIMSKY.
[GROVE 5=b.in Havana]

FLESCH, Ella. Budapest, Jun 16
1900-Jun 6 1957, New York
City. Soprano, voice teacher.
KUTSCH, THOMPSON. [THOMPSON=
b.1902]

FLETCHER, Alice Cunningham.
Cuba, Mar 15 1838-Apr 6 1923,
Washington, DC. Ethnologist,
ethnomusicologist, writer.
BAKER 5, ENCI MUS, ENCI SAL-
VAT, ENCY MUS, MGG, PRATT,
RIEMANN, RIEMANN ERG, THOMP-
SON. [BAKER 5 & ENCI MUS=
b.Mar 16; PRATT=b.1845 in
Boston]

FLETCHER, Jane. 19th-century
English contralto. BROWN
BRIT.

FLETCHER, Maud. 19th-century
English violoncellist.
BROWN BRIT.

FLICK, Hermine von see
Bosetti, Hermine

FLINN, Kate. 19th-century
English soprano. BROWN BRIT.

FLISSLER, Eileen. USA, 1929- .
Pianist. PAVLAKIS=p.261,
SANDVED.

FLISSLER, Joyce. USA, 1931- .
Violinist. SANDVED.

99 FONBLANQUE

FLODIN, Adée (Mrs. Karl
Theodor, born Leander).
Helsinki, May 29 1873-Jul
6 1935, Helsinki. Soprano.
ENCI MUS, RIEMANN.

FLORENCE, Amy (stage name=
Firenze). Edgbaston, Bir-
mingham, ?-?. 19-20th-cen-
tury English soprano.
BROWN BRIT.

FLORENCE, Evangeline (real
name=Houghton). Cambridge,
Mass., Dec 12 1873-Nov 1
1928, London. Soprano.
BAKER 5, BLOM, GROVE 5,
GROVE 5 SUP, PRATT=p.456,
THOMPSON.

FLOWER, Eliza. Harlow, Essex,
Apr 19 1803-Dec 12 1846,
London. Church composer,
composer, soprano, poet.
BROWN BIO, BROWN BRIT,
GROVE 5, SCHOLES, THOMPSON.

FLOWER, Sara (later Mrs.
W. B. Adams). ?-Aug 16 1865,
Melbourne, Australia.
Contralto. BROWN BIO,
BROWN BRIT=p.148 & 463.

FOCKE, Ria. Haarlem, Netherlands, Jun 29 1908- .
Contralto. ENCI MUS.

FODOR-MAINVIELLE, Henriette.
19th-century French singer.
ENCI MUS.

FODOR-MAINVIELLE, Joséphine.
Paris, Oct 13 1789-Aug 14
1870, Saint-Genis, nr.
Lyons. Soprano. BLOM, BROWN
BIO, CLAYTON=p.213, CORTE,
ENCI MUS, ENCI SALVAT, ENCY
MUS, GROVE 1, GROVE 5,
THOMPSON. [BROWN BIO &
GROVE 1=b.1793]

FOERSTEL (Forstel), Gertrude.
Cologne, Dec 4 1880-Jun 7

1950, Bad Godesburg, nr.
Bonn. Soprano. ENCI SALVAT,
ENCY MUS, KUTSCH. [KUTSCH=
b.Dec 21 1880 at Leipzig]

FOERSTER, Elsa Oehme- see
Oehme-Foerster, Elsa

FÖRSTER, Therese see Herbert,
Therese

FOERSTROVÁ-LAUTEREROVÁ, Berta
(sometimes Bertha Foerster-
Lauterer). Prague, Jan 11
1869-Apr 9 1936, Prague.
Soprano, voice teacher.
ENCI MUS, GROVE 5, KUTSCH.

FOGEL, Helen see Schnabel,
Helen

FOGLIAZZI, Teresa. ?-Oct 31
1790, Cormanno, Italy.
Dancer. ENCI MUS=v.1 p.76
(in article on the Angiolini
family).

FOHSTRÖM-RODE, Alma. Helsinki,
Jan 2 1856-Feb 20 1936,
Helsinki. Soprano. GROVE 5,
RIEMANN, THOMPSON.

FOLKES, Lucretia see Bradshaw, Lucretia

FOLKESTONE, Viscountess see
Radnor, Countess of

FOLVILLE, Juliette-Eugénie-
Émilie. Liège, Jan 5 1870-
Oct 28 1946, Dourgne, Tarn,
France. Composer, pianist,
piano teacher, conductor,
violinist. BAKER 1, BAKER 5,
ENCI MUS, ENCI SALVAT, ENCY
MUS, MGG, RIEMANN, THOMPSON.
[ENCI MUS & MGG=d.Oct 19
1949]

FOMPRÉ, Mme. de see De
Fompré, Mme.

FONBLANQUE, Ellen de see
Campbell, Ellen

FONDA, Mrs. G. A. see
Hensel, Octavia

FONDEN, Olly Folge (Mrs. Henk
Badings). 20th-century
Dutch violinist. ENCI MUS=
v.1 p.163.

FONTEYN, *Dame* Margot (pseud.
of Margaret Hookham). Rei-
gate, Surrey, May 18 1919- .
Dancer. ENCI SALVAT=v.2
p.529, ENCY MUS, RIEMANN,
RIEMANN ERG.

FONTYN, Jacqueline (Mrs.
Schmit). Antwerp, Dec 27
1930- . Composer. DICT
MUS, MGG SUP, RIEMANN ERG.

FOOT, Phyllis Margaret. London, Oct 15 1914- . Composer, teacher. CBC.

FORD, Ann (later Mrs. P.
Thicknesse). fl.1760. English harmonica player,
musical glasses player,
singer. BROWN BIO, BROWN
BRIT, GROVE 1.

FORMES, Pauline Greenwood.
19th-century American
singer. ENCI MUS.

FORNAROLI, Cia (Lucia).
Milan, Oct 16 1898-Aug 16
1954, Riberdale, Italy.
Dancer. ENCY MUS.

FORNIA-LABEY, Rita (born
Newman). San Francisco,
Jul 17 1878-Oct 27 1922,
Paris. Soprano, later mezzo-
soprano. BAKER 5, KUTSCH,
PRATT, THOMPSON.

FORQUERAY, Marie-Rose. Paris,
Jan 17 1717-?. Clavecinist.
ENCY MUS.

FORREST, Mary (Mrs. Rudolph
Ganz). 20th-century American

singer. ENCI MUS=v.2 p.274.

FORRESTER, Maureen Katherine
Stewart. Montréal, Jul 25
1930- . Contralto. KUTSCH,
RIEMANN ERG, *SANDVED,
THOMPSON, *ULLSTEIN.

FORST, Grete. Vienna, Dec 16
1880- . Soprano. KUTSCH.

FORSTEL, Gertrude see
Foerstel, Gertrude

FORSYTH, Josephine. Cleveland,
Jul 5 1889-May 24 1940,
Cleveland. Composer. BAKER 5.

FORTEY, Mary Comber. 19th-
century English composer,
pianist. BROWN BRIT.

FORTI, Helena. Berlin, Apr 25
1884-May 11 1942, Vienna.
Soprano. KUTSCH.

FOSSA, Amalia. Naples, 1852-
Dec 26 1911, Florence.
Soprano. ENCI MUS.

FOSTER, Fay. Leavenworth, Kan.,
Nov 8 1886-Apr 17 1960,
Bayport, New York. Composer,
light-opera composer. BAKER
5, BAKER 1971.

FOSTER, Megan. Tonypandy, Gla-
morgan, Wales, Jul 16 1898- .
Soprano. GROVE 5, *PALMER=
illus.p.188.

FOSTER, Muriel. Sunderland,
England, Nov 22 1877-Dec 23
1937, London. Contralto.
BAKER 5, BLOM, GROVE 5,
PRATT, THOMPSON. *[GROVE 5=*
mezzo-soprano]

FOURIE, Johanna Everdina
(born La Rivière). Zwolle,
Netherlands, Sep 17 1884- .
Ethnomusicologist. RIEMANN
ERG.

FORNEAU, Marie-Thérèse.
St.-Mandé, France, Apr 9
1924- . Pianist. ENCI
SALVAT, ENCY MUS.

FOURRIER, Janine. Rambouillet,
France, 1924- . Singer.
ENCI SALVAT, ENCY MUS.

FOWLES, Margaret F. Ryde,
Isle of Wight, ?-?. fl.
1870-90. Conductor, pianist,
organist, composer, church
composer. BROWN BRIT.

FOX, Charlotte (born Milligan).
Omagh, Ireland, 1860-Mar 26
1916, London. Amateur
composer, folklorist,
writer. BAKER 5, PRATT,
THOMPSON.

FRACCI, Carla (Mrs. Menegatti).
Milan, Aug 20 1936- .
Dancer. RIEMANN ERG.

FRANCA, Celia. London, Jun 25
1921- . Dancer. ENCI SAL-
VAT, ENCY MUS.

FRANCALUCCI, Augusta see
Boccabadati Francalucci,
Augusta

FRANCESCHI, Vera. San Francisco, May 5 1928-Jul 11
1966, New York City. Pia-
nist. PAVLAKIS=p.261.
*[PAVLAKIS=b.1926. Dates in
entry based on New York
Times obituary, Jul 13 1966,
p.43, col.1]*

"FRANCESCINA, La" see
Duparc, Elizabeth

FRANCHÈRE-DES ROSIERS, Roede
Lima. Montréal, Jan 6
1863-?. Pianist, teacher,
composer. CBC.

FRANCILLO-KAUFMANN (-Kauff-
mann), Hedwig (Hedi). Wies-

baden, Sep 30 1878-Apr 5
1948, Rio de Janeiro. Soprano,
voice teacher. ENCI SALVAT,
ENCY MUS, KUTSCH. *[KUTSCH=
b.in Vienna]*

FRANCKENSTEIN, Maria see
Nezadal, Maria

FRANCO, Rina. Venice, Dec 13
1893- . Pianist, piano
teacher. ENCI MUS.

FRANÇOIS, Jacqueline see
Guillemautot, Jacqueline

FRANO, Mlle. de see De
Frano, Mlle.

FRANTZ, Helena see Braun,
Helena

FRANZ, Marie see Hinrichs,
Marie

FRANZISKA, Maria Anna. 18th-
century German singer.
ENCI MUS=v.3 p.426 (brief
mention in article on
Johann Christoph Pez).

FRASER, Janet. Kirkcaldy,
Scotland, May 22 1911- .
Mezzo-soprano. ENCI MUS,
GROVE 5, THOMPSON.

FRASER, Marjory Kennedy- see
Kennedy-Fraser, Marjory

FRASI, Giulia. fl.1743-59.
Italian soprano. BROWN BIO,
ENCY MUS, GROVE 1, GROVE 5,
THOMPSON.

FRATESANTI, Signora. fl.1743.
English singer. GROVE 1.

FRAZZONI, Gigliola. Bologna,
Feb 22 1927- . Soprano.
ENCI MUS.

FREDERIKSEN, Tenna. Copenhagen,
May 16 1887- . Soprano.
THOMPSON.

FREER, Eleanor (born Everest).
Philadelphia, May 14 1864-
Dec 13 1942, Chicago.
Composer. BAKER 5, THOMPSON.

FREGE, Livia (born Gerhard).
Gera, Germany, Jun 13 1818-
Aug 22 1891, Leipzig. So-
prano. ENCI SALVAT, ENCY
MUS, GROVE 1, GROVE 5,
PRATT, RIEMANN, THOMPSON.

FREITAS, Violetta Coelho
Netto de. Rio de Janeiro,
1910- . Soprano. MARIZ.

FREMSTAD, Anna Augusta Olivia
(orig.=Petterson). Stock-
holm, Mar 14 1871-Apr 21
1951, Irvington-on-Hudson,
New York. Mezzo-soprano,
soprano, voice teacher.
BAKER 5, BLOM, CELLETTI,
ENCI MUS, ENCI SALVAT, ENCY
MUS, *EWEN LIVING, EWEN
NEW, GROVE 5, KUTSCH, MARIZ,
PRATT, RIEMANN, *SANDVED,
THOMPSON. [CELLETTI, ENCI
MUS, ENCI SALVAT, ENCY MUS=
b.1868; EWEN LIVING=b.1870;
PRATT=b.1870?; MARIZ &
SANDVED=b.1872]

FRENI, Mirella. Modena, Feb
27 1936- . Soprano. BAKER 5,
ENCI MUS, EWEN NEW, KUTSCH,
RIEMANN ERG, *ULLSTEIN.

FRÈRE, Marguerite Jeanne see
Hatto, Jeanne

FREUND, Marya. Wroclaw,
Poland, Dec 12 1876-May 21
1966, Paris. Soprano, voice
teacher. BAKER 5, BAKER
1971, CORTE, ENCI SALVAT,
ENCY MUS, GROVE 5, THOMPSON.

FREY, Hélène-Narcisse see
Couperin, Hélène-Narcisse

FREZZOLINI, Erminia (later

Mrs. Poggi). Orvieto, Italy,
Mar 27 1818-Nov 5 1884,
Paris. Soprano. BLOM, BROWN
BIO, CORTE, *ENCI MUS=illus.
fac.p.238, GROVE 1, GROVE 1
APP, GROVE 5, PRATT, SANDVED,
THOMPSON.

FRÍAS, Brigida see Buchardo,
Brigida

FRIAS, Duchess de see
Balfe, Victoire

FRICCI, Antonietta (pseud. of
Frietsche). Vienna, Jan 8
1840-Sep 7 1912, Turin.
Soprano. CORTE, ENCI MUS,
ENCI SALVAT, ENCY MUS.

FRICHE, Claire Alexandrine.
Brussels, Mar 2 1875-Feb 12
1968, Paris. Soprano. RIE-
MANN ERG.

FRICKENHAUS, Fanny (born
Evans). Cheltenham, England,
Jun 7 1849-Aug 8 1913,
London. Pianist. BAKER 1,
BROWN BRIT, GROVE 1 APP,
GROVE 5, PRATT, THOMPSON.

FRICKER, Anne (later Mrs.
Mogford). England, c1820-?.
Songwriter, poet. BROWN BIO,
BROWN BRIT.

FRIDERICI-JAKOWICKA, Teodozja.
Kielce, Poland, 1836-Nov 4
1889, Warsaw. Soprano.
GROVE 5, GROVE 5 SUP.

FRIDMAN-KOTSCHEWSKOJ, Sophie
de see Eckhardt-Gramatté,
Sophie Carmen

FRIEDBERG, Annie. Bingen-on-
Rhine, Germany, c1878-?.
Concert manager. THOMPSON.

FRIEDLÄNDER, Thekla. 19th-
century German soprano.
GROVE 5, THOMPSON.

103   *FUCHS*

FRIEDMAN-GRAMATTÉ, Sonia
  see Eckhardt-Gramatté,
  Sophie Carmen

FRIEDRICH, Amalie see
  Materna, Amalie

FRIEDRICH, Elisabeth. Karlsruhe, Germany, 1893- .
  Soprano. KUTSCH.

FRIETSCHE, Antonietta see
  Fricci, Antonietta

FRIJSH (Frysch), Povla (real
  name=Paula Frisch). Aarhus,
  Denmark, Aug 3 1881-Jul 10
  1960, Blue Hill, Me. Soprano,
  voice teacher, pianist. BAKER
  5, BAKER 1971, ENCI SALVAT=
  v.2 p.262, ENCY MUS, *EWEN
  LIVING, KUTSCH, *SANDVED,
  THOMPSON. [SANDVED=b.1885]

FRIND, Annie. Nixdorf, Bohemia,
  Feb 2 1900- . Soprano, voice
  teacher. KUTSCH.

FRITSCHER, Eleonore see
  Westenholz, Eleonore

FRÖHLICH, Anna see Fröhlich,
  Maria Anna

FRÖHLICH, Barbara Franziska.
  Vienna, Aug 30 1797-Jun 30
  1879, Vienna?. Contralto.
  BLOM, ENCI SALVAT, ENCY
  MUS, GROVE 1, GROVE 1 APP,
  GROVE 5, GROVE 5 SUP, MGG,
  PRATT, RIEMANN, THOMPSON.

FRÖHLICH, Josephine. Vienna,
  Dec 12 1803-May 7 1878,
  Vienna. Soprano. BLOM,
  ENCI SALVAT, ENCY MUS,
  GROVE 1, GROVE 1 APP,
  GROVE 5, GROVE 5 SUP, *MGG,
  PRATT, RIEMANN, THOMPSON.

FRÖHLICH, Katharina. Vienna,
  Jun 10 1800-Mar 3 1879,
  Vienna. Pianist. BLOM, ENCI

SALVAT, ENCY MUS, GROVE 1,
GROVE 1 APP, GROVE 5, *MGG,
PRATT, RIEMANN.

FRÖHLICH, Maria Anna (Nanette).
  Vienna, Sep 19 1793-Mar 11
  1880, Vienna. Pianist,
  soprano, voice teacher.
  BLOM, ENCI SALVAT, ENCY MUS,
  GROVE 1, GROVE 1 APP, GROVE 5,
  *MGG, PRATT, RIEMANN, THOMPSON.
  [ENCY MUS & RIEMANN=b.Nov 19]

FROLOWSKIJ, Nadeschda Filaretowna see Meck, Nadeschda
  Filaretowna

FROMM-MICHAELS, Ilse. Hamburg,
  Dec 30 1888- . Pianist,
  composer. ENCI SALVAT, ENCY
  MUS, MGG, MGG SUP, RIEMANN,
  RIEMANN ERG, THOMPSON.

FROST, Beatrice. 19-20th-century
  English soprano. BROWN BRIT.

FROST, Eliza (born Redford).
  19th-century English contralto. BROWN BRIT.

FRYSCH, Povla see Frijsh,
  Povla

FUÀ, Laura. Cogno di Valca-
  monica, Brescia, Italy,
  Nov 11 1916- . Critic.
  ENCI MUS.

FUCHS, Lillian. New York City,
  Nov 18 1910- . Viola player,
  composer, teacher. PAVLAKIS=
  p.275, RIEMANN ERG, THOMP-
  SON. [RIEMANN ERG=b.Nov 18
  1912]

FUCHS, Marta. Stuttgart, Jan 1
  1898-Sep 22 1974, Stuttgart.
  Soprano. CELLETTI, ENCI SAL-
  VAT, ENCY MUS, EWEN NEW,
  KUTSCH, RIEMANN, RIEMANN
  ERG. [Date and place of death
  based on obituary in Opera,
  Dec 1974, p.1098]

FUCHS, Sibylle Ursula. Kon-
stance-Wollmatingen, Ger-
many, Sep 8 1921- . Soprano,
voice teacher. RIEMANN,
RIEMANN ERG, ULLSTEIN.

FUCHSOVA, Liza. Brno, Moravia,
Mar 31 1913- . Pianist.
GROVE 5.

FÜRSCH-MADI, Emmy. Bayonne,
France, 1847-Sep 20 1894,
Warrenville, N.J. Soprano.
BAKER 1, BAKER 5, PRATT,
SANDVED, THOMPSON. [BAKER 5=
d.Warrenville, N.Y.]

FULLER, Loïe Marie-Louise.
Fullersburg, Ill., 1862-
Jan 1 1928, Paris. Dancer.
ENCI SALVAT, ENCY MUS.

FUOCO, Sofia (pseud. of Maria
Brambilla). Milan, Jan 16
1830-Jun 3 1916, Carate
Lario, Italy. Dancer.
ENCI SALVAT=v.1 p.404,
ENCY MUS.

FURMEDGE, Edith (Mrs. Dihn
Gilly). London, Mar 27
1898- . Contralto. ENCI MUS=
v.2 p.314, GROVE 5, PALMER.

FURTWÄNGLER, Gise. Berlin,
Sep 25 1917- . Dancer,
choreographer. RIEMANN ERG.

FUSCHI, Olegna. USA, 1934- .
Pianist. SANDVED.

FUX, Maria Anna. ?, 1771-1852,
?. Singer. GROVE 5=v.3
p.573 (brief mention in
article on father Florian
Leopold Gassmann).

G

GABARAIN, Marina de. San
Sebastián, Spain, 1926-
Jun 13 1972, Paris. Mezzo-
soprano. GROVE 5 SUP.

GABBI, Adalgisa. Parma, May 3
1857-Dec 16 1933, Milan.
Soprano. *ENCI MUS=illus.
fac.p.247.

GABBI, Leonilde. Parma, Apr 5
1863-Jan 8 1919, Parma.
Soprano. ENCI MUS.

GABRIEL, Marianne see
Davis, Marianne

GABRIEL, Mary Ann Virginia
(Mrs. George E. March).
Banstead, Surrey, Feb 7
1825-Aug 7 1877, London.
Composer, light-opera compo-
ser, pianist. BAKER 1,
BAKER 5, BROWN BIO, BROWN
BRIT, GROVE 1, GROVE 5,
PRATT, THOMPSON.

GABRIELI, Adriana (called
"La Ferrarese," "Ferraresi
del Bene," and "La Gabriel-
lina"; in some books confused
with Francesca Gabrielli,
q.v.). Ferrara, c1755-after
1799, Venice?. Soprano.
BAKER 1, BLOM=p.203, ENCI
MUS=v.2 p.183, ENCI SALVAT,
ENCY MUS, GROVE 5, THOMPSON.

GABRIELLI, Caterina (Catterina),
"La Coghetta," "La Cochetta,"
or "La Cuochetina." Rome,
Nov 12 1730-Feb 16 1796, Rome.
Soprano. BAKER 1, BAKER 5,
BLOM, BROWN BIO, CLAYTON=
p.71, CORTE, DICT MUS, *ENCI
MUS=illus.fac.p.255, ENCI
SALVAT, ENCY MUS, GROVE 1,
GROVE 5, *MGG, PRATT, RIE-
MANN, RIEMANN ERG, THOMPSON.
[BAKER 1, BROWN BIO, &
MGG=d.Apr 1796]

GABRIELLI, Checca see Gabrielli, Francesca

GABRIELLI, Francesca (Checca;
in some books confused with
Adriana Gabrieli, q.v.).

Ferrara, c1735-c1795, Venice. Mezzo-soprano. BAKER 1, CORTE, ENCI MUS, ENCI SALVAT, ENCY MUS, GROVE 5, MGG, PRATT, THOMPSON.

GABRILOWITSCH, Clara see Clemens, Clara

GABRY, Edith. Budapest, Jul 18 1927- . Singer. RIEMANN ERG.

GABUSSI, Rita see De Begnis, Rita

GADSKI (Gadsky), Johanna Emilia Agnes. Anclam, Pomerania, Jun 15 1872-Feb 22 1932, Berlin. Soprano. BAKER 5, BLOM, CELLETTI, EWEN NEW, GROVE 5, GROVE 5 SUP, KUTSCH, MARIZ, PRATT, RIEMANN, SANDVED, THOMPSON.

GÄHWILLER, Sylvia. Zürich, Jul 5 1909- . Singer, voice teacher. SCHUH.

GAFFORINI, Elisabetta. Milan, c1775-?. Singer. *ENCI MUS=illus.fac.p.256.

GAGGI, Elisa Luigia see Storti, Elisa Luigia

GAGLIARDI, Cecilia. Rome, c1890- . Soprano. THOMPSON.

GAGNEBIN, Ruth Schmid- see Schmid-Gagnebin, Ruth

GAĬGEROVA (Gaiguerova, Gajgerova), Varvara Adrianovna. Orekhovo-Zuevo, Russia, Oct 4 or 17 1903-Apr 6 1944, Moscow. Composer. BLOM, ENCI MUS, ENCI SALVAT, GROVE 5, RIEMANN, THOMPSON, VODARSKY.

GAÏL, Edmée Sophie (born Garre). Paris, Aug 28 1775-Jul 24 1819, Paris. Soprano, composer, opera composer. BAKER 1, BROWN BIO, DICT MUS, ENCI SALVAT, ENCY MUS, MGG, PRATT, RIEMANN, THOMPSON.

GAJGEROVA, Varvara Adrianovna see Gaĭgerova, Varvara Adrianovna

GÁL, Margit (Mrs. Franz Salmhofer). 20th-century Austrian pianist. ENCI MUS=v.4 p.98.

GALAJIKIAN, Florence Grandland. Maywood, Ill., Jul 29 1900- . Composer, pianist. BAKER 5, ENCI SALVAT, ENCY MUS, REIS, THOMPSON.

GALEOTTI, Marguerite. Munich, 1867-?. Pianist. THOMPSON.

GALERATTI, Catterina. fl.1714-21. English contralto. GROVE 1.

GALL (Galle), Yvonne Irma. Paris, Mar 6 1885-Summer 1972, Paris. Soprano. BAKER 1971, ENCI SALVAT, ENCY MUS, MARIZ, THOMPSON.

GALLETTI-GIANOLI, Isabella (stage name of Filomena Rustichelli). Bologna, Nov 11 1835-Aug 31 1901, Milan. Soprano, voice teacher. ENCI MUS, PRATT, THOMPSON. *[ENCI MUS=mezzo-soprano]*

GALLI, Caterina. Italy, c1727-1804, London. Mezzo-soprano. BLOM, BROWN BIO, ENCI SALVAT, ENCY MUS, GROVE 1, GROVE 5, THOMPSON.

GALLI, Rosina (Mrs. Giulio Gatti-Casazza). Italy, 1896-Apr 30 1940, Milan. Dancer. ENCI MUS=v.2 p.283.

GALLI-CAMPI, Amri. Honesdale, Pa., ?- . 20th-century American soprano. *EWEN LIVING.

GALLI-CURCI, Amelita. Milan, Nov 18 1882-Nov 26 1963, La Jolla, Calif. Soprano. BAKER 5, BAKER 1971, BLOM, CELLETTI, COOPER, CORTE, *ENCI MUS=illus.fac.p.263, ENCI SALVAT, ENCY MUS, EWEN LIV SUP, EWEN NEW, GROVE 5, KUTSCH, MARIZ, PRATT, RIEMANN, RIEMANN ERG, *SANDVED, THOMPSON, ULLSTEIN. *[CELLETTI, CORTE, EWEN LIV SUP, & PRATT= b.1889; MARIZ=b.1890]*

GALLI-MARIÉ, Célestine (Marié de l'Isle; Mrs. Galli). Paris, Nov 1840-Sep 22 1905, Vence, nr.Nice, France. Mezzo-soprano. BAKER 1, BAKER 5, BLOM, COOPER, CORTE, DICT MUS, *ENCI MUS= illus.fac.p.263, ENCI SAL-VAT, ENCY MUS, EWEN NEW, GROVE 1 APP, GROVE 5, MARIZ, PRATT, RIEMANN, SANDVED, THOMPSON.

GALLIA, Maria (Margherita?). fl.1703. Singer. GROVE 1, GROVE 5.

GALLIGNANI-BERNAU, Chiara. Athens, Jan 7 1852-Mar 11 1901, Milan. Soprano. ENCI MUS.

GALLMEYER, Joséphine. Leipzig, Feb 27 1838-Feb 3 1884, Vienna. Singer. ENCI SALVAT, ENCY MUS, RIEMANN ERG.

GALLYOT, Céleste see Boucher, Céleste

GALVANI, (Johanna) Magdalena see Willmann, (Johanna) Magdalena

GALVANY, Fanny Maria. Turin, 1858-?. Soprano. MARIZ.

GALVANY, Maria. Granada, 1878-Feb 2 1949, Rio de Janeiro. Soprano. CELLETTI, ENCI MUS, KUTSCH, MARIZ. *[CELLETTI & ENCI MUS=d.Nov 2 1949]*

GALVANY, Marisa. 20th-century American soprano. PAVLAKIS= p.288.

GAMBARINI, Elisabetta de see De Gambarini, Elisabetta

GAMBELL, Doris. Wallasey, Cheshire, England, Jun 6 1903- . Soprano. *PALMER= illus.p.188.

GANDINI, Signora see Para-vicini, Signora

GANEVAL, Emilienne see Machabey, Emilienne

GANNON, Helen C. Baltimore, Apr 13 1898- . Composer, pianist, piano teacher. THOMPSON.

GANZ, Mary Forrest see Forrest, Mary

GARA, Teresa Zylis- see Zylis-Gara, Teresa

GARABEDIAN-GEORGE, Edna. 20th-century American con-tralto. PAVLAKIS=p.297.

GARBIN, Adelina Stehle- see Stehle-Garbin, Adelina

GARBOUSOVA (Garbusova, Gar-buzova), Raya. Tiflis, Russia, Sep 12 or 25 1906- . Violoncellist. BAKER 5, ENCI MUS, ENCI SALVAT, *EWEN LIVING, GROVE 5, GROVE 5 SUP, RIEMANN, RIEMANN ERG, *SANDVED, THOMPSON,

VODARSKY. *[EWEN LIVING=*
b.1909]

GARCÍA, Eduarda Mansilla de.
Buenos Aires, 1835-1892, ?.
Composer. ARIZAGA.

GARCÍA, Eugénie (born Mayer).
Paris, 1818-Aug 12 1880,
Paris. Soprano, voice
teacher. BAKER 1, BAKER 5,
*ENCI MUS=illus.fac.p.270.

GARCIA, Maria-Felicita see
Malibran, Maria-Felicita

GARCIA, Pauline Viardot see
Viardot-Garcia, Michelle
Ferdinande Pauline

GARCÍA MUÑOZ, Carmen. Buenos
Aires, 1929- . Composer.
ARIZAGA.

GARCÍA ROBSON, Magda. Buenos
Aires, 1916- . Composer.
ARIZAGA.

GARDEL, Anne Jacqueline see
Coulon, Anne Jacqueline

GARDEL, Marie Élisabeth Anne
(born Houbert, known as
Miller). Auxonne, France,
Apr 8 1770-May 18 1823,
Paris. Dancer. DICT MUS,
ENCI SALVAT, ENCY MUS,
GROVE 5, *MGG=v.4 col.1379;
illus.fac.col.1408. *[ENCI*
SALVAT=d.Apr 18 1833]

GARDEL, Marie-Françoise-Lucie.
Metz, France, Apr 8 1755-?.
Dancer. DICT MUS, ENCI
SALVAT, ENCY MUS.

GARDEN, Mary. Aberdeen, Feb
20 1874 (not 1877)-Jan 3
1967, Aberdeen. Soprano,
voice teacher, impresario,
actress. BAKER 5, BAKER
1971, BLOM, *CELLETTI=illus.
foll.col.352, CORTE, ENCI

MUS, ENCI MUS, ENCI SALVAT,
ENCY MUS, *EWEN LIVING, EWEN
LIV SUP, EWEN NEW, GROVE 5,
KUTSCH, MARIZ, PRATT, RIE-
MANN, RIEMANN ERG, *SANDVED,
THOMPSON.

GARELLI DELLA MOREA, Vincenza.
Valeggio, Pavia, Italy,
Nov 1859-?. Composer.
ENCI MUS.

GARMO, Tilly de (orig.=Mathilde
Jonas). Dresden, Apr 3 1888?-
?. Soprano, voice teacher.
KUTSCH.

GARNIER, Genoveffa see
Canavasso, Genoveffa

GARRE, Edmée Sophie see
Gaïl, Edmée Sophie

GARRIGUES, Malvina see
Schnorr von Carolsfeld,
Malvina

GARRISON, Mabel. Baltimore,
Apr 24 1886-Aug 20 1963,
New York City. Soprano,
voice teacher. BAKER 5,
BAKER 1971, KUTSCH, THOMP-
SON. *[KUTSCH=d.Aug 15 1963*
in Northampton, Mass. Date
and place of death given in
entry confirmed in obituary
in Opera News, v.28, Nov 16
1963, p.35]

GARROW, Theodosia see
Abrams, Theodosia

GARULLI, Ernestina see
Bendazzi, Ernestina

GARUTA, Lucija. Riga, Latvia,
May 27 1902- . Composer,
pianist, teacher. RIEMANN
ERG.

GASKELL, Helen. Tring, Herts.,
England, Jan 14 1906- . English hornist, oboist. PALMER.

GASSIER, Josefa (born Fernán-
dez). Bilbao, Spain, 1821-
Nov 8 1866, Madrid. Soprano.
BLOM, GROVE 5, THOMPSON.

GASSMANN, Maria Anna. Vienna,
1771-Aug 27 1852, Vienna.
Singer. ENCI MUS.

GASSMANN, Maria Theresa (later
Rosenbaum). Vienna, Apr 1
1774-Sep 8 1837, Vienna.
Singer. ENCI MUS, GROVE 5.
[ENCI MUS=Gassmann, Therese
Maria]

GASTELL, Maria see Wilhelmj,
Maria

GATES, Lucy. St. George,
Utah, c1889- . Soprano,
administrator. THOMPSON.

GATTA, Dora. Foggia, Italy,
Nov 11 1928- . Soprano.
ENCI MUS.

GATTI, Clelia Aldrovandi
(sometimes Gatti-Aldrovandi).
Mantua, May 30 1901- .
Harpist. ENCI MUS, GROVE 5.

GATTI, Gabriella. Rome, Jul 5
1916- . Soprano. CELLETTI,
COOPER, ENCI MUS, ENCY MUS,
GROVE 5, KUTSCH.

GATTI-CASAZZA, Rosina see
Galli, Rosina

GAUDIN, Cathérine. 20th-cen-
tury French violinist.
ENCI MUS=v.1 p.422 (brief
mention in article on
Henri Casadesus).

GAULTIER, Juliette de la
Verendrye. Ottawa, ?- .
20th-century Canadian
singer. THOMPSON.

GAUTHIER, Eva. Ottawa, Sep 20
1885-Dec 26 1958, New York

City. Soprano, folklorist.
BAKER 5, BAKER 1971, *EWEN
LIVING, KUTSCH, SANDVED,
THOMPSON. [EWEN LIVING=
b.1886, contralto; THOMPSON=
mezzo-soprano]   ·

GAUTIER, Jeanne. Asnières,
France, Sep 18 1898- .
Violinist, teacher. ENCI
SALVAT, ENCY MUS.

GAUTIER, Judith Louise Charlotte Ernestine. Paris, Aug
25 1845-Dec 26 1917, St.-
Énogat, France. Writer.
DICT MUS=v.1 p.392, MGG=
v.4 col.1487, RIEMANN, RIE-
MANN ERG.

GAVEAU, Colette see Mal-
cuzynski, Colette

GAVIRATI, Giulia Oddone- see
Oddone-Gavirati, Giulia

GAY, María (Maria Pitchot).
Barcelona, Jun 13 1879-Jul 29
1943, New York City. Soprano,
contralto, voice teacher.
BAKER 5, BLOM, CELLETTI,
COOPER, ENCI MUS, ENCI SALVAT,
GROVE 5, KUTSCH, MARIZ,
PRATT, RIEMANN, THOMPSON.
[BAKER 5=b.Jun 10; CELLETTI=
b.Jun 17; ENCI SALVAT=b.1889]

GAYER, Catherine (Mrs. Ashkenasi)
Los Angeles, Feb 11 1939- .
Soprano. RIEMANN ERG, ULLSTEIN.
[ULLSTEIN=b.Feb 1 1937]

GAYLORD, Julia. New York City,
c1850-?, Brooklyn. Soprano,
voice teacher. THOMPSON.

GAYNOR, Jessie Love (born
Smith). St. Louis, Mo.,
Feb 17 1863-Feb 20 1921,
Webster Groves, Mo. Composer,
pianist. RIEMANN.

GAZZANIGA MALASPINA ALBITES,

Marietta. Voghera, Italy,
1824-Jan 2 1884, Milan.
Soprano. ENCI MUS.

GAZZUOLO, Cecilia see
Boccabadati Gazzuolo,
Cecilia

GEDALGE, Amélie Alexandrine
see Obigny de Ferrières,
Amélie Alexandrine d'

GEISER-PEYER, Barbara.
Zürich, Jul 27 1928- .
Violinist. SCHUH.

GEISTINGER, Marie Charlotte
Cäcilia. Graz, Jul 26 1836-
Sep 29 1903, Klagenfurt,
Austria. Soprano. BAKER 1,
BAKER 5, PRATT, RIEMANN
ERG, THOMPSON. *[Some sources
give place of death as
Rastenfeld, which RIEMANN
ERG corrects to Klagenfurt]*

GELLER-WOLTER, Luise. Rittergut Hohenborn, Hessen-
Kassel, Germany, Mar 27
1859-Oct 27 1934, Berlin.
Contralto. RIEMANN.

GELLING, Hilda Grace. Cork,
?- . 20th-century Irish
contralto, voice teacher.
THOMPSON.

GENAST, Doris see Raff,
Doris

GENAST, Emile. ?, 1833-1905,
?. German singer. PRATT.

GENCER, Leyla. Istanbul,
Oct 10 1928- . Soprano.
ENCI MUS, KUTSCH. *[KUTSCH=
b.1927 in Ankara]*

GENÉE, Adeline (born Anina
Jensen). Aarhus, Denmark,
Jan 6 1878-Apr 23 1970,
London. Dancer. RIEMANN
ERG.

GENHART, Cecile (born Staub).
Basel, ?- . 20th-century
Swiss pianist, piano teacher.
THOMPSON.

GENLIS, Stéphanie Félicité
(Comtesse de Marquise de
Sillery, born Du Crest).
Champcery, nr. Autun,
France, Jan 25 1746-Dec 31
1830, Paris. Music lover,
writer. BLOM, DICT MUS,
ENCI SALVAT, ENCY MUS,
*MGG=illus.fac.col.1760.

GENOVESE, Nana. Genoa, Nov 30
1882- . Mezzo-soprano.
THOMPSON.

GENTILE, Maria. Catania,
Sicily, Nov 17 1902- .
Soprano, voice teacher.
KUTSCH.

GENTILI BONURA, Giustina.
19th-century Italian singer.
ENCI MUS.

GENTILI VERONA, Gabriella.
Turin, Oct 17 1913- .
Cembalist. ENCI MUS.

GENTLE, Alice (Mrs. Jacob
Proebstel, born True).
Chatsworth, Ill., Jun 30
1888-Feb 28 1958, Oakland,
Calif. Mezzo-soprano.
THOMPSON.

GENTNER-FISCHER, Else. Frankfurt, Sep 5 1883-Apr 26
1943, Prienam-Chiemsee,
Germany. Soprano. KUTSCH.

GEON, Marcella. East Liverpool, Ohio, ?- . 20th-century
pianist, piano teacher.
THOMPSON.

GEORGE, Miss see Oldmixon,
Lady

GEORGI, Yvonne. Leipzig, Oct

29 1904- . Choreographer.
RIEMANN, RIEMANN ERG.

GERARD, Lidia Nikolaievna
Figner- see Figner-
Gerard, Lidia Nikolaievna

GERARD, Ruby. New York City,
May 7 1887- . Violinist.
THOMPSON.

GÉRARD DE FESTENBOURG, Stefania see Lobaczewska,
Stefania

GERHARD, Livia see Frege,
Livia

GERHARDT, Elena. Leipzig,
Nov 11 1883-Jan 11 1961,
London. Mezzo-soprano,
voice teacher. BAKER 5,
BAKER 1971, BLOM, COOPER,
*EWEN LIVING, EWEN LIV SUP,
GROVE 5, KUTSCH, MARIZ,
PRATT, RIEMANN, RIEMANN
ERG, *SANDVED, THOMPSON,
ULLSTEIN. *[EWEN LIVING=*
soprano]

GERHART, Maria. Vienna,
1896- . Soprano, voice
teacher. KUTSCH.

GERL, Barbara (Mrs. Franz
Xaver, born Reisinger).
Pressburg or Vienna, 1770-
May 25 1806, Mannheim.
Soprano. ENCI MUS.

GERLACH, Clara Anna see
Korn, Clara Anna

GERLICH, Clara see
Edwards, Clara

GERMAN, Priscilla see
Reed, Priscilla

GERMANI-CIOMAC, Muza.
Braila, Romania, 1891-
Pianist. THOMPSON.

GERMANO, Virginia Ferni see
Ferni Germano, Virginia

GERSON-KIWI, Esther Edith.
Berlin, May 13 1908- .
Musicologist, teacher,
writer. DICT MUS, ENCI MUS,
ENCI SALVAT, ENCY MUS,
GROVE 5, MGG, RIEMANN,
RIEMANN ERG, THOMPSON.

GERSTEIN, Chaia (orig.=
Adrienne). Milwaukee, Aug 10
1933- . Pianist. RIEMANN ERG.

GERSTER, Etelka (Mme. Gerster-
Gardini). Karschau, Hungary,
Jun 25 1855-Aug 20 1920,
Pontecchio, nr.Bologna.
Soprano, voice teacher,
administrator, writer.
BAKER 1, BAKER 5, BLOM,
BROWN BIO, ENCI MUS, EWEN
NEW, GROVE 1 APP, GROVE 5,
GROVE 5 SUP, MARIZ, PRATT,
RIEMANN, SANDVED, THOMPSON,
ULLSTEIN. *[BROWN BIO=b.*
Jun 16 1855 or 1857; GROVE 1
APP=b.1856; MARIZ & PRATT=
b.1857]

GERSTER, Rita Haldemann- see
Haldemann-Gerster, Rita

GERSTMAN, Blanche. Capetown,
Apr 2 1910- . Composer,
double bassist. BAKER 5,
GROVE 5, THOMPSON.

GERVILLE-RÉACHE, Jeanne.
Orthez, France, Mar 26 1882-
Jan 5 1915, New York City.
Contralto. BAKER 5, ENCI MUS,
ENCI SALVAT, ENCY MUS, EWEN
NEW, KUTSCH, PRATT, SANDVED,
THOMPSON.

GESELSCHAP, Marie. Batavia,
Java, 1874?-?. Pianist.
BAKER 1, PRATT.

GESZTY, Sylvia (Mrs. Duncker,

born Witkowsky). Budapest, Feb 28 1934- . Soprano. RIEMANN ERG.

GEYER, Steffi (Mrs. Walter Schulthess). Budapest, Jun 23 1888-Dec 11 1956, Zürich. Violinist. ENCI MUS=v.4 p.178, GROVE 5, GROVE 5 SUP, RIEMANN ERG, SCHUH=p.419, THOMPSON. *[SCHUH=b.Jun 28]*

GEYERSECK, Marianne von see Pirker, Marianne

GHIKA-COMANESTI, Ioana. 20th-century Romanian composer. THOMPSON.

GIACHETTI, Ada. 19-20th-century Italian singer. ENCI MUS.

GIACHETTI, Rina. Milan, Aug 26 1880-Jun 1 1959, Cerreto Guidi, Florence. Soprano. ENCI MUS.

GIANETTINI (Giannettini, Zanettini), Maria Caterina. 17-18th-century Italian singer. ENCI MUS.

GIANI, Nini. ?, 1907- . Italian contralto. KUTSCH.

GIANNETTINI, Maria Caterina see Gianettini, Maria Caterina

GIANNINI, Antonietta see Briglia, Antonietta

GIANNINI, Dusolina. Philadelphia, Dec 19 1902- . Soprano, voice teacher, administrator. BAKER 5, ENCI MUS, ENCY MUS, *EWEN LIVING, EWEN NEW, GROVE 5, KUTSCH, MARIZ, RIEMANN, RIEMANN ERG, SANDVED, THOMPSON, ULLSTEIN.

GIANOLI, Isabella Galletti- see Galletti-Gianoli, Isabella

GIBSON, Isabella Mary (Mrs. Patrick, born Scott). Edinburgh, 1786-Nov 28 1838, Edinburgh. Composer, singer, harpist. BROWN BIO, BROWN BRIT.

GIBSON, Louisa. London, 1833-?. Teacher, writer. BROWN BIO, BROWN BRIT.

GIDEON, Miriam. Greeley, Colo., Oct 23 1906- . Composer, teacher, musicologist. BAKER 5, BAKER 1971, PAVLAKIS=p.332, REIS, RIEMANN ERG, SANDVED, THOMPSON, VINTON.

GIEBEL, Agnes. Heerlen, Netherlands, Aug 10 1921- . Soprano. KUTSCH, RIEMANN, RIEMANN ERG, ULLSTEIN.

GIERSE, Edyth la see Tréville, Yvonne de

GIFFORD, Helen. Melbourne, 1935- . Composer, pianist. *MURDOCH=illus.foll.p.98.

GILBERT, Gloria Caroline see Trebelli (-Bettini), Zelia

GILCHRIST, Anne (Geddes). Manchester, England, Dec 8 1863-Jul 24 1954, nr. Lancaster, England. Music antiquarian, folklorist. BLOM, GROVE 5, GROVE 5 SUP.

GILLEBERT, Gloria Caroline see Trebelli (-Bettini), Zelia

GILLO, Miss see Carey, Mrs. George Saville

GILLY, Edith see Furmedge, Edith

GILMOUR, Doris Godson. Pretoria, Union of South Africa, Mar 21 1900- . Soprano. THOMPSON.

GINSTER, Ria. Frankfurt, Apr 15 1898- . Soprano, voice teacher. BAKER 5, ENCI SALVAT, ENCY MUS, *EWEN LIVING, EWEN LIV SUP, GROVE 5, KUTSCH, RIEMANN, RIEMANN ERG, SCHUH, THOMPSON.

GINZKEY, Julia Bertha von see Culp, Julia Bertha

GIORDANI, Emanuela see Cosmi, Emanuela

GIORGI, Brigitta see Banti, Brigitta

GIORGI, Rachele see D'Orta, Rachele

GIORGI, (Maria) Teresa see Belloc, (Maria) Teresa

GIORGI BANTI, Brigitta see Banti, Brigitta

GIORGI BRIZZI, Maria see Brizzi Giorgi, Maria

GIORGI-RIGHETTI, Geltrude see Brighenti, Maria

GIOVANNONI ZACCHI, Ginevra. Macerata, Italy, Jan 20 1839-Apr 7 1899, Bologna. Soprano. ENCI MUS.

GIPPS, Ruth. Bexhill-on-Sea, Sussex, Feb 20 1921- . Composer, pianist, oboist. BAKER 5, BLOM, DICT MUS, ENCI SALVAT, ENCY MUS, GROVE 5, *PALMER=illus. p.187, RIEMANN, RIEMANN ERG, THOMPSON.

GIRANEK, Franziska see Jiránek, Franziska

GIRARDEAU, Isabella (born Calliari?). fl.1700-20. Italian soprano. BLOM, GROVE 1, GROVE 5, THOMPSON.

GIRARDON, Renée-Madeleine see Masson, Renée-Madeleine

GIRELLI ANGUILLAR (Aguilar), Maria Antonia. 18th-century Italian soprano. GROVE 1, GROVE 5.

GIRÒ, Anna. Mantua or Venice, ?-?. 18th-century Italian singer, probably mezzo-soprano. ENCI MUS.

GIROD, Marie-Louise. Paris, Dec 10 1915- . Organist. ENCI SALVAT, ENCY MUS.

GISMONDI, Celeste ("Celeste" or "Celestina," later Mrs. Hempson). ?-Oct 28 1735, London. Mezzo-soprano. BLOM, GROVE 1, GROVE 5, THOMPSON.

GIUDICE, Maria (orig.=Maria Júdice da Costa). Lisbon, 1870-?. Contralto, soprano. KUTSCH.

GIULI BORSI, Teresa de see De Giuli Borsi, Teresa

GIULIANI, Cecilia (born Bianchi). fl.1788. Italian soprano. ENCI MUS, GROVE 1.

GIULIANI, Emilia. 19th-century Italian guitarist. DICT MUS.

GIURANNA, Elena Barbara. Palermo, Nov 18 1902- . Composer, pianist. CORTE, ENCI MUS, GROVE 5, RIEMANN, RIEMANN ERG, THOMPSON.

GIVEN, Thelma. Columbus, Ohio, Mar 9 1898- . Violinist. THOMPSON.

GJUNGJENAC, Zlata. Čazma, Croatia, Mar 11 1898- . Soprano. RIEMANN ERG.

GLADE, Coe. Chicago, Aug 12 1906- . Contralto. THOMPSON.

GLADKOWSKA, Konstancja. Warsaw, Jun 10 1810-Dec 20 1889, Skierniewice, Poland. Soprano. GROVE 5.

GLANVILLE-HICKS, Peggy. Melbourne, Dec 29 1912- . Composer, opera composer, critic, writer. BAKER 5, BAKER 1971, BLOM, ENCI MUS, ENCI SALVAT, ENCY MUS, EWEN NEW, GROVE 5, MGG, *MURDOCH= illus.foll.p.98, PAVLAKIS= p.332, RIEMANN, RIEMANN ERG, SANDVED, SCHOLES, THOMPSON, VINTON.

GLASER, Liv. Oslo, Sep 23 1935- . Pianist. RIEMANN ERG.

GLAZ, Herta (Hertha). Vienna, Sep 16 1914- . Contralto, voice teacher. BAKER 5, *EWEN LIVING, EWEN LIV SUP, EWEN NEW, KUTSCH, THOMPSON. [KUTSCH=b.1908]

GLEISS, Emile Feuge- se Feuge-Gleiss, Emile

GLEN, Annie. fl.1883. English soprano, writer. BROWN BRIT.

GLENN, Carroll see List, Carroll

GLENN, Mabelle. Oneida, Ill., ?- . 20th-century teacher, writer. THOMPSON.

GLINKA, Ludmilla Ivanova see Shestakova, Ludmilla Ivanova

GLOSSOP, Elizabeth (Mrs. Joseph, born Feron). ?, 1794?-May 9 1853, ?. English singer. BROWN BRIT.

GLOVER, Erminia (Mrs. Mackey). Dublin?, ?-Jun 1883, Dublin. Harpist. BROWN BRIT.

GLOVER, R. Ethel see Harraden, R. Ethel

GLOVER, Sarah Ann (Anna). Norwich, England, Nov 13 1786-Oct 20 1867, Malvern, England. Pianist, piano teacher, singer, voice teacher, writer. BAKER 1, BAKER 5, BROWN BIO, BROWN BRIT, GROVE 5, PRATT, RIE-MANN, THOMPSON. [BAKER 1, BROWN BIO, BROWN BRIT, & PRATT=b.1785]

GLUCK, Alma (real name=Reba Fiersohn). Bucharest, May 11 1884-Oct 27 1938, New York City. Soprano, voice teacher. BAKER 5, BLOM, EWEN NEW, GROVE 5, KUTSCH, PRATT, RIE-MANN, SANDVED, THOMPSON.

GLYN, Margaret Henrietta. Ewell, Surrey, Feb 28 1865-Jun 3 1946, Ewell, Surrey. Musicologist, composer, writer, editor. BAKER 5, DICT MUS, ENCI MUS, ENCI SALVAT, ENCY MUS, GROVE 5, MGG, RIEMANN, THOMPSON.

GMEINER, Luise Mysz- see Mysz-Gmeiner, Luise

GMEINER, Lulu Mysz- see Mysz-Gmeiner, Lulu

GNESSIN, Eléna Fabianovna. Rostov, Russia, May 30 1874-Jun 4 1967, Moscow. Pianist, composer, teacher. DICT MUS, ENCI MUS, RIEMANN, RIEMANN ERG.

GODDARD, Arabella (later Mrs.
J. W. Davison). St.-Servan,
nr.St.-Malo, France, Jan 12
1836-Apr 6 1922, Boulogne-
sur-Mer, France. Pianist,
composer. BAKER 1, BAKER 5,
BLOM, BROWN BIO, BROWN BRIT,
GROVE 1, GROVE 1 APP, GROVE
5, PRATT, RIEMANN=v.1 p.374,
THOMPSON. *[BAKER 1 & GROVE
1=b.1838]*

GODFREY, Batyah. 20th-century
American contralto. PAVLA-
KIS=p.297.

GODOY, Maria Lúcia. Belo
Horizonte, Brazil, Sep 2
1930- . Soprano. RIEMANN
ERG.

GÖHRINGER, Francilla see
Pixis, Francilla Göhringer

GÖRLIN, Helga Maria. Charlot-
tenberg, Värmland, Sweden,
Sep 26 1900- . Soprano.
GROVE 5=v.3 p.718, RIEMANN,
RIEMANN ERG.

GOERTZ, Gladys Davenport see
Davenport Goertz, Gladys

GÖTZE, Augusta. Weimar, Feb 24
1840-Apr 29 1908, Leipzig.
Singer, voice teacher.
THOMPSON.

GOETZE, Marie. Berlin, Nov 2
1865-Feb 18 1922, Berlin.
Contralto, mezzo-soprano,
administrator. KUTSCH,
PRATT.

GOFFAUX, Jeanne Maubourg-
see Maubourg-Goffaux,
Jeanne

GOHL-MÜLLER, Verena. Winterthur, Switzerland, Jul 6
1925- . Mezzo-soprano.
SCHUH.

GOLDBERG MARINI, Fanny see
Marini, Fanny Goldberg

GOLDSCHMIDT, Jenny see
Lind, Jenny

GOLDSTEIN, Ella. Harbin, Man-
churia, Jan 30 1927- .
Pianist. *EWEN LIV SUP.

GOLTZ, Christel. Dortmund,
Germany, Jul 8 1912- .
Soprano. ENCI MUS, ENCY MUS,
GROVE 5 SUP, KUTSCH, RIEMANN,
RIEMANN ERG, *ROSENTHAL=illus.
p.74, *SANDVED, THOMPSON,
*ULLSTEIN.

GOMES, Carmen. Rio de Janeiro,
1900- . Soprano. MARIZ.

GOMEZ, Alice (Mrs. T. Henry
Webb). Calcutta, ?-?. 19th-
century English mezzo-soprano, organist. BROWN BRIT.

GÓMEZ CARRILLO, Inés. Santiago
del Estero, Argentina,
1918- . Pianist. ARIZAGA.

GONZALO, Gisela Hernández-
see Hernández-Gonzalo,
Gisela

GOOD, Margaret. London, ?- .
20th-century English pianist.
PALMER.

GOODMAN, Miss see Burnett,
Mrs.

GOODSON, Katharine (Myra
Kate; Mrs. Arthur Hinton).
Watford, Herts., Jun 18
1872-Apr 14 1958, London.
Pianist. BAKER 5, BAKER 1971,
ENCI MUS=v.2 p.426, PRATT,
RIEMANN, RIEMANN ERG,
THOMPSON.

GOODWIN, Amina Beatrice. Manchester, England, Dec 5 1867-

Mar 10 1942, East Moseley, England. Pianist, piano teacher, composer. BAKER 1, BROWN BRIT, GROVE 5, PRATT, THOMPSON.

GOOSSENS, Marie Henriette. London, Aug 11 1894- . Harpist, teacher. ENCI MUS, GROVE 5, RIEMANN, RIEMANN ERG.

GOOSSENS, Sidonie. Liscard, Cheshire, England, Oct 19 1899- . Harpist, teacher. ENCI MUS, GROVE 5, *PALMER= illus.p.61, RIEMANN, RIE-MANN ERG.

GORDON, Cyrena van see Van Gordon, Cyrena

GORDON, Dorothy. New York City, Apr 4 1895- . Soprano. THOMPSON.

GORDON, Jeanne. Wallaceburg, Ontario, Canada, c1893-Feb 21 1952, Macon, Mo. Contralto. KUTSCH, THOMPSON. [KUTSCH=b.Feb 22]

GORR, Rita. Ghent, Feb 18 1926- . Mezzo-soprano, contralto. ENCI SALVAT, ENCY MUS, KUTSCH, RIEMANN ERG, *ROSENTHAL=illus.p.72, THOMPSON, ULLSTEIN.

GOTKOWSKY, Ida. Calais, Aug 26 1933- . Composer. ENCI SAL-VAT, ENCY MUS.

GOTTLIEB, Anna. Vienna, Apr 29 1774-Apr 7 1856, Vienna. Soprano, actress. ENCI MUS.

GOTTLIEB, Henriette. Berlin, 1884-1943, Berlin. Soprano. KUTSCH.

GOTTSCHALL, Liselotte Enck- see Enck-Gottschall, Liselotte

GOTTSCHED, Luise Adelgunde (Mrs. Johann Christoph). Danzig, Poland, ?-1762 Leipzig. Pianist, lutenist. *MGG.

GOUDARD, Sarah. ?-c1800, Paris. Writer. ENCI SALVAT=brief mention only, MGG.

GOUSSEAU, Lélia. Paris, Feb 11 1909- . Pianist. ENCI SALVAT, ENCY MUS.

GOUVERNÉ, Yvonne. Paris, Feb 6 1890- . Choral conductor, writer. ENCI SALVAT, ENCY MUS.

GOWARD, Mary Anne see Keeley, Mary Anne

GRABOWSKA, Klementyna. Poznań, Poland, 1771-1831, Paris. Pianist, composer. GROVE 5.

GRADDON, Miss. Bishop's Lydiard, nr. Taunton, England, 1804-?. Soprano. BROWN BIO, BROWN BRIT.

GRADOVA, Gitta. Chicago, ?- . 20th-century American pianist. THOMPSON.

GRAEVER, Madeleine (Madame Johnson). Amsterdam, 1830-?. Pianist, composer. BROWN BIO.

GRAF, Hedy. Barcelona, Oct 10 1926- . Singer. SCHUH.

GRAF, Meta. 20th-century pianist. ENCI MUS=v.2 p.432 (brief mention in article on Vagn Holmboe).

GRAHAM, Lucina Alexia see Grahn, Lucile

GRAHAM, Maria. fl.1852. Scottish writer. BROWN BIO, BROWN BRIT.

GRAHAM, Mary Ann (Madame Enders-

sohn). 19th-century English
soprano. BROWN BRIT.

GRAHN, Lucile (Lucina Alexia
Graham). Garnisons, nr.
Copenhagen, Jun 30 1819-
Apr 4 1907, Munich. Dancer.
RIEMANN ERG.

"GRAND, Le" see Scio,
Julie-Angélique

GRANDI, Margherita. Hobart,
Tasmania, Oct 10 1899- .
Soprano. CORTE, EWEN NEW,
GROVE 5, KUTSCH. *[CORTE &
GROVE 5=b.1907]*

GRANDVAL, Marie-Félicie-
Clémence de Reiset, Vicom-
tesse de. Saint-Rémy-des-
Monts, Sarthe, France,
Jan 21 1830-Jan 15 1907,
Paris. Composer, opera com-
poser. BAKER 1, BAKER 5,
ENCI SALVAT, RIEMANN, RIE-
MANN ERG, THOMPSON. *[BAKER
1=b.Jan 20]*

GRANFELT, (Lillian) Hanna von.
Sakkola, Finland, Jun 2
1884-Nov 3 1952, Helsinki.
Soprano. GROVE 5, KUTSCH,
RIEMANN, SOPRANO.

GRANGE, Anna Caroline de la
see La Grange, Anna Caro-
line de

GRANT, Miss see Molesworth,
Lady

GRANT, Lucy see Estcott,
Lucy

GRAS, Julie Aimée Josèphe
Dorus- see Dorus-Gras,
Julie Aimée Josèphe

GRASSI, Cecilia. Naples,
1746?-after 1782, ?.
Soprano. BLOM, ENCI MUS,
GROVE 1, GROVE 5, RIEMANN,
THOMPSON.

GRASSINI (Grassin), Giuseppina
Maria Camilla. Varese, Lom-
bardy, Italy, Apr 8 or 18
1773-Jan 3 1850, Milan. Con-
tralto, voice teacher,
actress. BAKER 5, BLOM, BROWN
BIO, CLAYTON=p.173, CORTE,
*ENCI MUS=illus.fac.p.346,
ENCI SALVAT, ENCY MUS, EWEN
NEW, GROVE 1, GROVE 1 APP,
GROVE 5, MGG, PRATT, RIEMANN
ERG, THOMPSON.

GRAUMANN, Dorothea see
Ertmann, Catharina Dorothea

GRAUMANN, Mathilde see
Marchesi de Castrone, Mathilde

GRAUPNER, Catherine (Mrs. Johann
Christian Gottlieb, born
Hillier). ?, 1770-1821, ?.
German singer. ENCI MUS.

GRAY, Edith Moxom. Boston, Jun
26 1890-Jul 13 1935, New York
City. Pianist. THOMPSON.

GRAY, Isabel Winton. Dundee,
Scotland, Sep 14 1898- .
Pianist, piano teacher.
THOMPSON.

GRAY, Louisa (Mrs. Abingdon
Compton). 19th-century
English light-opera composer,
composer. BROWN BRIT.

GRAZIELLA, Gina. Siena, Jan 12
1910- . Pianist. ENCI MUS=
v.3 p.497 (in article on the
Provvedi family).

GREBE, María Ester. Arica,
Chile, Jul 11 1928- . Musi-
cologist, writer. RIEMANN
ERG.

GREEF, Pelagie see Andriessen, Pelagie

GREEN, Eleanor see Baster,
Eleanor

GREENBAUM, Kyla (Betty).
Brighton, England, Feb 5
1922- . Pianist. GROVE 5,
PALMER.

GREENSPON, Muriel. 20th-
century American mezzo-
soprano. PAVLAKIS=p.295.

GREENWOOD, Pauline see
Formes, Pauline Greenwood

GREGG, Annie Jessy see
Curwen, Annie Jessy

GREGORI, Nininha. São Paulo,
Jan 20 1925- . Composer.
BAKER 5, THOMPSON.

GREIG, Maggie see Saint-
John, Florence

GRENVILLE, Lillian. New York
City, Nov 20 1888-1928,
Paris. Soprano. PRATT,
THOMPSON.

GRÉTRY, Lucile. Paris, Jul 16
1772-Aug 25 1790, Paris.
Composer, opera composer.
BLOM.

GREVER, Maria. Mexico City,
Aug 16 1894-Dec 15 1951,
New York City. Pianist,
violinist, guitarist,
soprano. ENCI MUS.

GREY, Annie (Mrs. Wade).
Edinburgh, Jul 4 1860-?.
Contralto. BROWN BRIT.

GREY, Madeleine. Villaines-
le-Juhel, France, Jun 11
1896- . Soprano. BAKER 5,
ENCI MUS, ENCI SALVAT,
ENCY MUS, GROVE 5, KUTSCH,
RIEMANN, RIEMANN ERG,
THOMPSON.

GRIEG, Nina (Mrs. Edvard,
born Hagerup). Nr. Bergen,
Nov 24 1845-Dec 9 1935,

Copenhagen. Soprano. BAKER 5,
BLOM, DICT MUS, ENCI MUS,
ENCY MUS, GROVE 5, *MGG,
RIEMANN, THOMPSON.

GRIERSON, Mary Gardner.
Edinburgh, Aug 25 1896-Mar 14
1964, Edinburgh. Conductor,
pianist, writer. RIEMANN ERG.

GRILLO, Joann. ?, 1939- .
American mezzo-soprano. PAV-
LAKIS=p.295.

GRIMANI, Maria Margherita.
fl.1715-18. Composer, court
musician. ENCI SALVAT, ENCY
MUS, MGG.

GRIMAUD, Yvette. Algiers, Jan
29 1920- . Composer, pianist.
BAKER 5, ENCI SALVAT, ENCY
MUS, THOMPSON. [BAKER 5 &
THOMPSON=b.1922]

GRISI, Carlotta. Visinada,
Istria, Italy, Jun 28 1819-
May 20 1899, St.-Jean, nr.
Geneva. Dancer, singer.
DICT MUS, ENCI SALVAT, ENCY
MUS, RIEMANN, RIEMANN ERG.

GRISI, Giuditta (Contessa
Barni). Milan, Jul 28 1805-
May 1 1840, Robecco d'Oglio,
nr. Cremona. Mezzo-soprano.
BAKER 1, BAKER 5, BLOM, BROWN
BIO, CORTE, DICT MUS, *ENCI
MUS=illus.fac.p.362, ENCI
SALVAT, ENCY MUS, GROVE 1,
GROVE 1 APP, GROVE 5, MGG,
PRATT, RIEMANN, RIEMANN ERG,
*SANDVED, THOMPSON, *ULLSTEIN.
[Some sources=d.May 2 1840,
which RIEMANN ERG corrects to
May 1 1840]

GRISI, Giulia (Comtessa Melcy).
Milan, Jul 28 1811-Nov 29
1869, nr. Berlin. Soprano.
BAKER 1, BAKER 5, BLOM,
BROWN BIO, *CLAYTON=p.363,
COOPER, CORTE, DICT MUS,

*ENCI MUS=illus.fac.v.2
p.362 & v.3 p.146, ENCI
SALVAT, ENCY MUS, EWEN NEW,
GROVE 1, GROVE 1 APP,
GROVE 5, *MGG, PRATT, RJE-
MANN, RIEMANN ERG, *SANDVED,
THOMPSON, *ULLSTEIN. [BROWN
BIO & GROVE 1=b.1812, d.Nov
25; ENCI MUS=b.Jul 18 1811]

GRIST, Reri. New York City,
?- . 20th-century soprano.
PAVLAKIS=p.288, RIEMANN
ERG, SANDVED.

GRISWOLD NEVINS, Marian see
MacDowell, Marian

GROB-PRANDL, Gertrud. Vienna,
Nov 7 1917- . Soprano.
CELLETTI, ENCI SALVAT,
ENCY MUS, KUTSCH.

GROCE, Catherine see Barre,
Catherine

GRÖNLUND, Adele Ester Merete
see Söderhjelm-Grönlund,
Adele Ester Merete

GROLL, Sophie. 19th-century
Hungarian? singer. ENCI
MUS=v.4 p.397 (brief men-
tion in article on the
Tomasini family).

GRØNDAHL, Agathe Ursula
Backer- see Backer-
Grøndahl, Agathe Ursula

GROSCHEWA, Jelena Andrejewna.
Baku, Azerbaidzhan, Sep 11
1908- . Writer. RIEMANN ERG.

GROSSI, Carlotta (real name=
Charlotte Grossmuck).
Vienna, Dec 23 1849-?.
Soprano. BAKER 1.

GROSSI, Eleonora. ?-1879,
Naples. Mezzo-soprano.
ENCI MUS.

GROSSMUCK, Carlotta see

Grossi, Carlotta

GROVES, Olive. Hampstead, London, 1899?-Jan 8 1974, ?.
Soprano. PALMER. [Death date
supplied from obituary in
Musical Times, Mar 1974,
p.243]

GRUBER, Lilo. Berlin, Jan 3
1915- . Dancer, choreographer. RIEMANN ERG.

GRUDZIŃSKA, Nina. Winnica,
Podolia, Poland, Jun 22
1904- . Mezzo-soprano.
GROVE 5.

GRÜMMER, Elisabeth. Nieder-
jeutz, now Yutz-Basse,
Moselle, Alsace-Lorraine,
Mar 31 1911- . Soprano.
BLOM, CELLETTI, KUTSCH,
RIEMANN, RIEMANN ERG,
*ROSENTHAL=illus.p.75,
THOMPSON, *ULLSTEIN.

GRÜN, Frederike. Mannheim, Jun
14 1836-Nov 1917, Mannheim.
Soprano. BAKER 1, THOMPSON.

GRÜNBAUM, Therese. Vienna,
Aug 24 1791-Jan 30 1876,
Berlin. Composer. ENCI
SALVAT, ENCY MUS, GROVE 5=
v.5 p.994 (brief mention in
article on father Wenzel
Müller).

GRUHN, Nora. London, Mar 6
1908- . Soprano. BAKER 5,
*PALMER=illus.p.169, THOMPSON.

GRUNDER, Anne-Marie. 20th-
century Swiss violinist.
SCHUH.

GSOVSKY, Tatiana (Tatjana).
Moscow, Mar 5 or 18 1901- .
Dancer. ENCI SALVAT, ENCY
MUS, RIEMANN, RIEMANN ERG,
THOMPSON. [Some sources=
b.1902, which RIEMANN ERG
corrects to 1901]

GUADAGNI, Lavinia Maria (Mrs. Felice Alessandri). Lodi, Nov 21 1735-c1790, Padua?. Singer. ENCI MUS= v.1 p.40 (in article on husband) & v.2 p.369 (in article on brother Gaetano), GROVE 1.

GUARDUCCI, Carolina. Leghorn, Italy, 1833-?. Singer. BROWN BIO.

GUARMANNI, Elisabetta Manfredini see Manfredini Guarmanni, Elisabetta

GUARNIERI, Guglielmina. 18-19th-century Italian violinist. ENCI MUS.

GUBAIDULINA, Sofia. Tsistopol, Tataria, USSR, Oct 24 1931- . Composer, motion picture composer, accompanist. VINTON.

GUBITOSI, Emilia. Naples, Apr 4 1887- . Composer, pianist. ENCI MUS, THOMPSON. *[THOMPSON=b.1889]*

GUBRUD, Irene. Minnesota, ?- . 20th-century soprano. PAV-LAKIS=p.288.

GÜDEL, Irene (Spittler-). Aegerten, nr.Biel, Switzerland, Jul 7 1930- . Violoncellist. SCHUH.

GÜDEN, Hilde (stage name of Hilde Herrmann). Vienna, Sep 15 1917- . Soprano. BAKER 5, BLOM, CELLETTI, CORTE, ENCI MUS, ENCI SALVAT, ENCY MUS, *EWEN LIV SUP, EWEN NEW, GROVE 5=v.3 p.836, GROVE 5 SUP=p.197, KUTSCH, RIEMANN, RIEMANN ERG, *ROSENTHAL=illus.p.76, *SANDVED=another illus. p.466, THOMPSON, *ULLSTEIN.

[Some sources=b.1922, others 1923; RIEMANN ERG corrects these to 1917]

GÜNTHER, Ida (Ilse, Inge) see Ivogün, Maria

GÜNTHER, Mizzi. Warnsdorf, Bohemia, Feb 8 1879-Mar 18 1961, Vienna. Soprano. KUTSCH.

GÜNTHER, Ursula (born Rösse). Hamburg, Jun 15 1927- . Musicologist, writer. RIEMANN ERG.

GÜNTHER-BACHMANN, Karoline. Düsseldorf, Feb 13 1816-Jan 17 1874, Leipzig. Actress, singer. BAKER 1, PRATT=p.407.

GUERRABELLA, Ginevra see Ward, (Lucy) Genevieve Teresa

GUERRE, Élisabeth Jacquet de la see La Guerre, Élisabeth Jacquet de

GUERRINA, Adriana. Florence, 1917- . Soprano. KUTSCH.

GUERRINI, Virginia. Brescia, Italy, Feb 21 1871-Feb 26 1948, Brescia, Italy. Mezzosoprano, contralto. CELLETTI, ENCI MUS. *[ENCI MUS=b.1872]*

GÜTHE, Dorothea see Wendling, Dorothea (II)

GUEYMARD, Pauline (born Lauters). Brussels, Dec 1 1834- . Mezzosoprano. BAKER 1, ENCI MUS.

GUGGENHEIMER, Minnie (Mrs. Charles S., born Schafer). New York City, Oct 22 1882-May 23 1966, New York City. Impresario. SANDVED. *[SANDVED= b.1881. Dates in entry based on New York Times obituary, May 24 1966, p.1, col.5]*

GUGLIELMI, Maria (later Leli).
fl.1770-72. Italian singer.
ENCI MUS, GROVE 1.

GUGLIEMETTI, Anna-Maria.
?, 1895?- . Soprano, voice
teacher. KUTSCH.

GUILBERT, Yvette. Paris, Jan
20 1867-Feb 2 1944, Aix-en-
Provence, France. Folklorist,
singer, actress. BAKER 5,
BLOM, COOPER, CORTE, DICT
MUS, ENCI MUS, *EWEN LIVING,
EWEN LIV SUP, GROVE 5, MARIZ,
THOMPSON, ULLSTEIN.

GUILFORD, Nanette. New York
City, Aug 17 1905- .
Soprano. THOMPSON.

GUILLAMAT, Ginette. Paris,
May 13 1911- . Pianist,
singer. ENCI SALVAT, ENCY
MUS.

GUILLEAUME, Margot. Hamburg,
Jan 12 1910- . Soprano,
voice teacher. KUTSCH,
RIEMANN, RIEMANN ERG,
ULLSTEIN.

GUILLEBERT, Gloria Caroline
see Trebelli (-Bettini),
Zelia

GUILLEMAUTOT, Jacqueline
(pseud.=Jacqueline François).
Paris, Jan 20 1922- . Singer.
ENCI SALVAT, ENCY MUS=v.2
p.167.

GUIMARD, Marie-Madeleine.
Paris, Dec 27 1743-May 4
1816, Paris. Dancer.
DICT MUS, ENCI SALVAT,
ENCY MUS.

GUIOMAR, Paule (Mrs. Michel,
born Chaillon). Paris, Nov
11 1927- . Music historian.
ENCI MUS.

GULBRANSON, Ellen (born Nor-
gren). Stockholm, Mar 8 1863-
Jan 2 1947, Oslo. Soprano.
BAKER 5, CELLETTI, ENCI MUS,
GROVE 5, KUTSCH, MARIZ, PRATT,
RIEMANN, THOMPSON.

GULLI, Enrica see Cavallo,
Enrica Gulli

GUMMER, Phyllis Mary. Kingston,
Ontario, Canada, Mar 12 1919- .
Composer, instrumentalist. CBC.

GUNGL (Gung'l), Virginia. Berlin,
c1850-?. Singer. BAKER 1, ENCI
MUS, ENCI SALVAT, ENCY MUS,
GROVE 5. *[ENCI SALVAT=b.in
Weimar; ENCY MUS=b.in Wei-
mar?]*

GUNN, Anne (Mrs. John, born
Young). 18th-century Scottish
pianist, writer. BROWN BIO,
BROWN BRIT, GROVE 5=v.3 p.851.

GUROWITSCH, Sara. New York City,
Feb 17 1892- . Violoncellist.
PRATT, THOMPSON.

GUSALEWICZ, Genia. Prague,
1902- . Contralto, voice
teacher. KUTSCH.

GUŠIĆ, Dora. Zagreb, Apr 11
1908- . Pianist. ENCI SALVAT,
RIEMANN.

GUSTAFSON, Lillian. Jamestown,
New York, ?- . 20th-century
soprano. THOMPSON.

GUSTL, Elisabeth Augusta see
Wendling, Elisabeth Augusta
(II)

GUTHEIL-SCHRÖDER, Marie.
Weimar, Feb 10 1874-Oct 4
1935, Ilmenau, Germany.
Mezzo-soprano, actress,
administrator. BAKER 5,
CELLETTI, ENCI SALVAT, ENCY

MUS, EWEN NEW, KUTSCH,
PRATT, RIEMANN, RIEMANN
ERG, *SANDVED, THOMPSON,
ULLSTEIN. *[Some sources=
b.Feb 16, which RIEMANN ERG
corrects to Feb 10]*

GUTHRIE, Augusta Amherst see
Austen, Augusta Amherst

GUTIÉRREZ, Lucía see Hol-
guín, Lucía

GUTZSCHBACH, Anna Marie see
Lissmann, Anna Marie

GYDE, Margaret. 19th-century
English pianist, composer.
BROWN BRIT.

GYENGES, Anna see Roselle,
Anne

GYURKOVICS, Mária. Budapest,
Jun 19 1913- . Soprano.
ENCI SALVAT, ENCY MUS,
RIEMANN, RIEMANN ERG.

H

HAAKE, Gail Martin (Mrs.
Charles J.). Liscomb, Iowa,
May 18 1884- . Pianist,
piano teacher. THOMPSON.

HAAS, Alma (born Hollaender).
Ratibor, Poland, Jan 31
1847-Dec 12 1932, London.
Pianist, administrator.
ENCI SALVAT, ENCY MUS,
GROVE 5, PRATT, RIEMANN,
THOMPSON.

HAAS, Monique (Mrs. Mihalo-
vici). Paris, Oct 20 1909- .
Pianist. BAKER 5, ENCI MUS,
ENCI SALVAT, ENCY MUS,
GROVE 5, RIEMANN, RIEMANN
ERG, *SANDVED, THOMPSON,
*ULLSTEIN.

HABICHT, Emma (Mrs. C.E.).
19th-century German writer.
BROWN BIO.

HACKETT, Maria. England, Nov 14
1783-Nov 5 1874, Hackney,
London. Writer. BROWN BRIT.

HADRABOVA, Eva. Lunza, nr.
Raknovic, Czechoslovakia,
Oct 12 1902- . Soprano.
KUTSCH.

HAEBLER, Ingrid. Vienna, Jun
20 1926 (not 1929)- . Pianist.
ENCI SALVAT, ENCY MUS, RIE-
MANN, RIEMANN ERG, THOMPSON,
*ULLSTEIN.

HAENDEL, Ida. Chelm, nr. Lublin,
Poland, Dec 15 1924 (not
1925)- . Violinist. COOPER,
CORTE, ENCI MUS, ENCY MUS,
GROVE 5, PALMER, RIEMANN,
RIEMANN ERG, SANDVED, THOMP-
SON, ULLSTEIN.

HÄNEL VON CRONENTHAL, Louisa
Augusta. Naumberg, Germany,
Jun 18 1836-Mar 9 1896,
Paris. Composer. BAKER 1=
p.249, PRATT=p.417, THOMPSON.
*[BAKER 1 & PRATT=b.1839
in Graz]*

HÄRTEL, Luise (born Hauffe).
Düben, Switzerland, Jan 2
1837-Mar 20 1882, Leipzig.
Pianist. BAKER 1=p.252.

HÄSER, Charlotte Henriette.
Leipzig, Jan 24 1784-May 1871,
Rome. Singer. BAKER 1, ENCI
SALVAT, ENCY MUS, MGG, PRATT.

HÄSSLER, Sophie (Mrs. Johann
Wilhelm, born Kiel). 18th-
century German singer. BAKER
1, ENCI MUS.

HAFGREN-DINKELA, Lilly Johanna
Maria. Stockholm, Oct 7 1884-
Feb 27 1965, Berlin. Soprano.
KUTSCH, RIEMANN, RIEMANN ERG.

HAGAN, Helen Eugenia. New Haven,
Conn., 1895- . Organist, pianist, composer. THOMPSON.

HAGEDORN, Meta. Beuthen, Poland, 1898- . Pianist. THOMPSON.

HAGELSTAM, Anna (born Silverberg). Turku, Finland, Mar 20 1883-May 2 1946, Helsinki. Singer. THOMPSON.

HAGEN, Betty-Jean. Canada, 1931- . Violinist. SANDVED.

HAGER, Mina. Madison, S.D., ?- . 20th-century mezzosoprano. THOMPSON.

HAGERUP, Nina see Grieg, Nina

HAGUE, Eleanor. ?, Nov 7 1875-?. Musicologist, folklorist, writer. THOMPSON.

HAGUE, Harriet. England, 1793-1816, England. Composer. BROWN BIO, BROWN BRIT.

HALBAN, Selma see Kurz, Selma

HALDEMANN-GERSTER, Rita. Gelterkinden, Baselland, Switzerland, Apr 14 1925- . Pianist, piano teacher. SCHUH

HALE, Jeannie M. (Mrs. William, born Stevens). 19th-century English pianist, piano teacher, singer. BROWN BRIT.

HALEY, Olga. Huddersfield, England, Nov 10 1898- . Mezzo-soprano. THOMPSON.

HALFAR, Eva see Badura-Skoda, Eva

HALIR, Theresa (Mrs. Karl, born Zerbst). 19-20th-century Bohemian soprano. ENCI MUS.

HALL, Alma Webster see Powell, Alma Webster

HALL, Elsie. Toowoomba, Australia, ?- . 20th-century pianist. GROVE 5.

HALL, Marie (Mary Pauline). Newcastle-on-Tyne, England, Apr 8 1884-Nov 11 1956, Cheltenham, England. Violinist. BAKER 5, BLOM, ENCI SALVAT, ENCY MUS, GROVE 5, GROVE 5 SUP, PRATT, RIEMANN, THOMPSON.

HALL, Pauline Margrete. Hamar, Norway, Aug 2 1890-Jan 23 1969, Oslo. Composer, pianist, critic. BAKER 5, BAKER 1971, ENCI MUS, ENCI SALVAT, ENCY MUS, MGG, RIEMANN, RIEMANN ERG, THOMPSON, VINTON. *[RIEMANN ERG=d.Jàn 24]*

HALLÉ, Wilma see Neruda, Wilma

HALLINGER, Marie Julie see Boulanger, Marie Julie

HALLSTEIN, Ingeborg (Mrs. Polanski). Munich, May 23 1937- . Soprano. KUTSCH, RIEMANN ERG, *ULLSTEIN= illus.p.222. *[KUTSCH=b.1931]*

HALSTEAD, Margaret. Pittsfield, Mass., 1904-Jan 6 1970, New York City. Soprano. *EWEN LIVING, THOMPSON.

HALVORSEN, Haldis. Dale, Söndfjord, Norway, Sep 22 1889-Aug 17 1936, Oslo. Soprano. THOMPSON.

HÄMÄLÄINEN, Armi see Klemetti, Armi

HAMARI, Julia (Mrs. Anlauf). Budapest, Nov 21 1942- . Contralto. RIEMANN ERG.

123 HARE

HAMATON, Adela. Denham,
Bucks., England, Aug 9
1884- . Pianist. GROVE 5.

HAMBACHER, Josepha   see
Dussek, Josepha

HAMEL, Margarethe Luise   see
Schick, Margarete Luise

HAMILTON, Catherine (Lady
Hamilton, born Barlow).
Colby, Pembrokeshire,
England, c1738-Aug 27 1782,
Portici, Italy. Pianist,
harpsichordist. *ENCI
SALVAT, ENCY MUS, GROVE 5,
MGG.

HAMILTON, Emily Drechsler   see
Woycke, Emily Drechsler

HAMILTON, Mrs. Gilbert   see
Cross, Mrs.

HAMLIN, Mary. Exeter, England,
Apr 18 1901- . Soprano.
PALMER.

HAMMOND, Joan Hood. Christ-
church, New Zealand, May
24 1912- . Soprano.
CELLETTI, GROVE 5, KUTSCH,
*PALMER=illus.p.134, RIE-
MANN, RIEMANN ERG, *ROSEN-
THAL=illus.p.85, THOMPSON.

HAMPTON, Hope. Houston, ?- .
20th-century soprano.
THOMPSON.

HANFSTÄNGEL, Marie (born
Schröder). Breslau, Silesia,
Apr 30 1848-Sep 5 1917,
Munich. Soprano. BAKER 1,
BAKER 5, PRATT, THOMPSON.
[BAKER 5=b.1846]

HANKA, Erika. Vinkovci, Croatia, Jun 18 1905- . Dancer,
choreographer. RIEMANN ERG.

HANNAH, Jane Osborn-   see
Osborn-Hannah, Jane

HANNIKAINEN, Mary Helena   see
Spennert, Mary Helena

HANSEN, Cecilia. Kamenskaia,
Russia, Feb 28 1897- .
Violinist, teacher. CORTE,
ENCI MUS, ENCI SALVAT, ENCY
MUS, RIEMANN, RIEMANN ERG,
THOMPSON, VODARSKY.

HANSEN, Kaja Andrea Karoline
Eidé   see   Noréna, Eidé

HANSEN, Nanny Matthison-   see
Matthison-Hansen, Nanny

HANSON, Louise B. M.   see
Dyer, Louise

HARCOURT, Marguerite Béclard
d'. Paris, Feb 24 1884-Aug 2
1964, Paris. Composer, folklorist, ethnomusicologist,
writer. BAKER 5, BAKER 1971,
DICT MUS=p.82, ENCI SALVAT=
v.1 p.333, ENCY MUS=p.364,
MGG, THOMPSON.

HARDELOT, Guy d' (Mrs. Rhodes).
Boulogne-sur-Mer, France,
?-?. 19th-century French
composer, light-opera composer. *BAKER 1.

HARDER, Hanna Stäblein-   see
Stäblein-Harder, Hanna

HARDIMAN, Ellena G. Canada,
1890-1949, Canada. Pianist,
composer. CBC.

HARDTMUTH, Hermine   see
Spies, Hermine

HARE, Amy. Taunton, Somerset,
England, ?-?. 19th-century
pianist. BROWN BRIT.

HARE, Elizabeth (I). ?-buried
Jul 8 1741, Islington, London. Music publisher. GROVE 5.

HARE, Elizabeth (II). ?-?, London. Music publisher. GROVE 5.

HARE, Maud Cuney- see
Cuney-Hare, Maud

HARICH-SCHNEIDER, Eta.
Oranienburg, nr. Berlin,
Nov 16 1897- . Harpsichor-
dist, writer, piano teacher.
ENCI SALVAT, ENCY MUS,
RIEMANN, RIEMANN ERG, THOMP-
SON, ULLSTEIN.

HARICLY DE HARTULARY, Hariclea
see Darclée, Hariclea

HARKNESS, Arma Leoretta see
Sankrah, Arma Leoretta

HARPER, Heather (Mary, Mrs.
Buck). Belfast, May 8
1930- . Soprano. BLOM,
GROVE 5 SUP, RIEMANN ERG.

HARRADEN, Beatrice. 19th-
century English violon-
cellist, composer, BROWN
BRIT.

HARRADEN, R. Ethel (Mrs.
Frank Glover). 19th-century
English light-opera compo-
ser, composer. BROWN BRIT.

HARRIERS-WIPPERN, Louise.
Hildesheim, Germany, Feb 28
1830-Oct 5 1878, Görbesdorf,
Silesia. Soprano. BAKER 1,
GROVE 1=v.4 p.476, GROVE 5,
PRATT, THOMPSON=p.2412.
[PRATT=b.1837]

HARRIS, Hilda. 20th-century
American mezzo-soprano.
PAVLAKIS=p.295.

HARRIS, Johanna Beula (Mrs.
Roy, born Duffey). Ottawa,
Jan 1 1913- . Pianist.
ENCI MUS.

HARRISON, Anita. Stockton-on-
Tees, England, Sep 1 1902-
Nov 1968, Stockholm. Pia-
nist. GROVE 5.

HARRISON, Annie Fortescue (Lady
Arthur William Hill). 19th-
century English composer,
light-opera composer. BAKER 1,
BROWN BRIT=p.198.

HARRISON, Beatrice. Roorke,
India, Dec 9 1892-Mar 10
1965, Smallfield, Surrey,
England. Violoncellist.
BAKER 5, BAKER 1971, GROVE 5,
PALMER, PRATT, THOMPSON.

HARRISON, Margaret. London,
?- . 20th-century violinist,
pianist. GROVE 5=v.4 p.114.

HARRISON, May. Roorke, India,
Mar 1891-Jun 8 1959, South
Nutfield, Surrey, England.
Violinist. BAKER 5, BAKER
1971, GROVE 5, GROVE 5 SUP,
PRATT, THOMPSON.

HARRISON, Teresa Maddalena
see Allegranti, Teresa
Maddalena

HARROP, Sarah see Bates,
Sarah

HARSANYI, Janice. Arlington,
Mass., Jul 15 1929- .
Soprano, voice teacher.
PAVLAKIS=p.288, RIEMANN ERG.

HARSHAW, Margaret. Narbeth,
Pa., May 12 1912- . Soprano,
contralto. BAKER 5, *EWEN LIV
SUP, KUTSCH, *ROSENTHAL=illus.
p.86, *SANDVED=another illus.
p.1027, THOMPSON.

HARTLAND, Lizzie. 19th-century
English accompanist, teacher,
composer. BROWN BRIT.

HARTMANN, Emma Sophie Amalie
(born Zinn). Copenhagen,
Aug 22 1807-Mar 6 1851,
Copenhagen. Soprano, actress.
ENCI MUS, ENCY MUS.

HARTOG, Henriette see
Melchers, Henriette

HARTULARY, Hariclea Haricly
de see Darclée, Hariclea

HARTY, Agnes see Nicholls,
Agnes

HARVEY, Mary (Lady Dering).
England, Aug 1629-1704,
England. Composer. BLOM,
ENCI SALVAT, ENCY MUS,
GROVE 5.

HARVEY, Mary Ann see
Davenport, Mary Ann

HASKIL, Clara. Bucharest,
Jan 7 1895-Dec 7 1960,
Brussels. Pianist. BAKER 5,
BAKER 1971, CORTE, DICT
MUS, *ENCI MUS=illus.fac.
p.399, ENCI SALVAT, ENCY
MUS, GROVE 5, RIEMANN,
RIEMANN ERG, SANDVED, SCHUH,
THOMPSON, *ULLSTEIN.

HASLBECK (Hasselbeck), Rosa
see Sucher, Rosa

HASSE, Faustina (born Bor-
doni). Venice, c1700-Nov 4
1781, Venice. Mezzo-soprano.
BAKER 1, BAKER 5, BLOM,
BROWN BIO, CLAYTON=p.52,
CORTE, *ENCI MUS=v.1 p.295
(illus.p.290), ENCI SALVAT=
v.1 p.393, ENCY MUS=p.429,
EWEN NEW, GROVE 1, GROVE 1
APP, GROVE 5=v.1 p.814,
*MGG, PRATT=p.421,447,
*SANDVED, SCHOLES, THOMPSON,
*ULLSTEIN. [CORTE, ENCY MUS,
& SCHOLES=b.1693; BAKER 1,
BROWN BIO, & CORTE=d.1783;
EWEN NEW, GROVE 5, & SAND-
VED=soprano]

HASSELBECK (Haslbeck), Rosa
see Sucher, Rosa

HASSELT-BARTH, Anna Maria

Wilhelmine (born van Hasselt).
Amsterdam, Jul 15 1813-Jan 6
1881, Mannheim. Soprano.
BAKER 1, PRATT, THOMPSON.

HASSINGER, Georgine see
Milinkovič, Georgine von

HASSLER, Henriette see
Eberwein, Henriette

HASTREITER, Hélène. Louisville,
Ky., Nov 14 1858-Aug 6 1922,
Varese, Italy. Contralto.

HATAŠ (Hattasch), Anna Fran-
tiška. Staré Benatky,
Bohemia, May 26 1728-1781,
Gotha, Bohemia. Soprano.
GROVE 5.

HATCHARD, Carolyn. Portsmouth,
England, 1883?-Jan 1970,
London. Soprano. THOMPSON.

HATTASCH, Anna Františka see
Hataš, Anna Františka

HATTO, Jeanne (stage name of
Marguerite Jeanne Frère).
Lyons, Jan 30 1879- .
Soprano. PRATT, THOMPSON.

HAUFFE, Luise see Härtel,
Luise

HAUK (Hauck), Minnie (orig.=
Amalia Mignon). New York
City, Nov 16 1851-Feb 6
1929, Triebschen, nr.Lucerne.
Soprano, actress, adminis-
trator. BAKER 1, BAKER 5,
BLOM, BROWN BIO, ENCI MUS,
ENCI SALVAT, ENCY MUS, EWEN
NEW, GROVE 1, GROVE 5, GROVE
5 SUP, MARIZ, PRATT, RIEMANN,
RIEMANN ERG, *SANDVED, THOMP-
SON. [Some sources=b.1852,
which RIEMANN ERG corrects
to 1851]

HAUPTMANN, Pauline Anna see
Milder-Hauptmann, Pauline Anna

HAUPTMANN, Susette (Mrs.
Moritz, born Hummel).
?, 1811-1892, ?. German
singer. ENCI MUS.

HAUSEGGER, Hertha (later
Ritter). ?-Jan 15 1913,
Hamburg. Singer. ENCI MUS.

HAVERGAL, Frances Ridley.
Astley Rectory, Worcester-
shire, Dec 14 1836-Jun 3
1879, Caswell Bay, Swansea,
England. Hymn writer. BROWN
BRIT, PRATT.

HAWES, Maria (Billington-
Hawes). London, Apr 1816-
Apr 24 1886, Ryde, Isle of
Wight. Contralto, composer.
BROWN BRIT, ENCI MUS, ENCY
MUS, GROVE 5, RIEMANN.

HAY, Louisa see Kerr, Louisa

HAYDEE, Marcia (orig.=Sala-
verry Pereira da Silva).
Niteroi, Brazil, Apr 18
1939- . Dancer. RIEMANN ERG.

HAYDEN, Ethyl. Washington,
Pa., ?- . 20th-century
American soprano. THOMPSON.

HAYDN, Maria Magdalena (Mrs.
Michael, born Lipp). ?,
1745-Jun 1827, ?. Austrian
soprano, court musician.
BLOM=p.378, ENCI MUS,
GROVE 5.

HAYES, Catherine (Mrs. William
Avery Bushnell). Limerick,
Oct 25 1825-Aug 11 1861,
Roccoles, Sydenham, London.
Soprano. BROWN BIO, BROWN
BRIT, CLAYTON=p.423, GROVE
1, GROVE 5, THOMPSON.

HAYNES, Elizabeth (born Broad,
"Mlle. Brétet"). 19th-century
English soprano. BROWN BRIT.

HAYWARD, Marjorie (Olive).
Greenwich, England, Aug 14
1885-Jan 10 1953, London.
Violinist. BLOM, GROVE 5,
PALMER, THOMPSON.

HEALE, Alice. London, Dec 15
1861-?. Contralto, voice
teacher. BROWN BRIT.

HEALE, Helene. London, Feb 14
1855-?. Pianist, piano
teacher, composer. BROWN
BRIT.

HEBBE, Signe Amanda Georgina.
Näsbyholm, Värnamo, Jönkö-
pings län, Sweden, Jul 30
1837-Feb 14 1925, Stockholm.
Soprano. RIEMANN ERG.

HEBER, Judith. Gol, Hallingdal,
Norway, Jun 27 1880-Oct 7
1919, Christiania, Norway.
Composer, pianist. THOMPSON.

HECKER, Margaret see Zöllner,
Margarete

HECKMANN, Marie (Mrs. Georg
Julius Robert). Greiz, Ger-
many, 1843-Jul 23 1890,
Cologne. Pianist. BAKER 1.

HECKSCHER, Céleste de Longpré
(born Massey). Philadelphia,
Feb 23 1860-Feb 18 1928,
Philadelphia. Composer,
opera composer, administrator.
BAKER 5, THOMPSON.

HEGAR, Valerie (Riggenbach).
Basle, Aug 7 1873-Jan 27
1953, ?. Soprano. ENCY MUS.

HÉGLON, Meyriane. Brussels,
1867-Jan 12 1942, Paris.
Soprano, contralto. PRATT,
THOMPSON. *[Information in
entry based on New York Times
obituary, Jan 13 1942, p.19,
col.4]*

HEGNER, Anna. Basle, Mar 1
1881-Feb 3 1963, Basle.
Violinist, teacher. GROVE 5,
RIEMANN, RIEMANN ERG, SCHUH,
THOMPSON.

HEIDERSBUCH, Käthe. Breslau,
Silesia, Oct 30 1897- .
Soprano, voice teacher.
KUTSCH.

HEILBRON, Marie. Anvers?,
France, 1851-1886, Nice.
Soprano. ENCI MUS.

HEILBRONNER, Rose. Paris,
1884- . Soprano. KUTSCH.

HEIM, Melitta. Vienna, Jan 7
1888- . Soprano. KUTSCH.

HEIMBURG, Helene von. Oldenburg, Germany, 1835-Nov 21
1904, New York City. Singer.
ENCI MUS=v.2 p.8 (brief
mention in article on the
Damrosch family).

HEINEFETTER, Clara   see
Heinefetter, Maria

HEINEFETTER, Eva. 19th-cen-
tury German singer. BAKER 1,
BAKER 5, ENCI SALVAT,
SANDVED.

HEINEFETTER, Fatima. fl.1834-
40. German singer. BAKER 1,
BAKER 5, ENCI MUS, ENCI
SALVAT, SANDVED.

HEINEFETTER, Katinka (Kathin-
ka). Mainz, 1820-Dec 20
1858, Freiburg. Singer.
BAKER 1, BAKER 5, ENCI MUS,
ENCI SALVAT, ENCY MUS,
GROVE 1 APP, GROVE 5, RIE-
MANN, SANDVED.

HEINEFETTER, Maria (Clara;
Mme. Stöckel). Mainz, Feb 16
1816-Feb 23 1857, Vienna.
Singer.   BAKER 1, BAKER 5,

ENCI MUS, ENCI SALVAT, ENCY
MUS, GROVE 1 APP, GROVE 5,
RIEMANN, SANDVED, THOMPSON.

HEINEFETTER, Nanette. fl.1829.
German singer. BAKER 1,
BAKER 5, ENCI MUS, ENCI
SALVAT, SANDVED.

HEINEFETTER, Sabina (Sabine).
Mainz, Aug 19 1809-Nov 18
1872, Illemau, Germany.
Soprano. BAKER 1, BAKER 5,
BROWN BIO, ENCI MUS, ENCI
SALVAT, ENCY MUS, GROVE 1
APP, GROVE 5, RIEMANN,
SANDVED, THOMPSON.

HEINEMANN, Käthe. Berlin-
Spandau, Nov 10 1891- .
Pianist. RIEMANN, RIEMANN
ERG.

HEINITZ, Eva. Berlin, Feb 2
1907- . Violoncellist,
gambist. RIEMANN ERG.

HEINRICH, Julia. Alabama,
1880?-Oct 18 1919, Louisiana.
Singer, voice teacher. KUTSCH.

HEINTZMANN, Cornelia   see
Richardson, Cornelia Heintzmann

HEINZE, Sarah (born Magnus).
Stockholm, 1838-1901, Dres-
den. Pianist. BAKER 1,
PRATT. *[PRATT=b.1836]*

HEITER, Amalie   see   Amalia
Friederike

HEKSCH, Alice. Vienna, Feb 12
1912-Aug 1 1957, Laren,
Netherlands. Pianist.
RIEMANN, RIEMANN ERG.

HELBLING, Maria. Winterthur,
Switzerland, Nov 30 1906- .
Soprano, voice teacher. SCHUH.

HELDY, Fanny (orig.=Marguerite

Deceuninck). Ath, Belgium, Feb 29 1888-Dec 18 1973, Paris. Soprano. CELLETTI, ENCI SALVAT, ENCY MUS, KUTSCH, RIEMANN ERG. *[Date and place of death based on obituary in Musical Times, Feb 1974, p.148]*

HELENE (JELENA) PAVLOVNA. Stuttgart, Jan 9 1807-Feb 2 1873, St. Petersburg. Patron. PRATT, RIEMANN, RIEMANN ERG.

HELLETSGRÜBER, Luise. Vienna, 1898?-Jan 1 1967, nr. Vienna. Soprano. KUTSCH.

HELLMESBERGER, Rosa. fl.1883. Austrian singer. BAKER 1.

HELM-SBISÁ, Anny. Vienna, 1903- . Soprano. ENCI MUS.

HELME, Harriot see Cabanel, Harriot

HEMMERLEIN, Eva Ursula. Born Bamberg, fl.1762. Singer, court musician. GROVE 5.

HEMPEL, Frieda. Leipzig, Jun 26 1885-Oct 7 1955, West Berlin. Soprano. BAKER 5, BLOM, CELLETTI, COOPER, ENCI MUS, ENCI SALVAT, ENCY MUS, *EWEN LIVING, EWEN LIV SUP, EWEN NEW, GROVE 5, GROVE 5 SUP, KUTSCH, MARIZ, MGG, PRATT, RIEMANN, *SANDVED, THOMPSON, *ULLSTEIN= illus.p.234.

HEMPSON, Celeste see Gismondi, Celeste

HENDERS, Harriet. Marengo, Iowa, 1904-May 8 1972, Carmel, New York. Soprano. THOMPSON.

HENDRICKX-VERMEULEN, Marie Louise. Amberes, France,

Aug 26 1921- . Soprano. ENCI SALVAT.

HENIUS, Carla. Mannheim, May 4 1919- . Mezzo-soprano. RIEMANN, RIEMANN ERG, ULLSTEIN.

HENNES, Therese. ?, Dec 21 1861-?. Pianist. THOMPSON.

HENNEY, Mme. de? see De Henney, Mme.?

HENRIOT-SCHWEITZER, Nicole. Paris, Nov 23 1925- . Pianist. BAKER 5, *EWEN LIV SUP, *SANDVED. *[SANDVED=b.1924]*

HENSCHEL, Helen. ?-1973, ?. English soprano, pianist. GROVE 5.

HENSCHEL, Lillian June (Mrs. Isidor Georg, born Bailey). Columbus, Ohio, Jan 17 1860-Nov 4 1901, London. Soprano. BAKER 1, BAKER 5, BLOM=p.42, GROVE 5=v.1 p.355, MGG, THOMPSON. *[GROVE 5 & THOMPSON=b.Jan 18]*

HENSEL, Fanny Cäcilia (or Cécile, born Mendelssohn). Hamburg, Nov 14 1805-May 14 1847, Berlin. Amateur composer, pianist. BAKER 1, BAKER 5, BLOM, BROWN BIO, DICT MUS=v.2 p.706, ENCI MUS= v.3 p.151, ENCI SALVAT, ENCY MUS, GROVE 1, GROVE 5=p.674, MARIZ, *MGG=v.9 col.73, PRATT, RIEMANN, RIEMANN ERG, SANDVED, THOMPSON. *[GROVE 5= d.May 17; BROWN BIO=d.May 17 1848]*

HENSEL, Octavia (real name=Mary Alice Ives Semour; pseud. of Mrs. G. A. Fonda). ?, 1837-May 12 1897, nr. Louisville, Ky. Writer. BAKER 1, BAKER 5, PRATT.

HENSHAW, Grace Mary Williams.

19th-century English pianist, piano teacher. BROWN BRIT.

HENSLER, Elise (Countess d'Edla). Boston, 1836-May 21 1929, Lisbon. Soprano. THOMPSON.

HENSLOWE, Cecilia Maria see Barthélemon, Cecilia Maria

HERBERT, Therese (Mrs. Victor, born Förster). ?, 1861-1927, ?. Soprano. BROWN BRIT, ENCI MUS.

HÉRITTE-VIARDOT, Louise see Viardot, Louise

HERMANN, Johanna see Müller-Hermann, Johanna

HERMANN, Miina. Ratshof, Estonia, Feb 9 1864-Nov 16 1941, Tartu, Estonia. Organist, composer, teacher. ENCI SALVAT, RIEMANN, RIEMANN ERG.

HERMES, Annie (Johanna Sophia). Hilversum, Netherlands, Sep 16 1906- . Contralto. RIEMANN, RIEMANN ERG.

HERNÁNDEZ-GONZALO, Gisela. Cárdenas, Matanzas, Cuba, Sep 15 1910- . Composer, choral conductor, administrator. ENCI MUS, ENCI SALVAT, ENCY MUS, GROVE 5, MGG, SLONIMSKY, VINTON.

HERR, Margaret(h)e see Stern, Margaret(h)e

HERRENBURG, Leopoldine see Tuček, Leopoldine

HERRMANN, Annelies Gabriele see Kupper, Annelies Gabriele

HERRMANN, Hilde see Güden, Hilde

HERRMANN, Klara. 19th-century German pianist. BAKER 1.

HERSCHEL, Caroline. 19th-century German singer. SCHOLES.

HERSEE, Rose (Mrs. Arthur Howell). London, 1845-Nov 26 1924, Wimbledon, England. Soprano. BROWN BIO, BROWN BRIT, GROVE 5, THOMPSON. [GROVE 5=d. London]

HERTZBERG-BEYRON, Olga Brita Lovisa. Norrköping, Sweden, Oct 19 1901- . Soprano. GROVE 5, RIEMANN, RIEMANN ERG, THOMPSON.

HERVIGNI, Mlle. d' see D'Hervigni, Mlle.

HERWIG, Käthe. Berlin, Dec 9 1891-Oct 28 1953, Berlin. Soprano, voice teacher. KUTSCH.

HERZ, Alice. Prague, Nov 26 1903- . Pianist. THOMPSON.

HERZOG, Colette. Strassburg, France, ?- . 20th-century soprano. RIEMANN ERG.

HERZOG, Emilie (Mrs. Heinrich Welti). Ermatigen, Switzerland, Dec 17 1859-Sep 16 1923. Aarburg, Switzerland. Soprano. BAKER 1, BAKER 5, KUTSCH, PRATT, RIEMANN, RIEMANN ERG, SCHUH=p.401, THOMPSON. [SCHUH=d.Sep 17]

HERZOG, Gerty see Blacher, Gerty

HERZOGENBERG, Elisabeth (born von Stockhausen). Paris, Apr 13 1847-Jan 7 1892, San Remo, Italy. Pianist. BAKER 1, CORTE, ENCI MUS, THOMPSON.

HESS, *Dame* Myra. London, Feb 25

1890-Nov 25 1965, London.
Pianist. BAKER 5, BAKER
1971, BLOM, ENCI SALVAT,
ENCY MUS, *EWEN LIVING,
EWEN LIV SUP, GROVE 5,
MARIZ, *PALMER=illus.p.79,
RIEMANN, RIEMANN ERG,
*SANDVED, THOMPSON, ULL-
STEIN. *[EWEN LIVING=b.*
1850 (!) at Hampstead]

HESSE, Johanna Elisabeth.
Braunschweig, Germany,
1690 or 1692-1774, Darm-
stadt. Singer. MGG.

HESSE, Ruth. Athens, Greece,
Sep 18 1940- . Contralto.
RIEMANN ERG.

HESSE-BUKOWSKA, Barbara.
Łódź, Poland, Jun 1 1930- .
Pianist. GROVE 5, RIEMANN
ERG.

HESSE-LILIENBERG, Davida
Augusta, Gäfle, Switzer-
land, Jan 29 1877-?.
Soprano. THOMPSON.

HEUSSNER, Amélie see
Nikisch, Amélie

HEUVEL, Elise see Boyle,
Elise

HEWITT, Elisa see Biscac-
cianti, Eliza

HEWITT, Helen Margaret.
Granville, New York, May 2
1900- . Musicologist,
organist, teacher, writer.
BAKER 5, ENCI SALVAT, ENCY
MUS, GROVE 5, GROVE 5 SUP,
RIEMANN, RIEMANN ERG,
THOMPSON.

HEWITT, Sophia Henriette.
18-19th-century English-
American organist, pianist,
singer. ENCI MUS.

HEYDE-DOHRN, Ellinor von der.
Kassel, Feb 23 1905- .
Organist, teacher. RIEMANN,
RIEMANN ERG.

HEYMAN, Katherine Ruth Willough-
by. Sacramento, 1877 or 1879-
Sep 28 1944, Sharon, Conn.
Pianist, composer, writer,
accompanist. BAKER 5, PRATT,
THOMPSON.

HEYNIS, Aafje. Krommenie,
Netherlands, May 2 1924- .
Contralto. KUTSCH, RIEMANN
ERG.

HICKENLOOPER, Olga see
Samaroff, Olga

HIDALGO, Elvira de. Valder-
robres, Aragón, Spain,
Dec 27 1892- . Soprano,
voice teacher. CELLETTI,
*ENCI MUS, EWEN NEW, KUTSCH,
RIEMANN ERG, SANDVED.

HIEDLER, Ida. Vienna, Aug 24
1867-Aug 8 1932, Berlin.
Soprano, voice teacher.
KUTSCH.

HIER, Ethel Glenn. Cincinnati,
Jun 25 1889- . Composer,
pianist, piano teacher.
BAKER 5, REIS, THOMPSON.

HILAIRE, Mlle. see Dupuy,
Hilaire

HILDACH, Anna (born Schubert).
Königsberg, Prussia, Oct 5
1852-?. Mezzo-soprano, voice
teacher. BAKER 1, PRATT.

HILDEGARD, Saint. Böckelheim,
Germany, 1098-Sep 17 1179,
Rupertsberg, nr. Bingen,
Germany. Poet, composer.
BLOM, ENCI MUS.

HILGERMANN, Laura. Vienna,

Oct 13 1867-1937, Vienna.
Contralto, soprano, voice
teacher. KUTSCH.

HILL, Annie Fortescue see
Harrison, Annie Fortescue

HILL, Eliza see Atkins,
Eliza

HILL, Mabel Wood- see
Wood-Hill, Mabel

HILLEBRECHT, Hildegard.
Hanover, Nov 26 1927- .
Soprano. KUTSCH, *ULLSTEIN.

HILLER, Tony Kwast- see
Kwast-Hiller, Tony

HILLIAR, Anne see Dibdin,
Anne

HILLIER, Catherine see
Graupner, Catherine

HILLIS, Margaret. Kokomo,
Ind., Oct 1 1921- .
Choral conductor, conductor.
BAKER 5, RIEMANN ERG,
SANDVED, THOMPSON.

HINCHLIFFE, Jessie see
Rawsthorne, Jessie

HINDERAS, Natalie. 20th-
century American pianist,
piano teacher. PAVLAKIS=
p.262.

HINNENBERG-LEFEBRE, Margot
see Stuckenschmidt,
Margot

HINRICHS, Marie (later Mrs.
Robert Franz). ?, 1828-
May 5 1891, Halle. Composer.
BAKER 1, ENCI MUS=v.2 p.232.

HINTON, Katharine see
Goodson, Katharine

HIRVENSALO, Anja Ignatius-

see Ignatius-Hirvensalo,
Anja

HIRZEL-LANGENHAN, Anna.
Lachen, Switzerland, Aug 20
1874-Dec 15 1951, Schloss
Berg, Switzerland. Pianist,
piano teacher. GROVE 5,
GROVE 5 SUP, RIEMANN, RIEMANN
ERG, SCHUH.

HISSARLIAN-LAGOUTTE, Pierrette.
Paris, Jun 17 1911- . Writer.
SCHUH.

HISSEM-DeMOSS, Mary. California, Ky., 1871-?. Soprano.
PRATT.

HITZELBERGER, Catharina
Elisabeth. Würzburg, 1777-
1795, Würzburg. Contralto,
pianist. ENCI SALVAT, MGG,
RIEMANN.

HITZELBERGER, Johanna (Mrs.
Bamberger). Würzburg, 1783-?,
Würzburg. Contralto. ENCI
SALVAT, MGG, RIEMANN.

HITZELBERGER, Kunigunde.
Würzburg, c1778-1795,
Würzburg. Soprano. ENCI
SALVAT, MGG, RIEMANN.

HITZELBERGER, Regina see
Lang, Regina

HITZELBERGER, Sabina (born
Renk). Randersacker, nr.
Würzburg, Nov 12 1755-after
1807, Würzburg?. Soprano,
court musician. ENCI SALVAT,
MGG, PRATT, RIEMANN, THOMPSON.

HLOUŇOVÁ, Marie. Kutná Hora,
Czechoslovakia, May 3 1912- .
Violinist. GROVE 5.

HOARE, Margaret. 19th-century
English soprano. BROWN BRIT.

HOBDAY, Ethel (Mrs. Alfred,

born Sharpe). Dublin, Nov 28
1872-Jul 10 1947, Tankerton,
Kent, England. Pianist.
BLOM, BROWN BRIT=p.368,
GROVE 5, THOMPSON=p.989,
2005.

HOBSON, Edna. Salford, Lancs.,
England, May 30 1914- .
Soprano. PALMER.

HODAPP, Frieda Kwast- see
Kwast-Hodapp, Frieda

HODGES, Faustina Hasse. ?-Feb
1896, New York City. Organist, composer. BAKER 1,
GROVE 5. *[GROVE 5=d.Feb 4*
1895 in Philadelphia]

HODGES-TANNER, Annie Louise
see Musin, Annie Louise

HODSDON, Margaret (Mrs. Alec).
20th-century virginal
player. GROVE 5.

HÖFFGEN, Marga. Mülheim,
Germany, Apr 26 1921- .
Contralto. KUTSCH, RIEMANN
ERG, ULLSTEIN.

HÖNGEN, Elisabeth. Gevels-
berg, Westphalia, Dec 7
1906- . Contralto, voice
teacher. CELLETTI, *ENCI
MUS, ENCI SALVAT, ENCY MUS,
GROVE 5=v.4 p.347, KUTSCH,
RIEMANN, RIEMANN ERG, *ROSEN-
THAL=illus.p.86, THOMPSON,
*ULLSTEIN. *[ENCI MUS=mezzo-*
soprano; GROVE 5=b. Dec 17]

HOEVEN, Dina van den see
Van den Hoeven, Dina

HOFF, Elizabeth von see
Von Hoff, Elizabeth

HOFFMANN, Grace. Cleveland,
Nov 14 1925- . Contralto.
KUTSCH, PAVLAKIS=p.295,
RIEMANN ERG, *ROSENTHAL=

illus.p.92, *ULLSTEIN.
[ULLSTEIN=b.Jan 14 1925]

HOFFMANN, Hildegard (Mrs. Henry
Holden Huss). 20th-century
American singer. ENCI MUS=
v.2 p.446.

HOFFMANN-BEHRENDT, Lydia.
Tiflis, Sep 1 1890-Feb 15
1971, Hanover, N.H. Pianist.
RIEMANN, RIEMANN ERG.

HOFMEISTER, Anna Sachse- see
Sachse-Hofmeister, Anna

HOGARTH, Helen (Mrs. Roney).
19th-century English singer,
voice teacher. BROWN BRIT.

HOHN, Maia see Bang, Maia

HOHNSTOCK, Adelaide. ?, 1856-
?. German pianist. PRATT.

HOLGUÍN, Lucía (Mrs. Guillermo
Uribe, born Gutiérrez). 20th-
century Colombian pianist.
ENCI MUS.

HOLLAENDER, Alma see Haas,
Alma

HOLLAND, Caroline. fl.1883.
English composer, choral
conductor. BROWN BRIT.

HOLLWEG, Ilse. Solingen, Ger-
many, Feb 23 1922- . Soprano.
KUTSCH, RIEMANN, RIEMANN ERG,
ULLSTEIN.

HOLM, Hanya (born Johanna
Eckert). Worms, Germany,
1898- . Dancer, choreographer,
dance teacher. RIEMANN ERG.

HOLM, Renate. Vienna, Aug 10
· 1931- . Soprano, actress.
KUTSCH.

HOLMAN ANDREWS, Gertrude see
Ashton, Gertrude Cave-

HOLMBOE, Meta see Graf,
Meta

HOLMÈS, Augusta Mary Anne
(orig.=Holmes; pseud.=
Hermann Zenta). Paris,
Dec 16 1847-Jan 28 1903,
Paris. Pianist, composer,
opera composer. *BAKER 1,
BAKER 5, BLOM, CORTE, DICT
MUS, ENCI MUS, ENCI SALVAT,
ENCY MUS, GROVE 1 APP,
GROVE 5, MARIZ, MGG, PRATT,
RIEMANN, RIEMANN ERG,
THOMPSON. [PRATT=b.1849]

HOLMES, Mary. fl.1851. English writer, composer.
BROWN BIO, BROWN BRIT.

HOLMSEN, Borghild. Oslo, Oct
22 1865-Dec 6 1938, Bergen.
Pianist, composer. RIEMANN.

HOLST, Imogen Clare. Richmond,
Surrey, England, Apr 12
1907- . Composer, pianist,
teacher. BLOM, ENCI MUS,
GROVE 5, MGG=v.6 col.652,
SCHOLES, THOMPSON.

HOLT, Gertrude. London, Sep
28 1912- . Mezzo-soprano.
*PALMER=illus.p.187.

HOLÚBOVÁ, Marie see Voldan,
Marie

HOLZBAUER, Rosalie (Mrs. Ignaz
Jacob, born Andreides). 18th-
century German singer. ENCI
MUS.

HOLZHAUSER, Theresia see
Reutter, Theresia

HOME, Anne see Hunter, Anne

HOMER, Louise (born Louise
Dilworth Beatty). Pitts-
burgh, Apr 28 1871-May 6
1947, Winter Park, Fla.
Contralto. BAKER 5, CELLET-
TI, COOPER, ENCI MUS, ENCI

SALVAT, ENCY MUS, *EWEN LIVING,
EWEN NEW, GROVE 5, KUTSCH,
MARIZ, PRATT, RIEMANN, RIEMANN
ERG, *SANDVED, THOMPSON. [GROVE
5 & THOMPSON=b.Apr 30 1871;
MARIZ=b.1870; SANDVED=b.1874;
CELLETTI=mezzo-soprano]

HONEGGER, Andrée see Vaurabourg, Andrée

HOOD, Helen. Chelsea, Mass.,
Jun 28 1863-Jan 22 1949,
Brookline, Mass. Composer.
BAKER 1, BAKER 5, PRATT,
THOMPSON.

HOOKE, Emelie. Melbourne, Sep
24 1912-Apr 1974, London.
Soprano. GROVE 5, PALMER.
[Date and place of death
based on obituary in Musical
Times, Jun 1974, p.502]

HOOKHAM, Margaret see
Fonteyn, Margot

HOOPER, Catherine see
Penna, Catherine

HOOTON, Florence. Scarborough,
England, Jul 8 1912- .
Violoncellist. GROVE 5,
*PALMER=illus. p.169.

HOOTON, Marie see Brans-
combe, Marie

HOPEKIRK, Helen. Edinburgh,
May 20 1856-Nov 19 1945,
Cambridge, Mass. Pianist,
piano teacher, composer.
BAKER 1, BAKER 5, BLOM,
BROWN BIO, BROWN BRIT,
GROVE 5, RIEMANN, RIEMANN
ERG, THOMPSON.

HOPKINS, Louisa (Mrs. Richard
Lloyd). ?-1880, Cheltenham,
England. Teacher. BROWN BRIT,
GROVE 5, MGG.

HOPKINS, Sophia. 19th-century

English musician. GROVE 5,
MGG.

HORÁKOVÁ, Ota. Budapest, Apr
29 1904- . Soprano. THOMPSON.

HORN, Maria (Mrs. Charles
Edward, born Horton). Bir-
mingham, England, 1811-Jan
1887, Morrisania, England.
Singer, voice teacher.
BROWN BRIT.

HORNE, Marilyn. Bradford, Pa.,
Jan 16 1929- . Mezzo-soprano.
BAKER 1971, EWEN NEW, KUTSCH,
PAVLAKIS=p.288, RIEMANN ERG.

HORROCKS, Amy Elsie. Rio-
Grande-do-Sul, Brazil, Feb
23 1867-?. Pianist, composer,
piano teacher. BROWN BRIT.

HORSLEY, Imogene. Seattle,
Oct 31 1919- . Musicologist,
writer. RIEMANN ERG.

HORTENSE, Queen (Hortense de
Beauharnais). Paris, Apr 10
1783-Oct 5 1837, Viry,
France. Amateur musician.
BROWN BIO, GROVE 1, GROVE 5.

HORTON, Maria see Horn,
Maria

HORTON, Priscilla see Reed,
Priscilla

HORVATH, Cecile (born Ayres).
Boston, 1889- . Pianist,
piano teacher. PRATT,
THOMPSON.

HOUBERT, Marie Élisabeth Anne
see Gardel, Marie Élisabeth
Anne

HOUGHTON, Evangeline Florence
see Florence, Evangeline

HOUSMAN, Rosalie. San Francisco, Jun 25 1888-Oct 28

1949, New York City. Composer.
BAKER 5.

HOUSTON, Elsie. Rio de Janeiro,
1902- . Soprano. MARIZ.

HOVEN, Cacteau van den see
Van den Hoven, Cacteau

HOWARD, Kathleen. Clifton,
Ontario, Canada, Jul 17 1884-
Aug 15 1956, Hollywood, Calif.
Contralto, actress, writer.
BAKER 5, KUTSCH, PRATT,
RIEMANN, RIEMANN ERG, THOMP-
SON.

HOWARD-JONES, Evelyn. London,
1877-Jan 4 1951, London.
Pianist, conductor. GROVE 5,
THOMPSON.

HOWE, Mary. Richmond, Va.,
Apr 4 1882-Sep 14 1964,
Washington, D.C. Composer,
pianist, patron. BAKER 5,
BAKER 1971, ENCI SALVAT,
ENCY MUS, REIS, RIEMANN,
RIEMANN ERG, SANDVED,
THOMPSON.

HOWELL, Dorothy. Handsworth,
nr. Birmingham, England,
Feb 25 1898- . Composer,
pianist, piano teacher.
BAKER 5, BLOM, ENCI MUS,
ENCI SALVAT, ENCY MUS,
GROVE 5, RIEMANN, RIEMANN
ERG, SCHOLES, THOMPSON.

HOWELL, Leily see Austin,
Leily

HOWELL, Rose see Hersee,
Rose

HOWSON, Emma see Albertazzi,
Emma

HOYER, Dore (Anna Dora). Dres-
den, Dec 12 1911-between
Dec 29 1967 and Jan 4 1968,
Berlin. Dancer, choreographer.
RIEMANN ERG.

HŘÍMALÁ, Felicita. Cernauti, Czechoslovakia, Jul 30 1890- . Singer, voice teacher. GROVE 5.

HŘÍMALÁ, Marie. Plzeň, Czechoslovakia, Apr 13 1839-May 13 1921, Salzburg. Singer, voice teacher. GROVE 5.

HUBER, Anna Gertrud. Zürich, Mar 4 1894- . Pianist, writer. GROVE 5, SCHUH.

HUBER, Marianne see Willmann, Marianne

HUBERT, Antonia (Mrs. Léonard, born Sitcher de Mendi). Talavera de la Reina, France, Oct 20 1827-Jun 1914, Maisons-Laffitte, France. Singer. ENCI MUS.

HUBI, Ethel see Newcombe, Ethel

HUBI, Georgeanne see Newcombe, Georgeanne

HUDDART, Fanny (Mrs. John Russell). ?-Jun 28 1880, London. Contralto. BROWN BRIT.

HUDSON, Mary. London, ?-Mar 28 1801, London. Organist, composer. BROWN BIO, BROWN BRIT, GROVE 5.

HÜNI-MIHACSEK, Felicie. Fünfkirchen, Hungary, Apr 3 1896- . Soprano, voice teacher. KUTSCH, RIEMANN. [KUTSCH=b.Apr 4]

HUGHES, Mrs. F. J. fl.1880. English writer. BROWN BIO, BROWN BRIT.

HUGHES, Rosemary Stella Middlemore (Mrs. Smith). Bromsgrove, Worcester,

Nov 26 1911- . Musicologist, writer. ENCI SALVAT, GROVE 5, RIEMANN, RIEMANN ERG.

HUGUET DE ARNOLD, Josephina. Barcelona, Sep 22 1871-1951, Barcelona. Soprano. CELLETTI, KUTSCH.

HULL, Frances. 20th-century American concertmistress. PAVLAKIS=p.138.

HUMBERT-SAUVAGEOT, Madeleine. 20th-century French musicologist, writer. ENCI SALVAT, ENCY MUS.

HUMBY, Betty see Beecham, Betty

HUMMEL, Elisabeth (Mrs. Johann Nepomuk, born Röckel). Augsburg, Germany, 1792-Mar 1883, Weimar. Singer. BAKER 1, ENCI MUS, GROVE 5. [BAKER 1= b.1793]

HUMMEL, Susette see Hauptmann, Susette

HUMPHREY, Doris (Mrs. Woodford). Oak Park, Ill., Oct 17 1895-Dec 29 1958, New York City. Dancer, choreographer, teacher. RIEMANN ERG.

HUMPHRY, Mary see Bateman, Mary

HUNT, Anna see Thillon, Sophie Anne

HUNT, Arabella. ?-Dec 26 1705, London. Singer, lutenist, teacher, court musician. BLOM, BROWN BRIT, GROVE 1, GROVE 5, GROVE 5 SUP, SCHOLES, THOMPSON.

HUNT, Sophie Anne see Thillon, Sophie Anne

HUNTER, Anne (born Home).
Scotland, 1742-1821, Scotland?. Amateur composer,
poet. BROWN BIO, GROVE 1,
GROVE 5.

HURLEY, Laurel. Allentown,
Pa., Feb 14 1927- . Soprano.
BAKER 5, *SANDVED=another
illus.p.559, THOMPSON.

HUSS, Hildegard see Hoffmann, Hildegard

HUSSA, Maria. Vienna, Dec 7
1894- . Soprano, voice
teacher. KUTSCH.

HUSSERI, Hortense see
Monath, Hortense

HUTCHINSON, Cecilia Mary.
India, ?-?. 19th-century
English soprano. BROWN BRIT.

HVIID, Mimi. Christiania,
Norway, ?- . 19-20th-century Norwegian soprano,
voice teacher. THOMPSON.

HVOSLEF, Agnes Eveline
Hanson. Christiania, Norway, Apr 4 1883- . Mezzosoprano. THOMPSON.

HYAM, Lottie. Sydney, Australia, 1864-?. Pianist.
BROWN BRIT.

HYDE, Margaret Field- see
Field-Hyde, Margaret

HYE, Louise Genevieve la
see La Hye, Louise
Genevieve

I

IACOPI, Valetta. Newcastle,
England, ?- . 20th-century
English mezzo-soprano.
*PALMER=illus.p.151.

IAKOLEVNA, Anna. Russia, 1816-
1901, Russia?. Mezzo-soprano.
ENCI MUS=v.4 p.542.

IBELS, Jacqueline. Paris, 1904-
1968, ?. Pianist. ARIZAGA.

IBSEN, Bergljot (born Björnson).
Aulestad, Gausdal, Norway,
Jun 16 1869-?. Singer.
THOMPSON.

IGNATIUS-HIRVENSALO, Anja.
Tampere, Finland, Jul 2
1911- . Violinist. RIEMANN,
RIEMANN ERG.

IJZENMAN, Jo see McArden,
Joy

ILGNER, Margarete Gerda (born
Schmidt). Magdeburg, Germany,
Aug 3 1914- . Musicologist,
archivist, writer. ENCY MUS,
GROVE 5.

ILITSCH, Daniza. Belgrade,
Feb 21 1914-Jan 17 1965,
Vienna. Soprano. BAKER 5,
BAKER 1971, KUTSCH, THOMPSON.

ILOSVAY, Maria von (sang under
name Esther von Ilosvay).
Budapest, May 18 1913- .
Contralto. KUTSCH, RIEMANN,
RIEMANN ERG.

IMER, Teresa see Cornelys,
Teresa

IMPENS, Clara see Clairbert,
Clara

IMPROTA, Ivy. Bauru, São Paulo,
Jan 3 1930- . Pianist.
RIEMANN ERG.

L'INCOGNITA (Violet Mount).
Australia, ?-?. Soprano.
KUTSCH.

"INFANT SAPPHO" see Vinning,
Louisa

INGRAM, Frances. Liverpool, Nov 5 1888- . Contralto. PRATT, THOMPSON.

INNES, Audrey. Edinburgh, Sep 29 1936- . Pianist, harpsichordist. RIEMANN ERG.

INVERARITY, Eliza (Mrs. Charles Martyn). Edinburgh, Mar 23 1813-Dec 27 1846, Newcastle-on-Tyne, England. Soprano, composer. BROWN BIO, BROWN BRIT.

IRACEMA-BRÜGELMANN, Hedy. Porto Alegre, Brazil, Aug 16 1881-Apr 9 1941, Karlsruhe, Germany. Soprano, voice teacher. KUTSCH.

IRETSKAIA (Ireckaja), Natalia Alexandrovna. Russia, 1845-1922, USSR. Singer, teacher. ENCI SALVAT, ENCY MUS.

IRION, Yolanda see Mérö-Irion, Yolanda

ISAAC, Adèle (later Lelong). Calais, Jan 8 1854-1915, Paris. Soprano. ENCI MUS.

ISAACS, Rebecca. London, 1828-Apr 21 1877, London. Singer, actress. BROWN BIO, BROWN BRIT. [BROWN BIO=d. Apr 24]

ISABELLA LEONARDA see Leonarda, Isabella

ISELIN, Dora J. see Rittmeyer-Iselin, Dora J.

ISIDOR, Rosina. 19th-century English soprano. BROWN BRIT.

ISLE, Jeanne Marié de l' see Marié de L'Isle, Jeanne

ISORI, Ida. Florence, 1875-Oct 1926, Naples. Soprano, voice teacher. CORTE, ENCI MUS, PRATT.

ISOUARD, Ninette. Paris, 1814-Oct 6 1876, Paris. Pianist. ENCI MUS.

ISOUARD, Sophie-Nicole. Paris?, Nov 27 1809-?, Paris?. Musician. ENCI MUS.

ISTEL, Janet (Mrs. Edgar, born Wylie). 20th-century singer. ENCI MUS.

ITURBI, Amparo. Valencia, Mar 12 1899-Apr 21 1969, Beverly Hills, Calif. Pianist. BAKER 5, BAKER 1971, *EWEN LIVING.

ITZIG, Sara see Levy, Sara

IVANOVA, Lidiya. 20th-century Russian composer, pianist. VODARSKY.

IVIMEY, Alice. Southampton, England, ?-?. 19th-century English pianist. BROWN BRIT.

IVIMEY, Ella Plaistowe. London, Dec 15 1883-Feb 29 1952, London. Pianist, arranger. ENCY MUS, GROVE 5.

IVOGÜN, Maria (real name=Inge, Ida, or Ilse von Günther; stage name of Maria Kempner). Budapest, Nov 18 1891- . Soprano, voice teacher. BAKER 5, CELLETTI, CORTE, ENCI MUS, ENCY MUS, GROVE 5, GROVE 5 SUP, KUTSCH, MARIZ, MGG, RIEMANN, RIEMANN ERG, *SANDVED, THOMPSON, *ULLSTEIN.

J

JACHMANN, Johanna Wagner- see Wagner-Jachmann, Johanna

JACKSON, Jane see Bianchi, Jane; Roeckel, Jane

JACKSON, Leonora. Boston, Feb 20 1879- . Violinist. PRATT, THOMPSON.

JACOB-LOEWENSON, Alice.
Berlin, Jun 12 1895-Sep 18
1967, Stans, Unterwalden,
Switzerland. Musicologist,
writer. ENCI SALVAT, RIE-
MANN, RIEMANN ERG.

JACOBI, Irene (Mrs. Frederick,
born Schwarz). 20th-century
pianist. ENCI MUS.

JACOBS-BOND, Carrie see
Bond, Carrie Jacobs

JACOBY, Josephine. New York
City, 1875-Nov 13 1948, New
York City. Contralto, voice
teacher. KUTSCH, THOMPSON.

JACQUET, Élisabeth de la
Guerre see La Guerre,
Élisabeth Jacquet de

JACZYNOWSKA, Katarzyna.
Stawle, Poland, 1875-1920,
Warsaw. Pianist, piano
teacher. GROVE 5, THOMPSON.

JAECKEL, Grace Ann see
Bumbry, Grace Ann

JAËLL-TRAUTMANN, Marie.
Steinseltz, nr. Weissenburg,
Alsace, Aug 17 1846-Feb 7
1925, Paris. Pianist, piano
teacher, composer. BAKER 1,
BAKER 5, CORTE, DICT MUS,
ENCI MUS, ENCI SALVAT,
ENCY MUS, GROVE 5=v.4 p.574,
*MGG=illus.of hands only,
PRATT, THOMPSON. [MGG=
d.Feb 4]

JAENIKE, Margrit. Zürich,
Apr 28 1896- . Pianist,
administrator. SCHUH.

JAFFÉ, Sophia. Odessa, Russia, 1872-?. Violinist.
PRATT.

JAIMES, Judith. San Antonio,
Venezuela, ?- . 20th-cen-
tury pianist. RIEMANN ERG.

JAKOWICKA, Teodozja Friderici-
see Friderici-Jakowicka,
Teodozja

JAMES, Bernice see De Pasquali, Bernice

JAMES, Dorothy. Chicago, Dec 1
1901- . Composer, teacher.
BAKER 5, ENCI SALVAT, ENCY
MUS, REIS, RIEMANN, RIEMANN
ERG, THOMPSON.

JAMES, Helen (Mrs. Ivor, born
Just). 20th-century English
violoncellist. GROVE 5.

JANACOPULOS, Vera. Petrópolis,
Brazil, Dec 20 1896- . Soprano, voice teacher. GROVE
5, MARIZ. [MARIZ=b.1892]

JANDA (Jander), Therese.
Hanover, Germany, 1827-
Oct 2 1884, Hanover?,
Germany. Singer, voice
teacher. ENCI MUS=v.3
p.111.

JANINA, Olga (Countess of).
19th-century Russian pia-
nist, piano teacher, composer. BROWN BIO.

JANKOVIĆ, Danica S. Lešnica,
Serbia, May 7 1898-Apr 18
1960, Belgrade. Folklorist,
writer. RIEMANN ERG.

JANKU, Hana. Brno, Moravia,
Oct 25 1940- . Soprano.
RIEMANN ERG.

JÄNNES, Annikki Uiomen see
Uiomen-Jännes, Annikki

JANOTHA, (Marie Cecilia)
Natalia. Warsaw, Jun 8
1856-Jun 9 1932, The Hague.
Pianist, composer, court
musician. BAKER 1, BLOM,
ENCI SALVAT, ENCY MUS,
GROVE 5, MGG, PRATT, RIE-
MANN, THOMPSON.

JANOWITZ, Gundula. Berlin, Aug 2 1937- . Soprano. KUTSCH, RIEMANN ERG, *ULLSTEIN.

JANSEN, Cornelia (Mrs. Simon Cornelis, born Reder). 20th-century Dutch violoncellist. GROVE 5.

JANUSCHOWSKY-NEUENDORFF, Georgine von. Austria, 1850-Sep 6 1914, New York City. Soprano. BAKER 1, THOMPSON. *[Information in entry based on New York Times obituary, Sep 8 1914, p.11, col.6]*

JAPHA, Louise Langhans. Hamburg, Feb 2 1826-Oct 13 1910, Wiesbaden. Composer, pianist. ENCI SALVAT, PRATT, RIEMANN, THOMPSON.

JAQUE, Rhene (Soeur Jacques-Rene). Beauharnois, Québec, Feb 4 1918- . Composer. NAPIER.

JARECKI, Louise (later Llewellyn). New York City, Dec 10 1889-Mar 6 1954, New York City. Soprano. ENCI MUS.

JÄRNEFELT, Liva (born Edstrom). Vänersborg, Sweden, Mar 18 1876-Sep 17 1971, Stockholm. Mezzo-soprano. ENCI MUS, ENCI SALVAT, MGG, THOMPSON.

JÄRNEFELT-PALMGREN, Maikki (born Pakarinen). Joensuu, Finland, Aug 26 1871-Jul 4 1929, Turku, Finland. Soprano. BAKER 5, ENCI MUS, ENCI SALVAT, GROVE 5=v.4 p.597, MGG, THOMPSON.

JARRED, Mary. Brotton, Cleveland, Yorkshire, England, Oct 9 1899- . Contralto. GROVE 5, PALMER, THOMPSON.

JASIŃSKA, Magdalena (born Lazańska). Podlasie, Poland, c1760-c1800, Warsaw. Singer. GROVE 5.

JASPER, Bella. Szöny, Hungary, Feb 18 1937- . Soprano. RIEMANN ERG.

JAWURECK, Constance. Paris, 1803-Jun 8 1858, Brussels. Singer. BROWN BIO.

JEAFFRESON, Rosa Harriet see Newmarch, Rosa Harriet

JEHIN, Blanche Deschamps- see Deschamps-Jehin, Blanche

JELENA PAVLOVNA see Helene Pavlovna

JENSEN, Anina see Genée, Adeline

JENSEN, Wilma. 20th-century American organist, teacher. PAVLAKIS=p.283.

JEPSON, Helen (Mrs. Dellera). Titusville, Pa., Nov 28 1904- . Soprano, voice teacher. BAKER 5, *EWEN LIVING, EWEN LIV SUP, EWEN NEW, KUTSCH, MARIZ, RIEMANN, RIEMANN ERG, *SANDVED, THOMPSON. *[Some sources= b.1905 or 1906, which RIEMANN ERG corrects to 1904]*

JEREA, Hilda. Iassi, Romania, Mar 17 1916- . Composer. ENCI MUS.

JERITZA, Maria (real name= Mizzi Jedlitzka). Brno, Moravia, Oct 6 1887- . Soprano. BAKER 5, BAKER 1971, BLOM, CELLETTI, COOPER, CORTE, ENCI MUS, ENCI SALVAT, ENCY MUS, *EWEN LIVING, EWEN NEW, GROVE 5, KUTSCH, MARIZ,

MGG, RIEMANN, RIEMANN ERG,
*SANDVED, THOMPSON, *ULL-
STEIN.

JESKE-CHOIŃSKA-MIKORSKA,
Ludmila. Poland, 1849-1898,
Warsaw. Singer, composer.
GROVE 5.

JESSNER, Irene. Vienna, c1910-.
Soprano. *EWEN LIVING, EWEN
NEW, KUTSCH, THOMPSON.
*[EWEN NEW & KUTSCH=b.1909;
EWEN LIVING & THOMPSON=
b.c1910]*

JEUNESSE see Albani, Emma

JEWSON, Mrs. Frederick Augustus (born Dunbar Perkins).
19th-century English vio-
linist. BROWN BRIT.

JEWSON, Mrs. Frederick Bowen
(born Kirkman). ?-Dec 24
1896, London. Pianist.
BROWN BRIT.

JIRÁNEK (Giránek), Franziska
(Mrs. Anton, later Mrs.
Koch, born Romana). Dresden,
1748-1796, Dresden. Dancer,
singer. RIEMANN.

JOACHIM, Amalie (born Schneeweiss, shortened to Weiss).
Marburg an der Drau, Hesse,
Styria, May 10 1839-Feb 3
1899, Berlin. Contralto,
soprano. BAKER 1, BAKER 5,
BLOM=p.765, ENCI MUS, GROVE
5=v.9 p.246, MGG, PRATT,
RIEMANN=v.2 p.907, THOMPSON.
*[GROVE 5, MGG, & RIEMANN=
d. 1898]*

JOACHIM, Irene. Paris, 1913-.
Soprano. KUTSCH.

JOB, Emma see Lübbecke-Job,
Emma

JODRY, Annie-Marie. Reims,

Oct 4 1935-. Violinist.
ENCI SALVAT.

JOESTEN, Aga. Remagen, Germany,
1912?-. Soprano. KUTSCH.

JOHANNESEN, Zara see Nel-
sova, Zara

JOHANSEN, Kirsten Malfrid see
Flagstad, Kirsten Malfrid

JOHNSON, Jane see Cibber,
Jane

JOHNSON, Madeleine see
Graever, Madeleine

JOHNSON, Patricia. London,
?-. 20th-century English
mezzo-soprano. RIEMANN ERG.

JOKI, Fritzi. Vienna, Mar 23
1895-. Soprano. KUTSCH.

JOLAS, Betsy. Paris, Aug 5
1926-. Composer, editor,
writer. BAKER 1971, RIEMANN
ERG, VINTON.

JONAS, Elizabeth G. Southwark,
London, c1825-?. Pianist,
piano teacher. BROWN BRIT.

JONAS, Maryla. Warsaw, May 31
1911-Jul 3 1959, New York
City. Pianist. BAKER 5,
BAKER 1971, *EWEN LIV SUP,
SANDVED.

JONAS, Mathilde see Garmo,
Tilly de

JONES, Esther see Young,
Esther

JONES, Evelyn Howard see
Howard-Jones, Evelyn

JONES, Frances Pelton- see
Pelton-Jones, Frances

JONES, Gwyneth. Pontnewynydd,

Wales, Nov 7 1936- . So-
prano. RIEMANN ERG.

JONES, Hannah. Skewen, nr.
Swansea, England, ?-?.
19th-century contralto.
BROWN BRIT.

JORAN, Elise. 19-20th-century
English pianist. BROWN BRIT.

JORAN, Pauline. Australia, ?-
?. 19th-century soprano,
violinist. BROWN BRIT.

JORDAN, Dora (born Dorothea
Bland). Waterford, England,
1762-Jul 3 1816, St. Cloud,
nr. Paris. Ballad composer,
actress, singer. BROWN
BRIT, HIGHFILL.

JORDAN, Frances Elizabeth
see Mosher, Frances
Elizabeth

JORDAN, Irene. USA, 1919- .
Soprano, mezzo-soprano,
voice teacher. PAVLAKIS=
p.288, SANDVED.

JORDAN, Mary. Cardiff, Wales,
Nov 27 1879-May 15 1961,
San Antonio, Texas. Con-
tralto, voice teacher.
BAKER 5, BAKER 1971, PRATT,
THOMPSON.

JOURDAN-MORHANGE, Hélène.
Paris, Jan 30 1892- . Vio-
linist, writer. ENCI SALVAT,
ENCY MUS, MGG.

JOY, Geneviève. Bernaville,
France, Oct 4 1919- .
Pianist, teacher. BAKER
1971, ENCI SALVAT, ENCY MUS.

JOYCE, Eileen. Nr.Zeehan,
Tasmania, 1912- . Pianist,
harpsichordist. GROVE 5,
MARIZ, *PALMER=illus.p.115,
SANDVED, THOMPSON.

JUÁREZ, Nena (María Lastenia
Juárez). Tucumán, Argentina,
1902- . Mezzo-soprano.
ARIZAGA.

JUCH, Emma (Antonia Joanna).
Vienna, Jul 4 1863-Mar 6
1939, New York City. Soprano,
manager. BAKER 5, EWEN NEW,
KUTSCH, PRATT, SANDVED,
THOMPSON. *[PRATT=b.1865]*

JÚDICE DA COSTA, Maria see
Giudice, Maria

JULER, Pauline. London, Apr 8
1914- . Clarinettist. PALMER.

JUNG, Doris. 20th-century
American soprano. PAVLAKIS=
p.288.

JUNGKURTH, Hedwig. Darmstadt,
Jun 22 1900- . Soprano.
KUTSCH.

JURINAC, Sena (orig.=Srebrenka).
Travnik, Bosnia, Yugoslavia,
Oct 24 1921- . Soprano. BLOM,
*CELLETTI=illus.fac.col.353,
*COOPER=illus.p.145, CORTE=
p.718, ENCI MUS, ENCI SALVAT,
ENCY MUS, *EWEN LIV SUP, GROVE
5, KUTSCH, RIEMANN, RIEMANN
ERG, *ROSENTHAL=illus.p.90-91,
SANDVED, THOMPSON, *ULLSTEIN.

JURJEWSKAYA, Zinaida. Russia,
1896?-Aug 3 1925, Andermatt,
Switzerland. Soprano. KUTSCH.

JUST, Helen see James, Helen

JUTZ, Louise Christine see
Mansfield, Louise Christine

JUYOL, Suzanne. Paris, Jan 1
1920- . Soprano. KUTSCH.

K

KABAYAO, Marcelita López.

Hacienda Faraón, Philippines,
Mar 10 1933- . Pianist.
ENCY MUS.

KABOS, Ilona. Budapest, Dec 7
1898-May 27 1973, London.
Pianist. ENCI SALVAT, ENCY
MUS, GROVE 5, RIEMANN ERG.

KAFENDOVÁ-ZOCHOVÁ, Anna.
Zarieč, nr. Púchov, Slo-
vakia, Jun 24 1894- .
Pianist, piano teacher.
GROVE 5.

KAHRER, Laura see Rappoldi,
Laura

KAINZ, Marianne Katharina
Theresia. Innsbruck, May 19
1800-Mar 21 1866, Brno,
Moravia. Soprano, voice
teacher. MGG.

KAINZ, Marie Holland. Riga,
Latvia, Mar 12 1833-Aug 6
1902, Stettin, Prussia.
Soprano, voice teacher.
MGG.

KAJANUS, Aino. Helsinki, May
14 1888-Jan 19 1951, Num-
mela, Finland. Harpist.
MGG.

KAJANUS, Elvi see Kajanus-
Sjöstedt, Elvi

KAJANUS, Lilly (Agnes). Helsinki, Aug 11 1885- .
Harpist, harp teacher. MGG.

KAJANUS, Selma (Maria).
Helsinki, Feb 8 1860-Jul 19
1935, Helsinki. Pianist.
MGG.

KAJANUS-SJÖSTEDT, Elvi.
Stockholm, Dec 12 1908- .
Harpist. MGG.

KALLIR, Lilian. Prague, 1931- .
Pianist. PAVLAKIS=p.263,
RIEMANN ERG, SANDVED.

KALTER, Sabine. Jaroslav,
Russia, Mar 28 1889- .
Contralto, voice teacher.
KUTSCH.

KAN, Suna. Adana, Turkey,
1936- . Violinist. RIEMANN
ERG.

KANNER-ROSENTHAL, Hedwig.
Budapest, Jun 3 1882-Sep 5
1959, Asheville, N.C.
Pianist, piano teacher.
BAKER 5, BAKER 1971.

KAPPEL, Gertrude. Halle, Ger-
many, Sep 1 1884-Apr 3 1971,
Munich. Soprano. BAKER 5,
BAKER 1971, CELLETTI, EWEN
LIVING, EWEN NEW, KUTSCH,
*SANDVED, THOMPSON. [EWEN
LIVING=b. c1895]

KAPRÁLOVÁ, Vítězslava. Brno,
Moravia, Jan 24 1915-Jun 16
1940, Montpellier, France.
Composer, conductor. BAKER 5,
BLOM, DICT MUS, ENCI MUS,
ENCI SALVAT, GARDAVSKY,
GROVE 5, MGG, THOMPSON.

KARNITZKAÏA (Karničkaja),
Nina Andréevna. Kiev,
May 5 1906- . Composer.
ENCI SALVAT, ENCY MUS.

KARP, Natalia. Cracow, Feb 27
1914- . Pianist. GROVE 5.

KARPELES, Maud. London, Nov 12
1885- . Musicologist, folklorist, writer. *ENCI SALVAT,
ENCY MUS, GROVE 5, MGG,
RIEMANN ERG, THOMPSON.

KARSAVINA, Tamara. St. Peters-
burg, Mar 9 1885- . Dancer.
ENCI SALVAT, ENCY MUS,
RIEMANN, RIEMANN ERG.

KASCHOWSKA, Felice. Warsaw,
May 12 1872-1951, Cracow.
Soprano, voice teacher.
KUTSCH.

KASILAG, Lucrecia. San Fer-
nando, La Union, Philippines,
Aug 31 1918- . Composer.
RIEMANN ERG.

KASKAS, Anna (orig.=Ona Katkauskaite). Bridgeport,
Conn., Jan 4 1909- . Con-
tralto. *EWEN LIVING, EWEN
LIV SUP, RIEMANN ERG.

KATKAUSKAITE, Ona see
Kaskas, Anna

KATSKI, (Maria) Eugénie de
see Kontski, (Maria)
Eugénie de

KATULSKAJA, Jelena Klimentjewna. Odessa, Jun 2 1888-
Nov 19 1966, Moscow. So-
prano, voice teacher.
KUTSCH, RIEMANN ERG. [KUTSCH=
b.in Moscow, d.Nov 22]

KATUNDA, Eunice. Rio de
Janeiro, Mar 14 1915- .
Pianist, composer.
RIEMANN ERG.

KATUŠIĆ, Biserka see
Cvejić, Biserka

KAUFMANN (Kauffmann), Hedwig
(Hedi) see Francillo-
Kaufman, Hedwig

KAUFMANN, Helen. New York
City, Feb 2 1887- . Writer.
BAKER 5, BAKER 1971,
THOMPSON.

KAYSER, Margarethe Susanna.
Germany?, fl.1716. Singer,
church musician. THOMPSON.

KAYSER, Sophie see Verocai,
Sophie

KAZURO-TROMBINI, Margerita.
Warsaw, Nov 19 1891- .
Pianist, harpsichordist,
teacher. GROVE 5=v.8 p.551,
RIEMANN ERG.

KEAN, Ellen see Tree, Ellen

KEARTON, Annie. 19-20th-century
English soprano. BROWN BRIT.

KEDDIE, Henrietta Sarah Tytler
(or Tyler). Cupar, Fife, Mar
4 1827-?. Writer. BROWN BIO,
BROWN BRIT.

KEELEY, Mary Anne (born Goward).
Ipswich, England, Nov 22
1805-Mar 12 1899, London.
Soprano, actress. BROWN BRIT,
GROVE 1 APP, GROVE 5, PRATT,
THOMPSON.

KEETMAN, Gunild. Elberfeld,
Prussia, Jun 5 1904- . Composer, teacher. RIEMANN ERG.

KEISER, Barbara see Oldenburg, Barbara

KELCH, Aline see Sanden,
Aline

KELLER, Ginette. Asnières,
France, May 16 1925- .
Composer. ENCI SALVAT,
ENCY MUS.

KELLER, Wilhelmine (born
Meierhofer). 19th-century
German singer. RIEMANN
(brief mention only).

KELLEY, Jessie Stillmann
(Mrs. Edgar S.). Chippewa
Falls, Wisc., 1866-Apr 3
1949, Dallas. Pianist,
piano teacher, administrator.
BAKER 5.

KELLOGG, Clara Louise. Sumter-
ville, S.C., Jul 9 1842-
May 13 1916, New Hartford,
Conn. Soprano, manager.
BAKER 1, BAKER 5, BAKER 1971,
BLOM, BROWN BIO, ENCI MUS,
EWEN NEW, GROVE 1, GROVE 5,
PRATT, RIEMANN, RIEMANN ERG,
*SANDVED, THOMPSON.

KELLY, Frances Maria. Brighton, England, Oct 15 1790-Dec 6 1882, Feltham, Middlesex. Singer, actress. BROWN BRIT.

KELSEY, Corinne Rider- see Rider-Kelsey, Corinne

KEMBLE, Adelaide (also sang under married name of Mrs. Sartoris). London, 1814-Aug 4 1879, Warash House, Hants., England. Soprano. BLOM, BROWN BIO, BROWN BRIT, GROVE 1=also v.3 p.229, GROVE 1 APP, GROVE 5, SANDVED, THOMPSON. *[GROVE 1= d.Aug 6]*

KEMBLE, Gertrude see Santley, Gertrude

KEMP, Angela Barbara (Mrs. Max von Schillings). Cochem, Mosel, Germany, Dec 12 1881 (not 1886)-Apr 17 1959, Berlin. Soprano, voice teacher. BAKER 5, BAKER 1971, ENCI MUS=v.4 p.156, ENCI SALVAT, ENCY MUS, KUTSCH, RIEMANN, RIEMANN ERG, THOMPSON, ULLSTEIN.

KEMPE, Anna Eliza see Bray, Anna Eliza

KEMPNER, Maria see Ivogün, Maria

KENNEDY, Daisy. Burra, Australia, Jan 16 1893- . Violinist. GROVE 5, THOMPSON.

KENNEDY, Helen (Mrs. Campbell). 19th-century English soprano. BROWN BRIT.

KENNEDY, Jessie see Matthay, Jessie

KENNEDY, Kate. England?, 1861-Mar 23 1881, England?. Contralto. BROWN BRIT.

KENNEDY, Lizzie. England, 1863-1881, England?. Soprano. BROWN BRIT.

KENNEDY, Margaret. fl.1890. English teacher. BROWN BRIT.

KENNEDY, Moira see Shearer, Moira

KENNEDY-FRASER, Marjory. Perth, Oct 1 1857-Nov 21 1930, Edinburgh. Contralto, pianist, folklorist, composer, writer, librettist, critic. BAKER 5, BLOM=p.219, BROWN BRIT=p.229, CORTE, ENCI MUS, ENCY MUS, GROVE 5, GROVE 5 SUP, PALMER= p.279, SANDVED, *SCHOLES= illus.p.364, THOMPSON. *[ENCI MUS, GROVE 5, PALMER, & THOMPSON=d.Nov 22; SANDVED= soprano]*

KENNEY, Margarita. Venado Tuerto, Argentina, 1920- . Mezzo-soprano. ARIZAGA.

KENNEY, Sylvia W. Tampa, Fla., Nov 27 1922- . Musicologist, writer. RIEMANN ERG.

KENT, Ada Twohy (Mrs. W. G.). Denver, Feb 8 1888- . Composer, pianist, organist. CBC, NAPIER.

KENWAY, Helen. 19th-century English teacher. BROWN BRIT.

KERN, Adele. Munich, Nov 25 1907- . Soprano. KUTSCH, RIEMANN ERG. *[KUTSCH=b.1901]*

KERR, Bessie Maude. Toronto, Jun 4 1888- . Composer, pianist, piano teacher. CBC.

KERR, Louisa (Mrs. Alexander, born Hay). 19th-century

English song-writer and
writer. BROWN BIO, BROWN
BRIT.

KERR, Mary Elizabeth Grainger.
Dundee, Scotland, Oct 12
1864-Feb 24 1955, London.
Contralto. GROVE 5, GROVE 5
SUP.

KERR, Muriel. Regina, Canada,
Jan 18 1911-Sep 19 1963,
Los Angeles. Pianist, piano
teacher. *EWEN LIVING,
THOMPSON. [Death date supplied from New York Times
obituary, Sep 20 1963, p.33,
col.4]

KERSENBAUM, Sylvia Haydée.
Buenos Aires, Dec 27 1941- .
Pianist. RIEMANN ERG.

KERSEY, Eda. Goodmayes, Essex,
England, May 15 1904-Jul 13
1944, Ilkley, Yorkshire,
England. Violinist. BLOM,
GROVE 5, PALMER=p.262,
THOMPSON.

KERTTU, Siviä see Niemelä,
Tii

KESTNER, Felicitas see
Kukuck, Felicitas

KETTLE, Lizzie. 19th-century
English teacher. BROWN BRIT.

KEUPRULIAN, Bronislava see
Wójcikóvna, Bronislava

KHAN, Svetlana see Berio-
sova, Svetlana

KIEL, Sophie see Hässler,
Sophie

KIÉNÉ, Marie see Bigot de
Morognes, Marie

KIEPURA, Marta see Eggerth,
Marta

KIESEWETTER, Irene. Vienna,
Mar 27 1811-Jul 7 1872,
Graz. Pianist. ENCI MUS, MGG.

KILBY, Muriel Laura. Toronto,
Nov 5 1929- . Pianist,
marimbist, composer. CBC.

KILLINEN, Lea Maire see
Piltti, Lea Maire

KILPINEN, Margarete ("Darling
Maria," born Alfthan).
Helsinki, May 25 1896- .
Pianist, piano teacher.
GROVE 5, MGG. [GROVE 5=
b.Feb 4 1892]

KIND, Silvia. Chur, Switzerland, Aug 15 1907- . Pianist,
piano teacher. RIEMANN,
RIEMANN ERG, SCHUH.

KINDERMANN, Hedwig see
Reicher-Kindermann, Hedwig

KINDERMANN, Lydia Maria
Theresia. Lódź, Poland,
1891-Jan 1954, Warsaw.
Contralto, voice teacher.
ARIZAGA, KUTSCH, MARIZ.
[ARIZAGA=1892-1953; MARIZ=
b.1895. Dates in entry confirmed by obituary in Opera,
v.5, p.238, Apr 1954]

KINDLER, Frieda see Dieren,
Frieda van

KING, Jessie. 19th-century
English contralto. BROWN
BRIT.

KING, Julie Rivé- see Rivé-
King, Julie

KING, Moira see Shearer,
Moira

KINGSTON, Marie Antoinette
(Baroness von Zedlitz).
19th-century English composer. BROWN BRIT.

KINKEL, Johanna (born Mockel or Matthieux). Bonn, Jul 8 1810-Nov 15 1858, London. Composer, light-opera composer. BAKER 1, BAKER 5, RIEMANN, RIEMANN ERG.

KINLOCK, Eliza (born Traubner). London, Mar 7 1796-Aug 11 1887, Long Branch, N.J. Soprano. BROWN BRIT.

KINSCELLA, Hazel Gertrude. Nora Springs, Iowa, Apr 27 1893- . Musicologist, writer, composer. GROVE 5.

KIRCHGESSNER, Marianne (Mrs. Joseph Aloys Schmittbauer). Waghäusel, nr. Rastatt, Baden, Germany, 1770-Dec 9 1809, Schaffhausen, Germany. Glass harmonica player. ENCI MUS=v.4 p.162, GROVE 1, GROVE 5, GROVE 5 SUP, SANDVED, THOMPSON. *[GROVE 1=d.1808]*

KIRK, Helen Drysdale. Scotland, c1844-Jan 30 1871, Glasgow. Contralto. BROWN BRIT.

KIRKBY-LUNN, Louise. Manchester, England, Nov 8 1873-Feb 17 1930, London. Contralto, voice teacher. BAKER 5, BLOM=p.388, CELLETTI=col.490, GROVE 5=v.5 p.429, KUTSCH, SANDVED, THOMPSON. *[KUTSCH=d.Feb 2; CELLETTI & SANDVED=mezzo-soprano]*

KIRKENDALE, Ursula. Dortmund, Germany, Sep 6 1932- . Musicologist, writer. RIEMANN ERG.

KIRKMAN, Miss see Jewson, Mrs. Frederick Bowen

KIRKMAN, Mrs. Joseph. 19th-century English teacher, writer. BROWN BIO, BROWN BRIT.

KIRSCHSTEIN, Leonore. Stettin, Prussia, Mar 29 1933- . Soprano. RIEMANN ERG.

KIRSTEN, Dorothy. Montclair, N.J., Jul 6 1917- . Soprano. BAKER 5, *EWEN LIV SUP, EWEN NEW, GROVE 5, KUTSCH, PAV-LAKIS=p.289, *SANDVED, THOMP-SON. *[SANDVED=b.1919]*

KISCH, Eve (Evelyn Myra). London, Mar 18 1912-Oct 15 1945, London. Musicologist, writer. GROVE 5.

KITTEL, Hermine. ?, 1876?-Mar 4 1938, Vienna. Contralto, actress, voice teacher. *ENCI SALVAT, KUTSCH.

KITTL, Ema see Destinn, Emmy

KITTLOVÁ, Ema Pavlína see Destinn, Emmy

KIURINA, Berta. Linz, Austria, Feb 19 1882-May 3 1933, Vienna. Soprano. KUTSCH, RIEMANN, RIEMANN ERG.

KIWI, Edith Gerson- see Gerson-Kiwi, Edith

KLAFSKY (Lohse-Klafsky), Katharina. Szt. János, Hungary, Sep 19 1855-Sep 22 1896, Hamburg. Mezzo-soprano, later soprano. BAKER 1, BAKER 5, BLOM, ENCI MUS, EWEN NEW, GROVE 5, PRATT, RIEMANN, SANDVED, THOMPSON.

KLAJN, Stana Djurić- see Djurić-Klajn, Stana

KLECHNIOWSKA, Anna Maria. Cracow, Apr 15 1888- . Pianist, composer. GROVE 5.

KLEEBERG, Clotilde. Paris,
Jun 27 1866-Feb 7 1909,
Brussels. Pianist. BAKER 1,
BLOM, GROVE 5, PRATT,
THOMPSON.

KLEIN, Anna Christina see
Schwindel, Anna Christina

KLEIN, Irmgard see Becker-
Glauch, Irmgard

KLEIN, Ivy Frances (born Salaman). London, Dec 23 1895- .
Composer, singer, voice
teacher. BAKER 5, GROVE 5.

KLEINMICHEL, Klara. 19th-
century German singer.
RIEMANN (brief mention only).

KLEMENSOWSKA, Zofia (born
Malhomme). 20th-century
Polish pianist, piano teacher. GROVE 5=v.5 p.902
(in footnote to article on
granddaughter and teacher,
Helena Morsztyn).

KLEMETTI, Armi (Elina, born
Hämäläinen). Helsinki,
Apr 12 1885- . Writer. MGG.

KLEMETTI, Dagmar. Kuortane,
Finland; Nov 4 1878-Nov 24
1952, Helsinki. Singer,
voice teacher, editor. MGG.

KLENCKE, Helmina von see
Chézy, Helmina

KLINCKERFUSS, Johanna (born
Schultz). Hamburg, Mar 22
1855-Dec 12 1924, Ludwigsburg, Germany. Pianist.
RIEMANN, RIEMANN ERG.

KLINCKERFUSS, Margarethe.
Stuttgart, Oct 18 1877-
Jan 31 1959, Göppingen,
Germany. Pianist. RIEMANN,
RIEMANN ERG.

KLINE, Olive. New York, 1885?- .
Soprano. KUTSCH.

KLOSE, Amelie. Karlsruhe, Ger-
many, Nov 13 1867-Mar 29 1947,
Karlsruhe, Germany. Pianist.
ENCI MUS, MGG.

KLOSE, Margarete Frida (Mrs.
Bültemann). Berlin, Aug 6
1902-Dec 14 1968, Berlin.
Mezzo-soprano. BAKER 1971,
CELLETTI, ENCI SALVAT, ENCY
MUS, EWEN NEW, KUTSCH, RIE-
MANN, RIEMANN ERG, SANDVED,
THOMPSON, ULLSTEIN.

KNAPP, Phoebe Palmer. New York
City, 1839-Jul 10 1908,
Poland Springs, Me. Hymn
writer, church composer.
BAKER 1971.

KNARDAHL, Eva. Oslo, May 10
1927- . Pianist. RIEMANN ERG.

KNEISEL, Henriette see
Righini, Henriette

KNIPLOVÁ, Nadežda. Ostrava,
Czechoslovakia, Apr 18 1932- .
Soprano. RIEMANN ERG.

KNOCKER, Editha (Grace). Ex-
mouth, England, Mar 2 1869-
Sep 19 1950, Glenvig, Inver-
ness, Scotland. Violinist,
teacher. GROVE 5.

KNYVETT, Deborah (Mrs. William,
born Travis). Shaw, nr. Oldham, Lancs., England, before
1813-Feb 10 1876, London?.
Singer. BLOM, BROWN BIO,
BROWN BRIT, GROVE 1, GROVE 5,
MGG.

KOCH, Emma. Mainz, Germany,
Nov 12 1860-?. Pianist,
piano teacher. PRATT, THOMP-
SON.

KOCH, Franziska see Jiránek,
Franziska

KOCHAŃSKA, Praxede Marcelline
see Sembrich, Marcella

KOČOVA, Míla. 20th-century
Czech soprano. THOMPSON.

KÖHLER-RICHTER, Emmy. Gera,
Germany, Feb 9 1918- .
Dancer, choreographer.
RIEMANN ERG.

KOENEN, Tilly (Mathilde
Caroline). Salatiga, Java,
Dec 25 1873-Jan 4 1941,
The Hague. Mezzo-soprano.
BAKER 5, GROVE 5, KUTSCH,
PRATT. [PRATT=b.1880?;
KUTSCH=contralto]

KÖSTER, Luise (born Schlegel).
Lübeck, Germany, Feb 22 1823-
Nov 2 1905, Schwerin, Ger-
many. Soprano. PRATT=p.503,
THOMPSON.

KÖSTLIN, Josephine Caroline
see Lang, Josephine Caroline

KÖTH, Erika. Darmstadt, Sep 15
1927- . Soprano. ENCI MUS,
EWEN NEW, KUTSCH, RIEMANN,
RIEMANN ERG, THOMPSON, *ULL-
STEIN.

KOHAN, Celina. Buenos Aires,
Jan 31 1931- . Composer,
pianist. ARIZAGA, RIEMANN
ERG.

KOHLER, Irene. London, Apr 7
1912- . Pianist. GROVE 5,
PALMER.

KOLASSI, Irma. Athens, May 28
1918- . Soprano, voice
teacher. ENCI SALVAT, ENCY
MUS, RIEMANN, RIEMANN ERG,
THOMPSON.

KOLB, Barbara. Hartford, Conn.,

Feb 10 1939- . Composer.
VINTON.

KOLESSA, Chrystia. Vienna,
1915- . Violoncellist,
teacher. ENCI MUS, ENCI
SALVAT.

KOLESSA, Lubka (Lioubka).
Lvov, Ukraine, May 19 1904- .
Pianist. ENCI MUS, ENCI
SALVAT, ENCY MUS, RIEMANN,
THOMPSON, ULLSTEIN.

KOLLMANN, Johanna Sophia.
London?, 1789-May 1849,
London. Organist. BROWN BRIT,
ENCI SALVAT, ENCY MUS, MGG.

KOMAROVA, Varvara Dmitrievna
(born Stassova). St. Petersburg, 1862-?. Writer, critic.
ENCI MUS=v.4 p.275 (brief
mention in article on uncle
Vladimir Stassov), VODARSKY.

KONETZNI, Anny (Anni)(Mrs.
Wiedmann). Weisskirchen,
Hungary, Feb 12 1902-Jun 9
1968, Vienna. Soprano, voice
teacher. ENCI MUS, EWEN NEW,
GROVE 5, KUTSCH, RIEMANN,
RIEMANN ERG, THOMPSON. [GROVE
5=b.Dec 12 1902, mezzo-so-
prano]

KONETZNI, Hilde. Vienna, Mar 21
1905- . Soprano, voice tea-
cher. ENCI MUS, EWEN NEW,
GROVE 5, KUTSCH, RIEMANN,
RIEMANN ERG, THOMPSON. [ENCI
MUS & GROVE 5=b.1908]

KONTSKI (Katski), (Maria)
Eugénie de. Cracow, Nov 22
1816-Dec 7 1899, Ivanici,
Novgorod, Russia. Pianist,
composer. ENCI MUS, EWEN
NEW=v.2 p.668, GROVE 5,
MGG=v.7 p.735.

KOPLEFF, Florence. 20th-century
American contralto. PAVLAKIS=
p.297.

KOPPMAYER, Gisela see
Staudigl, Gisela

KORCHINSKA, Marie. Moscow,
?- . 20th-century harpist.
GROVE 5, PALMER.

KORJUS, Miliza. Warsaw [pro-
bably actually born in
Wisconsin], Aug 8 1912- .
Soprano. KUTSCH, SANDVED.

KORN, Clara Anna (born Ger-
lach). Berlin. Jan 30 1866-
Jul 14 1940, New York City.
Composer, teacher, opera
composer. BAKER 5, PRATT,
THOMPSON.

KOROLEWICZ-WAYDOWA, Janina.
Warsaw, 1875-Jun 20 1955,
Cracow, Poland. Soprano,
opera director. GROVE 5,
GROVE 5 SUP, KUTSCH.

KORSOFF, Lucette. Genoa,
Feb 1 1876-Feb 14 1955,
Brussels. Soprano, voice
teacher. KUTSCH.

KOS, Koraljka. Zagreb, May 12
1934- . Musicologist,
writer. RIEMANN ERG.

KOSCHAK, Marie Leopoldine
see Pachler-Koschak, Marie
Leopoldine

KOSHETZ, Nina Pavlova. Kiev,
Dec 30 1894-May 14 1965,
Santa Ana, Calif. Soprano,
voice teacher, actress.
BAKER 5, BAKER 1971, *EWEN
LIVING, KUTSCH, SANDVED,
THOMPSON, VODARSKY.

KOSKIMIES, Tii see Niemelä,
Tii

KOSTIA, Raili. Juva, Finland,
Aug 14 1930- . Mezzo-soprano.
RIEMANN ERG.

KOTSCHEWSKOJ, Sophie Carmen

de Fridman- see Eckhardt-
Gramatté, Sophie Carmen

KOUZNETZOFF (Kuznetzova,
Kuznecova), Maria (Mariya)
Nicolaievna (Nikolayevna).
Odessa, Jul 24 1884-Apr 26
1966, Paris. Soprano, dancer,
actress. DICT MUS, ENCI MUS=
v.3 p.126, ENCY MUS, GROVE 5=
v.4 p.879, KUTSCH, PRATT=
p.516, THOMPSON=p.1153,
VODARSKY=p.74. [GROVE 5 &
KUTSCH=b.1880]

KOŽELUH (Kozeluch), Barbara.
Prague, 1784?-?. Pianist.
ENCI MUS, MGG.

KOŽELUH (Kozeluch), Katharina.
Vienna, 1790-1858?, Vienna.
Pianist. ENCI MUS, MGG.

KRALL, Heidi. 20th-century
American soprano. *SANDVED.

KRÁSNOHORSKÁ, Eliška. Prague,
Nov 18 1847-Nov 26 1926, ?.
Librettist. THOMPSON.

KRÁSOVÁ, Marta. Protovin,
Bohemia, Mar 16 1901-Feb 20
1970, Vráz, nr. Beroun,
Bohemia. Contralto. BAKER
1971, KUTSCH, RIEMANN,
RIEMANN ERG, THOMPSON.

KRAUS, Adrienne (Mrs. Felix
von, born Osborne, orig.=
Eisbein). Buffalo, New York,
Dec 2 1873-Jun 15 1951, Zell
am Ziller, Austria. Contralto.
BAKER 1=p.428, BAKER 5=p.1189,
KUTSCH, RIEMANN, THOMPSON.

KRAUS, Anna Katharina see
Wranitzky, Anna Katharina

KRAUS, Auguste Seidl- see
Seidl-Kraus, Auguste

KRAUS, Else C. Darmstadt,
Sep 14 1899- . Pianist.
RIEMANN, RIEMANN ERG, ULL-

STEIN. *[ULLSTEIN=b.Sep 14 1898]*

KRAUS, Lili. Budapest, Apr 3 1905- . Pianist, piano teacher. BAKER 5, COOPER, GROVE 5, GROVE 5 SUP, *SANDVED, THOMPSON. *[COOPER= b.1908]*

KRAUSS, (Marie) Gabrielle. Vienna, Mar 24 1842-Jan 6 1906, Paris. Soprano, voice teacher, actress. BAKER 1, BAKER 5, BLOM, BROWN BIO, ENCI MUS, EWEN NEW, GROVE 1 APP, GROVE 5, PRATT, RIEMANN, SANDVED, THOMPSON.

KRAUSS, Suzanne Renate see Ebner, Suzanne Renate

KRAUSS, Viorica see Ursuleac, Viorica

KREBS, Aloysia (Mrs. Karl August, born Michalesi). Prague, Aug 29 1826-Aug 5 1904, Dresden. Soprano. ENCI MUS.

KREBS, Marie (Frau Brenning). Dresden, Dec 5 1851-Jun 27 1900, Dresden. Pianist, piano teacher. BAKER 1, BROWN BIO, ENCI MUS, GROVE 1, GROVE 5.

KRETZSCHMAR, Clara see Meller, Clara

KREUTZER, Cäcilia. Vienna, 1820-?. Singer. ENCI MUS.

KRIBEL, Anna see Vanzo, Anna

KRIEGNER, Marta von see Linz von Kriegner, Marta

KROLOP, Vilma see Voggen-huber, Vilma von

KRONOLD, Selma. Cracow, 1866-

Oct 9 1920, New York City. Soprano, administrator. BAKER 5, EWEN NEW, *SANDVED, THOMPSON.

KROPIK, Helene see Wessely, Helene

KRÜGER, Emmy. Frankfurt, Nov 27 1886-?. Singer, voice teacher. SCHUH.

KRULL, Annie. Rostock, Germany, Jan 12 1876-Jun 14 1947, Schwerin, Germany. Soprano. KUTSCH.

KRUMBHAAR, Harriet see Ware, Harriet

KRUMPHOLTZ, Stekler (born Meyer). Metz, France, c1755-after 1824, London. Harpist. BROWN BIO, ENCI MUS, MGG.

KRUSZELNICKA (Krusceniski, Kruscenisca), Salomea. Tarnopol, Galicia, Russia, 1872-Nov 14 1952, Lvov, USSR. Soprano, voice teacher. *CELLETTI=illus.foll.col. 480, *ENCI MUS=illus.fac. p.550, KUTSCH, SANDVED. *[SANDVED=b.1875; CELLETTI & ENCI MUS=d.1953]*

KRZYZANOWSKA, Halina. Paris, 1860-?. Pianist, composer. GROVE 5.

KSCHESSINSKA, Mathilde (Matelda-Marija Felixowna Kschessin-skaja-Netschui, Princess Romanowska-Krassinska). St. Petersburg, Aug 31 1872-Dec 6 1971, Paris. Dancer. RIEMANN ERG.

KUBELÍK, Anita (Anna). Bohemia, Jun 19 1904- . Violinist. ENCI MUS, GROVE 5.

KUBELÍK, Ludmila (Lála; Mrs. Rafael, born Bertlová).

20th-century Czech violinist.
ENCI MUS, GROVE 5.

KUCHTA, Gladys. Chicopee,
Mass., Jun 16 1923- .
Singer. RIEMANN ERG, *ULL-
STEIN.

KÜHNE, Catherine Walter- see
Walter-Kühne, Catherine

KÜHNLOVÁ, Julie see
Reisserová, Julie

KUFFERATH, Antonia. Brussels,
Oct 28 1857-Oct 26 1939,
Shenley, England. Soprano.
GROVE 5, THOMPSON.

KUHROEBER, Hanna-Ulrike see
Vassal, Hanna-Ulrike

KUKUCK, Felicitas (born
Kestner). Hamburg, Nov 2
1914- . Composer. RIEMANN
ERG.

KUMER, Zmaga. Ribnica, Slo-
vakia, Apr 24 1924- .
Musicologist, writer.
RIEMANN ERG.

KUNC, Zinka see Milanov,
Zinka

KUNTZE, Henriette see
Voigt, Henriette

KUPFER-BERGER, Ludmilla.
Vienna, 1850-May 12 1905,
Vienna. Soprano. BAKER 1,
PRATT, THOMPSON.

KUPPER, Annelies Gabriele
(Mrs. Herrmann). Glatz,
Schleisen, Austria, Jul 21
1906- . Soprano, voice
teacher. KUTSCH, RIEMANN,
RIEMANN ERG, ULLSTEIN.
[KUTSCH=b.Aug 21]

KURENKO, Maria. Tomsk, Siberia, 1890- . Soprano.

*EWEN LIVING, KUTSCH, MARIZ,
SANDVED. [SANDVED=b.1889]

KURT, Melanie. Vienna, Jan 8
1880-Mar 11 1941, New York
City. Soprano, voice teacher.
BAKER 5, CELLETTI, EWEN NEW,
KUTSCH, PRATT, *SANDVED,
THOMPSON.

KURTZ, Elaine see Shaffer,
Elaine

KURZ, Selma (Kurz-Halban).
Bielitz, Silesia, Nov 15
1874-May 10 1933, Vienna.
Soprano. BAKER 5, BAKER 1971,
BLOM, CELLETTI, COOPER,
EWEN NEW, GROVE 5, KUTSCH,
RIEMANN, SANDVED, THOMPSON.

KURZMANN LEUCHTER, Henriette.
Vienna, 1900-1942, ?. Pianist, piano teacher. ARIZAGA.

KUSS, Margarita Iwanowna.
Rjasan, Russia, Oct 13 1921- .
Composer. RIEMANN ERG.

KUTSCHERA, Elsa. Vienna, Jun 1
1867-Dec 29 1945, Vienna.
Soprano. BAKER 1971, PRATT,
THOMPSON. [PRATT=b.1874 in
Prague; THOMPSON=b.Jun 10
1867 in Prague]

KUULA, Alma (Johanna, born
Silventoinen). St. Peters-
burg, Feb 5 1884-Oct 8 1941,
Lappee, Finland. Soprano.
MGG.

KUULA-MARTTINEN, Sinikka.
Helsinki, Apr 4 1917- .
Pianist. MGG.

KUYPER, Elisabeth. Amsterdam,
Sep 13 1877-Feb 26 1953,
Lugano. Composer, conductor.
BAKER 5, BAKER 1971, PRATT,
RIEMANN, RIEMANN ERG, THOMP-
SON.

KUZA, Valentina Ivanova
(orig. Christian name=
Euphrosina). 19-20th-century
Russian soprano. GROVE 5.

KUZNETZOVA (Kuznečova), Maria
Nicolaïevna see Kouznet-
zoff, Maria Nicolaïevna

KWALWASSER, Helen. Syracuse,
New York, Oct 11 1927- .
Violinist, violin teacher.
BAKER 5.

KWAST-HILLER, Tony (Antonie).
Cologne, Jul 14 1850-Feb 15
1931, Stuttgart. Actress.
MGG.

KWAST-HODAPP, Frieda. Bargen,
Schwarzwald, Germany, Aug
13 1880-Sep 14 1949, Bad
Wiessee, Germany. Pianist.
GROVE 5, MGG.

KYRIAKIDI, Alexandra see
Trianti-Kyriakidi, Alexandra

L

LA BARRE, Anne. Paris, bapt.
Jul 3 1628-Mar or Apr 1688,
Paris. Singer, court musi-
cian. DICT MUS, ENCI SALVAT,
ENCY MUS.

LABEY, Charlotte (later Sohy).
Paris, Jul 12 1887-Dec 19
1956, Paris. Composer.
DICT MUS, ENCI MUS. *[ENCI
MUS=b.Jul 7 1887, d.Oct 19
1955]*

LABEY, Rita Fornia- see
Fornia-Labey, Rita

LABIA, Fausta. Verona, Apr 3
1870-Oct 6 1935, Rome.
Soprano. BAKER 5, CELLETTI,
ENCI MUS, THOMPSON.

LABIA, Gianna see Perea
Labia, Gianna

LABIA, Maria. Verona, Feb 14
1880-Feb 10 1953, Malcesine
del Garda, Italy. Soprano,
voice teacher, actress.
BAKER 5, BAKER 1971, CELLETTI,
CORTE, ENCI MUS, KUTSCH,
PRATT, RIEMANN, SANDVED,
THOMPSON. *[CORTE=b.1889;
PRATT=b.1885; KUTSCH=d.in
Como, Italy]*

LABLACHE, Fanny Wyndham (born
Wilton). ?-Sep 23 1877,
Paris. Contralto, voice
teacher. BROWN BIO, BROWN
BRIT.

LABRECQUE, Albertine Morin-
see Morin-Labrecque, Albertine

LA BRUCHOLLERIE, Monique de
see Bruchollerie, Monique
de la

LACHNER, Christiane. Rain,
Germany, 1805-?, Rain, Ger-
many. Organist. BLOM, ENCI
MUS, GROVE 5.

LACHNER, Thekla. Rain, Ger-
many, c1800-?, Augsburg,
Germany. Organist. BLOM,
ENCI MUS, GROVE 5.

LACHOWSKA, Aga. Lwów, Poland,
1886- . Mezzo-soprano.
GROVE 5.

LA COINTRIE, Mme. de see
De la Cointrie, Mme.

LACOMBE, Claudine (born as
Duclairfait, known as Andrée
Favel). Voisinlieu, Oise,
France, Jan 17 1831-Sep 8
1902, St. Vaast-la-Hougue,
Netherlands. Singer. MGG.

LACOUR, Marcelle Antoinette
Eugénie de. Besançon, France,
Nov 6 1896- . Clavecinist.
ENCI SALVAT, ENCY MUS, RIE-
MANN.

LA CROIX, Mlle. de see
De la Croix, Mlle.

LACY, Jane see Bianchi,
Jane

LADA, Janina. Warsaw, 1876-
Mar 30 1947, Zakopane,
Poland. Pianist, piano
teacher. GROVE 5.

LADISLAV, Sophia Giustina
see Dussek, Sophia Giustina

LAFFAILLE, Anne Terrier- see
Terrier-Laffaille, Anne

LAFFITTE, Lucette. ?-Feb 29
1948, ?. French violinist.
ENCI MUS=v.1 p.422 (in
article on the Casadesus
family).

LAFFRA, Annie. Paris, Aug 24
1931- . Violoncellist.
SCHUH.

LAFLEUR, Lucienne (Soeur M.-
Thérèse-de-la-Sainte-Face).
Ste. Agathe-des-Monts,
Québec, Canada, Feb 8
1904- . Pianist, composer,
organist, teacher. CBC.

LAGERCRANTZ, (Anna) Ingeborg.
Vyborg, Russia, Mar 27
1913- . Musicologist,
writer. GROVE 5.

LA GIERSE, Edyth see
Tréville, Yvonne de

LAGOUTTE, Pierrette Hissar-
lian- see Hissarlian-
Lagoutte, Pierrette

LA GRANGE, Anna Caroline de
(Princess Stankowitch).
Paris, Jul 24 1825-Apr 23
1905, Paris. Soprano,
voice teacher. BAKER 1,
BROWN BIO, ENCI MUS, MGG,
PRATT, THOMPSON.

LA GUERRE (Laguerre), Elisabeth
Claude de (born Jacquet).
Paris, 1664?-Jun 27 1729,
Paris. Composer, organist,
clavecinist, opera composer,
harpsichordist, court
musician. BAKER 5, DICT MUS=
v.1 p.534, ENCI MUS=v.2
p.492, GROVE 5, GROVE 5 SUP,
PRATT, RIEMANN, THOMPSON=
p.1053.

LA HYE, Louise Genevieve (born
Rousseau). Charenton, France,
Mar 8 1810-Nov 17 1838,
Paris. Pianist, composer,
teacher. BROWN BIO.

LAIDLAW (Laidlow), Robena
Anna (later transposed to
Anna Robena; Mrs. Thomson).
Bretton, Yorkshire, England,
Apr 30 1819-May 29 1901,
London. Pianist, piano
teacher, court musician.
BAKER 1, BAKER 5, BLOM,
BROWN BIO, BROWN BRIT,
GROVE 1, GROVE 5, PRATT,
RIEMANN, THOMPSON.

LAIL, Lorri. Oslo, Feb 20
1904- . Mezzo-soprano.
BAKER 5.

LAJEUNESSE, Marie Louise
Cecilia Emma see Albani,
Emma

LALANDE, Henriette Clémentine
(Méric-Lalande). Dunkerque,
France, 1798-Sep 7 1867,
Chantilly, France. Soprano.
BAKER 1, BLOM=p.423, BROWN
BIO, CORTE, *ENCI MUS=illus.
v.2 fac.p.559, GROVE 1,
GROVE 5=v.5 p.715, MGG=
v.9 col.123, PRATT, THOMP-
SON. [BAKER 1, CORTE, &
PRATT=d.in Paris]

L'ALLEMAND, Pauline. Syracuse,
New York, 1862-?. Soprano.
THOMPSON.

LA MARA, Marie Lipsius see
Lipsius, Marie

LAMBERT, Emily Bardsley see
Farmer, Emily Bardsley

LAMMERS, Gerda. Berlin,
1919- . Soprano. GROVE 5
SUP, *ROSENTHAL=illus.
p.104, *SANDVED=illus.
p.402, THOMPSON.

LAMPE, Isabella see Young,
Isabella

LANCIA, Florence. London,
Mar 20 1840-?. Soprano,
voice teacher. BROWN BRIT.

LANDI, Camilla. Geneva, 1866-
?. Italian mezzo-contralto.
GROVE 5, PRATT, THOMPSON.

LANDOUZY, Lise (orig.=Elise
Besville). Le Cateau,
France, 1861-1943, Aix-les-
Bains. Soprano, voice
teacher. KUTSCH.

LANDOWSKA, Wanda. Warsaw, Jul
5 1879-Aug 16 1959, Lake-
ville, Conn. Harpsichordist,
pianist, teacher, writer.
BAKER 5, BAKER 1971, BLOM,
COOPER, CORTE, DICT MUS,
ENCI MUS, *ENCI SALVAT=
illus.is caricature, *ENCY
MUS, *EWEN LIVING, EWEN LIV
SUP, GROVE 5, GROVE 5 SUP,
MARIZ, MGG, PRATT, RIEMANN,
*SANDVED, SCHOLES, THOMPSON,
ULLSTEIN. *[COOPER & PRATT=
b.1877; CORTE=b.1881]*

LANDOWSKI, Alice-Wanda (Mme.
W.-L.). Paris, Nov 28 1899-
Apr 18 1959, Paris. Writer,
music historian, teacher.
BAKER 5, BAKER 1971.

LANDZETTEL, Helga see
Dernesch, Helga

LANE, Gloria. 20th-century
American mezzo-soprano.
*SANDVED.

LANG, Josephine Caroline
(Lang-Köstlin). Munich,
Mar 14 1815-Dec 2 1880,
Tübingen, Germany. Com-
poser. BAKER 1, BAKER 5,
GROVE 1, GROVE 1 APP,
GROVE 5, MGG, PRATT,
RIEMANN, THOMPSON.

LANG, Margaret Ruthven. Boston,
Nov 27 1867-May 30 1972,
Jamaica Plain, Mass. Com-
poser. BAKER 1, BAKER 5,
BAKER 1971, ENCI MUS, PRATT,
RIEMANN, THOMPSON.

LANG, Regina (born Hitzelber-
ger). Würzburg, Feb 15 1788-
May 10 1827, Munich. Soprano,
court musician. GROVE 1,
GROVE 5, *MGG=v.6 col.490,
RIEMANN=v.1 p.803, THOMPSON.

LANGAARD, Borghild Bryhn- see
Bryhn-Langaard, Borghild

LANGE, Aloysia see Weber,
Aloysia

LANGENDORFF, Frieda. Breslau,
Silesia, Mar 24 1868-Jun 11
1947, New York City. Con-
tralto. BAKER 5, KUTSCH,
RIEMANN, THOMPSON.

LANGENHAN, Anna Hirzel- see
Hirzel-Langenhan, Anna

LANGPRÜCKNER, Therese Maria
see Platti, Therese Maria

LANKHOUT, Caroline. Utrecht,
Jan 26 1892- . Pianist.
THOMPSON.

LANKOW, Anna. Bonn, Jan 13
1850-Mar 19 1908, Bonn.
Contralto, voice teacher,

writer. BAKER 5, PRATT,
RIEMANN, THOMPSON.

LANNER, Katherine (Katti).
Vienna, 1828?-Nov 15 1908,
London. Dancer, dance tea-
cher. GROVE 1, THOMPSON.
*[Information in entry based
on New York Times obituary,
Nov 16 1908, p.9, col.6]*

LAPEYRETTE, Ketty. Oloron,
France, Jul 23 1884-Oct 2
1960, Paris. Mezzo-soprano,
voice teacher. KUTSCH,
THOMPSON.

LARA, Adelina de   see   De
Lara, Adelina

LAREDO, Ruth. 20th-century
American pianist. PAVLA-
KIS=p.264.

LARGE, Eliza Rebecca (Mrs.
Henry Chatfield). England,
1815-Jul 30 1881, Brixton,
London. Singer. BROWN BRIT.

LA RIVIÈRE, Johanna Everdina
see   Fourie, Johanna
Everdina

"LARK ELLEN"   see   Yaw,
Ellen Beach

LARKCOM, Charlotte Agnes.
New Reading, England, ?-?.
19th-century soprano,
voice teacher. BROWN BRIT.

LARRIVÉE, Marie-Jeanne (Mrs.
Henri, born Le Mière).
Sedan, France, Nov 29 1733-
Oct 1786, Paris. Soprano.
ENCI MUS.

LARROCHA, Alicia de. Barcelona,
May 23 1923- . Pianist. BAKER
1971, ENCI SALVAT.

LARSÉN-TODSEN, Nanny (Isidora).
Hagby, Kalmar län, Sweden,
Aug 2 1884- . Soprano, voice

teacher. BAKER 5, CORTE, ENCI
MUS, EWEN LIVING, EWEN LIV SUP,
EWEN NEW, GROVE 5, GROVE 5 SUP,
KUTSCH, RIEMANN, THOMPSON.

LASCELLES, Ann   see   Catley,
Ann

LASCHI, Luisa   see   Mombelli,
Luisa

LASHANSKA, Hulda. New York City,
Mar 15 1893-Jan 17 1974, New
York City. Soprano. *EWEN
LIVING, MARIZ. [MARIZ=b.1890.
Date and place of death based
on obituary in New York Times,
Jan 20 1974, p.57, col.1]*

LASKINE, Lily. Paris, Aug 31
1893- . Harpist. CORTE,
ENCI SALVAT.

LASSIMORE, Denise. 20th-century
English pianist. PALMER.

LASZLÓ, Magda. Marosvásárhely,
Hungary, c1919- . Soprano.
ENCI MUS, EWEN NEW, KUTSCH,
ULLSTEIN. *[ENCI MUS=b.c1920]*

LASZTOCZ, Sara Sebeök von   see
Seeböck, Charlotte von

LATILLA, Domenica   see
Casarini, Domenica

LATTERMANN, Ottilie   see
Metzger-Lattermann, Ottilie

LAUDER, Isabelle   see   Nef,
Isabelle

LAUFER, Beatrice. New York
City, 1916- . Composer.
REIS.

LAUNAY, Denise. Paris, Oct 7
1906- . Musicologist.
ENCI SALVAT, ENCY MUS, MGG.

LAURENTI, Antonia Maria   see
Novelli Laurenti, Antonia
Maria

LAUTE-BRUN, Antoinette. Nimes, France, Jul 1 1876-?. Soprano. KUTSCH.

LAUTENBACHER, Susanne. Augsburg, Germany, Apr 19 1932- Violinist. ULLSTEIN.

LAUTERER, Berta see Foerstrová-Lautererová, Berta

LAUTERS, Pauline see Gueymard, Pauline

LA VALLE, Mme. de see De La Valle, Mme.

LAVANCHY, Magda. Zürich, Dec 20 1901- . Violinist, violin teacher, pianist. SCHUH.

LAVENU, Elizabeth. 19th-century English music publisher. GROVE 5.

LAVERS, Marjorie. England?, May 8 1916- . Violinist. PALMER.

LAVROVSKA, Elisaveta Andreyevna (Elizabeth Andrejevna Lawrowskaja, Yelizaveta Andreyevna Lavrovskaya, Princess Tzereteli or Zeretelev). Kaschin (Kashin), Tver, Russia, Oct 12 1845-Feb 4 1919, Petrograd. Soprano, voice teacher. BAKER 1, GROVE 1=v.4 p.506, GROVE 5, GROVE 5 SUP, PRATT, VODARSKY. *[GROVE 5=mezzosoprano]*

LAWRENCE, Elizabeth S. fl. 1842-77. English organist. BROWN BRIT.

LAWRENCE, Emily M. Rugby, England, 1854-?. Composer, pianist. BROWN BRIT.

LAWRENCE, Marjorie. Dean's

March, nr. Melbourne, Feb 17 1909- . Soprano, voice teacher. BAKER 5, ENCI MUS, *EWEN LIVING, EWEN LIV SUP, EWEN NEW, GROVE 5, GROVE 5 SUP, KUTSCH, MARIZ, RIEMANN, *SANDVED=another illus.p.524, THOMPSON. *[SANDVED=b.1908]*

LAWROWSKAJA, Elizabeth Andrejevna see Lavrovska, Elisaveta Andreyevna

LAWTON, Dorothy. Sheffield, England, Jul 31 1874-Feb 19 1960, Bournemouth, England. Music librarian, pianist, piano teacher. BAKER 5, BAKER 1971, GROVE 5, THOMPSON. *[GROVE 5=b.1881]*

LAYTON WALKER, Sarah-Jane see Cahier, Sarah-Jane

LAZAŃSKA, Magdalena see Jasińska, Magdalena

LAZZARINI, Adriana. Mantua, Feb 5 1933- . Mezzo-soprano. ENCI MUS.

LEANDER, Adée see Flodin, Adée

LEAR, Evelyn. New York City, Jan 18 1930- . Soprano. BAKER 1971, EWEN NEW, KUTSCH, PAVLAKIS=p.289, *ULLSTEIN. *[ULLSTEIN=b.1928]*

LEBEAU, Elisabeth. Paris, Feb 22 1900- . Musicologist, writer. ENCI SALVAT, ENCY MUS.

LE BEAU, Louise Adolpha. Rastatt, Baden, Germany, Apr 25 1850-Jul 2 1927, Baden-Baden, Germany. Composer, pianist, piano teacher. BAKER 1, PRATT, RIEMANN.

LEBRUN, Franziska (born
Danzi). Mannheim, Mar 24
1756-May 14 1791, Berlin.
Soprano, composer, pianist.
BAKER 1, BAKER 5, BLOM,
DICT MUS, ENCI MUS, ENCI
SALVAT, GROVE 1, GROVE 5,
RIEMANN, SANDVED, THOMPSON.

LEBRUN, Rosine (Mrs. Stent-
zsch). Munich, Apr 29 1783-
Jun 5 1855, Munich. Singer,
pianist, actress. ENCI MUS,
ENCI SALVAT, ENCY MUS,
GROVE 1, GROVE 5, RIEMANN.
*[GROVE 1 & GROVE 5=b.Apr 13
1785]*

LEBRUN, Sophie. London, Jun 20
1781-after 1815, ?. Pianist,
composer. ENCI MUS, ENCI
SALVAT, ENCY MUS, GROVE 5,
RIEMANN.

LECHNER, Irmgard. Bonn, Jul 5
1907- . Harpsichordist,
harpsichord teacher. RIE-
MANN, THOMPSON, ULLSTEIN.

LECLAIR, Jeanne. Lyon, France,
May 5 1699-?. Musician.
DICT MUS, ENCI SALVAT, ENCY
MUS.

LEDAN, Marie see Delna,
Marie

LEDERMAN, Minna. 20th-century
American editor, writer.
THOMPSON.

LEE, Ella. 20th-century
American soprano. PAVLAKIS=
p.289.

LEE, Harriet see Waylett,
Harriet

LEFEBRE, Margot Hinnenberg-
see Stuckenschmidt, Margot

LEFÉBURE, Yvonne Élise. Er-
mont, Seine-et-Oise, France,

Jun 29 1904- . Pianist, piano
teacher. CORTE, ENCI SALVAT,
ENCY MUS, GROVE 5, RIEMANN,
THOMPSON.

LEFÉBURE-WÉLY (Lefebvre),
Joséphine-Thérèse (born
Court). Paris, Nov 19 1825-
Jan 28 1876, Paris. Singer.
ENCI MUS, ENCI SALVAT,

LEFEBVRE, Constance Caroline
see Faure, Constance
Caroline

LE FÈVRE, Caroline see
Spivacke, Caroline

LEFEVRE, Elizabeth see
Bride, Elizabeth

LEFÈVRE, Louise-Rosalie see
Dugazon, Louise-Rosalie

LEFFLER-BRUCKARD, Martha.
Berlin, Jun 16 1865-May 14
1954, Wiesbaden. Soprano,
voice teacher. BAKER 5,
KUTSCH, PRATT, THOMPSON.
[PRATT=b.1870?]

LEGINSKA, Ethel (real name=
Liggins). Hull, England, Apr
13 1886-Feb 26 1970, Los
Angeles. Composer, pianist,
piano teacher, opera compo-
ser, conductor. BAKER 5,
BAKER 1971, CORTE, ENCI MUS,
PRATT, RIEMANN, SANDVED,
THOMPSON. *[PRATT=b.1883;
CORTE & SANDVED=b.1890]*

LE-GRAND, Angélique see
Scio, Julie-Angélique

LEHMANN, Lilli. Würzburg,
Nov 24 1848-May 17 1929,
Berlin. Soprano, voice
teacher, writer, editor,
administrator. BAKER 1,
BAKER 5, BLOM, *CELLETTI=
illus.foll.col.480, COOPER,
CORTE, DICT MUS, ENCI MUS,

ENCI SALVAT, ENCY MUS, EWEN
NEW, GROVE 1 APP, GROVE 5,
KUTSCH, MARIZ, MGG, PRATT,
RIEMANN, *SANDVED, THOMPSON,
*ULLSTEIN.

LEHMANN, Liza (orig.=Eliza-
betha Nina Mary Frederica;
Mrs. Herbert Bedford). Lon-
don, Jul 11 1862-Sep 19 1918,
Pinner, Middlesex. Soprano,
composer, light-opera com-
poser. BAKER 1, BAKER 5,
BLOM, BROWN BRIT, COOPER,
CORTE, ENCI MUS, GROVE 5,
GROVE 5 SUP, PRATT, RIEMANN,
SANDVED, SCHOLES, THOMPSON.

LEHMANN, Lotte (later Krause).
Perleburg, Germany, Feb 27
1888- . Soprano, voice
teacher. BAKER 5, BAKER
1971, BLOM, CELLETTI,
COOPER, CORTE, DICT MUS,
*ENCI MUS=illus.v.2 fac.
p.586, *EWEN LIVING, EWEN
LIV SUP, EWEN NEW, GROVE 5,
GROVE 5 SUP, KUTSCH, MARIZ,
MGG, RIEMANN, *SANDVED=
another illus.p.1169,
THOMPSON, *ULLSTEIN. *[Many
sources=b.Jul 2 1885, others
Feb 22 1888; Feb 27 1888
recurs most frequently,
however]*

LEHMANN, Marie. Hamburg, May
15 1851-Dec 9 1931, Berlin.
Soprano, voice teacher.
BAKER 5, ENCI MUS, ENCI
SALVAT, ENCY MUS, GROVE 5,
PRATT, RIEMANN, THOMPSON.

LEHRITTER, Anna Maria see
Righini, Anna Maria

LEIDER, Frida. Berlin, Apr 18
1888- . Soprano, voice
teacher. BAKER 5, CELLETTI,
DICT MUS, *EWEN LIVING,
EWEN LIV SUP, EWEN NEW,
GROVE 5, GROVE 5 SUP,

KUTSCH, MARIZ, RIEMANN,
*SANDVED, THOMPSON, *ULLSTEIN.

LEIDY, Helen (born Carter).
Philadelphia, Oct 1873-Feb 9
1933, Philadelphia. Soprano,
pianist, harpist, patron.
THOMPSON.

LEIGH, Adele. London, Jun 15
1928- . Soprano, actress.
GROVE 5, GROVE 5 SUP, *ROSEN-
THAL=illus.p.106, SANDVED.

LEISINGER, Bertha. Germany?,
1825-1913, Germany?. Singer.
THOMPSON.

LEISINGER, Elisabeth. Stuttgart,
May 17 1864-Dec 15 1933,
Stuttgart. Soprano. BAKER 1,
BAKER 5, THOMPSON.

LEISNER, Emmi. Flensburg,
Germany, Aug 8 1885-Jan 11
1958, Flensburg, Germany.
Contralto. KUTSCH, RIEMANN,
THOMPSON, ULLSTEIN.

LEIVISKÄ, Helvi (Lemmikki).
Helsinki, May 25 1902- .
Composer. GROVE 5.

LEJEUNE, Gabrielle. Liège,
?-?. 19-20th-century soprano.
GROVE 5, GROVE 5 SUP,
THOMPSON.

LELEU, Jeanne. Saint-Mihiel,
France, Dec 29 1898- .
Pianist, composer. CORTE,
DICT MUS, ENCI MUS, ENCY
MUS, GROVE 5, MGG, RIEMANN.

LELI, Maria see Guglielmi,
Maria

LELONG, Adèle see Isaac,
Adèle

LE MAURE, Catherine Nicole.
Paris, Aug 3 1704-1786,

Paris. Soprano. DICT MUS,
ENCI SALVAT, ENCY MUS.

LE MIÈRE, Marie-Jeanne see
Larrivée, Marie-Jeanne

LEMMENS, Ella. 19th-century
English singer. BROWN BRIT.

LEMMENS, Helen (Mrs. Nicolas
Jacques, born Sherrington).
Preston, Lancashire, Oct 4
1934-May 9 1906, Brussels.
Soprano, voice teacher,
composer. BLOM, BROWN BIO=
p.559, BROWN BRIT=p.370,
GROVE 5, RIEMANN.

LEMMENS, Mary. 19th-century
English singer. BROWN BRIT.

LEMNITZ, Tiana. Metz, Alsace,
Oct 26 1897- . Soprano.
BAKER 5, BLOM, CELLETTI,
EWEN LIVING, EWEN NEW,
KUTSCH, RIEMANN, THOMPSON,
ULLSTEIN.

LENHARDSON, Antonieta Silveyra de. ?, 1886-1961, ?.
Argentine singer, voice
teacher. ARIZAGA.

LENT, Sylvia. Washington,
D.C., ?- . 20th-century
violinist. THOMPSON.

LENYA, Lotte (orig.=Karoline
Blamauer). 20th-century
Viennese singer, actress.
*SANDVED=illus.p.1381,
THOMPSON=p.2384.

LEO, Maria. Berlin, Oct 18
1873-Sep 2 1942, Berlin.
Pianist, piano teacher.
RIEMANN, THOMPSON.

LEO, Rosa. 19th-century
Italian mezzo-soprano.
BROWN BRIT.

LEONARD, Helen Louise see
Russell, Lillian

LEONARD, Lotte. Hamburg, Dec 3
1884- . Soprano, voice teacher. CORTE, GROVE 5, KUTSCH,
RIEMANN, THOMPSON.

LEONARDA, Isabella. Novara,
Italy, 1620-Apr 1700, Novara,
Italy. Church composer. CORTE,
DICT MUS, *ENCI MUS=v.2 p.480,
ENCI SALVAT, ENCY MUS, GROVE
5, MGG, RIEMANN=v.1 p.570.
[GROVE 5=b. c1641]

LEONOVA (Leonowa), Darya Mik-
hailovna. Vyshny-Volotchok,
Russia, Mar 9 1829-Feb 6 1896,
St. Petersburg. Contralto.
BAKER 1, BAKER 5, BAKER 1971,
BLOM, ENCI MUS, GROVE 5, GROVE
5 SUP, PRATT, THOMPSON, VO-
DARSKY. *[BAKER 1, ENCI MUS,
THOMPSON, & VODARSKY=b.1825;
BAKER 1=d.Feb 10 1896; ENCI
MUS=b.at Tver, Russia]*

LEOPOLDO, Mary Ann see
De Micheli, Mary Ann

L'ÉPINE, Francesca Margherita
de (later Mrs. John Christopher Pepusch). ?-Aug 9 or 10
1746, London. Soprano. BLOM,
BROWN BIO=p.233, CLAYTON=
p.15, ENCI MUS=v.3 p.402,
GROVE 1, GROVE 5, GROVE 5
SUP, HIGHFILL=v.4 p.292,
PRATT=p.336, THOMPSON.

LERNER, Tina. Odessa, Russia,
Jun 5 1890- . Pianist.
PRATT, THOMPSON.

LE ROCHOIS, Marthe. Caën,
France, 1650-Oct 9 1728,
Sartrouville-sur-Seine,
Paris. Soprano. CLAYTON,
ENCI MUS=v.4 p.32, ENCI
SALVAT, ENCY MUS, MGG.
*[MGG=d.Oct 8; CLAYTON=
d.Oct 28; ENCI SALVAT &
ENCY MUS=d.Nov 8]*

LEROUX, Zulmé see Dabadie,
Zulmé

"LESTER, MISS" see Reeves, Constance Sims

LEUCHTER, Henriette see Kurzmann Leuchter, Henriette

LEUTNER, Minna see Peschka-Leutner, Minna

LEV, Ray (Rae). Rostov, Russia, May 8 1912-May 20 1968, New York City. Pianist. BAKER 5, *EWEN LIVING, *SANDVED, TH OMPSON.

LEVASSEUR, Rosalie (stage name of Marie Claude Josèphe Levasseur). Valenciennes, France, Oct 8 1749-May 6 1826, Neuwied, Germany. Soprano. BAKER 1, BAKER 5, BLOM, ENCI MUS, *ENCI SALVAT, *ENCY MUS, EWEN NEW, GROVE 5, MGG, PRATT, RIEMANN, SANDVED, THOMPSON.

LÉVÊQUE, Marie-Antoinette de. Mamers, Sarthe, France, Feb 2 1903- . Pianist. ENCI MUS= v.2 p.235.

LEVINA, Zara Aleksandrovna. Simferopol, Russia, Feb 5 1906- . Composer. THOMPSON, VODARSKY. [VODARSKY=b.1905 in China]

LEVY, Sara (born Itzig). Germany?, 1761-1854, Germany?. Harpsichordist. MGG.

LEWING, Adele. Hanover, Aug 6 1866-Feb 16 1943, New York City. Pianist, piano teacher, composer. PRATT, THOMPSON.

LEWIS, Brenda. Sunbury, Pa., ?- . 20th-century American soprano. *SANDVED, THOMPSON.

LEWIS, Mary. Hot Springs, Ark., Jan 7 1900-Dec 31

1941, New York City. Soprano. KUTSCH, MARIZ, SANDVED, THOMPSON.

LHÉVINNE, Rosina. Kiev, Mar 28 1880- . Pianist, piano teacher. BAKER 5, BAKER 1971, *SANDVED, THOMPSON.

LICETTE, Miriam. Chester, England, Sep 9 1892-Apr 11 1969, Twyford, England. Soprano. GROVE 5, GROVE 5 SUP, KUTSCH, THOMPSON.

LICHNOWSKY, Christine. ?, 1765-1841, ?. Austrian patron. DICT MUS.

LICHTENEGGER, Mathilde see Mallinger, Mathilde

LICHTENSTEIN, Pauline see Donalda, Pauline

LICHTMANN, Sina (born Shafran). Odessa, 1895- . Pianist, piano teacher. THOMPSON.

LIE, Erika see Lie-Nissen, Erika

LIEBE, Annelise. Halle, Germany, Dec 29 1911- . Musicologist, writer. RIEMANN.

LIEBENBERG, Eva. Stettin, Germany, Feb 15 1890- . Contralto. KUTSCH.

LIEBLING, Estelle. New York City, Apr 21 1880-Sep 25 1970, New York City. Soprano, voice teacher. BAKER 5, BAKER 1971, ENCI MUS, EWEN NEW, THOMPSON. [ENCI MUS, EWEN NEW, & THOMPSON=b.1884. Dates in heading based on obituary in Opera News, vol.35, Dec 5 1970, p.33]

LIE-NISSEN, Erika. Kongsvinger, nr. Christiania, Norway, Jan

17 1845-Oct 27 1903, Christiania, Norway. Pianist,
piano teacher. BAKER 1,
BAKER 5, BLOM, GROVE 5,
PRATT, THOMPSON=p.1208 &
1472 (double entry).

LIGABUE, Ilva. Reggio, Italy,
1928- . Soprano. KUTSCH.

LIGGINS, Ethel see Leginska,
Ethel

LIGHTSTONE, Pauline see
Donalda, Pauline

LIIVAK, Evi. Finland, ?- .
20th-century violinist.
PAVLAKIS=p.272.

LILIENBERG, Davida Augusta
Hesse- see Hesse-Lilien-
berg, Davida Augusta

LILJEBLAD, Ingeborg. Helsinki,
Oct 17 1887-Feb 28 1942,
Helsinki. Soprano, voice
teacher. BAKER 5, THOMPSON.
*[THOMPSON=mezzo-soprano &
contralto]*

LIMA CRUZ, Maria Antonieta de.
Lisbon, Nov 3 1901-1957,
Lisbon?. Composer, musicolo-
gist. ENCI SALVAT, ENCY MUS.

LINCOLN, Marianne. London,
1822-Oct 6 1885, Sydenham,
England. Soprano. BROWN
BRIT.

LIND, Jenny (Johanna Maria,
later Jenny Lind Gold-
schmidt). Stockholm, Oct 6
1820-Nov 2 1887, Wynd's
Point, Malvern Wells, England. Soprano, voice tea-
cher. BAKER 1, BAKER 5,
BAKER 1971, BLOM, BROWN
BIO, *CLAYTON=p.461, *COO-
PER=p.151, CORTE, DICT MUS,
*ENCI MUS=illus.v.2 fac.
p.191, v.3 fac.p.14, *ENCI

SALVAT, *ENCY MUS, EWEN NEW,
GROVE 1, GROVE 1 APP, GROVE
5, GROVE 5 SUP, MARIZ, *MGG,
PRATT, RIEMANN, *SANDVED,
THOMPSON, *ULLSTEIN.

LINDBERG, Alie (Alexandra).
Åland, Finland, May 5 1849-
Mar 19 1933, Stockholm.
Pianist. GROVE 5.

LINDELHEIM, Joanna Maria (stage
name="The Baroness"). fl.
1703-17. German singer.
BLOM, GROVE 5, *HIGHFILL=
v.1 p.298.

LINDERMEYER, Elisabeth. Munich,
1925- . Soprano. KUTSCH.

LINDSAY, Julia. Paris, 1878-?.
Soprano. KUTSCH.

LINEVA, Evgenia Eduardovna
(Jewgenija Eduardowna Linowa,
born Papritz). Brest-Litowsk,
Russia, Jan 9 1854-Jan 24
1919, Moscow. Folksong col-
lector, writer. BAKER 5, ENCI
SALVAT, GROVE 5, MGG, RIE-
MANN=v.2 p.76, THOMPSON,
VODARSKY.

LING (De Hernando Belmori),
Dorothy (Evelyn). London,
Oct 27 1906- . Musicologist,
teacher, writer. GROVE 5.

LINKO-MALMIO, Liisa (Elina).
Kakisalmi, Finland, May 28
1918- . Soprano. GROVE 5.

LINLEY, Eliza(beth) Ann (Maid
of Bath). Bath, Sep 7 1754-
Jun 28 1792, Bristol. Soprano.
BLOM, BROWN BIO, BROWN BRIT,
ENCI MUS, ENCI SALVAT, ENCY
MUS, GROVE 1, GROVE 5, MGG,
*SANDVED, THOMPSON. *[GROVE 5
& MGG=b.Sep 5]*

LINLEY, Maria. Bath, Sep or
Oct 1763-Sep 5 1784, Bath.

Soprano. BLOM, BROWN BIO,
BROWN BRIT, ENCI MUS, ENCI
SALVAT, ENCY MUS, GROVE 1,
GROVE 5, MGG.

LINLEY, Mary (Mrs. Richard
Tickell). Bath, Jan 4 1758-
Jul 27 1787, Clifton, nr.
Bristol, England. Soprano.
BLOM, BROWN BIO, BROWN BRIT,
ENCI SALVAT, ENCY MUS, GROVE
1, GROVE 5, MGG. *[BROWN BIO=
b.1759; BROWN BRIT=b.1756
or 1759]*

LINOWA, Jewgenija Eduardowna
see Lineva, Evigenia
Eduardovna

LINWOOD, Mary. Birmingham?,
England, 1755-Mar 2 1845,
Leicester, England. Compo-
ser. BROWN BIO, BROWN BRIT.
[BROWN BIO=b.in Leicester]

LINZ VON KRIEGNER, Marta.
Budapest, Dec 22 1898- .
Violinist, composer.
RIEMANN.

LIPKOVSKA, Lydia Yakovlevna.
Babino, Khotin, Bessarabia,
Russia, May 10 1884-Jan 22
1955, Beirut. Soprano, voice
teacher. BAKER 5, ENCI MUS,
GROVE 5, GROVE 5 SUP, KUTSCH,
SANDVED, THOMPSON, VODARSKY.
*[KUTSCH=b.1882, d.Jan 23;
THOMPSON=b.c1887 in Poltava,
Russia; VODARSKY=b.1886 in
Poltava, Russia]*

LIPP, Maria Magdalena see
Haydn, Maria Magdalena

LIPP, Wilma. Vienna, Apr 26
1925- . Soprano. CORTE,
ENCI MUS, GROVE 5 SUP,
KUTSCH, RIEMANN, *ROSENTHAL=
illus.p.107, SANDVED, THOMP-
SON, *ULLSTEIN.

LIPPINCOTT, Joan. 20th-century

American organist, teacher.
PAVLAKIS=p.283.

LIPSIUS, Marie (pseud.=La Mara).
Leipzig, Dec 30 1837-Mar 2
1927, Rittergut Schmölen,
nr. Wurzen, Saxony. Writer.
BAKER 1, BAKER 5, BLOM=p.353,
CORTE=p.332, DICT MUS, ENCI
MUS, ENCI SALVAT=v.3 p.138,
ENCY MUS=v.3 p.17, GROVE 5,
MGG, PRATT, RIEMANN, THOMP-
SON, ULLSTEIN. *[GROVE 5=
d.in Leipzig]*

LIPTON, Martha. New York City,
Apr 6 1915- . Mezzo-soprano,
voice teacher. *EWEN LIV SUP,
EWEN NEW, *SANDVED, THOMPSON.
*[SANDVED=b.1919; THOMPSON=
b.Apr 16 1916, contralto]*

LISI, Anna Maria. Florence,
?-Jan 7 1726, Vienna. Singer,
court musician. ENCI MUS=
v.1 p.162 (in article on the
Badia family).

L'ISLE, Jeanne Marié de see
Marié de L'Isle, Jeanne

LISLEY, Mrs. see Barsanti,
Jane

LISSA, Zofia. Lwów, Poland,
Oct 19 1908- . Musicologist,
teacher, writer. BAKER 5,
DICT MUS, ENCI MUS, ENCI
SALVAT, ENCY MUS, GROVE 5,
RIEMANN, THOMPSON.

LISSMANN, Anna Marie (Mrs.
Heinrich Fritz, born Gutz-
schbach). 19th-century
German soprano. BAKER 1.

LIST, Carroll (Mrs. Eugene,
born Glenn). Chester, S.C.,
Oct 28 1924- . Violinist.
GROVE 5, PAVLAKIS=p.272,
THOMPSON=p.801.

LITTA, Marie (born Marie

Eugenia von Elsner). Bloom-
ington, Ind., Jul 7 1856-
Jul 7 1883, Bloomington,
Ind. Soprano. THOMPSON.
*[Death date supplied from
New York Times obituary,
Jul 8 1883, p.7, col.5]*

LITTLE, Vera. Memphis, Tenn.,
Dec 10 1928- . Contralto.
KUTSCH.

LITVINNE (Litvinova), Félia
(Feliya) Vasilyevna (real
name=Françoise-Jeanne
Schütz). St. Petersburg,
1861-Oct 12 1936, Paris.
Soprano, voice teacher.
BAKER 5, CELLETTI, CORTE,
ENCI MUS, ENCI SALVAT, ENCY
MUS, EWEN NEW, GROVE 5,
GROVE 5 SUP, KUTSCH, MARIZ,
PRATT, SANDVED, THOMPSON,
VODARSKY. *[MARIZ=b.1860;
PRATT=b.1860?; ENCI SALVAT &
ENCY MUS=b.1863, d.Sep 12]*

LITZ, Gisela. Hamburg, Dec 14
1922- . Singer. ULLSTEIN.

LIVERMORE, Ann (Lapraik; born
Mason). London, ?- . 19th-
century singer, musicolo-
gist. GROVE 5.

LIWANOWA, Tamara Nikolajewna.
Kischinew, Russia, Apr 18
1909- . Writer, teacher.
MGG.

LJUNGBERG, Göta Albertina.
Sundsvall, Sweden, Oct 4
1893-Jun 28 1955, Lidingö,
nr. Stockholm. Soprano,
voice teacher. BAKER 5,
ENCI MUS, *EWEN LIVING,
EWEN NEW, GROVE 5 SUP,
KUTSCH, RIEMANN, *SANDVED,
THOMPSON. *[KUTSCH=d.Jun 30]*

LLACER, Maria (Casali). Valencia, c1887-Jul 5 1962,
Madrid. Soprano, voice tea-

cher. CELLETTI, ENCI MUS,
KUTSCH. *[KUTSCH=b.1889]*

LLANOVER, Lady. Llandover,
Wales?, Mar 21 1802-Jan 17
1896, Llandover, Wales?.
Patron. BROWN BRIT.

LLEWELLYN, Louise see
Jarecki, Louise

LLINOS see Williams, Maria
Jane

LOBACZEWSKA, Stefania (born
Gérard de Festenbourg).
Lwów, Poland, Jul 31 1894-
Jan 16 1963, Cracow. Musi-
cologist, writer. DICT MUS,
ENCI SALVAT, ENCY MUS,
GROVE 5, MGG, RIEMANN. *[DICT
MUS=b.1888; RIEMANN=b.1891]*

LOCKWOOD, Miss. ?-Feb 1897,
Hanley, Staffordshire, England. Harpist. BROWN BRIT.

LOCKWOOD, Anna. Christchurch,
New Zealand, Jul 29 1939- .
Experimental and avant-garde
composer. BAKER 1971.

LODER, Kate Fanny (Lady Henry
Thompson). Bath, Aug 21 1825-
Aug 30 1904, Headley, Surrey.
Pianist, composer, opera
composer, teacher. BLOM,
BROWN BIO, BROWN BRIT,
GROVE 1, GROVE 5, PRATT.
*[BROWN BRIT & GROVE 1=
b.Aug 21 1826; BROWN BIO=
b.Aug 22 1826; PRATT=d.in
London]*

LOEW, Andrée Wachsmuth- see
Wachsmuth-Loew, Andrée

LÖWE, Johanna Sophie. Olden-
burg, Germany, Mar 24 1816-
Nov 28 1866, Pest, Hungary.
Soprano. BROWN BIO, *ENCI
MUS, GROVE 1, GROVE 1 APP,
GROVE 5, THOMPSON. *[BROWN
BIO=b.1815, d.Nov 29]*

LOEWE, Sophie. ?, 1848-1926,
?. Soprano. GROVE 5=v.5,
p.363 (brief mention in
article on aunt Johanna
Sophie Loewe).

LOEWENSON, Alice Jacob- see
Jacob-Loewenson, Alice

LÖWY, Pauline Metzler- see
Metzler-Löwy, Pauline

LOHMAN (Lohmann), Alwina
Valleria see Valleria,
Alwina

LOHMANN, Franziska see
Martienssen-Lohmann,
Franziska

LOHR, Ina. Amsterdam, Aug 1
1903- . Musicologist,
writer. RIEMANN.

LOHSE-KLAFSKY, Katharina see
Klafsky, Katharina

LOLLI, Dorotea. Bologna, ?-?.
18th-century singer.
ENCI MUS.

LOLLI, Nanette (Mrs. Antonio,
born Sauveur). 19th-century
French ballerina. ENCI MUS.

LOMANTO, Toti de Muro see
Dal Monte, Toti

LOMBARDINI, Maddalena see
Sirmen, Maddalena

LONG, Kathleen. Bury St.
Edmunds, Suffolk, England,
Jul 7 1896-Mar 20 1968,
Cambridge, England. Pianist,
piano teacher. GROVE 5,
GROVE 5 SUP, PALMER, SAND-
VED, THOMPSON. *[PALMER=b.in
Brentford, Middlesex. Death
date supplied from New York
Times obituary, Mar 22 1968,
p.47, col.3]*

LONG, Marguerite (Marie Char-
lotte). Nîmes, France, Nov 13
1874-Feb 13 1966, Paris.
Pianist, piano teacher,
writer. BAKER 5, BAKER 1971,
COOPER, DICT MUS, ENCI MUS,
ENCI SALVAT, ENCY MUS, GROVE
5, MARIZ, RIEMANN, SANDVED,
THOMPSON. *[ENCI MUS & RIE-
MANN=b.1878]*

LONG, Marie-Jeanne-Pauline.
Geneva, Aug 17 1885-Feb 14
1953, Geneva. Musicologist,
writer. ENCI SALVAT, ENCY
MUS, MGG, SCHUH.

LONGAS, Margherita see
Salvi, Margherita

LONGO, Miriam. Naples, May 12
1918- . Pianist. ENCI MUS,
ENCI SALVAT, ENCY MUS.

LOŇOVÁ, Maria see Hlouňová,
Marie

LOOSE, Emmy. Oustí nab Labem,
nr. Aussig, Bohemia, Jan 22
1920- . Soprano. ENCI MUS,
GROVE 5 SUP, KUTSCH, RIEMANN,
THOMPSON, ULLSTEIN. *[ENCI
MUS, KUTSCH, & ULLSTEIN=
b.1914]*

LÓPEZ, Brigida see Buchardo,
Brigida

LÓPEZ GARCÍA, Victoria see
De los Angeles, Victoria

LOPUSKA-WYLEZYŃSKA, Helena.
Warsaw, 1877-1920, Warsaw.
Pianist, composer. GROVE 5.

LORENGAR, Pilar. Zaragoza,
Spain, Jan 16 1928- .
Soprano, earlier mezzo-
soprano. ENCI SALVAT,
KUTSCH, *ULLSTEIN.

LORETO GARCÍA Y GARCÍA, Maria

de. Madrid, Dec 10 1799-May
5 1866, Paris. Voice tea-
cher. ENCI MUS=v.1 p.559
(brief mention in article
on Lorenza Correa).

LORIOD, Yvonne. Houilles,
Seine-et-Oise, France, Jan
20 1924- . Pianist, compo-
ser. BAKER 5, CORTE, ENCI
MUS, ENCI SALVAT, ENCY MUS,
GROVE 5, RIEMANN, THOMPSON,
ULLSTEIN.

LORKOVIĆ, Melita. Zupanja,
Croatia, Nov 25 1940- .
Pianist. RIEMANN.

LORTZING, Rosina (Mrs. Gustav
Albert, born Ahles). Bietig-
heim, nr. Stuttgart, Dec 8
1799-Jun 13 1854, ?. Violoncellist. ENCI MUS.

LOS ANGELES, María de see
Angeles, María Morales de
los

LOS ANGELES, Victoria de see
De los Angeles, Victoria

LOTTI, Santa Stella. 17th-
century Italian singer.
ENCI MUS.

LOTTI DELLA SANTA, Marcella.
Mantua, Sep 1831-Feb 9
1901, Paratico, Brescia,
Italy. Soprano. BROWN BIO,
ENCI MUS. [BROWN BIO=b.
Dec 23 1833]

LOUIS, Jenny see Viard,
Jenny

LOUS, Astrid. Kristiansund,
Norway, Apr 12 1876-?.
Mezzo-soprano. THOMPSON.

LOVE, Shirley. 20th-century
American mezzo-soprano.
PAVLAKIS=p.295.

LØVEBERG, Aase (born Nordmo).
Målselv, Norway, Jun 10 1923- .
Soprano. BAKER 5, KUTSCH=p.
310, SANDVED, THOMPSON=p.
1227.

LOVERIDGE, Iris. London, Apr
10 1917- . Pianist. GROVE 5,
PALMER, RIEMANN.

LOWTHIAN, Caroline (Mrs. Cyril
A. Prescott). 19th-century
English composer. BAKER 1,
BROWN BRIT.

LUART, Emma. Brussels, Aug 14
1892- . Soprano, voice
teacher. KUTSCH.

LUBIN, Germaine Léontine
Angélique. Paris, Feb 1
1890- . Soprano. BAKER 5,
CELLETTI, DICT MUS, ENCI
SALVAT, ENCY MUS, EWEN
LIVING, EWEN LIV SUP, EWEN
NEW, GROVE 5, GROVE 5 SUP,
KUTSCH, RIEMANN, SANDVED,
THOMPSON.

LUBOSCHUTZ, Genia see
Nemenoff, Genia

LUBOSCHUTZ, Léa (real name=
Luboshits). Odessa, Russia,
Feb 22 1885-Mar 18 1965,
Philadelphia. Violinist,
teacher. BAKER 5, BAKER 1971,
*EWEN LIVING, THOMPSON,
VODARSKY. [VODARSKY=b.1888]

LUCAS, Helen (Mrs. Charles,
born Taylor). ?-Mar 8 1866,
London. Soprano. BROWN BRIT.

LUCAS, Mary Anderson. London,
May 24 1882-Jan 14 1952,
London. Composer. BLOM,
BAKER 5, GROVE 5.

LUCCA, Giovannina (Mrs. Francesco, born Strazza). Fontanella, Cernobbio, 1814-Aug 19

1894, Fontanella, Cernobbio. Editor. ENCI MUS.

LUCCA, Pauline. Vienna, Apr 25 1841-Feb 28 1908, Vienna. Soprano, court musician. BAKER 1, BAKER 5, BLOM, BROWN BIO, CORTE, *ENCI MUS, ENCI SALVAT, ENCY MUS, EWEN NEW, GROVE 1, GROVE 1 APP, GROVE 5, MARIZ, MGG, PRATT, RIEMANN, SANDVED, THOMPSON, ULLSTEIN. *[BROWN BIO & GROVE 1 APP=b.Apr 26]*

LUCCHESINA, Maria Antonia Marchesini. fl.1737-39. English mezzo-soprano. · GROVE 1.

LUCOMBE, Emma see Reeves, Emma

LUDWIG, Christa. Berlin, Mar 16 1924- . Mezzo-soprano. BAKER 1971, BLOM, EWEN NEW, KUTSCH, RIEMANN, THOMPSON, *ULLSTEIN. *[BAKER 1971, KUTSCH, & ULLSTEIN=b.1928; RIEMANN & THOMPSON=b.1932; KUTSCH=contralto & mezzo-soprano]*

LÜBBECKE-JOB, Emma. Bonn, Jul 19 1888- . Pianist. RIEMANN.

LUEDER, Florence Pauline see Wickham, Florence Pauline

LÜTHI-WEGMANN, Elvira. Saronno, Italy, Sep 8 1896- . Singer. SCHUH.

LUKOMSKA, Halina. Warsaw, Apr 25 1924- . Soprano. ENCI MUS.

LUND, Josephine Amalie. Denmark?, 1829-1919, Denmark?. Contralto. ENCI MUS= v.4 p.621.

LUND, Signe. Christiania, Norway, Apr 15 1868-Apr 6 1950, Oslo. Composer. BAKER 5, BAKER 1971, BLOM, GROVE 5, GROVE 5 SUP, THOMPSON.

LUNN, Louise Kirkby- see Kirkby-Lunn, Louise

LUSSAN, Zélie de. Brooklyn, New York, Dec 21 1862-Dec 18 1949, London. Soprano. BAKER 1=p.652, BAKER 5, CELLETTI, COOPER, GROVE 5, GROVE 5 SUP, KUTSCH, PRATT, SANDVED, THOMPSON. *[KUTSCH=b.1861; BAKER 1, COOPER, PRATT, SAND-VED, & THOMPSON=b.1863; GROVE 5, KUTSCH, & SANDVED= mezzo-soprano]*

LUTYENS, Elisabeth Agnes. London, Jul 9 1906- . Composer. BAKER 5, BAKER 1971, BLOM, COOPER, CORTE, DICT MUS, ENCI MUS, ENCI SALVAT, ENCY MUS, GROVE 5, GROVE 5 SUP, MGG, PALMER, RIEMANN, SCHOLES, THOMPSON, ULLSTEIN, VINTON.

LUTZER, Jenny see Dingel-stedt, Jenny

LYMPANY, Moura. Saltash, Cornwall, England, Aug 18 1916- . Pianist. CORTE, *EWEN LIV SUP, GROVE 5, *PALMER=illus. p.188, RIEMANN, SANDVED, THOMPSON.

LYNE, Felice. Slater, Mo., Mar 28 1887-Sep 1 1935, Allentown, Pa. Soprano. BAKER 5, BLOM, SANDVED, THOMPSON. *[THOMPSON= b.1891]*

LYS, Edith de see De Lys, Edith

LYSTER, Jane see Barsanti, Jane

LYTE, Eve Maxwell- see
Maxwell-Lyte, Eve

M

MAAS, Marguerite Wilson.
Baltimore, Md., 1888- .
Pianist, piano teacher,
composer. THOMPSON.

MAAZEL, Mimi (Mrs. Lorin,
born Sandbanck). 20th-cen-
tury Brazilian pianist.
ENCI MUS.

MABEE, Grace Widney. Woodhull,
Ill., Sep 6 1875-?. Singer,
voice teacher. THOMPSON.

McARDEN, Joy (Jo Ijzenman).
Diemerburg, nr. Amsterdam,
Jan 16 1893-Apr 17 1952,
Birmingham, England. Soprano.
GROVE 5, GROVE 5 SUP.

MACBETH, Florence. Mankato,
Minn., Jan 12 1891- .
Soprano, voice teacher.
BAKER 5, KUTSCH, PRATT,
THOMPSON.

MacCARTHY, Maud. Clonmel,
Ireland, Jul 4 1882- .
Violinist, singer, lecturer.
GROVE 5, THOMPSON. [GROVE 5=
b.1884]

MACCHERINI, Giuseppina. Bologna, 1745-Sep 15 1825,
Bologna. Singer. GROVE 1.

MACCHI, Maria de. Peruzzaro,
Italy, 1870-Jan 16 1909,
Milan. Soprano. KUTSCH.

McCOLLIN, Frances. Philadelphia, Oct 24 1892-Feb 26
1960, Philadelphia. Composer, lecturer. REIS, THOMP-
SON=p.1311. [Death infor-
mation supplied from New
York Times obituary, Feb 27
1960, p.19, col.3]

McCORMIC, Mary. Belleville,
Ark., ?- . 20th-century
soprano. THOMPSON=p.1312.

McCRACKEN, Sandra see
Warfield, Sandra

MacDONALD, Jeanette. Philadelphia, Jun 18 1907-Jan 14
1965, Houston. Soprano,
actress. KUTSCH, *SANDVED,
THOMPSON.

McDONALD, Susann. Rock Island,
Ill., May 26 1935- . Harpist.
BAKER 1971=p.156, PAVLAKIS=
p.281.

MacDOWELL, Marian (Mrs. Edward
A., born Griswold Nevins).
New York City, Nov 22 1857-
Aug 23 1956, Los Angeles.
Pianist. ENCI MUS. [Dates in
entry based on New York Times
obituary, Aug 25 1956, p.15,
col.3]

Mac FARREN (Macfarren), Clara
Natalia (born Andrae). Lü-
beck, Germany, 1827-Apr 19
1916, Bakewell, Derbyshire,
England. Contralto, voice
teacher, writer. BAKER 1,
BROWN BIO=p.405 & 624, BROWN
BRIT, DICT MUS, ENCI MUS,
ENCY MUS, GROVE 1, GROVE 5,
PRATT, SCHOLES, THOMPSON.
[ENCY MUS=b.1828, d.Apr 9]

MACFARREN, Emma Marie Bennett
(Mrs. John, pen-name=Jules
Brissac). London, Jun 19
1824-Nov 9 1895, London.
Pianist, piano teacher,
composer, writer. BROWN BRIT.

MACFLEURAY, Clotilde. 19th-
century ballerina. ENCI MUS=
v.1 p.282 (in article on
François Adrien Boïeldieu).

McGILL, Josephine. Louisville,
Ky., Oct 20 1877-Feb 24 1919,

Louisville, Ky. Composer, folklorist, writer. BAKER 5, THOMPSON=p.1312.

MACHABEY, Emilienne (Mrs. Armand, born Ganeval). Paris, 1886- . Music publisher. ENCI MUS.

MacINTOSH, G. A. (pen-name= Claire Harris MacIntosh). Londonderry, Nova Scotia, 1882- . Composer. CBC.

MACINTYRE, Margaret. India, c1865-Apr 1943, London. Soprano. BLOM, BROWN BRIT, CBC, GROVE 5, THOMPSON.

McINTYRE, Margaret. England, 1905- . Composer. NAPIER.

MACIRONE, Clara Angela. London, Jan 20 1821-?. Composer, pianist, piano teacher. BAKER 1, BROWN BIO, BROWN BRIT, PRATT.

MACKENNA, Carmela. Santiago, Chile, Jul 31 1879- . Composer. SLONIMSKY.

MACKENZIE (M'Kenzie). Marian, Plymouth, England, ?-?. 19th-century contralto. BROWN BIO, BROWN BRIT.

MACKENZIE, Mary. 20th-century American contralto. SANDVED.

MACKEY, Erminia see Glover, Erminia

McLACHLAN, Jessie Niven (Mrs. Robert Buchanan). Oban, Scotland, Jun 18 1866-?. Soprano. BROWN BRIT.

McMURRAY, Mary. 20th-century American mezzo-soprano. SANDVED=p.822.

MACNAGHTEN, Anne Catherine.

Whitwick, Leicestershire, England, Aug 9 1908- . Violinist. GROVE 5, RIEMANN.

MACONCHY, Elizabeth. Broxbourne, England, Mar 19 1907- . Composer, opera composer. BAKER 5, BAKER 1971, BLOM, COOPER, DICT MUS, ENCI MUS, ENCI SALVAT, ENCY MUS, GROVE 5, GROVE 5 SUP, MGG, PALMER, RIEMANN, THOMPSON.

MADEIRA, Jean (born Browning). Centralia, Ill., Nov 14 1924-Jun 10 1972, Warwick Neck, R.I. Mezzo-soprano. BAKER 1971, BLOM, *EWEN LIVING, EWEN NEW, KUTSCH, *ROSENTHAL= illus.p.117, *SANDVED, THOMPSON. *[THOMPSON=b.1922]*

MADI, Emmy Fürsch- see Fürsch-Madi, Emmy

MADRIGUERA, Paquita. Igualda, nr. Barcelona, Sep 15 1900- . Pianist, composer. THOMPSON.

MAFFEI, Francesca Festa see Festa, Francesca

MAGELSSEN, Ida Basilier. Uleåborg, Finland, Sep 10 1846-May 23 1928, Hegra, Norway. Singer, voice teacher. THOMPSON.

MAGNETTI, Ermelinda. 20th-century Italian pianist. ENCI MUS=v.1 p.443 (brief mention in article on Domenico Ceccarossi).

MAGNUS, Sarah see Heinze, Sarah

MAGRINI, Giuseppina Finzi- see Finzi-Magrini, Giuseppina

MAHLKNECHT, Marie see Payne, Marie

MAHON see also Ambrose, Mrs.; Munday, Mrs.; Second, Mary (or Sarah)

MAHON, Miss M. (later Mrs. Warton). 18th-century English singer. GROVE 5.

MAID OF BATH see Linley, Eliza Ann

MAIER, Amanda see Röntgen, Amanda

MAILLARD, Marie-Thérèse. 18-19th-century French singer. ENCI MUS=v.1 p.253 (brief mention in article on the Berton family).

MAINVIELLE, Enrichetta. fl. 1846-49. German singer. GROVE 1=v.1 p.538 (in article on mother Joséphine Fodor-Mainvielle).

MAINVIELLE, Henriette see Fodor-Mainvielle, Henriette

MAINVIELLE, Joséphine see Fodor-Mainvielle, Joséphine

MAIRONI DA PONTE, Carlotta see Ponte, Carlotta Maironi da

MAJDAN, Hildegard Rössel- see Rössel-Majdan, Hildegard

MAKAROVA, Nina Vladimirovna. Yurin-on-Volga, Russia, Aug 12 1908- . Composer. BAKER 5, BLOM, ENCI MUS, GROVE 5, GROVE 5 SUP, THOMPSON, VODARSKY. [VODARSKY=b.1909]

MAKAS, Maxine. Ohio, ?- . 20th-century soprano. PAVLAKIS= p.289.

MAKEBA, Miriam. Prospect, nr. Johannesburg, Mar 4 1932- . Singer. BAKER 1971.

MALANIUK, Ira. Stanislau, Poland, Jan 29 1923- . Contralto. KUTSCH, SCHUH, ULLSTEIN.

MALANOTTE, Adelaide. Verona, 1785-Dec 31 1832, Brescia. Contralto. CORTE, ENCI MUS.

MALASPINA ALBITES, Marietta Gazzaniga see Gazzaniga Malaspina Albites, Marietta

MALCUZYNSKI, Colette (Mrs. Witold, born Gaveau). 20th-century pianist. ENCI MUS.

MALHOMME, Zofia see Klemensowska, Zofia

MALIBRAN, Maria Felicità (born Garcìa). Paris, Mar 24 1808-Sep 23 1836, Manchester, England. Contralto, soprano, pianist, composer. BAKER 1, BAKER 5, BLOM, BROWN BIO, *CLAYTON= p.330, CORTE, DICT MUS=v.1 p.385, *ENCI MUS=illus.fac. p.78&80, *ENCI SALVAT, *ENCY MUS, EWEN NEW, *GROVE 1, GROVE 5, GROVE 5 SUP, MARIZ, *MGG=v.4 col.1368, illus.fac. col.1313, PRATT, RIEMANN, SANDVED, SCHOLES=p.393, THOMPSON, *ULLSTEIN=p.187, 329, illus.p.329.

MALKIN, Beata. Odessa, Russia, Apr 1901-Sep 25 1973, New York City. Soprano, voice teacher. THOMPSON, VODARSKY. [Date and place of death based on obituary in Opera News, Jan 12 1974, p.27, which also gives 1891 as year of birth]

MALLINGER, Mathilde (orig.= Lichtenegger). Zagreb, Feb 17 1847-Apr 19 1920, Berlin. Soprano, voice teacher. BAKER 1, BAKER 5, BLOM, BROWN BIO, CORTE, ENCI MUS, EWEN NEW, GROVE 1 APP, GROVE 5, PRATT, RIEMANN, THOMPSON.

MALMIO, Liisa see Linko-
Malmio, Liisa

MALOZIOMOVA, Sofiya Andreyevna.
St. Petersburg, 1845-1908,
?. Pianist, piano teacher.
VODARSKY.

MALTEN, Therese (real name=
Müller). Insterburg, East
Prussia, Jun 21 1855-Jan 2
1930, Neuzschieren, nr.
Dresden. Soprano, actress.
BAKER 1, BAKER 5, BLOM,
ENCI MUS, GROVE 1 APP,
GROVE 5, MARIZ, MGG, PRATT,
RIEMANN, THOMPSON.

MALZEWA (Maltzeva), Katharine
(Ekaterina) Alexeivna
(Alekseyevna). St. Peters-
burg, Apr 26 1883- .
Musicologist, writer.
THOMPSON, VODARSKY.

MAMO-BORGHI, Erminia see
Borghi-Mamo, Erminia

MANA-ZUCCA (real name=Augusta
Zuckermann). New York City,
Dec 25 1890- . Pianist,
composer, soprano. BAKER 5,
BAKER 1971, MARIZ, SANDVED,
THOMPSON. [MARIZ=b.1891]

MANDAC, Evelyn. 20th-century
American soprano. PAVLAKIS=
p.289.

MANDIKIAN, Arda. Smyrna,
Greece, ?- . 20th-century
soprano. GROVE 5, GROVE 5
SUP.

MANDL, Camilla (Mrs. Richard,
born Barda). ?, 1822-1922,
?. Moravian (?) pianist,
piano teacher, writer.
ENCI MUS.

MANFREDINI GUARMANNI, Elisabetta. Bologna, 1790-?.
Soprano. ENCI MUS.

MANGERN, Elsa Laura Seeman von
see Wolzogen, Elsa Laura

MANGOLD, Charlotte. Darmstadt?,
1794-1876, Darmstadt?. Singer,
voice teacher. ENCI SALVAT,
ENCY MUS.

MANNA, Carolina see Bassi,
Carolina

MANNERS, Fanny see Moody,
Fanny

MANNES, Clara (Mrs. David,
born Damrosch). Breslau,
Silesia, Dec 12 1869-Mar 16
1948, New York City. Pia-
nist, administrator. BAKER
5, ENCI MUS, PRATT, RIEMANN,
THOMPSON.

MANNING, Kathleen Lockhart.
Nr. Hollywood, Calif., Oct 24
1890-Mar 20 1951, Los Angeles.
Composer, opera composer,
singer. BAKER 5, THOMPSON.

MANSFIELD, Louise Christine
(Mrs. Orlando Augustus, born
Jutz). Switzerland, ?-?.
19th-century pianist.
BROWN BRIT.

MANSKI, Dorothée. New York
City, Mar 11 1895-Feb 24
1967, Atlanta. Soprano,
voice teacher. BAKER 5,
BAKER 1971, *EWEN LIVING,
KUTSCH, RIEMANN, THOMPSON.

MANTELLI, Eugenia. Lisbon,
1860-Mar 3 1926, Lisbon.
Contralto, soprano, voice
teacher. KUTSCH, THOMPSON.
[THOMPSON=d. in Oporto]

MANZIARLY, Marcelle de.
Kharkov, Russia, Oct 13
1900- . Pianist, composer.
GROVE 5.

MARA, La see Lipsius, Marie

MARA, Gertrud Elisabeth (born
Schmeling). Kassel, Germany,
Feb 23 1749-Jan 20 1833,
Reval, Russia. Soprano,
voice teacher. BAKER 1,
BAKER 5, BROWN BIO, CLAYTON=
p.97, CORTE, DICT MUS, ENCI
MUS, ENCI SALVAT, ENCY MUS,
GROVE 1, GROVE 1 APP, GROVE
5, MARIZ, *MGG=illus.v.8
fac.col.1601, 1607, PRATT,
RIEMANN, THOMPSON, ULLSTEIN.

MARAGLIANO MORI, Rachele.
Casteggio, Pavia, Italy,
Jun 15 1894- . Mezzo-so-
prano, voice teacher. CORTE,
ENCI MUS, GROVE 5, GROVE 5
SUP.

MARCEL, Lucille (orig.=Was-
self; Mrs. Felix Paul von
Weingartner). New York City,
c1887-Jun 22 1921, Vienna.
Soprano. BAKER 5, ENCI MUS=
v.4 p.569, KUTSCH, PRATT,
RIEMANN=v.2 p.904, THOMPSON.

MARCEL-DUBOIS, Claudie. Tours,
France, Jan 19 1913- .
Ethnomusicologist, writer.
MGG, RIEMANN.

MARCH, Mary Ann Virginia see
Gabriel, Mary Ann Virginia

MARCHAND, Colette. Paris,
1925- . Dancer. RIEMANN.

MARCHAND, Marguerite see
Danzi, Margarete

MARCHESI DE CASTRONE, Blanche
(Baroness Andre Caccamisi).
Paris, Apr 4 1863-Dec 15
1940, London. Soprano, voice
teacher, violinist. BAKER 5,
BLOM, COOPER, CORTE, DICT
MUS, ENCI MUS, ENCI SALVAT,
ENCY MUS, GROVE 5, KUTSCH,
MGG, PRATT, RIEMANN, THOMP-
SON. [COOPER=b.1862; PRATT=
b.1864]

MARCHESI DE CASTRONE, Mathilde
(born Graumann). Frankfurt,
Mar 24 1821-Nov 17 1913,
London. Mezzo-soprano, voice
teacher, writer. BAKER 5,
BROWN BIO, COOPER, DICT MUS,
ENCI MUS, ENCI SALVAT, ENCY
MUS, EWEN NEW, GROVE 1,
GROVE 5, MARIZ, MGG, PRATT,
RIEMANN, THOMPSON, ULLSTEIN.
[BROWN BIO & GROVE 1=b.Mar
26 1826; ENCI SALVAT, ENCY
MUS, & MGG=b.Mar 26 1821,
d. Nov 18 1913; BROWN BIO=
soprano]

MARCHI, Giuliana. Milan, Aug
29 1925- . Pianist. ENCI MUS.

MARCHISIO, Barbara. Turin, Dec
6 1833-Apr 19 1919, Mira,
Italy. Contralto, voice tea-
cher. CORTE, *ENCI MUS=illus.
foll.p.103, ENCI SALVAT, ENCY
MUS, RIEMANN, THOMPSON.
[CORTE=b.1834; ENCY MUS=b.
Dec 12 1834]

MARCHISIO, Carlotta. Turin,
Dec 8 1835-Jun 28 1872,
Turin. Soprano. CORTE, *ENCI
MUS=illus.fac.p.103, ENCI
SALVAT ENCY MUS, RIEMANN,
THOMPSON. [ENCY MUS=b.Dec 6
1836]

MARCOLINI, Marietta. Florence,
?-?. 18th-century Italian
mezzo-soprano. CORTE, ENCI
MUS.

MARENGO, Isabel. Buenos Aires,
1897- . Soprano. ARIZAGA,
MARIZ.

MARESCHI, Giovanna de see
Cara, Giovanna

MARGULIES, Adele. Vienna, Mar
7 1863-Jun 6 1949, New York
City. Pianist, piano teacher.
PRATT, THOMPSON.

MARHER, Elfriede. Berlin,
1885- . Soprano. KUTSCH.

"MARIA, Darling" see
Kilpinen, Margarete

MARIA, Geltrude di see
Di Maria, Geltrude

MARIA ANTONIA WALPURGIS
(Electress of Saxony; pseud.=
E. T. P. A.=Ermelinda Talea
Pastorella Arcada). Munich,
Jul 18 1724-Apr 23 1780,
Dresden. Patron, librettist.
BAKER 5, BLOM, ENCI MUS,
ENCI SALVAT=v.4 p.551, ENCY
MUS, GROVE 5, GROVE 5 SUP,
*MGG, PRATT, RIEMANN, THOMP-
SON.

MARIA-PETRIS, Jolanda di.
Pola, Italy, Sep 5 1910- .
Soprano. RIEMANN.

MARIANI, Rosa. Cremona, 1799- .
Contralto. ENCI MUS.

MARIANI MASI, Maddalena. Flo-
rence, 1850-Sep 25 1916,
Erba, Italy. Soprano. ENCI
MUS.

MARIĆ, Ljubica. Kragujevac,
Serbia, Mar 18 1909- .
Composer. BAKER 1971, DICT
MUS, ENCI SALVAT, ENCY MUS,
GROVE 5, MGG, VINTON. *[DICT
MUS, ENCI SALVAT, ENCY MUS,
& MGG=b.Mar 5 1909]*

MARIÉ DE L'ISLE, Jeanne. Paris,
1872-1926, Paris. Contralto,
voice teacher. KUTSCH.

MARIMON, Marie. Paris, 1835?-?.
Soprano. GROVE 1 APP, PRATT,
THOMPSON. *[GROVE 1 APP=
b.1839 in Liège]*

MARINI, Antonia Raineri- see
Raineri-Marini, Antonia

MARINI, Clarice see Sinico,
Clarice

MARINI, Fanny Goldberg. 19th-
century Italian singer.
GROVE 5=v.3 p.698 (brief
mention in article on
brother Joseph Goldberg).

MARIÑO, Nibya. Montevideo,
Uruguay, Mar 23 1920- .
Pianist. GROVE 5.

MARIO, Queena (real name=
Tillotson). Akron, Ohio,
Aug 21 1896-May 28 1951,
New York City. Soprano,
voice teacher. BAKER 5,
*EWEN LIVING, EWEN LIV SUP,
EWEN NEW, KUTSCH, THOMPSON.
[KUTSCH=d.1952]

MARIX, Jeanne. Luxembourg,
Jan 22 1895-Mar 24 1939,
Paris. Musicologist, writer.
DICT MUS, ENCI SALVAT, ENCY
MUS, RIEMANN. *[RIEMANN=b.
1894, d.Feb 5 1939]*

MARIX-SPIRE, Thérèse. Nancy,
France, Feb 5 1898- . Critic,
writer. DICT MUS, ENCI SAL-
VAT, ENCY MUS, RIEMANN.
[RIEMANN=b.Feb 9]

MARK, Paula. ?, c1870-?. 19th-
century soprano. BAKER 1.

MARKOVA, Alicia (pseud. for
Alice Marks). London, 1910- .
Dancer. RIEMANN.

MARKOVA, Gali Enbaeff de.
Simbirsk, Russia, 1890- .
Mezzo-soprano, voice teacher.
VODARSKY.

MARKS, Alice see Markova,
Alicia

MARLOWE, Sylvia. New York City,
Sep 26 1908- . Harpsichordist,
teacher. PAVLAKIS=p.279,
*SANDVED, THOMPSON.

MARRIOTT, Annie Augusta. Nottingham, England, May 26

1859-?. Soprano. BROWN BIO, BROWN BRIT.

MARSCHNER, Marianne (Mrs. Heinrich, born Wohlbrück). Dresden, 1826-1854, Dresden?. Singer. ENCI MUS.

MARSH, Jane. 20th-century American soprano. PAVLAKIS= p.289.

MARSH, Lucille see Crews, Lucille

MARSH, Lucy Isabelle. Ithaca, New York, Apr 10 1878-Jan 20 1956, Providence, R.I. Soprano, voice teacher. KUTSCH.

MARSHALL, Florence A. (Mrs. Julian, born Thomas). Rome, Mar 30 1843-?. Composer, conductor, writer. BROWN BIO, BROWN BRIT.

MARSHALL, Lois. Toronto, 1928?- . Soprano. KUTSCH, PAVLAKIS=p.289, THOMPSON.

MARSHALL, Mrs. William. 19th-century English composer. BROWN BRIT.

MARTENOT, Ginette (Geneviève). Paris, Jan 27 1902- . Ondes Martenot player. ENCI MUS= v.3 p.306 (in article on the ondes Martenot), ENCY MUS.

MARTI, Katharina. Grafenried, Bern, Switzerland. Feb 26 1917- . Singer, voice teacher. SCHUH.

MARTIENSSEN-LOHMANN, Franziska (born Meyer-Estorf). Bromberg, Germany, Oct 6 1887-Feb 2 1971, Düsseldorf. Singer, voice teacher, writer. DICT MUS, ENCI MUS, ULLSTEIN.

MARTIN, Amy Florence. 19-20th-century English contralto. BROWN BRIT.

MARTIN, Jenny see Viard, Jenny

MARTINELLI, Caterina ("La Romanina" or "Caterinuccia"). Rome, 1590-Mar 9 1608, Mantua. Singer. ENCI MUS, GROVE 5= v.3 p.542 (brief mention in article on Marco da Gagliano).

MARTINEZ, Alicia see Alonso, Alicia

MARTINEZ (Martines), Marianne de (von; born Anna Katharina). Vienna, May 4 1744-Dec 13 1812, Vienna. Amateur singer, composer, pianist. BAKER 1, BAKER 5, BLOM, CORTE, ENCI SALVAT, ENCY MUS, GROVE 1, GROVE 5, MGG, PRATT, RIEMANN, THOMPSON.

MARTINIS, Carla. Danculovice, Yugoslavia, 1924- . Soprano. KUTSCH.

MARTINO, Adriana. Aversa, Caserta, Italy, Jul 26 1931- . Soprano. ENCI MUS.

MARTINO, Miranda. 20th-century Italian singer. ENCI MUS.

MARTTINEN, Sinikka see Kuula-Marttinen, Sinikka

MARTYN, Eliza see Inverarity, Eliza

MARTZY, Johanna. Temesvár, Hungary, Oct 26 1924- . Violinist. BLOM, CORTE, ENCI MUS, RIEMANN, *SANDVED, SCHUH, THOMPSON, *ULLSTEIN.

MARUNOWICZ, Francizka see Pierozyńska, Franciszka

MARZORATI, Lucia (later Romanini). Chiusi, Italy, Jan 13 1929- . Teacher. ENCI MUS.

MASI, Maddalena Mariani see Mariani Masi, Maddalena

MASON, Ann see Livermore, Ann

MASON, Edith Barnes. St. Louis, Mo., Mar 22 1893-Nov 26 1973, San Diego, Calif. Soprano. KUTSCH, PRATT, THOMPSON. *[PRATT=b.1892]*

MASON, Marilyn. ?, 1929- . American organist, teacher. PAVLAKIS=p.283.

MASSART, Louise-Aglaë (born Masson). Paris, Jun 10 1827- Jul 26 1887, Paris. Pianist, piano teacher. BAKER 1=p.382 (in article on husband Lambert-Joseph Massart), DICT MUS.

MASSARY, Fritzi (orig.=Friederike Massaryk, later Mrs. Pallenberg). Vienna, Mar 31 1882-Jan 31 1969, Beverly Hills, Calif. Soprano. KUTSCH, RIEMANN.

MASSEY, Céleste see Heckscher, Céleste de Longpré

MASSON, Elizabeth. Scotland, 1806-Jan 9 1865, London. Contralto, voice teacher, composer, editor, teacher. BROWN BRIT, GROVE 1 APP, THOMPSON.

MASSON, Louise-Aglaë see Massart, Louise-Aglaë

MASSON, Renée-Madeleine (born Girardon). Cherbourg, France, Jan 20 1912- . Music librarian, writer. ENCI SALVAT, ENCY MUS, MGG=v.5 col.164.

MATERNA, Amalie. St.Georgen,

Steiermark, Austria, Jul 10 1844-Jan 18 1918, Vienna. Soprano, voice teacher. BAKER 1, BAKER 5, BLOM, BROWN BIO, CORTE, ENCI MUS, ENCI SALVAT, ENCY MUS, EWEN NEW, GROVE 1, GROVE 1 APP, GROVE 5, MARIZ, MGG, PRATT, RIEMANN, SANDVED, THOMPSON, ULLSTEIN. *[CORTE, ENCI SALVAT, MGG, & PRATT=b.1845; BAKER 1 & BROWN BIO=b.1847]*

MATERNA, Hedwig. Graz, 1871-?. Soprano, writer. PRATT.

MATHIS, Edith. Lucerne, Feb 11 1938- . Soprano. BAKER 1971, KUTSCH, SCHUH=p.421, *ULLSTEIN. [KUTSCH=b.1933]*

MATTEI, Colomba. fl.1754-60. Singer. GROVE 1.

MATTFELD, Marie. Munich, c1870-Sep 18 1927, USA?. Mezzo-soprano. THOMPSON.

MATTHAY, Jessie (Mrs. Tobias Augustus, born Kennedy). 19-20th-century Scottish (?) singer. BROWN BRIT.

MATTHEWS, Anna Isabella see Stapleton, Anna Isabella

MATTHEWS, Eileen see Ralf, Eileen

MATTHEWS, Julia. London, 1843- May 19 1876, St. Louis, Mo. Soprano, actress. BROWN BRIT. *[BROWN BRIT=b.Australia, d. New York City. Entry based on New York Times obituary, May 21 1876, p.6, col.7]*

MATTHIEUX, Johanna see Kinkel, Johanna

MATTHISON-HANSEN, Nanny. Roskilde, Denmark, Feb 26 1830- Jul 13 1915, Copenhagen. Pianist, composer. MGG.

MATUROVÁ, Růžena. Prague,
Sep 2 1869-Feb 25 1938,
Prague. Soprano. GROVE 5.

MATZENAUER, Margarete.
Temesvár, Hungary, Jun 1
1881-May 19 1963, Van Nuys,
Calif. Soprano, contralto,
voice teacher. BAKER 5,
BAKER 1971, CELLETTI, ENCI
MUS, *EWEN LIVING, EWEN LIV
SUP, EWEN NEW, GROVE 5,
GROVE 5 SUP, KUTSCH, MARIZ,
PRATT, RIEMANN, SANDVED,
THOMPSON. [MARIZ=mezzo-
soprano]

MAUBOURG-GOFFAUX, Jeanne.
Namur, Belgium, Nov 10
1875-?. Mezzo-soprano,
soprano, voice teacher.
PRATT, THOMPSON.

MAUPIN, Madame (born d'Aubigny). Marseilles?, c1673-
1707, Paris. Soprano. CLAY-
TON=p.46, ENCI SALVAT, ENCY
MUS. [CLAYTON=b.in Paris]

MAURE, Catherine Nicole le
see Le Maure, Catherine
Nicole

MAURI ARGILAGÓ, Rosita. Reus,
France, Dec 6 1855-1923,
Paris. Dancer. *ENCI SALVAT.

MAURICE, Paule. Paris, Sep 29
1910- . Composer, teacher.
ENCY MUS.

MAUSCH, Mariella see Wil-
helmj, Mariella

MAXWELL-LYTE, Eve. London,
Apr 25 1908-Aug 1955, nr.
Grenoble. Singer, actress.
GROVE 5.

MAY, Florence. London, Feb 6
1845-Jun 29 1923, London.
Pianist, writer, composer.
BAKER 5, BROWN BRIT, GROVE

5, GROVE 5 SUP, RIEMANN,
THOMPSON.

MAYER, Lady see Moulton,
Dorothy

MAYER, Eugenie see García,
Eugenie

MAYER, Marie. Graz, Dec 8 1838-
Dec 3 1882, Stuttgart. Soprano. ENCI MUS=v.2 p.254
(brief mention in article
on son Theodor Bertram).

MAYERHOFER, Elfie. Marburg an
der Drau, Austria, Mar 15
1923- . Soprano. RIEMANN.

MAYNOR, Dorothy. Norfolk, Va.,
Sep 3 1910- . Soprano.
BAKER 5, *EWEN LIVING, EWEN
LIV SUP, GROVE 5, KUTSCH,
MARIZ, RIEMANN, *SANDVED,
THOMPSON.

MAZZOLENI, Ester. Sebenico,
Dalmatia, Mar 12 1883- .
Soprano. *CELLETTI=illus.
foll.col.224, ENCI MUS,
KUTSCH. [KUTSCH=b.1884]

MAZZUCATO, Elisa. 19th-century
Italian opera composer.
ENCI MUS.

MC filed as MAC

MEAD, Olive. Cambridge, Mass.,
Nov 22 1874-Feb 27 1946, New
York City. Violinist. BAKER
1, PRATT, THOMPSON.

MEADOWS WHITE, Alice see
Smith, Alice Mary

MECHETTI, Therese. ?, 1788-
Jun 28 1855, Vienna. Music
publisher. MGG.

MECK, Nadeschda Filaretowna
von (born Frolowskij).
Snamenskoje, nr. Smolensk,

Feb 10 1831-Jan 31 1894,
Wiesbaden. Patron. BAKER 5,
RIEMANN, *SANDVED=illus.
only p.1363, THOMPSON.

MEDINA, Maria see Viganò,
Maria Medina

MEERTI, Elisa see Blaes,
Elisa

MEHLIG, Anna (later Falk).
Stuttgart, Jul 11 1843-
Jul 16 1928, Berlin. Pia-
nist. BAKER 1, BROWN BIO,
GROVE 1, GROVE 1 APP, GROVE
5, PRATT, RIEMANN, THOMPSON.
*[BAKER 1=b.Jun 11 1843;
BROWN BIO=b.Jun 11 1846;
THOMPSON=b.Jul 11 1843;
GROVE 1 & RIEMANN=b.Jul 11
1846; RIEMANN=d.Jul 26 1928]*

MEICHIK, Anna. St. Petersburg,
1878-1934, New York City.
Contralto, voice teacher.
VODARSKY.

MEIERHOFER, Wilhelmine see
Keller, Wilhelmine

MEI-FIGNER, Medea Ivanovna.
Florence, Mar 4 1859-Jul 16
1952, Paris. Soprano. CEL-
LETTI, ENCI MUS=v.2 p.193,
ENCY MUS=v.2 p.57, GROVE 5=
v.3 p.89, GROVE 5 SUP=p.130,
*SANDVED=p.447. *[ENCY MUS=
b.Apr 4 1859; CELLETTI,
ENCI MUS, ENCY MUS, & GROVE
5 SUP=d.Jul 8 1952]*

MEISLE, Kathryn. Philadelphia,
Oct 12 1899-Jan 17 1970, New
York City. Contralto. BAKER
5, *EWEN LIVING, KUTSCH,
THOMPSON.

MEISTER, Elsa Scherz- see
Scherz-Meister, Elsa

MELANDER, Stina Britt. Stockholm, Jun 12 1924- . Soprano. KUTSCH.

MELBA, Nellie (stage name of
Mrs. Helen Porter Armstrong,
born Mitchell). Richmond,
nr. Melbourne, May 19 1861-
Feb 23 1931, Sydney. Soprano.
BAKER 1, BAKER 5, BAKER 1971,
BROWN BRIT=p.13, *CELLETTI=
illus.fac.col.608, *COOPER,
CORTE, DICT MUS, ENCI MUS,
ENCI SALVAT, ENCY MUS, EWEN
NEW, GROVE 5, GROVE 5 SUP,
KUTSCH, MARIZ, MGG, PRATT,
RIEMANN, *SANDVED, SCHOLES,
THOMPSON, ULLSTEIN. *[COOPER,
ENCI SALVAT, EWEN NEW, &
THOMPSON=b.1859; BAKER 1=
b.1865; ENCI SALVAT & ENCY
MUS=d.Mar 23 1931; CORTE,
ENCI MUS, RIEMANN, & ULL-
STEIN=b.in Burnley, nr. Mel-
bourne]*

MELBA PONZILLO, Rosa see
Ponselle, Rosa

MEL-BONIS see Bonis, Melanie

MELCHERS, Henriette (Mrs.
Henrik Melcher, born Hartog).
20th-century Swedish pianist.
ENCI MUS.

MELCY, Contessa see Grisi,
Giulia

MELINI (Mellini), Grazia.
?, 1720-Feb 16 1781, Copenhagen. Singer. ENCI MUS=
v.4 p.128 (in article on
Paolo Scalabrini).

MELIS, Carmen. Cagliari, Sardinia, Aug 14 1885-Dec 19
1967, Longone al Segrino,
Italy. Soprano, voice teacher. BAKER 5, BAKER 1971,
CELLETTI, *ENCI MUS=illus.
fac.p.139, KUTSCH, PRATT,
THOMPSON. *[ENCI MUS=b.
Aug 16]*

MELLER, Clara (Mrs. Hermann
Kretzschmar). Clifton,
Bristol, England, Feb 3 .

1856-?. Pianist. BROWN
BRIT.

MELLINI, Grazia see Melini,
Grazia   .

MENDELSSOHN, Fanny see
Hensel, Fanny Cäcilia

MENDI, Antonia Sitcher de
see Hubert, Antonia

MENEGATTI, Carla see
Fracci, Carla

MENEGHEL, Antonietta see
Dal Monte, Toti

MENEGHINI CALLAS, Maria see
Callas, Maria Meneghini

MENGES, Isolde. Hove, England,
May 16 1893- . Violinist,
teacher. BAKER 5, *EWEN
LIVING, GROVE 5, PALMER,
PRATT, THOMPSON. [EWEN
LIVING & PRATT=b.1894 in
Brighton, England]

MENGOZZI, Anna see Benini,
Anna

MENOTTI, Tatiana. Boston,
Jun 24 1911- . Soprano.
KUTSCH.   ·

MENTER, Sophie (Mrs. David
Popper). Munich, Jul 29
1846-Feb 23 1918, Stockdorf,
nr. Munich. Pianist, piano
teacher, composer. BAKER 1,
BAKER 5, BLOM, BROWN BIO,
ENCI MUS=v.3 p.472, ENCI
SALVAT, GROVE 1=v.3 p.16,
GROVE 1 APP, GROVE 5, THOMP-
SON. [BAKER 1, BLOM, & BROWN
BIO=b.1848]

MENUHIN, Hephzibah. San Francisco, May 20 1920- . Pianist. BAKER 5, CORTE, DICT
MUS, ENCI MUS, SANDVED.

MENUHIN, Yaltah. 20th-century
American pianist. SANDVED.

MEO, Cléonine de. Paris, 1904-
Aug 1930, Paris. Soprano.
KUTSCH.

MERCANTINI, Giuseppina see
De Filippi, Giuseppina

MERCÉ, Antonia see Argen-
tina, La

MEREST, Mrs. see Hawes, Maria

MÉRIC-LALANDE, Henriette (Clémentine) see Lalande,
Henriette Clémentine

MERIGHI, Antonia. 18th-century
Italian contralto. BLOM,
GROVE 1, GROVE 5, THOMPSON.

MÉRÖ-IRION, Yolanda. Pest,
Hungary, Aug 30 1887-Oct 17
1963, New York City. Pianist.
BAKER 5, BAKER 1971, PRATT,
THOMPSON.

MERREM-NIKISCH, Grete. Düren,
Germany, Jul 7 1887- .
Soprano. KUTSCH.

MERRIMAN, Nan (Katherine-Ann).
Pittsburgh, Apr 28 1920- .
Mezzo-soprano. BAKER 1971,
BLOM, KUTSCH, PAVLAKIS=
p.295, *ROSENTHAL=illus.
p.117, *SANDVED, THOMPSON,
ULLSTEIN. [KUTSCH=contralto]

MESSAGER, Dotie see Temple,
Hope

METCALFE, Susan. ?, 1884?- .
Contralto. KUTSCH.

METZGER-LATTERMANN, Ottilie.
Frankfurt, Jul 15 1878-Feb
1943, Auschwitz prison camp,
Poland. Contralto, voice
teacher. KUTSCH, PRATT,

THOMPSON. *[THOMPSON=b.Jun
15 1878, d.in Terezin
(Theresienstadt), Bohemia]*

METZGER-VESPERMANN, Klara.
?, 1799-1827, ?. German
singer. ENCI MUS=v.4 p.585
(brief mention in article
on teacher Peter von Winter).

METZLER-LÖWY, Pauline. Terezin (Theresienstadt), Bohemia, 1850?-?. Contralto.
BAKER 1.

MEUNIEZ, Rose Lucille see
Caron, Rose Lucille

MEYER, Berta see Morena,
Berta

MEYER, Cora Canne see Canne
Meyer, Cora

MEYER, Jenny. Berlin, Mar 26
1834-Jul 20 1894, Berlin.
Contralto, voice teacher,
administrator. BAKER 1,
PRATT.

MEYER, Kerstin. Stockholm,
Apr 3 1928- . Contralto.
KUTSCH, *SANDVED, THOMPSON,
*ULLSTEIN. *[SANDVED=mezzo-
soprano]*

MEYER, Marcelle. Lille, France,
May 22 1897-Nov 17 or 18
1958, Paris. Pianist. CORTE,
ENCI SALVAT, ENCY MUS.

MEYER, Stekler see Krump-
holtz, Stekler

MEYER-BAER, Kathi. Berlin,
Jul 27 1892- . Musicologist,
music librarian, critic,
editor, teacher, writer.
BAKER 5, BAKER 1971, GROVE
5, RIEMANN, THOMPSON.

MEYER-ESTORF, Franziska see
Martienssen-Lohmann, Franziska

MEZARI, Maddalena (called La
Casulana). Vicenza, Italy,
c1540-?. Composer. ENCI
MUS=v.1 p.433, GROVE 5, MGG,
THOMPSON.

MICELLI, Caterina. 18th-century
Italian soprano. ENCI MUS.

MICHAELI (Michal), Louise.
Stockholm, 1830-1875, Stockholm. Soprano. PRATT.

MICHAELIS, Ruth. Posen, Prussia,
Feb 27 1909- . Contralto,
voice teacher. KUTSCH, RIE-
MANN, ULLSTEIN.

MICHAELS, Ilse Fromm- see
Fromm-Michaels, Ilse

MICHAÏLOWA, Maria (orig.=Maria
van Puteren). Kharkov, Russia, 1864-?. Soprano. KUTSCH.

MICHAL, Louise see Michaeli,
Louise

MICHALESI, Aloysia see Krebs,
Aloysia

MICHALSKY, Anne. Prague, Jul
19 1908- . Soprano, voice
teacher. KUTSCH.

MICHEAU, Janine. Toulouse,
Apr 17 1914- . Soprano.
ENCI MUS, ENCI SALVAT, ENCY
MUS, GROVE 5, GROVE 5 SUP,
KUTSCH, RIEMANN. *[ENCI MUS,
ENCI SALVAT, & ENCY MUS=
b.Jan 16 1914]*

MICHELI, Mary Ann de see
De Micheli, Mary Ann

MIDGLEY, Henrietta (Mrs.
Samuel, born Tomlinson).
19th-century English soprano.
BROWN BRIT.

MIELKE, Antonia. Berlin, c1852-
Nov 15 1907, Berlin. Soprano,
voice teacher. BAKER 5, PRATT.

MIÈRE, Marie-Jeanne le see
Larrivée, Marie-Jeanne

MIGLIETTI, Adrienne. Geneva,
Jul 22 1918- . Soprano.
SCHUH.

MIGNON, Amalia see Hauk,
Minnie

MIHACSEK, Felicie Hüni- see
Hüni-Mihacsek, Felicie

MIHALOVICI, Monique see
Haas, Monique

MIKLASHEVSKAYA (Speilberg),
Irina (Irma Sergeyevna).
Moscow, 1883- . Pianist.
VODARSKY.

MIKLASZEWICZ, Antonia see
Campi, Antonia

MIKORSKA, Ludmila Jeske-
Choińska see Jeske-Choiń-
ska-Mikorska, Ludmila

MIKUSCH, Margarethe von.
Baydorf, Austria, 1884-?.
Composer. PRATT. ·

MILANOLLO, Domenica Maria
Teresa. Savigliano, nr.
Turin, Aug 28 1827-Oct 25
1904, Paris. Violinist,
composer. BAKER 1, BLOM,
BROWN BIO, CORTE, *ENCI
MUS=illus.fac.p.183, GROVE
1, GROVE 1 APP, GROVE 5,
PRATT, RIEMANN.

MILANOLLO, Maria. Savigliano,
nr. Turin, Jul 19 1832-Oct
21 1848, Paris. Violinist.
BAKER 1, BLOM, BROWN BIO,
CORTE, *ENCI MUS=illus.fac.
p.183, GROVE 1, GROVE 1
APP, GROVE 5, PRATT, RIE-
MANN. [BROWN BIO, ENCI MUS,
& GROVE 1 APP=b.Jun 19]

MILANOLLO, Teresa see

Milanollo, Domenico Maria
Teresa

MILANOV, Zinka (orig.=Kunc).
Zagreb, May 17 1906- .
Soprano, voice teacher,
writer. BAKER 5, BLOM, CEL-
LETTI, ENCI MUS, *EWEN LIVING,
EWEN LIV SUP, EWEN NEW, GROVE
5 SUP, KUTSCH, MARIZ, PAVLA-
KIS=p.289, RIEMANN, *ROSEN-
THAL=illus.p.119, *SANDVED,
THOMPSON, ULLSTEIN. [MARIZ=
b.1908]

MILDE, Rosa (born Agthe). Wei-
mar, Jun 25 1827-Jan 26 1906,
Weimar. Soprano. ENCI MUS,
PRATT, RIEMANN.

MILDENBURG, Anna von see
Bahr-Mildenburg, Anna

MILDER-HAUPTMANN, Pauline
Anna (born Milder). Constan-
tinople, Dec 13 1785-May 29
1838, Berlin. Soprano, act-
ress. BAKER 1, BAKER 5,
BLOM, BROWN BIO, ENCI MUS,
ENCI SALVAT, ENCY MUS, EWEN
NEW, GROVE 1, GROVE 5,
GROVE 5 SUP, MARIZ, *MGG,
PRATT, RIEMANN, THOMPSON,
ULLSTEIN.

MILDMAY, Audrey (Mrs. John
Christie). Hurstmonceaux,
Sussex, Dec 19 1900-May 31
1953, London. Soprano,
administrator. BLOM, EWEN
NEW, GROVE 5=v.3 p.684 (in
article on Glyndebourne),
KUTSCH, THOMPSON=p.398.
[KUTSCH=b.in Vancouver,
d.in Glyndebourne]

MILDNER, Poldi (Leopoldine).
Vienna, Jul 27 1915- .
Pianist. BAKER 5, *EWEN
LIVING, THOMPSON. [EWEN
LIVING=b.1916]

MILETTE, Juliette. Montréal,

Jun 17 1900- . Composer, teacher. CBC.

MILINKOVIĆ, Georgine von (later Hassinger). Prague, Jul 7 1913- . Contralto. KUTSCH, RIEMANN, *ROSEN-THAL=illus.p.118-119.

MILKINA, Nina. Moscow, 1919- . Pianist. PALMER.

MILLAR, Marian. Manchester, England, ?-?. 19th-century pianist, piano teacher, teacher, writer. BROWN BRIT.

MILLARD, Mrs. Philip. 19th-century English composer. BROWN BRIT.

MILLE, Agnes de see De Mille, Agnes

MILLER, Agnes Elizabeth. Brierley Hill, Staffordshire, England, Apr 20 1857-?. Pianist, piano teacher. BROWN BRIT.

MILLER, Elizabeth see Baker, Elizabeth

MILLER, Marie Élisabeth Anne see Gardel, Marie Élisabeth Anne

MILLER, Mildred. Cleveland, Ohio, Dec 16 1924- . Mezzo-soprano. BAKER 5, PAVLAKIS=p.295, *SANDVED, THOMPSON. *[BAKER 5=soprano]*

MILLIGAN, Charlotte see Fox, Charlotte

MILLS, Miss see Brown, Mrs. J.

MILLS, Eleanor see Chalmers, Eleanor

MILLS, Isabella see Vincent, Isabella

MILON, Marie Jeanne see Trial, Marie Jeanne

MINGHETTI, Lisa. Vienna, Oct 17 1912- . Violinist. GROVE 5.

MINGHINI-CATTANEO, Irene. Nr. Ravenna, Italy, Apr 12 1892-Mar 24 1944, Rimini, Italy. Contralto. KUTSCH.

MINGOTTI, Regina Caterina (born Valentini). Naples, Feb 6 1722-Oct 1 1808, Neuburg, Bavaria. Soprano. BAKER 1, BLOM, BROWN BIO, CLAYTON= p.63, CORTE, DICT MUS, *ENCI MUS=illus.fac.p.186, ENCI SALVAT, ENCY MUS, GROVE 1, GROVE 5, PRATT, RIEMANN, THOMPSON. *[PRATT=b.1721; ENCI SALVAT & RIEMANN=b. Feb 16 1722; BAKER 1, BROWN BIO, & GROVE 5=b.1728; BROWN BIO & GROVE 5=d.1807]*

MIOLAN, Félix see Carvalho, Caroline

MITCHELL, Frederica. 19th-century Australian soprano. BROWN BRIT=p.13 (in article on sister Helen Porter Armstrong [Nellie Melba]).

MITCHELL, Helen Porter see Melba, Nellie

MITCHELL, Marjorie. 20th-century American pianist. PAVLAKIS=p.265, *SANDVED.

MITCHELL, Viola. Pittsburgh, Pa., Jul 11 1911- . Violinist. *EWEN LIVING.

MIURA, Tamaki. Tokyo, Feb 22 1884-May 26 1946, Tokyo. Soprano. KUTSCH, THOMPSON. *[THOMPSON=d.May 25 1946]*

MOBERG, Ida (Georgina). Helsinki, Feb 13 1859-Aug 2 1947, Helsinki. Composer, opera composer. GROVE 5.

MOCKE, Marie-Félicité-Denise see Pleyel, Marie-Félicité-Denise

MOCKEL, Johanna see Kinkel, Johanna

MÖDL, Martha. Nürnberg, Mar 22 1912- . Soprano. BLOM, CELLETTI, CORTE, ENCI MUS, ENCI SALVAT, ENCY MUS, EWEN NEW, GROVE 5 SUP, KUTSCH, RIEMANN, *ROSENTHAL=illus. p.120, *ULLSTEIN. *[ENCI MUS, ENCI SALVAT, & ENCY MUS=b. Mar 25 1912; KUTSCH, RIEMANN & ULLSTEIN=b.Mar 22 1913; ENCI MUS=mezzo-soprano & soprano]*

MOFFO, Anna. Wayne, Pa., Jun 27 1932- . Soprano. BAKER 1971, BLOM, CELLETTI, ENCI MUS, EWEN NEW, KUTSCH, PAV-LAKIS=p.289, *SANDVED, THOMPSON, ULLSTEIN. *[KUTSCH= b.1933; BLOM, EWEN NEW, & THOMPSON=b.1934; CELLETTI, ENCI MUS, & ULLSTEIN=b.1935]*

MOGFORD, Anne see Fricker, Anne

MOIR, Eleanor (Mrs. Frank Lewis, born Farnol). 19th-century English soprano. BROWN BRIT.

MOKE, Marie-Félicité-Denise see Pleyel, Marie-Félicité-Denise

MOKRZYCKA, Maria see Moscisca, Maria

MOLESWORTH, Lady (Mrs. William, and earlier Mrs. Temple West, born Carstairs; stage name= Miss Grant). England?, c1810-May 16 1888, England?. Soprano. BROWN BRIT.

MOLTENI, Benedetta Emilia see Agricola, Benedetta Emilia

MOMBELLI, Anna. Milan, 1795-?. Singer. ENCI MUS.

MOMBELLI, Ester. Bologna, 1794-?. Singer. ENCI MUS.

MOMBELLI, Luisa (later Laschi). Florence, ?-c1789, ?. Singer. ENCI MUS.

MOMBELLI, Vincenza (later Viganò). 18th-century Italian dancer. ENCI MUS.

MONATH, Hortense (born Husseri). Newark, N.J., 1904-May 20 1956, New York City. Pianist. *EWEN LIVING, EWEN LIV SUP. *[Dates in entry based on New York Times obituary, May 22 1956, p.33, col.2]*

MONBELLI, Marie. Cadiz, Feb 13 1843-?. Soprano. BAKER 1.

MONDOLFI, Anna. Pisa, Jul 13 1907- . Musicologist, pianist, piano teacher, writer. ENCI MUS, MGG.

MONHAUPT, Klara see Klein-michel, Klara

MONROE, Lucy. 20th-century American soprano. *EWEN LIVING.

MONTAGNEY, Marguerite-Joséphine Desirée see Artôt, Marguerite-Joséphine-Desirée

MONTE, Toti Dal see Dal Monte, Toti

MONTÈGRE, Gabriella Colombari de see Ferrari, Gabriella

MONTES, Lola Marie Dolores Eliza Rosanna Gilbert. Lime-rick, Ireland, 1818-Jan 17 1861, Astoria, Long Island, New York. Dancer. ENCI SAL-VAT. *[ENCI SALVAT=b. in*

Seville in 1818 or in Montrose, Spain, in 1820.
Information in entry based on New York Times obituary, Jan 21 1861, p.8, col.1]

MONTET, Charlotte Antoinette Pauline du see Duchambge, Charlotte Antoinette Pauline

MONTGEROULT, Hélène (born Nervo). Lyon, Mar 2 1764-Jun 20 1836, Florence. Pianist, piano teacher, composer. ENCI SALVAT, ENCY MUS=p.233.

MONTI, Anna Maria (sometimes called Marianna). Rome, 1704-?. Singer. ENCI MUS.

MONTI, Grazia. 18th-century Italian singer. ENCI MUS. .

MONTI, Laura. ?-1760, Naples. Singer. ENCI MUS.

MONTI, Marianna. Naples, 1730-1814, Naples. Singer. ENCI MUS.

MONTIGNY-RÉMAURY, Fanny Marceline Caroline. Pamiers, France, Jan 22 1843-Jun 29 1913, Pamiers, France. Pianist. BLOM, BROWN BIO, GROVE 1, GROVE 5, THOMPSON. *[GROVE 1=b.Jan 21]*

MONTMOLLIN, Marie-Lise de. Neuchâtel, Switzerland, Sep 30 1918- . Contralto. SCHUH.

MOODIE, Alma. Brisbane, Sep 12 1900-Mar 7 1943, Frankfurt. Violinist, teacher. BAKER 5, BLOM, GROVE 5, RIEMANN, ULLSTEIN.

MOODY, Fanny (later Mrs. Charles Manners). Redruth, Cornwall, England, Nov 23 1866-

Jul 21 1945, Dundrum, nr. Dublin. Soprano. BAKER 5, BLOM, BROWN BRIT, ENCI MUS, GROVE 5, PRATT, RIEMANN=v.2 p.143, THOMPSON. *[ENCI MUS= d.1954 (presumably misprint)]*

MOODY, Jacquelynne. 20th-century American soprano. SANDVED.

MOODY, Marie. 19th-century English composer. BROWN BRIT.

MOOKE, Marie-Félicité-Denise see Pleyel, Marie-Félicité-Denise

MOORE, Bertha. Brighton, England, Jan 19 1862-?. Soprano. BROWN BRIT.

MOORE, Grace. Jellico, Tenn., Dec 5 1901-Jan 26 1947, Copenhagen. Soprano, actress. BAKER 5, CELLETTI, ENCI MUS, *EWEN LIVING, EWEN LIV SUP, GROVE 5, KUTSCH, MARIZ, RIEMANN, *SANDVED, THOMPSON. *[EWEN LIVING=b.Dec 1; EWEN LIVING, GROVE 5, & RIEMANN= b.in Slabtown, Tenn.]*

MOORE, Mary Carr. Memphis, Aug 6 1873-Jan 11 1957, Ingleside, Calif. Composer, opera composer. BAKER 5, THOMPSON.

MORALES, María de los Angeles see Angeles, María Morales de los

MORALT, Sophia Giustina see Dussek, Sophia Giustina

MORAN, Dora. ?-May 27 1930, Berlin. Soprano. ENCI MUS.

MORAN-OLDEN, Fanny (real name= Tappenhorn). Oldenburg, Germany, Sep 28 1855-Feb 13 1905, Schöneberg, nr. Berlin. Soprano. BAKER 1, BAKER 5, ENCI MUS, PRATT.

MORANDI, Rosa (born Morolli).
Senegal, Jul 17 1782-May 6
1824, Milan. Soprano. CORTE,
*ENCI MUS=illus.fac.p.210,
RIEMANN.

MORDAUCH, Ida see Ekman,
Ida

MORE, Félicité see Pradher,
Félicité

MORE, Margaret (Elizabeth).
Harlech, England, Jun 26
1903- . Composer, opera
composer. GROVE 5.

MOREA, Vincenza Garelli
Della see Garelli Della
Morea, Vincenza

MOREL, Lottie. Geneva, Jul 24
1909- . Pianist. SCHUH.

MORELLI, Adelina. Buenos
Aires, 1898-1969, ?. So-
prano. ARIZAGA.

MORENA, Berta (orig.=Meyer).
Mannheim, Jan 27 1878-Oct 7
1952, Rottach-Egern, Ger-
many. Soprano, voice teacher.
BAKER 5, CORTE, ENCI MUS,
KUTSCH, PRATT, RIEMANN,
THOMPSON.

MORESCHI, Luigia see Pol-
zelli, Luigia

MORETTO, Nelly. Rosario,
Argentina, 1925- . Composer.
ARIZAGA.

"MORFIDA" see Ralph, Kate

MORGAN, Maud. New York City,
Nov 22 1860-Dec 2 1941,
Prince's Bay, New York.
Harpist, composer, teacher.
GROVE 5 SUP, PRATT, THOMPSON.

MORGAN, Sydney (Lady Thomas
Charles, born Owenson).

Dublin, 1783-Apr 14 1859,
London. Harpist, writer.
BROWN BRIT.

MORGANA, Nina. Buffalo, New
York, Nov 15 1895- . So-
prano. THOMPSON.

MORHANGE, Hélène Jourdan- see
Jourdan-Morhange, Hélène

MORI, Rachele Maragliano see
Maragliano Mori, Rachele

MORICHELLI-BOSELLO, Anna.
Reggio Emilia, Italy, c1745-
Oct 30 1800, Trieste. So-
prano. ENCI MUS, GROVE 1.

MORIN-LABRECQUE, Albertine.
Montréal, Jun 8 1896- .
Composer, opera composer.
NAPIER.

MORINI, Erica (orig.=Erika).
Vienna, Jan 5 1904- .
Violinist. BAKER 5, ENCI
MUS, *EWEN LIVING, GROVE 5,
GROVE 5 SUP, MARIZ, PAVLAKIS=
p.273, RIEMANN, *SANDVED,
THOMPSON. *[MARIZ=b.1906;*
EWEN LIVING=b.1908]

MORISON, Christina W. (born
Bogue). Dublin, 1840-?.
Composer, opera composer.
BROWN BIO, BROWN BRIT.

MORISON, Elsie (Jean). Balla-
rat, Australia, Aug 15 1924- .
Soprano. GROVE 5, *ROSEN-
THAL=illus.p.121.

MOROLLI, Rosa see Morandi,
Rosa

MOROZEWICZ, Ludwika see
Rywacka, Ludwika

MORRIS, Margaret (Mrs. Alfred).
Caerleon, Monmouthshire,
England, ?-?. 19th-century
soprano, conductor, organist,
administrator. BROWN BRIT.

MORSCH, Anna. Gransee, Prussia,
1841-1916, Wiesbaden. Pianist, piano teacher, editor,
administrator, writer. PRATT.

MORSZTYN, Helena. Warsaw,
Apr 23 1895-May 23 1954,
New York City. Pianist,
piano teacher. GROVE 5.
[Death date based on obi-
tuary in New York Times,
May 23 1954, p.89, col.2]

MORTELLARI, Marietta Augusta
(later Woolrych). 18-19th-
century Italian singer.
ENCI MUS.

MORTON, Charlotte Jane see
Chapman, Charlotte Jane

MOSCHELES, Charlotte (Mrs.
Ignaz). Detmold, Germany,
Dec 13 1889- . Writer.
BAKER 1.

MOSCISCA, Maria (orig.=
Mokrzycka). Poland, 1885?-
Soprano. KUTSCH.

MOSELEY, Caroline Carr. 19th-
century English composer.
BROWN BRIT.

MOSHER, Frances Elizabeth
(born Jordan). St. John,
New Brunswick, Oct 23
1911- . Composer. CBC.

MOSS, Mary Hissem-De see
Hissem-De Moss, Mary

MOSSMAN, Sheila. London,
Aug 1923- . Pianist, piano
teacher. PALMER.

MOTTL, Zdenka see Fass-
báender, Zdenka

MOULTON, Dorothy (Lady Mayer).
London, Aug 24 1886-Apr 2
1974, Henham, Essex. Soprano,
administrator. GROVE 5,
THOMPSON. [THOMPSON=b.1890.

Date and place of death based
on obituary in Musical Times,
Jun 1974, p.502]

MOUNSEY, Ann Sheppard (Mrs.
Bartholomew). London, Apr 17
1811-Jun 24 1891, London.
Composer, organist, pianist,
teacher. BLOM, BROWN BIO=
p.58, BROWN BRIT=p.33,
GROVE 1, GROVE 5, THOMPSON.

MOUNSEY, Elizabeth. London,
Oct 8 1819-Oct 3 1905,
London. Organist, composer.
BLOM, BROWN BIO, BROWN BRIT,
GROVE 1, GROVE 5, THOMPSON.

MOUNT, Violet see L'Incognita

MOUNTAIN, Sarah (or Sophia;
born Wilkinson; also known as
Rosoman). ?, c1768-Jul 3
1841, Hammersmith, London.
Soprano, actress. BROWN BIO,
BROWN BRIT, GROVE 5, THOMPSON=
p.2405. [BROWN BRIT=d.Jul 1]

MOZART, Konstanze (Maria Con-
stantia Caecilia Josepha
Aloisia, born Weber). Zell,
Austria, Jan 5 1762-Mar 6
1842, Salzburg. Singer,
pianist. *DICT MUS, ENCI MUS,
ENCI SALVAT, ENCY MUS, GROVE
1, GROVE 5=v.5 p.983 & v.9
p.195, GROVE 5 SUP, MARIZ=
p.241, *MGG=biography v.9 &
v.14 col.323, illus. v.9
col.763, PRATT, RIEMANN.

MOZART, Maria Anna Walburga
Ignatia ("Nannerl"). Salz-
burg, Jul 30 1751-Oct 29
1829, Salzburg. Pianist,
piano teacher. BAKER 1,
BAKER 5, BLOM, BROWN BIO,
CORTE, *DICT MUS, ENCI MUS,
ENCI MUS, ENCI SALVAT, ENCY
MUS, GROVE 5, MARIZ, *MGG=
illus.v.9 fac.cols.705 &
752, PRATT, RIEMANN, ULL-
STEIN.

MRAVINA (Mravinskaya), Evgenia Konstantinovna. ?, 1864-Oct 25 1914, Yalta, Russia. Soprano. GROVE 5, GROVE 5 SUP.

MÜLLER, Elisabeth Catharina (Mrs. August Eberhard, born Rabert). 19th-century German pianist. ENCI MUS.

MÜLLER, Maria. Litoméřice, Bohemia, Jan 29 1898-Mar 13 1958, Bayreuth. Soprano. BAKER 5, ENCI MUS, EWEN NEW, GROVE 5, KUTSCH, RIEMANN, THOMPSON, ULLSTEIN. *[KUTSCH & ULLSTEIN=b.in Terezín (Theresienstadt), Bohemia)]*

MÜLLER, Therese see also Malten, Therese

MÜLLER, Therese. Vienna, Aug 24 1791-Jan 30 1876, Berlin. Soprano. ENCI MUS.

MÜLLER, Verena Gohl- see Gohl-Müller, Verena

MÜLLER-HERMANN, Johanna. Vienna, Jan 15 1878-Apr 19 1941, Vienna. Composer, teacher. BAKER 5, BLOM, GROVE 5=v.5 p.992, PRATT= p.605.

MÜLLER VON ASOW, Hedwig (born Böhme). Dresden, Jan 13 1911- . Archivist. ENCI MUS, RIEMANN.

MUKLE, Anna. 20th-century English pianist. PRATT.

MUKLE, May Henrietta. London, May 14 1880- . Violoncellist, composer. GROVE 5, PALMER, PRATT, THOMPSON.

MULLEN, Adelaide (Mrs. Henry Beaumont). Dublin, ?-?. 19th-century Irish soprano. BROWN BRIT.

MUNDAY, Mrs. (born Mahon). 18-19th-century English soprano. GROVE 5=v.5 p.518.

MUNDAY, Eliza see Salmon, Eliza

MUNDELLA, Emma. Nottingham, 1858-Feb 20 1896, England. Pianist, piano teacher, composer. BROWN BRIT.

MUNGO, Mary see Dibdin, Mary

MUÑOZ, Carmen García see García Muñoz, Carmen

MUNSEL, Patrice Beverly. Spokane, Wash., May 14 1925- . Soprano, actress. BAKER 5, *EWEN LIV SUP, EWEN NEW, GROVE 5, KUTSCH, *SANDVED, THOMPSON. *[KUTSCH= b.May 12]*

MURO LOMANTO, Toti de see Dal Monte, Toti

MURSKA, Ilma de (di). Zagreb, 1836-Jan 14 1889, Munich. Soprano, actress. BAKER 1, BAKER 5, BLOM, BROWN BIO, ENCI MUS, GROVE 1, GROVE 5, PRATT, THOMPSON=p.547. *[THOMPSON=b.1835; BROWN BIO & GROVE 1=b.1843; BAKER 1= d.Jan 16]*

MUSGRAVE, Thea. Edinburgh, May 27 1928- . Composer. BAKER 1971, BLOM, DICT MUS, ENCI MUS, VINTON.

MUSI, Maria Maddalena, "la Mignatta." Bologna, Jun 18 1669-May 2 1751, Bologna. Singer. ENCI MUS.

MUSIN, Annie Louise (Mrs. Ovide; earlier Hodges-Tanner). Boston, Oct 3 1856-Feb 28 1921, Boston. Soprano. BAKER 5, PRATT.

MUSULIN, Branka. Zagreb,
Aug 6 1920- . Pianist.
RIEMANN, ULLSTEIN.

MUSZELY, Melitta. Vienna,
Sep 13 1927- . Soprano.
KUTSCH, *ULLSTEIN.
[KUTSCH=b.1928]

MUZIO, Claudia. Pavia, Italy,
Feb 7 1889-May 24 1936,
Rome. Soprano. BAKER 5,
BLOM, *CELLETTI=illus.foll.
col.608, CORTE=p.720, *ENCI
MUS=illus.v.3 fac.p.247 &
311, EWEN NEW, GROVE 5,
GROVE 5 SUP, KUTSCH, MARIZ,
PRATT, *SANDVED, THOMPSON.
[MARIZ, PRATT, SANDVED, &
THOMPSON=b.1892]

MYSZ-GMEINER, Ella. Brașov
[Kronstadt], Romania, Nov 12
1878-1954 or 1955, Stutt-
gart. Singer. RIEMANN.

MYSZ-GMEINER, Luise. Brașov
[Kronstadt], Romania, Feb 1
1885-Mar 11 1951, Berlin.
Pianist, piano teacher.
RIEMANN, ULLSTEIN=p.369.

MYSZ-GMEINER, Lulu (or Lula).
Brașov [Kronstadt], Romania,
Aug 16 1876-Aug 7 1948,
Schwerin, Germany. Contralto,
voice teacher. BAKER 5,
GROVE 5, GROVE 5 SUP, KUTSCH,
PRATT, RIEMANN, THOMPSON,
ULLSTEIN. [GROVE 5=mezzo-
soprano]

MYSZYNSKA-WOYCIECHOWSKA,
Leokadia. Lowicz, Poland,
1858-1930, Warsaw. Composer.
GROVE 5.

N

NAGRIN, Helen see Tamiris,
Helen

NALDI, Carolina. ?, 1801-Dec

25 1876, Haut-Frizay, France.
Soprano. ENCI MUS.

NAMARA, Marguerite. Cleveland,
Nov 19 1888- . Soprano.
THOMPSON.

NANSEN, Eva Helene (born Sars).
Christiania, Norway, Dec 7
1858-Dec 9 1907, Lysaker,
nr. Oslo. Singer, voice
teacher. THOMPSON.

NANTIER-DIDIÉE, Constance
Betzy Rosabella. Saint-Denis,
Île de Bourbon [now Île de
la Réunion], Nov 16 1831-
Dec 4 1867, Madrid. Mezzo-
soprano. BLOM, BROWN BIO,
ENCI MUS, GROVE 1, GROVE 5,
PRATT, THOMPSON.

NASCIMBENI, Maria Francesca.
Ancona, Italy, 1658-?.
Composer. ENCI MUS, GROVE 5.

NASSYROVA (Nasyrova), Khalima.
Kokanda, Russia, 1913- .
Soprano. ENCI SALVAT, ENCY
MUS.

NAST, Minnie. Karlsruhe, Germany, Oct 10 1874-Jun 20
1956, Füssen, Germany.
Soprano, voice teacher.
KUTSCH.

NASYROVA, Khalima see
Nassyrova, Khalima

NATOLA, Aurora. Buenos Aires,
Dec 11 1928- . Violoncellist.
SCHUH NACH.

NAU, Maria Dolores Benedicta
Josefina. New York City,
Mar 18 1818-Jan 1891,
Levallois, nr. Paris. So-
prano. BAKER 1, BAKER 5,
BROWN BIO, ENCI MUS, GROVE 1,
GROVE 5, PRATT, THOMPSON.

NAUMANN, Ida. ?-1897, Berlin.

Singer, composer. ENCI MUS,
ENCI SALVAT, ENCY MUS.

NAVONE-BETTI, Carolina. Turin,
Feb 24 1871-Mar 7 1950,
Levanto, Italy. Harpist,
teacher. CORTE.

NAYLOR, Blanche see Cole,
Blanche

NAYLOR, Ruth Winifred. Adelaide, Aug 3 1908- .
Soprano. GROVE 5.

NEBLETT, Carol. Calif., ?- .
20th-century soprano. PAV-
LAKIS=p.290.

NEEDHAM, Eleanor Creathorne
see Clayton, Eleanor
Creathorne

NEEFE, Felice. ?, 1782-1826, ?.
German singer. ENCI MUS.

NEEFE, Louise Frederika. ?,
1779-1846, ?. German singer.
ENCI MUS.

NEEFE, Maria (sometimes Susanne; Mrs. Christian
Gottlob, born Zink). ?,
1751-1821, ?. German singer,
actress. ENCI MUS, GROVE 5.

NEELEY, Marilyn. 20th-century
American pianist, teacher.
PAVLAKIS=p.265.

NEF, Isabelle (born Lauder).
Geneva, Sep 27 1898- .
Pianist, piano teacher.
ENCI SALVAT, ENCY MUS,
SCHUH.

NEGRI, Giuditta see Pasta,
Giuditta

NEGRI, Maria (Anna) Catterina.
Bologna, c1705-?. Contralto.
GROVE 1.

NEJDANOVA, Antonia Vassilevna
see Neždanova, Antonida
Vassilevna

NELLI, Herva. Florence, ?- .
20th-century soprano. *EWEN
LIV SUP.

NELSON, Allison. 20th-century
Australian pianist. *SANDVED.

NELSOVA, Zara (Mrs. Grant
Johannesen). Canada, ?- .
20th-century violoncellist.
PAVLAKIS=p.277, *SANDVED.

NEMENOFF, Genia (later Lubo-
schutz). Paris, Oct 23 1908- .
Pianist. RIEMANN=v.2 p.104,
SANDVED.

NEMETH, Maria. Körment, Hungary, Mar 13 1897-Dec 28 1967,
Vienna. Soprano, voice teacher. CELLETTI, KUTSCH.
[CELLETTI=b.1899 in Budapest]

NERUDA, Amalie. Brno, Moravia,
Mar 31 1834-?, Berlin. Pianist. ENCI MUS, MGG.

NERUDA, Anna Maria Rudolfina.
Brno, Moravia, Mar 26 1840-
1922, Stockholm. Pianist.
MGG.

NERUDA, Olga. ?, 1858-Dec 9
1945, Stockholm. Pianist.
MGG.

NERUDA, Wilhelmine (Wilma)
Maria Frantiska (Lady Hallé).
Brno, Moravia, Mar 21 1839-
Apr 15 1911, Berlin. Vio-
linist, court musician.
BAKER 1, BLOM, BROWN BIO,
CORTE, DICT MUS, ENCI MUS,
ENCI SALVAT, ENCY MUS, GROVE
1, GROVE 1 APP, GROVE 5=v.4
p.24 & v.6 p.50 (former
brief mention in article on
husband, Sir Charles Hallé),

MGG, THOMPSON. *[DICT MUS &
MGG=b.Mar 21 1838; BAKER 1=
b.Mar 29 1839; BROWN BIO=
b.Mar 21 1840]*

NERVO, Hélène see Mont-
geroult, Hélène

NESHDANOVA, Antonina Vassilevna see Nezdanova,
Antonida Vassilevna

NESPOULOS, Marthe. Paris,
May 1 1894-Aug 6 1962,
Paris. Soprano, voice
teacher. KUTSCH.

NEUENSCHWANDER, Leni. Bern,
Jul 9 1909- . Singer. SCHUH.

NEVADA, Emma (orig.=Wixom).
Alpha, nr. Nevada City,
Calif., Feb 7 1859-Jun 20
1940, Liverpool. Soprano.
BAKER 1, BAKER 5, BLOM,
CORTE, ENCI MUS, EWEN NEW,
GROVE 1=v.4 p.477, GROVE 5,
PRATT, THOMPSON. *[PRATT=
b.1862]*

NEVADA, Mignon Mathilde Marie.
Paris, Aug 14 1886-Jun 1971,
Long Melford, England. So-
prano. BAKER 5, ENCI MUS,
GROVE 5, GROVE 5 SUP,
KUTSCH, THOMPSON. *[KUTSCH=
b.1888]*

NEVEU, Ginette. Paris, Aug 11
1919-Oct 28 1949, plane
crash over Azores. Vio-
linist. BAKER 5, BLOM,
COOPER, CORTE, *ENCI SALVAT,
ENCY MUS, GROVE 5, GROVE 5
SUP, MGG, SANDVED, THOMPSON,
*ULLSTEIN.

NEVINS, Marian Griswold see
MacDowell, Marian

NEWAY, Patricia. Brooklyn,
Sep 30 1919- . Soprano,
actress. BAKER 1971, EWEN

NEW, GROVE 5, KUTSCH, *SAND-
VED=illus.p.304 & 961,
THOMPSON. *[KUTSCH=b.1920]*

NEWCOMB, Ethel. Whitney Point,
New York, Oct 30 1875-Jul 3
1959, Whitney Point, New
York. Pianist, piano teacher.
BAKER 5, BAKER 1971, PRATT,
THOMPSON. *[PRATT=b.1879]*

NEWCOMBE, Ethel (born Hubi).
19th-century English so-
prano. BROWN BRIT.

NEWCOMBE, Georgeanne (born
Hubi). London, Dec 18 1843-?.
Soprano, composer. BROWN
BRIT.

NEWLIN, Dika. Portland, Ore.,
Nov 22 1923- . Writer,
composer, teacher, administrator. BAKER 5, THOMPSON.

NEWMAN, Rita see Fornia-
Labey, Rita

NEWMARCH, Rosa Harriet (born
Jeaffreson). Leamington,
England, Dec 18 1857-Apr 9
1940, Worthing, England.
Writer, critic. BAKER 5,
COOPER, CORTE, ENCI MUS,
GROVE 5, MARIZ, MGG, PALMER=
p.263, PRATT, RIEMANN,
THOMPSON.

NEWSTEAD, Katherine see
Bacon, Katherine

NEWTON, Adelaide (or Emily;
Mrs. Alexander, born Ward).
London, 1821-Dec 22 1881,
London. Composer, soprano.
BROWN BRIT.

NEY, Elly. Düsseldorf, Sep 27
1882-Mar 31 1968, Tutzing,
Germany. Pianist, piano
teacher, administrator.
BAKER 5, BAKER 1971, BLOM,
*EWEN LIVING, EWEN LIV SUP,

GROVE 5, MARIZ, MGG, RIE-
MANN, THOMPSON, ULLSTEIN.

NEY, Jenny Bürde- see
Bürde-Ney, Jenny

NEZADAL, Maria (Mrs. Clemens
Franckenstein). Pardubice,
Bohemia, Feb 12 1897- .
Soprano. KUTSCH.

NEŽDANOVA (Nejdanova, Nezh-
danova, Neshdanova),
Antonida (Antonia) Vassi-
levna. Krivaya Balka, nr.
Odessa, Jul 29 1873-Jun 26
1950, Moscow. Soprano,
voice teacher. BAKER 1971,
CELLETTI, *ENCI SALVAT=v.3
p.440, ENCY MUS, KUTSCH,
THOMPSON, VODARSKY. [VODAR-
SKY=b.1875; KUTSCH=d.May 26]

NICHOLLS, Agnes (Mrs. Hamil-
ton Harty). Cheltenham,
England, Jul 14 1877-Sep 21
1959, London. Soprano.
BAKER 5, BAKER 1971, ENCI
MUS=v.2 p.398, GROVE 5,
GROVE 5 SUP, KUTSCH, PRATT,
RIEMANN, THOMPSON=p.902.
[KUTSCH=b.1876]

NICHOLS, Marie. Chicago, 1879-
Nov 20 1954, Newton, Mass.
Violinist, teacher. PRATT.
[Date and place of death
based on New York Times
obituary, Nov 23 1954, p.33,
col.1]

NICKEL, Matilda. 20th-century
American soprano. PAVLAKIS=
p.290.

NICOLAIDI, Elena see Nikolaidi, Elena

"NICOLINI, Mlle." see Ditters von Dittersdorf,
Nicolina

NIEDHART, Henriette see
Rust, Henriette

NIEKRASZOWA, Ilza Sternicka-
see Sternicka-Niekraszowa,
Ilza

NIELSEN, Alice. Nashville,
Tenn., Jun 7 1876-Mar 8
1943, New York City. So-
prano, voice teacher.
BAKER 5, ENCI MUS, EWEN
NEW, KUTSCH, PRATT, SANDVED,
THOMPSON.

NIELSEN, Flora (real name=Sybil
Crawley). Vancouver, Aug 28
1900- . Mezzo-soprano, formerly soprano. GROVE 5,
GROVE 5 SUP.

NIEMELÄ, Tii (Kerttu, Siviä;
Mrs. Pentti Koskimies).
?, Mar 20 1918- . Finnish
soprano. GROVE 5.

NIESSEN-STONE, Matja von.
Moscow, Dec 28 1870-Jun 8
1948, New York City. So-
prano, voice teacher,
administrator. BAKER 5,
PRATT, THOMPSON.

NIJINSKA see Nischinskij

NIKISCH, Amélie (Mrs. Arthur,
born Heussner). ?-Jan 1938,
Leipzig. Singer. ENCI MUS.

NIKISCH, Grete Merrem- see
Merrem-Nikisch, Grete

NIKOLAYEVNA (Nikolaieva,
Nikolaeva), Tatiana Petrovna.
Bezhitz, USSR, May 4 1924- .
Composer, pianist. BAKER 5,
ENCI SALVAT, ENCY MUS,
THOMPSON.

NIKOLAIDI, Elena. Smyrna,
Turkey, Jun 13 1914- .
Contralto. BAKER 5, ENCI
MUS=v.3 p.271, *EWEN LIV
SUP, EWEN NEW, GROVE 5,
GROVE 5 SUP, KUTSCH, RIE-
MANN, *SANDVED, THOMPSON.
[EWEN LIV SUP, GROVE 5, &

RIEMANN=b.1909; KUTSCH=
b.Sep 26 1912 at Sofia]

NILŞSON, Birgit see Nilsson,
Märta Birgit

NILSSON, Kristina (Christine).
Sjöabol, nr. Vexiö, Weders-
löf, Sweden, Aug 20 1843-
Nov 22 1921, Stockholm.
Soprano. BAKER 1, BAKER 5,
BLOM, BROWN BIO, COOPER,
CORTE=p.720, ENCI MUS, ENCI
SALVAT, EWEN NEW, GROVE 1,
GROVE 5, MARIZ, MGG, PRATT,
RIEMANN, SANDVED, THOMPSON.
[ENCI MUS=b.Aug 22]

NILSSON, Märta Birgit. Karup,
Sweden, May 17 1918- .
Soprano. BAKER 1971, BLOM,
CELLETTI, DICT MUS, ENCI
MUS, ENCI SALVAT, EWEN NEW,
GROVE 5 SUP, KUTSCH, RIE-
MANN, *ROSENTHAL, *SANDVED=
another illus.p.1094, THOMP-
SON, *ULLSTEIN. [EWEN NEW=
b.1922; SANDVED=b.1923]

NISCHINSKIJ (Nijinskij),
Bronislawa (Nischinska).
Warsaw or Minsk, Russia,
Jan 8 1891-Feb 21 1972,
Pacific Palisades, Calif.
Dancer. RIEMANN. [RIEMANN=
d.Dec 1971. According to
New York Times obituary
(Feb 23 1972, p.44, col.1)
most authorities indicate
birthplace as Warsaw,
although others suggest
Minsk]

NISCHINSKIJ (Nijinskij),
Kyra. Russia, 1914- .
Dancer. RIEMANN.

NISKA, Maralin. 20th-century
American soprano. PAVLAKIS=
p.290.

NISSEN, Erika Lie- see
Lie-Nissen, Erika

NISSEN-SALOMAN, Henriette.
Göteborg, Sweden, Mar 12
1819-Aug 27 1879, Bad Harz-
burg, Saxony. Soprano, voice
teacher. BAKER 1, BROWN BIO,
ENCI MUS=v.4 p.100 (brief
mention in article on husband Siegfried Saloman),
MGG, PRATT, RIEMANN, THOMP-
SON. [BROWN BIO=b.1822]

NIVA, Rosa see Stoltz, Rosine

NOBEL, Elizabeth see Craig,
Elizabeth

NÖB, Victorine see Stoltz,
Rosine

NOËL, Victoire see Stoltz,
Rosine

NOLTHENIUS, Hélène Wagenaar.
Amsterdam, Apr 19 1920- .
Musicologist, writer. ENCI
SALVAT, ENCY MUS.

NONI, Alda. Trieste, Apr 30
1920- . Soprano. CORTE,
ENCI MUS, GROVE 5, KUTSCH,
*PALMER=illus.only p.133.
[KUTSCH=b.Jun 30 1916]

NOORDEWIER-REDDINGIUS, Aaltje.
Deurne, Netherlands, Sep 1
1868-Apr 6 1949, Hilversum,
Netherlands. Soprano, voice
teacher. GROVE 5, KUTSCH,
RIEMANN.

NORBURY, F. Ethel (born Fall).
Liverpool, Apr 20 1872-?.
Composer, teacher. CBC.

NORDICA, Lillian (stage name
of Lillian Norton-Gower-
Doeme). Farmington, Me.,
Dec 12 1857-May 10 1914,
Batavia, Java. Soprano. BAKER
1, BAKER 5, BAKER 1971, BLOM,
CELLETTI, COOPER, CORTE,
ENCI MUS, EWEN NEW, GROVE 5,
GROVE 5 SUP, KUTSCH, MARIZ,

PRATT, RIEMANN, *SANDVED, THOMPSON. [ENCI MUS=b.May 12 1857; CORTE, MARIZ, & PRATT=b.1859; CORTE=b.in Farmington, N.Y.]

NORDMO, Aase see Lóveberg, Aase

NORÉNA, (Kaja) Eidé (born Kaja Andrea Karoline Eidé Hansen). Horten, Norway, Apr 26 1884-Nov 19 1968, Switzerland. Soprano. BAKER 5, BAKER 1971, CELLETTI, *EWEN LIVING, EWEN LIV SUP, EWEN NEW, GROVE 5 SUP, KUTSCH, MARIZ, THOMPSON. [CELLETTI, EWEN LIVING, & MARIZ=b.in Oslo]

NORGREN, Ellen see Gulbranson, Ellen

NORLEDGE, Annie E. Newark, Nottingham, England, ?-?. 19th-century soprano, violinist, viola player. BROWN BRIT.

NORMAN, Helen Standing see Standing, Helen

NORMAN, Jesseye. 20th-century American soprano. PAVLAKIS= p.290.

NORTON, Caroline Elizabeth Sarah (born Sheridan). London?, 1808-Jun 15 1877, London. Composer. BROWN BIO, BROWN BRIT. [BROWN BRIT=b.1809]

NORTON, Eunice. Minneapolis, Jun 30 1908- . Pianist. BAKER 5, *EWEN LIVING, THOMPSON.

NORTON, Lillian see Nordica, Lillian

NOSE, Elisabeth see Dreyschock, Elisabeth

NOVAÉS, Guiomar. São João da Boa Vista, nr. São Paulo, Brazil, Feb 28 1895- . Pianist. BAKER 5, *EWEN LIVING, EWEN LIV SUP, GROVE 5, GROVE 5 SUP, MARIZ, RIEMANN, *SANDVED, THOMPSON.

NOVÁKOVÁ, Jaromíra see Tomášek, Jaromíra

NOVARO, Luciana. Genova, Mar 3 1923- . Dancer, choreographer. ENCI MUS.

NOVELLI, Anna Maria Sofia. 18th-century Italian singer. ENCI MUS=v.1 p.162 (brief mention in article on the Badia family).

NOVELLI, Giulia see Viñas, Giulia

NOVELLI LAURENTI, Antonia Maria (called "la Coralli"). 17-18th-century Italian singer. ENCI MUS=v.2 p.576 (brief mention in article on the Laurenti family).

NOVELLO, Cecilia. ?-Oct 4 1877, ?. English singer. GROVE 1.

NOVELLO, Clara Anastasia. London, Jun 10 1818-Mar 12 1908, Rome. Soprano. BAKER 1, BAKER 5, BLOM, BROWN BIO, BROWN BRIT, CORTE, DICT MUS, ENCI MUS, ENCY MUS, GROVE 1, GROVE 5, GROVE 5 SUP, MGG, SCHOLES, THOMPSON. [ENCI MUS=b.Jun 18; BAKER 1=b. Jun 19]

NOVELLO, Clara Natalia see Mac Farren, Clara Natalia

NOVELLO, Mary Sabilla. London, 1821-Jan 8 1904, Genoa. Soprano, writer. BROWN BIO, BROWN BRIT, DICT MUS, ENCI MUS, ENCY MUS, GROVE 1, GROVE 5, MGG.

NOVELLO, Mary Victoria (later
Mrs. Mary Cowden Clarke).
London, Jun 22 1809-Jan 12
1898, Genoa. Writer. BROWN
BIO=p.167, BROWN BRIT=p.92,
DICT MUS, ENCI MUS, ENCY
MUS, GROVE 5, MGG.

NOVELLO-DAVIES, Clara. Cardiff, Wales, Apr 7 1861-
Mar 1 1943, London. Choral
conductor, singer, voice
teacher, composer. BAKER 5,
BAKER 1971, BROWN BRIT=
p.117, *CLAYTON=p.383,
THOMPSON.

NOVOTNÁ, Jarmila. Prague,
Sep 23 1903- . Soprano,
actress. BAKER 5, CORTE=
p.720, ENCI MUS, *EWEN
LIVING, EWEN LIV SUP, EWEN
NEW, GROVE 5, KUTSCH, MARIZ,
RIEMANN, SANDVED, THOMPSON,
ULLSTEIN. *[EWEN NEW & KUTSCH=
b.1907; EWEN LIVING, GROVE 5,
& MARIZ=b.1909]*

NOYES, Edith Rowena. Cam-
bridge, Mass., Mar 26 1875-?.
Pianist, piano teacher,
composer. PRATT, THOMPSON.

NÜESCH, Nina. Balgach (St.-
Galler Rheintal), Switzerland, Sep 10 1903- . Singer,
voice teacher. SCHUH.

NUNN, Elizabeth Annie. Eng-
land?, 1861?-Jan 7 1894,
Fallowfield, Manchester,
England. Composer. BROWN
BRIT.

NUNN, Gertrude. 19th-century
English singer, violon-
cellist. BROWN BRIT.

NUNN, Henrietta. 19th-century
English singer. BROWN BRIT.

NYFFENEGGER, Esther. Zürich,
Jul 20 1941- . Violoncel-
list. SCHUH.

O

OAKEY (Okey), Maggie (Marguerite)
(Mrs. Vladimir de Pachmann).
Sydney, 1864-Jul 3 1952, Paris.
Pianist, composer. BROWN BRIT,
ENCY MUS=v.3 p.378.

OATES, Miss   see   Delagarde,
Mrs. J.

OBER, Julia Fuqua (Mrs. Vincent
Hilles Ober). Norfolk, Va.,
Dec 20 1900- . Administrator.
THOMPSON.

OBER, Margaret Arndt. Berlin,
Apr 15 1885-Mar 17 1971, Bad
Sachs, Germany. Contralto,
voice teacher. BAKER 5,
KUTSCH, MARIZ, PRATT, THOMP-
SON, ULLSTEIN=p.28. *[BAKER 5=
soprano; PRATT=mezzo-soprano]*

OBIGNY DE FERRIÈRES, Amélie
Alexandrine d' (Mrs. André
Gedalge). Paris, Feb 21
1865-?. Music theorist.
ENCI MUS=v.2 p.288.

OBOUKHOVA (Obukhova, Obuhova),
Nadesha (Nadejda) Andreivna.
Moscow, Feb 22 1886-Aug 15
1961, Feodosia, USSR. Mezzo-
soprano, voice teacher. ENCI
SALVAT, ENCY MUS, KUTSCH.
[KUTSCH=contralto]

OBROVSKÁ, Jana. Prague, Sep 15
1930- . Composer. GARDAVSKY.

OBUKHOVA (Obuhova), Nadejda
Andreivna   see   Oboukhova,
Nadesha Andreivna

OCAMPO, Victoria. Argentina,
1890- . Writer. ARIZAGA.

OCCA, Sophie dall'   see
Schoberlechner, Sophie

ODDONE-GAVIRATI, Giulia. 19th-
century Italian mezzo-
soprano. ENCI MUS.

ODDONE SULLI-RAO, Elisabetta.
Milan, Aug 13 1878- . Com-
poser, singer. CORTE, ENCI
MUS, RIEMANN, THOMPSON.

OEHME-FOERSTER, Elsa. New York
City, Sep 23 1899- . So-
prano, voice teacher. KUTSCH.

OFFERS, Maartje. Koudekerke,
Netherlands, Feb 27 1892-
Jan 28 1944, Tholen, Nether-
lands. Contralto. KUTSCH.

OGDEN, Henrietta Maria see
Bullock, Henrietta Maria

OHE, Adèle aus der see
Aus der Ohe, Adèle

OHMS, Elisabeth (Elizabeth).
Arnhem, Netherlands, May 17
1896- . Soprano. GROVE 5,
GROVE 5 SUP, KUTSCH,
THOMPSON. [KUTSCH=b.1888]

OKEY, Maggie see Oakey,
Maggie

OLCZEWSKA, Maria see
Olszewska, Maria

OLDEN, Fanny see Moran-
Olden, Fanny

OLDENBURG, Barbara (Mrs.
Reinhard Keiser). 18th-
century German singer.
ENCI MUS=v.2 p.525.

OLDHAM, Miss E. 19th-century
English pianist, piano
teacher. BROWN BRIT.

OLDHAM, S. Emily. 19th-century
English composer. BROWN
BRIT.

OLDMIXON, Lady (born Georgina
Sidus). England?, 1768-1835
or 1836, England?. Soprano.
BROWN BIO, BROWN BRIT.

O'LEARY, Rosetta (Mrs. Arthur,
born Vinning). 19th-century
English composer, choral
conductor, voice teacher.
BROWN BIO, BROWN BRIT.

OLEJNITSCHENKO, Galina.
Nr. Odessa, Feb 23 1929- .
Soprano. KUTSCH.

OLÉNINE D'ALHEIM, Marie.
Istomino, Riazan, Russia,
Oct 2 1869-Aug 27 1970,
Moscow. Soprano, voice
teacher, writer. BAKER 5,
BAKER 1971, ENCI MUS, PRATT=
p.301, THOMPSON=p.36 & 1493
(double entry).

OLHEIM, Helen. Buffalo, New
York, ?- . 20th-century
contralto. THOMPSON.

OLITZKA, Rosa. Berlin, Sep 6
1873-Sep 29 1949, Chicago.
Contralto, voice teacher.
CELLETTI, KUTSCH, THOMPSON.
[CELLETTI=contralto & mezzo-
soprano]

OLIVEIRA, Jocy de. Curitiba-
Parana, Brazil, Apr 11 1936- .
Pianist, composer. BAKER 1971.

OLIVEIRA, Magdala da Gama.
Rio de Janeiro, 1908- .
Critic, teacher. MARIZ.

OLIVERA DE COWLING, Mercedes.
Montevideo, Uruguay, Feb 14
1919- . Pianist, harpsi-
chordist. THOMPSON.

OLIVERO, Magda. Saluzzo, Italy,
Apr 25 1916- . Soprano.
CELLETTI, ENCI MUS, EWEN NEW,
KUTSCH. [KUTSCH=b.1912 at
Turin; CELLETTI & EWEN NEW=
b.1914 at Saluzzo]

OLIVEROS, Pauline. Houston,
Tex., May 30 1932- . Avant-

garde and electronic music
composer, teacher. BAKER
1971, PAVLAKIS=p.345,
VINTON.

OLIVIERI-SANGIACOMO, Elsa
see Respighi, Elsa

OLSZEWSKA, Maria (born Marie
Berchtenbreiter). Ludwigs-
schwaige, nr. Augsburg,
Germany, Aug 12 1892-May 17
1969, Klagenfurt, Austria.
Contralto, voice teacher.
BAKER 5, BAKER 1971, CELLET-
TI, *EWEN LIVING, EWEN NEW,
GROVE 5=v.6 p.184, GROVE 5
SUP=p.331, KUTSCH, MARIZ,
RIEMANN, THOMPSON, ULLSTEIN.
*[EWEN LIVING & EWEN LIV
SUP=mezzo-soprano; GROVE 5=
mezzo-contralto]*

OLTRABELLA, Augusta. Savona,
Italy, Dec 27 1906- .
Soprano. ENCI MUS, KUTSCH.
[KUTSCH=b.1901]

ONÉGIN, Sigrid (born Hoffmann;
complete name=Elizabeth
Elfriede Emilie Sigrid).
Stockholm, Jun 1 1889-Jun
16 1943, Magliasco, Ticino,
Switzerland. Contralto.
BAKER 5, CELLETTI, ENCI MUS,
*EWEN LIVING, EWEN LIV SUP,
GROVE 5, GROVE 5 SUP, KUTSCH,
MARIZ, RIEMANN, THOMP-
SON, *ULLSTEIN. *[EWEN LIVING,
EWEN LIV SUP, GROVE 5, MARIZ,
RIEMANN, SCHUH, THOMPSON, &
ULLSTEIN=b.1891; EWEN LIV
SUP=d.Jun 17 1943 in Lugano;
CELLETTI=d.Jun 6 1943]*

O'NEIL, Adine (Mrs. Norman,
born Rückert). ?, 1875-
1947, ?. Pianist. ENCI MUS,
GROVE 5, RIEMANN.

O'NEILL, Eliza see Dennett,
Eliza

OOSTERZEE, Cornélie van.
Batavia, Java, Aug 16 1863-?.
Composer. PRATT, THOMPSON=
p.2287.

OPIENSKA, Lydia see Barblan-
Opienska, Lydia

OPPENS, Ursula. 20th-century
American pianist. PAVLAKIS=
p.265.

OPRAWNIK, Pauline see
Erdmannsdörffer, Pauline

ORAVEZ, Edith. Budapest, ?- .
20th-century soprano.
SCHUH NACH.

O'REILLY, Mrs. William see
Bailey, Mary Sophia

ORGENI (Orgenyi), Aglaja (real
name=Görger St. Jorgen; also
Anna Maria Aglaia Orgeni).
Rimaszombat, Galicia, Dec
17 1841-Mar 15 1926, Vienna.
Soprano, voice teacher,
court musician. BAKER 1,
BAKER 5, BROWN BIO, GROVE 1,
GROVE 1 APP, GROVE 5, GROVE
5 SUP, PRATT, RIEMANN, THOMP-
SON. *[BAKER 1, PRATT, &
THOMPSON=b.1843]*

ORGER, Caroline see Reinagle,
Caroline

ORLANDI, Elisa. Macerata, Italy,
1811-1834, Rovigo, Italy.
Mezzo-soprano. ENCI MUS.

ORRIDGE, Ellen Amelia. London,
Aug 14 1856-Sep 16 1883,
Guernsey, England. Contralto.
BROWN BIO, BROWN BRIT,
GROVE 1 APP.

ORTA, Rachele d' see D'Orta,
Rachele

ORTA, Rosina d' see D'Orta,
Rosina

ORTMANN, Carolyn. Savannah, Ga., May 23 1881- . Soprano, voice teacher. THOMPSON.

ORTOLANI, Angelica. Almenno, Bergamo, Italy, c1830-Dec 31 1913, Leghorn. Soprano. ENCI MUS=v.4 p.384.

OSBORN-HANNAH, Jane. Wilmington, Ohio, Jul 8 1873-Aug 13 1943, New York City. Soprano. BAKER 5, PRATT, THOMPSON. *[PRATT=b.1880?]*

OSBORNE, Adrienne see Kraus, Adrienne

OS DE VRIES, Rosa van see De Vries, Rosa van Os

OSELIO, Gina. Christiania, Norway, Nov 19 1858-May 5 1937, Oslo. Mezzo-soprano. THOMPSON.

OSGOOD, Emma Aline. Boston, 1849-Nov 8 1911, Philadelphia. Soprano, voice teacher. BROWN BIO, PRATT, THOMPSON.

OSMAN, Fanny Wilson. Reading, England, ?-?. 19th-century soprano. BROWN BRIT.

OSTEN, Eva von der. Helgoland, Germany, Aug 19 1881-1936, Dresden. Soprano, administrator. KUTSCH.

OSTINELLI, Elisa see Biscaccianti, Eliza

OSTLERE, May. 19th-century English composer. BROWN BRIT.

OTTEY, Sarah. London?, c1695-?. Violinist, viol player, harpsichordist. GROVE 5, THOMPSON.

OTTO, Lisa. Dresden, Nov 14 1919- . Soprano. BLOM, KUTSCH, RIEMANN, THOMPSON, *ULLSTEIN.

OTTO, Melitta (born Alvsleben). Dresden, Dec 16 1842-Jan 13 1893, Dresden. Soprano. BAKER 1, GROVE 1 APP, GROVE 5, PRATT, THOMPSON. *[GROVE 1 APP=b.1845]*

OURY, Anna Caroline (born de Belleville). Landshut, Bavaria, Jun 24 1808-Jul 22 1880, Munich. Pianist, composer, arranger. BAKER 1= p.53, BAKER 5, BROWN BIO, GROVE 1, GROVE 1 APP, GROVE 5, THOMPSON=p.187. *[BROWN BIO= b.Jan 24 1806; BAKER 1=b. in Munich]*

OWENSON, Sydney see Morgan, Sydney

P

PAALEN, Bella. Paszthó, Hungary, Jul 9 1881-Jul 28 1964, New York City. Contralto, voice teacher. KUTSCH.

PÅLSON-WETTERGREN, Gertrud see Wettergren, Gertrud

PACÁKOVÁ, Anna see Patzaková, Anna

PACETTI, Iva. Prato, Toscana, Italy, Dec 13 1900- . Soprano, voice teacher. ENCI MUS, KUTSCH. *[KUTSCH=b.1898]*

PACHECO, Catalina see Palomino, Catalina

PACHLER-KOSCHAK, Marie Leopoldine. Graz, Oct 2 1792-Apr 10 1855, Graz. Pianist. BAKER 5, ENCI SALVAT, PRATT, THOMPSON.

PACHMANN, Maggie de see Oakey, Maggie

PACINI, Regina (born de Alvear). Lisbon, Jan 6 1871-Sep 18 1965, Buenos Aires. Soprano. ARIZAGA= p.40, CELLETTI, KUTSCH.

PACKER, Ruth see Davies, Ruth

PADILLA, Lola Artôt de see Artôt de Padilla, Lola

PAER, Francesca see Riccardi, Francesca

PAGE, Kate Stearns. Brookline, Mass., Aug 21 1873-Jan 19 1963, New York City. Pianist, piano teacher, teacher. BAKER 5, BAKER 1971.

PAGE, Ruth. Indianapolis, ?- . 20th-century dancer. RIEMANN.

PAGLIUGHI, Lina. New York City, May 27 1911- . Soprano. CELLETTI, ENCI MUS, KUTSCH. *[CELLETTI= b. c1910; KUTSCH=b.1910 in San Francisco]*

PAIGE, Mrs. J. B. 19th century American (?) writer. BROWN BIO.

PAIGE, Kate. 19th-century English writer. BROWN BIO, BROWN BRIT.

PAIN, Mlle.? du see Du Pain, Mlle.?

PAISIBLE, Mary see Davis, Mary

PAKARINEN, Maikki see Järnefelt-Palmgren, Maikki

PAKHMUTOVA, Alexandra. Stalingrad, Nov 9 1929- . Composer. BAKER 1971.

PALAZZESI, Matilde. Monte-

carotto, Ancona, Italy, Mar 1 1802-Jul 3 1842, Barcelona. Soprano. ENCI MUS.

PALLA, Lia (or Cornelia). Venlo, Netherlands, Feb 7 1917- . Pianist. ENCI SALVAT.

PALLENBERG, Friederike see Massary, Fritzi

PALMER, Bessie (Elizabeth Annie). London, Aug 9 1831-Sep 1 1910, London. Contralto. GROVE 5, THOMPSON.

PALMER, Isabelle Perkins see Dibdin, Isabelle Perkins

PALMER, Jeanne. New York City, 1904- . Soprano. THOMPSON.

PALMGREN, Maikki see Järnefelt-Palmgren, Maikki

PALMGREN, Minna (Mrs. Selim, born Talvik). 20th-century Finnish singer. GROVE 5.

PALOMINO, Catalina (Mrs. José, born Pacheco, called "La Catuja"). 18th-century Spanish singer, actress. GROVE 5.

PAMPANINI, Rosetta (or Rosa). Milan, Sep 2 1900-Aug 2 1973, Corbola, Italy. Soprano. CELLETTI, *ENCI MUS=illus.v.3 fac.p.311 & v.4 p.366, ENCI SALVAT, ENCY MUS, GROVE 5, KUTSCH.

PANCERA, Gabriele (called Ella). Vienna, Aug 15 1876-May 10 1932, Bad Ischl, Austria. Pianist. RIEMANN, THOMPSON. *[THOMPSON=b.1875]*

PANDOLFINI, Angelica. Spoletto, Italy, Aug 21 1871-Jul 15 1959, Lenno, Como, Italy. Soprano. CELLETTI, ENCI MUS, KUTSCH.

PANTALEONI, Romilda. Udine, Italy, 1847-Apr 20 1917, Milan. Soprano. *ENCI MUS= illus.v.3 fac.p.366.

PANTHÈS, Marie. Odessa, Russia, Nov 4 1881- . Pianist. SCHUH NACH, THOMPSON.

PANUM, Hortense. Kiel, Mar 14 1856-Apr 26 1933, Copenhagen. Musicologist, teacher, writer. BLOM, CORTE, GROVE 5, PRATT, RIEMANN, THOMPSON.

PAPIER, Rosa. Baden, nr. Vienna, Sep 15 1858-Feb 9 1932, Vienna. Mezzo-soprano, voice teacher. BAKER 1, BAKER 5, ENCI MUS, RIEMANN, THOMPSON.

PAPPENHEIM, Eugenie. Vienna, 1849-Jun 1924, Los Angeles. Soprano. BROWN BIO, GROVE 1= v.3 p.54, THOMPSON.

PAPPRITZ, Juliane. ?, May 28 1767-Mar 16 1806, ?. Italian singer. ENCI MUS=v.4 p.615.

PAPRITZ, Evgenia Eduardovna see Lineva, Evgenia Eduardovna

PARADIS (Paradies), Maria Therese (Theresia, Teresia) von. Vienna, May 15 1759-Feb 1 1824, Vienna. Pianist, piano teacher, composer, singer, voice teacher, light-opera composer, organist. BAKER 1, BAKER 5, BLOM, BROWN BIO, DICT MUS, ENCI MUS, ENCI SALVAT, ENCY MUS, GROVE 1, GROVE 5, MGG, PRATT, RIEMANN, THOMPSON.

PARAVICINI, Signora (born Gandini). Turin, 1769-after 1832, Italy?. Violinist. THOMPSON.

PARENT, Charlotte-Francès-

Hortense. London, Mar 22 1837-Jan 12 1929, Paris. Pianist, piano teacher. CORTE, DICT MUS, ENCY MUS, MGG, PRATT, RIEMANN, THOMPSON.

PAREPA-ROSA, Euphrosyne (Mrs. Karl Rosa, born Parepa de Boyescu). Edinburgh, May 7 1836-Jan 21 1874, London. Soprano. BAKER 5, BLOM, BROWN BIO, BROWN BRIT, ENCI MUS, GROVE 1, GROVE 5, PRATT, RIEMANN=v.1 p.537, THOMPSON. *[BROWN BIO=b.1839]*

PARETO, Graziella. Barcelona, 1888- . Soprano. CELLETTI, ENCI MUS, ENCI SALVAT, KUTSCH, THOMPSON. *[KUTSCH= b.Mar 6 1889]*

PARIS, Nanine see Chevé, Nanine

PARKE, Maria Hester (Mrs. Beardmore). London, 1775-Aug 15 1822, London. Singer. BROWN BIO, BROWN BRIT, GROVE 1, GROVE 5, MGG.

PARKER, Denne. Edinburgh, Jun 22 1889- . Contralto. GROVE 5, THOMPSON. *[GROVE 5= mezzo-contralto]*

PARKER, Louise. 20th-century American contralto. PAVLAKIS= p.297.

PARKINA (Elizabeth Parkinson). Kansas City, Mo., Jun 11 1882-Jun 11 1922, Colorado Springs. Soprano. KUTSCH, PRATT, THOMPSON.

PARKYNS, Beatrice (born Crawford). Bombay, ?-?. 19th-century English composer. BROWN BRIT.

PARLAMAGNI, Annetta. 18-19th-century Italian singer. ENCI MUS.

PARLOW, Kathleen. Calgary,
Sep 20 1890-Aug 19 1963,
Oakville, Canada. Vio-
linist, teacher. BAKER 5,
BAKER 1971, PRATT, THOMPSON.

"PARMIGIANA, La" see
Cuzzoni, Francesca

PARODI, Teresa. Genoa, 1827-?.
Soprano. THOMPSON.

PARODY, Julia. Málaga, Spain,
1890- . Pianist. ENCI
SALVAT.

PARR, Gladys. Bury, Lancs.,
England, ?- . 20th-century
contralto. GROVE 5.

PARSI-PETINELLA, Armida. Nr.
Rome, Aug 30 1868-Sep 1
1949, Milan. Contralto.
KUTSCH.

PARSONS, Susan Reid- see
Reid-Parsons, Susan

PARTEGIOTTI, Rosa. Carpi,
Italy, 1747-May 13 1813,
Carpi, Italy. Organist,
singer. ENCI MUS=v.3 p.
401 (in article on Antonio
Tonelli).

PASINI, Camilla. Rome, Nov 6
1875-Oct 29 1935, Rome.
Soprano. ENCI MUS.

PASINI, Enrica. 19-20th-cen-
tury Italian mezzo-soprano.
ENCI MUS.

PASINI, Laura. Gallarate,
Italy, Jan 28 1894-Jun 30
1942, Rome. Soprano, pia-
nist. ENCI MUS, KUTSCH,
THOMPSON.

PASINI, Lina (Carolina).
Rome, Nov 8 1872-Nov 23
1959, Rome. Soprano. ENCI
MUS, KUTSCH. *[KUTSCH=b.1876]*

PASQUA, Giuseppina. Perugia,
Italy, Mar 19 1855-Feb 24
1930, Pieve di Budrio,
Bologna, Italy. Mezzo-soprano.
ENCI MUS.

PASQUALI, Bernice de see
De Pasquali, Bernice

PASTA, Giuditta (born Negri).
Saronno, nr. Milan, Apr 9
1798-Apr 1 1865, Blavio, nr.
Como, Italy. Soprano, voice
teacher. BAKER 1, BAKER 5,
BLOM, BROWN BIO, *CLAYTON=
p.246, COOPER, CORTE, DICT
MUS, *ENCI MUS=illus.v.3 fac.
p.387 & v.4 fac.p.350, *ENCI
SALVAT, ENCY MUS, EWEN NEW,
GROVE 1, GROVE 5, MARIZ,
*MGG, PRATT, RIEMANN, SANDVED,
THOMPSON. *[ENCI MUS=Oct 28
1797-Apr 1 1867; BAKER 1 &
GROVE 1=b.in Como]*

PATEY, Janet Monach (born
Whytock). London, May 1 1842-
Feb 28 1894, Sheffield,
England. Contralto. BAKER 1,
BAKER 5, BLOM, BROWN BIO,
BROWN BRIT, GROVE 1, GROVE 5,
PRATT, THOMPSON.

PATHY, Ilonka von. Budapest,
Mar 29 1894- . Pianist.
THOMPSON.

PATIÑO ANDRADE, Graciela.
Buenos Aires, 1920- . Composer. ARIZAGA.

PATON, Eliza. fl.1833. English
singer. GROVE 5.

PATON, Isabella. fl.1825. English singer. GROVE 5.

PATON, Mary Ann(e)(Mrs. Joseph
Wood). Edinburgh, Oct 1802-
Jul 21 1864, Bulcliffe Hall,
Chapelthorpe, nr. Wakefield,
Scotland. Soprano, actress.
BAKER 1, BAKER 5, BLOM, BROWN

BIO, BROWN BRIT, CLAYTON=
p.274, ENCI MUS, GROVE 1,
GROVE 1 APP, GROVE 5,
PRATT, THOMPSON.

PATTERSON, Ada. Plymouth,
England, ?-?. 19th-century
soprano. BROWN BRIT.

PATTERSON, Annie Wilson.
Lurgan, Ireland, Oct 27
1868-Jan 16 1934, Cork.
Folklorist, writer, com-
poser, organist, pianist.
BAKER 5, BROWN BRIT, GROVE
5, PRATT, RIEMANN, THOMPSON.

PATTI, Adelina (Adela Juaña
Maria). Madrid, Feb 19 1843-
Sep 27 1919, Craig-y-Nos,
Brecknock, Wales. Soprano.
BAKER 1, BAKER 5, BLOM,
BROWN BIO, *CELLETTI=illus.
foll.col.608, *COOPER=illus.
p.201, CORTE, DICT MUS,
*ENCI MUS=illus.v.3 fac.p.
390, *ENCI SALVAT, ENCY MUS,
EWEN NEW, GROVE 1, GROVE 1
APP, GROVE 5, KUTSCH, MARIZ,
*MGG, PRATT, RIEMANN, *SAND-
VED, SCHOLES, THOMPSON,
*ULLSTEIN. [BAKER 1, EWEN
NEW, & GROVE 5=b.Feb 10;
CELLETTI=b.Feb 18]

PATTI, Amalia (Amelia). ?,
1831-Dec 1915, Paris.
Singer. ENCI MUS, ENCI
SALVAT, ENCY MUS, THOMPSON.
[THOMPSON=1838-1916]

PATTI, Carlotta. Florence,
Oct 30 1835-Jun 27 1889,
Paris. Soprano, pianist.
BAKER 1, BAKER 5, BLOM,
BROWN BIO, CORTE, DICT MUS,
ENCI MUS, ENCY MUS, EWEN
NEW, GROVE 1, GROVE 5, MGG,
PRATT, RIEMANN, SCHOLES,
THOMPSON. [BAKER 1, BROWN
BIO, GROVE 1, MGG, & PRATT=
b.1840]

PATTI, Caterina Chiesa. Rome,
?-Sep 6 1870, Rome. Soprano.
ENCI MUS, ENCI SALVAT, ENCY
MUS.

PATZAKOVÁ (Pacáková), Anna
(born Jandová). Plzeň,
Czechoslovakia, Jun 6 1895- .
Critic, writer. GROVE 5.

PAUL, Lady Dean see Poldowski

PAUL, Isabella (Mrs. Howard,
born Featherstone). Dartford,
Kent, England, 1833-Jun 6
1879, London. Contralto,
actress. BROWN BIO, BROWN
BRIT.

PAUL, Marie-Rose see Didelot,
Marie-Rose

PAULEE, Mona. Alberta, ?- .
20th-century Canadian mezzo-
soprano. *EWEN LIV SUP.

PAULY, Rosa (stage name of
Rose Pollak). Prešov, Czecho-
slovakia, Mar 15 1895- .
Soprano, voice teacher.
BAKER 5, CELLETTI, *EWEN
LIVING, EWEN LIV SUP, EWEN
NEW, KUTSCH, RIEMANN,
THOMPSON. [CELLETTI &
KUTSCH=b.1894; EWEN LIVING=
b. c1905; CELLETTI=b.in
Ellgott in Teschen, Czecho-
slovakia]

PAUR, Marie (born Bürger).
Gegenbach, Germany, 1862-
Apr 27 1899, New York City.
Pianist. BAKER 1, ENCI MUS,
THOMPSON.

PAVLOVA, Anna Pavlova. St.
Petersburg, Jan 31 1882-
Jan 23 1931, The Hague.
Dancer. DICT MUS, *ENCI
SALVAT, ENCY MUS, RIEMANN.

PAYNE, Miss see Cook, Mrs.
Aynsley

PAYNE, Marie (Mrs. Albert,
born Mahlknecht). Vienna,
Oct 11 1845-Jan 10 1931,
Leipzig. Singer. ENCI MUS,
RIEMANN.

PEARL, Ruth. Liverpool, Feb
14 1916- . Violinist.
*PALMER=illus.p.169.

PEDERZINI, Gianna. Vò di Avio,
Trento, Italy, Feb 10 1906- .
Contralto, mezzo-soprano.
CELLETTI, CORTE, ENCI MUS,
KUTSCH. *[CELLETTI=b.1900;
ENCI MUS=b.1904; CORTE=
b.1908]*

PEINEMANN, Edith. Mainz, Mar 3
1937- . Violinist. PAVLAKIS=
p.273, RIEMANN, *ULLSTEIN.

PEJACSEVICH, Dora von. Budapest, Sep 10 1885-Mar 5
1923, Munich. Composer.
THOMPSON.

PÉLISSIER, Marie. Paris, 1707-
Mar 21 1749, Paris. Singer.
ENCI MUS, ENCY MUS, MGG.
*[MGG=b.1706 or 1707, d.
Mar 21 1759]*

PELLETAN, Fanny. Paris, Jul 28
1830-Aug 2 1876, Passy, nr.
Paris. Editor, music ama-
teur. BAKER 1, PRATT, THOMP-
SON. *[BAKER 1=d.in Paris]*

PELLETIER, Rose E. see
Bampton, Rose E.

PELTENBURG, Mia. Haarlem,
Netherlands, Sep 8 1897- .
Soprano. GROVE 5.

PELTON-JONES, Frances. Salem,
Ore., Dec 6 1863-Apr 24
1946, New York City.
Harpsichordist. BAKER 5.

PENAGOS, Isabel. Spanish
singer. ENCI SALVAT.

PÈNE, Léontine Marie see
Bordes-Pène, Léontine Marie

PENNA, Catherine (Mrs. M.
Hooper). ?-Jun 6 1894, ?.
Soprano, composer. BROWN
BIO, BROWN BRIT.

PENNA, Catherine Louisa. (Mrs.
Frederic, born Smith). ?-Dec
27 1880, London. Soprano.
BROWN BIO, BROWN BRIT.

PENTLAND, Barbara (Lally).
Winnipeg, Jan 2 1912- .
Pianist, composer, opera
composer, teacher. BAKER
1971, CBC, ENCI MUS, MGG,
NAPIER, VINTON.

PEPPERCORN, Gertrude. West
Horsley, Surrey, England,
Dec 1 1878- . Pianist.
PRATT, THOMPSON.

PEPUSCH, Francesca Margherita
see L'Épine, Francesca
Margherita de

PERALTA, Angela. Puebla, Mexico,
Jul 6 1845-Aug 30 1883,
Matzatlán, Mexico. Soprano,
composer. GROVE 5, THOMPSON.

PERALTA, Frances. Manchester,
England, ?-Dec 22 1933, New
York City. Soprano. THOMPSON.

PEREA LABIA, Gianna. Milan,
May 19 1908- . Soprano.
ENCI MUS=v.2 p.555 (in
article on the Labia family).

PEREIRA DA SILVA, Marcia
Salaverry see Haydee, Marcia

PERINI, Flora. Rome, Nov 20
1887- . Mezzo-soprano. BAKER
5, KUTSCH, PRATT, THOMPSON.
[KUTSCH=contralto]

PERKINS, Dunbar see Jewson,
Mrs. Frederick Augustus

PERNEL, Orrea. St. Mary's
Platt, Kent, England, Jul 9
1906- . Violinist. GROVE 5
SUP, THOMPSON.

PERRAS, Margherita. Saloniki,
Greece, Jan 15 1908- .
Soprano. KUTSCH, SCHUH=
p.421.

PERRAUD, Adélaïde. 18-19th-
century Italian ballerina.
ENCI MUS=v.3 p.344 (brief
mention in article on the
Taglioni family).

PERREN, Rhea. Southport,
Lancashire, England, Jul 2
1908- . Pianist. PALMER.

PERRONI, Anna see Ambreville,
Anna Maria Lodovica d'

PERRY, Clara see Davies,
Clara

PERRY, Julia. Lexington, Ky.,
Mar 25 1924- . Composer,
writer, teacher. VINTON.

PERSIANI, Fanny (born Tac-
chinardi). Rome, Oct 4 1812-
May 3 1867, Passy, nr. Paris.
Soprano. BAKER 1, BAKER 5,
BLOM, BROWN BIO, CLAYTON=
p.413, CORTE, DICT MUS,
*ENCI MUS, EWEN NEW, GROVE
1, MARIZ, *MGG, PRATT,
RIEMANN, THOMPSON. [ENCI
MUS=b.1813]

PESCHKA-LEUTNER, Minna.
Vienna, Oct 25 1839-Jan 12
1890, Wiesbaden. Soprano.
BAKER 1, BROWN BIO, GROVE 1,
GROVE 5, PRATT, THOMPSON.

PESSL, Yella (real Christian
names=Gabriela Elsa). Vienna, Jan 4 1906- . Harpsi-
chordist, organist, pianist,
teacher, writer. BAKER 5,

*EWEN LIVING, RIEMANN,
SANDVED, THOMPSON.

PETERBOROUGH, Countess of
see Robinson, Anastasia

PETERS, Roberta. New York City,
May 4 1930- . Soprano, act-
ress. BAKER 5, BLOM, ENCI
MUS, *EWEN LIV SUP, EWEN NEW,
KUTSCH, PAVLAKIS=p.290,
*ROSENTHAL=illus.p.135,
*SANDVED=another illus.p.466,
THOMPSON, *ULLSTEIN.

PETERSEN, Heddy see Björling,
Heddy

PETINA, Irra. St. Petersburg,
Fla., 1907- . Contralto,
soprano. KUTSCH.

PETINELLA, Armida Parsi- see
Parsi-Petinella, Armida

PETRELLA, Clara. Greco Mila-
nese, Italy, Mar 28 1914- .
Soprano, actress. CORTE=
p.721, ENCI MUS, KUTSCH,
*ROSENTHAL=illus.p.136.
[KUTSCH=b.1918?]

PETRELLA, Oliva. Teramo, Italy,
Apr 24 1881- . Soprano.
ENCI MUS.

PETRELLI (stage name of Eleanora
Louise Marianne Petrov, born
Wigström). Siemtuna, Sweden,
Apr 9 1835-Feb 21 1904,
Chicago. Soprano, composer,
administrator. BAKER 5,
PRATT, THOMPSON.

PETRINI, Marie Therese. Rheins-
berg, Germany, 1736-1824,
Schwerin, Germany. Singer,
court musician. MGG.

PETRIS, Jolanda di Maria- see
Maria-Petris, Jolanda di

PETROV, Eleanora Louisa
Marianne see Petrelli

PETROVA, Anna Iakovlevna
see Vorobieva-Petrova,
Anna Iakovlevna

PETTERSON, Anna Augusta
Olivia see Fremstad,
Anna Olivia

PETZ, Maria Anna see
Franziska, Maria Anna

PEYER, Barbara Geiser- see
Geiser-Peyer, Barbara

PEYRON, Gisèle. Bex, Switzerland, Oct 23 1904- . Singer,
voice teacher, writer. ENCI
SALVAT, ENCY MUS, SCHUH.

PEYSER, Ethel Rose. New York
City, Mar 6 1887-Sep 12
1961, New York City. Edi-
tor, critic, writer. BAKER
5, THOMPSON.

PEZ, Maria Anna see
Franziska, Maria Anna

PFEIFFER, Marianne see
Spohr, Marianne

PFEIL, Anna Doris. Copenhagen,
1847-?. Soprano. PRATT.

PFLUGHAUPT, Sophie (born
Stschepin or Shtchepin).
Dvinsk, Latvia, Mar 15
1837-Nov 10 1867, Aix-la-
Chapelle. Pianist. BAKER 1,
BAKER 5, THOMPSON.

PFUND, Leonore (born Thiele).
Glauchau, Germany, May 21
1877- . Composer. THOMPSON.

PHILIPPI, Maria Cäcilia
(Philippi-Cantador). Mül-
heim, Baden, Germany, Jul
26 1875-Jun 16 1944, Zürich.
Contralto, voice teacher.

KUTSCH, RIEMANN, SCHUH,
ULLSTEIN. [RIEMANN & ULL-
STEIN=b.in Basel, d.Jun 17]

PHILLIPPS (Phillips), Adelaide
("Signora Filippi"). Strat-
ford-on-Avon, England, Oct
26 1833-Oct 3 1882, Karlovy
Vary, Bohemia. Contralto.
BAKER 1, BAKER 5, BLOM,
BROWN BIO, BROWN BRIT, EWEN
NEW, GROVE 1 APP, GROVE 5,
GROVE 5 SUP, PRATT, THOMP-
SON. [BROWN BIO=b.in Bristol]

PHILLIPS, Alice. 19th-century
German singer. BROWN BRIT.

PHILLIPS, Anna Maria see
Crouch, Anna Maria

PHILLIPS, Florence. 19th-
century English singer.
BROWN BRIT.

PHILLIPS, Karen (Mrs. Walter
Trampler). 20th-century
American viola player.
PAVLAKIS=p.275.

PHILLIPS, Louisa (Louise).
Bath, England, 1857-1950,
Exeter, England. Mezzo-
soprano. BROWN BRIT, GROVE 5.
[BROWN BRIT=soprano]

PHILLIPS, Sarah. 18th-century
Welsh music engraver.
GROVE 5.

PHILLIS, Jenny see Boïel-
dieu, Jenny

PHILP, Elizabeth. Falmouth,
England, 1827-Nov 26 1885,
London. Singer, voice
teacher, composer. BAKER 1,
BROWN BIO, BROWN BRIT,
GROVE 1 APP, GROVE 5,
THOMPSON.

PHILPOT, Lucy see Anderson,
Lucy

PIAGGIO DE TARELLI, Elsa.
Buenos Aires, 1903- .
Pianist. ARIZAGA.

"PIANIAVIA" see Casadesus,
Jacqueline

PICCOLOMINI, Maria (Marietta).
Siena, Mar 15 1834-Dec 23
1899, Florence. Soprano.
BAKER 1, BLOM, BROWN BIO,
*CLAYTON=p.493, ENCI MUS,
GROVE 1, GROVE 1 APP,
GROVE 5, PRATT, THOMPSON.
*[BROWN BIO=b.1835 (also
given as 1834 & 1836);
BAKER 1 & GROVE 1 APP=
b.1836; ENCI MUS=d.Poggio
Imperiale]*

PICHÉ, Eudore. Montréal,
Feb 9 1906- . Organist,
composer, choral conductor.
CBC.

PICHLER, Karoline see
Valentin, Karoline

PICHT-AXENFELD, Edith.
Freiburg, Germany, Jan 1
1914- . Pianist, harpsi-
chordist. RIEMANN, *ULL-
STEIN.

PIERCY, Rosetta. Birmingham,
England, Nov 29 1838-?. Violinist, soprano. BROWN BRIT.

PIEROZYŃSKA, Franciszka (born
Marunowicz). ?-Sep 19 1816,
Warsaw. Soprano. GROVE 5.

PILARCZYK, Helga Katharina.
Schöningen, Germany, Mar 12
1925- . Soprano. BLOM, ENCI
MUS, KUTSCH, RIEMANN,
THOMPSON, *ULLSTEIN.

PILOU, Jeannette. Alexandria,
Egypt, ?- . 20th-century
soprano. EWEN NEW.

PILTTI, Lea Maire (Killinen).

Rautjärvi, Finland, Jan 2
1904- . Soprano, voice
teacher. GROVE 5, KUTSCH,
RIEMANN.

PINACCI, Anna see Bagnolesi,
Anna

PINKERT, Regina. Warsaw, 1869-
May 28 1931, Milan. Soprano.
CELLETTI, ENCI MUS, KUTSCH.

PINTER, Margot (orig.=Piroska
Margot Hatherly Pintér).
Sacramento, Calif., c1918- .
Pianist. RIEMANN.

PINTO, Amelia. Palermo, Sicily,
Jan 21 1876-Jun 21 1946,
Palermo, Sicily. Soprano.
CELLETTI, ENCI MUS, KUTSCH.
[KUTSCH=b.1878]

PINTO, Charlotte see Brent,
Charlotte

PIPOS, Aurelia Cionca- see
Cionca-Pipos, Aurelia

PIPPEO, Maria Teresa see
De Giuli Borsi, Teresa

PIRANI, Leila see Doubleday,
Leila

PIRAZZINI, Miriam. Vincenza,
Italy, 1918- . Contralto.
KUTSCH.

PIRKER (Pircker), Marianne
(born von Geyerseck). ?,
Jan 27 1717-Nov 10 1782,
Eschenau, nr. Heilbronn,
Germany. Singer. RIEMANN.

PISARONI, Benedetta Rosamunda.
Piacenza, Italy, Feb 6 1793-
Aug 6 1872, Piacenza, Italy.
Soprano, later contralto.
BLOM, BROWN BIO, CLAYTON=
p.238, ENCI MUS, GROVE 1,
GROVE 5, PRATT, RIEMANN,
THOMPSON. *[ENCI MUS=b.May 16]*

PITCHOT, Maria see Gay, Maria

PITROT, Carolina ("Signora Carolina"). 18-19th-century Italian dancer. ENCI MUS= v.1 p.77 (in article on the Angiolini family).

PITZINGER-DUPONT, Gertrude. Mährisch-Schönbern, Austria, Aug 15 1904- . Mezzo-soprano, voice teacher. BAKER 5, *EWEN LIVING, KUTSCH, RIEMANN, THOMPSON, ULLSTEIN. *[EWEN LIVING=b.1906]*

PIXIS, Franzilla Göhringer. Lichtenthal, nr. Baden, Germany, 1816-?. Mezzosoprano. BROWN BIO, ENCI MUS, ENCY MUS, GROVE 5, MGG, THOMPSON.

PLACE, Gertrude. 19th-century English writer. BROWN BIO, BROWN BRIT.

PLAHETKA, Marie Léopoldine see Blahetka, Marie Léopoldine

PLAICHINGER, Thila. Vienna, Mar 13 1868-Mar 19 1939, nr. Vienna. Soprano, voice teacher. GROVE 5, GROVE 5 SUP, KUTSCH, PRATT, THOMPSON.

PLAISTED, Grace. fl.1883-84. English singer. BROWN BRIT.

PLANTADA, Mercedes. Barcelona, 1892- . Soprano. ENCI SALVAT.

PLATTI, Therese Maria (Mrs. Giovanni Benedetto, born Langprückner). 18th-century German singer. ENCI MUS.

PLEYEL, Marie-Félicité-Denise (Mrs. Camille, born Mocke,

Moke, or Mooke). Paris, Jul 4 1811-Mar 30 1875, St.-Joose-ten-Noode, nr. Brussels. Pianist, piano teacher. BAKER 1=p.456, BAKER 5, BLOM=p.435, BROWN BIO, BROWN BRIT, CORTE, DICT MUS, ENCI MUS, ENCY MUS, GROVE 1, GROVE 5, MGG, THOMPSON.

PLÜMACHER, Hetty. Solingen, Germany, Dec 3 1922- . Contralto. KUTSCH, RIEMANN, ULLSTEIN. *[RIEMANN=mezzosoprano]*

PLUNKETT, Catherine. Dublin, 1725-?. Violinist. GROVE 5.

POBBE, Marcella. Montegalda, Venice, Jul 13 1927- . Soprano. CELLETTI, ENCI MUS, *SANDVED.

POCOCK, Cyrena see Van Gordon, Cyrena

PODVALOVA, Marie. Cakovice, Czechoslovakia, 1912- . Soprano. KUTSCH.

PÖLZL, Marie see Rénard, Marie

POGGI, Erminia see Frezzolini, Erminia

POHL, Johanna (born Eyth). Karlsruhe, Germany, Mar 19 1824-Nov 25 1870, Baden-Baden, Germany. Harpist. ENCI MUS, THOMPSON.

POHL, Luise. 19-20th-century German writer. THOMPSON.

POLANSKI, Ingeborg see Hallstein, Ingeborg

POLDOWSKI (pen-name of Irene Regine Wieniawska; by marriage Lady Dean Paul). Brussels, May 16 1880-

Jan 28 1932, London. Composer. BAKER 5, BLOM, ENCI MUS=v.4 p.579 (in article on the Wieniawski family), GROVE 5, GROVE 5 SUP, MGG= v.14 col.627, THOMPSON.

POLIGNAC, Armande de. Paris, Jan 8 1876-?. Composer, opera composer. ENCY MUS, THOMPSON.

POLIGNAC, Winaretta (Princess Edmond de Polignac, born Singer). Yonkers, New York, 1865-Nov 26 1943, London. Patron, pianist, organist. ENCY MUS. *[Information in entry based on New York Times obituary, Nov 27 1943, p.13, col.3]*

POLI RANDACCIO, Ernestina. Ferrara, Apr 13 1879-Feb 1 1956, Milan. Soprano. CELLETTI, *ENCI MUS=illus. v.3 fac.p.459, KUTSCH. *[CELLETTI=b. between 1880 & 1885; KUTSCH=b.1877]*

POLKO, Elise (born Vogel or Vogler). Leipzig, Jan 13 1822-May 15 1899, Munich. Mezzo-soprano, writer. BAKER 1, BAKER 5, BROWN BIO, THOMPSON. *[BAKER 1= b.Jan 31 at Wackerbarthsruhe, nr. Dresden; BROWN BIO=b.Jan 31]*

POLLAK, Anna. Manchester, England, May 1 1915- . Soprano. GROVE 5, GROVE 5 SUP, *ROSENTHAL=illus. p.137.

POLLAK, Rose see Pauly, Rosa

POLLET, Marie-Nicole. Paris, c1783-c1830, Châtillon, France. Harpist, court musician. ENCY MUS.

POLZELLI, Luigia (born Moreschi). Naples, c1760-1832, Košire, nr. Prague. Singer. ENCI MUS.

PONCHARD, Marie Sophie (Mrs. Louis Antoine Eléonore, born Callault). Paris, May 30 1792-Sep 19 1873, Paris. Soprano. BROWN BIO, DICT MUS, ENCI MUS.

PONCHIELLI, Teresa Brambilla see Brambilla, Teresa

PONS, Lily (Alice Joséphine Pons). Draguignan, Tolone, France, Apr 12 1904- . Soprano, actress. BAKER 5, BLOM, CELLETTI, CORTE, *ENCI MUS=illus.v.3 fac.p.109 & 471, ENCI SALVAT, ENCY MUS, *EWEN LIVING, EWEN LIV SUP, EWEN NEW, GROVE 5, KUTSCH, MARIZ, RIEMANN, *SANDVED= another illus.p.715, THOMPSON. *[KUTSCH & RIEMANN= b.Apr 13 1904; CELLETTI & CORTE=b.Apr 16 1904; EWEN LIVING=b.Apr 13 1905; CELLETTI, CORTE, ENCI SALVAT, EWEN LIVING, MARIZ, & RIEMANN=b.in Cannes; KUTSCH= b.nr.Cannes]*

PONSELLE, Carmela (real name= Ponzillo). Schenectady, New York, Jun 7 1892- . Mezzo-soprano, voice teacher. BAKER 5, ENCI MUS, *EWEN LIVING, EWEN NEW, KUTSCH, THOMPSON.

PONSELLE, Rosa (real name= Melba Ponzillo). Meriden, Conn., Jan 22 1897- . Soprano. BAKER 5, BLOM, CELLETTI, *COOPER=p.203, ENCI MUS, ENCI SALVAT, ENCY MUS, *EWEN LIVING, EWEN LIV SUP, EWEN NEW, GROVE 5, KUTSCH, MARIZ, *SANDVED, THOMPSON. *[EWEN LIV SUP= b.1894; MARIZ=p.1898]*

PONSIN, Marie Hippolyte see
Roze, Marie Hippolyte

PONTE, Carlotta Maironi da.
?, 1826-1873, ?. Italian
soprano. ENCI MUS=v.4 p.612.

PONTE, Giulia da see Da
Ponte, Giulia

PONTÉT, Susanne Elisabeth
see Zinck, Susanne Elisa-
beth

PONZILLO, Melba see Pon-
selle, Rosa

POOLE, Elizabeth. London,
Apr 5 1820-Jan 14 1906,
Langley, Bucks., England.
Mezzo-soprano, actress.
BAKER 5, BLOM, BROWN BIO,
BROWN BRIT, GROVE 1, GROVE
5, PRATT, THOMPSON.

POOLE, Fanny Kemble (born
Barnett). London, 1845-?.
Contralto. BROWN BRIT.

POOLE, Maria see Dickons,
Maria

POPATENKO, Tamara Alexandrovna. Moscow, Apr 9 1912- .
Composer. ENCI SALVAT.

POPE, Isabel (later Mrs.
Conant). Evanston, Ill.,
Oct 19 1901- . Musicologist,
writer. RIEMANN, THOMPSON.

POPP, Lucia. Bratislava,
1940- . Soprano. KUTSCH.

POPPER, Sophie see Menter,
Sophie

PORTER ARMSTRONG, Helen see
Melba, Nellie

PORTMANN, Karoline see
Schneider, Karoline

POSSELT, Ruth. Medford, Mass.,
Sep 6 1914- . Violinist.
BAKER 5, THOMPSON.

POSTANS, Mary see Shaw,
Mary

POSTON, Elizabeth. Highfield,
Herts., England, Oct 24
1905- . Pianist, composer,
administrator. BAKER 5,
BLOM, GROVE 5, MGG, SCHOLES,
THOMPSON.

POTTER, Anice see Terhune,
Anice

POULTON, (Edith Eleanor)
Diana. Storrington, Sussex,
England, Apr 18 1903- .
Lutenist. GROVE 5.

POVEY, Miss. Birmingham, England, 1804-?. Soprano.
BROWN BIO, BROWN BRIT.

POWELL, Alma Webster (born
Hall). Chicago, Nov 20
1874-?. Soprano. ENCI MUS=
v.3 p.445 (brief mention in
article on Eugenio Pirani),
THOMPSON.

POWELL, Maud. Peru, Ill., Aug
22 1868-Jan 8 1920, Union-
town, Pa. Violinist. BAKER
5, BLOM, CORTE, GROVE 5,
MARIZ, PRATT, THOMPSON.

POWERS, Marie. ?-Dec 28 1973,
New York City. Soprano.
*SANDVED=illus.only p.304 &
823.

POWNALL, Mary Ann (first known
as Mrs. Wrighten and Wrightson). England, Feb 1751-Aug
11 1796, Charleston, S.C.
Actress, singer, composer.
BAKER 5, THOMPSON=p.1673 &
2429 (double entry).

POZNAŃSKA, Zofia see
Rabcewicz, Zofia

POZZI, Pina. Lugano, Jun 14
1914- . Pianist. SCHUH.

POZZONI, Antonietta see
Anastasi Pozzoni, Antonietta

PRADHER (Pradère), Félicité
(Mrs. Louis Barthélemi;
born More). Carcassone,
France, Jan 6 1800-Nov 12
1876, Gray, France. Singer,
actress. BROWN BIO.

PRAHÁCS, Margit. Budapest,
Apr 12 1893- . Pianist,
piano teacher, writer.
ENCI SALVAT, ENCY MUS,
GROVE 5, MGG.

PRANDL, Gertrud Grob- see
Grob-Prandl, Gertrud

PRATTEN, Madam Sidney.
19th-century English composer, guitarist. BROWN BIO,
BROWN BRIT.

PREOBRAJENSKAIA (Preobrashens-
kaja), Olga. St. Petersburg,
1871-?. Dancer. ENCI SALVAT,
ENCY MUS.

PREOBRAJENSKAIA (Preobrashens-
kaja), Sofia. Leningrad,
Sep 1904- . Contralto, voice
teacher. KUTSCH.

PRESCOTT, Caroline see
Lowthian, Caroline

PRESCOTT, Oliveria Louisa.
London, Sep 3 1842-1919,
London. Composer, teacher,
writer. BROWN BIO, BROWN
BRIT, THOMPSON.

PRESTI, Ida. Suresnes, France,
May 31 1924-Apr 24 1967,
Rochester, New York. Com-
poser, guitarist, teacher.
ENCY MUS.

PRESTON, Adelina see
De Lara, Adelina

PREVOSTI, Franceschina.
Leghorn, Italy, May 13
1869-Dec 28 1938, Camogli,
Italy. Soprano. THOMPSON.

PRICE, Leontyne (Mrs. William
Warfield). Laurel, Miss.,
Feb 10 1927- . Soprano.
BAKER 1971, BLOM, CELLETTI,
ENCI MUS, EWEN NEW, GROVE 5=
v.9 p.178, KUTSCH, PAVLAKIS=
p.290, *SANDVED, THOMPSON,
*ULLSTEIN. [KUTSCH=b.1929;
SANDVED=b.1933]

PRIETO, María Teresa. Oviedo,
Spain, ?- . 20th-century
composer. GROVE 5.

PRINCE, Stella see Stocker,
Stella

PROCHÁZKA, Clementine see
Schuch, Clementine Proska

PROEBSTEL, Alice see
Gentle, Alice

PROSKA, Clementine see
Schuch, Clementine Proska

PROVVEDI, Corella see
Camaiti, Corella Provvedi

PROVVEDI, Gina see
Graziella, Gina

PRUCKNER, Karoline (Mrs.
Dionys). Vienna, Nov 4
1832-Jun 16 1908, Vienna.
Soprano, voice teacher,
writer. BAKER 1, BROWN BIO,
GROVE 1 APP, PRATT, THOMPSON.

PUENTE, Helen del see
Del Puente, Helen

PÜTZ, Ruth-Margaret. Krefeld,
Germany, Feb 26 1931- .
Soprano. KUTSCH, *ULLSTEIN.

PUGET, Loïsa (Louise) Françoise. Paris, Feb 11 1810-
1889, Paris. Composer,
light-opera composer. BAKER
5, DICT MUS, GROVE 1, GROVE
5, MGG, THOMPSON.

PUIG-ROGET, Henriette see
Roget, Henriette Puig-

PULITI SANTOLIQUIDO, Ornella.
Florence, Nov 6 1904- .
Pianist. ENCI MUS.

PURGOLD, Nadežda Nikolaievna
see Rimski-Korsakov,
Nadežda Nikolaievna

PUTEREN, Maria van see
Michailowa, Maria

PUZZI, Giacinta (Mrs. Giovanni, born Toso). 19th-
century Italian singer.
GROVE 5.

PYKE, Helen see Carner,
Helen

PYNE, Louisa Aubert (Mrs.
Wilmore). fl.1857. English
composer, organist. BROWN
BRIT.

PYNE, Louisa Fanny (Mrs.
Frank Bodda). England,
Aug 27 1832-Mar 20 1904,
London. Soprano, voice
teacher, administrator.
BAKER 1, BROWN BIO, BROWN
BRIT, CLAYTON=p.502, ENCI
MUS, GROVE 1, GROVE 5,
THOMPSON.

PYNE, Zoe. fl.1888. English
violinist. BROWN BRIT.

Q

QUAILE, Elizabeth. Omagh,
Ireland, Jan 20 1874-Jun
30 1951, South Kent, Conn.

Pianist, piano teacher.
BAKER 5.

QUARTARARO, Florence. San Francisco, May 31 1922- . Soprano.
KUTSCH.

QUELER, Eve. 20th-century
American conductor. PAVLAKIS=
p.133.

QUINTON, Jeanie see Rosse,
Jeanie

R

RABCEWICZ, Zofia (born Poznańska). Wilno, Poland, 1870-
Sep 3 1947, Warsaw. Pianist,
piano teacher. GROVE 5.

RABENIUS, Olena Ida Teresia
Falkman. Germany, Sep 22
1849-Sep 13 1928, Stockholm.
Contralto. THOMPSON.

RABERT, Elisabeth Catharine
see Müller, Elisabeth
Catharine

RABINOF, Sylvia (Mrs. Benno).
20th-century American pianist, composer, light-opera
composer. *SANDVED.

RADCLIFF, Pauline (Mrs. John,
born Rita). 19th-century
English singer. BROWN BRIT.

RADECKE, Luise Moore. Celle,
Germany, Jun 27 1847-?.
Soprano. BAKER 1, BROWN BIO,
THOMPSON. [BROWN BIO=b.at
Hanover]

RADEV, Marianna. Costanza,
Romania, Nov 21 1913-Sep 17
1973, Zagreb. Contralto.
ENCI MUS, KUTSCH, RIEMANN,
ULLSTEIN. [KUTSCH=b.1911]

RADNOR, Countess of (formerly

Viscountess Folkestone).
19th-century English amateur
composer, conductor, singer,
editor. BROWN BRIT.

RAFFTOR (Raftor), Catherine
see Clive, Catherine

RAINERI-MARINI, Antonia.
19th-century Italian so-
prano. ENCI MUS.

RAINFORTH, Elizabeth. England,
Nov 23 1814-Sep 22 1877,
Redland, Bristol, England.
Soprano, voice teacher.
BLOM, BROWN BIO, BROWN BRIT,
GROVE 1, GROVE 5, THOMPSON.

RAINIER, Priaulx. Howick,
Natal, South Africa, Feb 3
1903- . Composer, teacher,
violinist. BAKER 5, BAKER
1971, COOPER, ENCI SALVAT,
GROVE 5, MGG, RIEMANN,
SCHOLES, THOMPSON.

RAINS, Ida see Souez, Ina

RAISA, Rosa (born Rose Bur-
stein). Bialystok, Poland,
May 30 1893-Sep 28 1963,
Los Angeles. Soprano, voice
teacher, administrator.
BAKER 5, BAKER 1971, CEL-
LETTI, *ENCI MUS=illus.v.3
fac.p.526, EWEN NEW, KUTSCH,
MARIZ, PRATT, SANDVED,
THOMPSON.

RAISBECK, Rosina. Ballarat,
Australia, Feb 28 1918- .
Contralto, later soprano.
GROVE 5.

RAITZIN, Florencia. Buenos
Aires, 1926- . Pianist.
ARIZAGA.

RAJDL, Maria. 20th-century
Austrian soprano. THOMPSON.

RAKOWSKA, Elena (Mrs. Tullio

Serafin). Cracow, 1878-Jul
1965, Rome. Soprano. ENCI
MUS=v.3 p.530 & v.4 p.201.

RALF, Eileen (Mrs. Thomas
Matthews). Australia, Jun
25 1913- . Pianist. GROVE 5=
v.5 p.634 (brief mention in
article on husband), PALMER.

RALPH, Kate (Mrs. Francis,
born Roberts, "Morfida").
London, ?-?. 19th-century
pianist, composer. BROWN
BRIT.

RAMANN, Lina. Mainstockheim,
nr. Kitzingen, Bavaria, Jun
24 1833-Mar 30 1912, Munich.
Composer, editor, writer,
administrator. BAKER 1,
BAKER 5, BROWN BIO, CORTE,
ENCI MUS, GROVE 1, GROVE 1
APP, GROVE 5, GROVE 5 SUP,
MGG, PRATT, THOMPSON.

RAMM, Valentina Iosifovna
(Wally). Karkov, Russia,
Oct 22 1888- . Composer.
THOMPSON, VODARSKY.

RAMPONI, Virginia see
Andreini, Virginia

RANCZAK, Hildegard. Witkowitz,
Moravia, Dec 20 1895- .
Soprano. KUTSCH.

RANDACCIO, Ernestina Poli
see Poli Randaccio, Ernestina

RANDELL, Sheila. Hazlemere,
Bucks., England, Feb 21
1930- . Pianist. PALMER.

RANDLES, Elizabeth. Wrexham,
England, Aug 1 1800-1829,
Liverpool. Pianist, piano
teacher. BROWN BIO, BROWN
BRIT, THOMPSON.

RANGMAN-BJÖRLIN, Elli. Ylistaro, Finland, Apr 21 1882- . Pianist, piano teacher. THOMPSON.

RANKIN, Nell. Montgomery, Ala., 1926- . Mezzo-soprano. KUTSCH, PAVLAKIS=p.295, *SANDVED, THOMPSON.

RAO, Elisabetta Oddone Sulli- see Oddone Sulli-Rao, Elisabetta

RAPOPORT, Eda Ferdinand. Dvinsk, Latvia, 1900-May 9 1969, New York City. Com- poser, pianist. REIS.

RAPPOLD, Marie (later Mrs. Rudolf Berger, born Winter- roth). London, c1873-May 12 1957, North Hollywood, Calif. Soprano, voice tea- cher. BAKER 5, ENCI MUS, KUTSCH, PRATT, THOMPSON. *[PRATT=b.1880? in Brooklyn. New York Times obituary (May 14 1957, p.35, col.3) indicates birth in Brooklyn]*

RAPPOLDI, Laura (Mrs. Eduard, born Kahrer). Mistelbach, nr. Vienna, Jan 14 1853- Aug 17 1925, Dresden. Pia- nist, piano teacher, court musician. BAKER 1, BAKER 5, BROWN BIO, GROVE 5, RIEMANN, THOMPSON=p.1092 & 1740 (double entry). *[GROVE 5, RIEMANN, & THOMPSON=d. Aug 1]*

RASA, Lina Bruna. Padua, Sep 24 1907- . Soprano. *ENCI MUS=illus.v.3 fac.p.534.

RASKIN, Judith. New York City, Jun 21 1932- . So- prano. EWEN NEW, KUTSCH, PAVLAKIS=p.290, *SANDVED= another illus.p.885, THOMP- SON.

RATTI, Eugenia. Genoa, Apr 5 1935- . Soprano. *CELLETTI= illus.foll.col.480, ENCI MUS, KUTSCH. *[KUTSCH=b.1933]*

RAUTAWAARA, (Terttu) Aulikki. Helsinki, May 2 1906- . Soprano, voice teacher. ENCI MUS, GROVE 5, GROVE 5 SUP, KUTSCH, MGG, RIEMANN, THOMPSON, ULLSTEIN. *[ENCI MUS=b.in Vaasa; MGG=b.in Wasa]*

RAVEAU, Alice. ?, 1884?-1945, Paris. Contralto. KUTSCH.

RAWLINS, Bessie. London, 1898- . Violinist. THOMPSON.

RAWSTHORNE, Jessie (Mrs. Alan, born Hinchliffe). 20th-cen- tury English violinist. ENCI MUS.

RAY, Ruth. Alvin, Ill., Jul 19 1899- . Violinist. THOMPSON.

RAYMOND, Fanny see Ritter, Fanny

RAYMOND, Madeleine. Donnaconna, Quebec, Jul 5 1919- . Pia- nist, composer, improvisator. CBC.

REA, Emma Mary (or May; Mrs. William, born Woolhouse). ?-May 6 1893, Newcastle, England. Pianist. BROWN BRIT.

RÉACHE, Jeanne Gerville- see Gerville-Réache, Jeanne

RÉBEL, Anne. ?, 1688-1712, ?. French singer. ENCI MUS.

RÉBEL, Anne-Renée. Paris, 1662-May 5 1722, Paris. Singer, court musician. BLOM, DICT MUS, ENCI MUS, ENCY MUS, GROVE 5. *[ENCY MUS=b.1667]*

RÉBEL, Rose. ?, 1689-1712, ?. Singer. ENCI MUS.

RECLI, Giulia. Milan, Dec 4 1890- . Composer. ENCI MUS, MARIZ, THOMPSON.

REDAELLI, Francesca see Zuccari, Francesca

REDDINGIUS, Aaltje Noordewier-see Noordewier-Reddingius, Aaltje

REDEKER, Louise Dorette Auguste. Duingen, Hanover, Jan 19 1853-?. Contralto. BROWN BIO, GROVE 1.

REDELL, Emma. Baltimore, ?-Feb 2 1940, New York City. Soprano. THOMPSON.

REDENBURG, Anna Angermayer de see D'Angeri, Anna

REDER, Cornelia see Jansen, Cornelia

REDFORD, Eliza see Frost, Eliza

REDONNET, Ana Serrano see Serrano Redonnet, Ana

REED, Priscilla (Mrs. Thomas German, born Horton). Birmingham, England, Jan 1 1818-Mar 18 1895, Bexley Heath, England. Contralto, actress. BAKER 1, BROWN BIO, BROWN BRIT, GROVE 1, GROVE 5=v.3 p.605.

REES, Eleanor. Neath, Glamorganshire, Wales, ?-?. 19th-century contralto. BROWN BRIT.

REEVES, Constance Sims ("Miss Lester"). 19th-century English singer. BROWN BRIT.

REEVES, Emma (Mrs. John Sims, born Lucombe). ?, 1820?-Jun 10 1895, Upper Norwood, England. Soprano, voice teacher. BROWN BIO, BROWN BRIT.

REEVES, Maud (Mrs. Sims, born Rene). 19th-century English singer. BROWN BRIT.

REGAN, Anna see Schimon-Regan, Anna

REGGIANI, Hilde. Modena, 1914- . Soprano. *EWEN LIVING, KUTSCH. [KUTSCH=b.Nov 26 1911]

REGULES, Marisa. Rosario, Argentina, 1925?-Jul 13 1973, New York City. Pianist, conductor. ARIZAGA. [ARIZAGA=b.1914; birth date in entry taken from New York Times obituary (Jul 15 1973, p.47, col.3) indicating death at the age of 48]

REICHARDT, Luise. Berlin, Apr 11 1779-Nov 17 1826, Hamburg. Composer, soprano, voice teacher. BAKER 1, BAKER 5, BROWN BIO, ENCI MUS=v.1 p. 230 (brief mention in article on Benda family), GROVE 5, GROVE 5 SUP, MGG, THOMPSON. [BAKER 1=b.1788; BROWN BIO=b.1778]

REICHER-KINDERMANN, Hedwig. Munich, Jul 15 1853-Jun 2 1883, Trieste. Soprano. BAKER 5, BLOM, GROVE 1 APP, GROVE 5, PRATT, RIEMANN, THOMPSON.

REID-PARSONS, Susan. 20th-century American mezzo-soprano. PAVLAKIS=p.295.

REIMANN, Margarete. Schiltigheim, nr. Strassburg, Elsass,

Germany, Oct 17 1907- .
Musicologist, pianist,
piano teacher, writer.
MGG, RIEMANN.

REINAGLE, Caroline (born
Orger). London, 1818-Mar 11
1892, Tiverton, Devonshire,
England. Composer, pianist,
writer. BROWN BIO, BROWN
BRIT, ENCI MUS, GROVE 5.

REINER, Catherine. Budapest,
Jun 13 1906- . Soprano.
THOMPSON.

REINHARDT, Delia. Elberfeld,
Germany, Apr 27 1892- .
Soprano. KUTSCH.

REINING, Maria. Vienna, Aug 7
1905- . Soprano. CORTE,
KUTSCH, RIEMANN, THOMPSON.
[CORTE=b.1903]

REIS, Claire R. Texas, ?- .
20th-century writer, tea-
cher. THOMPSON.

REISENBERG, Nadia. Vilno,
Russia, Jul 14 1904- .
Pianist, piano teacher.
*EWEN LIVING, *SANDVED,
THOMPSON. *[THOMPSON=b.1905]*

REISET, Marie Félicie Clémence
de see Grandval, Marie
Félicie Clémence de Reiset

REISINGER, Barbara see
Gerl, Barbara

REISS, Thelma. Plymouth,
Devonshire, England, Jul 2
1906- . Violoncellist.
GROVE 5, PALMER, THOMPSON.

REISSEROVÁ, Julie (born
Kühnlová). Prague, Oct 9
1888-Feb 25 1938, Prague.
Composer. BAKER 5, GROVE 5,
MGG, THOMPSON.

RELLSTAB, Caroline. Berlin,
Apr 18 1794-Feb 17 1813,
Breslau. Singer. BROWN BIO=
p.504 (in article on brother
Heinrich Friedrich Ludwig),
ENCI MUS, ENCY MUS, GROVE 5,
MGG. *[BROWN BIO=d.1814]*

REMAN, Anne Loyse see
Thursfield, Anne Loyse

RÉMAURY, Fanny see Montigny-
Rémaury, Fanny

REMMERT, Martha. Gross-Schwein,
nr. Glogau, Poland, Aug 4
1864-?. Pianist, piano
teacher. BAKER 1, PRATT,
THOMPSON. *[BAKER 1=b.Sep 13
1854]*

RÉNARD, Marie (real name=
Pölzl). Graz, Jan 18 1863-
1939, Graz. Soprano. BAKER 1,
ENCI MUS, PRATT, THOMPSON.
*[BAKER 1=b.1864; ENCI MUS=
mezzo-soprano]*

RENARD, Rosita. Santiago,
Chile, Feb 8 1894-May 24
1949, Santiago, Chile.
Pianist, piano teacher.
GROVE 5, THOMPSON.

RENÉ, Anna E. Schoen- see
Schoen-René, Anna E.

RENE, Maud see Reeves, Maud

RENIÉ, Henriette. Paris, Sep
18 1875-Mar 1 1956, Paris.
Harpist, composer, teacher.
BAKER 5, BLOM, CORTE, DICT
MUS, ENCI MUS, ENCI SALVAT,
ENCY MUS, MGG, THOMPSON.

RENK, Sabina see Hitzel-
berger, Sabina

RENNÈS, Catharina van. Utrecht,
Aug 2 1858-Nov 23 1940,
Amsterdam. Composer, teacher,

singer. BLOM, GROVE 5, MGG, RIEMANN, THOMPSON=p.2287.

RENSHAW, Rosette. Montréal, May 4 1920- . Composer, pianist, organist. CBC.

RESNIK, Regina. New York City, Aug 30 1922- . Soprano, mezzo-soprano. BAKER 5, BLOM, ENCI MUS, *EWEN LIV SUP, EWEN NEW, GROVE 5 SUP, KUTSCH, PAVLAKIS=p.290, *ROSENTHAL=illus.p.138, *SANDVED=another illus. p.560, THOMPSON, *ULLSTEIN. [SANDVED=b.1921; ENCI MUS & GROVE 5 SUP=b.Aug 30 1921; EWEN NEW=b.Aug 20 1922; KUTSCH & ULLSTEIN= b.Aug 30 1923]

RESPIGHI, Elsa (born Olivieri-Sangiacomo). Rome, Mar 24 1894- . Composer, opera composer, singer. BAKER 5, BLOM, ENCI MUS, GROVE 5, RIEMANN, THOMPSON.

RESZKE, Josephine de. Warsaw, Jun 4 1855-Feb 22 1891, Warsaw. Soprano. BAKER 5= p.373, DICT MUS, ENCI SAL-VAT, ENCY MUS, EWEN NEW, GROVE 1 APP, GROVE 5, MGG, *SANDVED.

RETCHITZKA, Basia. Geneva, Sep 2 1920- . Soprano. SCHUH.

RETHBERG, Elisabeth (born Lisbeth Sättler). Schwarzen-berg/Erzgebirge, Saxony, Sep 22 1894- . Soprano. BAKER 5, BAKER 1971, CELLET-TI, COOPER, CORTE, ENCI MUS, *EWEN LIVING, EWEN LIV SUP, EWEN NEW, GROVE 5, GROVE 5 SUP, KUTSCH, MARIZ, MGG, RIEMANN, *SANDVED, THOMPSON, ULLSTEIN. [THOMPSON=b.Dec 22]

RÉTHY, Ester. Budapest, Oct 22 1912- . Soprano. KUTSCH.

REUSS-BELCE, Luise. Vienna, Oct 24 1860-Mar 5 1945, Aibach, Germany. Soprano, administrator, manager. BAKER 5, KUTSCH, PRATT, THOMPSON. [KUTSCH=b.1862; PRATT=b.1863]

REUTER, Sara Wennerberg- see Wennerberg-Reuter, Sara

REUTTER, Theresia (later Holz-hauser). Vienna, Oct 22 1708-Apr 7 1782, Vienna. Singer. BROWN BIO, ENCI MUS.

REVOIL, Fanély. Marseilles, Sep 25 1916- . Singer. ENCI SALVAT.

RÉVY, Aurelie. Kapsovar, Hungary, 1879-Oct 30 1957, Toronto. Soprano, voice teacher. KUTSCH.

REY, Mlle. (I). Early 18th-century French dancer, court musician. MGG.

REY, Mlle. (II). Late 18th-century French dancer. MGG.

REY, Mlle. (III). Late 18th-century French dancer, singer?. MGG.

REY, Louise (I). Late 18th-century French teacher. MGG.

REY, Louise (II). Late 18th-century French dancer. MGG.

REY, Mion. Late 18th-century French dancer. MGG.

REYER, Carolyn. 20th-century American mezzo-soprano. PAVLAKIS=p.295.

REYNOLDS, Eleanor. Penn.,
?-Aug 3 1954, Heidelberg.
Contralto. THOMPSON.

REYNOLDSON, Caroline see
Richings-Bernard, Caroline

RHIGINI, Countess de see
Russell, Ella

RHODES, Guy see Hardelot,
Guy d'

RHODES, Jane. Paris, 1930- .
Soprano. KUTSCH.

RICCARDI, Francesca. 18-19th-
century Italian singer.
ENCI MUS=v.3 p.352 (brief
mention in article on the
Paer family).

RICCIONI, Barbara ("la Romanina"). Bologna, ?-?.
18th-century singer. ENCI
MUS.

RICHARDS, Elizabeth Rebecca
see Edwin, Elizabeth
Rebecca

RICHARDS, Irene. Coulsdon,
Surrey, England, Jan 10
1911- . Violinist. PALMER.

RICHARDSON, Cornelia Heitz-
man. Waterloo, Ontario,
Canada, 1890- . Composer.
CBC.

RICHEZ, Céliny Chailley see
Chailley-Richez, Céliny

RICHINGS-BERNARD, Caroline
(adopted daughter of Peter
Richings and wife of Pierre
Bernard, born Reynoldson).
England, 1827-Jan 14 1882,
Richmond, Va. Pianist,
singer. THOMPSON.

RICHTER, Emmy Köhler- see
Köhler-Richter, Emmy

RICHTER, Marga. Wisc., 1926-
Composer. SANDVED.

RIDDICK, Kathleen. Epsom, England, Jul 17 1907- . Con-
ductor. PALMER.

RIDER-KELSEY, Corinne. Nr.
Batavia, New York, Feb 24
1877-Jul 10 1947, Toledo,
Ohio. Soprano. BAKER 5,
PRATT, THOMPSON. *[PRATT=
b.1879]*

RIDLEY, Elizabeth see
Dorman, Elizabeth

RIEGO, Teresa Clotilde del
see Del Riego, Teresa
Clotilde

RIES, Anna Maria. Bonn, c1745-
?. Soprano, court musician.
ENCI MUS, ENCI SALVAT, ENCY
MUS, GROVE 5.

RIGAL, Delia. Buenos Aires,
1920- . Soprano. ARIZAGA.

RIGHETTI GIORGI, Geltrude see
Giorgi-Righetti, Geltrude

RIGHINI, Anna Maria (Mrs.
Vincenzo, born Lehritter).
Würzburg, Feb 25 1762-1793,
?. Soprano. ENCI MUS,
RIEMANN.

RIGHINI, Henriette (Mrs.
Vincenzo, born Kneisel).
Stettin, Prussia, 1767-
Jan 25 1801, Berlin. Singer.
ENCI MUS, GROVE 5, RIEMANN.

RIHOUËT, Yvonne see Rokseth,
Yvonne

RILEY, Ellen see Wright,
Ellen

RILEY, Sarah see Shepley,
Sarah

RIMSKI-KORSAKOV, Nadežda
Nikolaievna (Mrs. Nikolai,
born Purgold). St. Petersburg, 1848-1919, St. Petersburg. Pianist, arranger.
ENCI MUS, RIEMANN, THOMPSON=
p.1716.

RIMSKI-KORSAKOV, Yuliya
Lazarevna see Weissberg,
Yuliya Lazarevna.

RINALDI, Ernestina. Genoa,
Mar 11 1880- . Pianist.
ENCI MUS.

RINALDI, Gioconda (Mrs. Giovanni, born Anfossi). 19th-
century Italian musician.
ENCI MUS.

RIO, Anita. Alameda, Calif.,
Jul 30 1873-?. Soprano.
PRATT, THOMPSON. *[PRATT=
b.1880]*

RIPLEY, Gladys. London, Jul 9
1908-Dec 21 1955, Chiches-
ter, England. Contralto.
GROVE 5, GROVE 5 SUP,
PALMER. *[GROVE 5=b.in
Forest Gate, Essex]*

RIPPER, Alice. Budapest, Mar
23 1889- . Pianist. RIE-
MANN, THOMPSON.

RITA, Pauline see Radcliff,
Pauline

RITCHIE, Margaret Willard.
Grimsby, England, Jun 7
1903-Feb 7 1969, London.
Soprano. GROVE 5.

RITTER, Fanny (Mrs. Frédéric
Louis, born Raymond).
Philadelphia, 1840-1890, ?.
Writer, poet. BAKER 1,
BROWN BIO, BROWN BRIT,
PRATT. *[BROWN BRIT=b.in
England]*

RITTER, Hertha see Hausegger,
Hertha

RITTER-CIAMPI, Cécile. La
Cadière, Var, France, Nov
22 1859-1939, St.-Briac,
Ile-et-Vilaine, France.
Pianist, singer. ENCI MUS.

RITTER-CIAMPI, Gabrielle.
Paris, Nov 2 1886- . Soprano,
voice teacher. ENCI MUS,
ENCY MUS, KUTSCH, RIEMANN,
THOMPSON.

RITTMEYER-ISELIN, Dora J.
Basel, Mar 6 1902- .
Musicologist, writer. SCHUH.

RIVÉ-KING, Julie (born Rivé).
Cincinnati, Oct 31 1857-Jul
24 1937, Indianapolis.
Pianist, piano teacher,
composer. BAKER 5, BROWN
BIO=p.359, PRATT, RIEMANN,
THOMPSON.

RIVERA, Graciela. Ponce, Puerto
Rico, Apr 17 1921- . Soprano.
ENCI MUS.

RIVIÈRE, Ann(a) see Bishop,
Ann(a)

RIVIÈRE, Johanna Everdina la
see Fourie, Johanna
Everdina

RIVOLI, Ludwika. Warsaw, 1814-
1878, Lwów. Soprano. GROVE
5, GROVE 5 SUP.

RIVOLI, Paulina. Warsaw, 1817-
Oct 12 1881, Warsaw. So-
prano. GROVE 5.

RIZZA, Gilda Dalla- see
Dalla-Rizza, Gilda

RIZZIERI, Elena. Rovigo,
Italy, Oct 1922- . Soprano.
*PALMER=illus.p.139.

RIZZOLI, Bruna. Bologna,
Mar 30 1925- . Soprano.
ENCI MUS, ULLSTEIN.

ROBERTI, Margherita. Iowa,
?- . 20th-century soprano.
THOMPSON.

ROBERTS, Juliane see
Walter, Juliane

ROBERTS, Kate see Ralph,
Kate

ROBERTS, Winifred. Lismore,
Australia, Nov 4 1923- .
Violinist. PALMER.

ROBERTSON, Ann Turner see
Robinson, Ann Turner

ROBERTSON, Ethel see
Bartlett, Ethel

ROBERTSON, Fanny. 19th-
century English contralto.
BROWN BRIT.

ROBERTSON, Sophie Maria.
Valparaiso, Chile, Jul 31
1854-?. Soprano. BROWN
BRIT.

ROBESON, Lila P. Cleveland,
Apr 4 1880-Dec 7 1960,
Euclid, Ohio. Contralto,
voice teacher. BAKER 5,
BAKER 1971, PRATT.

ROBIN, Mado (Madeleine).
Yzeures-sur-Creuse, France,
Dec 29 1918-Dec 10 1960,
Paris. Soprano. ENCI SAL-
VAT, ENCY MUS, KUTSCH.
[KUTSCH=b.in Tours]

ROBINA, Fanny see Stanis-
laus, Fanny

ROBINSON, Anastasia (Countess
of Peterborough). London,
c1698-Apr 26 1755, Southampton. Soprano. BLOM, BROWN

BIO, BROWN BRIT, CLAYTON=
p.26, ENCI MUS, GROVE !,
GROVE 5, *MGG=illus.v.11
fac.col.416, THOMPSON.
[BLOM, ENCI MUS, & MGG=
b.c1695]

ROBINSON, Ann Turner (Mrs.
John, born Robertson).
England, ?-Jan 5 1741,
London. Singer. BROWN BIO,
GROVE 5, MGG, THOMPSON.

ROBINSON, Edith. Manchester,
England, Oct 29 1867-Apr 18
1940, Manchester, England.
Violinist, teacher. THOMPSON.

ROBINSON, Elizabeth. London,
c1700-?. Singer. BLOM,
GROVE 5.

ROBINSON, Fanny (Mrs. Joseph,
born Arthur). Southampton,
England, Sep 1831-Oct 31
1879, Dublin. Pianist, composer. BROWN BIO, BROWN
BRIT, GROVE 1, GROVE 5,
THOMPSON.

ROBINSON, Faye. 20th-century
American soprano. PAVLAKIS=
p.290.

ROBINSON, Gail. Tenn., ?- .
20th-century soprano.
PAVLAKIS=p.290.

ROBINSON, Winifred. Boston,
Lincolnshire, England,
?-?. 19th-century violinist.
BROWN BRIT.

ROBSON, Magda García see
García Robson, Magda

ROCHAT, Andrée. Geneva, Jan
12 1900- . Composer. SCHUH.

ROCHOIS, Marthe le see
Le Rochois, Marthe

ROCKEFELLER, Martha Baird
see Baird, Martha

RODE, Alma see Fohström-
Rode, Alma

RODIO, Jolanda. Zürich, Mar
1 1914- . Singer, voice
teacher. SCHUH.

RODRIGO, María. Madrid, Mar
20 1888- . Composer, opera
composer, patron. RIEMANN.

RODRÍGUEZ, Esther. Manzanillo,
Cuba, Nov 29 1920- . Compo-
ser, pianist. ENCI MUS,
GROVE 5, SLONIMSKY.

RODWELL, Anne. 19th-century
English writer. BROWN BIO,
BROWN BRIT.

RÖCKEL, Elisabeth see
Hummel, Elisabeth

ROECKEL, Jane (Mrs. Joseph
Leopold, born Jackson;
pen-name=Jules de Sivrai).
19th-century English
pianist, composer. BROWN
BRIT.

ROEGER, Marie Soldat- see
Soldat-Roeger, Marie

RÖNTGEN, Amanda (born Maier).
Landskrona, Sweden, Feb 19
1853-Jul 15 1894, Amsterdam.
Violinist, composer. ENCI
MUS, RIEMANN, THOMPSON.

ROESELER, Marcella. Berlin,
1890-Jan 29 1957, Berlin.
Soprano, voice teacher.
KUTSCH.

ROESGEN-CHAMPION, Marguerite
Sara (pseud.=Jean Delysse).
Geneva, Jan 25 1894- . Com-
poser, pianist, harpsichor-
dist. BAKER 5, DICT MUS,
ENCI MUS, ENCI SALVAT, ENCY
MUS, *EWEN LIVING, RIEMANN,
THOMPSON.

RÖSSE, Ursula see Günther,
Ursula

RÖSSEL-MAJDAN, Hildegard.
Moosbierbaum, Austria, Jan
21 1921- . Contralto.
KUTSCH, RIEMANN, THOMPSON,
ULLSTEIN.

RÖSSLER, Ernestine see
Schumann-Heink, Ernestine

ROGERS, Clara Kathleen (born
Barnett). Cheltenham, Eng-
land, Jan 14 1844-Mar 8
1931, Boston. Soprano, voice
teacher, composer. BAKER 1,
BAKER 5, CORTE, ENCI MUS,
GROVE 5=v.1 p.443 (in
article on father John
Francis Barnett), PRATT,
THOMPSON.

ROGERS, Della. Denver, 1879-?.
Soprano. BAKER 1.

ROGET, Henriette Puig-. Bastia,
Corsica, Jan 9 1910- . Composer, organist, pianist.
BAKER 5, DICT MUS, ENCI MUS=
v.3 p.502 & v.4 p.36 (double
entry), ENCI SALVAT, ENCY
MUS, MGG, RIEMANN=v.1 p.447.

ROGGERO, Margaret. New York
City, Aug 4 1926- . Mezzo-
soprano. *SANDVED, THOMPSON.

ROGNER, Eva Maria. Zürich,
May 28 1928- . Soprano.
RIEMANN, SCHUH, *ULLSTEIN.
[SCHUH=b.May 31]

ROHS, Martha. Saarbrücken,
Germany, 1909-Jul 27 1963,
Vienna. Contralto. KUTSCH.

ROKSETH, Yvonne (born Rihouët).
Maisons-Laffitte, nr. Paris,
Jul 17 1890-Aug 23 1948,
Strasbourg, France. Musi-
cologist, writer, organist,

composer, editor, teacher, music librarian. BAKER 5, BLOM, CORTE, DICT MUS, ENCI MUS, ENCI SALVAT, ENCY MUS, GROVE 5, *MGG, RIEMANN, THOMPSON, ULLSTEIN. *[MGG= b.Strassburg; BAKER 5, MGG, & THOMPSON=d.Paris]*

ROLANDT, Hedwig (stage name of Hedwig Wachutta). Graz, Sep 2 1858-?. Soprano. BAKER 1.

ROLPH, Clara M. see Brickerhoff, Clara M.

ROMAN, Josette. Paris, ?- . 20th-century pianist. *SANDVED.

ROMAN, Stella. Cluj, Romania, 1910- . Soprano. KUTSCH, MARIZ. *[MARIZ=b.1905]*

ROMAN, Yvette. Paris, ?- . 20th-century pianist. *SANDVED.

ROMANA, Franziska see Jiránek, Franziska

"ROMANI" see Bland, Maria Theresa Catherine

"ROMANINA, La" see Archilei, Vittoria; Aschieri, Caterina; Benti Bulgarelli, Marianna; Martinelli, Caterina; Riccioni, Barbara

ROMANINI, Lucia see Marzorati, Lucia

ROMANOWSKA-KRASSINSKA, Princess see Kschessinska, Mathilde

"ROMANZINI" see Bland, Maria Theresa Catherine

ROMBERG, Angelica. Münster,

Germany, Jul 21 1775- . Soprano, pianist. MGG.

ROMBERG, Bernhardine. Hamburg, Dec 14 1803-Apr 26 1878, Hamburg. Singer. ENCI MUS, MGG.

ROMBERG, Therese. Münster, 1778-?. Singer, church musician. ENCI MUS, GROVE 1, GROVE 5, MGG. *[GROVE 1= b.1781; GROVE 5=b.1791]*

ROMELLI, Lina. Buenos Aires, 1896- . Soprano. ARIZAGA.

ROMER, Annie (Mrs. William Brough). England, 1829-Feb 1 1852, London. Soprano. BROWN BRIT.

ROMER, Emma. England, 1814- Apr 11 1868, Margate, England. Soprano. BROWN BIO, BROWN BRIT, GROVE 5, THOMPSON.

RONEY, Helen see Hogarth, Helen

RONZI, Giuseppina see Begnis, Giuseppina Ronzi de

ROOSEVELT, Emily. Stamford, Conn., Dec 19 1893- . Soprano. THOMPSON.

ROOTHAM, Mabel Margaret. 19th-century English pianist, piano teacher. BROWN BRIT.

ROQUER, Calvé de see Calvé, Rosa-Noémie-Emma

ROS, Maria (stage name of Maria Asuncion Aguilar). Alicante, Spain, May 16 1899- . Singer. ENCI MUS.

ROSA, Alba. Milan, 1889- . Violinist, teacher. THOMPSON.

219   *RUBINSTEIN*

ROSA, Euphrosyne see
Parepa-Rosa, Euphrosyne

ROSA, Lina see Balfe, Lina

ROSAY, Lily see Sás, Lily

ROSE, Clara see Samuell,
Clara

ROSE, Gloria. New York City,
May 20 1933- . Musicologist.
ENCI MUS.

ROSELLE, Anne (orig.=Anna
Gyenges). Budapest, Mar 20
1894- . Soprano, voice
teacher. KUTSCH.

ROSENBAUM, Maria Theresa
see Gassmann, Maria
Theresa

ROSENBERGER, Carol. 20th-
century American pianist.
PAVLAKIS=p.266.

ROSENTHAL, Hedwig Kanner-
see Kanner-Rosenthal,
Hedwig

ROSOMAN, Sarah (or Sophia)
see Mountain, Sarah

ROSS, Elinor. 20th-century
American soprano. PAVLAKIS=
p.291.

ROSS, Mrs. William see
Brown, Mrs. J.

ROSSE, Jeanie (Mrs. H. A.
Quinton). Notting Hill,
London, Jun 29 1860-?.
Contralto, voice teacher.
BROWN BRIT.

ROSSI, Countess see
Sontag, Henriette

ROSSINI, Isabella Angela
see Colbran, Isabella
Angela

ROSSINI, Maria Carbone see
Carbone Rossini, Maria

ROSZA, Anna. Temesvar, Romania,
1898- . Soprano. KUTSCH.

ROTHAUSER, Therese. Budapest,
Jun 10 1865-1942?, prison
camp at Auschwitz [Oświecim]
Poland. Contralto. KUTSCH.

ROTHENBERGER, Anneliese.
Mannheim, Jun 19 1926- .
Soprano. BLOM, KUTSCH,
RIEMANN, THOMPSON, *ULLSTEIN.
[KUTSCH & ULLSTEIN=b.1924]

ROUSSEAU, Esther see
Burney, Esther

ROUSSEAU, Louise Genevieve
see La Hye, Louise Genevieve

ROUSSELOIS, Marie Wilhelmine.
Vienna, Feb 26 1765-Nov 8
1850, Brussels. Soprano.
BROWN BIO.

ROWSON, Jane see Crowe, Jane

ROY, Berthe. Québec, Feb 8
1886-Nov 9 1951, Québec.
Pianist, piano teacher.
GROVE 5.

ROZE, Marie Hippolyte (born
Ponsin). Paris, Mar 2 1846-
Jun 21 1926, Paris. Soprano,
voice teacher. BLOM, BROWN
BIO, EWEN NEW, GROVE 1,
GROVE 1 APP, GROVE 5, PRATT,
SANDVED, THOMPSON.

RUATA, Ada Sassòli see
Sassòli Ruata, Ada

RUBINI, Adelaide (born Chomel).
?, 1794-Jan 30 1874, Milan.
Mezzo-soprano. BROWN BIO.

RUBINSTEIN, Erna. Naguszeben,
Hungary, Mar 2 1903- .
Violinist. THOMPSON.

RUBINSTEIN, Ida. Kharkov,
Russia, Oct 5 1885?-Sep 20
1960, Vence (Alpes-Mar),
France. Dancer. DICT MUS,
*ENCI MUS=illus.v.4 fac.
p.75, ENCI SALVAT, ENCY MUS,
RIEMANN. *[RIEMANN=b.c1880
in St. Petersburg, d.Oct 15
1960. Birth-date in entry
based on New York Times
obituary, Oct 18 1960, p.39,
col.4, indicating death at
age of 75]*

RUBIO, Consuelo. Spain,
1928- . Soprano. KUTSCH.

RUDERSDORFF, Hermine. Ivanov-
sky, Ukraine, Dec 12 1822-
Feb 26 1882, Boston. Soprano, voice teacher. BAKER 1,
BAKER 5, BLOM, BROWN BIO,
GROVE 1, GROVE 1 APP, GROVE
5, PRATT, THOMPSON.

RUDGE, Antonieta. São Paulo,
1886- . Pianist. MARIZ.

RÜCKERT, Adine see O'Neill,
Adine

RUEFF, Jeanine. Paris, Feb 5
1922- . Composer. DICT MUS,
ENCI SALVAT, ENCY MUS.

RUEGGER, Elsa (Mrs. Edmund
Lichtenstein). Lucerne,
Dec 6 1881-Feb 19 1924,
Chicago. Violoncellist,
teacher. PRATT, THOMPSON.

RÜHL, Maria see Schröter,
Maria

RUEL, Mme. du see Du Ruel,
Mme.

RÜNGER, Gertrude. Posen,
Prussia, 1899-Jun 10 1965,
Berlin. Contralto, soprano,
voice teacher. KUTSCH.

RÜSCHE-ENDORF, Cäcilie. Dort-

mund, Germany, Apr 8 1873-
Mar 13 1939, Leipzig. So-
prano. KUTSCH.

RUFER, Magdi. Münchenbuchsee,
Switzerland, Oct 19 1924- .
Pianist. SCHUH.

RUMMEL, Francisca. Wiesbaden,
Feb 4 1821-?. Singer, court
musician. GROVE 1, GROVE 5,
MGG.

RUMMEL, Josephine. Manzanaresi,
Spain, May 12 1812-Dec 19
1877, Wiesbaden. Pianist,
court musician. GROVE 1,
GROVE 5, MGG.

RUNGE, Gertrud. Brandenburg,
Germany, 1880-Aug 7 1948,
Weimar. Soprano. KUTSCH.

RUSS, Giannina (born Cerri).
Lodi, Italy, Mar 27 1873-
Feb 28 1951, Milan. Soprano,
voice teacher. CELLETTI,
CORTE, *ENCI MUS=illus.
v.4 fac.p.75, KUTSCH.
*[CORTE & KUTSCH=b.1878;
KUTSCH=d.Feb 26]*

RUSSELL, Ann see Bullock,
Ann

RUSSELL, Anna (stage name of
Claudia Anna Russell-Brown).
?, 1911- . Singer, come-
dienne. SANDVED.

RUSSELL, Ella (Countess de
Rhigini). Cleveland, Mar 30
1864-Jan 16 1935, Florence.
Soprano. GROVE 5, PRATT,
THOMPSON.

RUSSELL, Lillian (orig.=Helen
Louise Leonard). Clinton,
Iowa, Dec 4 1861-Jun 6 1922,
Pittsburgh. Soprano. THOMP-
SON.

RUSSELL, Louise (orig.=Lois

Crane). 20th-century American soprano. PAVLAKIS=
p.291.

RUSSELL-BROWN, Claudia Anna
see Russell, Anna

RUST, Henriette (Mrs. Friedrich Wilhelm, born Niedhart). 18th-century German
singer. ENCI MUS, GROVE 5.

RUSTICHELLI, Filomena see
Galletti-Gianoli, Isabella

RUSZKOWSKA, Elena (in Poland, sang under name of Helena Zboińska-Ruszkowska). Cracow, 1878-Nov 3 1948, Cracow. Soprano, voice teacher. GROVE 5, KUTSCH. *[GROVE 5=b.in Lwów]*

RUTA, Gilda. Naples, Oct 13 1853?-Oct 26 1932, New York City. Pianist, composer, opera composer, piano teacher. ENCI MUS. *[ENCI MUS=b.1856. Birth-date in entry based on New York Times obituary, Oct 27 1932, p.19, col.1, indicating death at age of 79]*

RUTHVEN, Margaret Lang see
Lang, Margaret Ruthven

RUZICZKA, Else (after 1934, Else Tegetthoff; Mrs. Hans Strobach). Vienna, 1898- . Contralto. KUTSCH.

RYBER, Dagmar de Corval. Baden, Germany, Sep 9 1890-Jul 22 1965, Garden City, Long Island, New York. Pianist, composer. THOMPSON.

RYLEK-STAŇKOVÁ, Blažena. Slivenec, nr. Prague, Feb 10 1888- . Composer, teacher. GROVE 5.

RYSANEK, Leonie (Louise). Vienna, Nov 14 1926- . Soprano. BAKER 1971, BLOM, CELLETTI, ENCI MUS, ENCI SALVAT, ENCY MUS, EWEN NEW, GROVE 5 SUP, KUTSCH, *ROSEN-THAL=illus.p.149, *SANDVED= illus.p.782, THOMPSON, *ULLSTEIN. *[ENCI MUS, EWEN NEW, & THOMPSON=b.Nov 12; KUTSCH= b.Nov 24; SANDVED=b.1928]*

RYSANEK, Lotte. Vienna, Mar 18 1928- . Soprano. RIEMANN, THOMPSON, ULLSTEIN.

RYWACKA, Ludwika (born Morozewicz). ?, 1817-Feb 23 1858, nr. Warsaw. Soprano. GROVE 5, GROVE 5 SUP.

S

SÁ E COSTA, Helena Moreira de. Oporto, Portugal, May 26 1913- . Pianist, piano teacher. GROVE 5.

SABATER, Rosa. Barcelona, 1929- . Pianist. *ENCI SALVAT.

SABATIER, Karoline see
Unger-Sabatier, Karoline

SACHSE-HOFMEISTER, Anna. Gumpoldskirchen, nr. Vienna, Jul 26 1852-?. Soprano. BAKER 1.

SACK, Erna Dorothea. Spandau-Berlin, Feb 6 1898-Mar 2 1972, Wiesbaden. Soprano. BAKER 5, ENCI SALVAT, ENCY MUS, *EWEN LIVING, KUTSCH, MARIZ, RIEMANN, SANDVED, THOMPSON. *[KUTSCH=b.1903; BAKER 5 & EWEN LIVING=b. 1906; ENCI SALVAT, ENCY MUS, MARIZ, & SANDVED= b.1908]*

SADERO, Geni see Scarpa, Eugenia

SADOVEN, Hélène. Finland, 1894- . Contralto. KUTSCH.

SÄTTLER, Lisbeth see Rethberg, Elisabeth

SAFFERY, Eliza (Mrs. Henry Shelton). 19th-century English composer. BROWN BRIT.

SAILER, Friederike. Regensburg, Germany, 1926- . Soprano. KUTSCH, RIEMANN.

SAINT-AUBIN, Alexandrine. Paris, 1793-Apr 1867, Saint Saulge, France. Soprano. BROWN BIO=brief mention only, GROVE 1, GROVE 5, MGG.

SAINT-AUBIN, Anne-Cécile-Dorlise (Mme. Duret). Lyon, 1785-1862, Paris. Soprano. BROWN BIO=brief mention only, GROVE 1, GROVE 5, MGG, THOMPSON.

SAINT-AUBIN, Jeanne-Charlotte (born Schroeder). Paris, Dec 9 1764-Sep 11 1850, Paris. Soprano, actress. BROWN BIO, GROVE 1, GROVE 5, MGG, THOMPSON.

SAINT-HUBERTY, Antoinette Cécile (born Anne-Antoinette Clavel). Toul, nr. Nancy, France, Dec 15 1756-Jul 22 1812, Barnes, nr. Richmond, England. Soprano, actress. BAKER 1, BROWN BIO, CLAYTON= p.91, ENCI MUS, ENCI SALVAT, ENCY MUS, GROVE 1, GROVE 5, PRATT, RIEMANN, THOMPSON.

SAINT-JOHN, Florence (stage name of Maggie Greig). Tavestock, Devonshire, England, 1854-Jan 30 1912, London. Singer, actress, pianist. BROWN BRIT. [In-

formation in entry based on *New York Times obituary, Jan 31 1912, p.11, col.4]*

SAINTON-DOLBY, Charlotte Helen (born Dolby). London, May 17 1821-Feb 18 1885, London. Contralto, composer, administrator. BAKER 1, BLOM, BROWN BIO, BROWN BRIT, GROVE 1, GROVE 1 APP, GROVE 5, PRATT, THOMPSON.

SAKHAROFF, Clotilde see Derp, Clotilde von

SALAMAN, Ivy Frances see Klein, Ivy Frances

SALAVERRY PEREIRA DA SILVA, Marcia see Haydee, Marcia

SALE, Mary Anne. 19th-century English musician. BROWN BIO, BROWN BRIT.

SALE, Sophia. ?-May 3 1869, London?. Musician. BROWN BIO=brief mention only, BROWN BRIT.

SALICOLI (Salicolo, Salicola, Salicola-Suini), Margherita ("la bella Margherita"). Bologna, c1660-1717, Bologna. Singer, court musician. ENCI MUS, GROVE 5, THOMPSON.

SALLÉ, Marie. ?, 1707-1756, Paris. Dancer. *ENCI SALVAT= v.4 p.216, ENCY MUS.

SALMHOFER, Margit see Gál, Margit

SALMON, Eliza (born Munday). Oxford, 1787-Jun 5 1849, Chelsea. Soprano. BLOM, BROWN BIO, BROWN BRIT, GROVE 1, GROVE 5, THOMPSON.

SALOMAN, Henriette see Nissen-Saloman, Henriette

SALOMON, Anna Jakobina.
18-19th-century singer.
ENCI MUS.

SALOMON, Anna Maria. 18-19th-
century singer. ENCI MUS.

SALQUIN, Hedy. Lucerne, Oct 13
1928- . Pianist, piano
teacher. SCHUH.

SALTER, Mary Elizabeth (Mrs.
Sumner, born Turner).
Peoria, Ill., Mar 15 1856-
Sep 12 1938, Orangeburg,
New York. Soprano, composer.
BAKER 5, PRATT, THOMPSON.
[THOMPSON=d.Sep 13]

SALTZMANN-STEVENS, Minnie.
Bloomington, Ill., 1879- .
Soprano. GROVE 5, KUTSCH,
PRATT, THOMPSON. [PRATT=
b.1885?]

SALVADOR, Josefina. 20th-
century Spanish violinist.
ENCI SALVAT.

SALVADOR, Matilde. Castellón
de la Plana, Spain, 1918- .
Composer, opera composer.
ENCI SALVAT.

SALVATINI, Mafalda. Nr. Naples,
Oct 17 1888- . Soprano,
actress. KUTSCH.

SALVI, Adelina Spech see
Spech Salvi, Adelina

SALVI, Margherita (Margarita;
Mrs. Federico Longas).
Milan, 1904- . Soprano.
GROVE 5=v.5 p.391, KUTSCH.

SALVINI DONATELLI, Fanny.
Florence, c1815-Jun 1891,
Milan. Soprano. ENCI MUS.

SAMAROFF, Olga (born Hickenlooper). San Antonio, Tex.,
Aug 8 1882-May 17 1948,

New York City. Pianist,
piano teacher, writer, critic.
BAKER 5, ENCI MUS, GROVE 5,
MARIZ, PRATT, RIEMANN, SAND-
VED, THOMPSON.

SAMPSON, Peggie. Edinburgh,
Feb 16 1912- . Violoncellist.
GROVE 5=v.2 p.98 (brief
mention in article on the
Carter String Trio), PALMER.

SAMUELL, Clara (later Mrs.
Henry Robert Rose). Manches-
ter, England, Aug 29 1857-?.
Soprano. BROWN BIO, BROWN
BRIT=p.355.

SAMWORTH, Elizabeth see
Bride, Elizabeth

SÁNCHEZ, Manuela Cornejo de.
Salta, Argentina, 1854-1902,
?. Composer. ARIZAGA.

SANCHEZ DE VELASCO, María see
Thompson, Marquita Sánchez de

SÁNCHEZ ELÍA, Magdalena Bengolea de. Argentina, 1889-
1962, ?. Singer. ARIZAGA.

SANCHIONI, Nunu. Cairo, Egypt,
Sep 17 1908- . Soprano.
KUTSCH.

SANDBANCK, Mimi see Maazel,
Mimi

SANDEN, Aline (orig.=Aline
Kelch). Berlin, Nov 26 1876-
May 8 1955, Berlin. Soprano,
voice teacher, actress.
KUTSCH.

SANDERS, Alma. 19th-century
English composer, pianist,
piano teacher. BROWN BRIT.

SANDERS, Ellen (Mrs. James).
?, 1826?-May 10 1891,
Liverpool. Choral conductor,
teacher. BROWN BRIT.

SANDERSON, Lillian. Sheboygan, Wisc., Oct 13 1867-?. Soprano, mezzo-soprano. BAKER 1, PRATT. *[BAKER 1= b. in Milwaukee]*

SANDERSON, Sibyl. Sacramento, Calif., Dec 7 1865-May 15 1903, Paris. Soprano. BAKER 1, BAKER 5, BLOM, ENCI MUS, EWEN NEW, GROVE 5, PRATT, SANDVED, THOMPSON.

SANDONI, Francesca see Cuzzoni, Francesca

SANDS, Mollie (Mrs. Brian Jaquet). London, Dec 20 1904- . Soprano, lecturer, writer. GROVE 5.

SANDUNOWA, Jelisaweta Semjonowna (born Fjodorowa). St. Petersburg, 1772-Nov 22 1826, Moscow. Mezzo-soprano. MGG.

SANGIACOMO, Elsa Olivieri- see Respighi, Elsa

SANGIORGI, Santina see Ferlotti, Santina

SANT ANGELO, Pauline. Manchester, England, ?-?. 19th-century English pianist. BROWN BRIT.

SANTA, Marcella della see Lotti della Santa, Marcella

SANTAOLALLA, Marta. Madrid, 1920- . Soprano, actress. ENCI SALVAT.

SANTI, Anna de see Andreozzi, Anna

SANTLEY, Edith. 19th-century English soprano. BAKER 1, BROWN BRIT.

SANTLEY, Gertrude (Mrs. Charles, born Kemble). ?-Sep 1 1882, England. Soprano. BAKER 1, BROWN BRIT.

SANTLEY, Kate. USA, 1837?- Jan 18 1923, Brighton, England. Singer, actress, producer of light operas. BROWN BRIT.

SANTLOW, Hester see Booth, Hester

SANTVIG, Marie see Sundelius, Marie

SAPORITI, Caterina. 18th-century Italian singer. ENCI MUS=v.1 p.187 (brief mention in article on Luigi Barilli).

SAPORITI, Teresa. ?, 1763-Mar 17 1869, Milan. Soprano. ENCI MUS.

"SAPPHO, Infant" see Vinning, Louisa

SARACENI, Adelaide. Rosario de Santa Fé, Argentina, Sep 25 1895- . Soprano, voice teacher. ENCI MUS, KUTSCH. *[KUTSCH=b.1898]*

SARDI, Dorotea. 18-19th-century Italian soprano. ENCI MUS=v.1 p.348.

SARENECKA, Jadwiga. Slawuta, Wolhynia, Poland, 1878-1913, Cracow. Pianist, composer. GROVE 5.

SARFATY, Regina Victoria. USA, 1934- . Mezzo-soprano. *SANDVED.

SARI, Ada (real name=Jadwiga

Szajerowa or Schayer).
Stary Sacz, nr. Lwów, Po-
land, Jun 30 1888-Jul 12
1968, Ciechocinek, Poland.
Soprano, voice teacher.
BAKER 1971, GROVE 5,
KUTSCH, RIEMANN.

SARRATT, Camilla see Dufour,
Camilla

SARS, Eva Helene see Nansen,
Eva Helene

SARSELLI, Elisabeth Augusta
see Wendling, Elisabeth
Augusta (I)

SARTORETTI. fl.1770 in Mantua. Noted only for the
unusual compliment she
paid the young Mozart when
he visited Mantua and for
providing him with pomade
for his severely chapped
hands. GROVE 1.

SARTORIS, Adelaide see
Kemble, Adelaide

SÁS, Lily (Mrs. Andrés,
born Rosay). 20th-century
Peruvian pianist. ENCI
MUS, GROVE 5.

SASS (Sax or Saxe), Marie-
Constance. Ghent, Jan 26
1838-Nov 8 1907, St.-
Périne, nr. Paris. So-
prano. BAKER 1, BLOM, BROWN
BIO, ENCI MUS, GROVE 5,
PRATT, THOMPSON.

SASSÒLI RUATA, Ada. Bologna,
Sep 25 1886-Dec 3 1946,
Rome. Harpist, teacher.
BAKER 5, CORTE, ENCI MUS,
GROVE 5, PRATT, THOMPSON.
[GROVE 5 & PRATT=b.1887]

SAUNDERS, Arlene. 20th-cen-
tury American soprano.
PAVLAKIS=p.291, SANDVED.

SAUREL, Emma. Palermo, 1850-?.
Singer. BAKER 1.

SAUVAGEOT, Madeleine Humbert-
see Humbert-Sauvageot,
Madeleine

SAUVEUR, Nanette see Lolli,
Nanette

SAVAGE, Jane. 18th-century
English composer, harpsi-
chordist. BROWN BRIT,
ENCI MUS, GROVE 5, MGG.

SAVILLE, Frances. San Francisco, Jan 6 1862-Nov 8
1935, Burlingame, Calif.
Soprano. BAKER 5, KUTSCH,
THOMPSON.

SAVONARI, Eugenia see
Tadolini, Eugenia

SAX(E), Marie-Constance see
Sass, Marie-Constance

SAYÃO, Bidú (orig.=Balduina
de Oliveira Sayão). Rio de
Janeiro, May 11 1902- .
Soprano. BAKER 5, CELLETTI,
ENCI MUS, *EWEN LIVING,
EWEN LIV SUP, EWEN NEW,
GROVE 5, KUTSCH, MARIZ,
RIEMANN, *SANDVED, THOMPSON.

SBISÁ, Anny Helm- see
Helm-Sbisá, Anny

SBRISCIA, Zelinda. Rome, 1819-
Jan 29 1898, Rome. Contralto.
ENCI MUS.

SCACCIATI, Bianca. Florence,
Jul 3 1894-Oct 15 1948,
Brescia, Italy. Soprano.
BAKER 1971, CELLETTI,
ENCI MUS, KUTSCH.

SCALABERNI, Luisa see
Tetrazzini, Luisa

SCALABRINI, Teresa (Mrs. Paolo,

born Torre or Torri). 18th-century Italian singer. ENCI MUS.

SCALCHI, Sofia. Turin, Nov 29 1850-Aug 22 1922, Rome. Mezzo-soprano, contralto. BAKER 1, BAKER 5, BLOM, BROWN BIO, ENCI MUS, EWEN NEW, GROVE 1, GROVE 5, PRATT, SANDVED, THOMPSON. *[THOMPSON=d.1921]*

SCARABELLI DIAMANTE, Maria ("La Diamantina"). Bologna, Oct 9 1675-?. Singer. ENCI MUS, ENCI SALVAT, ENCY MUS.

SCARISBRICK, Mrs. Thomas (born Whitnall). England?, 1829-1874, England?. Contralto. BROWN BRIT.

SCARLATTI, Anna Maria. Palermo, Dec 8 1661-Dec 14 1703, Naples. Singer. ENCI MUS, ENCI SALVAT, ENCY MUS, MGG, RIEMANN.

SCARLATTI, Barbara see Stabili, Barbara

SCARLATTI, Flaminia Anna Caterina. Rome, Apr 10 1683-c1725, Rome. Singer. ENCY MUS, RIEMANN.

SCARLATTI, Melchiorra Brigida. Palermo, Oct 5 1663-Dec 2 1736, Naples. Viola player, court musician. ENCI SALVAT, MGG, RIEMANN.

SCARLATTI, Rosa. Naples, May 5 1716-?. Singer. ENCI MUS.

SCARPA, Eugenia (pseud. of Geni Sadero). Constanti-nople. May 12 1886-Aug 7 1961, Milan. Folksong singer, composer. BAKER 5= p.1398, ENCI MUS. *[BAKER 5 =b.in Trieste]*

SCATES, Linda (Mrs. Dutton Cook). Dublin, Nov 16 1855-?. Pianist, piano teacher. BROWN BRIT.

SCHÄRNACK, Luise. Oldenburg, Germany, 1860-?. Mezzo-soprano. BAKER 1.

SCHÄRTEL, Elisabeth. Weiden, Germany, 1890-?. Contralto. KUTSCH.

SCHAFER, Minnie see Guggen-heimer, Minnie

SCHAK (Žák), Antonia. ?, 1784-1851, ?. Bohemian singer, court musician. ENCI MUS.

SCHAK (Žák), Elisabeth see Weinhold, Elisabeth

SCHARRER, Irene. London, Feb 2 1888-Jan 11 1971, London. Pianist, piano teacher. BAKER 5, BAKER 1971, GROVE 5 SUP, PALMER, PRATT, THOMPSON. *[PRATT=b.1880?]*

SCHARWENKA, Marianne (Mrs. Ludwig Philipp, born Stresov). ?, 1865-Dec 24 1918, ?. German violinist. ENCI MUS, GROVE 5, PRATT.

SCHAUROTH, Delphine (Adolphine) von. Magdeburg, Germany, 1814-after 1881, ?. Pianist, composer. GROVE 1, GROVE 1 APP.

SCHAYER, Jadwiga see Sari, Ada

SCHEBEST (Schebst or Schebesta), Agnese (Agnes). Vienna, Feb 10 1813-Dec 22 1869, Stuttgart. Mezzo-soprano. BAKER 1, BAKER 5, BROWN BIO, GROVE 1, PRATT, THOMPSON. *[BAKER 1, BROWN BIO, & GROVE 1=b.Feb 15]*

SCHECH, Marianne. Geitau, Bavaria, Jan 8 1915- .

Soprano. KUTSCH, THOMPSON.
[THOMPSON=b.Jan 1918]

SCHECHNER-WAAGEN, Anna
(Nanette). Munich, 1806-
Apr 29 1860, Munich.
Soprano. BLOM, BROWN BIO,
GROVE 5, GROVE 5 SUP,
PRATT, THOMPSON. [BROWN
BIO=d.Apr 30]

SCHEFF, Fritzi. Vienna, Aug
30 1879-Apr 8 1954, New
York City. Soprano. KUTSCH,
SANDVED, THOMPSON.

SCHEIDLER, Dorette see
Spohr, Dorette

SCHEIDLER, May. New York
City, 1890?- . Soprano.
PRATT.

SCHEIDT, Selma Vom. Bremen,
Jun 26 1874-Mar 1959,
Weimar. Soprano. KUTSCH.

SCHEIN, Ann. White Plains,
New York, Nov 10 1939- .
Pianist. THOMPSON.

SCHELLER ZEMBRANO, María.
Buenos Aires, 1917-1944, ?.
Composer. ARIZAGA.

SCHEPPAN, Hilde. Forst in der
Lausitz, Germany, Sep 17
1908-Sep 24 1970, Bayreuth.
Soprano, voice teacher.
KUTSCH, RIEMANN.

SCHERZ-MEISTER, Elsa. Langen-
thal, Switzerland, Jul 3
1901- . Soprano. GROVE 5,
SCHUH.

SCHEYER, Gerda. Vienna, Jul
18 1925- . Soprano. KUTSCH.

SCHICHT, Costanza (Mrs.
Johann Gottfried, born
Valdesturla). ?-Jul 19 1809.
Italian singer. ENCI MUS.

SCHICK, Margarete Luise (born
Hamel). Mainz, Apr 26 1773-
Apr 29 1809, Berlin. Soprano.
BAKER 1, BAKER 5, BLOM, BROWN
BIO, GROVE 5, MARIZ, MGG,
PRATT, RIEMANN, THOMPSON.
[RIEMANN=b.Apr 27 1768]

SCHICK, Philippine. Bonn,
Feb 9 1893- . Composer.
ENCI MUS, MGG, RIEMANN.

SCHIELOWA, Lucja Drége- see
Drége-Schielowa, Lucja

SCHILLER, Madeline. London,
?-after 1899, ?. Pianist.
BAKER 1.

SCHILLING, Berthe Agnes Lisette
see Bréval, Lucienne

SCHILLINGS, Angela Barbara see
Kemp, Angela Barbara

SCHIMON, Anna (born Regan).
Aich, nr. Karlsbad, Germany,
Sep 18 1841-Apr 18 1902,
Munich. Soprano, voice
teacher. BAKER 1, BAKER 5,
BROWN BIO, ENCI MUS, GROVE 5,
MGG, PRATT, THOMPSON.

SCHIØLER, Annette see
Telmányi, Annette

SCHIRA, Margherita. ?-Apr 1885,
Milan. Singer, voice teacher,
choral conductor. BROWN BIO,
ENCI MUS.

SCHIRMACHER, Dora. Liverpool,
Sep 1 1857-?. Pianist,
composer. BROWN BIO, BROWN
BRIT, GROVE 1.

SCHLAMME, Martha. Vienna, ?- .
20th-century soprano.
*SANDVED.

SCHLEGEL, Luise see Köster,
Luise

SCHLEMM, Anny. Neu-Isenburg, Germany, Feb 22 1929- . Soprano. KUTSCH, RIEMANN.

SCHLESINGER, Kathleen. Hollywood, nr. Belfast, Jun 27 1862-Apr 16 1953, London. Musicologist, writer. BAKER 5, BLOM, ENCY MUS, GROVE 5, THOMPSON. [BLOM & ENCY MUS= d.Apr 18]

SCHLESINGER, Therese see Devrient, Therese

SCHLETTERER, Hortensia (Mrs. Hans Michael, born Zirges). 19th-century German violinist. ENCI MUS.

SCHLÜTER, Erna. Oldenburg, Germany, Feb 5 1904-Feb 1 1969, Hamburg. Soprano. KUTSCH, RIEMANN, THOMPSON.

SCHMELING, Gertrud Elisabeth see Mara, Gertrud Elisabeth

SCHMID, Rosl. Munich, Apr 25 1911- . Pianist. RIEMANN.

SCHMID-GAGNEBIN, Ruth. Neuchâtel, Switzerland, Mar 5 1921- . Pianist. ENCI SALVAT=v.4 p.250, ENCY MUS.

SCHMIT, Jacqueline see Fontyn, Jacqueline

SCHMITT, Cornelia (born Czanyi). Debreczen, Hungary, Dec 6 1851-Oct 11 1906, Wismar, Mecklenburg, Germany. Singer. BLOM=brief mention only, ENCI MUS.

SCHMITTBAUER, Marianne see Kirchgessner, Marianne

SCHMUCK, Margarete see Stockhausen, Margarete

SCHNABEL, Helen (born Fogel).

?, 1911?-Sep 29 1974, Gravedona, Italy. Pianist. ENCI MUS, RIEMANN. [Date of birth based on New York Times obituary, Oct 10 1974, p.50, col.3, indicating death at the age of 63]

SCHNABEL, Therese (Mrs. Artur, born Behr). Stuttgart, Sep 14 1876-Jan 30 1959, Lugano. Contralto. ENCI MUS, GROVE 5= v.1 p.598, GROVE 5 SUP=p.29, KUTSCH, RIEMANN, THOMPSON.

SCHNABEL-TOLLEFSEN, Augusta (Mrs. Carl Henry Tollefsen, born Schnabel). Boise, Idaho, Jan 5 1885-Apr 9 1955, Brooklyn. Pianist. ENCI MUS=v.4 p.395, PRATT.

SCHNAPPER, Edith (Betty). Frankfurt, Oct 31 1909- . Musicologist, librarian, editor, writer. GROVE 5, MGG, THOMPSON.

SCHNÉEVOIGT, Sigrid Ingeborg (later Sundgren). Helsinki, Jun 17 1878-Sep 14 1953, Stockholm. Pianist, piano teacher. BAKER 5=p.1601, ENCI MUS, MGG, THOMPSON.

SCHNEEWEISS, Amalie see Joachim, Amalie

SCHNEIDER, Eta Harich- see Harich-Schneider, Eta

SCHNEIDER, Hortense Caroline Jeanne. Bordeaux, Apr 30 1833-May 6 1920, Paris. Soprano. DICT MUS, MGG.

SCHNEIDER, Jacklyn. 20th-century American soprano. PAVLAKIS=p.291.

SCHNEIDER, Karoline (later Portmann). 18th-century German singer. ENCI MUS.

SCHNEIDER, Maschinka see Schubert, Maschinka

SCHNEIDERHAN, Irmgard Seefried see Seefried, Irmgard

SCHNITZER, Germaine. Paris, May 28 1888- . Pianist. PRATT, THOMPSON.

SCHNORR VON CAROLSFELD, Malvina (Mrs. Ludwig, born Garrigues). Copenhagen, Dec 7 1825-Feb 8 1904, Karlsruhe, Germany. Soprano, voice teacher. BAKER 5, BLOM=p.231, CORTE, ENCI MUS, GROVE 5, MGG, PRATT=p.733, THOMPSON. *[BAKER 5, CORTE, & PRATT=b.1832]*

SCHOBERLECHNER, Sophie (born Dall'Occa). St. Petersburg, 1807-Jan 1864, Florence. Soprano. BROWN BIO, *ENCI MUS=illus.v.4 fac.p.163, GROVE 1, GROVE 5, MGG, PRATT. *[BROWN BIO, ENCI MUS, GROVE 1, & PRATT=d.1863]*

SCHODEL, Rozalie. Kolozsvar, Hungary, Sep 29 1811-Sep 19 1854, Nyaregyhaza, Hungary. Singer. ENCI SALVAT=v.4 p.255, ENCY MUS.

SCHOEN-RENÉ, Anna E. Coblenz, Germany, Jan 12 1864-Nov 13 1942, New York City. Singer, voice teacher. BAKER 5, EWEN NEW, THOMPSON.

SCHÖNE, Lotte. Vienna, Dec 15 1898- . Soprano, voice teacher. ENCI SALVAT=v.4 p.259, ENCY MUS, GROVE 5, KUTSCH, THOMPSON. *[KUTSCH=b.1894]*

SCHOENING, Alwina see Valleria, Alwina

SCHOLTE, Mona see Dahmen, Mona

SCHRÖDER, Cornelia (Cora; Mrs. Hanning, born Auerbach). Breslau, Aug 24 1900- . Teacher, writer. RIEMANN.

SCHROEDER, Jeanne-Charlotte see Saint-Aubin, Jeanne-Charlotte

SCHRÖDER, Marie see Hanfstängel, Marie

SCHRÖDER, Marie Gutheil- see Gutheil-Schröder, Marie

SCHRÖDER-DEVRIENT, Wilhelmine. Hamburg, Dec 6 1804-Jan 26 1860, Coburg, Germany. Soprano. BAKER 1, BAKER 5, BLOM, BROWN BIO, CLAYTON= p.288, CORTE, DICT MUS, *ENCI MUS=illus.v.4 fac.p. 171, *ENCI SALVAT=v.4 p.261, *ENCY MUS, EWEN NEW, GROVE 1, GROVE 1 APP, GROVE 5, MARIZ, *MGG, PRATT, RIEMANN, SANDVED, THOMPSON. *[GROVE 1= d.Jan 21]*

SCHRÖTER, Corona Elisabeth Wilhelmine. Gubin, Poland, Jan 14 1751-Aug 23 1802, Ilmenau, Germany. Soprano, composer, actress, court musician. BAKER 1, BAKER 5, BLOM, CORTE, DICT MUS, ENCI MUS, ENCI SALVAT=v.4 p.261, ENCY MUS, GROVE 1 APP, GROVE 5, *MGG=illus.v.12 fac.col.165, PRATT, RIEMANN, THOMPSON.

SCHRÖTER, Maria (Marie) Henriette (later Rühl). Leipzig, 1766-after 1804, Darmstadt?. Singer. ENCI MUS, MGG.

SCHUBERT, Anna see Hildach, Anna

SCHUBERT, Georgine. Dresden,
Oct 28 1840-Dec 26 1878,
Potsdam. Soprano. BAKER 1,
ENCI MUS, GROVE 5, MGG=
v.12 col.102, PRATT=brief
mention in article on
mother Maschinka, THOMPSON.
[ENCI MUS=d.in Strelitz]

SCHUBERT, Maschinka (born
Schneider). Reval, Estonia,
Aug 25 1815-Sep 20 1882,
Dresden. Soprano, actress.
BAKER 1, ENCI MUS, GROVE 5,
MGG=v.12 col.102, PRATT,
RIEMANN, THOMPSON. [ENCI
MUS=b.in Tallinn]

SCHUCH, Clementine Proska
(real name=Procházka).
Sopron, nr. Vienna, Feb 12
1853-Jun 18 1932, Kötz-
schenbroda, nr. Dresden.
Soprano. BAKER 5, BLOM,
ENCI MUS, GROVE 5, GROVE
5 SUP, RIEMANN, THOMPSON.
[BAKER 5=b.1850; GROVE 5=
b.in Vienna; THOMPSON=
d.Jun 11]

SCHUCH, Liesel von. Dresden,
Dec 12 1891- . Soprano.
BAKER 5, ENCI MUS, RIEMANN.

SCHÜRHOFF, Else. Wuppertal,
Germany, 1898-Mar 17 1961,
Hamburg. Contralto, voice
teacher. KUTSCH.

SCHÜTZ, Françoise-Jeanne see
Litvinne, Félia Vasilyevna

SCHULTHESS, Steffi see
Geyer, Steffi

SCHULTZ, Ann(a) see
Bishop, Ann(a)

SCHULTZ, Johanna see
Klinckerfuss, Johanna

SCHULTZ-ADAÏEWSKA, Ella von
see Adaïewska, Ella von

SCHULTZ VON BECKERATH, Lulu.
19-20th-century German
pianist. ENCI MUS=v.1 p.213
(brief mention in article on
son Hermann von Beckerath).

SCHUMANN, Clara Josephine
(born Wieck). Leipzig, Sep
13 1819-May 20 1896, Frankfurt. Pianist, piano teacher,
composer, editor. BAKER 1,
BAKER 5, BAKER 1971, BLOM,
BROWN BIO, *COOPER=p.253,
CORTE, ENCI MUS, *ENCI
SALVAT=v.4 p.272ff, *ENCY
MUS, GROVE 1, GROVE 1 APP,
GROVE 5=v.7 p.600 & v.9
p.286, MARIZ, *MGG=illus.
v.7 opp.col.64, v.12 col.
263, 265 & opp.col.288,
PRATT, RIEMANN, *SANDVED=
illus.p.1235-36, 1239,
*SCHOLES=p.800, THOMPSON.

SCHUMANN, Elisabeth. Merseburg,
Germany, Jun 13 1885-Apr 23
1952, New York City. Soprano,
voice teacher. BAKER 5, BLOM,
CELLETTI, *COOPER=illus.p.
252, ENCI MUS, ENCI SALVAT=
v.4 p.272, ENCY MUS, *EWEN
LIVING, EWEN LIV SUP, EWEN
NEW, GROVE 5, GROVE 5 SUP,
KUTSCH, MARIZ, MGG, RIEMANN,
*SANDVED, THOMPSON. [BLOM,
CELLETTI, ENCI MUS, GROVE
5 SUP, MARIZ, & THOMPSON=
b.1888; MGG & SANDVED=b.
1891; CELLETTI=d.Apr 24]

SCHUMANN-HEINK, Ernestine
(born Rössler). Lieben, nr.
Prague, Jun 15 1861-Nov 17
1936, Hollywood, Calif.
Contralto. BAKER 1, BAKER 5,
BLOM, CELLETTI, COOPER, ENCI
MUS, EWEN NEW, GROVE 5,
GROVE 5 SUP, KUTSCH, MARIZ,
MGG, PRATT, RIEMANN, *SAND-
VED, THOMPSON. [BLOM &
EWEN NEW=d.Nov 16; PRATT=
soprano]

SCHUR, Adelaide see
Bishop, Adelaide

SCHUYLER, Philippa. USA,
1933- . Pianist. SANDVED.

SCHWADKE, Fraulein see
Sebald, Frau von

SCHWAIGER, Rosl. Alm im
Pinzgau, Austria, Sep 5
1918-Apr 19 1970, Munich.
Soprano. KUTSCH, RIEMANN,
THOMPSON. [KUTSCH=b.in
Saalfelden]

SCHWARZ, Bianca see
Bianchi, Bianca

SCHWARZ, Friederike. Prague,
1910- . Composer, pianist.
THOMPSON.

SCHWARZ, Irene see Jacobi,
Irene

SCHWARZ, Vera. Zagreb, Jul 10
1889-Dec 4 1964, Vienna.
Soprano, voice teacher.
BAKER 1971, KUTSCH. [KUTSCH=
b.1888]

SCHWARZKOPF, Elisabeth. Jarot-
schin, nr. Poznań, Poland,
Dec 9 1915- . Soprano. BAKER
5, BLOM, *CELLETTI=illus.
fac.col.736, COOPER, CORTE,
DICT MUS, ENCI MUS, ENCI
SALVAT=v.4 p.279, ENCY MUS,
*EWEN LIV SUP, EWEN NEW,
GROVE 5, GROVE 5 SUP, KUTSCH,
RIEMANN, *ROSENTHAL=illus.
p.151, *SANDVED, THOMPSON.

SCHWEITZER, Nicole see
Henriot-Schweitzer, Nicole

SCHWINDEL (Schwindl), Anna
Christina (later Klein).
?, 1759-Mar 6 1795, Cologne.
Soprano. ENCI MUS, MGG.

SCHYMBERG, Hjördis Gunborg.

Alnö, Västernorrlands län,
Sweden, Apr 24 1909- .
Soprano. GROVE 5, KUTSCH,
RIEMANN, THOMPSON.

SCHYTTE, Frida (Frida Scotta).
Copenhagen, Mar 31 1871-
Apr 29 1948, Ohlstadt,
Bavaria. Violinist. RIEMANN.

SCIO, Julie-Angélique ("Le-
Grand"). Lille, 1768-Jul 14
1807, Paris. Soprano.
ENCI MUS.

SCIUTTI, Graziella. Turin,
Apr 17 1932- . Soprano.
BLOM, CELLETTI, ENCI MUS,
ENCI SALVAT=v.4 p.238,
ENCY MUS, GROVE 5 SUP,
KUTSCH, RIEMANN, *ROSENTHAL=
illus.p.152, THOMPSON.

SCOTNEY, Evelyn. Ballarat,
Australia, Jul 11 1896-Aug 5
1967, London. Mezzo-soprano.
KUTSCH.

SCOTT, Alicia Ann (Lady John
Douglas, born Spottiswoode).
Spottiswoode, Berwickshire,
Scotland, 1810-Mar 12 1900,
Spottiswoode, Berwickshire,
Scotland. Amateur composer.
BROWN BRIT, GROVE 5, MARIZ.

SCOTT, Isabella see Young,
Isabella

SCOTT, Isabella Mary see
Gibson, Isabella Mary

SCOTT, Marion Margaret. Syden-
ham, London, Jul 16 1877-
Dec 24 1953, London. Musi-
cologist, writer. BAKER 5,
BLOM, GROVE 5, GROVE 5 SUP,
THOMPSON.

SCOTTA, Frida see Schytte,
Frida

SCOTTO, Renata. Savona, Italy,

Feb 24 1934- . Soprano.
BLOM, CELLETTI, ENCI MUS,
EWEN NEW, KUTSCH. *[KUTSCH=
b.1933]*

SCOVOTTI, Jeanette. New York
City, Dec 5 1933- . Soprano.
THOMPSON.

SCRIABINE, Marina. Moscow,
Jan 30 1911- . Composer,
writer. BAKER 1971.

SCUDERI, Sara. Catania,
Sicily, Dec 11 1906- .
Soprano. KUTSCH.

SCUDÉRY, Madeleine. Le Havre,
1607-Jun 2 1701, Paris.
Writer. DICT MUS.

SEBALD, Frau von (born Schwadke). Berlin?, 1791-?. Contralto. GROVE 1.

SEBALD, Amalie. Berlin?,
1801-?. Soprano. GROVE 1,
GROVE 5=v.1 p.545 (in
article on Beethoven).

SEBALD, Auguste. Berlin?,
1802-?. Soprano. GROVE 1=
in article on sister Amalie
Sebald

SEBASTIANI, Pía. Buenos Aires,
1925- . Pianist, composer.
ARIZAGA.

SEBAULT, Pauline Thys- see
Thys-Sebault, Pauline

SECOND, Mary (or Sarah)(born
Mahon). Oxford, c1771-Oct 16
1805, London. Soprano. BROWN
BIO, BROWN BRIT, GROVE 5=
v.5 p.518.

SEDIE, Margherita delle see
Tizzoni, Margherita

SEDLMAIR, Sophie. Hanover,
Jan 25 1857-1939, Hanover.

Soprano, voice teacher.
KUTSCH.

SEEBÖCK, Charlotte von (orig.=
Sara Sebeök von Lasztocz).
Satoraljaujhely, Hungary,
1886- . Soprano, voice
teacher. KUTSCH.

SEEFRIED, Irmgard (later Schnei-
derhan). Köngetried, nr. Wöris-
hofen, Bavaria, Oct 9 1919- ,
Soprano. BAKER 5, BLOM, *CEL-
LETTI=illus.foll.col.736,
COOPER, CORTE, ENCI MUS, ENCI
SALVAT, ENCY MUS, *EWEN LIV
SUP, EWEN NEW, GROVE 5, GROVE
5 SUP, KUTSCH, MGG=v.11 col.
1909, RIEMANN, *ROSENTHAL=
illus.p.153, *SANDVED, THOMP-
SON.

SEEGER, Ruth Porter see
Crawford, Ruth Porter

SEEMAN VON MANGERN, Elsa Laura
see Wolzogen, Elsa Laura

SÉGUIN, Ann (Mrs. Arthur Edward
Sheldon, born Childe). London,
1814-Aug 24 1888, New York
City. Soprano, voice teacher.
BROWN BIO, BROWN BRIT, GROVE
1, GROVE 1 APP, GROVE 5,
THOMPSON.

SEGUIN, Elizabeth. London, 1815-
1870, London. Singer. BROWN
BIO, BROWN BRIT, ENCI MUS=
v.3 p.373 (in article on
Euphrosyne Parepa-Rosa),
GROVE 5, THOMPSON.

SEHLBACH, Irma (Mrs. Erich,
born Zucca). 20th-century
German pianist. ENCI MUS.

SEIDL-KRAUS, Auguste. Vienna,
Aug 28 1853-Jul 17 1939,
Kingston, New York. Soprano.
THOMPSON.

SEIDLER, Karoline see
Wranitzky, Karoline

SEILER, Emma. Würzburg, 1821-
after 1875, ?. Singer, voice
teacher, writer. BROWN BIO,
PRATT.

SEINEMEYER, Meta. Berlin,
Sep 5 1895-Aug 19 1929,
Dresden. Soprano. KUTSCH.

SELLICK, Phyllis. Newbury
Park, Essex, England, Jun
16 1911- . Pianist. GROVE
5, PALMER.

SELVA, Blanche. Brive, Cor-
rèze, France, Jan 29 1884-
Dec 3 1942, St.-Amand-
Tallende, Puy-de-Dôme,
France. Pianist, piano
teacher. BAKER 5, BLOM,
CORTE, DICT MUS, ENCI MUS,
ENCI SALVAT, ENCY MUS,
GROVE 5, MGG, RIEMANN,
THOMPSON.

SEMBRICH, Marcella (Marzella;
real name=Praxede Marcelline
Kochańska). Wisniewczyk,
Galicia, Poland, Feb 15
1858-Jan 11 1935, New York
City. Soprano, voice tea-
cher. BAKER 1, BAKER 5,
BLOM, BROWN BIO, CELLETTI,
COOPER, CORTE, ENCI MUS,
EWEN NEW, GROVE 1, GROVE 5,
KUTSCH, MARIZ, MGG, PRATT,
RIEMANN, *SANDVED, THOMPSON.
*[EWEN NEW & GROVE 5=b.Feb
18; BROWN BIO=b.in Lemberg
(Lwów), Poland]*

SEMINO, Norina. Nr. Turin,
?- . 20th-century violon-
cellist. PALMER.

SEMOUR, Mary Alice Ives   see
Hensel, Octavia

SENGER-BETTAQUE, Katharina.
Berlin, 1862-?. Soprano,
court musician. KUTSCH.

SENKRAH, Arma Leoretta (Lo-

retta; born Harkness). New
York City, Jun 6 1864-1900,
?. Violinist. BAKER 1,
PRATT.

SENPIERE, Maria Dorothea   see
Wendling, Maria Dorothea

SENS, Gina   see   Cigna, Gina

SEPPILLI, Anna   see   Coen,
Anna Seppilli

SEPÚLVEDA, María Luisa.
Chillán, Chile, Aug 14 1898-?.
Pianist, viola player, singer,
conductor, composer. GROVE 5.

SERAFIN, Elena   see   Rakowska,
Elena

SERASSI, Maria Caterina.
Bergamo, Sep 18 1723-Dec 11
1756, Gandino, Bergamo.
Organist, nun. ENCI MUS,
MGG.

SERATO, Cleopatra. Bologna,
Jul 22 1879- . Harpist,
teacher. ENCI MUS.

SERGEYEVNA, Irma   see
Miklashevskaya, Irina

SÉRIEYX, Jeanne (Mrs. Auguste,
born Taravant). ?-1920,
Montreux, France. Pianist.
ENCI MUS.

SEROEN, Berthe. Mechelen,
Belgium, Nov 27 1882- .
Singer. GROVE 5, THOMPSON.

SEROV (Serova, Sierova),
Valentine Semenovna (born
Bergmann). Moscow, 1846-
1927, ?. Composer, opera
composer, editor, writer.
BAKER 5, ENCI MUS, GROVE 5,
PRATT, RIEMANN, THOMPSON,
VODARSKY.

SERRANO REDONNET, Ana. Buenos

Aires, 1914- . Composer.
ARIZAGA.

SESSI, Anna Maria. Rome, 1790-
Jun 9 1864, Vienna. Singer.
ENCI MUS.

SESSI, Imperatrice. Rome,
1784-Oct 25 1808, Florence.
Singer. *ENCI MUS=illus.
fac.p.206.

SESSI, Maria Teresa. 19th-
century Italian singer.
ENCI MUS.

SESSI, Marianna. Rome, 1776-
Mar 10 1847, Vienna. So-
prano, composer, court
musician. BROWN BIO, *ENCI
MUS=illus.fac.p.206.

SEYDEL, Irma. Boston, Sep 27
1896- . Violinist. THOMPSON.

SHACKLOCK, Constance. Sher-
wood, Nottingham, England,
Apr 16 1913- . Mezzo-so-
prano. GROVE 5, GROVE 5
SUP, *ROSENTHAL=illus.p.154,
THOMPSON.

SHAFFER, Elaine (Mrs. Efrem
Kurtz). Pa., 1926-Feb 19
1973, London. Flutist.
CORTE=p.723, PAVLAKIS=
p.280 & 751.

SHAFIR, Shulamith. Odessa,
May 1 1923- . Pianist.
GROVE 5, PALMER, THOMPSON.
[PALMER=b.1922]

SHAFRAN, Sina see Licht-
mann, Sina

SHARP, Mary. 19th-century
English harpist. BROWN
BRIT.

SHARP, Mrs. William. 19th-
century English writer.
BROWN BRIT.

SHARPE, Ethel see Hobday,
Ethel

SHAW, Mary (Mrs. Alfred, born
Postans). London, 1814-Sep 9
1876, Hadleigh Hall, Suffolk,
England. Contralto, voice
teacher. BAKER 5, BLOM,
BROWN BIO, BROWN BRIT, ENCI
MUS, GROVE 1, GROVE 5, PRATT,
THOMPSON. *[BLOM, BROWN BRIT,
ENCI MUS, & GROVE 5=b.in
Lee (Lea), Kent]*

SHEARER, Moira (born King,
married Kennedy). Dunfermline,
Fifeshire, Scotland, Jan 17
1926- . Dancer. RIEMANN.

SHELTON, Eliza see Saffery,
Eliza

SHEPLEY, Sarah (Mrs. Daniel
Sutton, born Riley). England?,
1861?-Jul 12 1894, Brixton,
England. Contralto. BROWN
BRIT.

SHERIDAN, Caroline Elizabeth
Sarah see Norton, Caroline
Elizabeth Sarah

SHERIDAN, Helen Selina see
Dufferin, Helen Selina

SHERIDAN, Margaret. Castlebar
Ireland, Oct 15 1889-Apr 16
1958, Dublin. Soprano.
CELLETTI, COOPER, ENCI MUS,
GROVE 5, GROVE 5 SUP, KUTSCH,
THOMPSON. *[KUTSCH=b.1899]*

SHERRINGTON, Ella see
Lemmens, Ella

SHERRINGTON, Helen see
Lemmens, Helen

SHERRINGTON, Jose. Rotterdam,
Oct 27 1850-?. Soprano.
BROWN BRIT.

SHERRINGTON, Mary see
Lemmens, Mary

SHERWIN, Amy. Tasmania, ?-?.
19th-century soprano. BROWN
BRIT.

SHESTAKOVA, Ludmilla Ivanova
(born Glinka). Russia,
1816?-1906, Russia?. Writer,
critic. VODARSKY.

SHINNER, Emily. Cheltenham,
England, Jul 7 1862-Jul 17
1901, London. Violinist.
BROWN BRIT, GROVE 1 APP,
GROVE 5, THOMPSON.

SHIREBURN, Frances see
Cross, Frances

SHIRREFF, Jane (Mrs. Thomas
Walcott). London?, 1811-
Dec 23 1883, London. So-
prano. BROWN BIO, BROWN
BRIT, GROVE 1, GROVE 1 APP,
GROVE 5, THOMPSON.

SHORE, Catherine see Cibber,
Catherine

SHTCHEPIN, Sophie see
Pflughaupt, Sophie

SHUARD, Amy. London, Jul 19
1924-Apr 18 1975, London.
Soprano. BLOM, CELLETTI,
ENCI MUS, GROVE 5 SUP,
KUTSCH, *ROSENTHAL=illus.
p.155. [Death date from
Variety, Apr 23 1975,
p.71]

SHURTLEFF, Elizabeth Sprague
see Coolidge, Elizabeth
Sprague

SHUTTLEWORTH, Barbara. Canada,
?- . 20th-century soprano.
PAVLAKIS=p.291.

SIBONI, Johanna Frederika
(Mrs. Erik Anton Waldemar,
born Crull). Rostock,
Germany, Jan 30 1839-?.
Pianist. BROWN BIO.

SIDUS, Georgina see Oldmixon,
Lady

SIEBERT, Dorothea. Königsberg,
Germany, 1921- . Soprano.
KUTSCH.

SIEDLE, Philippine see
Edwards, Philippine

SIEMS, Margarethe. Dresden,
Dec 30 1879-May 13 1952,
Dresden. Soprano, voice
teacher. GROVE 5 SUP, KUTSCH.
[KUTSCH=b.in Breslau]

SIEROVA, Valentine Semenovna
see Serov, Valentine
Semenovna

SIEWERT, Ruth. Viersen, Germany,
1911?- . Contralto. KUTSCH.

SILJA, Anja. Berlin, Apr 7
1940- . Soprano. KUTSCH.

SILK, Dorothy. Alvechurch,
England, 1884-Jul 30 1942,
Alvechurch, England. Soprano.
BROWN BIO, GROVE 5, THOMPSON.

SILLS, Beverly (real name=
Belle Silverman). Brooklyn,
May 25 1929- . Soprano.
BAKER 1971, EWEN NEW, PAVLA-
KIS=p.291, SANDVED.

SILVA, Marcia Salaverry Pereira
da see Haydee, Marcia

SILVENTOINEN, Alma see Kuula,
Alma

SILVER, Millicent. London, Nov
17 1905- . Pianist, harpsichordist. GROVE 5, PALMER,
THOMPSON. [PALMER=b.1910]

SILVERBERG, Anna see Hagelstam, Anna

SILVERMAN, Belle see Sills,
Beverly

SIMIONATO, Giulietta. Forlì, Italy, Dec 15 1910- . Mezzo-soprano. BLOM, CEL- LETTI, CORTE, ENCI MUS, EWEN NEW, GROVE 5 SUP, KUTSCH, RIEMANN, *ROSEN- THAL=illus.p.166-67, THOMP- SON. [CELLETTI=b.May 12]

SIMON, Alicja (Alicia). War- saw, Nov 13 1879-May 23 1957, Łódź, Poland. Musi- cologist, editor, writer, teacher. BAKER 5, BAKER 1971, ENCI SALVAT, ENCY MUS, GROVE 5 SUP, MGG, THOMPSON.

SIMON, Joanna. 20th-century American mezzo-soprano. PAVLAKIS=p.296.

SIMONEAU, Pierrette see Alarie, Pierrette

SIMONS, Amélie-Julie see Candeille, Amélie-Julie

SINGER, Teresina. Bohemia, c1850-Jan 9 1928, Florence. Soprano. CORTE, *ENCI MUS= illus.fac.p.226.

SINGER, Winaretta see Polignac, Winaretta

SINGLETON, Esther. Baltimore, Nov 4 1865-Jul 2 1930, Stonington, Conn. Writer. BAKER 5, PRATT, THOMPSON.

SINICO, Clarice (later Campo- bello, born Marini). fl. 1864-67. Italian soprano. GROVE 1.

SINISCALCHI, Tina Filippone- see Filippone-Siniscalchi, Tina

SIRMEN (Syrmen), Maddalena Laura (born Lombardini). Venice, 1735-c1800, Venice. Violinist, composer, singer.

BLOM, BROWN BIO, DICT MUS, ENCI MUS=v.4 p.336, ENCI SALVAT, ENCY MUS, GROVE 1, GROVE 5, GROVE 5 SUP, MGG= v.13 col.13, PRATT, RIEMANN= v.2 p.762, THOMPSON=p.2036 & 2166 (double entry).

SISLEY, Mme. de see De Sis- ley, Mme.

SITCHER DE MENDI, Antonia see Hubert, Antonia

SIVRAI, Jules de (pen-name) see Roeckel, Jane

SJÖGREN, Berta (Mrs. Emil, born Dahlman). 19-20th- century Swedish pianist. GROVE 5=brief mention only.

SJÖSTEDT, Elvi Kajanus- see Kajanus-Sjöstedt, Elvi

SKILONDZ, Adelaide von. St. Petersburg, Jan 21 1888- . Soprano, voice teacher. KUTSCH.

SKINNER, Florence Marian (Mrs. Stuart Stresa). 19th-century English opera composer. BROWN BRIT.

SKINNER, Mrs. Robert see Bristow, Mrs.

SKRHOVÁ, Jitka Snižková- see Snižková-Skrhová, Jitka

SLADEN, Victoria. London, May 24 1910- . Soprano. COOPER, GROVE 5, GROVE 5 SUP, *PAL- MER=illus.p.169.

SLAVINA, Maria Alexandrovna. Russia, 1858-?. Mezzo-sopra- no. ENCI MUS.

SLENCZYNSKA, Ruth. Sacramento, Calif., Jan 15 1925- . Pia- nist. BAKER 5, *EWEN LIVING,

EWEN LIV SUP, PAVLAKIS=
p.268, *SANDVED, THOMPSON.

SLOBODSKAYA, Oda. Vilna,
Lithuania, Nov 28 1889-
Jul 30 1970, London. So-
prano, voice teacher. BAKER
1971, COOPER, GROVE 5,
GROVE 5 SUP, KUTSCH, PALMER,
RIEMANN. *[GROVE 5, KUTSCH, &
RIEMANN=b.1895; birth date
in entry based on obituary
in Opera (vol.21, p.870-71,
Sep 1970) indicating death
at age 81]*

SMART, Harriet Anne (later
Mrs. William Callow). London, Oct 20 1817-Jun 30
1883, London. Amateur
composer. BROWN BRIT.

SMITH, Alice Mary (Mrs.
Frederick Meadows White).
London, May 19 1839-Dec 4
1884, London. Composer.
BAKER 1, BAKER 5, BLOM,
BROWN BIO, BROWN BRIT, ENCI
MUS, GROVE 1=v.4 p.451,
GROVE 1 APP, GROVE 5, PRATT,
RIEMANN=v.2 p.919, SCHOLES,
THOMPSON.

SMITH, Carol. 20th-century
American contralto. PAV-
LAKIS=p.298, SANDVED.

SMITH, Catherine Louisa see
Penna, Catherine Louisa
Smith

SMITH, Clara Ann see Dixon,
Clara Ann

SMITH, Elizabeth see Arnold,
Elizabeth

SMITH, Jessie Love see
Gaynor, Jessie Love

SMITH, Julia. 19th-century
English singer. BROWN BRIT=

p.316 (in article on brother-
in-law Frederic Penna).

SMITH, Julia. Denton, Tex.,
Jan 25 1911- . Composer,
pianist, writer, adminis-
trator. PAVLAKIS=p.353,
VINTON.

SMITH, Laura Alexandrine. 19th-
century English composer,
writer. BROWN BRIT.

SMITH, Mabel (Mrs. William
Braxton, born Berrey). 19th-
century English soprano.
BROWN BRIT.

SMITH, Nellie Curzon. 19th-
century English pianist.
GROVE 5=v.2 p.589 (brief
mention in article on great-
grandfather William Dance).

SMITH, Rosemary see Hughes,
Rosemary

SMOLENSKAYA, Eugenia. Donets
Basin, Ukraine, 1919- .
Soprano. KUTSCH.

SMYTH(E), *Dame* Ethel Mary.
Foots Gray, Kent, England,
Apr 23 1858-May 9 1944,
Woking, Surrey, England.
Composer, opera composer,
light-opera composer. BAKER
5, BAKER 1971, BLOM, BROWN
BRIT, COOPER, CORTE, DICT
MUS, ENCI MUS, ENCI SALVAT,
ENCY MUS=v.3 p.709, GROVE 5,
GROVE 5 SUP, PALMER, PRATT,
*SANDVED, *SCHOLES, THOMPSON.
*[Some sources=d.May 8; date
in entry, confirmed by most
sources, based on New York
Times obituary, May 10 1944,
p.19, col.3]*

SNEDDON, Janet C. 19th-century
English contralto. BROWN
BRIT.

SNIŽKOVÁ-SKRHOVÁ, Jitka.
Prague, Sep 14 1924- .
Pianist, composer. GAR-
DAVSKY.

SNOW, Sophia see Baddeley,
Sophia

SOBIESKI (Sobieska), Jadwiga
(Mrs. Marian, born Pietru-
szyńska). Warsaw, Oct 14
1910- . Musicologist,
ethnologist. DICT MUS, ENCI
SALVAT, GROVE 5, MGG.
[GROVE 5=b.1909]

SÖDERHJELM-GRÖNLUND, Adele
Ester Merete. Viipuri,
Finland, Aug 24 1910-
Pianist. GROVE 5.

SÖDERMAN, Greta Lisa. Göteborg, Sweden, Nov 13 1891-
Soprano. ENCI MUS, MGG=
v.12 col.822.

SÖDERMAN, Ingalill. 20th-
century Swedish singer.
MGG=v.12 col.823.

SÖDERMAN, Karin. 20th-century
Swedish violinist. MGG=
v.12 col.823.

SÖDERMAN, Tova. 20th-century
Swedish singer. MGG=v.12
col.823.

SOEDERSTROEM, Elisabeth.
Stockholm, May 7 1927- .
Soprano. BLOM, ENCI MUS,
GROVE 5 SUP, KUTSCH,
*SANDVED, THOMPSON.
[KUTSCH & SANDVED=b.1926]

SOHY, Charlotte see Labey,
Charlotte

SOLDAT-ROEGER, Marie. Graz,
Mar 25 1863-Sep 30 1955,
Graz. Violinist. BAKER 1,
BAKER 5, GROVE 5, GROVE 5
SUP, PRATT, RIEMANN, THOMP-
SON. [BAKER 1, GROVE 5,

PRATT, & THOMPSON=b.1864]

SOLDENE, Emily. Islington,
London, 1840-Apr 8 1912,
London. Soprano, actress.
BROWN BIO, BROWN BRIT.

SOLOMON, Mirrie. Sydney,
1893- . Pianist, composer,
teacher. THOMPSON.

SOMELLERA, Josefa. Buenos
Aires, 1810-1885, ?. Pianist,
composer. ARIZAGA.

SOMER, Hilde. Vienna, Feb 11
1930- . Pianist. BAKER 1971,
PAVLAKIS=p.268.

SOMIGLI, Franca (stage name of
Marian Bruce Clarke). New York
City, Mar 18 1907-May 14 1974,
Trieste. Soprano. ENCI MUS,
EWEN LIVING. [Date and place
of death based on obituary in
Opera News, Nov 1974, p.63]

SOMIS, Cristina. 18th-century
Italian singer. ENCI MUS.

SONTAG, Henriette (real name=
Gertrud Walburga or Walpur-
gis Sonntag, later Countess
Rossi). Coblenz, Germany,
Jan 3 1806-Jun 17 1854,
Mexico City. Soprano. BAKER
1, BAKER 5, BAKER 1971,
BLOM, BROWN BIO, *CLAYTON=
p.296, CORTE, DICT MUS, *ENCI
MUS=illus.fac.p.251, *ENCI
SALVAT, ENCY MUS, EWEN NEW,
GROVE 1, *GROVE 1 APP,
GROVE 5, GROVE 5 SUP, *MGG,
PRATT, RIEMANN, *SANDVED,
THOMPSON. [BAKER 1=b.1804;
BLOM=d.Jun 3; DICT MUS=
d.Jul 9]

SOPHIE, Elisabeth. Güstrow,
Germany, Aug 20 1613-Jul 12
1676, Lüchow, Germany.
Composer. MGG.

SORACE, Anna Selina see
Storace, Anna Selina

SOREL, Claudette. 20th-century American pianist. SANDVED.

SOROLDONI, Carlotta see Bellincioni, Carlotta

SOUEZ, Ina (orig.=Ida Rains). Windsor, Canada, 1908- . Soprano. KUTSCH, THOMPSON.

SOUKOUPOVÁ, Vera. Prague, Apr 12 1932- . Contralto. KUTSCH.

SOULAGE, Marcelle. Lima, Peru, Dec 12 1894- . Composer, pianist. ENCI SALVAT, ENCY MUS, MGG, RIEMANN.

SOUTHAM, Ann. Winnipeg, Feb 4 1937- . Composer, electronic music composer. NAPIER.

SPAETH, Helen see Vanni, Helen

SPANI, Hina (orig.=Higínia Tunon). Puán, Argentina, Feb 15 1896-Jul 1969, Buenos Aires. Soprano, voice teacher, administrator. ARIZAGA, KUTSCH.

SPEAKS, Margaret. Columbus, Ohio, ?- . 20th-century soprano. *EWEN LIVING.

SPECH SALVI, Adelina. Milan, Aug 18 1811-Aug 1886, Bologna. Soprano. *ENCI MUS=illus.fac.p.262.

SPECKNER, Anna Barbara. Munich, Oct 20 1902- . Harpsichordist. RIEMANN.

SPENA, Lita. Buenos Aires, 1904- . Composer. ARIZAGA.

SPENCE, Sarah. fl.1810. English writer. BROWN BIO, BROWN BRIT.

SPENCER, Annie Jessy see Curwen, Annie Jessy

SPENCER, Eleanor. Chicago, Nov 30 1890-Oct 12 1973, Locarno. Pianist. PRATT, THOMPSON.

SPENCER, Marguerita. Glace Bay, Nova Scotia, 1892- . Pianist, organist, composer, violoncellist. CBC.

SPENNERT, Mary Helena. ?, Dec 1 1901- . Soprano. ENCI MUS= v.2 p.394 (brief mention in article on the Hannikainen family).

SPEZIA, Maria see Aldighieri, Maria

SPIER, Rosa. The Hague, Nov 7 1891- . Harpist. RIEMANN, THOMPSON.

SPIES, Hermine (later Hardtmuth). Löhneberger Hütte, nr. Weilburg, Germany, Feb 25 1857-Feb 26 1893, Wiesbaden. Contralto. BAKER 1, BAKER 5, BLOM, GROVE 5, MGG, PRATT, RIEMANN, THOMPSON.

SPINNEY, Mattie (Mrs. Beesley). 19th-century English organist, pianist, teacher. BAKER 1, BROWN BRIT.

SPIRE, Thérèse Marix- see Marix-Spire, Thérèse

SPITTA, Klara. Odessa, Russia, May 9 1886- . Pianist, piano teacher. ENCI MUS, THOMPSON.

SPITTLER-GÜDEL, Irene see Güdel, Irene

SPIVACKE, Caroline (Mrs. Harold, born Le Fèvre). 20th-century American violinist. ENCI MUS.

SPLETTER, Carla. Flensburg,
Germany, Nov 9 1911-Oct 19
1953, Hamburg. Soprano.
KUTSCH.

SPOHR, Dorette (Mrs. Louis,
born Scheidler). Gotha,
Germany, Dec 2 1787-Nov 20
1834, Kassel, Germany.
Harpist. ENCI MUS, RIEMANN.

SPOHR, Marianne (Mrs. Louis,
born Pfeiffer). Kassel,
Germany, Jun 17 1807-Jan 3
1892, Kassel, Germany.
Pianist. ENCI MUS, RIEMANN.

SPOHR, Rosalie. Braunschweig,
Germany, Jan 22 1829-Jan 11
1919, Berlin. Harpist.
ENCI MUS, RIEMANN.

SPOONENBERG, Erna. Jogjakarta,
Java, 1925- . Soprano.
KUTSCH.

SPOTTISWOODE, Alicia Ann see
Scott, Alicia Ann

SPOURNI, Dorothea see
Wendling, Dorothea (I)

SPURNI, Dorothea see
Wendling, Dorothea (I)

SQUIRE, Emily. 19th-century
English soprano. BROWN BRIT.

STABILI, Barbara. 18th-century
Italian singer. ENCI MUS=
v.4 p.131 (in article on
the Scarlatti family).

STADE, Frederica von see
Von Stade, Frederica

STADELMANN, Li. Würzburg,
Feb 2 1900- . Harpsichor-
dist, pianist. RIEMANN.

STADER, Maria. Budapest, Nov
5 1915- . Soprano, voice
teacher. BLOM, ENCI MUS,

GROVE 5, GROVE 5 SUP, KUTSCH,
RIEMANN, *SANDVED, SCHUH,
THOMPSON. *[SCHUH=b.1911;*
KUTSCH=b.1918]

STÄBLEIN-HARDER, Hanna. Altona,
Prussia, Jan 14 1929- .
Musicologist, writer. MGG.

STAGNO-BELLINCIONI, Bianca
see Bellincioni, Bianca

STAHLMAN, Sylvia. Nashville,
Tenn., Mar 5 1929- . So-
prano. KUTSCH, PAVLAKIS=
p.291, *SANDVED=illus.only
p.1004.

STAIR, Patty. Cleveland, Ohio,
Nov 12 1869-Apr 26 1926,
Cleveland, Ohio. Organist,
composer, light-opera composer. BAKER 5, THOMPSON.

STANDING, Helen (Madame Helen
Standing Norman, known as
Helen Standish). ?-Jan 1891,
London. Contralto. BROWN
BRIT.

STANDISH, Helen see Standing,
Helen

STANISLAUS, Fanny (Mrs. Frederick, born Robina). 19th-
century English singer.
BROWN BRIT.

STAŇKOVÁ, Blažena Rylek- see
Rylek-Staňková, Blažena

STANKOWITCH, Princess see
La Grange, Anna Caroline de

STANLEY, Helen. Cincinnati,
Ohio, Feb 24 1889- .
Soprano. THOMPSON.

STAPLETON, Anna Isabella
(born Matthews). ?-Mar 23
1885, London. Teacher.
BROWN BRIT.

STARCK, Ingeborg see Bronsart von Schellendorf, Ingeborg von

STARK, Helen Mary see Trust, Helen Mary

STARR, Susan. 20th-century American pianist. PAVLAKIS= p.268.

STASSOVA, Varvara Dmitrievna see Komarova, Varvara Dmitrievna

STAUB, Cecile see Genhart, Cecile

STAUDIGL, Gisela (Mrs. Joseph, Jr., born Koppmayer). 19th-century Austrian contralto. GROVE 5.

STAVENHAGEN, Agnes (Mrs. Bernhard, born Denis). 19-20th-century singer. GROVE 5=brief mention only.

STEBER, Eleanor. Wheeling, W.Va., Jul 17 1916- . Soprano, voice teacher. BAKER 5, BLOM, ENCI MUS, *EWEN LIV SUP, EWEN NEW, GROVE 5, GROVE 5 SUP, KUTSCH, PAVLAKIS=p.291, *ROSENTHAL=illus.p.168, *SANDVED, THOMPSON.

ŠTĚBETOVA, Veronica see Dussek, Veronica

STEELE, Janet. 20th-century American soprano. PAVLAKIS= p.292.

STEELE, Mary Sarah. ?, 1816?- Mar 26 1881, London. Singer, voice teacher, administrator. BROWN BRIT=p.274 (in article on Elizabeth Masson).

STEENKISTE, Julie-Aimée-Josèphe van see Dorus-Gras, Julie-Aimée-Josèphe

STEFANI, Eleonora. Warsaw?, 1802-1831, Warsaw?. Soprano. MGG.

STEFANI, Karolina. Warsaw, 1784-1803, Warsaw. Soprano. ENCI MUS, GROVE 5, MGG.

STEFAŃSKA, Halina Czerny- see Czerny-Stefańska, Halina

STEFFAK, Hanny. Biala, Poland, Dec 12 1930- . Soprano. KUTSCH.

STEHLE, Sophie. Hohenzollern-Sigmaringen, Germany, May 15 1838-Oct 4 1921, Schloss Harterode, nr. Hanover. Soprano. BAKER 5, ENCI MUS, PRATT, RIEMANN, THOMPSON.

STEHLE-GARBIN, Adelina. Graz, 1865-Dec 24 1945, Milan. Soprano, voice teacher. CELLETTI, *ENCI MUS=illus. fac.p.283, KUTSCH. [ENCI MUS=b.1863; KUTSCH=b.in Trieste]

STEIN, Grace Maxwell see Wallace, Grace Maxwell

STEIN, Maria Anna (Nannette). Augsburg, Germany, Jan 2 1769-Jan 16 1833, Vienna. Pianist, piano maker. DICT MUS, ENCI MUS, GROVE 1, GROVE 5, MGG, THOMPSON. [GROVE 1=d.Jan 16 1835; THOMPSON=d.Jan 15 1833]

STEIN, Rose. Strasbourg, France, Sep 9 1907- . Harpist. RIEMANN.

STEINGRUBER, Ilona. Vienna, Feb 8 1912-Dec 10 1962, Vienna. Soprano, voice teacher. BAKER 5, BAKER 1971, ENCI MUS=v.4 p.580 (brief mention in article on husband, Friedrich Wildgans), KUTSCH, MGG=v.14

col.650, THOMPSON.

STELLA, Antonietta. Perugia,
Italy, Mar 15 1929- .
Soprano. CELLETTI, ENCI
MUS, GROVE 5 SUP, KUTSCH,
*ROSENTHAL=illus.p.169,
*SANDVED. *[GROVE 5 SUP &
ROSENTHAL=b.1930]*

STENHAMMAR, Elsa Elfrida
Marguerite. Stockholm, May
23 1866-1960, Stockholm.
Choral conductor. MGG.

STENHAMMAR, Fredrika (born
Andrée). Visby, Gotland,
Sweden, Sep 19 1836-Oct 7
1880, Stockholm. Soprano,
voice teacher. MGG.

STENTZSCH, Rosine see
Lebrun, Rosine

STEPHENS, Catherine (Countess
of Essex; known as Kitty
Stephens). London, Sep 18
1794-Feb 22 1882, London.
Soprano. BAKER 1, BLOM,
BROWN BIO, BROWN BRIT,
CLAYTON=p.267, GROVE 1,
GROVE 5, *MGG, PRATT,
THOMPSON. *[BAKER 1=b.Dec 18
1791 or perhaps Sep 18 1794;
BROWN BIO & BROWN BRIT=b.
Dec 18 1791]*

STERLING, Antoinette. Ster-
lingville, New York, Jan
23 1850-Jan 9 1904, London.
Contralto. BAKER 1, BAKER
5, BLOM, BROWN BIO, GROVE
1, GROVE 5, PRATT, THOMPSON.

STERLING, Clara Ann see
Dixon, Clara Ann

STERN, Margaret(h)e (born
Herr). Dresden, Nov 25 1857-
Oct 4 1899, Dresden. Pia-
nist. BAKER 1, THOMPSON.

STERNICKA-NIEKRASZOWA, Ilza.
?, Sep 20 1898-Jun 27 1932,

Warsaw. Composer. GROVE 5,
GROVE 5 SUP.

STEVENS, Jeannie M. see
Hale, Jeannie M.

STEVENS, Minnie Saltzmann- see
Saltzmann-Stevens, Minnie

STEVENS, Risë. New York City,
Jun 11 1913- . Mezzo-soprano.
BAKER 5, BLOM, ENCI MUS,
*EWEN LIVING, EWEN LIV SUP,
EWEN NEW, GROVE 5, GROVE 5
SUP, KUTSCH, MARIZ, *ROSEN-
THAL=illus.p.172, *SANDVED,
THOMPSON. *[MARIZ=b.1910;
EWEN NEW=contralto; SANDVED=
soprano]*

STEWART, Harriet see Wainwright, Harriet

STEWART, Nellie. Melbourne,
1860-Jun 20 1931, ?. Soprano.
BROWN BRIT.

STHAMER, Pelagie see
Andriessen, Pelagie

STICH-RANDALL, Teresa. West
Hartford, Conn., Dec 24
1927- . Soprano. BLOM,
CELLETTI, ENCI MUS, EWEN
NEW, KUTSCH, *ROSENTHAL=
illus.p.170, *SANDVED,
THOMPSON. *[ENCI MUS=b.1930;
CELLETTI=b.c1933]*

STIGNANI, Ebe. Naples, Jul 10
1904-Oct 5 1974, Imola, Italy.
Mezzo-soprano. CELLETTI,
CORTE, *ENCI MUS=illus.fac.
p.291, *EWEN LIV SUP, EWEN
NEW, GROVE 5, KUTSCH, MARIZ,
RIEMANN, *ROSENTHAL=illus.
p.171, SANDVED, THOMPSON.
*[KUTSCH=b.Jul 11 1904; ENCI
MUS & RIEMANN=b.Jul 11 1907.
Date and place of death
based on obituary in Musical
Times, Dec 1974, p.1071, which
indicates death at age 70, so
birth in 1904 appears correct]*

STILES-ALLEN, Lilian. London,
Jul 28 1896- . Soprano.
GROVE 5, PALMER, THOMPSON.

STIRLING, Elizabeth (Mrs.
Frederick A. Bridge).
Greenwich, England, Feb 26
1819-Mar 25 1895, London.
Organist, composer. BAKER 1,
BAKER 5, BLOM, BROWN BIO,
BROWN BRIT, GROVE 1, GROVE
5, PRATT, SCHOLES, THOMPSON.

STOCKER, Stella (born Prince).
Jacksonville, Ill., Apr 3
1858-?. Composer, opera
composer. THOMPSON.

STOCKHAUSEN, Elisabeth von
see Herzogenberg, Elisa-
beth

STOCKHAUSEN, Ella. Dortmund,
Germany, Oct 1 1883- .
Pianist. RIEMANN.

STOCKHAUSEN, Margarete (born
Schmuck). Gebweiler, Alsace,
1803-Oct 6 1877, Colmar,
Germany. Soprano. BLOM,
BROWN BIO, ENCI MUS, ENCY
MUS, GROVE 1, GROVE 5,
THOMPSON.

STÖHR, Maria. Vienna, May 4
1905- . Music historian,
writer. MGG.

STÖWE, Charlotte Karoline
Wilhelmine see Bachmann,
Charlotte Karoline Wil-
helmine

STOKES, Nancy. 20th-century
American soprano. PAVLAKIS=
p.292.

STOLTZ, Rosine (real name=
Victoire Noël or Victorine
Nöb; assumed names of Rosa
Niva, Mlle. Ternaux, and
Mlle. Heloise Stoltz).
Paris, Feb 13 1815-Jul 28

1903, Paris. Mezzo-soprano,
actress. BAKER 1, BAKER 5,
BLOM, BROWN BIO, CORTE, ENCI
MUS, EWEN NEW, GROVE 1,
GROVE 5, PRATT, RIEMANN,
THOMPSON. *[ENCI MUS=b.Jan
13; PRATT & THOMPSON=soprano]*

STOLZ, Fanny (Francesca). 19th-
century Bohemian singer.
ENCI MUS.

STOLZ, Lidia (Ludmila). Kostelec nad Labem, Czechoslovakia, May 8 1827-?. Soprano.
ENCI MUS.

STOLZ (STOLZOVÁ), Teresa (Tere-
sina). Kostelec nad Labem,
Czechoslovakia, Jun 2 1834-
Aug 23 1902, Milan. Soprano.
BAKER 5, CORTE, *ENCI MUS=
illus.fac.p.294, EWEN NEW,
GROVE 5, THOMPSON. *[ENCI MUS=
b.Jun 5]*

STOLZENBERG, Hertha. Cologne,
1889-Mar 20 1960, Obertsdorf,
Germany. Soprano. KUTSCH.

STOLZOVÁ, Teresa see Stolz,
Teresa

STONE, Matja von Niessen- see
Niessen-Stone, Matja von

STORACE, Anna Selina (also
known as Nancy). London,
1766-Aug 24 1817, Dulwich,
London. Soprano. BAKER 1,
BAKER 5, BLOM, BROWN BIO,
BROWN BRIT, CLAYTON=p.138,
*ENCI MUS=illus.fac.p.294,
ENCI SALVAT, ENCY MUS,
GROVE 1, GROVE 5, MARIZ,
PRATT, RIEMANN, SANDVED,
THOMPSON. *[THOMPSON=b.1776]*

STORCHIO, Rosina. Venice, May
19 1876-Jul 24 1945, Milan.
Soprano. BAKER 1971, *CEL-
LETTI=illus.foll.col.736,
CORTE, *ENCI MUS=illus.fac.

p.295, KUTSCH, *SANDVED=
illus.only p.369.

STORTI, Elisa Luigia (Mrs.
Gaggi). Fano, Italy, Apr 25
1802-May 10 1887, Fano,
Italy. Soprano, teacher.
ENCI MUS, ENCY MUS. *[ENCY
MUS=b.1800]*

STORY, Emma Hayden see
Eames, Emma Hayden

STOSKA, Polyna. Worcester,
Mass., 1914- . Soprano.
KUTSCH.

STRADA, Anna Maria ("La
Stradina"). 18th-century
Italian soprano. BLOM, ENCI
MUS, GROVE 5, THOMPSON.

STRÄSSER, Barbara see
Fischer, Barbara

STRAKOVÁ, Theodora. Vienna,
Dec 21 1915- . Musicolo-
gist, writer. RIEMANN.

STRALIA, Elsa (born Fischer).
Adelaide, Australia, 1880-
Aug 5 1945, Melbourne.
Soprano, voice teacher.
KUTSCH.

STRATAKI, Anastasia see
Stratas, Teresa

STRATAS, Teresa (real name=
Anastasia Strataki).
Toronto, May 26 1938- .
Soprano. BAKER 1971,
KUTSCH, *SANDVED, THOMPSON.

STRAUSS, Pauline (Mrs. Richard,
born De Ahna). ?-May 13
1950, Garmisch-Partenkirchen,
Germany. Soprano. GROVE 5=
v.2 p.620 & v.8 p.124-25.

STRAZZA, Giovannina see
Lucca, Giovannina

STREICH, Rita (Mrs. Berger).
Barnaul, Siberia, Dec 18
1926- . Soprano. BLOM,
ENCI MUS, KUTSCH, RIEMANN,
*ROSENTHAL=illus.p.184,
*SANDVED, THOMPSON. *[BLOM
& KUTSCH=b.1920]*

STREICHER, Lyubov Lvovna.
Vladikavkaz, Russia, 1887- .
Composer, light-opera com-
poser, violinist. VODARSKY.

STREPPONI, Clelia Maria
Josepha (later Giuseppina
Verdi). Lodi, Italy, Sep 18
1815-Nov 14 1897, Busseto,
Italy. Soprano, voice tea-
cher. BAKER 1=p.599, BAKER 5,
CORTE, *ENCI MUS=illus.fac.
p.314, ENCI SALVAT, ENCY MUS,
EWEN NEW, GROVE 5=v.8 p.730,
737, *MGG=illus.v.13 col.
1429, PRATT, SANDVED, THOMP-
SON.

STRESA, Florence Marian see
Skinner, Florence Marian

STRESOV, Marianne see
Scharwenka, Marianne

STRICKLAND, Lily Teresa.
Anderson, S.C., Jan 28 1887-
Jun 6 1958, Hendersonville,
N.C. Composer. THOMPSON.

STRIGGIO, Virginia (later
Vagnoli). 16th-century
Italian lutenist. ENCI MUS.

STRINASACCHI, Regina (Anna).
Ostiglia, nr. Mantua, 1764-
c1823, Gotha, Germany.
Violinist, guitarist. BLOM,
CORTE, ENCI MUS, ENCY MUS,
GROVE 1, GROVE 5, GROVE 5
SUP, THOMPSON. *[BLOM=d.1839
in Dresden]*

STRINASACCHI, Teresa. Ostiglia,
nr. Mantua, 1768-after 1838,

Italy?. Soprano. CORTE,
ENCI MUS.

STROBACH, Else see Ruzicka,
Else

STRÖSSER, Caroline see
Waltershausen, Caroline von

STRONG, Susan. Brooklyn, Aug
3 1870-Nov 3 1946, London.
Soprano. KUTSCH, PRATT,
THOMPSON. [PRATT=b.1875?]

STROZZI, Barbara. Venice,
c1620-?, Venice. Singer,
composer. BLOM, CORTE, DICT
MUS, ENCI SALVAT, ENCY MUS,
GROVE 5, PRATT=p.890, RIE-
MANN, THOMPSON.

STROZZI, Violetta de. Zagreb,
1895- . Soprano. KUTSCH.

STSCHEPIN, Sophie see
Pflughaupt, Sophie

STUART, Lía (Amalia D'Urbano
de Colombo). Buenos Aires,
1889- . Soprano. ARIZAGA.

STUCEVSKI, Julia (Mrs. Joachim,
born Bliudz). Tsarskoie Selo,
nr.St. Petersburg, Oct 25
1908- . Singer. ENCI MUS.

STUCKENSCHMIDT, Margot (Mrs.
Hans Heinz, born Hinnen-
berg-Lefebre). 20th-century
Austrian soprano. ENCI MUS.

STUCKI, Aida. Cairo, Egypt,
Feb 19 1921- . Violinist.
SCHUH NACH.

STUCKI, Rosemarie. Berne,
Switzerland, Dec 11 1918- .
Pianist. GROVE 5, SCHUH.

STUDER, Carmen Weingartner-
see Weingartner-Studer,
Carmen

STÜCKGOLD, Grete (born Sch-

neidt). London, Jun 6 1895- .
Soprano, administrator. BAKER
5, ENCI MUS=v.4 p.177 (brief
mention in article on Schüt-
zendorf brothers), *EWEN
LIVING, EWEN NEW, KUTSCH,
SANDVED, THOMPSON. [EWEN NEW=
b.Jul 6]

STÜSSI, Else. Wadenswil, Switzerland, Nov 29 1904- .
Violinist. SCHUH.

STÜZNER, Elisa. Thuringia,
Germany, 1888?- . Soprano,
voice teacher. KUTSCH.

SUÁREZ, Aurea. 20th-century
Cuban pianist. ENCI MUS=v.3
p.112 (brief mention in
article on Edgardo Martín).

SUART, Evelyn (Lady Harcourt).
Sindapore [Singapore?], Apr
30 1881-Oct 24 1950, London.
Pianist. GROVE 5, THOMPSON.

SUBLIGNY, Marie Thérèse Perdou
de. 1666-c1736. French
dancer. DICT MUS.

SUCHER, Rosa (Mrs. Joseph, born
Hasselbeck or Hasslbeck). Vel-
burg, Upper Palatinate, Feb 23
1849-Apr 16 1927, Eschweiler,
nr.Aachen, Germany. Soprano,
voice teacher. BAKER 1, BAKER
5, BLOM, ENCI MUS, EWEN NEW,
GROVE 1, GROVE 1 APP, GROVE 5,
PRATT, SANDVED, THOMPSON.

SUDDABY, Elsie. Yorkshire, ?- .
20th-century soprano. THOMPSON.

SUGGIA, Guilhermina. Oporto,
Portugal, Jun 27 1888-Jul 31
1950, Oporto, Portugal. Vio-
loncellist. BAKER 5, BLOM,
*COOPER, CORTE, ENCI MUS,
GROVE 5, GROVE 5 SUP, RIEMANN,
THOMPSON. [CORTE=d.in London]

SULIOTIS, Elena. Athens, Greece,
1943- . Soprano. KUTSCH.

SULLI-RAO, Elisabetta Oddone
see Oddone Sulli-Rao,
Elisabetta

SUMAC, Yma (orig.=Emperatriz
Chavarri). Ycochán, Peru,
Sep 10 1927- . Singer.
BAKER 5, ENCI SALVAT, ENCY
MUS, SANDVED, THOMPSON.

SUNDELIUS, Marie (orig.=Marie
Sandtvig). Karlstad, Sweden,
Feb 4 1884-Jun 26 1958,
Boston. Soprano, voice tea-
cher. BAKER 5, KUTSCH,
SANDVED, THOMPSON. *[KUTSCH=*
d.Jun 27]

SUNDERLAND, Susan (born Sykes).
Brighouse, Yorkshire, Eng-
land, Apr 30 1819-May 6
1905, Brighouse, Yorkshire,
England. Soprano. BLOM,
BROWN BRIT, GROVE 1 APP=
v.4 p.797, GROVE 5, THOMP-
SON.

SUNDGREN, Sigrid Ingeborg see
Schnéevoigt, Sigrid Ingeborg

SUPERVÍA, Conchita. Barcelona,
Dec 8 1899-Mar 30 1936, Lon-
don. Mezzo-soprano. BAKER 5,
BAKER 1971, BLOM, CELLETTI,
COOPER, CORTE, *ENCI MUS=
illus.fac.p.326, ENCY MUS,
EWEN NEW, GROVE 5, KUTSCH,
MARIZ, SANDVED, THOMPSON.
[BAKER 1971, CELLETTI, ENCI
MUS, EWEN NEW, & KUTSCH=
b.1895]

SUTHERLAND, Joan. Point Piper,
Sydney, Nov 7 1926- . So-
prano. BAKER 1971, BLOM,
*CELLETTI=illus.foll.col.
736, *ENCI MUS=illus.fac.
p.330, EWEN NEW, GROVE 5
SUP, KUTSCH, *ROSENTHAL=
illus.p.181-82, *SANDVED,
THOMPSON. *[ENCI MUS=b.1928;*
EWEN NEW=b.1929]

SUTHERLAND, Margaret. Adelaide?,
Australia, Nov 20 1897- .
Composer, teacher. *MURDOCH=
illus.foll.p.146, VINTON.

SUTRO, Florence Edith (born
Clinton). ?, May 1 1865-Apr
29 1906, New York City.
Teacher, writer, administrator. BAKER 5, THOMPSON.

SUTRO, Ottilie. Baltimore,
Jan 4 1872-?. Pianist.
BAKER 5, GROVE 5, PRATT,
THOMPSON.

SUTRO, Rose Laura. Baltimore,
Sep 15 1870-Jan 11 1957,
Baltimore. Pianist. BAKER 5,
GROVE 5, GROVE 5 SUP, PRATT,
THOMPSON.

SUTTER, Anna. Wil, Switzerland,
Nov 26 1871-Jun 29 1910,
Stuttgart. Soprano. KUTSCH.

SVICHER, Isabella. Florence,
1865-?. Soprano. CELLETTI.

SWAIN, Freda. Portsmouth,
England, Oct 31 1902- .
Pianist, composer. BAKER 5,
BAKER 1971, BLOM, ENCI MUS,
GROVE 5, SCHOLES, THOMPSON.
[BAKER 5 & THOMPSON=b.Oct 13]

SWARTHOUT, Gladys. Deepwater,
Mo., Dec 25 1904-Jul 8 1969,
La Ragnaia, nr. Florence.
Contralto. BAKER 5, BAKER
1971, *EWEN LIVING, EWEN
LIV SUP, EWEN NEW, GROVE 5,
GROVE 5 SUP, KUTSCH, MARIZ,
RIEMANN, *SANDVED=another
illus.p.853, THOMPSON.

SWEPSTONE, Edith. 19th-century
English composer, teacher.
BROWN BRIT.

SWOL, Gérarda Demphina van
see Brouwenstijn, Gré

SYKES, Susan see Sunder-
land, Susan

SYLVA, Marguerite Alice
Helene Smith. Brussels,
Jul 10 1875-Feb 21 1957,
Glendale, Calif. Soprano,
voice teacher. KUTSCH.

SYNGE, Mary Helena. Parsons-
town, Ireland, ?-?. 19th-
century pianist, composer.
BROWN BRIT.

SYRMEN, Maddalena see
Sirmen, Maddalena

SZAJEROWA, Jadwiga see
Sari, Ada

SZALIT, Paulina. Lwów, Poland,
1886- . Pianist, composer.
GROVE 5.

SZANTHO, Enid. Budapest, 1907-
. Contralto, voice teacher.
*EWEN LIVING, KUTSCH, THOMP-
SON.

SZARBO, Luisa. Budapest, 1904-
Nov 19 1934, Budapest.
Soprano. KUTSCH.

SZAREWICZ, Helena. ?-Oct 11
1801, Warsaw. Soprano.
GROVE 5.

SZARVADY, Wilhelmine see
Clauss-Szarvady, Wilhelmine

SZCZEPAŃSKA, Maria Klementyna.
Złoczów, nr. Lwów, May 13
1902-Oct 18 1962, Posen,
Poland. Musicologist, tea-
cher, writer. ENCI SALVAT,
ENCY MUS, GROVE 5, MGG,
THOMPSON.

SZEGÖ, Julia. Beregszás, Hungary, Apr 19 1900- . Singer,
musicologist, writer. ENCI
SALVAT, ENCY MUS.

SZÖNI (Szönyi), Erzsébet
(Elisabeth). Budapest, Apr
25 1924- . Composer, teacher.
ENCI SALVAT, ENCY MUS.

SZTOJANOVITS, Adrienne. Budapest, Jan 5 1890- . Teacher.
ENCY MUS.

SZTOJANOVITS, Edith. Budapest,
Sep 12 1891- . Soprano,
mezzo-soprano. ENCY MUS.

SZTOJANOVITS, Lily. Budapest,
Aug 2 1894- . Soprano.
ENCY MUS.

SZUMOWSKA, Antoinette (Anto-
nina; Mrs. Joseph Adamowska).
Lubin, Poland, Feb 22 1868-
Aug 18 1938, Rumson, N.J.
Pianist, piano teacher.
BAKER 1, BAKER 5, GROVE 5,
PRATT, THOMPSON.

SZYMANOWSKA, Filipina see
Brzezińska, Filipina

SZYMANOWSKA, Maria Agata (born
Wolowska). Warsaw, Dec 14
1789-Jul 24 1831, St. Peters-
burg. Pianist, piano teacher,
composer, court musician.
BAKER 1, BAKER 5, BLOM, DICT
MUS, ENCI SALVAT, ENCY MUS,
GROVE 5, GROVE 5 SUP, MGG,
RIEMANN, THOMPSON. *[BAKER 1=
b.1790; ENCI SALVAT, ENCY
MUS, & MGG=d.Jul 25 1831;
THOMPSON=d.1832]*

T

TACCHINARDI, Elisa. 19th-
century Italian pianist.
ENCI MUS.

TACCHINARDI, Fanny see
Persiani, Fanny

TADEO-ADANI, Laura see
Adani, Mariella

TADOLINI, Eugenia (Mrs. Giovanni, born Savorini).
Forli, Italy, 1809-after
1848, Naples. Soprano.
BLOM, *ENCI MUS=illus.fac.
p.338.

TAGLIAFERRO, Magda(lena).
Petrópolis, Brazil, 1890- .
Pianist. ENCI SALVAT, ENCY
MUS, *EWEN LIVING, MARIZ.
[ENCI SALVAT=b.1892]

TAGLIANA, Emilia. Milan,
1854-?. Soprano. BAKER 1,
PRATT, THOMPSON.

TAGLIONI, Adélaïde see
Perraud, Adélaïde

TAGLIONI, Maria. Stockholm,
Apr 23 1804-Apr 27 1884,
Marseille. Dancer. CORTE,
DICT MUS, *ENCI MUS=illus.
v.4 fac.p.342-43, *ENCI
SALVAT, *ENCY MUS. *[ENCY
MUS=b.Apr 24]*

TAILLEFERRE, Germaine. Parc-
de-St.-Maur, nr. Paris,
Apr 19 1892- . Composer.
BAKER 5, BLOM, COOPER,
CORTE, *DICT MUS=illus.v.1
fac.p.433, *ENCI MUS=illus.
v.2 fac.p.367 & v.1 fac.p.
502, *ENCI SALVAT=illus.v.2
p.423, ENCY MUS, GROVE 5,
GROVE 5 SUP, RIEMANN, *SAND-
VED=illus.p.1158 & 1276,
THOMPSON, ULLSTEIN.

TAIT, Annie. ?-Feb 24 1886,
Eastbourne, England. Pia-
nist, composer. BROWN BRIT.

TALLEY, Marion. Nevada, Mo.,
Dec 20 1907- . Soprano.
BAKER 5, *EWEN LIVING,
KUTSCH, THOMPSON. *[KUTSCH=
b.1906; EWEN LIVING=b.in
Kansas City, Mo.]*

TALMA, Louise. Archachon,

France, Oct 31 1906- . Composer, opera composer, teacher. BAKER 5, BAKER 1971,
PAVLAKIS=p.355, REIS, SAND-
VED, THOMPSON, VINTON.

TALVIK, Minna see Palmgren,
Minna

TAMBLYN, Bertha Louise.
Oshawa, Ontario, Canada,
?- . 20th-century composer.
CBC.

TAMIRIS, Helen (Mrs. Daniel
Nagrin, born Becker). New
York City, 1902-Aug 4 1966,
New York City. Dancer,
choreographer. RIEMANN.
*[RIEMANN=b.1905; birthdate
in entry based on New York
Times obituary (Aug 5 1966,
p.31, col.1) indicating
death at age of 64]*

TANGEMAN, Nell. Columbus,
Ohio, Dec 23 1917-Feb 15
1965, Washington, D.C.
Mezzo-soprano. GROVE 5,
THOMPSON.

TANNER-MUSIN, Annie Louise
see Musin, Annie Louise

TAPPENHORN, Fanny see
Moran-Olden, Fanny

TAPPER, Bertha (born Feiring).
Christiania, Norway, Jan 25
1859-Sep 2 1915, New York
City. Pianist, piano teacher,
editor. BAKER 5, THOMPSON.

TARAVANT, Jeanne see Sérieyx,
Jeanne

TARELLI, Elsa Piaggio de see
Piaggio de Tarelli, Elsa

TARJUS, Blanche. Courbevoie,
France, Jun 17 1932- .
Violinist. ENCI SALVAT,
ENCY MUS.

TARQUINI, Tarquinia see
Zandonai, Tarquinia

TARRAGÓ, Renata. Barcelona,
1927- . Guitarist. ENCI
SALVAT.

TARTAGLIA, Lydia. Rome, Oct
20 1898- . Pianist. THOMP-
SON.

TARTAGLINI, Rosa see Tibaldi, Rosa

TAS, Helen Teschner. New York
City, May 24 1889- . Vio-
linist. *EWEN LIVING, THOMP-
SON.

TASKIN, Arlette. Paris, Sep
16 1880- . Contralto.
DICT MUS, ENCI MUS. *[ENCI
MUS=b.1881]*

TASSINARI, Domenica (Pia).
Modigliana di Faenza, Italy,
Sep 15 1909- . Soprano,
mezzo-soprano. ENCI MUS,
KUTSCH, ULLSTEIN. *[ENCI
MUS=b.1903]*

TASSOPULOS, Anna. Patras,
Greece, Dec 17 1917- .
Soprano. RIEMANN.

TATE, Margaret see Teyte,
Maggie

TATE, Phyllis Margaret Duncan.
Gerrards Cross, Bucks.,
England, Apr 6 1911- .
Composer, light-opera com-
poser. BAKER 5, BAKER 1971,
BLOM, ENCI MUS, ENCI SALVAT,
GROVE 5, GROVE 5 SUP, RIE-
MANN, SCHOLES, THOMPSON.

TAUBEROVÁ, Maria. Vysoké Mýto,
Czechoslovakia, 1914- .
Soprano. KUTSCH.

TAUSIG, Seraphine (Mrs. Carl,
born von Vrabely). ?-Sep 2

1931, Dresden. Pianist.
ENCI MUS, RIEMANN.

TAVARES, Stella. Lourenço
Marques, Mozambique, Aug
1913- . Mezzo-soprano.
GROVE 5.

TAYBER, Elisabeth see Teyber,
Elisabeth

TAYBER, Therese see Teyber,
Therese

TAYLOR, Elizabeth see Bayzand, Elizabeth

TAYLOR, Helen see Lucas,
Helen

TAYLOR, Laura W. (Mrs. Tom,
born Barker). Thirkleby,
Yorkshire, England, 1819-
1905, Coleshill, nr. Amersham,
England. Composer. BROWN BIO,
BROWN BRIT, GROVE 5.

TCHERKASSKAYA, Marianna Borisovna. Russia, 1892- .
Soprano. GROVE 5.

TEBALDI, Renata. Pesaro, Italy,
Feb 1 1922- . Soprano.
BAKER 5, BLOM, *CELLETTI=
illus.foll.col.736, CORTE,
*ENCI MUS=illus.v.4 fac.p.
363, *ENCI SALVAT, ENCY MUS,
*EWEN LIV SUP, EWEN NEW,
GROVE 5 SUP, KUTSCH, RIEMANN,
*ROSENTHAL=illus.p.185-86,
*SANDVED, THOMPSON, *ULLSTEIN.

TEDESCA, Fernanda. Nr. Baltimore, 1860-1885, ?. Violinist.
BAKER 1.

TEGETHOFF, Else see Ruziczka,
Else

TELLINI, Ines Alfani-. Florence,
1900?- . Soprano, voice
teacher. KUTSCH.

TELMÁNYI, Annette (Mrs. Emil, born Schiøler). ?, Jan 17 1904- . Hungarian (?) pianist. ENCI MUS.

TELVA, Marion. St. Louis, Mo., Sep 26 1897-Oct 23 1962, Norwalk, Conn. Contralto. *EWEN LIVING, EWEN NEW, KUTSCH, THOMPSON. *[KUTSCH= b.Dec 26 1897]*

TEMPLE, Hope (pseud. for .Dotie Davies; Mrs. André Messager). Dublin, 1859-May 10 1938, Folkestone, England. Composer. BAKER 1, BROWN BRIT, ENCI MUS=v.3 p.163, THOMPSON.

TENCH, Rose see Cullen, Rose

TENNEY, Gena see Branscombe, Gena

TENTONI, Rosa. Buhl, Minn., ?- . 20th-century American soprano. *EWEN LIVING, THOMPSON.

TEODORINI, Elena see Theodorini, Elena

TERHUNE, Anice (born Potter). Hampden, Mass., Oct 27 1873-Nov 9 1964, Pompton Lakes, N.J. Pianist, composer. BAKER 5, BAKER 1971, THOMPSON.

TERNAUX, Rosine see Stoltz, Rosine

TERNINA, Milka. Veziscě, nr. Zagreb, Dec 19 1863-May 18 1941, Zagreb. Soprano, voice teacher. BAKER 5, BLOM, CELLETTI, COOPER, CORTE, ENCI MUS, EWEN NEW, GROVE 5, GROVE 5 SUP, KUTSCH, SANDVED, THOMPSON. *[CELLETTI, COOPER, & ENCI MUS=b.1864; COOPER & CORTE= d.1940]*

TERRIER-LAFFAILLE, Anne. Laval, France, Jul 22 1904- . Composer. ENCI SALVAT, ENCY MUS.

TERVANI, Irma (born Ackté). Helsinki, Jun 4 1887-Oct 29 1936, Berlin. Contralto. GROVE 5, KUTSCH, RIEMANN, THOMPSON. *[GROVE 5=d.1935]*

TERZIÁN, Alicia. Córdoba, Argentina, 1936- . Composer. ARIZAGA.

TESCHEMACHER, Marguerite. Cologne, Mar 3 1903-May 19 1959, Tegernsee, Germany. Soprano. EWEN NEW, KUTSCH, RIEMANN, THOMPSON, *ULLSTEIN. *[KUTSCH=d.in Bad Weisse, Germany]*

TESCHNER, Salomea see Deszner, Salomea

TESI-TRAMONTINI, Vittoria. Florence, Feb 13 1700-May 9 1775, Vienna. Contralto, court musician. BAKER 1, BAKER 5, BLOM, BROWN BIO, *ENCI MUS=illus.v.4 fac.p. 374, ENCI SALVAT, ENCY MUS, GROVE 1, GROVE 5, PRATT, RIEMANN, THOMPSON. *[GROVE 1= b.1690; BAKER 1=b.c1695; BROWN BIO=soprano]*

TESS, Guilia. Milan, Feb 19 1889- . Soprano. ENCI MUS.

TETHERINGTON, Catherine see Collet, Catherine

TETRAZZINI, Eva. Milan, Mar 1862-Oct 27 1938, Salsomaggiore, Italy. Soprano. BAKER 5, CORTE, ENCI MUS, ENCI SALVAT, ENCY MUS, RIEMANN, THOMPSON.

TETRAZZINI, Luisa (later Scalaberni). Florence, Jun 28 or 29 1871-Apr 28

1940, Milan. Soprano. BAKER 5, BLOM, CELLETTI, CORTE, *ENCI MUS=illus.v.4 fac. p.375, ENCI SALVAT, ENCY MUS, EWEN NEW, GROVE 5, KUTSCH, MARIZ, PRATT, RIEMANN, *SANDVED, THOMPSON, ULLSTEIN. *[PRATT=b.1874]*

TEYBER (Tayber), Elisabeth. Vienna, Sep 16 1744-May 9 1816, Vienna. Soprano. DICT MUS, ENCI MUS, RIEMANN. *[ENCI MUS & RIEMANN=b.1746 or 1747]*

TEYBER (Tayber), Therese. Vienna, Oct 15 1760-Apr 5 1830, Vienna. Soprano. DICT MUS, ENCI MUS, RIEMANN.

TEYSSEIRE-VUILLEUMIER, Hélène. Geneva, Jan 30 1898- . Violinist. SCHUH.

TEYTE, Maggie (orig.=Margaret Tate). Wolverhampton, England, Apr 17 1888- . Soprano. BAKER 5, BLOM, COOPER, CORTE=p.724, *EWEN LIV SUP, EWEN NEW, GROVE 5, GROVE 5 SUP, KUTSCH, PALMER, PRATT, RIEMANN, *SANDVED, THOMPSON. *[KUTSCH, PRATT, & RIEMANN=b.1889; PALMER=b.1890]*

THALBERG, Zaré (actually Ethel Western). Derbyshire, England, Apr 16 1858-1915, Finchley, nr. London. Soprano. BLOM, GROVE 5, THOMPSON.

THEBOM, Blanche. Monessen, Pa., Sep 19 1918- . Mezzo-soprano. BAKER 5, ENCI MUS, *EWEN LIV SUP, EWEN NEW, GROVE 5 SUP, KUTSCH, PAVLAKIS=p.296, RIEMANN, *ROSENTHAL=illus.p.187, *SANDVED, THOMPSON, ULLSTEIN. *[EWEN NEW, GROVE 5,*

& SANDVED=b.1919; RIEMANN & ULLSTEIN=b.1922]

THEGERSTRÖM, Hilda (Aurora). Stockholm, Sep 17 1838-Dec 9 1907, Stockholm. Pianist, piano teacher, composer. GROVE 5.

"THEODORE, Mme." see D'Auberval, Mme. Jean

THEODORINI (Teodorini), Elena (Helena)(stage name of Elena Theodorides). Craiova, Romania, Mar 25 1857-Feb 27 1926, Bucharest. Soprano, voice teacher. BAKER 5, BAKER 1971, CELLETTI, KUTSCH, PRATT, THOMPSON. *[CELLETTI & KUTSCH=b.1858; PRATT & THOMPSON=b.1862; CELLETTI=d.1925; THOMPSON=d.Mar 1926]*

THIBAUD, Gladys see Casadesus, Gladys

THIBAULT, Geneviève (Comtesse de Chambure). Neuilly-sur-Seine, France, May 20 1902- . Musicologist, writer. BAKER 5, DICT MUS, ENCI MUS, ENCI SALVAT, ENCY MUS, GROVE 5 SUP, RIEMANN, THOMPSON.

THICKNESSE, Ann see Ford, Ann

THIELE, Leonore see Pfund, Leonore

THILLON, Sophie Anne (Anna; born Hunt). Calcutta or London, 1819-May 5 1903, Torquay, France. Soprano. BAKER 1, BLOM, BROWN BIO, BROWN BRIT, GROVE 1, GROVE 5, PRATT, THOMPSON. *[PRATT= b.1816?]*

THIRWALL, Annie. London, 1830-Oct 19 1881, London. Soprano. BROWN BRIT=p.102 & 408, GROVE 1, GROVE 5.

THOM, Ruth see Dusseau,
Jeanne

THOMA, Therese see Vogl,
Therese

THOMÁN, Maria. Budapest, Jul
12 1909- . Violinist.
THOMPSON.

THOMÁN, Valerie. Budapest,
Aug 16 1878- . Singer.
THOMPSON.

THOMAS, Adelaide Louisa.
Clapham, London, ?-?.
19th-century pianist,
composer, administrator.
BROWN BRIT.

THOMAS, Florence A. see
Marshall, Florence A.

THOMAS, Frances. 19th-century
English clarinettist.
BROWN BRIT.

THOMAS, Virginia Carrington
see Carrington-Thomas,
Virginia

THOMPSON, Fanchon. 19-20th-
century American mezzo-
soprano. THOMPSON.

THOMPSON, Lady Henry see
Loder, Kate Fanny

THOMPSON, Marquita Sánchez de
(born María Sánchez de
Velasco). Buenos Aires,
1786-1881, ?. Poet. ARIZAGA.

THOMSEN, Marie (Elisabeth).
1789-1823. Danish soprano.
ENCI MUS=v.4 p.621.

THOMSON, Mrs. see Laidlaw,
Robena Anna

THOMSON, Alexandra. 19th-
century English composer.
BROWN BRIT.

THORBORG, Kerstin. Venjan,
Dalekarlia (Kopparberg),
Sweden, May 19 1896-Apr 12
1970, Falum, Sweden. Con-
tralto, voice teacher,
court musician, actress.
BAKER 5, BAKER 1971, *EWEN
LIVING, EWEN LIV SUP, EWEN
NEW, GROVE 5, KUTSCH, MARIZ,
RIEMANN, *SANDVED, THOMPSON,
ULLSTEIN. *[THOMPSON=b.May 18;
MARIZ=b.in Stockholm; BAKER
1971=d.in Hedemora, Sweden]*

THORNE, Beatrice. London, Apr
14 1878- . Pianist, composer.
BROWN BRIT.

THORNTON, Edna. Bradford, Yorkshire, England, 1875-1958,
Brighton, England. Contralto,
voice teacher. KUTSCH, THOMP-
SON.

THUDICHUM, Charlotte. Kensing-
ton, London, ?-?. 19th-cen-
tury soprano. BROWN BRIT.

THUE, Hildµr Fjord. Christiania,
Norway, Jan 26 1870-Nov 30
1936, Oslo. Soprano. THOMPSON.

THURAU, Elfriede Antonie see
Feudel, Elfriede Antonie

THURBER, Jeanette Meyer. New
York City, 1851-Jan 2 1946,
Bronxville, New York. Patron.
THOMPSON.

THURLOW, Lady see Bolton,
Mary Catherine

THURSBY, Emma Cecilia. Brook-
lyn, New York, Feb 21 1844-
Jul 4 1931, New York City.
Soprano, voice teacher.
BAKER 1, BAKER 5, BROWN BIO,
GROVE 1, GROVE 5, GROVE 5
SUP, PRATT, SANDVED, THOMP-
SON. *[GROVE 5 SUP & SANDVED=
b.1845; BAKER 1, BROWN BIO, &
GROVE 1=b.Nov 17 1857; GROVE
5 SUP=d.Feb 4]*

THURSFIELD, Anne Loyse (born
Reman). New York City, Mar
28 1885-Jun 5 1945, London.
Mezzo-soprano. BLOM, GROVE
5, GROVE 5 SUP, THOMPSON.

THYBO, Kerstin (Mrs. Leif,
born Wagrell). 20th-century
Danish singer. ENCI MUS.

THYS-SEBAULT, Pauline. France?,
1836-?. Composer, opera composer. BROWN BIO.

TIBALDI, Rosa (Mrs. Giuseppe
Luigi, born Tartaglini).
?-Nov 17 1775, Bologna.
Singer, composer. ENCI MUS.

TIBALDI CHIESA, Maria. Milan,
Apr 28 1896- . Writer.
BAKER 5, ENCI MUS, THOMPSON.

TICKELL, Mary see Linley,
Mary

TIETJENS (Titiens), Therese
Cathline Johanna Alexandra.
Hamburg, Jul 17 1831-Oct 3
1877, London. Soprano.
BAKER 1, BAKER 5, BLOM,
BROWN BIO, CLAYTON=p.507,
GROVE 1, GROVE 5, PRATT,
SANDVED, THOMPSON. [BROWN
BIO=b.1831 or 1833; GROVE 1=
b.1831 or 1834; BAKER 5=
d.1888]

TIKALOVÁ, Drahomira. Berlin,
May 9 1915- . Soprano.
KUTSCH.

TILBURY, Adelina see De Lara,
Adelina

TILLOTSON, Queena see Mario,
Queena

TILLY, Margaret. Maidenhead,
England, Sep 15 1900- .
Violinist, pianist, music
therapist, lecturer.
GROVE 5.

TIMANOVA (Timanoff), Vera
Victorovna. Ufa, Russia,
Feb 18 1855-1942, Leningrad.
Pianist, piano teacher.
BAKER 1, BAKER 5, GROVE 1,
PRATT, THOMPSON, VODARSKY.
[BAKER 5=b.1885 (obvious
misprint)]

TIPO, Maria. Naples, Dec 23
1931- . Pianist. ENCI MUS.

TISZAY, Magda. Békéscaba,
Hungary, Apr 4 1919- .
Mezzo-soprano. RIEMANN.

TITIENS, Therese Cathline
Johanna Alexandra see
Tietjens, Therese Cathline
Johanna Alexandra

TIZZONI, Margherita see
Delle Sedie, Margherita

TODI, Luiza Rosa (born d'Ag-
uiar). Setúbal, Portugal,
Jan 9 1753-Oct 1 1833,
Lisbon. Mezzo-soprano.
BAKER 1, BAKER 5, BLOM,
CORTE, ENCI MUS, ENCI SALVAT,
ENCY MUS, GROVE 5, PRATT,
RIEMANN, THOMPSON.

TODI, Maria Francesca. Portugal,
1748-Jun 1793, Lisbon. Contralto. BROWN BIO, GROVE 1.

TODSEN, Nanny Larsén- see
Larsén-Todsen, Nanny

TÖMLICH, Antoinette see
Wolf, Antoinette

TÖPPER, Hertha. Graz, Apr 19
1924- . Contralto. KUTSCH,
RIEMANN, THOMPSON, *ULLSTEIN.

TOFTS, Catherine ("Camilla").
?-1756, Venice. Soprano.
BLOM, BROWN BIO, BROWN BRIT,
CLAYTON=p.15, GROVE 1,
GROVE 5, THOMPSON. [BROWN
BRIT=d.c1760]

TOGNOLI VERNI, Antonia. 18th-
century Italian singer.
ENCI MUS=v.4 p.491 (brief
mention in article on the
Verni family).

TOLLEFSEN, Augusta see
Schnabel-Tollefsen, Augusta

TOLLETT, Henrietta Maria
see Crisp, Henrietta Maria

TOMÁŠEK, Jaromíra (Mrs. Jaroslav, born Nováková). Jaro-
měr, Bohemia, May 23 1892- .
Singer. ENCI MUS.

TOMEONI, Irene. 18th-century
singer. ENCI MUS=v.2 p.109
(brief mention in article
on Pierre Dutillieu).

TOMLINSON, Henrietta see
Midgley, Henrietta

TOMLINSON, Marion. 19th-cen-
tury English contralto.
BROWN BRIT=p.280 (in article
on brother-in-law Samuel
Midgley).

TONELLI, Rosa see Parte-
giotti, Rosa

TONNE, Mary Anne see Dibdin,
Mary Anne

TORRÁ, Celia. Concepción del
Uruguay, Argentina, Sep 18
1889-1962, ?. Violinist,
conductor, composer.
ARIZAGA, GROVE 5, SLONIMSKY.

TORRE, Teresa see Scalabrini,
Teresa

TORRESELLA, Fanny. Tiflis,
1856-May 2 1914, Rome.
Soprano. CELLETTI.

TORRI, Rosina. Guastalla,
Italy, Dec 20 1898- .
Soprano. KUTSCH.

TORRI, Teresa see Scalabrini,
Teresa

TORRIANI, Ottavia. fl.1873.
Italian soprano. THOMPSON.

TÓRTOLA VALENCIA, Carmen.
Seville, Jun 18 1882-Feb 13
1955, Barcelona. Dancer.
ENCI SALVAT.

TOSI, Adelaide. Milan, ?-Mar
27 1859, Naples. Soprano.
ENCI MUS.

TOSO, Giacinta see Puzzi,
Giacinta

TOUR, Anna El- see El-Tour,
Anna

TOUREL, Jennie. Montréal, Jun
22 1910-Nov 23 1973, New
York City. Mezzo-soprano,
soprano, voice teacher.
BAKER 5, BLOM, CORTE, ENCI
MUS, *EWEN LIV SUP, EWEN NEW,
GROVE 5, KUTSCH, MARIZ,
PAVLAKIS=p.296, *SANDVED,
THOMPSON. [MARIZ=b.1905 in
Russia; PAVLAKIS=b.in Russia]

TOWNSEND, Mrs. 19th-century
English writer. BROWN BIO,
BROWN BRIT.

TOWNSEND, Pauline D. 19th-
century English writer.
BROWN BRIT.

TRACEY, Minnie. Albany, New
York, c1870-Jan 29 1929,
Cincinnati. Soprano, voice
teacher. THOMPSON.

TRAMONTINI, Vittoria Tesi- see
Tesi-Tramontini, Vittoria

TRAMPLER, Karen see Phillips,
Karen

TRAUBEL, Helen. St. Louis, Mo.,
Jun 20 1899-Jul 29 1972,

Santa Monica, Calif. So-
prano. BAKER 5, BLOM,
CELLETTI, *EWEN LIVING,
EWEN LIV SUP, EWEN NEW,
GROVE 5, GROVE 5 SUP,
KUTSCH, MARIZ, *SANDVED,
THOMPSON. [CELLETTI=b.
Jun 16 1899; MARIZ=b.1900]

TRAUBMAN, Sophie. New York
City, May 12 1867-Aug 16
1951, New York City.
Soprano. THOMPSON.

TRAUBNER, Eliza see Kinlock,
Eliza

TRAUTMANN, Marie see Jäell-
Trautmann, Marie

TRAVERS, Patricia. Clifton,
N.J., Dec 5 1927- . Vio-
linist. BAKER 5, THOMPSON.

TRAVIS, Deborah see Knyvett,
Deborah

TREBELLI, Antoinette (later
Antonia Dolores). 19th-
century French singer.
GROVE 5.

TREBELLI (-Bettini), Zelia
(stage name of Gloria
Caroline Gillebert, Guillebert, or Gilbert). Paris,
1838-Aug 18 1892, Étretat,
France. Mezzo-soprano.
BAKER 1, BAKER 5, BLOM,
BROWN BIO, ENCI MUS, GROVE
1, GROVE 5, PRATT, THOMPSON.

TREE, Anna Maria (Mrs. James
Bradshaw). London, Aug 1801
or 1802-Feb 17 1862, Queen's
Gate Terrace, London. Mezzo-
soprano, actress. BLOM,
BROWN BRIT, GROVE 1 APP=
v.4 p.800, GROVE 5, THOMP-
SON.

TREE, Ellen (Mrs. Charles
Kean). Ireland, Dec 1805-

Aug 20 1880, London?. Singer,
actress. BROWN BRIT.

TREHERNE, Georgina see
Weldon, Georgina

TREMBLAY, Amedée. Montréal,
Apr 14 1876-1949, ?. Com-
poser. NAPIER.

TRENCK, Nicolina see Ditters
von Dittersdorf, Nicolina

TRENTINI, Emma. Mantua, Apr 12
1878-Mar. 23 1959, Milan.
Soprano. KUTSCH.

TRÉVILLE, Yvonne de (real name=
Edyth La Gierse). Galveston,
Texas, Aug 25 1881-Jan 25
1954, New York City. Soprano,
voice teacher. BAKER 5, KUTSCH,
PRATT, THOMPSON=p.534.

TREW, Susan (Mrs. Charles A.).
19th-century English pianist,
composer. BROWN BRIT.

TRIAL, Marie Jeanne (born
Milon). Paris, Aug 1 1746-
Feb 13 1818, Paris. Soprano.
BLOM, ENCI MUS, GROVE 5.
[ENCI MUS=d.Feb 11 1814]

TRIANTI-KYRIAKIDI, Alexandra.
Athens, Greece, Jan 9 1901- .
Mezzo-soprano. GROVE 5,
RIEMANN. [GROVE 5=b.Jan 23
1903]

TRIBOLET, Madame see Willmann, (Anna Maria Antonetta)
Marianne

TRIEPEL, Susanne see Dessoir,
Susanne

TRIGONA, Rose de Ader see
Ader, Rose

TRIMBLE, Joan. Enniskillen,
Ulster, Ireland, Jun 18
1915- . Pianist, composer.
GROVE 5, PALMER, THOMPSON.

TRIMBLE, Valerie. Enniskillen, Ulster, Ireland, Aug 20 1917- . Pianist. GROVE 5, PALMER.

TRÖTSCHEL, Elfriede. Dresden, Jul 16 1913-Jun 20 1958, Berlin. Soprano. ENCI MUS, RIEMANN, *ULLSTEIN.

TROMBETTA, Maria Teresa see Belloc, Maria Teresa

TROMBINI, Margerita Kazuro- see Kazuro-Trombini, Margerita

TROUP, Emily Josephine. 19th- century English composer. BROWN BRIT.

TROWBRIDGE, Leslie. 19th- century English soprano, composer. BROWN BRIT.

TROYANOS, Tatiana. 20th- century American mezzo- soprano. PAVLAKIS=p.296.

TROYON-BLAESI, Emmy. Solecure, Switzerland, May 10 1873- Mar 14 1956, Lausanne. Pianist, accompanist. SCHUH.

TRUE, Alice see Gentle, Alice

TRUST, Helen Mary (born Stark). Norwich, England, ?-?. 19th-century soprano. BROWN BRIT.

TSCHACHTLI, Marie-Madeleine. Morat, Switzerland, Sep 8 1925- . Violinist. SCHUH.

TUA, Teresina (real name=Maria Felicità; Sister May di Gesù). Turin, May 22 1867- Oct 29 1955, Rome. Vio- linist, teacher. BAKER 1, BAKER 5, BAKER 1971, BROWN BIO, CORTE, *ENCI MUS=illus.

v.4 fac.p.431, GROVE 1, GROVE 5, PRATT, THOMPSON. *[CORTE= b.1866; THOMPSON=b.Apr 23 1866; ENCI MUS=b.Apr 24 1866; GROVE 5=b.May 22 1866; ENCI MUS=d.Oct 28 1956]*

TUBB, Carrie (Caroline Eliza- beth). London, May 17 1876-?. Soprano. GROVE 5, THOMPSON.

TUBBS, Elizabeth see Arnold, Elizabeth

TUCCI, Gabriella. Rome, Aug 4 1932- . Soprano. KUTSCH, THOMPSON.

TUČEK (Tuczek), Leopoldine (Tuczek-Herrenburg). Vienna, Nov 11 1821-Oct 20 1883, Baden, nr. Vienna. Soprano. ENCI MUS, GROVE 1, GROVE 5, THOMPSON.

TUCZEK, Clara see Bruch, Clara

TUCZEK, Leopoldine see Tuček, Leopoldine

TUNON, Higínia see Spani, Hina

TURECK, Rosalyn. Chicago, Dec 14 1914- . Pianist, harpsi- chordist, teacher. BAKER 5, BLOM, CORTE=p.724, *EWEN LIVING, PAVLAKIS=p.268, RIEMANN, *SANDVED, THOMPSON.

TURNER, Claramae. Dinuba, Calif., Oct 28 1920- . Contralto. *EWEN LIV SUP, EWEN NEW, PAVLAKIS=p.296, SANDVED, THOMPSON. *[SANDVED= b.1900 (!); EWEN LIV SUP= b.in Eureka, Calif.]*

TURNER, Eva. Oldham, Lancs., England, Mar 10 1892- . Soprano, voice teacher. BLOM, CELLETTI, COOPER,

EWEN NEW, GROVE 5, KUTSCH,
PALMER, SANDVED, THOMPSON.
[COOPER=b.1899]

TYLER, Sarah see Keddie,
Henrietta Sarah Tytler

TYLER, Veronica. 20th-century
American soprano. PAVLAKIS=
p.292.

TYRRELL, Agnes. Brno, Moravia,
Sep 20 1846-Apr 18 1883,
Brno, Moravia. Pianist, com-
poser. THOMPSON.

TYTLER, Sarah see Keddie,
Henrietta Sarah Tytler

TZERETELI, Princess see
Lavrovska, Elisaveta
Andreyevna

TZVEYCH, Biserka see Cvejič,
Biserka

U

UCKO, Paula. Berlin, Oct 22
1875-Oct 14 1932, Berlin.
Soprano. THOMPSON.

UDOVICK, Lucille. Denver,
1920- . Soprano. KUTSCH.

UGALDE, Delphine (born Beaucé).
Paris, Dec 3 1829-Jul 19
1910, Paris. Soprano, voice
teacher, light-opera com-
poser. BAKER 1, BAKER 5,
BLOM, BROWN BIO, ENCI MUS,
GROVE 1, GROVE 5, PRATT,
THOMPSON.

UGALDE, Marguerite (stage name
of Marie Varcollier). Paris,
Jun 30 1862-Jul 6 1940,
Paris. Soprano. ENCI MUS.

UIOMEN-JÄNNES, Annikki. Kuopio, Finland, 1891-Jun 10
1937, Kuopio, Finland.
Mezzo-soprano. THOMPSON.

ULRICA, Friederica Louise.
Lübeck, Germany, Feb 15
1765-May 4 1839, Ludwigs-
lust, Germany. Singer,
court musician. MGG=v.7
col.1902 & 1908 (brief
mention in article on the
Kunzen family).

UMIŃSKA, Eugenia. Warsaw,
Oct 4 1910- . Violinist.
GROVE 5, RIEMANN.

UNGER-SABATIER, Karoline (in
Italy known as Carlotta
Ungher). Székesfehérvár,
nr. Pest, Oct 28 1803-Mar
23 1877, La Concezione, nr.
Florence. Contralto, so-
prano, voice teacher, actress.
BAKER 1, BAKER 5, BLOM, BROWN
BIO, CORTE, DICT MUS, *ENCI
MUS=illus.fac.p.447, ENCI
SALVAT, ENCY MUS, EWEN NEW,
GROVE 1, GROVE 5, MGG, PRATT,
RIEMANN, THOMPSON, ULLSTEIN.
[BLOM, MGG, RIEMANN, & ULL-
STEIN=b.in Vienna]

UNSCHULD, Marie von. Olmütz,
Austria, May 17 1881- .
Pianist, composer, writer.
THOMPSON.

UPTON, Emily. London, Sep 5
1864-?. Pianist, administrator. BROWN BRIT.

URBANEK, Carolyn. Lowell, Mass.,
?- . 20th-century soprano.
*EWEN LIVING.

URIBE HOLGUÍN, Lucía see
Gutiérrez, Lucía

URSO, Camilla. Nantes, France,
Jun 13 1842-Jan 20 1902,
New York City. Violinist.
BAKER 1, BAKER 5, PRATT,
THOMPSON.

URSULEAC, Viorica (Mrs. Clemens
Krauss). Czernowitz, Buko-

wina, Romania, Mar 26 1899- .
Soprano. BAKER 5, CORTE,
ENCI MUS=v.2 p.545, EWEN
NEW, GROVE 5=v.4 p.837,
KUTSCH, RIEMANN, THOMPSON,
*ULLSTEIN. [KUTSCH=b.Mar 23]

URUSOVA, Olga (Mrs. Henry
Wood). ?-Dec 20 1909, ?.
Soprano. ENCI MUS=v.4
p.593.

USTVOLSKAYA, Galina Ivanovna.
Petrograd, Jul 17 1919- .
Composer, teacher. BAKER
1971, VINTON.

V

VAGNOLI, Virginia see
Striggio, Virginia

VALDA, Giulia. Boston, c1855-
Nov 26 1925, Paris. So-
prano, voice teacher.
THOMPSON.

VALDESTURLA, Costanza see
Schicht, Costanza

VALENCIA, Carmen Tórtola
see Tórtola Valencia,
Carmen

VALENTE, Benita. 20th-century
American soprano. PAVLAKIS=
p.292.

VALENTIN, Karoline (born
Pichler). Frankfurt, May
17 1855-May 26 1923,
Frankfurt. Writer. THOMPSON.

VALENTINE, Ann. 18th-century
English composer. BROWN
BRIT.

VALENTINI, Regina Caterina
see Mingotti, Regina
Caterina

VALESI, Anna. 1776-1792.
Bavarian singer. ENCI MUS.

VALESI, Crescentia. ?, 1791-?.
Bavarian singer. ENCI MUS.

VALESI, Magdalena. ?, 1782-?.
Bavarian singer. ENCI MUS.

VALESI, Thekla. ?, 1786-?.
Bavarian singer. ENCI MUS.

VÄLKKI, Anita. Sääksmäki,
Finland, Oct 25 1926- .
Soprano. KUTSCH.

VALLANDRI, Aline. Paris, 1878-
May 30 1952, Paris. Soprano.
KUTSCH.

VALLE, Mme. de la see De La
Valle, Mme.

VALLERIA, Alwina (in London
known under name Lohman or
Lohmann; real name=Schoe-
ning). Baltimore, Oct 12
1848-Feb 17 1925, Nice.
Soprano. BAKER 5, BROWN BIO,
EWEN NEW, GROVE 1, GROVE 5,
PRATT, THOMPSON.

VALLIN, Ninon (stage name of
Eugénie Vallin-Pardo).
Montalieu-Vercin, Isère,
France, Sep 9 1886-Nov 22
1962, Lyon. Soprano, voice
teacher. CELLETTI, COOPER,
*ENCI MUS=illus.fac.p.459,
ENCY MUS, KUTSCH, MARIZ,
THOMPSON. [CELLETTI=b.Sep 8;
ENCI MUS=d.1961 in Millery,
Rhône]

VAN BARENTZEN, Aline. Somer-
ville, Mass., Jul 7 1897- .
Pianist, singer, voice
teacher. ENCI SALVAT, ENCY
MUS, THOMPSON=p.146.

VAN DEN BOORN-COCLET, Henriette. Liège, Jan 15 1866-
Mar 6 1945, Liège. Composer,
teacher. BAKER 5, PRATT,
THOMPSON.

VAN DEN BOSCH, Betty. Rotterdam, Mar 19 1906- . Soprano.
THOMPSON.

VAN DEN HOEVEN, Dina. Amsterdam, Oct 16 1874-?. Pianist.
THOMPSON.

VAN DEN HOVEN, Cacteau. Amsterdam, Sep 20 1879- .
Violoncellist. THOMPSON.

VAN DE WIELE, Aimée. Brussels,
Mar 8 1907- . Harpsichor-
dist, composer. ENCI SALVAT,
ENCY MUS, GROVE 5=v.9 p.287.

VAN DIEREN, Frieda see
Dieren, Frieda van

VAN DRESSER, Marcia. Memphis,
Dec 4 1877-Jul 11 1937,
London. Soprano, actress.
BAKER 5, GROVE 5=v.2 p.766,
THOMPSON.

VANERI, Pauline see Filippi,
Pauline

VAN GORDON, Cyrena (orig.=
Pocock). Camden, Ohio, Sep
4 1896-Apr 4 1964, New York
City. Contralto. *EWEN
LIVING, KUTSCH=p.165,
THOMPSON. [KUTSCH=b.1893]

VAN HASSELT, Anna Maria Wilhelmine see Hasselt-Barth,
Anna Maria Wilhelmine

VANIER, Jeannine. Laval,
Québec, Canada, Aug 21
1929- . Composer. NAPIER.

VANINI, Francesca see
Boschi, Francesca

VANNI, Helen (born Helen
Spaeth). Davenport, Iowa,
Jan 30 1924- . Mezzo-so-
prano. PAVLAKIS=p.296,
*SANDVED, THOMPSON.

VANONI, Ornella. Milan, Sep 22
1935- . Singer, actress.
ENCI MUS.

VAN OOSTERZEE, Cornélie see
Oosterzee, Cornélie van

VAN PUTEREN, Maria see
Michailowa, Maria

VAN RENNÈS, Catharina see
Rennès, Catharina van

VAN STEENKISTE, Julie-Aimée-
Josèphe see Dorus-Gras,
Julie-Aimée-Josèphe

VAN SWOL, Gérarda Demphina
see Brouwenstijn, Gré

VAN ZANDT, Jennie (Mme. Vanzini). ?, c1840-?. Italian
soprano. ENCI MUS=v.4 p.607,
THOMPSON.

VAN ZANDT, Marie. Brooklyn?,
New York, Oct 8 1861-Dec 31
1919, Cannes. Soprano.
BAKER 5, ENCI MUS=v.4 p.607,
GROVE 1=v.4 p.499, GROVE 5=
v.9 p.398, SANDVED=p.1511,
THOMPSON. [ENCI MUS & GROVE
1=b.in New York City]

VAN ZANTEN, Cornelia. Dordrecht,
Netherlands, Aug 2 1855-Jan
10 1946, The Hague. Soprano,
voice teacher, composer,
writer. BAKER 5, ENCI MUS=
v.4 p.609, THOMPSON.

VANZINI, Jennie see Van
Zandt, Jennie

VANZO, Anna (Mrs. Vittorio
Maria, born Kribel). 20th-
century Italian singer.
ENCI MUS.

VARCOLLIER, Marie see
Ugalde, Marguerite

VARESI, Elena see Boccabadati Varesi, Elena

VARESI, Giulia see Bocca-
badati Varesi, Giulia

VARNAY, Ibolyka Astrid Maria.
Stockholm, Apr 25 1918- .
Soprano, actress. BAKER 5,
BLOM, COOPER, CORTE, ENCI
MUS, ENCI SALVAT, ENCY MUS,
*EWEN LIV SUP, EWEN NEW,
GROVE 5, KUTSCH, RIEMANN,
*ROSENTHAL=illus.p.190,
*SANDVED=another illus.
p.470, THOMPSON, *ULLSTEIN=
illus.p.572. [CORTE=b.1920]

VARRO, Marie-Aimée. Brunoy,
France, Feb 18 1915-Sep 14
1971, Neuchâtel, France.
Pianist. BAKER 1971.

VARTENISSIAN, Shakeh. 20th-
century Syrian soprano.
*SANDVED.

VASSAL, Hanna-Ulrike (orig.=
Kuhroeber). Bonn, Oct 13
1920- . Soprano. RIEMANN.

VAUCHER-CLERC, Germaine.
Geneva, Dec 6 1918- .
Pianist, clavecinist.
SCHUH.

VAURABOURG, Andrée (Mrs.
Arthur Honegger). Toulouse,
France, Sep 8 1894- .
Pianist, composer. BAKER 5=
p.733, BLOM, ENCI MUS=v.2
p.436, GROVE 5=v.4 p.345 &
v.7 p.826, RIEMANN, THOMP-
SON.

VAURENVILLE, Louise Deschalliez de see Deschalliez,
Louise

VEGA, Silvia Eisenstein de
see Eisenstein de Vega,
Silvia

VEISBERG, Yuliya Lazarevna
see Weissberg, Yuliya
Lazarevna

VELASCO, María Sánchez see
Thompson, Marquita Sánchez
de

VELIČKOVA, Ljuba see Welitsch,
Ljuba

VENABLES, Ann see Arne, Ann

VENGEROVA, Izabella Afanasyevna.
Minsk, Russia, Mar 1 1877-
Feb 7 1956, New York City.
Pianist, piano teacher. BAKER
5, SANDVED, THOMPSON, VODAR-
SKY. [VODARSKY=b.1879 in
Vilna]

VENORA, Lei. 20th-century
American soprano. PAVLAKIS=
p.292.

VERBITSKAYA, Eugenia. Kiev,
1904- . Contralto. KUTSCH.

VERDI, Giuseppina see Strepponi, Clelia Maria Josepha

VÈRE, Clémentine Duchêne de
(de Vère-Sapio; real name=
Wood de Vère). Paris, Dec 12
1864-Jan 19 1954, Mt. Vernon,
New York. Soprano, voice
teacher. BAKER 1, BAKER 5,
ENCI MUS, THOMPSON.

VERGIN, Eugénie Elise see
Colonne, Eugénie Elise

VERLET, Alice. Belgium, 1873-
1934, Paris. Soprano, voice
teacher. KUTSCH.

VERMEULEN, Marie Louise Hen-
drickx- see Hendrickx-
Vermeulen, Marie Louise

VERNA, Mary Curtis- see
Curtis-Verna, Mary

VERNE, Adela (orig.=Wurm).
Southampton, England, Feb
27 1877-Feb 5 1952, London.
Pianist, piano teacher.
BAKER 5, BLOM, GROVE 5,
RIEMANN, THOMPSON.

VERNE, Alice Verne Bredt
(orig.=Wurm). Southampton,
England, Aug 9 1868-Apr 12
1958, London. Pianist,
piano teacher, composer.
BAKER 5, BROWN BRIT=p.460,
GROVE 5, RIEMANN=v.2 p.952,
THOMPSON.

VERNE, Mathilde (orig.=Wurm).
Southampton, England, May
25 1865-Jun 4 1936, London.
Pianist, piano teacher.
BAKER 5, BROWN BIO, BROWN
BRIT=p.460, GROVE 5, RIE-
MANN=v.2 p.952, THOMPSON.

VERNEUIL, Mimi de see De
Verneuil, Mimi

VERNI, Antonia see Tognoli
Verni, Antonia

VERNI, Maria. fl.1804. Italian
singer. ENCI MUS.

VERNIER, Josepha see Fischer,
Josepha

VERNILLAT, France Marie
Elisabeth. Nancy (Meurthe-
et-Moselle), France, Jan 1
1912- . Music historian,
writer. MGG.

VERNON, Dorothy. Heaton Park,
Manchester, England, May
1923- . Soprano. PALMER.

VEROCAI, Sophie (Mrs. Giovanni,
born Kayser). 18th-century
German violinist. ENCI MUS.

VERONA, Gabriella Gentili
see Gentili Verona, Gab-
riella

VEROVIO, Verovia. 17th-century
Italian singer. ENCI MUS.

VERRETT, Shirley. New Orleans,
c1933- . Mezzo-soprano,
contralto. EWEN NEW, KUTSCH,
PAVLAKIS=p.296. *[KUTSCH=
b.1938]*

VESPERMANN, Klara Metzger-
see Metzger-Vespermann,
Klara

VESTFALI, Felicja (real name=
Westfalowicz). Cracow, 1834-
1863, New York City. Con-
tralto. GROVE 5.

VESTRIS, Lucia Elizabeth (Eliza
Lucy; Mrs. Armand, born Bartolozzi). London, Jan 3 or Mar 2
1797-Aug 8 1856, Fulham, London. Contralto, actress,
manager. BLOM, BROWN BIO,
BROWN BRIT, *ENCI MUS=illus.
v.4 fac.p.559, EWEN NEW,
GROVE 1, GROVE 1 APP=v.4
p.812, GROVE 5, PRATT.

VESTRIS, Maria Caterina Violante (Marie Catherine Violante [Violantina]). Florence,
c1732-Apr 23 1791, Paris.
Singer, dancer, court musician. GROVE 5.

VIALTZEVA, Anastasia. ?, 1871-
Feb 4 1913, St. Petersburg.
Contralto. KUTSCH.

VIARD, Jenny (Mrs. Nicolas
Louis, born Martin). Carcas-
sonne, France, Sep 29 1831-?.
Pianist, piano teacher.
BROWN BIO, GROVE 1=v.4 p.342
& 812.

VIARDOT, Louise (Pauline Marie)
Héritte de la Tour. Paris,
Dec 14 1841-Jan 17 1918,
Heidelberg. Contralto, voice
teacher, composer, opera
composer. BAKER 1=p.267 &

601, BLOM=p.283, ENCI MUS,
ENCI SALVAT, GROVE 5, PRATT,
RIEMANN, ULLSTEIN=p.187
(in article on the García
family).

VIARDOT-GARCIA, Michelle
Ferdinande Pauline. Paris,
Jul 18 1821-May 18 1910,
Paris. Mezzo-soprano, voice
teacher, composer, light-
opera composer, actress.
BAKER 1, BAKER 5, BAKER
1971, BLOM, BROWN BIO,
*CLAYTON=p.398, CORTE,
DICT MUS=v.1 p.385, *ENCI
MUS=illus.fac.p.495, ENCI
SALVAT, ENCY MUS, EWEN NEW,
GROVE 1, GROVE 5, MARIZ,
MGG=v.4 col.1368, illus.
fac.col.1313, RIEMANN,
*SANDVED, SCHOLES=p.393,
THOMPSON, *ULLSTEIN=p.187.

VIEUXTEMPS, Josephine (Mrs.
Henri, born Eder). Vienna,
Dec 15 1815-Jun 29 1868,
Celle St.-Cloud, nr. Paris.
Pianist. ENCI MUS, RIEMANN.

VIGANÒ, Maria Medina. Paris,
1883- . Dancer. DICT MUS,
ENCI MUS.

VIGANÒ MOMBELLI, Vincenza
see Mombelli, Vincenza

VILDA, Maria see Wilt,
Marie

VILLANI, Luisa. San Francisco,
c1890- . Soprano, voice
teacher. KUTSCH, THOMPSON.
[KUTSCH=b.c1885?]

VILLENEUVE, Marie-Louise-
Diane. St. Anne des Plaines,
Québec, Canada, ?- . 20th-
century pianist, organist,
composer, choral conductor,
teacher. CBC.

VIÑAS, Giulia (Mrs. Francisco,

born Novelli). Rome, 1860-
Jul 21 1932, Moyá, Spain.
Mezzo-soprano. ENCI MUS.

VINCENT, Isabella (born Burchell, later Mrs. Mills).
Surrey?, England, 1735-Jun
9 1802, London. Soprano.
GROVE 5.

VINCENT, Johanna Maria. Amsterdam, Mar 8 1898- . Soprano,
voice teacher. GROVE 5,
KUTSCH. *[GROVE 5=b.Mar 6]*

VINCENT, Ruth. Yarmouth, Nor-
folk, England, Mar 22 1877-
Jul 8 1955, London. Soprano.
ENCI MUS.

VINETTE, Alice. Saint-Urbain,
Québec, Canada, Apr 24 1894- .
Pianist, composer, organist.
CBC.

VINING, Helen Sherwood. Brook-
lyn, New York, Jul 4 1855-?.
Pianist, piano teacher.
BAKER 1.

VINNING, Louisa (as child=
"Infant Sappho"). Kingsbridge,
Devon, England, Nov 10 1836-
1904, London. Soprano, har-
pist. BLOM, BROWN BRIT,
GROVE 1, GROVE 5.

VINNING, Rosetta see O'Leary,
Rosetta

VINOGRADOVA, Vera. 20th-century
Russian pianist, composer.
VODARSKY.

VIOLLIER, Renée. Geneva, May 15
1894- . Musicologist, editor,
writer. SCHUH.

VISEUR, Suzanne Cesbron see
Cesbron-Viseur, Suzanne

VISHNEVSKAYA, Galina. Leningrad, Oct 25 1926- . Soprano.

263 VON MANGERN

ENCI MUS=v.4 p.65, EWEN
NEW, KUTSCH, *SANDVED,
THOMPSON.

VITALI, Giuseppina see
Ferlotti, Giuseppina

VITELLARO, Rosalia see
Cammarano, Rosalia

VITO, Gioconda de see
De Vito, Gioconda

VIVANTE, Ginevra. Nr. Venice,
?- . 20th-century soprano.
ENCI MUS.

VIX, Geneviève (born Brouwer).
Nantes, France, Dec 31 1879-
Aug 25 1939, Paris. Soprano,
actress. BAKER 5, KUTSCH,
PRATT, THOMPSON. [PRATT=
b.1887; KUTSCH=b.in Le
Havre]

VOGEL, Elise see Polko,
Elise

VOGGENHUBER, Vilma von (Mrs.
Franz Krolop). Budapest,
1845-Jan 11 1888, Berlin.
Soprano, court musician.
BAKER 1, PRATT, THOMPSON.

VOGL, Therese (born Thoma).
Tutzing, Bavaria, Nov 12
1845-Sep 29 1921, Munich.
Soprano. BAKER 1, BLOM,
ENCI MUS, GROVE 1, GROVE 5.
[GROVE 1=b.1846]

VOIGT, Henriette (born Kuntze).
Leipzig, Nov 24 1808-Oct 15
1839, Leipzig. Amateur pia-
nist. BAKER 5, GROVE 1,
PRATT, RIEMANN, THOMPSON.
[GROVE 1=b.1809]

VOLAVY, Marguerite. Brno,
Moravia, Dec 28 1886- .
Pianist. PRATT, THOMPSON.

VOLDAN, Marie (Mrs. Bedřich,

born Holúbová). Bohemia?,
Jan 9 1928- . Violinist.
ENCI MUS.

VOLKOVA, Avdotia see Vorobiev, Avdotia

VOLKSTEIN, Pauline. Quedlin-
burg, Germany, Jan 19 1849-
May 6 1925, Weimar. Composer.
THOMPSON.

VON ALPENHEIM, Ilse see
Alpenheim, Ilse von

VON ARNIM, Bettina see
Brentano, Bettina

VON ASOW, Hedwig Müller see
Müller von Asow, Hedwig

VON BECKERATH, Lulu see
Schultz von Beckerath, Lulu

VON DACH, Charlotte see
Dach, Charlotte von

VON FLICK, Hermine see
Bosetti, Hermine

VON GEYERSECK, Marianne see
Pirker, Marianne

VON GINZKEY, Julia Bertha
see Culp, Julia Bertha

VON HOFF, Elizabeth (Mrs.
Henry, born Chamberlaine).
19th-century English pianist,
organist, composer, teacher.
BROWN BRIT.

VON KLENCKE, Helmina see
Chézy, Helmina

VON KRAUS, Adrienne see
Kraus, Adrienne

VON KRIEGNER, Marta see
Linz von Kriegner, Marta

VON MANGERN, Elsa Laura Seeman
see Wolzogen, Elsa Laura

VON NIESSEN-STONE, Matja
see Niessen-Stone, Matja
von

VON SCHILLINGS, Angela Barbara see Kemp, Angela
Barbara

VON SCHULTZ, Ella see
Adaĭewska, Ella von

VON SEBALD, Frau see
Sebald, Frau von

VON STADE, Frederica. N.J.,
?- . 20th-century American
mezzo-soprano. PAVLAKIS=
p.296.

VON STOCKHAUSEN, Elisabeth
see Herzogenberg, Elisa-
beth

VON VOGGENHUBER, Vilma see
Voggenhuber, Vilma von

VON VRABELY, Seraphine see
Tausig, Seraphine

VON WALTERSHAUSEN, Caroline
von see Waltershausen,
Caroline von

VON WEINGARTNER, Lucille see
Marcel, Lucille

VON ZEDLITZ, Baroness see
Kingston, Marie Antoinette

VORLOVÁ, Slávka. Náchod,
Czechoslovakia, Mar 15
1894- . Composer. ENCI MUS,
GROVE 5.

VOROBIEV, Avdotia (Mrs. Iakob,
born Volkova). 18th-century
Russian singer. ENCI MUS.

VOROBIEVA-PETROVA, Anna
Iakovlevna. Russia, 1816-
1901, Russia. Contralto.
ENCI MUS, ENCI SALVAT=
v.3 p.614.

VOTIPKA, Thelma. Cleveland,
Ohio, 1898?-Oct 24 1972,
New York City. Soprano.
KUTSCH, SANDVED. *[KUTSCH=*
b.1906; SANDVED=birth-date
not given. Birth-date in
entry based on obituary in
Opera, Dec 1972, p.1115,
indicating death at age of
74]

VRABELY, Seraphine von see
Tausig, Seraphine

VRETBLAD, Karin (born Bodman).
Sweden?, Dec 29 1883- .
Violinist, viola player.
THOMPSON.

VRIES, Rosa van Os de see
De Vries, Rosa van Os

VRONSKY, Vitya (real name=
Victoria Vronsky). Evpa-
toria, Crimea, Aug 22 1909-
Pianist. BAKER 5, ENCI MUS=
v.1 p.150 (brief mention in
article on husband Victor
Babin), EWEN LIVING, GROVE
5=v.1 p.281 (brief mention
in article on husband Victor
Babin), *SANDVED, THOMPSON.

VUILLEUMIER, Hélène Teysseire-
see Teysseire-Vuilleumier,
Hélène

VULPUS, Jutta. Weimar, Dec 31
1937- . Soprano. KUTSCH.

VYALTZEVA, Anastasiya Dimitri-
yevna. Russia?, 1871-1913,
Russia?. Gypsy singer.
VODARSKY.

VYVYAN, Jennifer. Broadstairs,
Kent, England, Mar 13 1925-
Apr 5 1974, London. Soprano.
BLOM, GROVE 5, KUTSCH, SAND-
VED, ULLSTEIN. *[ULLSTEIN=*
b.1924. Date and place of
death based on obituary in
Musical Times, Jun 1974, p.502]

W

WAAGEN, Anna see Schechner-
Waagen, Anna

WACHSMUTH-LOEW, Andrée. La
Chaux-de-Fonds, Switzerland,
Jan 7 1911- . Harpsichor-
dist. SCHUH.

WACHUTTA, Hedwig see Rolandt,
Hedwig

WADE, Annie see Grey, Annie

WAGELE BERNASCONI, Antonia
see Bernasconi, Antonia
Wagele

WAGNER, Cosima. Bellaggio, on
Lake Como, Italy, Dec 24
1837-Apr 1 1930, Bayreuth.
Patron, writer, administra-
tor. BAKER 5, BAKER 1971,
BROWN BIO=p.605, CORTE, ENCI
MUS, *ENCI SALVAT=illus.v.4
p.544, EWEN NEW, MGG, RIE-
MANN=v.2 p.877, *SANDVED=
illus.p.1450-51, THOMPSON.
[ENCI MUS, RIEMANN, & THOMP-
SON=b.Dec 25]

WAGNER, Johanna see Wagner-
Jachmann, Johanna

WAGNER, Mathilde see Wesendonck, Mathilde

WAGNER, Sieglinde. Linz, Apr 21
1921- . Contralto. KUTSCH.

WAGNER-JACHMANN, Johanna.
Seelze, nr.Hanover, Oct 13
1826-Oct 16 1894, Würzburg.
Soprano, voice teacher, act-
ress. BAKER 1, BAKER 5,
BROWN BIO, CORTE, ENCI MUS,
EWEN NEW, GROVE 1, GROVE 1
APP=v.4 p.814, GROVE 5, GROVE
5 SUP, MGG, PRATT, RIEMANN=
v.1 p.874, THOMPSON. [BROWN
BIO, CORTE, GROVE 1, MGG,
PRATT, & RIEMANN=b.1828]

WAGRELL, Kerstin see Thybo,
Kerstin

WAINWRIGHT, Harriet (later
Mrs. Colonel Stewart). fl.
1780-1840. Composer, writer.
BROWN BIO=p.577, BROWN BRIT,
GROVE 5, THOMPSON.

WAKEFIELD, (Augusta) Mary.
Sedgwick, nr.Kendal, West-
morland, England, Aug 19
1853-Sep 16 1910, Grange-
over-Sands, Lancs., England.
Contralto, composer, editor,
writer. BLOM, BROWN BRIT,
ENCI MUS, GROVE 5, PRATT,
THOMPSON.

WALCOTT, Jane see Shirreff,
Jane

WALDMANN, Maria. Vienna, 1844-
Nov 6 1920, Ferrara. Mezzo-
soprano. BLOM, *ENCI MUS=
illus.fac.p.551, GROVE 5,
*MGG=illus.v.8 col.1513.
[ENCI MUS=b.1842]

WALENN, Dorothea. 19th-century
English violinist, teacher.
BROWN BRIT.

WALEVSKA, Christine. Los Angeles, ?- . 20th-century
violoncellist. PAVLAKIS=
p.278.

WALKER, Bettina. ?-Feb 4 1893,
Fulham, England. Pianist,
writer. BROWN BRIT.

WALKER, Edyth. Hopewell, nr.
Rome, New York, Mar 27 1867-
Feb 19 1950, New York City.
Mezzo-soprano, voice teacher.
BAKER 5, ENCI MUS, EWEN NEW,
GROVE 5, GROVE 5 SUP, KUTSCH,
PRATT, RIEMANN, *SANDVED,
THOMPSON.

WALKER, Sarah-Jane-Layton see
Cahier, Sarah-Jane

WALL, Joan. 20th-century
American mezzo-soprano.
SANDVED.

WALLACE, Eliza. ?-Aug 1878,
Sydney, Australia. Singer,
violinist, voice teacher.
BROWN BRIT.

WALLACE, Grace Maxwell (born
Stein). Edinburgh, c1800-
Mar 12 or 13 1878, New
York City. Writer, trans-
lator. BROWN BIO, BROWN
BRIT, GROVE 1, GROVE 5,
MGG, PRATT, THOMPSON.
[BROWN BRIT & PRATT=b.
c1815]

WALLACE, Lucille (Mrs. Clif-
ford Curzon). Chicago, Feb
22 1898- . Harpsichordist,
pianist. ENCI MUS=v.1 p.583
(brief mention in article
on husband), GROVE 5, PAL-
MER, SANDVED, THOMPSON.

WALLMANN, Margherita. Vienna,
Jun 22 1904- . Dancer,
choreographer, opera pro-
ducer. *ENCI MUS=illus.
v.4 fac.p.135 & v.3 fac.
p.555, EWEN NEW.

WALLNER, Bertha Antonia.
Munich, Aug 20 1876-Oct 29
1956, Munich. Musicologist,
writer. MGG, PRATT, RIEMANN.

WALPURGIS, Maria Antonia
see Maria Antonia Walpurgis

WALSWORTH, Joan see Davies,
Joan

WALTER, Ida. 19th-century
English composer. BROWN
BRIT.

WALTER, Juliane (Mrs. Ignaz,
born Roberts). 18-19th-
century singer. GROVE 5.

WALTER, Minna. 19th-century
Bohemian singer. GROVE 5=
v. 9 p.154 (brief mention
in article on father Gustav
Walter).

WALTER-KÜHNE, Catherine (Adol-
fowna). St. Petersburg, May
13 1870-Feb 19 1931, Rostock.
Harpist. MGG.

WALTERSHAUSEN, Caroline von
(Mrs. Hermann, born Strösser).
?, Jan 3 1900- . German
pianist. ENCI MUS.

WANNE, Kerttu. Turku, Finland,
Jul 26 1905- . Violinist.
GROVE 5.

WARD, Adelaide see Newton,
Adelaide

WARD, Clementine. 19th-century
English organist, composer,
singer. BROWN BRIT.

WARD, Eliza A. 19th-century
English pianist, singer,
teacher. BROWN BRIT.

WARD, Emily see Newton,
Adelaide

WARD, Evelyn. Hampstead, England, Jan 9 1865-?. Soprano.
BROWN BRIT.

WARD, Genevieve Teresa see
Ward, (Lucy) Genevieve
Teresa

WARD, Jessie. 19th-century
English contralto. BROWN
BRIT.

WARD, Lily. 19th-century
English soprano. BROWN BRIT.

WARD, (Lucy) Genevieve Teresa
(earlier sang under name
Ginevra Guerrabella). New

York City, Mar 27 1833-
Aug 18 1922, Hampstead,
London. Soprano. THOMPSON.

WARE, Harriet (Mrs. Hugh M.
Krumbhaar). Waupun, Wisc.,
Aug 26 1884-Feb 9 1962,
New York City. Pianist,
composer. BAKER 5, BAKER
1971, PRATT, THOMPSON.
*[Some sources=b.1877. Birth
date in entry based on
obituary in New York Times
(Feb 11 1962, p.86, col.7)
indicating death at age 84]*

WARE, Helen. Woodbury, N.J.,
Sep 9 1887- . Violinist,
composer. PRATT, THOMPSON.

WARENSKJOLD, Dorothy. San
Leandro, Calif., 1932- .
Soprano. *SANDVED.

WARFIELD, Leontyne see
Price, Leontyne

WARFIELD, Sandra (Mrs. James
McCracken). 20th-century
American mezzo-soprano,
writer. PAVLAKIS=p.297.

WARNER, Sylvia Townsend.
Harrow on the Hill, London,
Dec 6 1893- . Composer,
editor, writer. BAKER 5,
RIEMANN, THOMPSON.

WARNOTS, Elly. Liège, 1857-?.
Soprano. BAKER 1, BROWN
BIO, GROVE 5, PRATT. *[BAKER
1=b.1862]*

WARRELL, Eliza see Atkins,
Eliza

WARREN, Elinor Remick. Los
Angeles, Feb 23 1905- .
Pianist, composer. BAKER 5,
THOMPSON.

WARROT, Marie-Aimée. Brunoy,

France, Feb 18 1915- .
Pianist, piano teacher.
ENCI SALVAT, ENCY MUS.

WARTEL, Atale (Alda) Thérèse
Annette (born Adrien). Paris,
Jul 2 1814-Nov 6 1865, Paris.
Pianist, composer. ENCI MUS,
GROVE 5, THOMPSON.

WARTON, Mrs. see Mahon,
Miss M.

WARWICK, Alexandra (later Mrs.
Ehrenberg). England, 1863?-
Sep 2 1896, England. Con-
tralto. BROWN BRIT.

WARWICK, Giulia. 19th-century
English soprano, voice
teacher. BROWN BRIT.

WASSELF, Lucille see Marcel,
Lucille

WASTERLAIN, Viola. 20th-century
American violinist. THOMPSON.

WATERMAN, Constance Dorothy.
London, ?- . 19-20th-century
pianist, composer, accompanist. CBC.

WATSON, Claire. New York City,
1927- . Soprano. KUTSCH,
PAVLAKIS=p.292, *SANDVED=
illus.only p.1357.

WATSON, Elizabeth see Boman,
Elizabeth

WATSON, Hilda see Wilson,
Matilda Ellen

WATTS, Helen. Pembrokeshire,
England, Dec 1927- . Con-
tralto. GROVE 5 SUP, KUTSCH.

WAYDA, Giannina see Koro-
lewicz-Wayda, Janina

WAYDOWA, Janina Korolewicz-

see Korolewicz-Waydowa,
Janina

WAYLETT, Harriet (later Mrs.
George Alexander Lee, born
Cooke). Bath, England, Feb
7 1800-Apr 26 1851, Ken-
sington, England. Soprano,
actress. BROWN BIO, BROWN
BRIT, GROVE 1 APP=v.4 p.
817, GROVE 5, THOMPSON.
[BROWN BIO=d.Apr 19]

WEATHERS, Felicia. St. Louis,
Mo., Aug 13 1937- . So-
prano. EWEN NEW, KUTSCH,
PAVLAKIS=p.292. *[KUTSCH=*
b.1939?]

WEBB, Alice see Gomez,
Alice

WEBER, Aloysia see Weber,
Maria Aloysia Louise
Antonia

WEBER, Carolina (Lina)(Mrs.
Carl Maria Friedrich Ernst
von, born Brandt). Bonn,
Nov 19 1794-Feb 23 1852,
Dresden. Singer. RIEMANN.

WEBER, Costanze see Mozart,
Konstanze

WEBER, Josepha see Weber,
Maria Josepha

WEBER, Konstanze see Mozart,
Konstanze

WEBER, Margrit. Ebnat-Kappel,
Switzerland, Feb 24 1924- .
Pianist. BAKER 1971, SCHUH.

WEBER, Maria Aloysia Louise
Antonia. Zell, Baden, Aus-
tria, 1761-Jun 8 1839,
Salzburg. Soprano. BLOM,
ENCI SALVAT, ENCY MUS,
GROVE 1, GROVE 5 SUP, MGG,
PRATT. *[PRATT=b.1750; ENCI*
SALVAT & ENCY MUS=b.in
Mannheim, d.in Frankfurt]

WEBER, Maria Josepha. Zell,
Baden, Austria, 1759-Dec 29
1819, Vienna. Singer. ENCI
MUS, GROVE 1, GROVE 5,
MARIZ, MGG.

WEBER, Maria Sophie (Sophia).
Zell, Baden, Austria, Oct
1763-Oct 26 1846, Salzburg.
Singer. GROVE 1, GROVE 5,
MGG. *[GROVE 1=b.1764, d.*
1843; GROVE 5=b.1767]

WEBER, Sophie see Weber,
Maria Sophie

WEBER-BELL, Susanne. Lucerne,
1857-?. Singer, voice teacher, inventor. PRATT.

WEBSTER, Clarinda Augusta.
London, ?-?. 19th-century
English pianist, teacher,
writer. BROWN BRIT.

WEBSTER, Elizabeth see
Davies, Elizabeth

WEBSTER-POWELL, Alma see
Powell, Alma Webster

WEDEKIND, Erika. Hanover,
Nov 13 1868-Oct 10 1944,
Zürich. Soprano. BAKER 1,
GROVE 5, KUTSCH, PRATT,
RIEMANN, SCHUH, THOMPSON.
[RIEMANN=b.Nov 3; BAKER 1 &
PRATT=b.1872]

WEED, Marion. Rochester, New
York, 1866?-Jun 22 1947,
Rochester, New York. So-
prano, voice teacher. THOMP-
SON. *[THOMPSON=b.1870. Birth*
date in entry based on New
York Times obituary (Jun 23
1947, p.23, col.5) indicating
death at age 81]

WEGMANN, Elvira see Lüthi-
Wegmann, Elvira

WEGMANN, Maria Anna (later
Ebert). Frankfurt, Feb 27

1764-Oct 24 1802, Frankfurt.
Organist, church musician.
MGG.

WEGNER, Walburga. Iserlohn,
nr. Cologne, Aug 25 1913- .
Soprano. KUTSCH, RIEMANN.

WEICHSEL, Elizabeth see
Billington, Elizabeth

WEIDT, Lucy. Troppau, Silesia,
1880-Jul 28 1940, Vienna.
Soprano, voice teacher.
BAKER 5, CORTE, ENCI MUS,
GROVE 5, KUTSCH, PRATT,
THOMPSON. *[KUTSCH=b.1879]*

WEIGL, Vally. Vienna, Sep 11
1899- . Composer, music
therapist. ENCI MUS, MGG,
RIEMANN. *[MGG=b.1894]*

WEILL, Janine. Paris, Jan 13
1903- . Pianist, adminis-
trator. ENCI SALVAT, ENCY
MUS.

WEINGAND, Amelia Cocq- see
Cocq-Weingand, Amelia

WEINGARTNER, Lucille von see
Marcel, Lucille

WEINGARTNER-STUDER, Carmen.
Winterthur, Switzerland,
Mar 25 1907- . Conductor,
composer, writer. SCHUH.

WEINHOLD, Elisabeth. 18th-
century German singer.
ENCI MUS=v.4 p.148 (brief
mention in article on
Benedikt Emanuel Schak).

WEISBERG, Yuliya Lazarevna
see Weissberg, Yuliya
Lazarevna

WEISE, Dagmar. Kulmbach, Germany, 1926- . Musicologist,
writer. ENCI SALVAT, ENCY
MUS.

WEISS, Amalie see Joachim,
Amalie

WEISS, Georgiana Ansell (Mrs.
Willoughby Hunter, born
Barnett). Gloucester, Eng-
land, 1826-Nov 6 1880,
Brighton, England. Soprano.
BROWN BRIT, GROVE 1, GROVE 5.

WEISS, Margrit see Bagdasarjanz-Weiss, Margrit

WEISSBERG (Weisberg, Veisberg),
Yuliya Lazarevna (Julia
Lazarewna; Mrs. Nikolai
Rimski-Korsakov). Orenburg,
Kirghisia, Russia, Dec 25
1878-Mar 1 1942, Leningrad.
Composer, opera composer,
editor. BAKER 5, BAKER 1971,
BLOM, CORTE, ENCI MUS=v.4
p.570, ENCI SALVAT, GROVE 5,
GROVE 5 SUP, RIEMANN=v.2
p.516, THOMPSON, VODARSKY=
p.140. *[GROVE 5 & THOMPSON=
b.Dec 23; RIEMANN=d.May 1]*

WELCKER, Mary. ?-1778, London.
English music printer and
seller. GROVE 5.

WELDON, Georgina (born Treherne). London, May 24 1837-
Jan 11 1914, Brighton, England. Soprano, composer,
choral conductor. BAKER 5,
BROWN BIO, BROWN BRIT, ENCI
MUS, GROVE 1, GROVE 5, PRATT,
SCHOLES, THOMPSON. *[THOMPSON=
b.in Clapham, England]*

WELITSCH, Ljuba (orig.=Velič-
kova or Welitschkowa). Bor-
risovo, nr. Varna, Bulgaria,
Jul 10 1913- . Soprano.
BAKER 5, BLOM, COOPER, CORTE,
ENCI MUS, *EWEN LIV SUP, EWEN
NEW, GROVE 5, RIEMANN, *SAND-
VED, THOMPSON.

WELLITSCH, Ingeborg see
Borkh, Inge

WELLS, Patricia. Louisiana, ?- . 20th-century American soprano. PAVLAKIS=p.293.

WELLS, Madame Thaddeus. ?-Mar 1885, London. Contralto. BROWN BRIT.

WELSH, Mary Ann see Wilson, Mary Ann

"WELSH NIGHTINGALE" see Wynne, Sarah Edith

WELTI-HERZOG, Emilie see Herzog, Emilie

WÉLY, Joséphine-Thérèse see Lefébure-Wély, Joséphine-Thérèse

WEND, Flore. Geneva, Mar 31 1909- . Singer. SCHUH.

WENDLING, Dorothea (I)(born Spurni or Spourni). Stuttgart, Mar 21 1736-Aug 20 1811, Munich. Soprano, voice teacher. DICT MUS, ENCI MUS, GROVE 5, MGG, RIEMANN. *[GROVE 5 & RIEMANN=b.1737]*

WENDLING, Dorothea (II)(later Güthe). Mannheim, Jan 27 1767-May 19 1839, Munich. Singer. MGG.

WENDLING, Elisabeth Augusta (I)(born Sarselli; called Lisl). Mannheim, Feb 20 1746-Jan 10 1786, Munich. Singer. DICT MUS, ENCI MUS, GROVE 5, MGG, RIEMANN. *[RIEMANN=d.1794; DICT MUS, ENCI MUS, & GROVE 5=d.Feb 18 1794]*

WENDLING, Elisabeth Augusta (II)(called Gustl). Mannheim, Oct 4 1752-Feb 18 1794, Munich. Soprano, voice teacher. MGG, RIEMANN.

WENDLING, Maria Dorothea (born Senpiere). 18th-century German lutenist. ENCI MUS.

WENNERBERG-REUTER, Sara (Margareta Eugenia Eufrosyne). Ottersted, Skaraborgs län, Sweden, Feb 11 1875-?. Organist, composer. GROVE 5.

WENSLEY, Frances Foster. 19th-century English pianist, composer. BROWN BRIT.

WERBER, Mia. Vienna, Nov 10 1876-1943, Terezín [Theresienstadt] Bohemia. Soprano. KUTSCH.

WERTHEIM, Rosy. Amsterdam, Feb 19 1888-May 27 1949, Laren, Netherlands. Composer. THOMPSON.

WERTHEMANN, Helene. Basel, Apr 18 1928- . Writer. SCHUH.

WESENDONCK, Mathilde (orig.=Agnes; bron Luckemeyer). Elberfeld, Germany, Dec 23 1828-Aug 31 1902, Villa Traunblick nr. Altmünster, Austria. Poetess. BAKER 5, CORTE, ENCI MUS=v.4 p.550 (in article on husband Richard Wagner), RIEMANN, *SANDVED= illus.only p.1446, THOMPSON.

WESSELY, Helene (born Kropik). Vienna, Jul 29 1924- . Musicologist, writer. ENCI MUS, MGG.

WEST, Clara (born Ainsworth). Chatham, England, Sep 9 1844-?. Soprano. BROWN BRIT.

WEST, Lottie. South Hackney, England, Nov 5 1865-?. Contralto, pianist, composer, teacher. BROWN BRIT.

WEST, Mrs. Temple see Molesworth, Lady

WESTENHOLZ, Barbara Lucietta
Fricemelica (born Affabili).
Venice, 1725-Sep 20 1776,
Ludwigslust, Germany. Singer,
court musician. MGG.

WESTENHOLZ, Eleonore Sophia
Maria (born Fritscher).
Neubrandenburg, Germany,
Jul 10 1759-Oct 4 1838,
Ludwigslust, Germany. Sin-
ger, court musician. MGG.

WESTERN, Ethel see Thalberg,
Zaré

WESTFALOWICZ, Felicja see
Vestfali, Felicja

WESTFIELD, Carolyn see
Beebe, Carolyn

WESTROP, Kate. 19th-century
English composer, organist,
pianist. BROWN BRIT.

WETTERGREN, Gertrud (born
Pålson). Eslöv län, Malmö-
hus, Sweden, Feb 17 1897- .
Contralto. BAKER 5, *EWEN
LIVING, EWEN LIV SUP, GROVE
5=v.6 p.532, KUTSCH, THOMP-
SON.

WHEATLEY, Julia. New York
City, 1817-c1875, ?. Con-
tralto. THOMPSON.

WHITE, Alice Mary see Smith,
Alice Mary

WHITE, Carolina (Carolyn).
Dorchester, Mass., Dec 23
1886-Oct 5 1961, Rome.
Soprano. KUTSCH, PRATT,
THOMPSON. [THOMPSON=b.1883]

WHITE, Colbourne see Baber,
Colbourne

WHITE, Kitty see Burden,
Kitty

WHITE, Mary Louise. Sheffield,
England, Sep 2 1866-Jan 1955,
London. Composer, teacher.
BAKER 5, THOMPSON. [THOMPSON=
d.1935]

WHITE, Maude Valérie. Dieppe,
Jun 23 1855-Nov 2 1937,
London. Composer. BAKER 1,
BAKER 5, BLOM, BROWN BIO,
BROWN BRIT, GROVE 1, GROVE 5,
MGG, PRATT, SCHOLES, THOMPSON.

WHITEHURST, Carolyn see Beebe,
Carolyn

WHITESIDE, Abby. S.D., 1881-
Dec 10 1956, Menlo Park,
Calif. Pianist, piano tea-
cher. THOMPSON.

WHITING, Virginia. New York
City, c1840-?. Soprano.
THOMPSON.

WHITNALL, Miss see Scarisbrick, Mrs. Thomas.

WHITTALL, Gertrude Clark.
Bellevue, Neb., Oct 7 1867-
Jun 29 1965, Washington,
D.C. Patron. BAKER 5,
BAKER 1971.

WHOMES, Clara. England?,
1853?-1884, Sydney. Pianist.
BROWN BRIT.

WHOMES, Emma. 19th-century
English organist. BROWN
BRIT.

WHYTOCK, Janet Monach see
Patey, Janet Monach

WICHERN, Karoline. Nr. Hamburg, 1836-1906, Nr. Ham-
burg. Soprano, choral conductor, teacher, editor.
PRATT.

WICKHAM, Florence Pauline
(Mrs. E. Lueder). Beaver,
Pa., 1882-Oct 20 1962,
New York City. Contralto,
light-opera composer,
composer. BAKER 5, BAKER
1971, PRATT, THOMPSON.
*[Some sources=b.1880; date
in entry based on New York
Times obituary (Oct 21 1962,
p.89, col.1) indicating
death at age 82]*

WICKS, Camilla. Long Beach,
Calif., Aug 9 1928- .
Violinist. RIEMANN, SANDVED,
THOMPSON.

WIECK, Clara Josephine see
Schumann, Clara Josephine

WIECK, Marie. Leipzig, Jan 17
1832-Nov 2 1916, Dresden.
Pianist, piano teacher,
court musician. BAKER 1,
BAKER 5, BROWN BIO, ENCI
MUS, GROVE 5, MGG, PRATT.
[BAKER 1=b.1835]

WIEDMANN, Anny see Konetzni,
Anny

WIELE, Aimée van de see
Van de Wiele, Aimée

WIENIAWSKA, Irene Regine see
Poldowski

WIERUSZOWSKI, Lili. Cologne,
Dec 10 1899- . Organist,
choral conductor, composer.
SCHUH.

WIETROWETZ, Gabriele. Ljubljana, Yugoslavia, Jan 13
1866-Apr 6 1937, Berlin.
Violinist, teacher. GROVE 5,
PRATT, THOMPSON.

WIGMAN, Mary. Hanover, Germany,
Nov 13 1886-Sep 18 1973,
Dahlem, Berlin. Dancer,
choreographer. THOMPSON.

*[Dates in entry based on New
York Times obituary, Sep 20
1973, p.50, col.1]*

WIGSTRÖM, Eleanora Louise
Marianne see Petrelli

WILD, Margaret. 19th-century
English pianist. BROWN BRIT.

WILDBRUNN, Helene. Vienna,
Apr 8 1882-Apr 10 or 11 1972,
Vienna. Soprano, contralto,
voice teacher. KUTSCH, RIE-
MANN, THOMPSON.

WILDGANS, Ilona see Steingruber, Ilona

WILFORD, Mary see Bulkley,
Mary

WILHELMJ, Maria (born Gastell).
Mainz, Jul 27 1856-Feb 27
1930, Wiesbaden. Soprano.
BAKER 1, ENCI MUS, RIEMANN.

WILHELMJ, Mariella (born
Mausch). 19-20th-century
German pianist. ENCI MUS.

WILHORST, Cora de. New York
City, ?-?. 19th-century
soprano. THOMPSON.

WILKINSON, Sarah see Mountain,
Sarah

WILKOMIRSKA, Wanda. Warsaw,
1929- . Violinist. THOMPSON.

WILLAUER, Marguerite. Charleston, S.C., ?- . 20th-century
soprano. *SANDVED.

WILLEMS, Elizabeth see
Addison, Elizabeth

WILLENT, Luisa see Bordogni-
Willent, Luisa

WILLER, Luise. Munich, 1888- .
Contralto. KUTSCH.

273   *WILSON*

WILLIAMS, Anna. London, Aug 6
1845-Sep 3 1924, London.
Soprano, voice teacher.
BLOM, BROWN BIO, BROWN
BRIT, GROVE 1, GROVE 5,
PRATT, THOMPSON.

WILLIAMS, Anne. Bitterley,
Salop, England, 1818-?.
Singer. BROWN BRIT, GROVE 1.

WILLIAMS, Annie. ?-Oct 16 1890,
London. Welsh contralto,
organist. BROWN BRIT.

WILLIAMS, Camilla. Danville,
Va., 1925- . Soprano.
*EWEN LIV SUP, KUTSCH,
PAVLAKIS=p.293, *SANDVED,
THOMPSON.

WILLIAMS, Grace   see also
Arthur, Grace

WILLIAMS, Grace. Barry, Glamorganshire, Wales, Feb 19
1906- . Composer. BLOM,
ENCI MUS, ENCY MUS, GROVE 5,
MGG, RIEMANN.

WILLIAMS, Maria Jane (Llinos).
Glamorganshire, Wales, Oct
9 1793-Nov 10 1873, Gla-
morganshire, Wales. Soprano,
editor. BROWN BRIT, GROVE 5,
THOMPSON.

WILLIAMS, Martha. Bitterley,
Salop, England, 1821-?.
Contralto. BROWN BRIT,
GROVE 1.

WILLIS, Mary. 19th-century
English mezzo-soprano.
BROWN BRIT.

WILLMANN, (Anna Maria An-
tonetta) Marianne (Madame
Tribolet). Paderborn, Prussia, Feb 17 1768-Apr 21
1813, Klosterneuburg, Austria. Singer, court musician. GROVE 1, MGG. *[GROVE
1=d.1812]*

WILLMANN, (Johanna) Magdalena
(born Galvani). Forchtenberg,
Hohenlohe, nr. Bonn, Sep 13
1771-Dec 23 1801, Vienna.
Contralto, court musician.
GROVE 1, MGG, PRATT, RIEMANN.

WILLMANN, (Maria Anna Magdalena) Caroline. Vienna, Feb
25 1796-1860, Vienna?.
Pianist, soprano. GROVE 1,
MGG.

WILLMANN, Marianne (born Huber).
?, 1770-?. Austrian pianist,
court musician. RIEMANN.

WILLMANN, (Maximiliana Valentina) Walburga. Bonn, May 18
1769-Jul 27 1835, Mainz.
Pianist. GROVE 1, MGG.

WILMORE, Louisa Aubert   see
Pyne, Louisa Aubert

WILSON, Agnes. Gloucester,
England, Oct 8 1864-Apr 27
1907, London. Contralto,
voice teacher. BROWN BRIT,
GROVE 5, THOMPSON.

WILSON, Mrs. Cornwall Baron.
England, 1797?-Jan 12 1846,
London. Composer, poet.
BROWN BRIT.

WILSON, Florence Mary   see
Austral, Florence Mary

WILSON, Hilda   see   Wilson,
Matilda

WILSON, Marie. London, Nov 30
1903- . Violinist. GROVE 5,
PALMER.

WILSON, Mary Ann (Mrs. Thomas
Welsh). London, 1802-Dec 13
1867, Goudhurst, Kent, England. Soprano. BROWN BIO=
p.612, BROWN BRIT, GROVE 1,
GROVE 5, THOMPSON.

WILSON, Matilda Ellen (known

as Hilda Watson). Monmouth,
England, Apr 7 1860-Dec 1
1918, Boscombe, Hants.,
England. Contralto. BROWN
BRIT, GROVE 5, PRATT,
THOMPSON.

WILT, Marie (in Italy known
as Maria Vilda; born Lieben-
thaler). Vienna, Jan 30
1833-Sep 24 1891, Vienna.
Soprano. BAKER 1, BLOM,
BROWN BIO, GROVE 1, GROVE 5,
PRATT, THOMPSON. *[GROVE 1=
b.c1835; BROWN BIO=b.1838]*

WILTON, Fanny Wyndham see
Lablache, Fanny Wyndham

WINDSOR, Alicia see Daniels,
Alicia

WINN, Florence. 19th-century
English contralto. BROWN
BRIT.

WINSTON, Jeannie (stage name
of Janet Bruce). Liverpool,
1845-Oct 29 1929, Washington, D.C. Soprano. THOMPSON.

WINTER, Pattie. 19th-century
English soprano. BROWN BRIT.

WINTERNITZ-DORDA, Martha.
Vienna, 1885- . Soprano,
voice teacher. KUTSCH.

WINTERROTH, Marie see
Rappold, Marie

WIPPERN, Louise see Harriers-
Wippern, Louise

WIRZ-WYSS, Clara. Lenzburg,
Switzerland, Jan 6 1881- .
Pianist, soprano, voice
teacher. SCHUH.

WISE, Patricia. 20th-century
American soprano. PAVLAKIS=
p.293.

WISSMAN, Lore. Neckartailfingen,
Württemberg, Germany, Jun 22
1922- . Soprano. KUTSCH, RIE-
MANN.

WITHALL, Kathleen Mary see
Fitzwilliam, Kathleen Mary

WITKOWSKA, Nadja. 20th-century
soprano. PAVLAKIS=p.293.

WITKOWSKY, Sylvia see Geszty,
Sylvia

WITTICH, Marie. Giessen, Germany, May 27 1868-Aug 4 1931,
Dresden. Soprano. EWEN NEW,
PRATT, THOMPSON. *[THOMPSON=
b.1862]*

WIXOM, Emma see Nevada, Emma

WOFFINGTON, Margaret (or Peg).
Dublin, 1718-Mar 28 1760,
London. Singer, actress.
BROWN BRIT.

WOHLBRÜCK, Marianne see
Marschner, Marianne

WÓJCIKÓVNA, Bronislava (later
Keuprulian). Lvov, Poland,
Aug 6 1890-1934, Warsaw.
Musicologist, writer. RIE-
MANN, THOMPSON.

WOLF, Anna Mrasek. ?, Nov 15
1774-Jun 2 1808, Vienna.
Pianist. MGG.

WOLF, Antoinette (Mrs. Endré,
born Tömlich). 20th-century
pianist. GROVE 5 SUP.

WOLFF, Beverly. 20th-century
American mezzo-soprano.
PAVLAKIS=p.297.

WOLFF, Henny. Cologne, Feb 3
1896- . Soprano. RIEMANN.

WOLOWSKA, Maria see Szymanowska, Maria

WOLTER, Luise Geller- see
Geller-Wolter, Luise

WOLZOGEN, Elsa Laura (later
Seeman von Mangern). Dresden, Aug 5 1876-?. Singer,
lutenist. ENCI MUS.

WOOD, Anne. Crawley, Sussex,
England, Aug 2 1907- .
Contralto. GROVE 5.

WOOD, Mary Anne see Paton,
Mary Anne

WOOD, Mary Knight. East Hampton, Mass., Apr 7 1857-Dec
20 1944, Florence. Pianist,
composer. BAKER 1, BAKER 5,
THOMPSON.

WOOD, Mary Louisa. 19th-cen-
tury English organist,
choral conductor, teacher.
BROWN BRIT.

WOOD, Olga see Urusova,
Olga

WOOD DE VÈRE, Clémentine
Duchêne de see Vère,
Clémentine Duchêne de

WOODFORD, Doris see Humphrey,
Doris

WOOD-HILL, Mabel. Brooklyn,
Mar 12 1870-Mar 1 1954,
Stamford, Conn. Composer.
BAKER 5, REIS=p.183, THOMP-
SON=p.948 & 2425.

WOODYATT, Emily. Hereford,
England, 1814-?. Singer.
BROWN BRIT, GROVE 1, GROVE
5, THOMPSON.

WOOLF, Sophia Julia. London,
1831-Nov 20 1893, West
Hampstead, England. Pianist,
composer. BROWN BRIT.

WOOLHOUSE, Emma Mary see
Rea, Emma Mary

WOOLRYCH, Marietta Augusta
see Mortellari, Marietta
Augusta

WORALECK, Josephine see
Cannabich, Josephine

WORGAN, Mary. 18th-century
English composer. BROWN BRIT.

WORRELL, Marie (born Duval).
London?, Mar 3 1856-Feb 12
1895, Tulse Hill, London.
Soprano. BROWN BRIT.

WOUD, Annie. Haarlem, Netherlands, Sep 21 1901- . Contralto. THOMPSON.

WOYCIECHOWSKA, Leokadia Myszyn-
ska see Myszynska-Woyciechowska, Leokadia

WOYCKE, Bertha. 19th-century
English violinist. BROWN BRIT.

WOYCKE, Emily Drechsler (born
Hamilton). Edinburgh, ?-?.
19th-century violinist.
BAKER 1, BROWN BRIT.

WOYTOWICZ, Stefania. Orynin,
Poland, 1926- . Soprano.
KUTSCH.

WRANITZKY, Anna Katharina
(born Kraus). Vienna, Aug 6
1801-Jun 23 1851, Vienna.
Singer. ENCI MUS, GROVE 5,
MGG, RIEMANN, THOMPSON.

WRANITZKY, Karoline (born
Seidler). Vienna, 1794-Sep 4
1872, Vienna. Soprano. ENCI
MUS, GROVE 5, MGG, RIEMANN,
THOMPSON.

WRIGHT, Charlotte see Blanchard, Charlotte

WRIGHT, Elizabeth see Arne,
Elizabeth

WRIGHT, Ellen (born Riley).

London, ?-?. 19-20th-century composer. BROWN BRIT.

WRIGHTEN, Mary Ann see Pownall, Mary Ann

WRIGHTSON, Mary Ann see Pownall, Mary Ann

WURM, Adela see Verne, Adela

WURM, Alice Verne Bredt see Verne, Alice Verne Bredt

WURM, Mary J. A. Southampton, England, May 18 1860-Jan 21 1938, Munich. Pianist, composer, light-opera composer, conductor. BAKER 1, BAKER 5, BLOM, BROWN BRIT, GROVE 5, PRATT, RIEMANN, THOMPSON.

WURM, Mathilde see Verne, Mathilde

WYCKOFF, Lou Ann. 20th-century American soprano. PAVLAKIS= p.293.

WYLEZYŃSKA, Helena see Lopuska-Wylezyńska, Helena

WYLIE, Janet see Istel, Janet

WYNNE, Kate. Holywell, Flintshire, Wales, ?-?, Birmingham, England. 19th-century contralto. BROWN BRIT, GROVE 5.

WYNNE, Sarah Edith (known as "Eos Cymru Pencerddes" or the "Welsh Nightingale"). Holywell, Flintshire, Wales, Mar 11 1842-Jan 24 1897, London. Soprano. BLOM, BROWN BRIT, GROVE 1 APP=v.4 p.815, GROVE 5, THOMPSON. *[BROWN BRIT=d. Jan 23]*

WYSS, Clara Wirz- see Wirz-Wyss, Clara

WYSS, Colette see Feschotte, Colette

WYSS, Sophie. Neuveville, Jura, Switzerland, Jul 5 1897- . Soprano. GROVE•5, PALMER.

Y

YALKOVSKY, Isabelle. Philadelphia, Dec 24 1907- . Pianist. THOMPSON.

YARICK, Doris. 20th-century American soprano. *SANDVED.

YAVOR, Maria. ?, 1889- . Soprano. ENCI MUS=v.4 p.471 (brief mention in article on the Várnay family).

YAW, Ellen Beach (Mrs. Franklin D. Cannon, known as "Lark Ellen"). Boston, New York, Sep 18 1869-Sep 9 1947, West Covina, Calif. Soprano, voice teacher. KUTSCH.

YEEND, Frances. Vancouver, 1918- . Soprano. *EWEN LIV SUP, KUTSCH, *PAVLAKIS=illus. p.402 & 1506, THOMPSON.

YOUNG, Anne see Biggs, Anne; Gunn, Anne

YOUNG, Cecilia see Arne, Cecilia

YOUNG, Elizabeth see Dorman, Elizabeth

YOUNG, Esther (or Hester). 18th-century English singer. ENCI MUS, GROVE 5.

YOUNG, Harriet Maitland. 19th-century English composer, light-opera composer. BROWN BRIT.

YOUNG, Hester see Young,
Esther

YOUNG, Isabella ("Mrs. Scott").
England?, ?-1791, England.
Contralto or mezzo-soprano.
ENCI MUS, GROVE 5.

YOUNG, Isabella (Mrs. Johann
Friederich Lampe). 18th-
century English soprano.
BLOM, BROWN BRIT, ENCI MUS,
GROVE 5.

YOUNG, Mary see Young, Polly

YOUNG, Polly (or Mary; Mrs.
François Hippolyte). London,
c1745-Sep 20 1799, London.
Soprano, voice teacher.
BAKER 5, BLOM, BROWN BRIT,
ENCI MUS, GROVE 5.

YOUNGER, Margaret see Bicknell, Margaret

Z

ZACCHI, Ginevra see Giovannoni Zacchi, Ginevra

ZACCHI, Rosina. 19th-century
Italian soprano. ENCI MUS=
v.2 p.318 (in article on
Ginevra Giovannoni Zacchi).

ZADEK, Hilde. Bromberg, Germany, Dec 15 1917- . So-
prano. KUTSCH, RIEMANN,
ULLSTEIN. [RIEMANN=b.1921]

ŽÁK, Antonia see Schak,
Antonia

ŽÁK, Elisabeth see Weinhold,
Elisabeth

ZAMBELLI, Carlotta. Milan,
Nov 4 1877-?. Dancer,
dance teacher. ENCI MUS,
ENCI SALVAT, ENCY MUS.
[ENCI MUS=b.1875]

ZAMBONI, Maria. Peschiera del
Garda, Italy, Jun 25 1895- .
Soprano. ENCI MUS, KUTSCH.
[KUTSCH=b.Jul 25 1898]

ZANAZZIO, Cesira see Ferrani
Cesira

ZANDONAI, Tarquinia (Mrs. Ric-
cardo, born Tarquini). 20th-
century Italian singer.
ENCI MUS.

ZANDT, Jennie van see Van
Zandt, Jennie

ZANDT, Marie Van see Van
Zandt, Marie

ZANETTI, Emilia. Florence,
Dec 4 1915- . Musicologist,
writer. CORTE, ENCI MUS,
ENCI SALVAT, ENCY MUS,
RIEMANN. [RIEMANN=b.Mar 4]

ZANETTINI, Maria Caterina
see Gianettini, Maria
Caterina

ZANTEN, Cornelia van see
Van Zanten, Cornelia

ZAREMBA, Sylvia. 20th-century
American pianist. *SANDVED.

ZARESKA, Eugenia. Lwów, Poland,
1910- . Ukrainian mezzo-
soprano. ENCI MUS, GROVE 5,
KUTSCH.

ZBOIŃSKA-RUSZKOWSKA, Helena
see Ruszkowska, Elena

ZBRUJEWA, Eugenia. Moscow,
1869-1936, Moscow. Contralto,
voice teacher. KUTSCH.

ZEANI, Virginia. Bucharest,
Oct 21 1928- . Soprano.
CELLETTI, ENCI MUS, KUTSCH,
*ROSENTHAL=illus.p.204.

ZEDLITZ, Baroness von see
Kingston, Marie Antoinette

ZEISLER, Fannie Bloomfield.
Bielitz, Silesia, Jul 16
1863-Aug 20 1927, Chicago.
Pianist. BAKER 1=p.71,
BAKER 5, GROVE 5, PRATT,
THOMPSON. *[BAKER 1=b.1866]*

ZELTER, Juliane see Pappritz,
Juliane

ZEMBRANO, María Scheller see
Scheller Zembrano, María

ZENTA, Hermann see Holmès,
Augusta Mary Anne

ZENTAY, Mary (Marie Zimmer).
Budapest, Jul 30 1897- .
Violinist. THOMPSON.

ZEPILLI, Alice. Italy, 1884- .
Soprano, voice teacher.
KUTSCH.

ZERBST, Theresa see Halir,
Theresa

ZERETELEV, Princess see
Lavrovska, Elisaveta
Andreyevna

ZERR, Anna. Baden-Baden,
Germany, Jul 26 1822-Jul
14 1881, Winterbach, nr.
Oberkirch, Baden, Germany.
Soprano. ENCI MUS, GROVE 1,
GROVE 5, THOMPSON.

ZIEGLER, Anne. Liverpool,
?- . Soprano, actress.
*PALMER=p.37 (illus.p.97).

ZIERITZ, Grete von. Vienna,
Mar 10 1899- . Composer,
pianist. ENCI MUS, RIEMANN,
ULLSTEIN.

ZILLI, Emma. Fagagna, Udine,
Italy, Nov 11 1864-Jan
1901, L'Avana, Italy. So-

prano. CORTE, *ENCI MUS=
illus.v.4 fac.p.619.

ZIMBALIST, Mary Louise see
Curtis, Mary Louise

ZIMMER, Marie see Zentay,
Mary

ZIMMERMANN, Agnes Marie Jacobina. Cologne, Jul 5 1847-
Nov 14 1925, London. Composer, pianist, editor. BAKER
1, BAKER 5, BAKER 1971,
BROWN BIO, ENCI MUS, GROVE 1,
GROVE 5, PRATT, THOMPSON.

ZINCK, Marie Elisabeth see
Thomsen, Marie Elisabeth

ZINCK, Susanne Elisabeth (later
Pontét). ?, c1745-1832, ?.
Singer. ENCI MUS.

ZINETTI, Giuseppina. Milan,
1800?-?. Contralto. KUTSCH.

ZINK, Maria see Neefe, Maria

ZINN, Emma Sophie Amalie see
Hartmann, Emma Sophie Amalie

ZIRGES, Hortensia see
Schletterer, Hortensia

ZOCHOVÁ, Anne Kafendová- see
Kafendová-Zochová, Anna

ZÖLLNER, Margarete (Mrs. Richard, born Hecker). Braun-
schweig, Germany, Jul 22
1907- . Violinist. ENCI MUS.

ZORIAN, Olive. Manchester,
England, Mar 16 1916-May 17
1965, London?. Violinist.
GROVE 5, PALMER.

ZUCCA, Irma see Sehlbach,
Irma

ZUCCARI, Francesca (Mrs. Carlo,
born Redaelli). 18th-century
amateur singer. ENCI MUS.

ZUMSTEEG, Emilie. Stuttgart,
Dec 9 1796-Aug 1 1857,
Stuttgart. Composer, tea-
cher. ENCI MUS, RIEMANN.

ZYLIS-GARA, Teresa. Vilno,
Poland, Jan 23 1937- .
Soprano. EWEN NEW.

CLASSIFIED LIST OF WOMEN MUSICIANS

283

ACCOMPANISTS

Gubaidulina, Sofia
Hartland, Lizzie
Heyman, Katherine Ruth Wil-
  loughby
Troyon-Blaesi, Emmy
Waterman, Constance Dorothy

ACTRESSES

Abegg, Mrs.
Abrams, Miss G.
Adams, Mrs.
Addison, Elizabeth
Allison, Maria
Alpar, Gitta
Andreini, Virginia
Andrews, Miss
Arkwright, Mrs. Robert
Arnaud, (Germaine) Yvonne
Arnold, Elizabeth
Arthur, Grace
Atherton, Miss
Atkins, Eliza
Ayliff, Mrs.
Baddeley, Sophia
Bailey, Mary Sophia
Baker, Mrs.
Baker, Elizabeth
Baker, Mrs. J. S.
Barnes, Miss
Barnet, Mrs.
Barnett, Catherine
Barowby, Miss
Barre, Catherine
Barrett, Miss
Barrett, Mrs.
Barsanti, Jane
Baster, Eleanor
Bateman, Mary
Bates, Sarah
Bennet, Elizabeth
Benson, Mrs.
Besanzoni, Gabriella
Besford, Esther
Bicknell, Margaret
Biggs, Anne
Bishop, Mrs.
Bithmere, Marie Françoise
Blanchard, Charlotte
Blurton, Mary
Böhm Cartellieri, Elisabeth

Boimaison, Mrs.
Bolla, Maria
Boman, Mrs.
Boman, Elizabeth
Bond, Jessie
Booth, Hester
Booth, Ursula Agnes
Bracegirdle, Anne
Bradshaw, Lucretia
Braithwaite, Ann
Bramwell, Georgiana
Brett, Elizabeth
Brett, Hannah
Bride, Elizabeth
Bridges, Mrs.
Brigg, Mrs.
Britton, Mrs.
Broadhurst, Miss
Brooks, Patricia
Brown (Brawn), Miss
Brown, Mrs. (fl.1790-97)
Brown, Mrs. J.
Brunette, Miss
Budgell, Anne Eustace
Bulkley, Mary
Bullock, Henrietta Maria
Burden, Kitty
Burn, Miss
Burnett, Miss
Burnett, Mrs.
Butler, Mrs.
Butler, Charlotte
Byrne, Mrs.
Campbell, Mrs.
Candeille, Amélie-Julie
Cantrell, Miss
Cantrell, Mrs.
Careless, Elizabeth
Cargill, Ann
Carnevale, Signora Pietro
Carter, Miss
Catley, Ann(e)
Cavalieri, Lina
Chalmers, Eleanor
Chambers, Elizabeth
Chambers, Isabella
Chapman, Charlotte Jane
Chapman, Frances R.
Chapman, Hannah
Chatterley, Miss
Chetwood, Anne
Cibber, Catherine
Cibber, Jane

Cibber, Susanna Maria
Claire, Marion
Clark, Mrs. (fl.1695-1723)
Clark, Miss (fl.1736)
Clark, Miss (fl.1736-47)
Clarke, Mrs. Nathaniel
Clendining, Elizabeth
Clive, Catherine
Coates, Mrs.
Coates, Edith Mary
Cole, Miss
Colles, Hesther
Collet, Mrs. Ann
Collet, Catherine
Connard, Miss
Cooke, Mary
Cooper, Miss
Copin, Elizabeth
Correa, Lorenza
Courtenay, Miss
Cox, Mrs.
Cox, Miss
Cranford, Miss
Crisp, Henrietta Maria
Crofts, Miss
Cross, Mrs. John Cartwright
Cross, Frances
Cross, Letitia
Crouch, Anna Maria
Cullen, Rose
Dall, Miss
Dancey, Mrs.
Dancey, Miss
Daniels, Alicia
Darley, Anne
Davenport, Mary Ann
Davies, Elizabeth
Davis, Miss (fl.1739-62)
Davis, Mrs. (fl.1799-1803)
Davis, Mary
Davis, Sarah
Dawson, Miss
De Camp, Adelaide
De Fompré, Mme.
Delagarde, Mrs. J.
Delorme, Mlle.
Delpini, Signora Carlo Antonio
Dennett, Miss B.
Dennett, Eliza
Dennett, Miss F.
Destinn, Emmy
Deszner, Salomea
D'Evelyn, Miss

De Verneuil, Mimi
Dibdin, Anne
Dibdin, Mary
Didier, Margaret
Dixon, Clara Ann
Dodd, Martha
Dodson, Miss
Dodson, Mrs.
Dorman, Elizabeth
Dove, Elizabeth
Dubellamy, Frances Maria
Dudley, Miss
Dufour, Camilla
Dugazon, Louise-Rosalie
Dunstall, Mary
Dyer, Harriet
Edwin, Elizabeth Rebecca
Eggerth, Marta
Favart, Marie-Justine-Benoîte
Fenton, Lavinia
Fitzwilliam, Kathleen Mary
Garden, Mary
Gottlieb, Anna
Grassini, Giuseppina Maria
  Camilla
Günther-Bachmann, Karoline
Guilbert, Yvette
Gutheil-Schröder, Marie
Hartmann, Emma Sophie Amalie
Hauk (Hauck), Minnie
Holm, Renate
Howard, Kathleen
Isaacs, Rebecca
Jordan, Dora
Keeley, Mary Anne
Kelly, Frances Maria
Kittel, Hermine
Koshetz, Nina Pavlova
Kouznetzoff, Maria Nicolaïevna
Krauss, (Marie) Gabrielle
Kwast-Hiller, Tony
Labia, Maria
Lebrun, Rosine
Leigh, Adele
Lenya, Lotte
MacDonald, Jeanette
Malten, Therese
Matthews, Julia
Maxwell-Lyte, Eve
Milder-Hauptmann, Pauline Anna
Moore, Grace
Mountain, Sarah
Munsel, Patrice Beverly

285   *AMATEUR MUSICIANS*

Murska, Ilma de
Neefe, Maria
Neway, Patricia
Novotná, Jarmila
Palomino, Catalina
Paton, Mary Ann
Paul, Isabella
Peters, Roberta
Petrella, Clara
Pons, Lily
Poole, Elizabeth
Pownall, Mary Ann
Pradher, Félicité
Reed, Priscilla
Saint-Aubin, Jeanne-Charlotte
Saint-Huberty, Antoinette
   Cécile
Saint-John, Florence
Salvatini, Mafalda
Sanden, Aline
Santaolalla, Marta
Santley, Kate
Schröter, Corona Elisabeth
   Wilhelmine
Schubert, Maschinka
Soldene, Emily
Stoltz, Rosine
Thorborg, Kerstin
Tree, Anna Maria
Tree, Ellen
Unger-Sabatier, Karoline
Van Dresser, Marcia
Vanoni, Ornella
Varnay, Ibolyka Astrid Maria
Vestris, Lucia Elizabeth
Viardot-Garcia, Michelle
   Ferdinande Pauline
Vix, Geneviève
Wagner-Jachmann, Johanna
Waylett, Harriet
Woffington, Margaret
Ziegler, Anne

ADMINISTRATORS

Baur, Bertha
Bliss, Ilsa Foerstel
Boese, Helen
Côte, Hélène
Cross, Joan
Delmas, Solange
Diller, Angela
Dreyschock, Elisabeth

Gates, Lucy
Gerster, Etelka
Giannini, Dusolina
Goetze, Marie
Gutheil-Schröder, Marie
Haas, Alma
Hauk (Hauck), Minnie
Heckscher, Céleste de Longpré
Hernández-Gonzalo, Gisela
Jaenike, Margrit
Kelley, Jessie Stillmann
Kronold, Selma
Lehmann, Lilli
Mannes, Clara
Meyer, Jenny
Mildmay, Audrey
Morris, Margaret
Morsch, Anna
Moulton, Dorothy
Newlin, Dika
Ney, Elly
Niessen-Stone, Matja von
Ober, Julia Fuqua
Osten, Eva von der
Petrelli
Poston, Elizabeth
Pyne, Louisa Fanny
Raisa, Rosa
Ramann, Lina
Reuss-Belce, Luise
Sainton-Dolby, Charlotte Helen
Smith, Julia
Spani, Hina
Steele, Mary Sarah
Stückgold, Grete
Sutro, Florence Edith
Thomas, Adelaide Louisa
Upton, Emily
Wagner, Cosima
Wallmann, Margherita
Weill, Janine

AMATEUR MUSICIANS

Amalia Catharina (Princess of
   Erbach)
Anspach, Elizabeth, Margravine
   of
Drinker, Sophie Hutchinson
Fox, Charlotte
Hensel, Fanny Cäcilia
Hortense, Queen
Hunter, Anne

Martinez, Marianne de
Pelletan, Fanny
Radnor, Countess of
Scott, Alicia Ann
Smart, Harriet Anne
Voigt, Henriette

ARCHIVISTS

Ilgner, Margarete Gerda
Müller von Asow, Hedwig

ARRANGERS

Cadzow, Dorothy
Ivimey, Ella Plaistowe
Oury, Anna Caroline
Rimski-Korsakov, Nadežda
Nikolaievna

CHOREOGRAPHERS

Argentina, La
Cerrito, Fanny
Charrat, Janine
Chladek, Rosalia
Cullberg, Birgit
Furtwängler, Gise
Georgi, Yvonne
Gruber, Lilo
Hanka, Erika
Holm, Hanya
Hoyer, Dore
Humphrey, Doris
Köhler-Richter, Emmy
Novaro, Luciana
Tamiris, Helen
Wallmann, Margherita
Wigman, Mary

CLARINETTISTS

Juler, Pauline
Thomas, Frances

COMPOSERS

See also electronic music
composers; light-opera com-
posers; motion-picture music
composers; opera composers.

Abrams, Harriet

Ackland, Jeanne Isabel Dorothy
Ackland, Jessie Agnes
Adaïewska (Adajewska), Ella
  (Elisabeth) von
Agnesi Pinottini, Maria Teresa d'
Ahlefeldt, Maria Theresia
  (Countess)
Aleotti, Raffaela
Aleotti, Vittoria
Alessandra, Caterina
Allitsen, Frances
Alter, Martha
Amalia, Marie A. Friederike
Ames, Marie Mildred
Andrée, Elfrida
Andrews, Jenny
Anida, Maria Luisa
Anna Amalia, Duchess of Saxe-
  Weimar
Anna Amalia, Princess of Prussia
Anspach (Ansbach), Elizabeth,
  Margravine of
Appeldoorn, Dina
Araujo, Gina de
Archer, Violet Balestreri
Aretz de Ramón y Rivera,
  Isabelle
Arizti, Cecilia
Arkwright, Marian Ursula
Arkwright, Mrs. Robert
Arrieu, Claude
Aspri (Asperi), Orsola
Assandra, Caterina
Auernhammer, Josepha Barbara von
Aulin, Laura Valborg
Aus der Ohe, Adele
Austen, Augusta Amherst
Auster, Lidia Martinowna
Axtens, Florence E.
Bacewicz, Grazyna
Bach, Maria
Bachmann, Charlotte Karoline
  Wilhelmine
Backer-Grøndahl, Agathe Ursula
Badarzewska-Baranowska, Tekla
Ballou, Esther Williamson
Baratta, Maria de
Barblan-Opienska, Lydia
Barbour, Florence Newell
Barnard, Charlotte
Barnett, Alice
Barnett, Emma
Barns, Ethel

Baron Supervielle, Susana
Baroni-Cavalcabo, Julie
Barraine, Jacqueline Elsa
Bassett, Karolyn Wells
Bauer, Emilie Frances
Bauer, Marion Eugenie
Bauld, Alison
Bawr, Alexandrine Sophie Coury
  de Champgrand
Bayon, Mme. Louis
Beach, Amy Marcy
Beaton, Isabella
Beaumesnil, Henriette Adélaide
  Villard de
Beecroft, Norma (Marian)
Behrend, Jeanne
Bembo, Antonia
Benavente, Regina
Benda, Juliana
Benoit, Francine
Berberian, Cathy
Berckman(n), Evelyn
Bertin, Louise-Angélique
Bertrand, Aline
Bialkiewicz de Langeron, Irena
Billington, Elizabeth
Biltcliffe, Florence
Binet, Jocelyne
Bisset, Elizabeth Anne
Blahetka (Plahetka), Marie
  Léopoldine
Blake, Dorothy Gaynor
Bliss, Mrs. J. Worthington
Blomfield-Holt, Patricia
Boese, Helen
Bond, Carrie Jacobs
Bonis, Mélanie
Bordewijk Roepman, Johanna
Borek, Minuetta
Borkowiczówna, Maria
Borton, Alice
Bosmans, Henriëtta
Boucher, Lydia
Boulanger, Lili Juliette Marie
  Olga
Boulanger, Nadia Juliette
Bourges, Clementine de
Boyce, Ethel Mary
Boyd, Anne
Branscombe, Gena
Brentano, Bettina
Bright, Dora Estella
Britain, Radíe

Brizzi Giorgi, Maria
Brjussowa, Nadeschda Jakowlewna
Broadwood, Lucy E.
Brogue, Roslyn
Bronsart von Schellendorf,
  Ingeborg von
Bruckshaw, Kathleen
Brzezińska, Filipina
Buchanan, Annabel Morris
Buck, Era Marguerite
Buckley, Beatrice Barron
Burchell, H. Louise
Caccini, Francesca, La Cecchina
Cadoret, Charlotte
Cadzow, Dorothy
Calcagno, Elsa
Calegari, Maria Caterina
Campbell, Mary Maxwell
Campmany, Montserrat
Canal, Marguerite
Canales, Marta
Candeille (Simons), Amélie-
  Julie
Cantelo, Annie
Capsir-Tanzi, Mercedes
Carmichael, Mary Grant
Carreño, Maria Teresa
Carrington-Thomas, Virginia
Carrique, Ana
Carvalho, Dinorá de
Carwithen, Doreen
Casadesus, Regina Patorni
Casson, Margaret
Catunda, Eunice
Chamberlayne, Miss E. A.
Chaminade, Cécile Louise-
  Stéphanie
Chittenden, Kate Sara
Cianchettini, Veronica
  Elizabeth
Cimaglia-Espinosa, Lía
Claman, Dolores Olga
Clark, Florence Durell
Clarke, Rebecca
Clostre, Adrienne
Coccia, Maria Rosa
Cohen, Dulcie
Colbran, Isabella Ángela
Cole, Charlotte
Coleridge-Taylor, Avril
Collet, Sophia Dobson
Colonna, Vittoria
Coolidge, Elizabeth Sprague

Corri, Ghita
Côte, Hélène
Coulombe-Saint-Marcoux,
  Micheline
Coulthard, Jean
Cozzolani, Chiara Margherita
Crawford, Ruth Porter
Crews, Lucille
Curran, Pearl Gildersleeve
Curubeto Godoy, María Isabel
Dach, Charlotte von
Dahmen, Mona
Dale, Kathleen
Dall, Miss
Dancla, Alphonsine-Geneviève-
  Lore
Daneau, Suzanne
Daniels, Mabel Wheeler
Davenport Goertz, Gladys
Davies, Llewela
Davis, Miss
Davis, Marianne
Davy, Ruby Claudia Emily
Deacon, Marie Conner
Decaix, Marianne Ursule
Decarie, Reine
De Gambarini, Elisabetta
Delaborde, Élie Miriam
De Lara, Adelina
Delorme, Isabelle
Del Riego, Teresa Clotilde
Demarquez, Suzanne
Demessieux, Jeanne
Desportes, Yvonne Berthe
  Melitta
Deyo, Ruth Lynda
Dianda, Hilda
Dibdin, Isabelle Perkins
Dickson, Ellen
Dillon, Fannie Charles
Dlugoszewski, Lucia
Donátová, Narcisa
Drége-Schielowa, Lucja
Drynan, Margaret
Duchambge, Charlotte Antoinette
  Pauline
Dufferin, Helen Selina
Dugal, Madeleine
Dulcken, Sophie
Dunlop, Isobel
Dussek, Josepha
Dussek, Olivia
Dussek, Sophia Giustina

Duval, Mlle.
Eberlin, Maria Cäcilia Barbara
Eckhardt-Gramatté, Sophie
  Carmen
Edwards, Clara
Eggar, Katharine Emily
Eggleston, Anne
Ellicott, Rosalind Frances
Erhart, Dorothy Agnes Alice
Escobar, Maria Luisa
Estrella, Blanca
Fahrbach, Henriette
Faisst, Clara Mathilde
Faltis, Evelyn
Farmer, Emily Bardsley
Farrenc, Jeanne Louise
Farrenc, Victorine Louise
Ferrari, Carlotta
Ferrari, Gabriella
Fine, Vivian
Fisher, Charlotte E.
Fleites, Virginia
Flower, Eliza
Folville, Juliette-Eugénie-
  Émilie
Fontyn, Jacqueline
Foot, Phyllis Margaret
Forsyth, Josephine
Fortey, Mary Comber
Foster, Fay
Fowles, Margaret F.
Fox, Charlotte
Franchère-Des Rosiers, Roede
  Lima
Freer, Eleanor
Fromm-Michaels, Ilse
Fuchs, Lillian
Gabriel, Mary Ann Virginia
Gaïgerova, Varvara Adrianovna
Galajikian, Florence Grandland
Gannon, Helen C.
García, Eduarda Mansilla de
García Muñoz, Carmen
García Robson, Magda
Garelli Della Morea, Vincenza
Garuta, Lucija
Gaynor, Jessie Love
Gerstman, Blanche
Ghika-Comanesti, Ioana
Gibson, Isabella Mary
Gideon, Miriam
Gifford, Helen
Gipps, Ruth

Giuranna, Elena Barbara
Glanville-Hicks, Peggy
Glyn, Margaret Henrietta
Gnessin, Eléna Fabianovna
Goddard, Arabella
Goodwin, Amina Beatrice
Gotkowsky, Ida
Grabowska, Klementyna
Graever, Madeleine
Grandval, Marie-Félicie-Clé-
  mence de Reiset
Gray, Louisa
Gregori, Nininha
Grétry, Lucile
Grimani, Maria Margherita
Grimaud, Yvette
Grünbaum, Therese
Gubaidulina, Sofia
Gubitosi, Emilia
Gummer, Phyllis Mary
Gyde, Margaret
Hänel von Cronenthal, Louisa
  Augusta
Hagan, Helen Eugenia
Hague, Harriet
Hall, Pauline Margrete
Harcourt, Marguerite Béclard d'
Hardelot, Guy d'
Hardiman, Ellena G.
Harraden, Beatrice
Harraden, R. Ethel
Harrison, Annie Fortescue
Hartland, Lizzie
Harvey, Mary
Hawes, Maria
Heale, Helene
Heber, Judith
Heckscher, Céleste de Longpré
Hensel, Fanny Cäcilia
Hermann, Miina
Hernández-Gonzalo, Gisela
Heyman, Katherine Ruth
  Willoughby
Hier, Ethel Glenn
Hildegard, Saint
Hinrichs, Marie
Hodges, Faustina Hasse
Holland, Caroline
Holmès, Augusta Mary Anne
Holmes, Mary
Holmsen, Borghild
Holst, Imogen Clare
Hood, Helen

Hopekirk, Helen
Horrocks, Amy Elsie
Housman, Rosalie
Howe, Mary
Howell, Dorothy
Hudson, Mary
Hunter, Anne
Inverarity, Eliza
Ivanova, Lidiya
Jaell-Trautmann, Marie
James, Dorothy
Janina, Olga
Janotha, Natalia
Japha, Louise Langhans
Jerea, Hilda
Jeske-Choińska-Mikorska,
  Ludmila
Jolas, Betsy
Jordan, Dora
Kaprálová, Vítězslava
Karnitzkaïa, Nina Andréevna
Kasilag, Lucrecia
Katunda, Eunice
Keetman, Gunild
Keller, Ginette
Kennedy-Fraser, Marjory
Kent, Ada Twohy
Kerr, Bessie Maude
Kilby, Muriel Laura
Kingston, Marie Antoinette
Kinkel, Johanna
Kinscella, Hazel Gertrude
Klechniowska, Anna Maria
Klein, Ivy Frances
Knapp, Phoebe Palmer
Kohan, Celina
Kolb, Barbara
Kontski, (Maria) Eugénie de
Korn, Clara Anna
Krzyzanowska, Halina
Kukuck, Felicitas
Kuss, Margarita Iwanowna
Kuyper, Elisabeth
Labey, Charlotte
Lafleur, Lucienne
La Guerre, Elisabeth Claude de
La Hye, Louise Genevieve
Lang, Josephine Caroline
Lang, Margaret Ruthven
Laufer, Beatrice
Lawrence, Emily M.
Le Beau, Louise Adolpha
Lebrun, Franziska

Lebrun, Sophie
Leginska, Ethel
Lehmann, Liza
Leivinskä, Helvi
Leleu, Jeanne
Lemmens, Helen
Leonarda, Isabella
Levina, Zara Alexsandrovna
Lewing, Adele ·
Lima Cruz, Maria Antonieta de
Linwood, Mary
Linz von Kriegner, Marta
Loder, Kate Fanny
Lopuska-Wylezyńska, Helene
Loriod, Yvonne
Lowthian, Caroline
Lucas, Mary Anderson
Lund, Signe
Lutyens, Elisabeth Agnes
Maas, Marguerite Wilson
McCollin, Frances
Macfarren, Emma Marie Bennett
McGill, Josephine
MacIntosh, G. A.
McIntyre, Margaret
Macirone, Clara Angela
Mackenna, Carmela
Maconchy, Elizabeth
Madriguera, Paquita
Makarova, Nina Vladimirovna
Malibran, Maria Felicità
Mana-Zucca
Manning, Kathleen Lockhart
Manziarly, Marcelle de
Marić, Ljubica
Marshall, Florence A.
Marshall, Mrs. William
Martinez, Marianne de
Masson, Elizabeth
Matthison-Hansen, Nanny
Maurice, Paule
May, Florence
Menter, Sophie
Mezari, Maddalena
Mikusch, Margarethe von
Milanollo, Domenica Maria
  Teresa ·
Milette, Juliette
Millard, Mrs. Philip
Moberg, Ida
Montgeroult, Hélène
Moody, Marie
Moore, Mary Carr

More, Margaret
Moretto, Nelly
Morgan, Maud
Morin-Labrecque, Albertine
Morison, Christina W.
Moseley, Caroline Carr
Mosher, Frances Elizabeth
Mounsey, Ann Sheppard
Mounsey, Elizabeth
Müller-Hermann, Johanna
Mukle, May Henrietta
Mundella, Emma
Musgrave, Thea
Myszynska-Woyciechowska,
  Leokadia
Nascimbeni, Maria Francesca
Naumann, Ida
Newcombe, Georgeanne
Newlin, Dika
Newton, Adelaide
Nikolayevna, Tatiana Petrovna
Norbury, F. Ethel
Norton, Caroline Elizabeth
  Sarah
Novello-Davies, Clara
Noyes, Edith Rowena
Nunn, Elizabeth Annie
Oakey, Maggie
Obrovská, Jana
Oddone Sulli-Rao, Elisabetta
Oldham, S. Emily
O'Leary, Rosetta
Oliveira, Jocy de
Oliveros, Pauline
Oosterzee, Cornélie van
Ostlere, May
Oury, Anna Caroline
Pakhmutova, Alexandra
Paradis, Maria Therese von
Parkyns, Beatrice
Patiño Andrade, Graciela
Patterson, Annie Wilson
Pejacsevich, Dora von
Penna, Catherine
Pentland, Barbara
Peralta, Angela
Perry, Julia
Petrelli
Pfund, Leonore
Philp, Elizabeth
Piché, Eudore
Poldowski
Polignac, Armande de

Popatenko, Tamara Alexandrovna
Poston, Elizabeth
Pownall, Mary Ann
Pratten, Madam Sidney
Prescott, Oliveria Louisa
Presti, Ida
Prieto, María Teresa
Puget, Loïsa Françoise
Pyne, Louisa Aubert
Rabinof, Sylvia
Radnor, Countess of
Rainier, Priaulx
Ralph, Kate
Ramann, Lina
Ramm, Valentina Iosifovna
Rapoport, Eda Ferdinand
Raymond, Madeleine
Recli, Giulia
Reichardt, Luise
Reinagle, Caroline
Reisserová, Julie
Renié, Henriette
Rennès, Catharina van
Renshaw, Rosette
Respighi, Elsa
Richardson, Cornelia Heitzman
Richter, Marga
Rivé-King, Julie
Robinson, Fanny
Rochat, Andrée
Rodrigo, María
Rodríguez, Esther
Roeckel, Jane
Röntgen, Amanda
Roesgen-Champion, Marguerite
  Sara
Rogers, Clara Kathleen
Roget, Henriette Puig-
Rokseth, Yvonne
Rueff, Jeanine
Ruta, Gilda
Ryber, Dagmar de Corval
Rylek-Stanková, Blažena
Saffery, Eliza
Sainton-Dolby, Charlotte Helen
Salter, Mary Elizabeth
Salvador, Matilde
Sánchez, Manuela Cornejo de
Sanders, Alma
Sarenecka, Jadwiga
Savage, Jane
Scarpa, Eugenia
Schauroth, Delphine von

Scheller Zembrano, María
Schick, Philippine
Schirmacher, Dora
Schröter, Corona Elisabeth
  Wilhelmine
Schumann, Clara Josephine
Schwarz, Friederike
Scott, Alicia Ann
Scriabine, Marina
Sebastiani, Pia
Sepúlveda, María Luisa
Serov, Valentine Semenovna
Serrano Redonnet, Ana
Sessi, Marianna
Sirmen, Maddalena Laura
Smart, Harriet Anne
Smith, Alice Mary
Smith, Julia
Smith, Laura Alexandrine
Smyth(e), Dame Ethel Mary
Snižková-Skrhová, Jitka
Solomon, Mirrie
Somellera, Josefa
Sophie, Elisabeth
Soulage, Marcelle
Southam, Ann
Spena, Lita
Spencer, Marguerita
Stair, Patty
Sternicka-Niekraszowa, Ilza
Stirling, Elizabeth
Stocker, Stella
Streicher, Lyubov Lvovna
Strickland, Lily Teresa
Strozzi, Barbara
Sutherland, Margaret
Swain, Freda
Swepstone, Edith
Synge, Mary Helena
Szalit, Paulina
Szöni, Erzsébet
Szymanowska, Maria Agata
Tailleferre, Germaine
Tait, Annie
Talma, Louise
Tamblyn, Bertha Louise
Tate, Phyllis Margaret Duncan
Taylor, Laura W.
Temple, Hope
Terhune, Anice
Terrier-Laffaille, Anne
Terzián, Alicia
Thegerström, Hilda

Thomas, Adelaide Louisa
Thomson, Alexandra
Thorne, Beatrice
Thys-Sebault, Pauline
Tibaldi, Rosa
Torrá, Celia
Tremblay, Amedée
Trew, Susan
Trimble, Joan
Troup, Emily Josephine
Trowbridge, Leslie
Tyrrell, Agnes
Unschuld, Marie von
Ustvolskaya, Galina Ivanovna
Valentine, Ann
Van den Boorn-Coclet, Henriette
Van de Wiele, Aimée
Vanier, Jeannine
Van Zanten, Cornelia
Vaurabourg, Andrée
Verne, Alice Verne Bredt
Viardot, Louise Héritte de la
   Tour
Viardot-Garcia, Michelle
   Ferdinande Pauline
Villeneuve, Marie-Louise-Diane
Vinette, Alice
Vinogradova, Vera
Volkstein, Pauline
Von Hoff, Elizabeth
Vorlová, Slávka
Wainwright, Harriet
Wakefield, (Augusta) Mary
Walter, Ida
Ward, Clementine
Ware, Harriet
Ware, Helen
Warner, Sylvia Townsend
Warren, Elinor Remick
Wartel, Atale Thérèse Annette
Waterman, Constance Dorothy
Weigl, Vally
Weingartner-Studer, Carmen
Weissberg, Yuliya Lazarevna
Weldon, Georgina
Wennerberg-Reuter, Sara
Wensley, Frances Foster
Wertheim, Rosy
West, Lottie
Westrop, Kate
White, Mary Louise
White, Maude Valérie
Wickham, Florence Pauline

Wieruszowski, Lili
Williams, Grace
Wilson, Mrs. Cornwall Baron
Wood, Mary Knight
Wood-Hill, Mabel
Woolf, Sophia Julia
Worgan, Mary
Wright, Ellen
Wurm, Mary J. A.
Young, Harriet Maitland
Zieritz, Grete von
Zimmermann, Agnes Marie
   Jacobina
Zumsteeg, Emilie

CONCERTINA PLAYER

Binfield, Louisa

CONDUCTORS, CHORAL

Boulanger, Nadia Juliette
Branscombe, Gena
Brassuer, Élisabeth
Brico, Antonia
Burchell, H. Louise
Campbell, Edith May
Dessoff, Margarete
Fahrbach, Henriette
Gouverné, Yvonne
Hernández-Gonzalo, Gisela
Hillis, Margaret
Holland, Caroline
Novello-Davies, Clara
O'Leary, Rosetta
Piché, Eudore
Sanders, Ellen
Schira, Margherita
Stenhammar, Elsa Elfrida
   Marguerite
Villeneuve, Marie-Louise-Diane
Weldon, Georgina
Wichern, Karoline
Wieruszowski, Lili
Wood, Mary Louisa

CONDUCTORS, INSTRUMENTAL

Aspri (Asperi), Orsola
Boulanger, Nadia Juliette
Branscombe, Gena
Brico, Antonia
Coleridge-Taylor, Avril

Dianda, Hilda
Erhart, Dorothy Agnes Alice
Evrard, Jane
Fischer, Ivana
Folville, Juliette-Eugénie-
　Émilie
Fowles, Margaret F.
Grierson, Mary Gardner
Hillis, Margaret
Howard-Jones, Evelyn
Kaprálová, Vítězslava
Kuyper, Elisabeth
Leginska, Ethel
Marshall, Florence A.
Morris, Margaret
Queler, Eve
Radnor, Countess of
Regules, Marisa
Riddick, Kathleen
Sepúlveda, María Luisa
Torrá, Celia
Weingartner-Studer, Carmen
Wurm, Mary J. A.

CONTRALTOS

Abrams, Theodosia
Ahlin, Cvetka
Albertazzi, Emma
Alberts, Eunice
Alboni, Marietta
Albuzzi-Todeschini, Teresa
Alcock, Merle
Alessio, Aurora d'
Allitsen, Emma
Alvarez, Marguerite d'
Amparan, Belen
Anday, Rosette
Anderson, Marian
Angri, Elena
Arangi-Lombardi, Giannina
Archipova, Irina
Aylward, Leila J.
Bagnolesi, Anna
Balfour, Margaret
Bampton, Rose E.
Barnett, Alice
Baroni, Andriana
Bassi, Carolina
Bauermeister, Mathilde
Beckmann, Friedel
Bellincioni, Carlotta
Bérat, Louise

Berglund, Ruth
Berry, Sarah
Bertin, Louise-Angélique
Bertolli, Francesca
Besanzoni, Gabriella
Biancolini Rodriguez, Marietta
Boese, Ursula
Bond, Jessie
Bornemann, Eva
Bourgignon, Jane
Bouvier, Hélène
Bowden, Pamela
Boys, Margaret
Brambilla, Marietta
Brandt, Marianne
Branscombe, Marie
Branzell Reinshagen, Karin
　Maria
Braslau, Sophie
Brema, Marie
Brice, Carol
Bridgman, Nanie
Brighenti, Maria
Brohly, Suzanne
Brunskill, Muriel
Butt, Dame Clara
Butterworth, Annie
Cahier, Sarah-Jane
Capuana, Maria
Cariaga, Marvellee
Cary, Annie Louise
Casazza, Elvira
Casei, Nedda
Castagna, Bruna
Cavelti, Elsa
Cernay, Germaine
Červená, Sona
Chambers, Lucy
Chavanne, Irene von
Chookasian, Lili
Cibber, Susanna Maria
Clemens, Clara
Coates, Edith Mary
Cole, Belle
Conrad-Amberg, Margrit
Cook, Mrs. Aynsley
Cossotto, Fiorenza
Creser, Amelia
Croiza, Claire
Crossley, Ada
Cushman, Charlotte Saunders
Damian, Grace
Davidova, Vera

Davis, Jessie Bartlett
Delna, Marie
Deroubaix, Jeanne
Deschamps-Jehin, Blanche
Desmond, Astra
Devallier, Lucienne
Dews, Elizabeth
Doe, Doris
Dominguez, Oralia
Dougall, Lilly
Doyle, Ada
Dreyschock, Elisabeth
Duchêne, Maria
Fabbri, Guerrina
Falk, Lina
Fassbáender, Brigette
Ferlendis, Signora
Ferrier, Kathleen
Finnilä, Birgit
Fischer, Res
Fletcher, Jane
Flower, Sara
Focke, Ria
Forrester, Maureen
Foster, Muriel
Fröhlich, Barbara Franziska
Frost, Eliza
Furmedge, Edith
Galeratti, Catterina
Garabedian-George, Edna
Gay, María
Geller-Wolter, Luise
Gelling, Hilda Grace
Gerville-Réache, Jeanne
Giani, Nini
Giudice, Maria
Glade, Coe
Glaz, Herta
Godfrey, Batyah
Goetze, Marie
Gordon, Jeanne
Gorr, Rita
Grassini, Giuseppina Maria
  Camilla
Grey, Annie
Guerrini, Virginia
Gusalewicz, Genia
Hamari, Julia
Harshaw, Margaret
Hastreiter, Hélène
Hawes, Maria

Heale, Alice
Héglon, Meyriane
Hermes, Annie
Hesse, Ruth
Heynis, Aafje
Hilgermann, Laura
Hitzelberger, Catharina
  Elisabeth
Hitzelberger, Johanna
Höffgen, Marga
Höngen, Elisabeth
Hoffmann, Grace
Homer, Louise
Howard, Kathleen
Huddart, Fanny
Ilosvay, Maria von
Ingram, Frances
Jacoby, Josephine
Jarred, Mary
Joachim, Amalie
Jones, Hannah
Jordan, Mary
Kalter, Sabine
Kaskas, Anna
Kennedy, Kate
Kennedy-Fraser, Marjory
Kerr, Mary Elizabeth Grainger
Kindermann, Lydia Maria
  Theresia
King, Jessie
Kirk, Helen Drysdale
Kirkby-Lunn, Louise
Kittel, Hermine
Kopleff, Florence
Krásová, Marta
Kraus, Adrienne
Lablache, Fanny Wyndham
Landi, Camilla
Langendorff, Frieda
Lankow, Anna
Leisner, Emmi
Leonova, Darya Mikhailovna
Liebenberg, Eva
Little, Vera
Lund, Josephine Amalie
Mac Farren, Clara Natalia
Mackenzie, Marian
MacKenzie, Mary
Malaniuk, Ira
Malanotte, Adelaide
Malibran, Maria Felicità

Mantelli, Eugenia
Marchisio, Barbara
Mariani, Rosa
Marié de L'Isle, Jeanne
Martin, Amy Florence
Masson, Elizabeth
Matzenauer, Margarete
Meichik, Anna
Meisle, Kathryn
Merighi, Antonia
Metcalfe, Susan
Metzger-Lattermann, Ottilie
Metzler-Löwy, Pauline
Meyer, Jenny
Meyer, Kerstin
Michaelis, Ruth
Milinkovič, Georgine von
Minghini-Cattaneo, Irene
Montmollin, Marie-Lise de
Mysz-Gmeiner, Lulu
Negri, Maria (Anna) Catterina
Nikolaidi, Elena
Ober, Margaret Arndt
Offers, Maartje
Olheim, Helen
Olitzka, Rosa
Olszewska, Maria
Onégin, Sigrid
Orridge, Ellen Amelia
Paalen, Bella
Palmer, Bessie
Parker, Denne
Parker, Louise
Parr, Gladys
Parsi-Petinella, Armida
Patey, Janet Monach
Paul, Isabella
Pederzini, Gianna
Petina, Irra
Philippi, Maria Cäcilia
Phillipps, Adelaide
Pirazzini, Miriam
Pisaroni, Benedetta Rosamunda
Plümacher, Hetty
Poole, Fanny Kemble
Preobrajenskaia, Sofia
Rabenius, Olena Ida Teresia
  Falkman
Radev, Marianna
Raisbeck, Rosina
Raveau, Alice
Redeker, Louise Dorette
  Auguste

Reed, Priscilla
Rees, Eleanor
Reynolds, Eleanor
Ripley, Gladys
Robertson, Fanny
Robeson, Lila P.
Rössel-Majdan, Hildegard
Rohs, Martha
Rosse, Jeanie
Rothauser, Therese
Rünger, Gertrude
Ruziczka, Else
Sadoven, Hélène
Sainton-Dolby, Charlotte Helen
Sbriscia, Zelinda
Scalchi, Sofia
Scarisbrick, Mrs. Thomas
Schärtel, Elisabeth
Schnabel, Therese
Schürhoff, Else
Schumann-Heink, Ernestine
Sebald, Frau von
Shaw, Mary
Shepley, Sarah
Siewert, Ruth
Smith, Carol
Sneddon, Janet C.
Soukoupová, Věra
Spies, Hermine
Standing, Helen
Staudigl, Gisela
Sterling, Antoinette
Swarthout, Gladys
Szantho, Enid
Taskin, Arlette
Telva, Marion
Tervani, Irma
Tesi-Tramontini, Vittoria
Thorborg, Kerstin
Thornton, Edna
Todi, Maria Francesca
Töpper, Hertha
Tomlinson, Marion
Turner, Claramae
Unger-Sabatier, Karoline
Van Gordon, Cyrena
Verbitskaya, Eugenia
Verrett, Shirley·
Vestfali, Felicja
Vestris, Lucia Elizabeth
Vialtzeva, Anastasia
Viardot, Louise Héritte de la
  Tour

Vorobieva-Petrova, Anna
  Iakovlevna
Wagner, Sieglinde
Wakefield, (Augusta) Mary
Ward, Jessie
Warwick, Alexandra
Watts, Helen
Wells, Madame Thaddeus
West, Lottie
Wettergren, Gertrud
Wheatley, Julia
Wickham, Florence Pauline
Wildbrunn, Helene
Willer, Luise
Williams, Annie
Williams, Martha
Willmann, (Johanna) Magdalena
Wilson, Agnes
Wilson, Matilda Ellen
Winn, Florence
Wood, Anne
Woud, Annie
Wynne, Kate
Young, Isabella
Zbrujewa, Eugenia
Zinetti, Giuseppina

COURT MUSICIANS

Balbi, Rosina
Bembo, Antonia
Benson, Mrs.
Boschetti, Teresa
Couperin, Marguerite-
  Antoinette
Erdmannsdörffer, Pauline
Essipova, Anna Nikolaevna
Grimani, Maria Margherita
Haydn, Maria Magdalena
Hemmerlein, Eva Ursula
Hitzelberger, Sabina
Hunt, Arabella
Janotha, Natalia
La Barre, Anne
La Guerre, Elisabeth Claude de
Laidlaw, Robena Anna
Lang, Regina
Lisi, Anna Maria
Lucca, Pauline
Neruda, Wilhelmine Maria
  Frantiska
Orgeni, Aglaja
Petrini, Marie Therese

Pollet, Marie-Nicole
Rappoldi, Laura
Rébel, Anne-Renée
Rey, Mlle.
Ries, Anna Maria
Rummel, Francisca
Rummel, Josephine
Salicoli, Margherita
Scarlatti, Melchiorra Brigida
Schak, Antonia
Schröter, Corona Elisabeth
  Wilhelmine
Senger-Bettaque, Katharina
Sessi, Marianna
Szymanowska, Maria Agata
Tesi-Tramontini, Vittoria
Thorborg, Kerstin
Ulrica, Friederica Louise
Vestris, Maria Caterina
  Violante
Voggenhuber, Vilma von
Westenholz, Barbara Lucietta
  Fricemelica
Westenholz, Eleonore Sophia
  Maria
Wieck, Marie
Willmann, (Anna Maria Antonetta)
  Marianne
Willmann, (Johanna) Magdalena
Willmann, Marianne

CRITICS

Bauer, Emilie Frances
Benoit, Francine
Bienenfeld, Elsa
Bokesová-Hanáková, Zdenka
Chissell, Joan Olive
Demarquez, Suzanne
Fuà, Laura
Glanville-Hicks, Peggy
Hall, Pauline Margrete
Kennedy-Fraser, Marjory
Komarova, Varvara Dmitrievna
Marix-Spire, Thérèse
Meyer-Baer, Kathi
Newmarch, Rosa Harriet
Oliveira, Magdala da Gama
Patzaková, Anna
Peyser, Ethel Rose
Samaroff, Olga
Shestakova, Ludmilla Ivanova

Adams, Miss E.
Adams, Miss H.
Adams, Miss S.
Alonso, Alicia
Amaya, Carmen
Angiolini, Madame
Angiolini, Fortunata
Archilei, Vittoria
Argentina, La
Atherton, Miss
Baker, Mrs.
Baker, Elizabeth
Baker, Mrs. J. S.
Balbi, Rosina
Bambridge, Mrs.
Banti, Signora
Banti, Felicità
Barcavelle, Mrs.
Barnes, Miss
Barowby, Miss
Barré, Mlle.
Barrett, Mrs.
Bassan, Miss
Baston, Miss
Batchelor, Miss
Bates, Miss
Beaulieu, Mrs.
Bedini, Signora
Belfort, Mrs.
Bell, Mrs.
Bennet, Elizabeth
Beriosova, Svetlana
Besford, Esther
Besford, Mrs. Joseph
Beswick, Mrs.
Bettini, Signora
Bicknell, Margaret
Biddy, Miss
Bilsingham, Miss
Binety, Anna
Birt (Bert), Miss S.
Bishop, Mrs.
Bithmere, Mme. Augustine Louis
Bithmere, Marie Françoise
Blagden, Miss
Blake, Mrs.
Blanchard, the Misses
Boccherini, Anna Matilda
Boccherini, Maria Ester
Boisgérard, Mme.
Bologna, Barbara

Bologna, Mrs. Louis
Bologna, Mrs. Pietro
Boman, Mrs.
"Bombastini, Signora"
Bonneval, Mlle.
Bonomi, Giac(inta?)
Booth, Hester
Boronat Fabra, Teresina
Boudet, Mme.
Boudet, Mlle.
Bougier, Mlle.
Bourgeois, Mlle.
Bourk, Elizabeth
Boyce, Mrs. Thomas
Braithwaite, Ann
Brett, Elizabeth
Bride, Elizabeth
Brider, Miss
Brigg, Mrs.
Britton, Mrs.
Brookes, Miss
Brown (Brawn), Miss
Brown, Sarah
Browning, Miss
Bruce, Mrs.
Brunette, Miss
Buckinger, Miss
Bugiani, Elizabetta
Bulkley, Mary
Bullock, Miss
Bullock, Ann
Bullock, Henrietta Maria
Burn, Miss
Bury, Miss
Butler, Charlotte
Byrne, Mrs. (d.1782)
Byrne, Miss (fl.1784-87)
Byrne, Mrs. (fl.1785-1800)
Cabanel, Eliza
Cabanel, Harriot
Camargo, Sophie
Campanini, Barbarina
Campion, Mary Anne
Campioni, Signora
Cantrell, Miss
Capdeville, Mlle. (fl.1754-71)
Capdeville, Miss (fl.1762)
Capitani, Polly
"Capuchino, Signora"
Carlini, Rosa
Carne, Miss
Carr, Mrs.
Carré, Marie-Thérèse

Carter, Mrs.
Casagli, Serafina
Casaia, Miss
Casimere, Mme.
Catley, Ann(e)
Cerail (Crail), Mlle.
Cerrito, Fanny
Chapman, Hannah
Charon, Mme.
Charrat, Janine
Chateauneuf (Chatin), Marie
Chauviré, Yvette
Cherrier, Miss
Chetwood, Anne
Chevigny, Mlle.
Chiringhelli, Signora
Chise, Mme.
Chladek, Rosalia
Chollet, Constance
Clamakin, Mrs.
Clark, Mrs.
Clary, Mme.
Closson, Mlle.
"Codgerino, Signora"
Cole, Miss
Collet, Catherine
Colombe, Émilie
Como, Signora Antonio
Connelly, Miss
Constance, Mlle.
Constantini, Signora
Conti, Anna
Cook, Mrs. (fl.1740-41)
Cook, Mrs. (fl.1763)
Coombes, Miss
Cooper, Miss
Cope, Mrs.
Copeland, Mrs.
Coradini, Signora
Costanza, Signora
Coulon, Anne Jacqueline
Cox, Miss
Cox, Mrs.
Cramerer, Mlle.
Cranfield, Mrs.
Crauford, Mrs.
Crawford (Craford), Mrs.
Crespi, Signora
Crisp, Henrietta Maria
Crofts, Miss
Cross, Letitia
Crowe, Jane
Crozier, Miss

Cullberg, Birgit
Curtz, Mlle.
Dancey, Mrs.
Dancey, Miss
Danilova, Alexandra Dionisjewna
D'Auberval, Mme. Jean
Dause, Mrs.
Davis, Miss (fl.1739-62)
Davis, Miss (fl.1795)
Davis, Mrs. K.
Davis, Mary
Daw, Miss
Dawson, Nancy (1730?-67)
Dawson, Nancy (fl.1785)
De Amicis, Anna Lucia
Dearl, Mrs.
De Camp, Adelaide
De Camp, Sophia (fl.1776-77)
De Camp, Sophia (b.1785)
De Fompré, Mme.
De Franco, Mlle.
D'Egville, Fanny
D'Egville, Sophia
De Henney, Mme.
De la Cointre, Mme.
De la Croix, Mlle.
Delagarde, Mrs. Charles
Delagarde, Mrs. J.
Del Caro, Mlle. (fl.1794-1803)
Del Caro, Mlle. (fl.1790-1815)
Delfevre, Mme.
Deligny, Louise
De l'Isle, Mlle.
Delorme, Mme.
Delorme, Mlle.
De Mille, Agnes
Dennett, Miss B.
Dennett, Eliza
Dennett, Miss F.
Dennis, Mrs.
Dennison, Mrs.
Dents, Miss
Dents, De Long
Derp, Clotilde von
Desbarques, Mlle.
Desbarques, Mme.
Deschalliez, Louise
Desdechina, Signora
De Verneuil, Mimi
D'Hervigni, Mlle.
Dibdin, Miss
Didelot, Marie-Rose
Dixon, Mrs. Cornelius

Dodson, Miss
Dolmetsch, Mabel Johnston
Dominique, Mme.
Domitilla, Miriamne
Dorival, Anne Marguerite
Dorival à Corifet
Dorsion, Mlle.
Dove, Elizabeth
Drake, Miss
Dromat, Marianne
Duchemin, Mlle.
Duchesne, Mme.
Dudley, Miss
Dulisse, Mme.
Dulisse, Mlle.
Dumont, Mme.
Dumont, Mlle. (fl.1748)
Dumont, Mlle. (fl.1781)
Duncan, Isadora
Du Pain, Mlle.
Dupré, Mme.
Dupré, Éléonore
Durand, Mlle.
Durham, Miss
Du Ruel, Mme.
Duval, Mlle.
Duval, Mme.
Dyer, Harriet
Elssler, Fanny
Elssler, Therese
Fabbri, Flora
Ferraris, Amalia
Fogliazzi, Teresa
Fonteyn, Dame Margot
Fornaroli, Cia (Lucia)
Fracci, Carla
Franca, Celia
Fuller, Loïe Marie-Louise
Fuoco, Sofia
Furtwängler, Gise
Galli, Rosina
Gardel, Marie Élisabeth Anne
Gardel, Marie Françoise Lucie
Genée, Adeline
Grahn, Lucile
Grisi, Carlotta
Gruber, Lilo
Gsovsky, Tatiana
Guimard, Marie-Madeleine
Hanka, Erika
Haydee, Marcia
Holm, Hanya
Hoyer, Dore

Humphrey, Doris
Jiránek, Franziska
Karsavina, Tamara
Köhler-Richter, Emmy
Kouznetzoff, Maria Nicolaïevna
Kschessinska, Mathilde
Lanner, Katherine
Lolli, Nanette
Macfleuray, Clotilde
Marchand, Colette
Markova, Alicia
Mauri Argilagó, Rosita
Mombelli, Vincenza
Montes, Lola Marie Dolores
  Eliza Rosanna Gilbert
Nischinskij, Bronislawa
Nischinskij, Kyra
Novaro, Luciana
Page, Ruth
Pavlova, Anna Pavlova
Perraud, Adélaïde
Pitrot, Carolina
Preobrajenskaia, Olga
Rey, Mlle. (I)
Rey, Mlle. (II)
Rey, Mlle. (III)
Rey, Louise
Rey, Mion
Rubinstein, Ida
Sallé, Marie
Shearer, Moira
Subligny, Marie-Thérèse
  Perdou de
Taglioni, Maria
Tamiris, Helen
Tórtola Valencia, Carmen
Vestris, Maria Caterina Violante
Viganò, Maria Medina
Wallmann, Margherita
Wigman, Mary
Zambelli, Carlotta

DOUBLE BASSIST

Gerstman, Blanche

EDITORS

Abert, Anna Amalie
Anderson, Emily
Arblay, Frances d'
Bate, Mrs. J. D.
Bauer, Emilie Frances

Broadwood, Lucy E.
Caland, Elisabeth
Cecil, Theophania
Clercx-Lejeune, Suzanne
Diller, Angela
Estcourt, Mary Jane
Fisher, Charlotte E.
Glyn, Margaret Henrietta
Jolas, Betsy
Klemetti, Dagmar
Lederman, Minna
Lehmann, Lilli
Lucca, Giovannina
Masson, Elizabeth
Meyer-Baer, Kathi
Morsch, Anna
Pelletan, Fanny
Radnor, Countess of
Ramann, Lina
Rokseth, Yvonne
Schnapper, Edith
Schumann, Clara Josephine
Serov, Valentine Semenovna
Simon, Alicja
Tapper, Bertha
Viollier, Renée
Wakefield, (Augusta) Mary
Warner, Sylvia Townsend
Weissberg, Yuliya Lazarevna
Wichern, Karoline
Williams, Maria Jane
Zimmermann, Agnes Marie
  Jacobina

ELECTRONIC MUSIC COMPOSERS

Beecroft, Norma (Marian)
Boyd, Anne
Coulombe-Saint-Marcoux,
  Micheline
Oliveros, Pauline
Southam, Ann

ENGLISH HORNIST

Gaskell, Helen

ENGRAVERS

Balls, Eliza
Phillips, Sarah

ETHNOMUSICOLOGISTS

Aretz de Ramón y Rivera,
  Isabelle
Czekanowska, Anna
Densmore, Frances
Eisenstein de Vega, Silvia
Ellis, Catherine Joan
Fletcher, Alice Cunningham
Fourie, Johanna Everdina
Harcourt, Marguerite Béclard d'
Marcel-Dubois, Claudie
Sobieski, Jadwiga

FLUTISTS

Cardigan, Cora
Dolmetsch, Marie
Shaffer, Elaine

FOLKLORISTS

Alford, Violet
Alvarenga, Oneyda
Babaĭan, Marguerite
Baratta, María de
Broadwood, Lucy E.
Cabrera, Ana S. de
Coelho, Olga Praguer
Densmore, Frances
Fox, Charlotte
Gauthier, Eva
Gilchrist, Anne
Guilbert, Yvette
Hague, Eleanor
Harcourt, Marguerite Béclard d'
Jankovič, Danica
Karpeles, Maud
Kennedy-Fraser, Marjory
Lineva, Evgenia Eduardovna
McGill, Josephine
Patterson, Annie Wilson

GLASS HARMONICA PLAYERS

Cartwright, Miss
Davies, Marianne
Kirchgessner, Marianne

GUITARISTS

Anida, María Luisa
Brondi, Maria Rita

Cabrera, Ana S. de
Coelho, Olga Praguer
Costanzo, Irma
Giuliani, Emilia
Grever, Maria
Pratten, Madam Sidney
Presti, Ida
Strinasacchi, Regina
Tarragó, Renata

HARMONICA PLAYER

Davies, Marianne

HARMONIUM PLAYER

Alexandre, Charlotte

HARPISTS

Balcells, Rosa
Baroni, Caterina
Barthélemon, Cecilia Maria
Bertrand, Aline
Binfield, Hannah Rampton
Bisset, Elizabeth Anne
Boucher, Céleste
Cariven-Martel, Edith
Couperin, Antoinette Victoire
David, Annie Louise
De la Valle, Mme.
Dibdin, Mary Anne
Dilling, Mildred
Du Park, Miss
Dupree, Miss
Dussek, Olivia
Dussek, Sophia Giustina
Dussek, Veronica
Ferrari, Francisca
Gatti, Clelia Aldrovandi
Gibson, Isabella Mary
Glover, Erminia
Goossens, Marie Henriette
Goossens, Sidonie
Kajanus, Aino
Kajanus, Lilly (Agnes)
Kajanus-Sjöstedt, Elvi
Korchinska, Marie
Krumpholtz, Stekler
Laskine, Lily
Leidy, Helen
Lockwood, Miss

McDonald, Susann
Morgan, Maud
Morgan, Sydney
Navone-Betti, Carolina
Pohl, Johanna
Pollet, Marie-Nicole
Renié, Henriette
Sassòli Ruata, Ada
Serato, Cleopatra
Sharp, Mary
Spier, Rosa
Spohr, Dorette
Spohr, Rosalie
Stein, Rose
Vinning, Louisa
Walter-Kühne, Catherine

HARPSICHORDISTS

Ahlgrimm, Isolde
Aleotti, Vittoria
Anna Amalia, Princess of Prussia
Attwood, Miss
Aubert, Pauline
Barthélemon, Cecilia Maria
Bartlett, Ethel
Baston, Miss
Bayon, Mme. Louis
Benda, Maria Carolina
Berghout, Sophie Rose
Bilgram, Hedwig
Bliss, Ilsa Foerstel
Bloch, Suzanne
Burney, Esther
Cambert, Marie-Anne
Campion, Mary Anne
Casadesus, Regina Patorni
Casson, Margaret
Certain, Marie-Françoise
Chaplin, Nellie
Couperin, Elisabeth-Antoinette
Couperin, Marguerite-Antoinette
Couperin, Marguerite-Louise
Davies, Marianne
Davis, Miss
Ehlers, Alice
Erhart, Dorothy Agnes Alice
Fabrizio, Margaret
Forqueray, Marie-Rose
Gentili Verona, Gabriella
Hamilton, Catherine
Harich-Schneider, Eta
Hodsdon, Margaret

Innes, Audrey
Joyce, Eileen
Kazuro-Trombini, Marguerita
Lacour, Marcelle Antoinette
  Eugénie de
La Guerre, Elisabeth Claude de
Landowska, Wanda
Lechner, Irmgard
Levy, Sara
Marlowe, Sylvia
Olivera de Cowling, Mercedes
Ottey, Sarah
Pelton-Jones, Frances
Pessl, Yella
Picht-Axenfeld, Edith
Roesgen-Champion, Marguerite
  Sara
Savage, Jane
Silver, Millicent
Speckner, Anna Barbara
Stadelmann, Li
Tureck, Rosalyn
Van de Wiele, Aimée
Vaucher-Clerc, Germaine
Wachsmuth-Lowe, Andrée
Wallace, Lucille

HORNIST

See also English hornist

"Bombastini, Signorina"

IMPRESARIOS

Friedberg, Annie
Garden, Mary
Guggenheimer, Minnie

INSTRUMENTALISTS
(unspecified further)

Boucher, Lydia
Gummer, Phyllis Mary

LIBRARIANS

Allan, Jean Mary
Becker-Glauch, Irmgard
Bridgman, Nanie
Lawton, Dorothy
Masson, Renée-Madeleine
Meyer-Baer, Kathi

Rokseth, Yvonne
Schnapper, Edith

LIBRETTISTS

Chézy, Helmina von
Kennedy-Fraser, Marjory
Krásnohorská, Eliška
Maria Antonia Walpurgis

LIGHT-OPERA COMPOSERS

Ahlefeldt, Maria Theresia
Amalia, Marie A. Friederike
Arrieu, Claude
Candeille (Simons), Amélie-
  Julie
Carmichael, Mary Grant
Foster, Fay
Gabriel, Mary Ann Virginia
Gray, Louisa
Hardelot, Guy d'
Harraden, R. Ethel
Harrison, Annie Fortescue
Kinkel, Johanna
Lehmann, Liza
Paradis, Maria Therese von
Puget, Loïsa Françoise
Rabinof, Sylvia
Smyth(e), Dame Ethel Mary
Stair, Patty
Streicher, Lyubov Lvovna
Tate, Phyllis Margaret Duncan
Ugalde, Delphine
Viardot-Garcia, Michelle
  Ferdinande Pauline
Wickham, Florence Pauline
Wurm, Mary J. A.
Young, Harriet Maitland

LUTENISTS

Archilei, Vittoria
Baroni, Eleanora
Bloch, Suzanne
Brondi, Maria Rita
Chanot, Florentine
Gottsched, Luise Adelgunde
Hunt, Arabella
Poulton, (Edith Eleanor) Diana
Striggio, Virginia
Wendling, Maria Dorothea
Wolzogen, Elsa Laura

MANAGERS

Baylis, Lilian
Bovy, Vina
Catalani, Angelica
Chateauneuf (Chatin), Marie
Friedberg, Annie
Juch, Emma
Kellogg, Clara Louise
Reuss-Belce, Luise
Vestris, Lucia Elizabeth

MARIMBISTS

Chenoweth, Vida
Kilby, Muriel Laura

MEZZO-SOPRANOS

Abbadia, Luigia
Alió, Myriam
Allen, Betty
Anderson, Josephine
Artôt, Marguerite-Joséphine-
   Desirée
Baker, Janet Abbott
Baldwin, Marcia
Barbi, Alice
Barbieri, Fedora
Belloc, Maria Teresa
Belocca, Anna de
Berganza, Teresa
Bertana, Luisa
Bible, Frances
Bohé, Marie-Luce
Bonazzi, Elaine
Borghi-Mamo, Adelaide
Bressler-Gianoli, Clotilde
Brighenti, Maria
Bumbry, Grace Ann
Campodonico, Armanda
Canasi, Ida
Canne Meyer, Cora
Caplan, Joan
César, Sara
Cisneros, Eleanora de
Claessens, Maria
Claussen, Julia
Clegg, Edith Kate
Coates, Edith Mary
Cole, Susanna
Coltellini, Céleste
Corri-Paltoni, Frances

Cossira, Emma
Culp, Julia Bertha
Curry, Corinne
Cvejić, Biserka
Dalis, Irene
Davidson, Joy
Davies, Mary
De Ahna, Eleanora
Del Puente, Helen
Dolmetsch, Cécile
Doluchanowa, Sara
Dunn, Mignon
Durigo, Ilona
Eberhart, Constance
Elias, Rosalind
Elmo, Cloe
Evans, Nancy
Fabbri, Vittorina
Fornia-Labey, Rita
Fraser, Janet
Fremstad, Anna Augusta Olivia
Gabarain, Marina de
Gabrielli, Francesca
Galli, Caterina
Galli-Marié, Célestine
Genovese, Nana
Gentle, Alice
Gerhart, Elena
Girò, Anna
Gismondi, Celeste
Goetze, Marie
Gohl-Müller, Verena
Gomez, Alice
Gorr, Rita
Greenspon, Muriel
Grillo, Joann
Grisi, Giuditta
Grossi, Eleonora
Grudzińska, Nina
Guerrini, Virginia
Gueymard, Pauline
Gutheil-Schröder, Marie
Hager, Mina
Haley, Olga
Harris, Hilda
Hasse, Faustina
Henius, Carla
Hildach, Anna
Holt, Gertrude
Horne, Marilyn
Hvoslef, Agnes Eveline Hanson
Iacopi, Valetta
Iakolevna, Anna

Järnefelt, Liva
Johnson, Patricia
Jordan, Irene
Juárez, Nena
Kenney, Margarita
Klafsky, Katharina
Klose, Margarete Frida
Koenen, Tilly
Kostia, Raili
Lachowska, Aga
Lail, Lorri
Landi, Camilla
Lane, Gloria
Lapeyrette, Ketty
Lazzarini, Adriana
Leo, Rosa
Lipton, Martha
Lorengar, Pilar
Lous, Astrid
Love, Shirley
Lucchesina, Maria Antonia
  Marchesini
Ludwig, Christa
McMurray, Mary
Madeira, Jean
Maragliano Mori, Rachele
Marchesi de Castrone, Mathilde
Marcolini, Marietta
Markova, Gali Enbaeff de
Mattfeld, Marie
Maubourg-Goffaux, Jeanne
Merriman, Nan
Miller, Mildred
Nantier-Didiée, Constance
  Betzy Rosabella
Nielsen, Flora
Oboukhova, Nadesha Andreivna
Oddone-Gavirati, Giulia
Orlandi, Elisa
Oselio, Gina
Papier, Rosa
Pasini, Enrica
Pasqua, Giuseppina
Paulee, Mona
Pederzini, Gianna
Perini, Flora
Phillips, Louisa
Pitzinger-Dupont, Gertrude
Pixis, Franzilla Göhringer
Polko, Elise
Ponselle, Carmela
Poole, Elizabeth
Rankin, Nell

Reid-Parsons, Susan
Resnik, Regina
Reyer, Carolyn
Roggero, Margaret
Rubini, Adelaide
Sanderson, Lillian
Sandunowa, Jelisaweta Semjonowna
Sarfaty, Regina Victoria
Scalchi, Sofia
Schärnack, Luise
Schebest, Agnese
Scotney, Evelyn
Shacklock, Constance
Simionato, Giulietta
Simon, Joanna
Slavina, Maria Alexandrovna
Stevens, Risë
Stignani, Ebe
Stoltz, Rosine
Supervia, Conchita
Sztojanovits, Edith
Tangeman, Nell
Tassinari, Domenica
Tavares, Stella
Thebom, Blanche
Thompson, Fanchon
Thursfield, Anne Loyse
Tiszay, Magda
Todi, Luiza Rosa
Tourel, Jennie
Trebelli (-Bettini), Zelia
Tree, Anna Maria
Trianti-Kyriakidi, Alexandra
Troyanos, Tatiana
Uiomen-Jännes, Annikki
Vanni, Helen
Verrett, Shirley
Viardot-Garcia, Michelle
  Ferdinande Pauline
Viñas, Giulia
Waldmann, Maria
Walker, Edyth
Wall, Joan
Warfield, Sandra
Willis, Mary
Wolff, Beverly
Young, Isabella
Zareska, Eugenia

MOTION PICTURE MUSIC COMPOSERS

Barraine, Jacqueline Elsa
Gubaidulina, Sofia

MUSIC HISTORIANS

Guiomar, Paule
Landowski, Alice-Wanda
Stöhr, Maria
Vernillat, France Marie
    Elisabeth

MUSICAL GLASSES PLAYERS

*See Glass harmonica
    players*

MUSICIANS
(unspecified further)

Bach, Maria Barbara
Bacon, Louisa Mary
Binfield, Louisa
Brixi, Dorota
Campbell, Lady Archibald
Cauvini, -----
Eberlin, Maria Josepha
    Catharina
Ebner, Suanne Renate
Hopkins, Sophia
Isouard, Sophie-Nicole
Leclair, Jeanne
Rinaldi, Gioconda
Sale, Mary Anne
Sale, Sophia

MUSICOLOGISTS

Aarburg, Ursula
Abert, Anna Amalie
Alvarenga, Oneyda
Anderson, Emily
Aretz de Ramón y Rivera,
    Isabelle
Arnheim, Amalie
Badura-Skoda, Eva
Bauer, Marion Eugenie
Becker-Glauch, Irmgard
Bokesová-Hanáková, Zdeňka
Bragard, Anne-Marie
Brenet, Michel
Bridgman, Nanie
Brockhoff, Maria Elisabeth
Busch-Weise, Dagmar von
Chissell, Joan Olive
Clercx-Lejeune, Suzanne
Curtiss, Mina

Cuyler, Louise Elvera
Czekanowska, Anna
Dale, Kathleen
Densmore, Frances
Dikenmann-Balmer, Lucie
Donà, Mariangela
Droz, Eugènie
Ellis, Catherine Joan
Engelbrecht, Christiane
Fellinger, Imogen
Gerson-Kiwi, Esther Edith
Gideon, Miriam
Glyn, Margaret Henrietta
Grebe, María Ester
Günther, Ursula
Hague, Eleanor
Hewitt, Helen Margaret
Horsley, Imogene
Hughes, Rosemary Stella
    Middlemore
Humbert-Sauvageot, Madeleine
Ilgner, Margarete Gerda
Jacob-Loewenson, Alice
Karpeles, Maud
Kenney, Sylvia W.
Kinscella, Hazel Gertrude
Kirkendale, Ursula
Kisch, Eve (Evelyn Myra)
Kos, Koraljka
Kumer, Zmaga
Lagercrantz, (Anna) Ingeborg
Launay, Denise
Lebeau, Elisabeth
Liebe, Annelise
Lima Cruz, Maria Antonieta de
Ling, Dorothy
Lissa, Zofia
Livermore, Ann
Lobaczewska, Stefania
Lohr, Ina
Long, Marie-Jeanne-Pauline
Malzewa, Katharine Alexeivna
Marix, Jeanne
Meyer-Baer, Kathi
Mondolfi, Anna
Nolthenius, Hélène Wagenaar
Panum, Hortense
Pope, Isabel
Reimann, Margarete
Rittmeyer-Iselin, Dora J.
Rokseth, Yvonne
Rose, Gloria
Schlesinger, Kathleen

Schnapper, Edith
Scott, Marion Margaret
Simon, Alicja
Sobieski, Jadwiga
Stäblein-Harder, Hanna
Straková, Theodora
Szczepańska, Maria Klementyna
Szegö, Julia
Thibault, Geneviève
Viollier, Renée
Wallner, Bertha Antonia
Weise, Dagmar
Wessely, Helene
Wójcikóvna, Bronislava
Zanetti, Emilia

OBOISTS

Barbirolli, Evelyn
Gaskell, Helen
Gipps, Ruth

ONDES MARTENOT PLAYER

Martenot, Ginette

OPERA COMPOSERS

Agnesi Pinottini, Maria
  Teresa d'
Amalia, Marie A. Friederike
Andrée, Elfrida
Barraine, Jacqueline Elsa
Beaton, Isabella
Bertin, Louise-Angélique
Blahetka (Plahetka), Marie
  Léopoldine
Boulanger, Nadia Juliette
Bright, Dora Estella
Bronsart von Schellendorf,
  Ingeborg von
Caccini, Francesca
Deyo, Ruth Lynda
Donátová, Narcisa
Ferrari, Carlotta
Glanville-Hicks, Peggy
Grandval, Marie-Félicie-
  Clémence de Reiset
Grétry, Lucile
Heckscher, Céleste de Longpré
Holmès, Augusta Mary Anne
Korn, Clara Anna
La Guerre, Elisabeth Claude de

Leginska, Ethel
Loder, Kate Fanny
Maconchy, Elizabeth
Manning, Kathleen Lockhart
Mazzucato, Elisa
Moberg, Ida
Moore, Mary Carr
More, Margaret
Morin-Labrecque, Albertine
Morison, Christina W.
Pentland, Barbara
Polignac, Armande de
Respighi, Elsa
Rodrigo, María
Ruta, Gilda
Salvador, Matilde
Serov, Valentine Semenovna
Skinner, Florence Marian
Smyth(e), Dame Ethel Mary
Stocker, Stella
Talma, Louise
Thys-Sebault, Pauline
Viardot, Louise Héritte de la
  Tour
Weissberg, Yuliya Lazarevna

ORGANISTS

Ackland, Jeanne Isabel Dorothy
Alain, Marie-Claire
Aleotti, Raffaela
Andrée, Elfrida
Andreoli, Maria
Austen, Augusta Amherst
Bilgram, Hedwig
Binfield, Hannah Rampton
Bonwick, Miss
Boschetti, Teresa
Boulanger, Nadia Juliette
Bransden, Lillie Juliette
Brizzi Giorgi, Maria
Buchanan, Annabel Morris
Buck, Era Marguerite
Burchell, H. Louise
Calegari, Maria Caterina
Campbell, Edith May
Carrington-Thomas, Virginia
Cecil, Theophania
Clark, Florence Durell
Clarke, Jane
Couperin, Antoinette Victoire
Couperin, Elisabeth-Antoinette
Couperin, Marie-Madeleine-Cécile

Crozier, Catherine
Day, Ellen
Deacon, Marie Conner
Deacon, Mary Ann
De Gambarini, Elisabetta
Demessieux, Jeanne
Dowding, Emily
Dufour, Marie
Dussek, Olivia
Fowles, Margaret F.
Girod, Marie-Louise
Gomez, Alice
Hagan, Helen Eugenia
Hermann, Miina
Hewitt, Helen Margaret
Hewitt, Sophia Henriette
Heyde-Dohrn, Ellinor von der
Hodges, Faustina Hasse
Hudson, Mary
Jensen, Wilma
Kent, Ada Twohy
Kollmann, Johanna Sophia
Lachner, Christiane
Lachner, Thekla
Lafleur, Lucienne
La Guerre, Elisabeth Claude de
Lawrence, Elizabeth S.
Lippincott, Joan
Mason, Marilyn
Morris, Margaret
Mounsey, Ann Sheppard
Mounsey, Elizabeth
Paradis, Maria Therese von
Partegiotti, Rosa
Patterson, Annie Wilson
Pessl, Yella
Piché, Eudore
Polignac, Winaretta
Pyne, Louise Aubert
Renshaw, Rosette
Roget, Henriette Puig-
Rokseth, Yvonne
Serassi, Maria Caterina
Spencer, Marguerita
Spinney, Mattie
Stair, Patty   ·
Stirling, Elizabeth
Villeneuve, Marie-Louise-
    Diane
Vinette, Alice
Von Hoff, Elizabeth
Ward, Clementine
Wegmann, Maria Anna
Wennerberg-Reuter, Sara

Westrop, Kate
Whomes, Emma
Wieruszowski, Lili
Williams, Annie
Wood, Mary Louisa

PATRONS

Baird, Martha
Coolidge, Elizabeth Sprague
Curtis, Mary Louise
Dyer, Louise
Elizalde, Elena Sansinena de
Helene (Jelena) Pavlovna
Howe, Mary
Leidy, Helen
Lichnowsky, Christine
Llanover, Lady
Maria Antonia Walpurgis
Meck, Nadeschda Filaretowna von
Polignac, Winaretta
Rodrigo, María
Thurber, Jeanette Meyer
Wagner, Cosima
Whittall, Gertrude Clark

PIANISTS

Ackland, Jeanne Isabel Dorothy
Ackland, Jessie Agnes
Adaïewska (Adajewska), Ella
    (Elisabeth) von
Adler, Agnes Charlotte Dagmar
Agnesi Pinottini, Maria Teresa d'
Aïtoff, Irène
Alpenheim, Ilse von
Alter, Martha
Alvarez, Carmen
Ambrož (Ambrosch), Wilhelmine
Ancell, Sarah
Andersen, Hildur
Andersen, Lucy
Andersen, Stell
Andreoli, Maria
Andreoli, Rosa
Ansorge, Margarethe
Antonelli, Pina
Appeldoorn, Dina
Archer, Violet Balestreri
Arco, Annie d'
Aretz de Ramón y Rivera, Isabelle
Argerich, Martha
Arnaud, (Germaine) Yvonne
Arrieu, Claude

Ashton, Diana Uvedale
Auerbach, Nanette
Aulin, Laura Valborg
Aus der Ohe, Adele
Austin, Miss
Aylward, Janetta
Aylward, Leila J.
Baccara, Luisa
Bachauer, Gina
Bache, Constance
Bachmann, Charlotte Karoline
  Wilhelmine
Backer-Grøndahl, Agathe Ursula
Bacon, Katherine
Badura-Skoda, Eva
Bailey-Apfelbeck, Marie Louise
Baird, Martha
Ballek, Daniela
Barbour, Florence Newell
Barnes, Philippa
Barnett, Emma
Baroni-Cavalcabo, Julie
Bartlett, Ethel
Bates, Mona
Bauer, Emilie Frances
Beach, Amy Marcy
Beaton, Isabella
Becker, Jeanne
Beebe, Carolyn
Beecham, Betty
Behrend, Jeanne
Benois, Marie
Berg, María
Bergmann, Maria
Bernáthová, Eva
Bernette, Yara
Bertin, Louise-Angélique
Berwald, Astrid Maria Beatrice
Bialkiewicz de Langeron, Irena
Bianco-Lanzi, Maria
Bidal, Denise
Bigot de Morognes, Marie
Biltcliffe, Florence
Binfield, Fanny Jane
Binfield, Hannah Rampton
Biret, Idil
Bisset, Catherine
Bizzozero, Julieta
Blacher, Gerty
Blahetka (Plahetka), Marie
  Léopoldine
Blancard, Jacqueline
Blomfield-Holt, Patricia

Boese, Helen
Bohrer, Sophie
Bonneau, Jacqueline
Bordes-Pène, Léontine Marie
Bordino, Maria
Borek, Minuetta
Borgatti, Renata
Borton, Alice
Boschi, Hélène
Bosmans, Henriëtta
Bosmans, Sara
Botez, Manya
Boyce, Ethel Mary
Brandes, Emma
Branscombe, Gena
Bright, Dora Estella
Brizzi Giorgi, Maria
Brodsky, Vera
Bronsart von Schellendorf,
  Ingeborg von
Bruchollerie, Monique de la
Bruckshaw, Kathleen
Brzezińska, Filipina
Buchanan, Annabel Morris
Buck, Era Marguerite
Buckley, Beatrice Barron
Burrowes, Katharine
Buxton, Eugenia
Byrn, Adelaide C.
Cadoret, Charlotte
Caffaret, Lucie
Caland, Elisabeth
Calcagno, Elsa
Camaiti, Corella Provvedi
Caminals, Rosa Maria
Canals, María R.
Canela, María
Cannabich, Rosine Therese
  Petronelle
Cantelo, Annie
Carbonell, María
Carmichael, Mary Grant
Carner, Helen
Carreño, Maria Teresa
Carreras, Maria Avani
Carvalho, Dinorá de
Carwithen, Doreen
Casadesus, Gaby
Casadesus, Gladys
Casadesus, Regina Patorni
Casadesus, Rose
Caspar, Helene
Cavallo, Enrica Gulli

Chailley-Richez, Céliny
Chaminade, Cécile Louise-
  Stéphanie
Chaplin, Nellie
Chase, Mary Wood
Christie, Winifred
Cianchettini, Veronica
  Elizabeth
Cimaglia-Espinosa, Lía
Cionca-Pipos, Aurelia
Claman, Dolores Olga
Clark, Florence Durell
Clauss-Szarvady, Wilhelmine
Cleve, Berit
Cocorascu, Madeleine
Cocq-Weingand, Amelia
Coen, Anna Seppilli
Cohen, Dame Harriet
Coolidge, Elizabeth Sprague
Coons, Minnie
Côte, Hélène
Cottlow, Augusta
Coulthard, Jean
Couperin, Céleste-Thérèse
Crawford, Ruth Porter
Cuney-Hare, Maud
Curubeto Godoy, María Isabel
Curwen, Annie Jessy
Czartoryska, Marcelline
Czerny-Stefańska, Halina
Dacosta, Janine
Dahmen, Mona
Dale, Kathleen
Daneau, Suzanne
Darré, Jeanne-Marie
Davies, Fanny
Davies, Joan
Davies, Llewela
Davies, Marianne
Davy, Ruby Claudia Emily
Dawidowitsch, Bella Michajlowna
Day, Ellen
Dayas, Karin Elin
Deacon, Marie Conner
Deacon, Mary Ann
De Blasis, Teresa
De Filippi, Giuseppina
Delaborde, Élie Miriam
De Lara, Adelina
De la Valle, Mme.
Del Corona, Itala
Delorme, Isabelle
Descaves, Lucette

Dessoir, Susanne
Devèze, Germaine
Deyo, Ruth Lynda
Dieren, Frieda van
Diller, Angela
Djurić-Klajn, Stana
Dlugoszewski, Lucia
Dorfmann, Ania
Drége-Schielowa, Lucja
Drewett, Nora
Droucker, Sandra
Duchambge, Charlotte Antoinette
  Pauline
Dufour, Marie
Dugal, Madeleine
Dulcken, Marie Luise
Dulcken, Sophie
Dunning, Carre Louise
Durno, Jeannette
Dussek, Josepha
Dussek, Olivia
Dussek, Sophia Giustina
Dussek, Veronica Rosaria
Eckhardt-Gramatté, Sophie
  Carmen
Eggar, Katharine Emily
Ehlers, Alice
Eibenschütz, Ilona
Eissler, Emma
Ellegaard, France Marguerite
Ellicott, Rosalind Frances
Erdmannsdörffer, Pauline
Erikson, Märta Greta
Erkin, Ferhunde
Ertmann, Catharina Dorothea
Essipova, Anna Nikolaevna
Eyre, Margaret
Fahrbach, Johanna
Fahrbach, Josephine
Farmer, Dinah
Farnadi, Edith
Farrenc, Jeanne Louise
Farrenc, Victorine Louise
Fay, Amy
Ferrari, Gabriella
Filippone-Siniscalchi, Tina
Fine, Vivian
Fischer, Annie
Fisher, Charlotte E.
Fisher, Esther
Flissler, Eileen
Folville, Juliette-Eugénie
  Emilie

Fortey, Mary Comber
Fourneau, Marie-Thérèse
Fowles, Margaret F.
Franceschi, Vera
Franchère-des Rosiers,
  Roede Lima
Franco, Rina
Frickenhaus, Fanny
Frijsh, Povla
Fröhlich, Katharina
Fröhlich, Maria Anna
Fromm-Michaels, Ilse
Fuchsova, Liza
Fuschi, Olegna
Gabriel, Mary Ann Virginia
Gál, Margit
Galajikian, Florence Grandland
Galeotti, Marguerite
Gannon, Helen C.
Garuta, Lucija
Gaynor, Jessie Love
Genhart, Cecile
Geon, Marcella
Germani-Ciomac, Muza
Gerstein, Chaia
Geselschap, Marie
Gipps, Ruth
Giuranna, Elena Barbara
Glaser, Liv
Glover, Sarah Ann
Gnessin, Eléna Fabianovna
Goddard, Arabella
Goldstein, Ella
Gómez Carrillo, Inés
Good, Margaret
Goodson, Katharine
Goodwin, Amina Beatrice
Gottsched, Luise Adelgunde
Gousseau, Lélia
Grabowska, Klementyna
Gradova, Gitta
Graever, Madeleine
Graf, Meta
Gray, Edith Moxom
Gray, Isabel Winton
Graziella, Gina
Greenbaum, Kyla
Grever, Maria
Grierson, Mary Gardner
Grimaud, Yvette
Gubitosi, Emilia
Guillamat, Ginette
Gunn, Anne

Gušić, Dora
Gyde, Margaret
Haake, Gail Martin
Haas, Alma
Haas, Monique
Haebler, Ingrid
Härtel, Luise
Hagan, Helen Eugenia
Hagedorn, Meta
Haldemann-Gerster, Rita
Hale, Jeannie M.
Hall, Elsie
Hall, Pauline Margrete
Hamaton, Adela
Hamilton, Catherine
Hardiman, Ellena G.
Hare, Amy
Harris, Johanna Beula
Harrison, Anita
Harrison, Margaret
Haskil, Clara
Heale, Helene
Heber, Judith
Heckmann, Marie
Heinemann, Käthe
Heinze, Sarah
Heksch, Alice
Hennes, Therese
Henriot-Schweitzer, Nicole
Henschel, Helen
Hensel, Fanny Cäcilia
Henshaw, Grace Mary Williams
Herrmann, Klara
Herz, Alice
Herzogenberg, Elisabeth
Hess, Dame Myra
Hesse-Bukowska, Barbara
Hewitt, Sophia Henriette
Heyman, Katherine Ruth
  Willoughby
Hier, Ethel Glenn
Hinderas, Natalie
Hirzel-Langenhan, Anna
Hitzelberger, Catharina
  Elisabeth
Hobday, Ethel
Hoffmann-Behrendt, Lydia
Hohnstock, Adelaide
Holguín, Lucía
Holmès, Augusta Mary Anne
Holmsen, Borghild
Holst, Imogen Clare
Hopekirk, Helen

Lübbecke-Job, Emma
Lympany, Moura
Maas, Marguerite Wilson
Maazel, Mimi
MacDowell, Marian
Macfarren, Emma Marie Bennett
Macirone, Clara Angela
Madriguera, Paquita
Magnetti, Ermelinda
Malcuzynski, Colette
Malibran, Maria Felicità
Maloziomova, Sofiya Andreyevna
Mana-Zucca
Mandl, Camilla
Mannes, Clara
Mansfield, Louise Christine
Manziarly, Marcelle de
Marchi, Giuliana
Margulies, Adele
Mariño, Nibya
Martinez, Marianne de
Massart, Louise-Aglaë
Matthison-Hansen, Nanny
May, Florence
Mehlig, Anna
Melchers, Henriette
Meller, Clara
Menter, Sophie
Menuhin, Hephzibah
Menuhin, Yaltah
Mérö-Irion, Yolanda
Meyer, Marcelle
Miklashevskaya, Irina
Mildner, Poldi
Milkina, Nina
Millar, Marian
Miller, Agnes Elizabeth
Mitchell, Marjorie
Monath, Hortense
Mondolfi, Anna
Montgeroult, Hélène
Montigny-Rémaury, Fanny
  Marceline Caroline
Morel, Lottie
Morsch, Anna
Morsztyn, Helena
Mossman, Sheila
Mounsey, Ann Sheppard
Mozart, Konstanze
Mozart, Maria Anna Walburga
  Ignatia
Müller, Elisabeth Catharina
Mukle, Anna

Mundella, Emma
Musulin, Branka
Mysz-Gmeiner, Luise
Neeley, Marilyn
Nef, Isabelle
Nelson, Allison
Nemenoff, Genia
Neruda, Amalie
Neruda, Anna Maria Rudolfina
Neruda, Olga
Newcomb, Ethel
Ney, Elly
Nikolayevna, Tatiana Petrovna
Norton, Eunice
Novaës, Guiomar
Noyes, Edith Rowena
Oakey, Maggie
Oldham, Miss E.
Oliveira, Jocy de
Olivera de Cowling, Mercedes
O'Neill, Adine
Oppens, Ursula
Oury, Anna Caroline
Pachler-Koschak, Marie Leo-
  poldine
Page, Kate Stearns
Palla, Lia
Pancera, Gabriele
Panthès, Marie
Paradis, Maria Therese von
Parent, Charlotte-Francès-
  Hortense
Parody, Julia
Pasini, Laura
Pathy, Ilonka von
Patterson, Annie Wilson
Patti, Carlotta
Paur, Marie
Pentland, Barbara
Peppercorn, Gertrude
Perren, Rhea
Pessl, Yella
Pflughaupt, Sophie
Piaggio de Tarelli, Elsa
Picht-Axenfeld, Edith
Pinter, Margot
Pleyel, Marie-Félicité-Denise
Polignac, Winaretta
Poston, Elizabeth
Pozzi, Pina
Prahács, Margit
Puliti Santoliquido, Ornella
Quaile, Elizabeth

Rabcewicz, Zofia
Rabinof, Sylvia
Raitzin, Florencia
Ralf, Eileen
Ralph, Kate
Randell, Sheila
Randles, Elizabeth
Rangmann-Björlin, Elli
Rapoport, Eda Ferdinand
Rappoldi, Laura
Raymond, Madeleine
Rea, Emma Mary
Regules, Marisa
Reimann, Margarete
Reinagle, Caroline
Reisenberg, Nadia
Remmert, Martha
Renard, Rosita
Renshaw, Rosette
Richings-Bernard, Caroline
Rimski-Korsakov, Nadežda
    Nikolaievna
Rinaldi, Ernestina
Ripper, Alice
Ritter-Ciampi, Cécile
Rivé-King, Julie
Robinson, Fanny
Rodríguez, Esther
Roeckel, Jane
Roesgen-Champion, Marguerite
    Sara
Roget, Henriette Puig-
Roman, Josette
Roman, Yvette
Romberg, Angelica
Rootham, Mabel Margaret
Rosenberger, Carol
Roy, Berthe
Rudge, Antonieta
Rufer, Magdi
Rummel, Josephine
Ruta, Gilda
Ryber, Dagmar de Corval
Sá e Costa, Helena Moreira de
Sabater, Rosa
Saint-John, Florence
Salquin, Hedy
Samaroff, Olga
Sanders, Alma
Sant Angelo, Pauline
Sarenecka, Jadwiga
Sás, Lily
Scates, Linda

Scharrer, Irene
Schauroth, Delphine von
Schein, Ann
Schiller, Madeline
Schirmacher, Dora
Schmid, Rosl
Schmid-Gagnebin, Ruth
Schnabel, Helen
Schnabel-Tollefsen, Augusta
Schnéevoigt, Sigrid Ingeborg
Schnitzer, Germaine
Schultz von Beckerath, Lulu
Schumann, Clara Josephine
Schuyler, Philippa
Schwarz, Friederike
Sebastiani, Pia
Sehlbach, Irma
Sellick, Phyllis
Selva, Blanche
Sepúlveda, María Luisa
Sérieyx, Jeanne
Shafir, Shulamith
Siboni, Johanna Frederika
Silver, Millicent
Sjögren, Berta
Slenczynska, Ruth
Smith, Julia
Smith, Nellie Curzon
Snižková-Skrhová, Jitka
Söderhjelm-Grönlund, Adele
    Ester Merete
Solomon, Mirrie
Somellera, Josefa
Somer, Hilde
Sorel, Claudette
Soulage, Marcelle
Spencer, Eleanor
Spencer, Marguerita
Spinney, Mattie
Spitta, Klara
Spohr, Marianne
Stadelmann, Li
Starr, Susan
Stein, Maria Anna
Stern, Margaret(h)e
Stockhausen, Ella
Stucki, Rosemarie
Suárez, Aurea
Suart, Evelyn
Sutro, Ottilie
Sutro, Rose Laura
Swain, Freda
Synge, Mary Helena

Szalit, Paulina
Tacchinardi, Elisa
Tagliaferro, Magda(lena)
Tait, Annie
Tapper, Bertha
Tartaglia, Lydia
Tausig, Seraphine
Telmányi, Annette
Terhune, Anice
Thegerström, Hilda
Thomas, Adelaide Louisa
Thorne, Beatrice
Tilly, Margaret
Timanova, Vera Victorovna
Tipo, Maria
Trew, Susan
Trimble, Joan
Trimble, Valerie
Troyon-Blaesi, Emmy
Tureck, Rosalyn
Tyrrell, Agnes
Unschuld, Marie von
Upton, Emily
Van Barentzen, Aline
Van den Hoeven, Dina
Varro, Marie-Aimée
Vaucher-Clerc, Germaine
Vaurabourg, Andrée
Vengerova, Izabella Afanasyevna
Verne, Adela
Verne, Alice Verne Bredt
Verne, Mathilde
Viard, Jenny
Vieuxtemps, Josephine
Villeneuve, Marie-Louise-Diane
Vinette, Alice
Vining, Helen Sherwood
Vinogradova, Vera
Voigt, Henriette
Volavy, Marguerite
Von Hoff, Elizabeth
Vronsky, Vitya
Walker, Bettina
Wallace, Lucille
Waltershausen, Caroline von
Ward, Eliza A.
Ware, Harriet
Warren, Elinor Remick
Warrot, Marie-Aimée
Wartel, Atale Thérèse Annette
Waterman, Constance Dorothy
Weber, Margrit
Webster, Clarinda Augusta

Weill, Janine
Wensley, Frances Foster
West, Lottie
Westrop, Kate
Whiteside, Abby
Whomes, Clara
Wieck, Marie
Wild, Margaret
Wilhelmj, Mariella
Willmann, (Maria Anna Magda-
  lena) Caroline
Willmann, Marianne
Willmann, (Maximiliana Valen-
  tina) Walburga
Wirz-Wyss, Clara
Wolf, Anna Mrasek
Wolf, Antoinette
Wood, Mary Knight
Woolf, Sophia Julia
Wurm, Mary J. A.
Yalkovsky, Isabelle
Zaremba, Sylvia
Zeisler, Fannie Bloomfield
Zieritz, Grete von
Zimmermann, Agnes Marie
  Jacobina

PIANO MANUFACTURER

Stein, Maria Anna

PIANO TEACHERS

Ackland, Jessie Agnes
Adler, Agnes Charlotte Dagmar
Andersen (Anderson), Lucy
Andersen, Stell
Andreoli, Rosa
Appeldoorn, Dina
Bacon, Katherine
Bartlett, Ethel
Bates, Mona
Bauer, Emilie Frances
Bigot de Morognes, Marie
Bordes-Pène, Léontine Marie
Borgatti, Renata
Bosmans, Sara
Burrowes, Katharine
Caland, Elisabeth
Camaiti, Cornelia Provvedi
Carreras, Maria Avani
Carwithen, Doreen
Casadesus, Regina Patorni

Parent, Charlotte-Francès-
  Hortense
Pleyel, Marie-Félicité-Denise
Práhacs, Margit
Quaile, Elizabeth
Rabcewicz, Zofia
Randles, Elizabeth
Rangman-Björlin, Elli
Rappoldi, Laura
Reimann, Margarete
Reisenberg, Nadia
Remmert, Martha
Renard, Rosita
Rivé-King, Julie
Rootham, Mabel Margaret
Roy, Berthe
Ruta, Gilda
Sá e Costa, Helena Moreira de
Salquin, Hedy
Samaroff, Olga
Sanders, Alma
Scates, Linda
Scharrer, Irene
Schnéevoigt, Sigrid Ingeborg
Schumann, Clara Josephine
Selva, Blanche
Spitta, Klara
Szumowska, Antoinette
Szymanowska, Maria Agata
Tapper, Bertha
Thegerström, Hilda
Timanova, Vera Victorovna
Vengerova, Izabella Afanas-
  yevna
Verne, Adela
Verne, Alice Verne Bredt
Verne, Mathilde
Viard, Jenny
Vining, Helen Sherwood
Warrot, Marie-Aimée
Whiteside, Abby
Wieck, Marie

POETS

Alvarenga, Oneyda
Barnard, Charlotte
Baroni, Caterina
Bourges, Clementine de
Brentano, Bettina
Chézy, Helmina
Costa, Margarita de
Flower, Eliza

Fricker, Anne
Hildegard, Saint
Hunter, Anne
Ritter, Fanny
Thompson, Marquita Sánchez de
Wesendonck, Mathilde
Wilson, Mrs. Cornwall Baron

PRINTER

Welcker, Mary

PUBLISHERS

Balls, Eliza
Castagneri, Marie-Anne
Dillon, Fannie Charles
Dyer, Louise
Fentum, Catherine
Fentum, Mary Ann
Hare, Elizabeth (I)
Hare, Elizabeth (II)
Lavenu, Elizabeth
Machabey, Emilienne
Mechetti, Therese

SINGERS
(unspecified further)

Abrams, Eliza
Abrams, Flora
Abrams, Miss G.
Abrams, Jane
Adams, Mrs.
Adams, Miss E.
Adams, Miss H.
Adams, Miss S.
Adcock, Miss
Addison, Elizabeth
Agnetta, Signora
Ahnger, Alexandra
Albergotti, Vittoria
Albrici, Leonora
Allinson, Mrs.
Allison, Maria
Allitsen, Frances
Ambrosini, Antonia
Amicis (Buonsollazzi), Rosalba
  Baldacci
Amoretti, Giustina
Andersen, Lale
Andreini, Virginia
Andrews, Miss

Andrews, Jenny
Angelelli, Augusta
Angelica, Mrs.
Angelo, Signora
Anna, Signora
Antier, Maria
Anunciati, Signora
Araujo, Gina de
Archilei, Vittoria
Arne, Ann
Arnold, Elizabeth
Arthur, Grace
Aschieri, Caterina
Aspri (Asperi), Orsola
Atherton, Miss
Atkins, Eliza
Aubert, Isabella
Audinot, Mlle.
Avoglio, Christina Maria
Ayliff, Mrs.
Babaïan, Marguerite
Babbi, Giovanna (fl.1739)
Babbi, Giovanna (fl.1797)
Bachmann, Charlotte Karoline
  Wilhelmine
Baddeley, Sophia
Badini, Signora
Baglioni, Camilla
Baglioni, Clementina
Baglioni, Costanza
Baglioni, Giovanna
Baglioni, Rosina
Baglioni, Vincenza
Bailey, Mary Sophia
Baini, Cecilia
Baker, Mrs.
Baker, Miss
Baker, Elizabeth
Baker, Mrs. J. S.
Baldwin, Mary
Ball, Mrs.
Bandiera, Anna
Barbier, Jane
Barnes, Miss
Barnet, Mrs.
Barnett, Catherine
Baroni, Caterina
Baroni, Eleanora
Barre, Catherine
Barrett, Miss
Barrett Mrs.
Barro, Mathilde
Barsanti, Jane

Bartelman, Mrs.
Barthélemon, Cecilia Maria
Baster, Eleanor
Bateman, Mary
Bates, Miss
Bawr, Alexandrinę Sophie Coury
  de Champgrand
Bayley, Mrs.
Bayon, Mme. Louis
Bayzand, Elizabeth
Beaufort, Miss
Beaumesnil, Henriette Adélaide
  Villard de
Beaumont, Mrs.
Belisani, Cecchina (Cecilia)
Belloli, Marianna
Benda, Mme.
Benda, Maria Carolina
Bendidio, Isabella
Bendidio, Lucrezia
Bennet, Elizabeth
Bennett, Maria
Benson, Mrs. (fl.1675)
Benson, Mrs. (fl.1784-86)
Berg, Anna Lisa
Bernardi, Signora
Berton, Liliane
Bicknell, Mrs.
Biggs, Anne
Bigi, Giacinta
Biscaccianti, Eliza
Bisgaard, Astri Udnaes
Bishop, Mrs.
Björling, Heddy
Blanchard, Charlotte
Blurton, Mary
Boccabadati Francalucci,
  Augusta
Boccabadati Gazzuolo, Cecilia
Boccabadati Varesi, Giulia
Boïeldieu, Jenny
Boimaison, Mrs.
Bolla, Maria
Bologna, Mrs. Pietro
Boman, Mrs.
Boman, Elizabeth
Booth, Miss
Booth, Ursula Agnes
Bordogni-Willent, Luisa
Borselli, Elisabetta
Boschi, Francesca
Botarelli, Mrs.
Bower, Mrs.

Boyle, Elise
Bracegirdle, Anne
Bradford, Mrs.
Bradley, Mrs. M.
Bradshaw, Lucretia
Brambilla, Annetta
Brambilla, Francesca
Brambilla, Laura
Bramwell, Georgiana
Branèze, Maria
Brett, Hannah
Bricklayer, Miss
Brickler, Miss
Bridges, Mrs.
Brigg, Mrs.
Bristow, Mrs.
Broadhurst, Miss
Brown, Mrs. (fl.1786-87)
Brown, Mrs. (fl.1790-97)
Brown, Mrs. J.
Browning, Miss
Bruch, Clara
Brumaire, Jacqueline
Brumen, Miss
Buckley, Beatrice Barron
Budgell, Anne Eustace
Bugamelli, Teresita
Burden, Kitty
Burnett, Miss
Burnett, Mrs. William
Buroni, Signora
Burr, Mrs.
Bussani, Carolina
Butler, Mrs.
Butler, Charlotte
Butler, Mrs. William
Byre, Mrs.
Caccini, Francesca
Caccini, Settimia
Calegari, Maria Caterina
Calvert, Mrs.
Calvesi, Teresa
Camati (Camal), Maria
Cammarano, Rosalia
Campbell, Mrs.
Campion, Mary Anne
Campolini, Signora
Canali, Isabella
Canavasso, Genoveffa
Cantrell, Mrs.
Cantrell, Miss
Capper, Miss
Cara, Giovanna

Carara, Signora Antonio
Cardarelli (Cardelli), Signora
Cardi, Signora
Careless, Elizabeth
Carey, Mrs. George Saville
Cargill, Ann
Carli, Miss
Carmignani, Giovanna
Carnevale, Signora Pietro
Carreño, Maria Teresa
Carter, Mrs.
Carter, Miss (fl.1741-42)
Carter, Miss (fl.1759-65)
Cartwright, Mrs.
Casaccia, Gaetana
Casadesus, Jacqueline
Caselli, Signora
Casey, Polly
Casson, Margaret
Castelle (Cartell, Castelli),
    Mrs.
Castelli, -----
Castelli, Anna
Catenacci, Signora Maria
Catley, Ann(e)
Celestino, Signora Eligio
Celotti, Ziuliana
Celson, Miss
Cemmitt, Miss
Cerail (Crail), Mlle.
Chabran, Margherita
Chabran, Marianna
Chailley, Marie-Thérèse
Chalmers, Eleanor
Chambers, Elizabeth
Chambers, Isabella
Chapman, Charlotte Jane
Chapman, Frances R.
Chateauneuf (Chatin), Marie
Chatterley, Miss
Chimenti, Margherita
Chippendale, Mrs. William
Cibber, Catherine
Cibber, Jane
Clark, Mrs. (fl.1695-1723)
Clark, Miss (fl.1736)
Clark, Miss (fl.1736-47)
Clark, Mrs. (fl.1789)
Clarke, Mrs. Nathaniel
Clendining, Elizabeth
Cléricy Blanc du Collet, Marie
    Camille Joséphine

Clive, Catherine
Coates, Mrs.
Coats, Miss
Cole, Miss
Colles, Hesther
Collet, Mrs. Ann
Colombati, Elisabetta
Colon, Marguerite
Coltellini, Anna
Connard, Miss
Contini, Giovanna
Cook, Alice Aynsley
Cooke, Mary
Cooper, Miss
Cooper, Margaret
Copin, Elizabeth
Cornelys, Teresa
Correa, Lorenza
Correia, Lourença Nunes
Corri, Signora Domenico
Cosmi, Emanuela
Costa, Margarita de
Costantini, Signora
Cotterel, Miss
Couperin, Antoinette Victoire
Couperin, Céleste-Thérèse
Couperin, Marguerite-Louise
Courtenay, Miss
Couvand, Chérie
Cox, Mrs. (fl.1760)
Cox, Mrs. (fl.1781-82)
Cox, Miss
Cozzolani, Chiara Margherita
Craig, Elizabeth
Cranford, Miss
Crawford, Miss
Cremonini, Clementina
Crisp, Henrietta Maria
Crofts, Miss
Crosby, Miss
Cross, Mrs. John Cartwright
Cross, Frances
Cross, Letitia
Crozier, Miss
Cruvelli, Friederike Marie
Cullen, Rose
Curioni, Rosa
Custonelli, Signora
Dall, Miss
Daniels, Alica
Darley, Anne
Davenport, Mary Ann
Davies, Miss

Davies, Elizabeth
Davies, Marianne
Davis, Mrs. (fl.1726-45)
Davis, Miss (fl.1739-62)
Davis, Miss (fl.1794)
Davis, Miss (fl.1795)
Davis, Mrs. (fl.1799-1803)
Davis, Mary
Davis, Sarah
Dawson, Miss
De Amicis, Anna Lucia
De Caro, Giulia
De Fesch, Mrs. William
D'Egville, Miss
Del'Acqua, Teresa
Delicati, Margherita
Delpini, Signora Carlo Antonio
Demera, Signora
De Micheli, Mary Ann
Dennis, Mrs. (fl.1720)
Dennis, Mrs. (fl.1752-70)
Dennison, Mrs.
De Sisley, Mme.
Deszner (Teschner), Salomea
Dettey, Miss
D'Evelyn, Miss
Devrient, Therese
Dibdin, Anne
Dibdin, Mary
Didier, Margaret
Dighton, Mrs. Robert
Di Maria, Geltrude
Dietters von Dittersdorf,
  Nicolina
Dixon, Clara Ann
Dodd, Martha
Dodson, Mrs.
Dominique, Mme.
Donadieu, Miss
Dorman, Elizabeth
D'Orta, Rachele
D'Orta, Rosina
Dotti, Anna
Dowson, Ann
Drake, Miss
Draper, Miss
Dubellamy, Frances Maria
Ducrast, Mme.
Dufour, Camilla
Dugazon, Louise-Rosalie
Dumont, Mrs.
Dunstall, Mary
Duport, Miss
Dupuy, Hilaire

Dussek, Josepha
Dussek, Sophia Giustina
Duval, Mlle.
Dyer, Mrs.
Eberlin, Maria Francisca
  Veronika
Edwin, Elizabeth Rebecca
Ernst, Anna Katherina
Evers, Katinka
Fabri, Anna Maria
Fahrbach, Maria Johanna
Farmer, Anna Maria
Farnese, Marianna
Favart, Marie-Justine-Benoîte
Fei-Liu-Li
Fel, Marie Antoinette Fran-
  çoise
Férès, Maria Simone
Ferlotti, Claudia
Fernández, María Antonio
Ferrabasco, Elizabeth
Ferrandini, Anna Maria
  Elisabetta
Ferrari, Sofia
Feschotte, Colette
Festa, Francesca
Filippi, Pauline
Finck, Hermine
Fischer, Barbara
Fischer, Josepha
Fischer, Louise
Fischer, Therese Wilhelmine
Fitzwilliam, Kathleen Mary
Fleischer, Eva
Fodor-Mainvielle, Henriette
Ford, Ann
Formes, Pauline Greenwood
Forrest, Mary
Fourrier, Janine
Franziska, Maria Anna
Fratesanti, Signora
Fux, Maria Anna
Gabry, Edith
Gähwiller, Sylvia
Gafforini, Elisabetta
Gallia, Maria
Gallmeyer, Joséphine
Gassmann, Maria Anna
Gassmann, Maria Theresa
Gaultier, Juliette de la
  Verendrye
Genast, Emile
Gentili Bonura, Giustina

Giachetti, Ada
Gianettini, Maria Caterina
Gibson, Isabella Mary
Glossop, Elizabeth
Glover, Sarah Ann
Götze, Augusta
Graf, Hedy
Graupner, Catherine
Grisi, Carlotta
Groll, Sophie
Guadagni, Lavinia Maria
Guarducci, Carolina
Günther-Bachmann, Karoline
Guglielmi, Maria
Guilbert, Yvette
Guillamat, Ginette
Guillemautot, Jacqueline
Gungl (Gung'l), Virginia
Häser, Charlotte Henriette
Hässler, Sophie
Hagelstam, Anna
Hale, Jeannie M.
Hauptmann, Susette
Hausegger, Hertha
Heimburg, Helene von
Heinefetter, Eva
Heinefetter, Fatima
Heinefetter, Katinka
Heinefetter, Maria
Heinefetter, Nanette
Heinrich, Julia
Hellmesberger, Rosa
Hemmerlein, Eva Ursula
Herschel, Caroline
Hesse, Johanna Elisabeth
Hewitt, Sophia Henriette
Hoffmann, Hildegard
Hogarth, Helen
Holzbauer, Rosalie
Horn, Maria
Hřimalá, Felicita
Hřimalá, Marie
Hubert, Antonia
Hummel, Elisabeth
Hunt, Arabella
Ibsen, Bergljot
Iretskaia, Natalia Alexandrovna
Isaacs, Rebecca
Istel, Janet
Janda, Therese
Jasińska, Magdalena
Jawureck, Constance
Jeske-Choińska-Mikorska, Ludmila

Jiránek, Franziska
Jordan, Dora
Kayser, Margarethe Susanna
Keller, Wilhelmine
Kelly, Frances Maria
Klein, Ivy Frances
Kleinmichel, Klara
Klemetti, Dagmar
Knyvett, Deborah
Kreutzer, Cäcilia
Krüger, Emmy
Kuchta, Gladys
La Barre, Anne
Lacombe, Claudine
Large, Eliza Rebecca
Lebrun, Rosine
Lefébure-Wély (Lefebvre),
 Joséphine-Thérèse
Leisinger, Bertha
Lemmens, Ella
Lemmens, Mary
Lenhardson, Antonieta
 Silveyra de'
Lenya, Lotte
Lindelheim, Joanna Maria
Lisi, Anna Maria
Litz, Gisela
Livermore, Ann
Lolli, Dorotea
Lotti, Santa Stella
Lüthi-Wegmann, Elvira
Mabee, Grace Widney
MacCarthy, Maud
Maccherini, Giuseppina
Magelssen, Ida Basilier
Mahon, Miss M.
Maillard, Marie-Thérèse
Mainvielle, Enrichetta
Makeba, Miriam
Mangold, Charlotte
Manning, Kathleen Lockhart
Marini, Fanny Goldberg
Marschner, Marianne
Marti, Katharina
Martienssen-Lohmann, Franziska
Martinelli, Caterina
Martinez, Marianne de
Martino, Miranda
Mattei, Colomba
Matthay, Jessie
Maxwell-Lyte, Eve
Melini, Grazia
Metzger-Vespermann, Klara

Mombelli, Anna
Mombelli, Ester
Mombelli, Luisa
Monti, Anna Maria
Monti, Grazia
Monti, Laura
Monti, Marianna
Mortellari, Marietta Augusta
Mozart, Konstanze
Musi, Maria Maddalena
Mysz-Gmeiner, Ella
Nansen, Eva Helene
Naumann, Ida
Neefe, Felice
Neefe, Louise Frederika
Neefe, Maria
Neuenschwander, Leni
Nikisch, Amélie
Novelli, Anna Maria Sofia
Novelli Laurenti, Antonia Maria
Novello, Cecilia
Novello-Davies, Clara
Nüesch, Nina
Nunn, Gertrude
Nunn, Henrietta
Oddone Sulli-Rao, Elisabetta
Oldenburg, Barbara
Palmgren, Minna
Palomino, Catalina
Pappritz, Juliane
Paradis, Maria Therese von
Parke, Maria Hester
Parlamagni, Annetta
Partegiotti, Rosa
Paton, Eliza
Paton, Isabella
Patti, Amalia
Payne, Marie
Pélissier, Marie
Penagos, Isabel
Petrini, Marie Therese
Peyron, Gisèle
Phillips, Alice
Phillips, Florence
Philp, Elizabeth
Pirker, Marianne
Plaisted, Grace
Platti, Therese Maria
Polzelli, Luigia
Pownall, Mary Ann
Pradher, Félicité
Puzzi, Giacinta
Radcliff, Pauline

Radnor, Countess of
Rébel, Anne
Rébel, Anne-Renée
Rébel, Rose
Reeves, Constance Sims
Reeves, Maud
Rellstab, Caroline
Rennès, Catharina van
Respighi, Elsa
Reutter, Theresia
Revoil, Fanély
Rey, Mlle. (III)
Riccardi, Francesca
Riccioni, Barbara
Richings-Bernard, Caroline
Righini, Henriette
Ritter-Ciampi, Cécile
Robinson, Ann Turner
Robinson, Elizabeth
Rodio, Jolanda
Romberg, Bernhardine
Romberg, Therese
Ros, Maria
Rummel, Francisca
Russell, Anna
Rust, Henriette
Saint-John, Florence
Salicoli, Margherita
Salomon, Anna Jakobina
Salomon, Anna Maria
Sánchez Elía, Magdalena
  Bengolea de
Santley, Kate
Saporiti, Caterina
Saurel, Emma
Scalabrini, Teresa
Scarabelli Diamante, Maria
Scarlatti, Anna Maria
Scarlatti, Flaminia Anna
  Caterina
Scarlatti, Rosa
Scarpa, Eugenia
Schak, Antonia
Schicht, Costanza
Schira, Margherita
Schmitt, Cornelia
Schneider, Karoline
Schodel, Rozalie
Schoen-René, Anna E.
Schröter, Maria Henriette
Seguin, Elizabeth
Seiler, Emma
Sepúlveda, María Luisa

Seroen, Berthe
Sessi, Anna Maria
Sessi, Imperatrice
Sessi, Maria Teresa
Sirmen, Maddalena Laura
Smith, Julia
Söderman, Ingalill
Söderman, Tova
Stanislaus, Fanny
Stavenhagen, Agnes
Steele, Mary Sarah
Stolz, Fanny
Strozzi, Barbara
Stucevski, Julia
Sumac, Yma
Szegö, Julia
Thomán, Valerie
Thybo, Kerstin
Tibaldi, Rosa
Tognoli Verni, Antonia
Tomášek, Jaromíra
Tomeoni, Irene
Trebelli, Antoinette
Tree, Ellen
Ulrica, Friederica Louise
Valesi, Anna
Valesi, Crescentia
Valesi, Magdalena
Valesi, Thekla
Van Barentzen, Aline
Vanoni, Ornella
Vanzo, Anna
Verni, Mariå
Verovio, Verovia
Vestris, Maria Caterina
  Violante
Vorobiev, Avdotia
Vyaltzeva, Anastasiya
  Dimitriyevna
Wallace, Eliza
Walter, Juliane
Walter, Minna
Ward, Clementine
Ward, Eliza A.
Weber, Carolina
Weber, Maria Josepha
Weber, Maria Sophie
Weber-Bell, Susanne
Weinhold, Elisabeth
Wend, Flore
Wendling, Dorothea (II)
Wendling, Elisabeth Augusta (I)
Westenholz, Barbara Lucietta

Fricemelica
Westenholz, Eleonore Sophia
  Maria
Williams, Anne
Willmann, (Anna Maria Anto-
  netta) Marianne
Woffington, Margaret
Wolzogen, Elsa Laura
Woodyatt, Emily
Wranitzky, Anna Katharina
Young, Esther
Zandonai, Tarquinia
Zinck, Susanne Elisabeth
Zuccari, Francesca

SOPRANOS

Abarbanell, Lina
Abbott, Emma
Abegg, Mrs.
Abendroth, Irene
Abott (Abbott), Bessie Pickens
Abrams, Harriet
Achsel, Wanda
Achté, Emmy
Ackté, Aïno
Adami Corradetti, Iris
Adams, Suzanne
Adani, Mariella
Addison, Adele
Ader, Rose
Adini (Adiny), Ada
Agai, Karola
Agostinelli Quiroli, Adelina
Agricola, Benedetta Emilia
Agujari (Ajugari), Lucrezia
Aimaro, Lina
Alarie, Pierrette
Alban-Wilk, Judith
Albanese, Licia
Albani, Emma
Alberghetti, Anna Maria
Albertini-Baucardé, Augusta
Alda, Frances
Aldighieri, Maria
Aldrich, Mariska
Alemán, Fedora
Allegranti, Teresa Maddalena
Allen, Mildred
Alpar, Gitta
Alsen, Elsa
Alsop, Ada
Alten, Bella

Altman, Karen
Amara, Lucine
Ambreville, Anna Maria Lodovica
  d'
Ambreville, Rosa Teresa Giovanna
  Lodovica d'
Ambrose, Mrs.
Ambrož (Ambrosch), Wilhelmine
Ameling, Elly
Amicis (Buonsollazzi), Anna
  Lucia de
Amiet, Doris
Amstad, Marietta
Amstad, Martha
Anastasi Pozzoni, Antonietta
Andreozzi, Anna
Andriessen, Pelagie
Angeles, Maria Morales de los
Angelici, Marta
Angelo, Gianna d'
Angerer, Margit
Anitúa, Fanny
Antoine, Josephine
Antti, Aune
Arangi-Lombardi, Giannina
Arkel, Teresa
Armhold, Adelheid
Armstrong, Karen
Arne, Cecilia
Arne, Elizabeth
Arnold, Irmgard
Arnoldson, Sigrid
Arnould, Madeleine Sophie
Arral, Blanche
Arroyo, Martina
Artner, Josephine von
Artôt de Padilla, Lola
Ashton, Gertrude Cave-
Astrua, Giovanna
Attwood, Martha
Austral, Florence Mary
Averino, Olga
Aylward, Gertrude
Ayton, Fanny
Baber, Miss Colbourne
Bäumer, Margaret
Bahr-Mildenburg, Anna
Baillie, Isobel
Baldanza, Romana
Baldassare-Tedeschi, Giuseppina
Balducci, Maria
Balfe, Lina
Balfe, Victoire

Balguerìe, Suzanne Madeleine
Bampton, Rose E.
Bandin, Sofìa
Bandrowska-Turska, Ewa
Banti, Brigitta
Barabas, Sari
Barbany, Marìa Rosa
Barbato, Elisabetta
Barbieri-Nini, Marianna
Barilli, Marianna Bondini
Barlow, Klara
Barrera, Giulia
Barrientos, Marìa
Barsova, Valeria Vladimirovna
Bartolomasi, Valentina
Basabilbaso de Catelin,
  Henriette
Basilier-Magelssen, Ida
Bassett, Karolyn Wells
Bates, Sarah
Bathori, Jane
Bau Bonaplata, Carmen
Bauermeister, Mathilde
Bayan, Daria
Beardslee, Bethany
Beaujon, Marise
Beeth, Lola
Begnis, Giuseppina Ronzi de
Beilke, Irma Käthe Else
Bellincioni, Bianca
Bellincioni, Gamma Cesira
  Matilda
Belling, Susan
Belmas, Xenia
Benda, Anna Franciska
Bendazzi, Ernestina
Bendazzi, Luigia
Benini, Anna
Ben-Sedira, Leila
Benti Bulgarelli, Marianna
Benza Nagy, Ida
Benzell, Mimi
Beralta, -----
Berberian, Cathy
Bergé, Laure
Berger, Erna
Berlendi, Livia
Bernard, Annabelle
Bernasconi, Antonia Wagele
Berthon, Mareille
Bertinotti-Radicati, Teresa
Bettendorf, Emmy
Bialkiewicz de Langeron, Irena

Bianchi, Jane
Bianchi, Valentine
Bianchi Charitas, Bianca
Billington, Elizabeth
Bindernagel, Gertrude
Birch, Charlotte Ann
Birch, Eliza Ann
Bishop, Adelaide
Bishop, Ann(a)
Bjoner, Ingrid
Blaes, Elisa
Bland, Elsa
Bland, Maria Theresa Catherine
Blauvelt, Lillian Evans
Blegen, Judith
Blume, Bianka
Blyth, May
Boatright, Helen
Boccabadati, Luigia
Boccabadati Carignani, Virginia
Boccabadati Varesi, Elena
Boccolini, Ebe
Bodanya, Natalie
Böhm Cartellieri, Elisabeth
Boerner, Charlotte
Bogard, Carole
Bokor, Margit
Bolska, Adelaida Yulianovna
Bolton, Eliza
Bolton, Mary Catherine
Boninsegna, Celestina
Bonwick, Miss
Borelli Angelini, Medea
Borghi-Mamo, Erminia
Bori, Lucrezia
Borkh, Inge
Boronat, Olimpia
Boschetti, Signora Mengis
Bosetti, Hermine
Bosio, Angiolina
Boué, Géorgi
Boulanger, Marie Julie
Bovy, Vina
Bozzi Lucca, Irma
Brambilla, Amalia
Brambilla, Giuseppina
Brambilla, Teresa
Brambilla, Teresa (Mrs. Amil-
  care Ponchielli)
Brancato, Rosemarie
Brandt-Forster, Ellen
Braun, Helena
Bréjean-Silver, Georgette

Brent, Charlotte
Brereton, Sarah
Bréval, Lucienne
Briem, Tilla
Brighenti, Maria
Brinkerhoff, Clara M.
Broggini, Cesy
Bronskaja, Eugenia
Brooks, Patricia
Brothier, Yvonne
Brouwenstijn, Gré
Bruna-Rasa, Lina
Bruno, Joanna
Bryhn-Langaard, Borghild
Buchardo, Brigida
Buckel, Ursula
Buckman, Rosina
Bürde-Ney, Jenny
Bugg, Madeleine
Bunlet, Marcelle
Burguet Díaz, Iris Zenaida
Burke, Hilda
Burns, Georgina
Burzio, Eugenia
Butler, Joan
Caballé, Montserrat
Cabel (Cabu), Marie Josephe
Callas, Maria Meneghini
Calori (Calari), Angiola
Calvé, Rosa-Noémie-Emma
Campbell, Ellen
Campi, Antonia
Campiña, Fidela
Camporese, Violante
Campredon, Jeanne
Candeille (Simons), Amélie-
  Julie
Caniglia, Maria
Cannabich, Josephine
Cantelo, April
Cappelletti, Theresa Poggi
Capsir-Tanzi, Mercedes
Caracciolo, Juanita
Caradori-Allan, Maria Caterina
  Rosalbina
Carbone Rossini, Maria
Carelli, Emma
Carena, Maria
Carew, Miss
Caron, Rose Lucille
Carosio, Margherita
Carracciolo, Juanita
Carré, Marguerite

Carrera, Avelina
Carroll, Joan
Carteri, Rosanna
Carvalho, Caroline
Casarini, Signora
Casarini, Domenica
Case, Anna
Castellan, Jeanne Anaïs
Catalani, Angelica
Catley, Gwen
Cavalieri, Katharina
Cavalli, Floriana
Cavan, Marie
Cavelti, Elsa
Cebotari, Maria
Cerquetti, Anita
Cervi Caroli, Ersilde
Cesbron-Viseur, Suzanne
Chalabala, Běla
Chalia, Rosalia
Chenal, Marthe
Cigna, Gina
Clairbert, Clara
Claire, Marion
Cobelli, Giuseppina
Coelho, Olga Praguer
Coertse, Mimi
Colbran, Isabella Ángela
Cole, Blanche ·
Cole, Charlotte
Collier, Joan
Collier, Marie Elisabeth
Colonne, Eugénie Elise
Colonnese, Elvira
Concato, Augusta
Conner, Nadine
Conrad, Barbara Smith
Corona, Leonora
Correia, Arminda
Corri, Ghita
Corri, Rosálie
Corridori, Lucia
Corsi, Emilia
Cortesi, Adelaide
Costa, Mary
Coward, Hilda
Cowper, Miss
Crader, Jeannine
Craft, Marcella
Crespin, Régina
Cristoforeanu, Florica
Cross, Joan
Crouch, Anna Maria

Cruvelli, Johanne Sophie
  Charlotte
Cruz-Romo, Gilda
Cunitz, Maud
Curtin, Phyllis
Curtis-Verna, Mary
Cuzzoni (Catzoni), Francesca
Dabadie, Zulmé
Dalla-Rizza, Gilda
Dal Monte, Toti
Damoreau, Laure Cinthie
Danco, Suzanne
D'Angeri, Anna
Danzi, Margarete
Da Ponte, Giulia
Darbo, Erica
Darclée, Hariclea
Davelli, Marthe
Davies, Cecilia
Davies, Clara
Davies, Margaret
Davies, Mary
Davies, Ruth
Davis, Agnes
Davis, Ellabelle
Davrath, Netania
Davy, Gloria
De Begnis, Rita
Debicka, Hedwig von
De Blasis, Virginia
Debogis, Marie Louise
De Cecco, Disma
De Gambarini, Elisabetta
De Giuli Borsi, Teresa
Del Campo, Sofia
Della Casa-Debeljevic, Lisa
Delmas, Solange
De los Angeles, Victoria
De Lys, Edith
Demeur, Anne Arsène
Demougeot, Marcella
Denera, Erna
Denya, Marcelle
De Pasquali, Bernice
Dernesch, Helga
Derschniskaya, Xenia
Dessoir, Susanne
Destinn, Emmy
Devriès, Fidès
Devriès, Jeanne
De Vries, Rosa van Os
Dibdin, Isabelle Perkins
Dickons (Dickens), Maria

Dickson, Muriel
Dieman, Ursula Van
Dietrich, Marie
Diez, Sophie
Dingelstedt, Jenny
Dirkens, Annie
Dobbs, Mattiwilda
Domaninská, Libuše
Donadio, Bianca
Donalda, Pauline
Donath, Helen
Dorus-Gras, Julie-Aimée-Josèphe
Dosia, Elen
Dow, Dorothy
Dowiakowska, Karolina
Dragonette, Jessica
Dufau, Jenny
Dumesnil, Suzanne
Duparc, Elizabeth
Durand, Marie
Duranstanti, Margherita
Dusseau, Jeanne
Dustmann, Marie Luise
Dux, Claire
Dvořáková, Ludmila
Dyer, Lorely
Eadie, Noël
Eames, Emma Hayden
Easton, Florence Gertrude
Ebel-Wilde, Minna
Ebers, Clara
Eberwein, Henriette
Edvina, Marie Louise Lucienne
  Juliette Martin
Edwards, Philippine
Egerton, Grace
Eggerth, Marta
Ehrenberg, Eleanora
Eipperle, Trude
Ekman, Ida
Ellinger, Désirée
Elliott, Carlotta
Elliott, Victoria
El-Tour, Anna
Enck-Gottschall, Liselotte
Endich, Saramae
Engle, Marie
Estcott, Lucy
Fabris, Amanda
Faccio, Chiarina
Fahberg, Antonio
Fahrni, Helene
Falchi, Cortini Zaira

Falcon, Marie-Cornélie
Farley, Carole
Farneti, Maria
Farrar, Geraldine
Farrell, Eileen
Fassbáender, Zdenka
Faull, Ellen
Faure, Constance Caroline
  Lefebvre
Favero, Mafalda
Fay, Maude
Féart, Rose
Fel, Marie
Felbermayer, Annie
Fenton, Lavinia
Féraldy, Germaine
Ferlotti, Giuseppina
Ferlotti, Santina
Ferni, Carolina
Ferni, Vincenzina
Ferni Germano, Virginia
Ferrani, Cesira
Feuge, Elisabeth
Feuge-Gleiss, Emile
Field-Hyde, Margaret
Figner-Gerard, Lidia
  Nikolaievna
Fillunger, Marie
Fineschi, Onelia
Finneberg, Laelia
Finzi-Magrini, Giuseppina
Fioretti Ciampoli, Elena
Fisher, Susanne
Fisher, Sylvia
Fitziu, Anna
Flagstad, Kirsten Malfrid
Fleischer, Editha
Fleischer-Edel, Katharina
Flesch, Ella
Flinn, Kate
Flodin, Adée
Florence, Amy
Florence, Evangeline
Flower, Eliza
Fodor-Mainvielle, Joséphine
Foerstel, Gertrude
Foerstrová-Lautererová, Berta
Fohström-Rode, Alma
Fornia-Labey, Rita
Forst, Grete
Forti, Helena
Fossa, Amalia
Foster, Megan

Francillo-Kaufmann, Hedwig
Frasi, Giulia
Frazzoni, Gigliola
Frederiksen, Tenna
Frege, Livia
Freitas, Violeta Coelho Netto de
Fremstad, Anna Augusta Olivia
Freni, Mirella
Freund, Marya
Frezzolini, Erminia
Fricci, Antonietta
Friche, Claire Alexandrine
Friderici-Jakowicka, Teodozja
Friedländer, Thekla
Friedrich, Elisabeth
Frijsh, Povla
Frind, Annie
Fröhlich, Josephine
Fröhlich, Maria Anna
Frost, Beatrice
Fuchs, Marta
Fuchs, Sibylle Ursula
Fürsch-Madi, Emmy
Gabbi, Adalgisa
Gabbi, Leonilde
Gabrieli, Adriana
Gabrielli, Caterina
Gadski, Johanna Emilia Agnes
Gagliardi, Cecilia
Gail, Edmée Sophie
Gall (Galle), Yvonne Irma
Galletti-Gianoli, Isabella
Galli-Campi, Amri
Galli-Curci, Amelita
Gallignani-Bernau, Chiara
Galvany, Fanny Maria
Galvany, Maria
Galvany, Marisa
Gambell, Doris
García, Eugénie
Garden, Mary
Garmo, Tilly de
Garrison, Mabel
Gassier, Josefa
Gates, Lucy
Gatta, Dora
Gatti, Gabriella
Gauthier, Eva
Gay, Maria
Gayer, Catherine
Gaylord, Julia
Gazzaniga Malaspina Albites,
  Marietta

Geistinger, Marie Charlotte
  Cäcilia
Gentile, Maria
Gentner-Fischer, Else
Gerhart, Maria
Gerl, Barbara
Gerster, Etelka
Geszty, Sylvia
Giachetti, Rina
Giannini, Dusolina
Giebel, Agnes
Gilmour, Doris Godson
Ginster, Ria
Giovannoni Zacchi, Ginevra
Girardeau, Isabella
Girelli Anguillar, Maria
  Antonia
Giudice, Maria
Giuliani, Cecilia
Gjungjenac, Zlata
Gladkowska, Konstancja
Glen, Annie
Gluck, Alma
Godoy, Maria Lúcia
Görlin, Helga Maria
Goltz, Christel
Gomes, Carmen
Gordon, Dorothy
Gottlieb, Anna
Gottlieb, Henriette
Graddon, Miss
Graham, Mary Ann
Grandi, Margherita
Granfelt, (Lillian) Hanna von
Grassi, Cecilia
Grenville, Lillian
Grever, Maria
Grey, Madeleine
Grieg, Nina
Grisi, Giulia
Grist, Reri
Grob-Prandl, Gertrud
Grossi, Carlotta
Groves, Olive
Grümmer, Elisabeth
Grün, Frederike
Gruhn, Nora
Gubrud, Irene
Güden, Hilde
Günther, Mizzi
Guerrina, Adriana
Gugliemetti, Anna-Maria
Guilford, Nanette

Guilleaume, Margot
Gulbranson, Ellen
Gustafson, Lillian
Gyurkovics, Mária
Hadrabova, Eva
Hafgren-Dinkela, Lilly Johanna
  Maria
Halir, Theresa
Hallstein, Ingeborg
Halstead, Margaret
Halvorsen, Haldis
Hamlin, Mary
Hammond, Joan Hood
Hampton, Hope
Hanfstängel, Marie
Harper, Heather
Harriers-Wippern, Louise
Harsanyi, Janice
Harshaw, Margaret
Hartmann, Emma Sophie Amalie
Hasselt-Barth, Anna Maria
  Wilhelmine
Hataš (Hattasch), Anna Františka
Hatchard, Carolyn
Hatto, Jeanne
Hauk (Hauck), Minnie
Hayden, Ethyl
Haydn, Maria Magdalena
Hayes, Catherine
Haynes, Elizabeth
Hebbe, Signe Amanda Georgina
Hegar, Valerie
Héglon, Meyriane
Heidersbuch, Käthe
Heilbron, Marie
Heilbronner, Rose
Heim, Melitta
Heinefetter, Sabina
Helbing, Maria
Heldy, Fanny
Helletsgrüber, Luise
Helm-Sbisá, Anny
Hempel, Frieda
Henders, Harriet
Hendrickx-Vermeulen, Marie
  Louise
Henschel, Helen
Henschel, Lillian June
Hensler, Elise
Herbert, Therese
Hersee, Rose
Hertzberg-Beyron, Olga Brita
  Lovisa

Herwig, Käthe
Herzog, Colette
Herzog, Emilie
Hesse-Lilienberg, Davida
  Augusta
Hidalgo, Elvira de
Hiedler, Ida
Hilgermann, Laura
Hillebrecht, Hildegard
Hissem-DeMoss, Mary
Hitzelberger, Kunigunde
Hitzelberger, Sabina
Hoare, Margaret
Hobson, Edna
Hollweg, Ilse
Holm, Renate
Hooke, Emelie
Horáková, Ota
Houston, Elsie
Hüni-Mihacsek, Felicie
Huguet de Arnold, Josephina
Hurley, Laurel
Hussa, Maria
Hutchinson, Cecilia Mary
Hviid, Mimi
Ilitsch, Daniza
L'Incognita (Violet Mount)
Inverarity, Eliza
Iracema-Brügelmann, Hedy
Isaac, Adèle
Isidor, Rosina
Isori, Ida
Ivogün, Maria
Janacopulos, Vera
Janku, Hana
Janowitz, Gundula
Januschowsky-Neuendorff,
  Georgine von
Jarecki, Louise
Järnefelt-Palmgren, Maikki
Jasper, Bella
Jepson, Helen
Jeritza, Maria
Jessner, Irene
Joachim, Amalie
Joachim, Irene
Joesten, Aga
Joki, Fritzi
Jones, Gwyneth
Joran, Pauline
Jordan, Irene
Juch, Emma
Jung, Doris

Jungkurth, Hedwig
Jurinac, Sena
Jurjewskaya, Zinaida
Juyol, Suzanne
Kainz, Marianne Katharina
  Theresia
Kainz, Marie Holland
Kappel, Gertrude
Kaschowska, Felice
Katulskaja, Jelena Klimentjewna
Kearton, Annie
Keeley, Mary Anne
Kellogg, Clara Louise
Kemble, Adelaide
Kemp, Angela Barbara
Kennedy, Helen
Kennedy, Lizzie
Kern, Adele
Kinlock, Eliza
Kirschstein, Lenore
Kirsten, Dorothy
Kiurina, Berta
Klafsky, Katharina
Kline, Olive
Kniplová, Nadežda
Kočova, Míla
Köster, Luise
Köth, Erika
Kolassi, Irma
Konetzni, Anny
Korjus, Miliza
Korolewicz-Waydowa, Janina
Korsoff, Lucette
Koshetz, Nina Pavlova
Kouznetzoff, Maria Nicolaïevna
Krall, Heidi
Krauss, (Marie) Gabrielle
Krebs, Aloysia
Kronold, Selma
Krull, Annie
Kruszelnicka, Salomea
Kufferath, Antonia
Kupfer-Berger, Ludmilla
Kupper, Annelies Gabriele
Kurenko, Maria
Kurt, Melanie
Kurz, Selma
Kutschera, Elsa
Kuula, Alma
Kuza, Valentina Ivanova
Labia, Fausta
Labia, Maria
La Grange, Anna Caroline de

Lalande, Henriette Clémentine
L'Allemand, Pauline
Lammers, Gerda
Lancia, Florence
Landouzy, Lise
Lang, Regina
Larkcom, Charlotte Agnes
Larrivée, Marie-Jeanne
Larsén-Todsen, Nanny
Lashanska, Hulda
Laszló, Magda
Laute-Brun, Antoinette
Lavrovska, Elisaveta Andreyevna
Lawrence, Marjorie
Lear, Evelyn
Lebrun, Franziska
Lee, Ella
Leffler-Bruckard, Martha
Lehmann, Lilli
Lehmann, Liza
Lehmann, Lotte
Lehmann, Marie
Leider, Frida
Leidy, Helen
Leigh, Adele
Leisinger, Elisabeth
Lejeune, Gabrielle
Le Maure, Catherine Nicole
Lemmens, Helen
Lemnitz, Tiana
Leonard, Lotte
L'Épine, Francesca Margherita
   de
Le Rochois, Marthe
Levasseur, Rosalie
Lewis, Brenda
Lewis, Mary
Licette, Miriam
Liebling, Estelle
Ligabue, Ilva
Liljeblad, Ingeborg
Lincoln, Marianne
Lind, Jenny
Lindermeyer, Elisabeth
Lindsay, Julia
Linko-Malmio, Liisa
Linley, Eliza(beth) Ann
Linley, Maria
Linley, Mary
Lipkovska, Lydia Yakovlevna
Lipp, Wilma
Lissmann, Anna Marie
Litta, Marie

Litvinne, Félia Vasilyevna
Ljungberg, Göta Albertina
Llacer, Maria
Löwe, Johanna Sophie
Loewe, Sophie
Loose, Emmy
Lorengar, Pilar
Lotti della Santa, Marcella
Løveberg, Aase
Luart, Emma
Lubin, Germaine Léontine
   Angélique
Lucas, Helen
Lucca, Pauline
Lukomska, Halina
Lussan, Zélie de
Lyne, Felice
McArden, Joy
Macbeth, Florence
Macchi, Maria de
McCormic, Mary
MacDonald, Jeanette
Macintyre, Margaret
McLachlan, Jessie Niven
Makas, Maxine
Malibran, Maria Felicità
Malkin, Beata
Mallinger, Mathilde
Malten, Therese
Mana-Zucca
Mandac, Evelyn
Mandikian, Arda
Manfredini Guarmanni, Elisabetta
Manski, Dorothée
Mantelli, Eugenia
Mara, Gertrud Elisabeth
Marcel, Lucille
Marchesi de Castrone, Blanche
Marchisio, Carlotta
Marengo, Isabel
Marher, Elfriede
Maria-Petris, Jolanda di
Mariani Masi, Maddalena
Marimon, Marie
Mario, Queena
Mark, Paula
Marriott, Annie Augusta
Marsh, Jane
Marsh, Lucy Isabelle
Marshall, Lois
Martinis, Carla
Martino, Adriana
Mason, Edith Barnes

Massary, Fritzi
Materna, Amalie
Materna, Hedwig
Mathis, Edith
Matthews, Julia
Maturová, Růžena
Matzenauer, Margarete
Maubourg-Goffaux, Jeanne
Maupin, Madame
Mayer, Marie
Mayerhofer, Elfie
Maynor, Dorothy
Mazzoleni, Ester
Mei-Figner, Medea Ivanovna
Melander, Stina Britt
Melba, Nellie
Melis, Carmen
Menotti, Tatiana
Meo, Cléonine de
Merrem-Nikisch, Grete
Micelli, Caterina
Michaeli, Louise
Michailowa, Maria
Michalsky, Anne
Micheau, Janine
Midgley, Henrietta
Mielke, Antonia
Miglietti, Adrienne
Milanov, Zinka
Milde, Rosa
Milder-Hauptmann, Pauline Anna
Mildmay, Audrey
Mingotti, Regina Caterina
Mitchell, Frederica
Miura, Tamaki
Mödl, Martha
Moffo, Anna
Moir, Eleanor
Molesworth, Lady
Monbelli, Marie
Monroe, Lucy
Moody, Fanny
Moody, Jacquelynne
Moore, Bertha
Moore, Grace
Moran, Dora
Moran-Olden, Fanny
Morandi, Rosa
Morelli, Adelina
Morena, Berta
Morgana, Nina
Morichelli-Bosello, Anna
Morison, Elsie

Morris, Margaret
Moscisca, Maria
Moulton, Dorothy
Mountain, Sarah
Mravina, Evgenia Konstantinovna
Müller, Maria
Müller, Therese
Mullen, Adelaide
Munday, Mrs.
Munsel, Patrice Beverly
Murska, Ilma de
Musin, Annie Louise
Muszely, Melitta
Muzio, Claudia
Naldi, Carolina
Namara, Marguerite
Nassyrova, Khalima
Nast, Minnie
Nau, Maria Dolores Benedicta
    Josefina
Naylor, Ruth Winifred
Neblett, Carol
Nelli, Herva
Nemeth, Maria
Nespoulos, Marthe
Nevada, Emma
Nevada, Mignon Mathilde Marie
Neway, Patricia
Newcombe, Ethel
Newcombe, Georgeanne
Newton, Adelaide
Nezadal, Maria
Neždanova, Antonida
Nicholls, Agnes
Nickel, Matilda
Nielsen, Alice
Nielsen, Flora
Niemelä, Tii
Niessen-Stone, Matja von
Nilsson, Kristina
Nilsson, Märta Birgit
Niska, Maralin
Nissen-Saloman, Henriette
Noni, Alda
Noordewier-Reddingius, Aaltje
Nordica, Lillian
Noréna, (Kaja) Eidé
Norledge, Annie E.
Norman, Jesseye
Novello, Clara Anastasia
Novello, Mary Sabilla
Novotná, Jarmila
Oehme-Foerster, Elsa

Ohms, Elisabeth
Oldmixon, Lady
Olejnitschenko, Galina
Olénine d'Alheim, Marie
Olivero, Magda
Oltrabella, Augusta
Oravez, Edith
Orgeni, Aglaja
Ortmann, Carolyn
Ortolani, Angelica
Osborn-Hannah, Jane
Osgood, Emma Aline
Osman, Fanny Wilson
Osten, Eva von der
Otto, Lisa
Otto, Melitta
Pacetti, Iva
Pacini, Regina
Pagliughi, Lina
Palazzesi, Matilde
Palmer, Jeanne
Pampanini, Rosetta
Pandolfini, Angelica
Pantaleoni, Romilda
Pappenheim, Eugenie
Parepa-Rosa, Euphrosyne
Pareto, Graziella
Parkina (Elizabeth Parkinson)
Parodi, Teresa
Pasini, Camilla
Pasini, Laura
Pasini, Lina
Pasta, Giuditta
Paton, Mary Ann
Patterson, Ada
Patti, Adelina
Patti, Carlotta
Patti, Caterina Chiesa
Pauly, Rosa
Peltenburg, Mia
Penna, Catherine
Penna, Catherine Louisa
Peralta, Angela
Peralta, Frances
Perea Labia, Gianna
Perras, Margherita
Persiani, Fanny
Peschka-Leutner, Minna
Peters, Roberta
Petina, Irra
Petrella, Clara
Petrella, Oliva
Petrelli

Pfeil, Anna Doris
Piccolomini, Maria
Piercy, Rosetta
Pierozyńska, Franciszka
Pilarczyk, Helga Katharina
Pilou, Jeannette
Piltti, Lea Maire
Pinkert, Regina
Pinto, Amelia
Pisaroni, Benedetta Rosamunda
Plaichinger, Thila
Plantada, Mercedes
Pobbe, Marcella
Podvalova, Marie
Poli Randaccio, Ernestina
Pollak, Anna
Ponchard, Marie Sophie
Pons, Lily
Ponselle, Rosa
Ponte, Carlotta Maironi da
Popp, Lucia
Povey, Miss
Powell, Alma Webster
Powers, Marie
Prevosti, Franceschina
Price, Leontyne
Pruckner, Karoline
Pütz, Ruth-Margaret
Pyne, Louisa Fanny
Quartararo, Florence
Radecke, Luise Moore
Raineri-Marini, Antonia
Rainforth, Elizabeth
Raisa, Rosa
Raisbeck, Rosina
Rajdl, Maria
Rakowska, Elena
Ranczak, Hildegard
Rappold, Marie
Rasa, Lina Bruna
Raskin, Judith
Ratti, Eugenia
Rautawaara, (Terttu) Aulikki
Redell, Emma
Reeves, Emma
Reggiani, Hilde
Reichardt, Luise
Reicher-Kindermann, Hedwig
Reiner, Catherine
Reinhardt, Delia
Reining, Maria
Rénard, Marie
Resnik, Regina

Reszke, Josephine de
Retchitzka, Basia
Rethberg, Elisabeth
Réthy, Ester
Reuss-Belce, Luise
Révy, Aurelie
Rhodes, Jane
Rider-Kelsey, Corinne
Ries, Anna Maria
Rigal, Delia
Righini, Anna Maria
Rio, Anita
Ritchie, Margaret Willard
Ritter-Ciampi, Gabrielle
Rivera, Graciela
Rivoli, Ludwika
Rivoli, Paulina
Rizzieri, Elena
Rizzoli, Bruna
Roberti, Margherita
Robertson, Sophie Maria
Robin, Mado
Robinson, Anastasia
Robinson, Faye
Robinson, Gail
Roeseler, Marcella
Rogers, Clara Kathleen
Rogers, Della
Rogner, Eva Maria
Rolandt, Hedwig
Roman, Stella
Romberg, Angelica
Romelli, Lina
Romer, Annie
Romer, Emma
Roosevelt, Emily
Roselle, Anne
Ross, Elinor
Rosza, Anna
Rothenberger, Anneliese
Rousselois, Marie Wilhelmine
Roze, Marie Hippolyte
Rubio, Consuelo
Rudersdorff, Hermine
Rünger, Gertrude
Rüsche-Endorf, Cäcilie
Runge, Gertrud
Russ, Giannina
Russell, Ella
Russell, Lillian
Russell, Louise
Ruszkowska, Elena
Rysanek, Leonie

Rysanek, Lotte
Rywacka, Ludwika
Sachse-Hofmeister, Anna
Sack, Erna Dorothea
Sailer, Friederike
Saint-Aubin, Alexandrine
Saint-Aubin, Anne-Cécile-Dorlise
Saint-Aubin, Jeanne-Charlotte
Saint-Huberty, Antoinette Cécile
Salmon, Eliza
Salter, Mary Elizabeth
Saltzmann-Stevens, Minnie
Salvatini, Mafalda
Salvi, Margherita
Salvini Donatelli, Fanny
Samuell, Clara
Sanchioni, Nunu
Sanden, Aline
Sanderson, Lillian
Sanderson, Sibyl
Sands, Mollie
Santaolalla, Marta
Santley, Edith
Santley, Gertrude
Saporiti, Teresa
Saraceni, Adelaide
Sardi, Dorotea
Sari, Ada
Sass, Marie-Constance
Saunders, Arlene
Saville, Frances
Sayão, Bidú
Scacciati, Bianca
Schech, Marianne
Schechner-Waagen, Anna
Scheff, Fritzi
Scheider, May
Scheidt, Selma vom
Scheppan, Hilde
Scherz-Meister, Elsa
Scheyer, Gerda
Schick, Margarete Luise
Schimon, Anna
Schlamme, Martha
Schlemm, Anny
Schlüter, Erna
Schneider, Hortense Caroline
  Jeanne
Schneider, Jacklyn
Schnorr von Carolsfeld, Malvina
Schoberlechner, Sophie
Schöne, Lotte
Schröder-Devrient, Wilhelmine

Schröter, Corona Elisabeth
  Wilhelmine
Schubert, Georgine
Schubert, Maschinka
Schuch, Clementine Proska
Schuch, Liesel von
Schumann, Elisabeth
Schwaiger, Rosl
Schwarz, Vera
Schwarzkopf, Elisabeth
Schwindel, Anna Christina
Schymberg, Hjördis Gunborg
Scio, Julie-Angélique
Sciutti, Graziella
Scotto, Renata
Scovotti, Jeanette
Scuderi, Sara
Sebald, Amalie
Sebald, Auguste
Second, Mary
Sedlmair, Sophie
Seeböck, Charlotte von
Seefried, Irmgard
Séguin, Ann
Seidl-Kraus, Auguste
Seinemeyer, Meta
Sembrich, Marcella
Senger-Bettaque, Katharina
Sessi, Marianna
Sheridan, Margaret
Sherrington, Jose
Sherwin, Amy
Shirreff, Jane
Shuard, Amy
Shuttleworth, Barbara
Siebert, Dorothea
Siems, Margarethe
Silja, Anja
Silk, Dorothy
Sills, Beverly
Singer, Teresina
Sinico, Clarice
Skilondz, Adelaide von
Sladen, Victoria
Slobodskaya, Oda
Smith, Mabel
Smolenskaya, Eugenia
Söderman, Greta Lisa
Soederstroem, Elisabeth
Soldene, Emily
Somigli, Franca
Sontag, Henriette
Souez, Ina

Spani, Hina
Speaks, Margaret
Spech Salvi, Adelina
Spennert, Mary Helena
Spletter, Carla
Spoonenberg, Erna
Squire, Emily
Stader, Maria
Stahlman, Sylvia
Stanley, Helen
Steber, Eleanor
Steele, Janet
Stefani, Eleonora
Stefani, Karolina
Steffak, Hanny
Stehle, Sophie
Stehle-Garbin, Adelina
Steingruber, Ilona
Stella, Antonietta
Stenhammar, Fredrika
Stephens, Catherine
Stewart, Nellie
Stich-Randall, Teresa
Stiles-Allen, Lilian
Stockhausen, Margarete
Stokes, Nancy
Stolz, Lidia
Stolz, Teresa
Stolzenberg, Hertha
Storace, Anna Selina
Storchio, Rosina
Storti, Elisa Luigia
Stoska, Polyna
Strada, Anna Maria
Stralia, Elsa
Stratas, Teresa
Strauss, Pauline
Streich, Rita
Strepponi, Clelia Maria Josepha
Strinasacchi, Teresa
Strong, Susan
Strozzi, Violetta de
Stuart, Lía
Stuckenschmidt, Margot
Stückgold, Grete
Stüzner, Elisa
Sucher, Rosa
Suddaby, Elsie
Suliotis, Elena
Sundelius, Marie
Sunderland, Susan
Sutherland, Joan
Sutter, Anna

Svicher, Isabella
Sylva, Marguerite Alice
   Helene Smith
Szarbo, Luisa
Szarewicz, Helena
Sztojanovits, Edith
Sztojanovits, Lily
Tadolini, Eugenia
Tagliana, Emilia
Talley, Marion
Tassinari, Domenica
Tassopulos, Anna
Tauberová, Maria
Tcherkasskaya, Marianna
   Borisovna
Tebaldi, Renata
Tellini, Ines Alfani-
Tentoni, Rosa
Ternina, Milka
Teschemacher, Marguerite
Tess, Guilia
Tetrazzini, Eva
Tetrazzini, Luisa
Teyber, Elisabeth
Teyber, Therese
Teyte, Maggie
Thalberg, Zaré
Theodorini, Elena
Thillon, Sophie Anne
Thirwall, Annie
Thomsen, Marie
Thudichum, Charlotte
Thue, Hildur Fjord
Thursby, Emma Cecilia
Tietjens, Therese Cathline
   Johanna Alexandra
Tikalová, Drahomira
Tofts, Catherine
Torresella, Fanny
Torri, Rosina
Torriani, Ottavia
Tosi, Adelaide
Tourel, Jennie
Tracey, Minnie
Traubel, Helen
Traubman, Sophie
Trentini, Emma
Tréville, Yvonne de
Trial, Marie Jeanne
Trötschel, Elfriede
Trowbridge, Leslie
Trust, Helen Mary
Tubb, Carrie

Tucci, Gabriella
Tuček, Leopoldine
Turner, Eva
Tyler, Veronica
Ucko, Paula
Udovick, Lucille
Ugalde, Delphine
Ugalde, Marguerite
Unger-Sabatier, Karoline
Urbanek, Carolyn
Ursuleac, Viorica
Urusova, Olga
Valda, Giulia
Valente, Benita
Välkki, Anita
Vallandri, Aline
Valleria, Alwina
Vallin, Ninon
Van den Bosch, Betty
Van Dresser, Marcia
Van Zandt, Jennie
Van Zandt, Marie
Van Zanten, Cornelia
Varnay, Ibolyka Astrid Maria
Vartenissian, Shakeh
Vassal, Hanna-Ulrike
Venora, Lei
Vère, Clémentine Duchêne de
Verlet, Alice
Vernon, Dorothy
Villani, Luisa
Vincent, Isabella
Vincent, Johanna Maria
Vincent, Ruth
Vinning, Louisa
Vishnevskaya, Galina
Vivante, Ginevra
Vix, Geneviève
Voggenhuber, Vilma von
Vogl, Therese
Votipka, Thelma
Vulpus, Jutta
Vyvyan, Jennifer
Wagner-Jachmann, Johanna
Ward, Evelyn
Ward, Lily
Ward, (Lucy) Genevieve Teresa
Warenskjold, Dorothy
Warnots, Elly
Warwick, Giulia
Watson, Claire
Waylett, Harriet
Weathers, Felicia

Weber, Maria Aloysia Louise Antonia
Wedekind, Erika
Weed, Marion
Wegner, Walburga
Weidt, Lucy
Weiss, Georgiana Ansell
Weldon, Georgina
Welitsch, Ljuba
Wells, Patricia
Wendling, Dorothea (I)
Wendling, Elisabeth Augusta (II)
Werber, Mia
West, Clara
White, Carolina
Whiting, Virginia
Wichern, Karoline
Wildbrunn, Helene
Wilhelmj, Maria
Wilhorst, Cora de
Willauer, Marguerite
Williams, Anna
Williams, Camilla
Williams, Maria Jane
Willmann, (Maria Anna Magdalena) Caroline
Wilson, Mary Ann
Wilt, Marie
Winston, Jeannie
Winter, Pattie
Winternitz-Dorda, Martha
Wirz-Wyss, Clara
Wise, Patricia
Wissman, Lore
Witkowska, Nadja
Wittich, Marie
Wolff, Henny
Worrell, Marie
Woytowicz, Stefania
Wranitzky, Karoline
Wyckoff, Lou Ann
Wynne, Sarah Edith
Wyss, Sophie
Yarick, Doris
Yavor, Maria
Yaw, Ellen Beach
Yeend, Frances
Young, Isabella
Young, Polly
Zacchi, Rosina
Zadek, Hilde
Zamboni, Maria

Zeani, Virginia
Zepilli, Alice
Zerr, Anna
Ziegler, Anne
Zilli, Emma
Zylis-Gara, Teresa

TEACHERS

See also   piano teachers;
voice teachers

Abel-Struth, Sigrid
Ackland, Jessie Agnes
Alter, Martha
Archer, Violet Balestreri
Arizti, Cecilia
Austin, Florence
Bacewicz, Grazyna
Bache, Constance
Ballou, Esther Williamson
Bang, Maia
Barstow, Vera
Bauer, Marion Eugenie
Baur, Bertha
Behrend, Jeanne
Bicking, Ada Elizabeth
Bilgram, Hedwig
Biltcliffe, Florence
Binet, Jocelyne
Blake, Dorothy Gaynor
Blomfield-Holt, Patricia
Borek, Minuetta
Boucher, Lydia
Boulanger, Nadia Juliette
Boyd, Anne
Branscombe, Gena
Brasseur, Élisabeth
Burchell, H. Louise
Burrowes, Katharine
Bustabo, Guila
Cadzow, Dorothy
Calle, Isabel de la
Campany, Montserrat
Candeille (Simons), Amélie-Julie
Carrington-Thomas, Virginia
Charrat, Janine
Chissell, Joan Olive
Chittenden, Kate Sara
Chladek, Rosalia
Cimaglia-Espinosa, Lía
Couperin, Marguerite-Antoinette
Crozier, Catherine

Cuney-Hare, Maud
Curwen, Annie Jessy
Cuyler, Louise Elvera
Dale, Kathleen
Dancla, Alphonsine-Geneviève-
  Lore
Deacon, Mary Ann
Delle Sedie, Margherita
Delorme, Isabelle
Demarquez, Suzanne
Demessieux, Jeanne
Denéréaz, Marguerite
Desportes, Yvonne Berthe
  Melitta
Dessoff, Margarete
Dianda, Hilda
Dibdin, Mary Anne
Diller, Angela
Dilling, Mildred
Dlugoszewski, Lucia
Donátová, Narcisa
Ehlers, Alice
Ellis, Catherine Joan
Estrella, Blanca
Fabrizio, Margaret
Fahrbach, Henriette
Fennings, Sarah
Feudel, Elfriede Antonie
Fine, Vivian
Foot, Phyllis Margaret
Franchère-Des Rosiers, Roede
  Lima
Fuchs, Lillian
Garuta, Lucija
Gautier, Jeanne
Gerson-Kiwi, Esther Edith
Gibson, Louisa
Gideon, Miriam
Glenn, Mabelle
Gnessin, Eléna Fabianovna
Goossens, Marie Henriette
Goossens, Sidonie
Hansen, Cecilia
Hartland, Lizzie
Hegner, Anna
Hermann, Miina
Hewitt, Helen Margaret
Heyde-Dohrn, Ellinor von der
Holm, Hanya
Holst, Imogen Clare
Hopkins, Louisa
Humphrey, Doris
Hunt, Arabella

Iretskaia, Natalia Alexandrovna
James, Dorothy
Jensen, Wilma
Joy, Geneviève
Kajanus, Lilly (Agnes)
Kazuro-Trombini, Margerita
Keetman, Gunild
Kennedy, Margaret
Kenway, Helen
Kettle, Lizzie
Kirkman, Mrs. Joseph
Knocker, Editha
Kolessa, Chrystia
Korn, Clara Anna
Kwalwasser, Helen
Lafleur, Lucienne
La Hye, Louise Genevieve
Landowska, Wanda
Landowski, Alice-Wanda
Lanner, Katherine
Lavanchy, Magda
Lechner, Irmgard
Lhévinne, Rosina
Ling, Dorothy
Lippincott, Joan
Lissa, Zofia
Liwanowa, Tamara Nikolajewna
Loder, Kate Fanny
Luboschutz, Léa
MacCarthy, Maud
McCollin, Frances
Marlowe, Sylvia
Marzorati, Lucia
Mason, Marilyn
Masson, Elizabeth
Maurice, Paule
Menges, Isolde
Meyer-Baer, Kathi
Milette, Juliette
Millar, Marian
Moodie, Alma
Morgan, Maud
Mounsey, Ann Sheppard
Müller-Hermann, Johanna
Navone-Betti, Carolina
Neeley, Marilyn
Newlin, Dika
Nichols, Marie
Norbury, F. Ethel
Oliveira, Magdala da Gama
Oliveros, Pauline
Page, Kate Stearns
Panum, Hortense

Parlow, Kathleen
Pentland, Barbara
Perry, Julia
Pessl, Yella
Prescott, Oliveria Louisa
Presti, Ida
Rainier, Priaulx
Reis, Claire R.
Renié, Henriette
Rennès, Catharina van
Rey, Louise (I)
Robinson, Edith
Rokseth, Yvonne
Rosa, Alba
Ruegger, Elsa
Rylek-Staňková, Blažena
Sanders, Ellen
Sands, Mollie
Sassòli Ruata, Ada
Schröder, Cornelia
Serato, Cleopatra
Simon, Alicja
Solomon, Mirrie
Spinney, Mattie
Stapleton, Anna Isabella
Storti, Elisa Luigia
Sutherland, Margaret
Sutro, Florence Edith
Swepstone, Edith
Szczepańska, Maria Klementyna
Szöni, Erzsébet
Sztojanovits, Adrienne
Talma, Louise
Tilly, Margaret
Tua, Teresina
Tureck, Rosalyn
Ustvolskaya, Galina Ivanovna
Van den Boorn-Coclet,
  Henriette
Villeneuve, Marie-Louise-Diane
Von Hoff, Elizabeth
Walenn, Dorothea
Ward, Eliza A.
Webster, Clarinda Augusta
West, Lottie
White, Mary Louise
Wichern, Karoline
Wietrowetz, Gabriele
Wood, Mary Louisa
Zambelli, Carlotta
Zumsteeg, Emilie

THEORBIST

See Lutenists

THEORIST

Obigny de Ferrières, Amélie
Alexandrine d'

THERAPISTS

Tilly, Margaret
Weigl, Vally

VIOL PLAYER

Ottey, Sarah

VIOLA PLAYERS

Clark, Florence Durell
Clarke, Rebecca
Copperwheat, Winifred
Dolmetsch, Nathalie
Fuchs, Lillian
Norledge, Annie E.
Phillips, Karen
Scarlatti, Melchiorra Brigida
Sepúlveda, María Luisa
Vretblad, Karin

VIOLA DA GAMBISTS

Baroni, Eleanora
Dolmetsch, Hélène
Dolmetsch, Mabel Johnston
Dolmetsch, Marie
Heinitz, Eva

VIOLA D'AMORE PLAYER

Chaplin, Kate

VIOLINISTS

Abel, Jenny
Ackland, Jeanne Isabel Dorothy
Afferni, Mary
Andrade, Janine
Arányi, Jelly d'
Astruc, Yvonne
Austin, Florence

Bacewicz, Grazyna
Bagdasarjanz, Ursula
Bagdasarjanz-Weiss, Margrit
Bang, Maia
Barns, Ethel
Barstow, Vera
Baylis, Lilian
Bernard, Claire
Binet, Jocelyne
Bobesco, Lola-Anna-Maria
Breuning-Storm, Gunna
Briglia, Antonietta
Buck, Era Marguerite
Bustabo, Guila
Canales, Marta
Carmirelli, Pina
Carter, Mary
Cervera, Montserrat
Chaplin, Kate
Chemet, Réné
Clark, Florence Durell
Clarke, Rebecca
Clench, Leonora
Cserfalvi, Elise
D'Albore, Lilia
Davenport Goertz, Gladys
Delorme, Isabelle
De Vito, Gioconda
Doubleday, Leila
Dubiska, Irena
Dunlop, Isobel
Du Val, Lorraine
Eaton, Sybil Evelyn
Eckhardt-Gramatté, Sophie
  Carmen
Edinger, Christiane
Eissler, Marianne
Fachiri, Adila
Fairless, Margaret
Fennings, Sarah
Ferni, Carolina
Ferni, Vincenzina
Fisher, Charlotte E.
Flissler, Joyce
Folville, Juliette-Eugénie-
  Émilie
Fonden, Olly Folge
Gaudin, Cathérine
Gautier, Jeanne
Geiser-Peyer, Barbara
Gerard, Ruby
Geyer, Steffi
Given, Thelma

Grever, Maria
Grunder, Anne-Marie
Guarnieri, Guglielmina
Haendel, Ida
Hagen, Betty-Jean
Hall, Marie
Hansen, Cecilia
Harrison, Margaret
Harrison, May
Hayward, Marjorie
Hegner, Anna
Hlouňová, Marie
Hull, Frances
Ignatius-Hirvensalo, Anja
Jackson, Leonora
Jaffé, Sophia
Jewson, Mrs. Frederick Augustus
Jodry, Annie-Marie
Joran, Pauline
Jourdan-Morhange, Hélène
Kan, Suna
Kennedy, Daisy
Kersey, Eda
Knocker, Editha
Kubelík, Anita
Kubelík, Ludmila
Kwalwasser, Helen
Laffitte, Lucette
Lautenbacher, Susanne
Lavanchy, Magda
Lavers, Marjorie
Lent, Sylvia
Liivak, Evi
Linz von Kriegner, Marta
List, Carroll
Luboschutz, Léa
MacCarthy, Maud
Macnaghten, Anne Catherine
Marchesi de Castrone, Blanche
Martzy, Johanna
Mead, Olive
Menges, Isolde
Milanollo, Domenica Maria
  Teresa
Milanollo, Maria
Minghetti, Lisa
Mitchell, Viola
Moodie, Alma
Morini, Erica
Neruda, Wilhelmine Maria
  Frantiska
Neveu, Ginette
Nichols, Marie

Norledge, Annie E.
Ottey, Sarah
Paravicini, Signora
Parlow, Kathleen
Pearl, Ruth
Peinemann, Edith
Pernel, Orrea
Piercy, Rosetta
Plunkett, Catherine
Posselt, Ruth
Powell, Maud
Pyne, Zoe
Rainier, Priaulx
Rawlins, Bessie
Rawsthorne, Jessie
Ray, Ruth
Richards, Irene
Roberts, Winifred
Robinson, Edith
Robinson, Winifred
Röntgen, Amanda
Rosa, Alba
Rubinstein, Erna
Salvador, Josefina
Scharwenka, Marianne
Schletterer, Hortensia
Schytte, Frida
Senkrah, Arma Leoretta
Seydel, Irma
Shinner, Emily
Sirmen, Maddalena Laura
Söderman, Karin
Soldat-Roeger, Marie
Spivacke, Caroline
Streicher, Lyubov Lvovna
Strinasacchi, Regina
Stucki, Aida
Stüssi, Else
Tarjus, Blanche
Tas, Helen Teschner
Tedesca, Fernanda
Teysseire-Vuilleumier, Hélène
Thomán, Maria
Tilly, Margaret
Torrá, Celia
Travers, Patricia
Tschachtli, Marie-Madeleine
Tua, Teresina
Umińska, Eugenia
Urso, Camilla
Verocai, Sophie
Voldan, Marie
Vretblad, Karin

Walenn, Dorothea
Wallace, Eliza
Wanne, Kerttu
Ware, Helen
Wasterlain, Viola
Wicks, Camilla
Wietrowetz, Gabriele
Wilkomirska, Wanda
Wilson, Marie
Woycke, Bertha
Woycke, Emily Drechsler
Zentay, Mary
Zöllner, Margarete
Zorian, Olive

VIOLONCELLISTS

Austin, Leily
Butler, Antonia
Casals, Pilar
Chaplin, Mabel
Christiani, Élise
Coetmore, Peers
Croxford, Eileen
Dickson, Joan
Dolmetsch, Hélène
DuPré, Jacqueline
Flachot, Reine
Fletcher, Maud
Garbousova, Raya
Güdel, Irene (Spittler-)
Gurowitsch, Sara
Harraden, Beatrice
Harrison, Beatrice
Heinitz, Eva
Hooton, Florence
James, Helen
Jansen, Cornelia
Kolessa, Chrystia
Laffra, Annie
Lortzing, Rosina
Mukle, May Henrietta
Natola, Aurora
Nelsova, Zara
Nunn, Gertrude
Nyffenegger, Esther
Reiss, Thelma
Ruegger, Elsa
Sampson, Peggie
Semino, Norina
Spencer, Marguerita
Suggia, Guilhermina
Van den Hoven, Cacteau
Walevska, Christine

VOICE TEACHERS

Abbadia, Luigia
Achsel, Wanda
Ader, Rose
Adini (Adiny), Ada
Agostinelli Quiroli, Adelina
Ahnger, Alexandra
Aimaro, Lina
Albani, Emma
Alcock, Merle
Alda, Frances
Allitsen, Emma
Alsen, Elsa
Alten, Bella
Amstad, Marietta
Amstad, Martha
Andrews, Jenny
Anitúa, Fanny
Antoine, Josephine
Arangi-Lombardi, Giannina
Arkel, Teresa
Arnoldson, Sigrid
Artner, Josephine von
Artôt, Marguerite-Joséphine-
  Desirée
Artôt de Padilla, Lola
Auerbach, Nanette
Austral, Florence Mary
Bäumer, Margaret
Bahr-Mildenburg, Anna
Baldanza, Romana
Baldassare-Tedeschi, Giuseppina
Bandrowska-Turska, Ewa
Barsova, Valeria Vladimirovna
Bathori, Jane
Beeth, Lola
Beilke, Irma Käthe Else
Bellincioni, Gemma Cesira
  Mathilda
Belmas, Xenia
Berger, Erna
Bertinotti-Radicati, Teresa
Besanzoni, Gabriella
Bianchi Charitas, Bianca
Biscaccianti, Eliza
Blaes, Elisa
Bland, Elsa
Blauvelt, Lillian Evans
Boccabadati, Luigia
Bordogni-Willent, Luisa
Boronat, Olimpia

Bosetti, Hermine
Bourgignon, Jane
Brambilla, Marietta
Brandt, Marianne
Branzell Reinshagen, Karin Maria
Bréjean-Silver, Georgette
Brema, Marie
Bréval, Lucienne
Bronskaja, Eugenia
Brothier, Yvonne
Cahier, Sarah-Jane
Campodonico, Armanda
Caron, Rose Lucille
Carré, Marguerite
Casazza, Elvira
Castagna, Bruna
Catalani, Angelica
Cavan, Marie
Cesbron-Viseur, Suzanne
Chailley, Marie-Thérèse
Cigna, Gina
Cisneros, Eleanora de
Claussen, Julia
Cléricy Blanc du Collet, Marie
  Camille Joséphine
Cole, Charlotte
Cole, Susanna
Colonne, Eugénie Elise
Colonnese, Elvira
Corridori, Lucia
Couperin, Céleste-Thérèse
Craft, Marcella
Craig, Elizabeth
Croiza, Claire
Crossley, Ada
Dalla-Rizza, Gilda
Dal Monte, Toti
Damoreau, Laure Cinthie
Debicka, Hedwig von
Décarie, Reine
De Lys, Edith
Denera, Erna
Dershniskaya, Xenia
Dessoir, Susanne
Dieman, Ursula van
Dietrich, Marie
Donalda, Pauline
Durigo, Ilona
Dustmann, Marie Luise
El-Tour, Anna
Ernst, Anna Katherina
Falk, Lina

Féart, Rose
Féraldy, Germaine
Ferrani, Cesira
Figner-Gerald, Lidia Niko-
  laievna
Filippi, Pauline
Fitziu, Anna
Fleischer, Editha
Flesch, Ella
Foerstrová-Lautererová, Berta
Francillo-Kaufmann, Hedwig
Fremstad, Anna Augusta Olivia
Freund, Marya
Frijsh, Povla
Frind, Annie
Fröhlich, Maria Anna
Fuchs, Sibylle Ursula
Gähwiller, Sylvia
Galletti-Gianoli, Isabella
García, Eugénie
Garden, Mary
Garmo, Tilly de
Garrison, Mabel
Gay, Maria
Gaylord, Julia
Gelling, Hilda Grace
Gentile, Maria
Gerhardt, Elena
Gerhart, Maria
Gerster, Etelka
Giannini, Dusolina
Ginster, Ria
Glaz, Herta
Glover, Sarah Ann
Gluck, Alma
Götze, Augusta
Grassini, Giuseppina Maria
  Camilla
Gugliemetti, Anna-Maria
Guilleaume, Margot
Gusalewicz, Genia
Harsanyi, Janice
Heale, Alice
Heidersbuch, Käthe
Heinrich, Julia
Helbling, Maria
Herwig, Käthe
Hidalgo, Elvira de
Hiedler, Ida
Hildach, Anna
Hilgermann, Laura
Höngen, Elisabeth

Hogarth, Helen
Horn, Maria
Hřímalá, Felicita
Hřímalá, Marie
Hüni-Mihacsek, Felicie
Hussa, Maria
Hviid, Mimi
Iracema-Brügelmann, Hedy
Isori, Ida
Ivogün, Maria
Jacoby, Josephine
Janacopulos, Vera
Janda, Therese
Jepson, Helen
Jordan, Irene
Jordan, Mary
Kainz, Marianne Katharina
  Theresia
Kainz, Marie Holland
Kalter, Sabine
Kaschowska, Felice
Katulskaja, Jelena Klimentjewna
Kemp, Angela Barbara
Kindermann, Lydia Maria Theresia
Kirkby-Lunn, Louise
Kittel, Hermine
Klein, Ivy Frances
Klemetti, Dagmar
Kolassi, Irma
Konetzni, Anny
Konetzni, Hilde
Korsoff, Lucette
Koshetz, Nina Pavlova
Krauss, (Marie) Gabrielle
Krüger, Emmy
Kruszelnicka, Salomea
Kupper, Annelies Gabriele
Kurt, Melanie
Labia, Maria
Lablache, Fanny Wyndham
La Grange, Anna Caroline de
Lancia, Florence
Landouzy, Lise
Lankow, Anna
Lapeyrette, Ketty
Larkcom, Charlotte Agnes
Larsén-Todsen, Nanny
Lavrovska, Elisaveta Andreyevna
Lawrence, Marjorie
Leffler-Bruckard, Martha
Lehmann, Lilli
Lehmann, Lotte

Lehmann, Marie
Leider, Frida
Lemmens, Helen
Lenhardson, Antonieta Silveyra
  de
Leonard, Lotte
Liebling, Estelle
Liljeblad, Ingeborg
Lind, Jenny
Lipkovska, Lydia Yakovlevna
Lipton, Martha
Litvinne, Félia Vasilyevna
Ljungberg, Göta Albertina
Llacer, Maria
Loreto García y García,
  Maria de
Luart, Emma
Mabee, Grace Widney
Macbeth, Florence
Mac Farren, Clara Natalia
Magelssen, Ida Basilier
Malkin, Beata
Mallinger, Mathilde
Mangold, Charlotte
Manski, Dorothée
Mantelli, Eugenia
Mara, Gertrud Elisabeth
Maragliano Mori, Rachele
Marchesi de Castrone, Blanche
Marchesi de Castrone, Mathilde
Marchisio, Barbara
Marié de L'Isle, Jeanne
Mario, Queena
Markova, Gali Enbaeff de
Marsh, Lucy Isabelle
Marti, Katharina
Martienssen-Lohmann, Franziska
Masson, Elizabeth
Materna, Amalie
Matzenauer, Margarete
Maubourg-Goffaux, Jeanne
Meichik, Anna
Melis, Carmen
Metzger-Lattermann, Ottilie
Meyer, Jenny
Michaelis, Ruth
Michalsky, Anne
Mielke, Antonia
Milanov, Zinka
Morena, Berta
Mysz-Gmeiner, Lulu
Nansen, Eva Helene
Nast, Minnie

Nemeth, Maria
Nespoulos, Marthe
Neždanova, Antonida
Nielsen, Alice
Niessen-Stone, Matja von
Nissen-Saloman, Henriette
Noordewier-Reddingius, Aaltje
Novello-Davies, Clara
Nüesch, Nina
Ober, Margaret Arndt
Oboukhova, Nadesha Andreivna
Oehme-Foerster, Elsa
O'Leary, Rosetta
Olénine d'Alheim, Marie
Olitzka, Rosa
Olszewska, Maria
Orgeni, Aglaja
Ortmann, Carolyn
Osgood, Emma Aline
Paalen, Bella
Pacetti, Iva
Papier, Rosa
Paradis, Maria Therese von
Pasta, Giuditta
Pauly, Rosa
Peyron, Gisèle
Philippi, Maria Cäcilia
Philp, Elizabeth
Piltti, Lea Maire
Pitzinger-Dupont, Gertrude
Plaichinger, Thila
Ponselle, Carmela
Preobrajenskaia, Sofia
Pruckner, Karoline
Pyne, Louisa Fanny
Rainforth, Elizabeth
Raisa, Rosa
Rappold, Marie
Rautawaara, (Terttu) Aulikki
Reeves, Emma
Reichardt, Luise
Révy, Aurelie
Ritter-Ciampi, Gabrielle
Robeson, Lila P.
Rodio, Jolanda
Roeseler, Marcella
Rogers, Clara Kathleen
Roselle, Anne
Rosse, Jeanie
Roze, Marie Hippolyte
Rudersdorff, Hermine
Rünger, Gertrude
Russ, Giannina

WRITERS ON MUSIC

Kerr, Louisa
Kinscella, Hazel Gertrude
Kirkendale, Ursula
Kirkman, Mrs. Joseph
Kisch, Eve (Evelyn Myra)
Klemetti, Armi
Komarova, Varvara Dmitrievna
Kos, Koraljka
Kumer, Zmaga
Lagercrantz, (Anna) Ingeborg
Landowska, Wanda
Landowski, Alice-Wanda
Lankow, Anna
Lebeau, Elisabeth
Lederman, Minna
Lehmann, Lilli
Liebe, Annelise
Lineva, Evgenia Eduardovna
Ling, Dorothy
Lipsius, Marie
Lissa, Zofia
Liwanowa, Tamara Nikolajewna
Lobaczewska, Stefania
Lohr, Ina
Long, Marguerite
Long, Marie-Jeanne-Pauline
Mac Farren, Clara Natalia
Macfarren, Emma Marie Bennett
McGill, Josephine
Malzewa, Katharine Alexeivna
Mandl, Camilla
Marcel-Dubois, Claudie
Marchesi de Castrone,
    Mathilde
Marix, Jeanne
Marix-Spire, Thérèse
Marshall, Florence A.
Martienssen-Lohmann,
    Franziska
Masson, Renée-Madeleine
Materna, Hedwig
May, Florence
Meyer-Baer, Kathi
Milanov, Zinka
Millar, Marian
Mondolfi, Anna
Morgan, Sydney
Morsch, Anna
Moscheles, Charlotte
Newlin, Dika
Newmarch, Rosa Harriet
Nolthenius, Hélène Wagenaar
Novello, Mary Sabilla

Novello, Mary Victoria
Ocampo, Victoria
Olénine d'Alheim, Marie
Paige, Mrs. J. B.
Paige, Kate
Panum, Hortense
Patterson, Annie Wilson
Patzaková, Anna
Perry, Julia
Pessl, Yella
Peyron, Gisèle
Peyser, Ethel Rose
Place, Gertrude
Pohl, Luise
Polko, Elise
Pope, Isabel
Prahács, Margit
Prescott, Oliveria Louisa
Pruckner, Karoline
Ramann, Lina
Reimann, Margarete
Reinagle, Caroline
Reis, Claire R.
Ritter, Fanny
Rittmeyer-Iselin, Dora J.
Rodwell, Anne
Rokseth, Yvonne
Samaroff, Olga
Sands, Mollie
Schlesinger, Kathleen
Schnapper, Edith
Schröder, Cornelia
Scott, Marion Margaret
Scriabine, Marina
Scudéry, Madeleine
Seiler, Emma
Serov, Valentine Semenovna
Sharp, Mrs. William
Shestakova, Ludmilla
Simon, Alicja
Singleton, Esther
Smith, Julia
Smith, Laura Alexandrine
Spence, Sarah
Stäblein-Harder, Hanna
Stöhr, Maria
Straková, Theodora
Sutro, Florence Edith
Szczepańska, Maria Klementyna
Szegö, Julia
Thibault, Geneviève
Tibaldi Chiesa, Maria
Townsend, Mrs.

Townsend, Pauline D.
Unschuld, Marie von
Valentin, Karoline
Van Zanten, Cornelia
Vernillat, France Marie
  Elisabeth
Viollier, Renée
Wagner, Cosima
Wainwright, Harriet
Wakefield, (Augusta) Mary
Walker, Bettina
Wallace, Grace Maxwell
Wallner, Bertha Antonia
Warfield, Sandra
Warner, Sylvia Townsend
Webster, Clarinda Augusta
Weingartner-Studer, Carmen
Weise, Dagmar
Werthemann, Helene
Wessely, Helene
Whiteside, Abby
Wójcikóvna, Bronislava
Zanetti, Emilia